Praise from
A Workbook Companion

"If the Text of *A Course in Miracles* is to get the message clear in our heads, the Workbook is to bring it home to our hearts. In their *Workbook Companion* series, Allen and Robert speak straight to our hearts, complementing the spirit and meaning behind the lessons. Their work resonates with intellectual honesty, building our relationship with the Course on the solid ground of their years of dedicated study."
—TIM SCHOENFELDER, M.D.

"Sometimes it seems as though Allen is reading my mind when he writes his Workbook commentary for the day. He has an uncanny way of addressing precisely the questions and objections that occur to me. I find Allen's commentaries unique in spanning the distance between the peace and truth of the real world and the dramatic distractions of the illusory world of separation. He is never just theoretical; he knows the terrain on this path, and he is a great travelling companion."
—MILLI GRAVEL

"Encouraging, stimulating…a beautiful and extremely important work."
—ARMANDO BRONS

"The return of the Workbook commentaries is like the return of a long departed friend. When I started the Course several years ago, the commentaries got me through the difficult but very rewarding process of completing the Workbook."
—DENNIS WESTON

"Robert and Allen are companions in a very real sense. Robert's support in terms of practice, and Allen's inspired commentaries, have been my travelling friends in my study of the Course for nearly two

years. They deliver genuine and often mind-expanding insights throughout the series. I keep the *Workbook Companion* alongside my copy of the Course."
—CLIVE BAYNE

"The lesson commentaries have been very helpful. I have been doing the Workbook for over fifteen years, and the additional insight has expanded my understanding of the Course. Thank you very much!"
—JUDY JUNGHANS

"Since I started to use these lesson commentaries, I have gained a much deeper understanding of the Course's teachings. Allen's brilliant insights have helped me immensely, opening many new doors of understanding for me. He one of the most down to earth, loving, gifted Course scholars living today."
—REV. LEE POEPPING, UNITY CHURCH OF SANTA CLARITA

"I have found the *Workbook Companion* books to be valuable tools in helping me gain a greater understanding of each lesson. They reinforce the goal for the day and encourage dedication to the actual exercise instructions so we can apply them to 'in the world' use. The commentaries enrich and enhance what can initially feel unclear. Any confusion about what each lesson might mean or how to apply it is clarified beautifully. I highly recommend these tools to anyone who has an interest in using the lessons in their daily lives."
—KATHY SMITH

"Allen brings a perspective to the lessons that has helped me to understand them at a deeper level. I have also found that his references to appropriate sections of the Text have deepened my appreciation for the importance of the Text to understanding the messages in the Workbook. Instruction in how to practice the lessons also makes a wonderful contribution. A very valuable aid to anyone starting out with the Course."
—SARAH HUEMMERT

"Allen's explanations and commentaries are so helpful. When I am not clear about a lesson I can refer to the practice summary and lesson commentary. What a godsend they are. The *Workbook Companion* books are valuable and important tools in my understanding and living *A Course in Miracles*."

—ALLISON CRAIG

A Workbook Companion

Volume II

A Workbook Companion

Commentaries on the Workbook
for Students from *A Course in Miracles*

Volume II
Lessons 181 - 365

Second Edition
Revised and Expanded

Lesson Commentaries by Allen Watson
Practice Instructions and Cameo Essays by Robert Perry

Published by Circle Publishing
A division of The Circle of Atonement Teaching and Healing Center
P.O. Box 4238 • West Sedona, AZ 86340
(928) 282-0790 • Fax: (928) 282-0523
E-mail: info@circleofa.org • Website: www.circleofa.org

Cover design by George Foster; www.fostercovers.com
Design and layout by Phillips Associates UK Ltd
Printed in the USA

ISBN-13: 978-1-886602-25-0
ISBN-10: 1-886602-25-5

Library of Congress Cataloging-in-Publication Data

Watson, Allen, 1940-
  A workbook companion : commentaries on the Workbook for students from
A course in miracles, second edition, revised and expanded / lesson
commentaries by Allen Watson ; practice instructions and cameo essays
by Robert Perry.
        p. cm.
  Summary: "A practice aid for students doing the Workbook of A Course
in Miracles, containing lesson commentaries, practice summaries, and
essays on practice methods"--Provided by publisher.
  Includes bibliographical references.
  ISBN 1-886602-24-7 -- ISBN 1-886602-25-5
  1. Spiritual life--New Age movement. I. Course in miracles. Workbook
for students. II. Perry, Robert, 1960- III. Title.
  BP605.C68W37 2005
  299'.93--dc22
                            2005005515

A Workbook Companion

*The goal is clear, but now you need
specific methods for attaining it.
The speed by which it can be reached depends
on this one thing alone; your willingness to practice every step.
Each one will help a little, every time it is attempted.
And together will these steps lead you from dreams of judgment
to forgiving dreams and out of pain and fear.*

Text, Introduction to Chapter 30

Contents

Contents

A note on reading Course references

All references are given for the Second Edition of the Course, and are listed according to the numbering in the Course, rather than according to page numbers. Each reference begins with a letter, which denotes the particular volume or section of the Course and its extensions (T = Text, W = Workbook for Students, M = Manual for Teachers, C = Clarification of Terms, P = *Psychotherapy*, and S = *Song of Prayer*). After this letter comes a series of numbers, which differ from volume to volume:

T, P, or S-chapter.section.paragraph:sentence; e.g., T-24.VI.2:3–4
W-part (I or II).lesson.paragraph:sentence; e.g., W-pI.182.4:1–2
M or C-section.paragraph:sentence; e.g., C-2.5:2

A Workbook Companion
Volume II

I

Introduction
and Lessons 181 - 200

INTRODUCTION

You'll recall that we have twice been told we're now in preparation for the second part of the Workbook. This introduction is telling us a little more specifically how the next twenty lessons are meant to prepare us.

First of all, the overall goal is to strengthen our commitment and unify our goals into one intent.

The immediate goal of our practicing these lessons is *experience* of the peace, liberation, and freedom that unified commitment can bring; holy instants when we have a foretaste of right-mindedness.

The method of making such experience available is a focus on the remaining blocks to it, with the intent of, even if just briefly, lifting those blocks.

If the *overall goal* is to firm up our willingness to commit ourselves more strongly to the Course's path, then obviously the Workbook is recognizing that at this point, about halfway through the Workbook, our willingness is probably still a bit irresolute, and our commitment less than complete. "You are not asked for total dedication all the time as

3

yet" (1:2). There are probably a few of us that are quite relieved to hear that. I think it is likely that, if the Course is not yet asking for total, continual dedication at this stage, it would be unwise and counterproductive to be asking it of ourselves. We have to bear in mind those two little words "as yet," indicating that "total dedication all the time" lies somewhere in our future; it is where we are being led. But we should not berate ourselves for not having that total dedication *now*.

What *is* being asked of us is to practice. The experience of the holy instant at this point in our spiritual growth is not expected anything more than "intermittently" (1:3). Notice how that idea is repeated several times in these three paragraphs. We are lifting the blocks "however briefly" (2:2). We aim to go past our defenses "for a little while each day" (3:4). We are practicing, each day, to bypass one major block to the awareness of love's presence, just for a short time. We aren't supposed to be worrying about making this our permanent mental state—not yet. It is the cumulative experience of these holy instants that will provide the motivation to make that total dedication; we aren't sufficiently motivated without that.

> It is experiencing this that makes it sure that you will give your total willingness to following the way the course sets forth. (1:4)

> Your motivation will be so intensified that words become of little consequence. You will be sure of what you want, and what is valueless. (2:5–6)

> No more than this [little while each day] is asked, because no more than this is needed. It will be enough to guarantee the rest will come. (3:5–6)

In Chapter 13 of the Text we are admonished: "Be you content with healing" (T-13.VIII.7:1). And as we progress through the Workbook we need to be content with practicing—same thing. Our experience of grace at this stage may still be intermittent, just a little while each day; that's okay, and we can be at peace with its being so. Just that little while each day will be enough to *guarantee* the rest will come, so there need be no panic nor discouragement. Just do the practice and full enlightenment will surely follow; that is the promise being made here.

4

LESSON 181 ✦ JUNE 30
"I trust my brothers, who are one with me."

Practice instructions

Purpose: To go past the special block of focusing on the mistakes of others, and so experience your own sinlessness. This experience will intensify your motivation and strengthen your commitment.

Morning/evening quiet time: At least five minutes; ideally, thirty or more.

The practice is a meditation aimed at experiencing the sinlessness in you. Close your eyes and hold in mind nothing but your great desire to see your own sinlessness, to experience the pure goodness that is your reality. Make this focus your only intent.

To do this, you will need to set aside your focus on the mistakes of others. This focus has been disastrous. It has caused those mistakes to fill your vision and show you a sinful world. This sinful world has then acted as a constant witness to the sinfulness in you. To see the sinlessness in you, then, you will have to banish from your mind any thought of the errors of others. If, during your meditation, your mind starts dwelling on someone's wrongdoing, quickly repeat, *"It is not this that I would look upon. I trust my brothers, who are one with me."*

You will also need to set aside all concerns about past and future. Don't let your ego tell you that the goal of seeing your sinlessness is just too different from your past goals and that this new goal, by eclipsing your old goals, will threaten your happiness. Don't let it tell you that, even if you should gain a glimpse of your holiness, "you will inevitably lose your way again" (4:3). Such concerns about past and future are really just subtle defenses against "present change" (5:3).

Refuse to let your mind be drawn off into these defenses. Hold an absolutely single focus. "We enter in the time of practicing with one intent; to look upon the sinlessness within" (5:7).

Hourly remembrance: One or two minutes as the hour strikes (reduce if circumstances do not permit).

Do a short version of morning/evening meditation, aimed at experiencing the sinlessness in you. Then thank God for His gifts in the previous hour and ask Him for His guidance in the coming hour.

Response to temptation: Whenever you want to focus on someone's mistakes.

Repeat, *"It is not this that I would look upon. I trust my brothers, who are one with me."* Realize that your focus on his mistakes is an obstruction blocking the vision of your own sinlessness (7:3). Dispel this obstruction not for any long-range purpose, but simply to relieve the misery that comes from focusing on sin.

Commentary

This lesson is not encouraging naive blindness to people's flaws. It isn't saying that you should unlock your house and car and leave your money lying in the street, trusting no one will steal it. It is talking about looking *beyond* others' errors and mistakes (their egos) to see their sinlessness. It is speaking of being aware of a person's mistakes (and taking them into practical account), while at the same time looking past them to their perfect innocence. Not seeing the mistakes as *sins* to be condemned and punished. As my friend Lynne once said of a man who had previously been abusive to her, "I may love a rattlesnake, but that doesn't mean I sleep with it."

The "block" this lesson is helping us to lift (however briefly) is our focus on the sins of our brothers and sisters. The lesson is telling us not to look for what is wrong in people, but what is right. The point behind this is that by focusing on the sins of others, we block their true Self from our sight, and thereby block the Self within us from our sight as well. If I cannot overlook the mistakes of my brothers, I cannot overlook my own. "Perception has a focus" (2:1). We need to change our focus. "Remove your focus on your brother's sins, and you experience the peace that comes from faith in sinlessness" (2:5). Remember the aim of these twenty lessons: to remove a block and thus *experience* something different; in this case, "faith in sinlessness."

As the introduction said, we are not trying to do this for all time!

(Not yet anyhow.) Not even for all day; just for a brief period. Do you have someone you feel you cannot forgive? How about trying to "practice" forgiving them, just for five minutes? Just for a brief period, be willing to let go of your judgments about them, to forget the past and to forget the future, and to look for the innocence in them, to see them as a holy child of God, deserving of His Love. How about trying, even for five minutes, just to be *willing* for this kind of experience? Don't worry about the fact that for the last month, or year, or however long, you've wanted to kill them; don't worry about the fact that ten minutes from now you will be fantasizing about how they will get what is coming to them. Maybe so. "How could this matter?" (5:1). The concerns we have about the past or the future "are but defenses against present change of focus in perception" (5:3). If we can let ourselves experience, even for a brief moment, what it feels like to see past their sins to innocence, that experience will be enough to motivate us to go all the way.

I encourage us all to bear these instructions in mind, not just for today's lesson, but for all the rest of the Workbook. When you sit down for a quiet time, put aside how you felt just before, and don't worry about how you will feel afterwards. "We do not seek for long-range goals" (7:2). All we are looking for is the experience of an instant of release, because that is all that is needed. At any moment during the day we can stop and say, "This instant is our willing one with His" (9:8). That instant is all we need.

Somehow, we seem to think that we can shift from total egoity to immediate spirituality. We think that if we spend five minutes with God in the morning, the rest of the day ought to be totally transformed, immediately. Our resistance is simply too great for that to happen; we have *overlearned* the ego's lessons, and unlearning them will take some effort. The ego tells us, "It isn't working," because we "forgave" our brother in those five minutes in the morning and spent half the rest of the day dreaming up ways to make him, or her, suffer. But something is happening; the ego is trying to make us guilty because it *knows* something is happening. Those five minutes when we lay our judgment aside bring us an experience of inner peace that we have never known before, and we know a good thing when we see it. Our motivation to forgive will grow, and grow, and grow. The experience of "surcease an instant from the misery the focus upon sin will bring" (7:3) will be such a relief that we will seek it again and again, until it grows to encompass our entire mind, all the time. All it takes is the willingness to practice.

LESSON 182 ✦ JULY 1
"I will be still an instant and go home."

Practice instructions

Purpose: To go past your defensiveness and briefly go home with the Christ Child in you. To have an experience of the eternal innocence in you. This experience will firm up your willingness to follow "the way the course sets forth" (W-pI.In.181-200.1:4).

Morning/evening quiet time: At least five minutes; ideally, thirty or more.

The exercise today is clearly a meditation. Begin by repeating the idea and then stilling your mind. Lay aside all your sense of defensiveness, all your need to protect yourself against an alien world that cares not about your needs. Throughout the meditation, whenever your thoughts wander, respond by repeating the idea.

The more you still your mind, the more, perhaps, you get in touch with a call in you, an inner pull to experience a sense of home that nothing in this world can provide. This pull is actually the call of the Christ Child in you, an element of your true Self Who feels dragged down into this world's smoggy atmosphere by the weight of your sleeping mind, and Who "desires to go home so deeply, so unceasingly, His voice cries unto you to let Him rest a while" (5:3).

Let this inner pull draw you to your real home, which lies deep within. As the Text says, "You do not remember how to look within for you do not believe your home is there" (T-12.IV.5:4). Let this Child take you there. Let Him carry you to your Father's house, and then rest there with Him "in perfect stillness, silent and at peace, beyond all words, untouched by fear and doubt, sublimely certain that you are at home" (8:3).

Hourly remembrance: One or two minutes as the hour strikes (reduce if circumstances do not permit).

Do a brief version of the longer practice. Be still an instant and go home with the Christ Child. You may also want to ask for guidance for the next hour and thank God for His gifts in the last hour.

Commentary

Another lesson about the holy instant. Notice how the thread about "instants," "moments," and "intervals" of stillness, quiet, and withdrawal from the world, begun in the introduction to this series of lessons and in Lesson 181, carries through nearly every lesson up to Lesson 200, the end of this series. It wasn't until my third or fourth time through these lessons that I realized they were all instructions in consciously setting aside short periods every day and attempting to enter the holy instant. The themes seem to differ, but all the difference lies in which block to our awareness of love's presence is being considered. The aim is always the same: a short suspension of that block, and the experience of a new awareness that comes when the block is momentarily removed.

The block being considered today is simply the temptation to find satisfaction, or to feel at home, in this world. We spend most of our lives in an attempt to adjust to the world, or to adjust the world to ourselves. It seems quite natural to us to try to be comfortable here, and we expend a great deal of effort trying to do so. This lesson appeals to us to set that effort aside, just for a brief while, and to recognize the childlike voice within us that is crying to go home—home to Heaven. We need to acknowledge that "this world you seem to live in is not home to you" (1:1). And, recognizing this is so, to take time each day to allow this Child within us to "rest a while" (5:3) and, for "just a few instants of respite...[to] return to breathe again the holy air that fills His Father's house" (5:4).

This lesson is perhaps the most poetically beautiful lesson in the entire Workbook. Some of you have heard, perhaps, the poignant reading of most of this lesson by Beverly Hutchinson on the tape *The Forgotten Song*. It is hard for me to listen without tears, and I don't bother trying. Tears are fine, but not enough; we need to hear the appeal and to act upon it: "Rest with Him frequently today" (9:1). "Go home with Him from time to time today" (10:3). "Be still an instant and go home with Him, and be at peace a while" (12:9).

The thought of this lesson has had a powerful effect in my life. Sometimes when I am feeling my lowest—dry, dull, and discouraged—

just quietly closing my eyes and saying, "I want to go home" is enough to break the spell and allow the peace of God into my mind.

Another passage, towards the end of the lesson, has had an equally powerful effect on me:

> You have not lost your innocence. It is for this you yearn. This is your heart's desire. This is the voice you hear, and this the call which cannot be denied.   (12:1–4)

When I remember these words, I seem to be always surprised at the soothing effect they have. I had not realized, until I repeated them, how deeply I was feeling that I *had* lost my innocence, how much the source of my depression was a hidden belief in my own loss of innocence. I suddenly realize that, yes, this *is* what I am yearning for; this *is* my heart's desire.

If you can, right now as you read this, stop, and be still and instant, and go home with me. It is so easy to do. Why delay an instant longer?

LESSON 183 ✦ JULY 2

"I call upon God's Name and on my own."

Practice instructions

Purpose: To go past the defense of valuing other gods, of valuing the idols of the world, and so experience the true God. This will intensify your motivation and strengthen your commitment.

Morning/evening quiet time: At least five minutes; ideally, thirty or more.

This lesson is the introduction of what I call Name of God Meditation. This meditation (which is described more fully in the cameo essay on page 14) can be summarized in the following way:

- Choose a name for God that you will use. You may want to ask within for this.
- Close your eyes and repeat the idea for today just once.
- After that, simply "repeat God's Name slowly again and still again" (6:1). Do not, however, repeat it as a mere word. Repeat it as a heartfelt invitation to God. Fully expect Him to hear. "And God will come, and answer it Himself" (7:2). You are asking, then, for the experience of God, and of your true Self, which is part of Him. Repeat the Name, then, with all the desire you have to know God and yourself. Repeat it as "the only wish [you] have" (6:6).
- Whenever your mind wanders and starts thinking about the idols of the world, repeat the Name to dispel those thoughts. It will help if you repeat it with the awareness that the Name is everything and the things you were thinking about are nothing.

Hourly remembrance: One or two minutes as the hour strikes (reduce if circumstances do not permit).

Do a short version of the morning/evening exercise. Close by asking for God's guidance for the coming hour and thanking Him for His gifts in the past hour.

Response to temptation: When tempted to cherish an idol, a valueless thing of this world.

Repeat God's Name, realizing that this Name signifies everything you want, while the idol is nothing.

Commentary

God's Name, as the term is used in this lesson and the next, symbolizes His Identity and our identity with Him. God's name is not Jehovah, or Krishna, or Allah. Yet any of those symbols could be used to represent Him. When this lesson urges us to "repeat God's Name," what, then, do we say? The actual word we use does not matter; it is the concept of His Identity that is to be foremost in our minds. We might say the word "God" over and over, or "Father," or "Divine Mother," or whatever word best symbolizes for us the Identity of God.

The general practice outlined in this lesson is very similar to practices in Eastern religions of repeating the Name of God over and over, and the intent is very much the same. In the Eastern spiritual practices, this often takes the form of chanting. The Hare Krishna religion, for instance, gains its name from the practice of repeatedly and seemingly endlessly chanting, "Hare Krishna, Hare Rama," which (I think) basically means "Praise Krishna. Praise Rama," with Krishna and Rama being names of God. A Christian group I once belonged to had a major emphasis on the practice of repeating the words "O Lord Jesus" for extended periods of time, with exactly the same kind of intent, and with often remarkable results. Although this kind of practice is not a major emphasis of the Course, clearly it is one means offered by the Course for helping us find the holy instant. The one difference I see here is that (in 5:4) the repetitions are meant to be *silent* and done "within your quiet mind," rather than aloud.

By focusing on God's Identity, we loosen the hold that all lesser names have on our minds. We counter the illusion of separation in recognizing the one Name that represents everything there is: "There is one Name for all there is, and all that there will be" (8:5).

Many results are attributed in this lesson to repeating the Name of God: it reminds us of our identity with Him (1:5); it invites the angels to surround us and keep us safe, recognizing the holiness we share with God (2:2); it prompts the world to lay down all illusions (3:1); it causes all idols to fall (4:1, 3–4); it calls upon our Self, the extension of God that we are (5:1); it acknowledges God as sole Creator of reality (8:1).

We are encouraged, almost as an aside, to do this practice with someone else, sitting together in silence and repeating God's Name in our minds; this seems to have particular merit, for by it we establish "an altar which reaches to God Himself and to His Son" (5:4). This is the only place I am aware of in the Course in which meditation with another person is even mentioned, but it is a very favorable mention, and indicates there is some added value in joining with others in meditation.

The primary idea of the practice seems to be that the thought of God replaces every other idea in our minds, and if other ideas enter, we can respond to them with God's Name (8:3–5). Instead of praying for any specific thing, or any specific persons (all of which have names that distinguish them from everything else), we repeat the Name of God which includes them all. "No prayer but this is necessary, for it holds them all within it" (10:2). As we repeat God's Name we can alter our mental state to experience the gift of grace (9:1); eventually we come to a place where "the universe consists of nothing but the Son of God, who calls upon His Father" (11:4).

NAME OF GOD MEDITATION

We in the West, primarily through the influx of Eastern spiritualities, are slowly discovering that meditation is an extremely powerful tool. If one wants to scale the heights of the Divine, attempting this without meditation might be the mountain-climbing equivalent of forgetting your gear, and your hiking boots as well. If this practice is so central to our journey home, what does *A Course in Miracles* have to say about it?

I have argued for many years that one of the major goals of the Course's Workbook is to train us in meditation. This training begins early on, in Lessons 41 and 44, after which meditation instruction becomes a staple of Workbook practice. The technique taught in the 40s is something I have written about several times. However, there is another method of meditation which is distinctly different from that one. This one is not introduced until Lesson 183. This technique is not only accorded great importance in that lesson (and in Lesson 184), but is a practice we are apparently expected to continue in Part II of the Workbook (see W-pII.In.10:4 and W-pII.222.2:1). It is a practice of entering into God's

Presence by repeating His Name over and over, to the exclusion of all else.

This is a method I have tried to use over the years, and have received some benefit from. Yet it never quite clicked into place for me until a few months ago when I took a personal retreat. One of the goals I had for this retreat was to really "get" this method—both in theory and in practice—in part because our group here in Sedona would soon be practicing Workbook Lesson 183. Oddly enough, I just happened to take my retreat at a Catholic retreat center which, I discovered upon arrival, is very focused on Centering Prayer, a contemporary form of Christian meditation which is rooted in the medieval mystical text, *The Cloud of Unknowing—and* which is very similar (though not identical) to the method taught in Lesson 183. The focus at the retreat center on Centering Prayer gave me a feeling of support and a renewed motivation. Then, while there, I did a close study of Lesson 183, which really clarified its method in my mind, so that when I went to practice it, it began to work much better than it had before. As a result, I enjoyed many wonderful meditations with this method during my retreat, and since then it has become my preferred technique.

The purpose of this essay is to clarify this technique to Course students so that they can make use of it, or make better use of it if they are practicing it already. The rest of the essay is divided into three parts: theory, technique, and instructions.

Theory

This method of meditation is grounded in a teaching which makes this meditation seem like the most logical and natural thing one can do with one's mind.

Our attention is naturally drawn to those things we think can bring us happiness, or at least protect us from pain. When our eyes look at a particular scene, don't they automatically gravitate to perceived sources of pleasure? To put this differently, we give our attention to what we think can answer our prayers. Attention, then, is an expression of desire, and desire is prayer. When we place our attention on the things of this world—which is where we usually place it—we are in essence praying to those things, hoping that they can fill our needs and make us safe. Yet can they really answer our prayers? Can they bring us true happiness? According to the Course, the answer is an emphatic "no." Only God can bring us true joy. He is the only true Object of our desires. By giving our attention to things of this world, we are making them into false gods, substitutes for the only One Who can truly reward our attention. We are behaving like

15

the ancient worshipper who prayed to a lifeless piece of stone that could neither hear nor answer his prayers.

We also give our attention to what we think is real. We don't spend a lot of our time, for instance, thinking about pink elephants—they're not real. Instead, we spend it thinking about the events and situations that face us in our day, precisely *because* we regard these as real. The Course, however, teaches that the world is a dream; only God is real. Certainly you and I are also real (Workbook Lesson 132 has us say, "For I am real because the world is not"), but our reality is *part* of God's. His reality encompasses ours, as well as the reality of all things.

This means that the characters we see walking around in the world have two aspects to them, a real aspect and an unreal one. They have the outer face they show us—their body and personality—which, the Course tells us, is unreal. And then behind this outer face lies their eternal spirit, the only thing truly real. And that spirit is part of God. Therefore, by placing our attention on God, we are simultaneously placing it on the truth within others, even while we are *withdrawing* our attention from the face they present the world.

In summary, we place our attention on what we think is real and will make us happy. The things of the world (in their outer aspect, the aspect we are generally focused on) are unreal and cannot make us happy. Only God is real ("only" because He encompasses all things real) and only He can make us happy.

This has obvious implications for where to put our attention. It implies that the most honest and appropriate thing we can do with our attention is to remove it from the outer realm and place it on God. And that is the essence of this meditation technique. We can see this as having several aspects. We transfer our attention from the outer to the inner, removing it from the sensory realm and placing it on God's Presence deep within. We transfer our attention from the many to the One, withdrawing it from the numberless external bodies and placing it on the One Spirit. We transfer our attention from the thousand nameless things of the world (nameless, because only real things deserve names) to the one Name, which stands for all of reality. We remove our desire from the little gods of the world, since they cannot answer our prayers, and we give it to the One God, Who yearns to answer all our prayers with the priceless gift of Himself.

An important element of this technique is that it uses only one word. This is part of the Workbook's focus in the latter half of its year, where it sets the goal of gradually going beyond words. Ultimately, we will not need words at all for our practice. With a single motion of our will, we will be instantly ushered into God's Presence. Reducing our practice from many words to just one is an important step towards this goal. Given that using only one word is central to this technique, I would not recommend using multiple names for God within a single meditation.

Technique

1. Selecting a name

Select a name of God to use (since the Workbook does not dictate which name you use for God). It can be any word that signifies God to you, but it should be a single word—preferably a short word of one or two syllables. It should have maximum personal meaning to you, maximum ability to evoke your desire and love for God. You may want to ask within for guidance on what word to choose.

2. Beginning the meditation

Sit comfortably. Close your eyes. The meditation consists in repeating the Name, slowly and intentionally, over and over. You can repeat it constantly, or regularly every several seconds (synchronized with your breath, if you like), or irregularly, whenever you feel moved to. The Workbook is silent on these issues and generally considers such matters unimportant.

3. Focusing only on repeating the Name

Draw your attention in from everything else and put all your attention and desire on the Name:

> Practice but this today; repeat God's Name slowly again and still again. Become oblivious to every name but His. Hear nothing else. Let all your thoughts become anchored on This. No other word we use except at the beginning, when we say today's idea but once. And then God's Name becomes our only thought, our only word, the only thing that occupies our minds, the only wish we have, the only sound with any meaning, and the only Name of everything that we desire to see; of everything that we would call our own.
>
> (W-pI.183.6:1–8)

4. Repeating the Name as a call for everything real and desirable

The meaning, the feeling, you place in this Name is important (as you can see in the above quote). Some suggestions about that:

4a. Don't say God's Name just as a word

Speak it directly to God, as a communication from you to Him. Expect Him to hear and respond. "Thus do we give an invitation which can never be refused. And God will come, and answer it Himself" (W-pI.183.7:1).

4b. Repeat the Name as a call, which calls out for a response from God

- You are calling to God to come and reveal Himself to you in direct experience. Let this call contain all your desire to experience Him.
- You are calling to your true Identity, Which is part of God. You are asking to know Who you really are.
- You are calling to all things real—including the reality of your brothers—since everything real is a part of God.
- You are calling for everything you truly want, since God is the only One you really want. As the Course asks us to pray, "Yet is Your Love the only thing I seek, or ever sought. For there is nothing else that I could ever really want to find" (W-pII.231.1:3).

In other words, with this one single word, you are calling for *everything*. You are calling for everything that is real and everything you truly want. Don't try to consciously include all of the above meanings in your mind. It is important to repeat the Name gently, without strain. However, while you do, also say it with meaning. Make it the appeal of your heart. As *The Cloud of Unknowing* (a medieval mystical text) put it, make this repetition into "a dart of longing love."

5. Drawing your mind back from wandering

Whenever your thought wanders to something of the world, or to anything besides God's Name, respond by repeating the Name. This wandering will be a regular occurrence, so don't be distressed by it. Expect it. Simply be ready to respond by repeating the Name and so dispelling the extraneous thought. Do this as often as you need to. *If you spend the whole time doing this and nothing else, the time will have been well spent.*

> Sit silently, and let His Name become the all-encompassing idea that holds your mind completely. Let all thoughts be still except this one. And to all other thoughts respond with this,

and see God's Name replace the thousand little names you gave your thoughts, not realizing that there is one Name for all there is, and all that there will be.   (W-pl.183.8:3–5)

In repeating the Name to dispel wandering thoughts, it helps if you remember that what you were thinking about is essentially nothing—it is unreal and unsatisfying, and that God's Name represents everything—all that is real and all that you really want. So, when you notice a wandering thought, repeat God's Name in the awareness that it represents everything and what you were thinking about is nothing.

Induction Process

I have found the following instructions useful for beginning the meditation. They are a way of turning the Name into a full and heartfelt call. Since they only take a few minutes, they are just there to get you started on the right foot.

At the beginning of the meditation, repeat God's Name two or three times, as a way of addressing Him directly. Treat Him as a real Person. Expect Him to hear.

And now repeat God's Name as an act of calling on Him, calling Him to come to you and reveal Himself to you in direct experience.

And now repeat the Name as a way of calling on the awareness of your true Identity. By calling on God you also call on your true Self, for They are one.

Now repeat the Name as a way of calling on all of reality, including the reality of your brothers, for everything real is part of God.

And now repeat God's Name as a prayer that asks for everything you truly want, a prayer that contains all possible prayers. Say it as the prayer of your heart.

And now repeat His Name in love; as "a dart of longing love."

Now let all of these meanings blend together into one, so that by speaking this one word you are calling on everything—everything real and everything you truly want. As you continue the meditation, continue repeating His Name in this spirit.

And whenever your mind wanders to something besides His Name, repeat the Name gently as a way of drawing your mind back to focus. Repeat it as an affirmation that God's Name represents everything, while the thing you were thinking about is really nothing.

LESSON 184 ✦ JULY 3

"The Name of God is my inheritance."

Practice instructions

Purpose: To go past the inheritance you gave yourself—the little, separate things of the world, each with its own name—and experience the inheritance that God gave you: everything, all of Heaven. This experience will help "make your weak commitment strong; your scattered goals blend into one intent" (W-pI.In.181-200.1:1).

Morning/evening quiet time: At least five minutes; ideally, thirty or more.

The practice in this lesson is the same as yesterday—what I call Name of God Meditation—with perhaps a slightly modified emphasis:

- Close your eyes and repeat today's idea one time.
- After that, simply "repeat God's Name slowly again and still again" (W-pI.183.6:1). As you repeat this Name (remember you can use a name of your own choosing), realize that you are calling upon the awareness of all of reality, including the true reality of all your brothers. You are really asking for the inheritance God gave you as His Son. He has passed on to you everything He has, which is everything there is. This is what you are asking for, so ask with desire.
- When your mind wanders to all the little names that denote the things of this world, use God's Name to dispel those names, remembering that everything that is real has only one Name.

Hourly remembrance: One or two minutes as the hour strikes (reduce if circumstances do not permit).

Do a short version of the morning/evening exercise. Close by asking for God's guidance for the coming hour and thanking Him for His gifts in the past hour.

Commentary

There is a lot we could think about in this lesson. The way names, which are symbols, are based on separation and distancing of things. The way that perception is built up by these names and distinctions. How all of this forces us to view wholeness as an enemy. The way that the learning of the world consists primarily in learning all these names and ways of classifying things.

All of this is in contrast to the reality that is represented by the Name of God. The Name of God stands for wholeness, oneness, "the one Identity Which all things share" (10:2). Our perception has taught us an illusion, based on thousands of names for discrete parts we see as separate things; reality, however, is wholeness, undifferentiated, unseparated. The picture of parts we have manufactured hides the reality of the wholeness from us.

So, then, are we to attempt to completely set aside our perception of parts with separate names, and to live, somehow, seeing only the oneness? Is it somehow "wrong" for us to use the names and symbols of the world, to act as though Marilyn is different from Bob? Are we to treat a bluebird like our own baby? No. The lesson affirms the absolute truth, but it does not insist we attempt to make this world fit into that picture.

First, it says quite clearly that learning all the little names and symbols of separation "is a phase of learning everyone who comes must go through" (7:2). As some teachers of transpersonal psychology (the branch of psychology that teaches that ultimate wholeness transcends individual ego development) have said, you cannot transcend the ego until you have developed a healthy ego. Ego development seems to be a necessary step in our overall growth. Children have to become healthy, adult egos before they can successfully go beyond the ego. If an adult is still wrestling with problems of personality development that, in "normal" growth, should have been handled in childhood or adolescence, those problems probably need to be addressed, on their own level, before the person seeks to transcend their ego entirely.

I am extrapolating on the lesson a good deal here, and expressing what have to be classed as opinions, not necessarily something taught by the Course. But I do think this section comes pretty close to implying this: *everyone* has to pass through the "teaching of the world" (7:1) stage before they can begin to question its premises. We do not want to stop short at the teaching of the world (7:4), but it does seem we have to pass through it. "In its proper place, it serves but as a starting point from which another kind of learning can begin" (7:5).

Not only do we all need to pass through the world's kind of learning as a starting point, but after we have begun to "go beyond all symbols of the world," there is still reason for us to continue to use them: we have a teaching function (9:1). We still continue, for instance, to call people by name, to treat them as individuals with individual needs, but we are "not deceived" (9:3) by these apparent differences. The names and symbols of the world are necessary for purposes of communication, but "they become but means by which you can communicate in ways the world can understand, but which you recognize is not the unity where true communication can be found" (9:5). We are using the symbols of the world to communicate the fact of wholeness; we are using symbols to undo the symbols.

This is a tricky game. It is easy, remaining in the world and playing by the rules of separation, so to speak, to forget the reality these symbols of separation are hiding. That is exactly why the practice of holy instants is so important!

> Thus what you need are intervals each day in which the learning of the world becomes a transitory phase; a prison house from which you go into the sunlight and forget the darkness. Here you understand the Word, the Name which God has given you; the one Identity which all things share; the one acknowledgment of what is true. And then step back to darkness, not because you think it real, but only to proclaim its unreality in terms which still have meaning in the world that darkness rules. (10:1–3)

Practicing with the Name of God enables us to let go of "all foolish separations...which kept us blind" (14:3). In our quiet times we remember the wholeness and forget the differences. We may still see differences, but what we see has not changed the truth (13:3). All things still have one Name. In our practicing we renew this awareness, and then we "step back to darkness"; we return to the world of symbols and dreams in order to proclaim to it the reality we have experienced in the holy instant:

Father, our Name is Yours. In It we are united with all living things, and You Who are their one Creator.

(15:1–2)

THINK NOT YOU MADE THE WORLD

There is a very puzzling statement in Workbook Lesson 184, so puzzling that I have been asked about it several times:

Think not you made the world. Illusions, yes! But what is true in earth and Heaven is beyond your naming.

(W-pl.184.8:1-3)

The apparent problem with this passage is obvious: The Course tells us many times that we made the world, yet here it says with great emphasis that we should *not* think we made the world. What's more, it suggests that there are "true" things in the world, the very world we have been repeatedly told is an illusion!

How can we harmonize this passage with the rest of the Course? It's too easy just to ignore it, to pass it off as Helen having a bad day, a glitch in taking down the Course, or that the Course is just inconsistent. I think such a passage calls for a serious attempt to reconcile what is said with the rest of the Course.

Our first impulse when facing this kind of issue is often to draw upon our overall understanding of the Course. We ask ourselves: Based on the Course's overall thought system, how can I explain this passage? Many readers, no doubt, have already asked themselves this question in the course of reading this article.

I think there is a far better way. The answer to this kind of question almost always lies in *immediate context*, in the material immediately before and after the puzzling passage. Read that material very carefully, looking for words and ideas that also occur in your puzzling passage. So let's do that with the passage we are looking at here. You might even want to go to Lesson 184 and read it from the start through paragraph 8, where our passage occurs.

If you read the lesson from the beginning, you notice a central topic which also occurs in our passage: the topic of *naming* ("naming" being the last word of our passage). The beginning paragraphs of the lesson talk about our process of giving names to everything around us. We are told that assigning something a special name appears to "carve it out of unity" (1:4), making it seem to be "a separate entity" (1:3) with its own "special attributes" (1:5). In the wake of this naming project, we end up with a "reality" composed of distinct entities separated by the unnamed space between them. The naming process is thus really a *making* process, whereby we become (at least in part) the author of what we name—which is why there is so much pride in inventing a name that sticks. This discussion of naming concludes by saying, "This is the way reality is made by partial vision, purposefully set against the given truth" (4:1).

Do you notice anything important about this sentence? Here we have another idea found in our passage: the idea of us making our own reality. This lesson appears to be talking about a somewhat different concept of making the world. Usually, the Course seems to be referring to us making the world through an unconscious process of dreaming time and space into "existence." Here, the Course is talking about a process closer to the surface: using names to separate our perceptual field into distinct and separate entities.

Let's now go on to the lines immediately following the passage we are trying to explain:

> When you call upon a brother, it is to his body that you make appeal. His true Identity is hidden from you by what you believe he really is. His body makes response to what you call him, for his mind consents to take the name you give him as his own. And thus his unity is twice denied, for you perceive him separate from you, and he accepts this separate name as his. (8:4–7)

To explain our puzzling passage, we need to answer a specific question: What are the illusions we made and what are the true things we didn't make? The answer to this question is right there in the lines just quoted. They contain a clear contrast between two things, one illusory and one real. Can you spot these two things? The illusory thing is the body, which merely *seems* to be what our brother is. The real thing is our brother's "true Identity," who he *really* is, which (as we know from elsewhere in the Course) is the Christ, a bodiless, boundless spiritual Self.

So, very simply, the illusions we made are bodies, the forms of this world, the visible aspect of this world. Yet behind each illusion is a brother, who is an invisible, spiritual mind, and who ultimately is the Christ Himself. This brother is real. He was not made by us but created by God. He is not even really in this world. His true location is Heaven. He seems to be here, however, trapped inside this body. That, I believe, is why our confusing passage speaks of "what is true in earth and Heaven." The true things in this earth are not really in the earth at all; they are part of Heaven.

The confusion in our passage is really explained by now. But before pulling together what we have discovered, I would like to uncover a little more, just to show how much meaning there is here. Notice, in the lines quoted above, how the process of naming is carried further than before. A whole process is sketched, which goes something like this: You have in front of you a human body. You believe that this body is who your brother is. You express this belief by calling your brother by the name the world has given him. This name does not designate his true Identity, Which is one with all things and so could not have a special name. This name stands for a particular separate entity moving through space and time. It stands for a physical body. Thus, simply by calling him this name, you affirm that he is a separate body. Then, upon hearing your call, he accepts this name as his own. His mind thinks, "Yes, that is me. I am the body with that particular name." As a result, his body responds to you, standing in for his actual identity and playing its role. This is how "his unity is twice denied." By calling him a unique name, you have denied his true state of oneness with all reality. When he accepts this name as actually referring to him, he too has denied his oneness.

Now we are in a position to understand our initially puzzling passage with complete clarity. All we need to do is pull together all the things we have discovered through inspecting its immediate context. Here again is the passage:

> Think not you made the world. Illusions, yes! But what is true in earth and Heaven is beyond your naming.
>
> (W-pI.184.8:1-3)

And here is what we have discovered that it means:

> First, you made a world of separate bodies in order to hide the unified field of minds which lay behind those bodies. Then, you *named* each body, further cementing the idea that this separate body—rather than the mind behind it—was the true person. Through this double process (of making forms then naming the forms) you made the world you see. But you think you made much more than this. Through this process, you think you made your brother (one of those unified minds) into the creature you see before you. You think you carved him out of unity; changed him from a boundless,

25

unified spirit into a separate physical creature, designated by a special name. What an arrogant thought! For you only made the illusions of the world. Your brother was not made by you and so cannot properly be named by you, nor shaped and molded by your naming. He is far beyond all that. His reality may seem to be encased in a body, may seem to be part of this world, but in truth he abides in Heaven, where God placed him.

If we look carefully at the immediate context of any passage in the Course, we not only gain clarity, we also gain a much fuller meaning than we saw before.

LESSON 185 ✦ JULY 4

"I want the peace of God."

Practice instructions

Purpose: To let go your attachment to the things of the world, so that you can unify your intent behind the peace of God, realizing that His peace is the only thing you ever really wanted.

Morning/evening quiet time: At least five minutes; ideally, thirty or more.

- Search your mind carefully for the dreams—the things in this world—you still cherish. Locate them not by the words you use, but by your desire for them. "Consider but what you believe will comfort you, and bring you happiness" (8:4). In other words, be honest in your search. However, don't be dismayed by what your honesty uncovers. You may feel shame over certain dreams and be tempted to conceal them. Instead, realize that all dreams are one. Of every dream you thus uncover, ask this question: *"Is this what I would have, in place of Heaven and the peace of God?"*

- The goal is to reach a place where you can say with real sincerity, *"I want the peace of God."* To really mean this, you must also mean that you *don't* want the things of this world, for the two are mutually exclusive. It also helps to realize that "I want the peace of God" does not mean "I have come to want His peace," but "I have come to realize that His peace is the only thing I ever wanted."

Remarks: The point today is to unify your intent. "You have been weak at times, uncertain in your purpose, and unsure of what you wanted, where to look for it, and where to turn for help in the attempt" (10:5). Today, try to have a single intent. Ask for God's peace and mean it. "Make this request with deep sincerity" (10:3). Make the request for everyone, not just yourself, for this is what everyone wants. Realize that you are uniting your intent with the call of every heart and with the Will of God Himself.

Hourly remembrance: One or two minutes as the hour strikes (reduce if circumstances do not permit).

Do a short version of the morning/evening exercise. Close by asking for God's guidance for the coming hour and thanking Him for His gifts in the past hour.

Commentary

Kind of interesting that a lesson about the peace of God falls on the day that celebrates a revolution (Independence Day in the USA). Our local Unity minister suggested that instead of "Independence Day" we should celebrate "Inner-dependence Day," which I thought was a nice play on words and quite appropriate.

This lesson teaches two seemingly opposing things. First, it teaches us that we do not yet really mean it when we say, "I want the peace of God." For if we meant it, we would have it. "No one can mean these words and not be healed" (2:1).

> Many have said these words. But few indeed have meant them. You have but to look upon the world you see around you to be sure how very few they are. (2:6–8)

Indeed, all you need to do is watch the evening news. Or spend one day at your job.

Second, it teaches us that, in spite of our obvious dedication to things other than peace, at heart we *really do* want the peace of God. All of us do. "We want the peace of God. This is no idle wish" (7:2–3). "You want the peace of God. And so do all who seem to seek for dreams" (10:1–2).

The task the Course sets before us is uncovering and fully accepting *both* of these facts. To accept them fully, they must be accepted as true of everyone, not just of ourselves. Underneath all the seeking for illusions, everyone wants peace. This is something that is universally true, a fact that can be totally depended upon. It is true, as the line I quoted in the last paragraph asserts, even of those who seem to be seeking for something else. They may not be *aware* that the peace of God is what they really want, but it is true, nevertheless (10:4). Our job in interacting with others is to remember this universal longing of every heart, and to join ourselves with it in the other person, even when they are totally unaware of it themselves.

Yet before we can firmly believe that we, and everyone, want the peace of God above all else, we have to face the fact that we have foolishly believed we wanted something else more than peace. For if we wanted only peace, we would have only peace; that is how the power of our minds works. So there must be something, or some things, that we have valued more than peace. Our first job, then, is uncovering these competing desires, assessing them honestly, recognizing that they are only idle wishes, and letting them go in favor of peace.

We want the most amazingly trivial things instead of peace. I watch a young child burst into tears and throw a tantrum because he cannot have his favorite breakfast, and I think, "The only difference between him and me is that I have developed sophisticated ways of camouflaging my tantrums." I share a house with Robert Perry and his family and another single man, and we often have guests. I have found myself losing my peace over empty ice cube trays and vanishing rolls of toilet paper. I have given away my peace in concern about who last emptied the garbage.

Perhaps, today, we can all stop ourselves when these "little" moments of separation occur and ask ourselves, "Is this what I would have, in place of Heaven and the peace of God?" (8:8). Do I really value a roll of toilet paper more than God's peace?

Let me point out one more interesting observation of this lesson: you cannot have peace alone. "The mind which means that all it wants is peace must join with other minds, for that is how peace is obtained" (6:1). To have peace we have to be willing to let the other person into our hearts. We have to recognize their desire for peace equally with our own.

The temptation is always to think, "I want peace; the problem is with the other person." Always remember, though: if you want peace, you will have it. No one else can take it from you. If you cannot be at peace when the other person seems to want something besides peace, what you are teaching that person is that your peace depends on their changing. This just reinforces the same belief in the other person, and they continue to believe that their peace depends on them changing you.

Our job is to see past the competing desires in that other person to the universal reality that lies underneath. However we respond to them, if we are to teach peace, our actions must affirm to that person that peace already lies within them, ready for them as soon as they are willing to receive it. We join our own intent with what they seek above all things (10:4). By our faith in that intent, however hidden it may appear, we draw it out of them; we give them the opportunity to recognize it within themselves and align their mind with it:

> It is this one intent we seek today, uniting our desires with the need of every heart, the call of every mind, the hope that lies beyond despair, the love attack would hide, the brotherhood that hate has sought to sever, but which still remains as God created it. (14:1)

LESSON 186 ✦ JULY 5

"Salvation of the world depends on me."

Practice instructions

Purpose: To go past both your self-made roles and your doubts about your worth and adequacy, and hear and accept your assigned role in God's plan for salvation. This will unify your scattered energies behind a single goal.

Morning/evening quiet time: At least five minutes; ideally, thirty or more.

Today's practice consists of listening to the Holy Spirit, asking for Him to tell you what your role in His plan is (this is similar to Lesson 135). To really listen, you will need to set aside your notions of your roles in life, realizing how shifting they are and how much they scatter your energies. You will need to open your mind to the fact that you have an essential role in the Holy Spirit's plan for the salvation of the world. Don't let your ego tell you that such an idea is arrogant, that you cannot possibly be worthy, that you are not strong enough, wise enough, or holy enough. Banish this arrogant chatter from your mind. Let go of all words. Open your mind and listen in genuine humility. Let the Voice for God reveal to you what He would have you do in His plan. Trust that the role He has selected for you suits you perfectly, that you can do it, because He knows you better than you know yourself. If the role you hear sounds beyond your capabilities, ask yourself who is more likely to be right: your ego's voice or God's Voice?

If you hear nothing, keep repeating your question with genuine desire. And keep setting aside the ego's chatter as it intrudes. Know that you are at the very least drawing closer the day when the answer will be yours.

End the practice period by trying to genuinely "accept the function given you" (10:1). If you have received a sense of what it is, try to accept that as your role in life. If you haven't received anything, try to accept your role in advance.

31

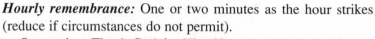

> *Hourly remembrance:* One or two minutes as the hour strikes
> (reduce if circumstances do not permit).
>
> Suggestion: Thank God for His gifts to you in the hour gone
> by. Then let go of your notions of your role in the coming hour,
> and ask God's Voice what role He has selected for you in that
> hour.

Commentary

Our individual salvation and our happiness depends on our accepting
what this lesson teaches: the salvation of the world depends on us. Our
function is to save the world, to bring the light and joy and peace of God
to every mind within our reach—which is a far greater number than we
imagine.

The lesson is not simply saying that it would be a good idea for us to
accept this thought. It is saying that acceptance is imperative to our own
personal freedom:

> There is one way, and only one, to be released from the
> imprisonment your plan to prove the false is true has
> brought to you. Accept the plan you did not make instead.
>
> (5:1–2)

The Course is often so uncompromising: "one way, and only one." If
we want to experience our own wholeness, if we want to find our Self,
we *must* accept that salvation of the world depends on us. Why?
Because the nature of Who we are demands it. If I am an extension of
God, and if Love, which created me, is what I am, then how can I
possibly accept that fact and *not* accept that my function is to give
myself to the world? Giving is what Love does!

To take our place among the saviors of the world is not arrogance, if
we are as God created us. It is merely accepting what has been given to
us by our Creator: "We did not establish [our function]. It is not our
idea" (2:2–3). In fact it is arrogant *not* to acknowledge this as our
function. The self-image we make in arrogance pictures us as weak,
ignorant, and helpless (6:3–4). It seems humble, but it is mountainous
arrogance masquerading as humility. This self-image thumbs its nose at
the Creator and says, "I am what I make of myself, and not what You
created me to be."

The last week or so I have frequently been finding myself feeling at loose ends. I seem to drift from one task to another, and to have a great deal of difficulty concentrating on anything. The description in 10:4 seems to describe me exactly: "The functions which the world esteems are so uncertain that they change ten times an hour at their most secure." And as I read this lesson I recognize that I have been trying to define my function for myself, instead of simply accepting the one God gave me. I have been fighting my function. Yet when it is accepted, it is so unambiguous that life simply straightens out, and all the confusion is gone: "In lovely contrast, certain as the sun's return each morning to dispel the night, your truly given function stands out clear and wholly unambiguous" (11:1).

So then, let me today stop resisting my function. Let me stop listening to my self-made image, which trembles as God speaks to me of my true function, sensing that the basis of its existence is being cut away (7:1–2). Let me simply let go of my plans for myself and surrender to the plan I did not make, trusting that everything I need to fulfill it has been given me; trusting that I am worthy to be counted among the saviors of the world; trusting that all my needs are answered by God, even though He does not see them, in whatever form is most useful at the moment (13:4–5).

> Salvation of the world depends on you who can forgive.
> Such is your function here.   (14:5–6)

LESSON 187 ✦ JULY 6

"I bless the world because I bless myself."

Practice instructions

Purpose: To bless yourself by looking upon the purity in you, and then to bless the world with that same purity. To give the world the lilies of forgiveness you find on the altar within you, and then to find those lilies returned to you, thereby dispelling your belief that giving is sacrifice.

Morning/evening quiet time: At least five minutes; ideally, thirty or more.

This is another meditation aimed at experiencing the purity within you, like Lessons 181 and 182. The lesson speaks of this using the imagery of a holy altar within you, and you may want to use this imagery in your meditation. Quiet your mind and go to find that holy altar in you. You might imagine, as other lessons suggest, that you are traveling through thick fog, until it clears and you reach the altar. Be unafraid to look upon it. There on the altar, you will see the lilies of forgiveness your brother has given you and you have given him. There before the altar, you stand united with all your brothers. With them, repeat the Name of God, for this altar is the place in you that is perfectly devoted to your Father. How can you possibly fear Him when such purity abides in you? This is your true nature, which is so pure and so blessed that looking on it will leave you enraptured. You will forget about all earthly gifts, as the gift of your holiness becomes the only thing you want.

Remarks: This is how you bless yourself, by looking on this holy altar. Now that you have received blessing, you can give it. "Now we are blessed, and now we bless the world" (11:1). So spend the day taking the lilies of forgiveness from your inner altar and giving them to your brothers. The lesson expects that this will often take concrete form: giving of your time, your abilities, and even your material means. If you fear that this is sacrifice, you can afford to laugh at that thought, for whatever you give you receive. Picture the outer gift you are giving as a lily of forgiveness, and realize that this lily will then be laid on *your* altar, as further testament to your purity. From there, this lily will manifest in your life in the "form most helpful" to you (5:7).

Hourly remembrance: One or two minutes as the hour strikes (reduce if circumstances do not permit).

Do a short version of the morning/evening exercise. Close by asking for God's guidance for the coming hour and thanking Him for His gifts in the past hour.

Response to temptation: When tempted to believe you are making a sacrifice.

Repeat the idea and then take the blessing you have been given within, and give it to your brother. All thought of sacrifice will vanish in the face of the receiving and giving of blessing.

Commentary

We find it easy to understand that in order to give a thing, you first must have it. That's obvious. We find it more difficult to believe that giving actually increases what you have.

The key to understanding this, says the lesson, lies in the fact that "things but represent the thoughts that make them" (2:3). To understand how giving away what we have increases it, we have to begin to recognize that "things" are not real; what is real are the thoughts behind them. This is not necessarily saying that if I give $100 to a brother in need I will immediately receive $200 in return from some other source. However, it is saying that when I give $100 away knowing that money is just an idea, I will be increasing the thought that brought money to me in the first place. Therefore, that will eventually result in more money, or more "wealth and abundance" in some form. The form may be identical or it may not:

> Perhaps the form in which the thought seems to appear is changed in giving. Yet it must return to him who gives. Nor can the form it takes be less acceptable. It must be more.
>
> (2:5–8)

In other words, what is returned is always greater than what is given.

I have begun to learn this by giving away ideas directly, in my study group and in my writing. I have indeed found it true that as I give away these ideas, they increase in me. I get at least as much, if not more, benefit than anyone who is "receiving" from me. I am quite aware that I am blessing the world because I am blessing myself; I am doing this for my own benefit.

It is harder when it comes to material things. It is not so easy to make the connection that money is just an idea, or a tape is just an idea, a book is just an idea, a car is just an idea. I learn in little ways. I give away newsletters that cost me money, believing that it will return to me eventually. I give hours of my time to the study group, believing that the return will come. I still *feel* that as basically giving it away. The return has only just begun.

I think when I learn this lesson fully it will be no big deal to give up the idea of ownership entirely and to share everything I possess with anyone who needs it. But I am a long way from that as yet.

The next paragraph is very important:

> Ideas must first belong to you, before you give them. If you are to save the world, you first accept salvation for yourself. But you will not believe that this is done until you see the miracles it brings to everyone you look upon. Herein is the idea of giving clarified and given meaning. Now you can perceive that by your giving is your store increased. (3:1–5)

To give salvation I must first accept it for myself. But to know I have it, I have to give it away. That must mean that I have to start giving before I know I have it! The gift that giving brings is knowing that I have the gift I give.

The lesson advises us to protect what we have by giving it away. It warns, "Yet value not its form" (4:3). In other words, you may not get it back in the exact form you give it. If I give $100 cash, I may receive a gift in a different form: a tape player, computer software, a burst of physical energy, or whatever. If I give away a particular book, I may not ever receive that particular form again, and I have to learn not to value the form, but the thought behind the form. It is foolish to value forms. "No form endures" (4:5). Remember:

> What [the giver] seems to lose is always something he will value less than what will surely be returned to him. (5:8)

Every gift I give is always a gift to myself. I never lose! I gain, and so does the recipient of my gift, especially if he or she learns from me to give again. "Who understands what giving means must laugh at the idea of sacrifice" (6:2). Laugh, because there is no such thing as sacrifice. What I give is given to myself; I never lose, I always gain. How can that be called sacrifice!

The lesson clearly applies this to all forms of "giving" and all forms of "sacrifice," including pain and loss, sickness, grief, poverty, starvation, and death. When I "give up" a relationship in the form I thought I wanted, according to this lesson I receive something I will value far more. Perhaps I may learn to accept the gift of self-sufficiency, for instance.

I'm sure the same will be true as I make other "sacrifices." Mistakenly I fear the "loss" I will feel with these things absent from my life. There will be no loss, no sacrifice. What I gain will far exceed the apparent loss. And in reality I lose nothing except a false identification.

For instance, I think I get a certain satisfaction and comfort from eating a nice meal. The pleasure of the taste; the pleasure of being full. I falsely identify these feelings with the object, the food. But pleasure, satisfaction, and comfort are just the ideas behind the food. If I were to dissociate food from those ideas, I would not be giving up those ideas; I would be affirming them. I retain them, and they grow. There will be pleasure, satisfaction, and comfort in other forms, more lasting and more generalized. I have gained the general form by giving up the specific identification of those ideas with "food."

In general, we will go through many iterations of apparent giving up, apparent sacrifice, until we learn that the thing is not the idea, that no particular form can be identified with the idea behind it. We will learn, eventually, to hold on to no form, but to always value not the form, but the thought behind it.

Ultimately we go beyond the idea of many different thoughts to see only one Thought—the innocent Son of God, the Christ. We see that Thought within ourselves, and "what we have looked upon we would extend, for we would see it everywhere" (11:2). "To ensure this holy sight is ours, we offer it to everything we see" (11:5).

LESSON 188 ✦ JULY 7
"The peace of God is shining in me now."

Practice instructions

Purpose: To go past thoughts of the outer world and so experience the peace of God shining in you now. This brief taste of your goal will strengthen your resolve to reach it completely.

Morning/evening quiet time: At least five minutes; ideally, thirty or more.

This is a meditation in which you seek to contact the peace of God shining in you now. To make sense of the discussion of thoughts in paragraphs 6-9, you might imagine that your thought is a stream or current that stretches all the way from the world outside, which is where your thoughts are focused now, to its source at the center of your being. At the outside of the stream, your thoughts are tainted "by the dream of worldly things outside yourself" (6:6), full of "strange desires and disordered wishes" (9:6). As the stream moves inward, however, your thoughts become "honest thoughts" (6:6) that actually "lead you back to peace" (7:5). They seek the light in you, the peace of God in you. Finally, at the inmost part of the stream, they become "the thoughts we share with God" (9:2), thoughts that are at one with His peace.

Your task in this meditation is to follow this stream inward, to move your thought—your attention—from the stream's outermost place to its innermost place. Begin by withdrawing your thoughts from their focus outside. As you withdraw them, they become washed clean, and they will start to draw you inward, for they feel the call of God. Now "let your thoughts fly to the peace within" (6:4). Trust that "they know the way" (6:5). Let them draw you along that stream until you reach its source, and rest in God.

As your thought reaches the peace of God within, know that that peace will extend from your heart around the world, blessing each living thing and returning to you with all the gifts you gave.

38

"From you salvation radiates with gifts beyond all measure, given and returned" (4:2).

Hourly remembrance: One or two minutes as the hour strikes (reduce if circumstances do not permit).

Repeat, *"The peace of God is shining in me now. Let all things shine upon me in that peace. And let me bless them with the light in me."* Then draw your attention inward and seek the peace of God in you. Finish by thanking God for His gifts in the hour gone by and asking for His guidance in the hour to come.

Response to temptation: When tempted to blame the world for what you thought it did to you.

Realize that the world hasn't done anything to you; what you see is what you chose. So choose that the world be pure and innocent, and lay your "saving blessing on it" (10:5) by repeating, *"The peace of God is shining in me now. Let all things shine upon me in that peace. And let me bless them with the light in me."*

Commentary

I always seem to hear the emphasis in this sentence on the last word, "now." It speaks to me of the holy instant. It tells me that whatever storms seem to be raging in my mind, whatever chaotic circumstances I find myself in, there is within me a constant beacon of peace, forever shining, uninterrupted and uninterruptible. It calls me to stop for a moment, withdraw my attention from all the turmoil that makes up my "life" in this world, and reconnect to that peace. Somewhere within me, there is a place that is always at perfect peace, like the eye of a hurricane. And I can find that place any time I choose to do so, truly desiring to find it.

The Course is consistent in its vision. Nothing separates us from the Love of God. Complete salvation, perfect peace, pure joy, and full forgiveness are always available right now. "Enlightenment is but a recognition, not a change at all" (1:4). What we call enlightenment is simply recognizing the presence of the light, which has never left us. It is realizing that the only reason we cannot see the light is that we have our hands over our eyes. That is why we "need do nothing." We don't have to *do*, we simply *un*do. We stop blocking the light, which is always there.

The particular block being addressed in this lesson (you'll recall that this series of lessons was billed as directly addressing certain specific blocks) is simply the tendency to see enlightenment as a future thing. The opening words sound the keynote: "Why wait for Heaven?" (1:1). "Why wait to find it in the future, or believe it has been lost already, or was never there?" (2:2). All that we need do to discover its reality is to look for it within ourselves, where it has always been.

But the peace of God is not only *within* me, it is *shining in* me. "The peace of God is shining in you now, and from your heart extends around the world" (3:1). I may feel as bottled up as Custer at the Last Stand; I may feel as fertile as the Sahara. But from within my being, nevertheless, the peace of God is being broadcast like a universal beacon to the entire world. My right mind is extending itself in global beneficence to all creation, pausing "to caress each living thing" (3:2) (what a beautiful image that brings to my mind!), and leaving an everlasting blessing with whatever it touches. That is part of what I am bringing to my awareness; that is part of the picture of my Self that I am learning to recognize each time I stop, become quiet, and look within. When the Course tells me that I am among the saviors of the world, it isn't telling me about something I have to *achieve*, it is telling me what I already am.

Within me there is, even now, and even in my darkest moments, a living flow of thoughts of light. There is a heavenly current constantly surging through me to extend love and blessing to the world, and to myself. That flow of thoughts is something I can, in the holy instant, become aware of and tune in to.

"Accept His Word for what you are" (8:2); that is what this lesson is calling on us to do. We read of the Christ, we read of the Buddha and his heart of compassion. The Buddha is you. And that is Jesus' message to us, that we are as he is. "He that saith he abideth in him ought himself also so to walk, even as he walked" (1 Jn 2:6). We are the Christ; that is what we are; that is what we need to accept. It seems too high, too far beyond our concept of ourselves. But in the holy instant, in the quiet, when we withdraw from the world and "let [our] thoughts fly to the peace within" (6:4), we can know ourselves in this way. We can sense the depth of love that wants to express itself through us.

Oh, we may not do such a great job, just yet, at letting that love out. We may get in the way more often than not. But the love that would embrace the world, heal its wounds, and dry its tears is in us, and *is* us. We all know that is so, if we are willing to look at it. We can look upon the whole world today and everyone within it, and we can say:

> We will forgive them all, absolving all the world from what we thought it did to us....Now we choose that it be innocent, devoid of sin and open to salvation. And we lay our saving blessing on it, as we say:

> *The peace of God is shining in me now. Let all things shine upon me in that peace, And let me bless them with the light in me.* (10:2, 4–7)

LESSON 189 ✦ JULY 8
"I feel the Love of God within me now."

Practice instructions

Purpose: To go past all your thoughts of self, world, and God and so experience the Love of God within you now. This will go far towards enabling you to give your total willingness to the Course's way.

Morning/evening quiet time: At least five minutes; ideally, thirty or more.

This is an exercise in what I call "Open Mind Meditation" (for more on this form of meditation, see the cameo essay on page 91). Follow the instructions in paragraph 7 (you may even want to use them as an induction process): Empty your mind of all thoughts and try to let go of all your beliefs as well, including your highest spiritual beliefs. Even ideas from the Course must not be allowed into your mind. "Empty your mind of everything" (7:2). And then stand there, with your mental hands completely open, ready to receive God's Love. Trust that He "knows the way to you" (8:1), and that all you need do is remove the obstacles and "His love will blaze its pathway" (9:4) into your mind. As always, whenever any words or thoughts intrude, repeat the idea and then return to waiting empty-handed for God's Love.

Hourly remembrance: One or two minutes as the hour strikes (reduce if circumstances do not permit).

Do a short version of the morning/evening exercise. Close by asking for God's guidance for the coming hour and thanking Him for His gifts in the past hour.

Commentary

By this point in the Workbook, any time we see the word "now" we should be seeing it as a probable reference to the holy instant. The word "feel" also has significance, directing our attention to the realm of experience, as opposed to conceptual understanding. Given these two points we can realize that this lesson is about entering a holy instant in which we have an experience of God's Love within us.

"There is a light in you the world can not perceive" (1:1). The lesson begins by referring, as did yesterday's lesson, to the light that is within us, inherent in our creation. It is not something visible to the body's sense organs (1:2), but quite visible to a different kind of sight. To see this light and to feel the Love of God are synonymous (1:7). We are being directed to experience this other kind of seeing.

We can see "through darkened eyes of malice and of fear" (3:2), or with a mind permeated with the experience of Love's presence within the mind. What we see within determines how we see the world. Based on our state of mind, we see either a world poised to attack us, or a world that reaches out to bless us. Either picture of the world makes the other picture inconceivable to us (3:5; 4:1).

If I am seeing "a world of hatred rising from attack" (3:5), the description of the world given in paragraph 2 seems to be no more than wishful thinking. People encountering the teaching of the Course for the first time often raise this objection. For instance, I once heard a man who had listened to a lecture on forgiveness say, "You people must be crazy! All you have to do is walk down the street in New York and you can't possibly maintain that love is all there is." He was seeing a world of hatred rising from attack; there was no room left in his mind to see anything else.

If I am seeing the world of hatred, how can I possibly see a world of love? No logical argument will ever change my mind. What is required is something that will change what my mind is seeing within itself, because the world I see is nothing more than a reflection of that, "the outside picture of an inward condition" (T-21.In.1:5). If I am seeing a world of attack it is because within myself I am seeing an attacking mind. "What they have felt in them they look upon, and see its sure reflection everywhere" (4:3). The holy instant can, and does, change that self-perception. "I feel the Love of God within me now." That experience will literally transform the way I see the world. "If you feel the Love of God within you, you will look out on a world of mercy and of love" (5:5).

This is why we are asked to "lay aside all thoughts of what [we] are" (7:1), to be still, and to allow something else to enter our minds. We are being asked to set aside every conclusion we have ever made about

43

anything, to allow—for a moment at least—that all of it may be misinformed and misguided, and to "come with wholly empty hands unto your God" (7:5). In asking us to forget even "this course" (7:5), the lesson is not saying that intellectual comprehension of the Course is not useful, but it is saying that only something that transcends the intellect can truly turn the tide of our wrong perception. Even our understanding of the Course is bound to be distorted when it is based on a mind firmly rooted in fear and in the concept of self we have built up. We may mistakenly use that imperfect understanding to dictate to God the way He should come to us. So we are asked to set even this aside, and to allow God to come to us in whatever way He wants to come.

To forget the Course is not a permanent principle, but a temporary expedient to be practiced in our moments of stillness, designed to allow a new kind of experience. It is merely part of removing the barriers to the experience of ourselves as Love, for even our ego-based "understanding" of the Course can interfere with the experience of its true meaning. So we are being told, when seeking the holy instant, to lay aside any assumption that we understand anything at all. Let everything be open to change. If we are willing to do this, "His Love will blaze its pathway of itself" (9:4).

We cannot force ourselves to see the world differently. But if we can, just for an instant, see *ourselves* differently, and feel the Love of God within ourselves, the way we see the world will change of itself, because the way we see the world *is* the way we see ourselves.

LESSON 190 ✦ JULY 9
"I choose the joy of God instead of pain."

Practice instructions

Purpose: To realize that pain is deceptive illusion, and that joy is reality and truth. To go past pain and experience the joy that lies beyond it. This will help "your scattered goals blend into one intent" (W-pI.In.181-200.1:1).

Morning/evening quiet time: At least five minutes; ideally, thirty or more.

This is a meditation in which you set aside all thought of attack and defense, all judgment and all assault. These are simply attempts to hide your holiness. Lay down these thoughts of war and sink into the stillness of Heaven's peace. In this holy place, you will feel the joy of God arise in you. Here, you will realize that pain, not joy, is the naive illusion. You will understand that joy is reality, it is awakening, and it is truth.

Hourly remembrance: One or two minutes as the hour strikes (reduce if circumstances do not permit).

Do a short version of the morning/evening exercise. Close by asking for God's guidance for the coming hour and thanking Him for His gifts in the past hour.

Response to temptation: (Suggestion) when tempted to think that the world causes your pain.

Realize this is a judgment, and that this judgment is a sword you hold against your throat. Then repeat the idea; choose the joy of God instead of pain.

Commentary

This is a tough lesson. It confronts us with another of those blocks we've been talking about: the apparent reality of pain. As the lesson very clearly states, pain seems to bear witness to "a nightmare of abandonment by an Eternal Love" (2:5). "It witnesses to God the Father's hatred of His Son" (1:7).

45

Anyone who has experienced serious pain knows what this is talking about. Anyone who has had a loved one endure deep, constant pain knows the questions it raises in the mind. "How could God allow this to happen, if He is love?" Even the milder forms of pain tell the same story, raise the same questions.

I am not going to pretend that I have entirely succeeded in removing this block from my mind. I find it hard to write about this lesson because I recognize that a very present part of me still sees pain as real, rather than illusion. Yet, I do believe that what the lesson says is true. I choose to believe it, and I want to believe it. So I do not see myself as being in conflict over this issue. I am learning, more and more, to look my fears straight in the face, and to recognize that I still do believe, in large measure, that pain is real. And if this lesson is true, this must mean that part of me believes there is no God (3:3–4), that the impossible has happened, and Eternal Love has abandoned me. If I have been reading the Text with any discernment, this is not news to me.

What then? Do I need to wallow in guilt because my mind has not yet been entirely renewed? Of course not:

> The time has come to laugh at such insane ideas. There is
> no need to think of them as savage crimes, or secret sins
> with weighty consequence. (4:2–3)

If the way to remember the Love of God is to look without judgment on my denial of Him, then seeing these "insane ideas" in my mind is a necessary part of the process, and an indication of progress, not regression. And the cure is not guilt, but laughter!

Basically, we have two choices in regard to pain. Either it is caused by something outside of us, which means ultimately that we are innocents suffering at the hands of an angry God (or that there is no God and we are subject to blind fate), or it is caused by myself, my own thoughts. If the former is true I have no hope of escape. If the latter is true, I *can* escape by changing my thoughts. I prefer to believe the latter! Even if I am wrong, what have I got to lose?

The Course's position is crystal clear:

> It is your thoughts alone that cause you pain. Nothing
> external to your mind can hurt or injure you in any way....
> No one but yourself affects you. (5:1–2, 4)

It takes some practice to learn to use these thoughts without any guilt. We are responsible, but not guilty; the Course is very clear on that as well. It also takes practice, perhaps even more, to use these thoughts when interacting with someone else who is in pain. May God forbid that we should ever use this line of reasoning to make someone guilty for their pain! The Course is equally clear that if we are unable as yet to fully accept this, if our level of fear is still too high to rely solely upon the mind to relieve pain, a compromise approach is necessary. To attempt to forgo medication, for instance, when to do so increases our fear, is counterproductive (see T-2.IV.3–5 and T-2.V.2). Healing is the release from fear; what increases fear cannot be healing.

Let me, then, learn to increasingly apply this lesson in ways that my level of fear can tolerate. Let me realize, for instance, that the person who cuts me off in traffic has not hurt me; only my thoughts about it hurt me. Let me realize that the person who seems to reject my love has not brought me any pain; only my thoughts about it cause me pain. Let me practice with physical pain as well as I can; if I have a headache, upset stomach, or cold, let me realize that my thoughts are the source, not anything outside of my mind. Let me realize that if I take medication I am masking the symptom, not curing the problem, and let me give equal attention to the healing of my mind. If I experience more severe or chronic pain, let me deny what it seems to witness to (God's anger or nonexistence), laugh at the idea that God is angry, and realize that the pain is only showing me that my mind is mistaken in what I think I am (2:3). Let me not focus on making the pain go away, but on healing the thinking that causes it. Using "magic" (physical means) to alleviate the pain while I devote myself to retraining my mind simply makes sense, and frees my mind to do what it needs to do.

And let me take frequent holy instants, to "come without defense into the quiet place where Heaven's peace holds all things still at last" (9:1). Let me feel the Love of God within me, and set aside my unmerciful self-judgment (9:4), even if I can do so only momentarily. I can testify to having experienced this, at least; I have seen pain disappear during the holy instant, both in myself and in a friend who was in chronic pain. These holy instants can train us to experience deeper and more lasting release from all pain, and liberate the joy that has been smothered by our pain.

> Pain is illusion; joy, reality. Pain is but sleep; joy is awakening. Pain is deception; joy alone is truth.   (10:4–6)

LESSON 191 ✦ JULY 10
"I am the holy Son of God Himself."

Practice instructions

Purpose: To go past your self-perception as weak, frail, and afraid—which comes from the denial of your Identity—and remember that you are the holy Son of God Himself. This will release you and will save the world from suffering.

Morning/evening quiet time: At least five minutes; ideally, thirty or more.

There are no specific instructions for the longer practice periods, just a strong focus on the use of these lines: *"I am the holy Son of God Himself ["Himself," by the way, refers to God]. I cannot suffer, cannot be in pain; I cannot suffer loss, nor fail to do all that salvation asks."* By saying and meaning these lines, you reverse your denial of your Identity. You accept the power and glory that is your true nature. You typically see the world as your jailer, filled with enemies massed against you. Yet this role is not inherent in the world. Rather, your denial of your Identity turns the world into this in order to support your false identity. Your denial imprisons the world. Thus, when you reverse that denial (through the words of today's practice), you set the world free. By unveiling your glory as God's Son, you release those in chains, those who see no mercy in the world, those who suffer pain, and even those who die. This is your motivation to practice today—their release and your release.

Beyond devoting some time to repeating these words, with as much certainty and sincerity as possible, the rest of the practice period is up to you—to your inspiration and your guidance from the Holy Spirit. You can't go wrong with meditation, especially since nine of the last eleven lessons have been devoted to it.

Hourly remembrance: One or two minutes as the hour strikes (reduce if circumstances do not permit).

Do a short version of the morning/evening exercise. Close by asking for God's guidance for the coming hour and thanking Him for His gifts in the past hour.

Commentary

Once again the Course sounds its keynote: You are as God created you. Anything God creates is like Himself—holy, sinless, guiltless, an endless spring of love, and immortal. To put a different twist on a familiar saying, we are not human beings seeking a spiritual experience; we are spiritual beings who *think* we are having a human experience. We did not suddenly spring into existence at birth, and we do not pass out of existence when the body stops functioning. We are aspects of an immortal being, existing entirely outside of time. "I am the holy Son of God Himself."

How we see ourselves determines how we see the world. It may not be obvious at first, but if we see ourselves as other than the holy Son of God, we are "giving to the world the role of jailer to the Son of God" (1:3). If we see ourselves as separate, isolated beings, we are inevitably cast in the role of victim. We become a mote of dust in a hurricane, whirled about by the universe without any consideration for our wellbeing (3:2).

The world then takes on an appearance that reflects this mistaken identity we have assumed. The whole world witnesses to our frailty; all our experience here seems to testify that death is certain, and loss inevitable (2:5–6). That is what projection does. The world becomes our jailer, our victimizer. If we deny our Identity as the holy Son of God, as God created us, we make the world into a place of chaos, evil, sin, and death. We then resent the world for it, although we have laid this role on the world! As I look at the world today, let me ask myself, "What have I done that this should be my world?" And let me answer myself, "I have denied my Identity as God's Son." Thus, to accept my Identity is to forgive the world for what it did not do to me.

Rectify that single mistake, and we have changed the world we see. The world cannot truly be as we see it, because Identity cannot truly be denied. Our imagined identity as *not-the-Son-of-God* is no more than a silly game, with no real effects and no real consequences. If we can begin to accept our Identity, all illusions that derive from this error disappear (4:1–6).

Again we are asked to "practice" recognizing our Identity in the holy instant. For a brief time, we "let today's idea find a place among [our] thoughts" (5:1). In that holy instant we rise far above the world (5:1) into a place of safety, where we recognize the impossibility of the world's victimizing us, because we see our own eternal, invulnerable nature. And from that place of safety we *return* to the world and set it free (5:2). Notice the similarity of this description to the earlier one in Lesson 184 (paragraph 10). In the holy instant we accept Atonement for ourselves, we recognize our true Identity. And then we return to bring the message of this shared Identity to all the world, that it may be free with us.

The realization of our Identity is enough to free us from every problem forever, and to free the world with us. To cling to our little, individual identity is to perpetuate "a devastating image of yourself walking the world in terror, with the world twisting in agony because your fears have laid the mark of death upon its heart" (6:5). Do I really want to go on playing this silly, tragic game? Do I want to continue to hold the world to task because it has not met my needs, but has denied me what is my right? Or will I recognize today that I have done this, I have denied my Self and blamed the world for it?

In the latter part of this lesson it speaks in glowing terms of "the Son of God" Who "has come in glory to redeem the lost" (8:3). Who is this "Son of God"? It is not speaking of Jesus. It is speaking of *you and me*. It appeals to us to realize that our glory is the light that saves the world, and asks us not to withhold it (10:5–6). It asks us to see the suffering in the world (not to brush over it, saying, "It's only an illusion!"), and to find it in our hearts to respond to it (10:7–8).

How can we release our brothers from suffering? By accepting our own release, by finding our own Identity (11:1–5).

> You are the holy Son of God Himself. Remember this, and all the world is free. Remember this, and earth and Heaven are one. (11:6–8)

LESSON 192 ✦ JULY 11
"I have a function God would have me fill."

Practice instructions

Purpose: To fulfill your function by forgiving your brother his sins and so experiencing that you are what he is: the Son of God. This experience will firm up "your willingness to make your weak commitment strong" (W-pI.In.181-200.1:1).

Morning/evening quiet time: At least five minutes; ideally, thirty or more.

As with yesterday, there are no specific instructions for today's practice. Begin, as always, by repeating the idea, and then spend the time doing practice that you have found helpful and that you feel prompted from within to do. You may want to meditate, using either Down-and-Inward Meditation, Name of God Meditation, or Open Mind Meditation. Or you may want to focus on forgiving those people whom you are holding prisoner.

Hourly remembrance: One or two minutes as the hour strikes (reduce if circumstances do not permit).

Spend the first minute or so as you choose, perhaps in quiet meditation or focusing on forgiveness. Close by asking for God's guidance for the coming hour and thanking Him for His gifts in the past hour.

Response to temptation: When a brother tempts you to be angry. "Realize you hold a sword above your head" (9:4). You may even picture this in your mind. Choose to avert the sword by repeating the idea, which means that your function on earth is to forgive, to let go of anger. Realize that you owe this brother thanks, for he has given you a blessed opportunity to choose right and free yourself.

Commentary

In Heaven we have a high and holy function: it is creation. The first paragraph describes it as well as it can be put into words, although when it comes down to it we on earth cannot even truly conceive of what it is (3:1). Creation is to complete God, to extend Love in His Name. What does that mean? We cannot fully know until we are there again, experiencing its meaning directly.

On earth, therefore, we have "a function in the world in its own terms" (2:1), something we can grasp and understand in the context in which we find ourselves. "Forgiveness represents your function here" (2:3). "Forgiveness is the closest it [creation] can come to earth" (3:3). Creation is formless; forgiveness is creation translated into form, a kindly dream so close to Heaven that, when we fully enter into it, our eyes are "already opening [to] behold the joyful sights" (3:6) the happy dreams are offering us.

Forgiveness as presented in the Course is far more than just letting go of specific grievances we hold against those we feel have wronged us. It is a radical shift in our perception of the entire world. The basic stance of the ego is to see the world as the cause of our unhappiness. There seems to be ample reason for such a view. How can we ever be content when nothing lasts, when pain and suffering seem to be everywhere, when things and persons dear to us are snatched away by fate, and when, no matter what we do, death awaits us at the end? Forgiveness means that we set aside such a view of the world, and allow the Holy Spirit to replace it all with a new perception. It includes even a reassessment of our own bodies, in which we disidentify with them and no longer see ourselves as bound to them. We come to see the body as "a simple teaching aid, to be laid by when learning is complete, but hardly changing him who learns at all" (4:3). We realize that we are, in reality, a "mind without a body" (5:1). "Only forgiveness can relieve the mind of thinking that the body is its home" (5:5).

That is the goal to which the Course is leading us. Yet although forgiveness is far more than letting go of specific grievances, it begins there. Through working with the specifics we learn the principles, and gradually learn to generalize them and apply them to the entire world, including our physical cages.

It may seem we are being asked to give up a lot. Indeed, we are being asked, eventually, to give up the entire world, including our bodies; this entire "life" in which we think we live. Yet, when it has been achieved, when our anger at the world is gone, we

will perceive that, for Christ's vision and the gift of sight, no sacrifice was asked, and only pain was lifted from a sick and tortured mind. Is this unwelcome? Is it to be feared?

(6:1–3)

If we can come to forgive the world, we will see it as the illusion it has always been, and let it go gladly, aware that it was never more than a nightmare of pain and death. Paradoxically, if we have not forgiven it, we end up "worshipping what is not there" (7:4). We value it precisely because it punishes us, because in our insanity of guilt we secretly believe we deserve it.

Our anger at the world imprisons us. We become the jailer, vigilant to hold the world at fault, and in so doing condemning ourselves to prison with the prisoners we are watching. Unless the "jailer" forgives "everyone he sees or thinks of or imagines" (8:1), he has to live in the jail keeping watch on the criminals. This is the very thing that holds us to this world; not its beauty, not its potential, but our anger at it for not being what we think it should be. Our anger is holding a sword above our own heads (9:4).

Therefore, the way out of prison is to release all the prisoners. We can learn this by recognizing that every time we are tempted to be angry, which can be anything from intense fury to a mild twinge of annoyance (see W-pI.21.2:5), we are being offered an opportunity to release ourselves. We can be merciful instead of wrathful. We can forgive. We can even be grateful for the opportunity (9:7). This is our only true function here (10:6). This is *the* lesson all of life is teaching us. This is *A Course in Miracles*.

LESSON 193 ✦ JULY 12
"All things are lessons God would have me learn."

Practice instructions

Purpose: To learn the lesson that God would have you learn in every situation: forgiveness. To "overcome a thousand seeming obstacles to peace in just one day" (10:1) by applying forgiveness to every painful, worrisome situation.

Morning/evening quiet time: At least five minutes; ideally, thirty or more.

Repeat the idea. Then search your mind for all the things you kept to solve by yourself, instead of giving them to the Holy Spirit. With each one you uncover, turn it over to Him by repeating, *"I will forgive, and this will disappear"* (or by saying to yourself, *"Forgive, and you will see this differently"*). Realize that any pain in the situation that seems real comes from your own unforgiveness, not from the situation itself, and that as you forgive, the pain will disappear. This is how you learn the lessons contained in each situation.

Remarks: Give as much time to your morning and evening practice as you can, and then "give a little more" (11:1). "Do not let the time be less than meets your deepest need" (10:6), for you can free yourself from a thousand obstacles to peace today and go in haste to your Father's house. This is time's true purpose.

Hourly remembrance: One or two minutes as the hour strikes (reduce if circumstances do not permit).

We begin a new form of hourly practice today. Search your mind for any happenings of the previous hour that have any negative feeling attached to them. Apply the lesson to each one, saying either *"I will forgive, and this will disappear"* or *"Forgive, and you will see this differently."* By doing this, you enter each new hour free of the old one. "Thus will you remain unbound, in peace eternal in the world of time" (12:5).

Response to temptation: Whenever pain seems real, whenever you feel apprehension, care, terror, or distress.

Remember that "there is a way to look on everything that lets it be to you another step to Him, and to salvation of the world" (13:1). Then repeat, *"I will forgive, and this will disappear"* or *"Forgive, and you will see this differently."* These words "give you power over all events that seem to have been given power over you" (6:3). They "release all minds from bondage" (6:2). They are the key to Heaven's gate.

Commentary

The central thought of this lesson sounds similar to things said in many spiritual teachings: There is a lesson in everything, if we are open to see it and to learn. But the meaning here is quite different. Many people believe that every event, even every adversity, carries some meaning for us. "What is the lesson in this for me?" is the natural question when something seems to go wrong. If we follow this line of thinking, we can spend a great deal of our time trying to figure out the answer to that question, over and over, and we can become quite puzzled at times when we cannot seem to find what "the lesson" is.

But this Workbook lesson is quite forthright in telling us, flat out, that the lesson is always the same in content, no matter what the form. We do not need to waste our efforts trying to figure out what the lesson is. There is only one lesson. It is always the same:

> Each lesson has a central thought, the same in all of them.
> The form alone is changed, with different circumstances
> and events; with different characters and different themes,
> apparent but not real. They are the same in fundamental
> content. It is this:
>
> *Forgive, and you will see this differently.*   (3:3–7)

Lest we miss the point, it is stated again in slightly different words towards the end of the lesson:

> This is the lesson God would have you learn: There is a
> way to look on everything that lets it be to you another step
> to Him, and to salvation of the world. To all that speaks of
> terror, answer thus:

55

I will forgive, and this will disappear.   (13:1–3)

Forgiveness is the central theme of the Course. It entails, as we saw yesterday, a radical shift in our perception, one that allows the light of Heaven to shine upon everything we see. Forgiveness is the one lesson that everything, literally everything, is teaching us. Everything can teach us this lesson because, in our madness, we have a grievance against the universe. What the Course is teaching us is a different way of looking on everything, a way that allows us to see it not as a threat, not as some kind of loss, not as an attack that deprives us of our happiness, but as a step to God, and to the salvation of the world.

When the Course tells us, as it did in earlier lessons, that forgiveness offers everything we want, that forgiveness is the key to happiness, we cannot at first understand. We are confused by the message because we do not see unforgiveness as a major problem in our lives. The lesson recognizes this:

Certain it is that all distress does not appear to be but unforgiveness. Yet that is the content underneath the form.
(4:1–2)

The consistent direction of the Course's instruction is towards helping us to recognize, in all the wide variety of forms of distress in our lives, this same underlying content. Gradually, as we study the Course and apply it to our daily lives, we begin to recognize the one, unique problem that besets us, whatever form it may appear to take: unforgiveness. Forgiveness is the answer to every problem, the "hidden" lesson in every distressing event of our lives.

I am not saying that you had a flat tire because you got angry at the grocery clerk, nor that you suffer lack of success in your relationships because you haven't forgiven your mother or father. Although sometimes such things may be true, the lesson God is trying to teach us is more far-reaching than that. What ultimately must be corrected is our unforgiveness of everything and everyone in the world, everything that appears to be outside of our own minds. Our general attitude towards the world is at issue here.

When I first read this lesson, I thought it was saying that whenever something went wrong in my life I had to start searching my heart for what or whom I had not forgiven. Often that search was just as frustrating as trying to figure out "What is the lesson in this?" I went through a period in which, one by one, I dug up every imaginable grievance I had against anyone, and tried to let it go. That can be a useful exercise, but it is only scratching the surface of what real forgiveness means. Forgiveness is aimed at transforming my perception of everything I see.

What does the Course mean by unforgiveness, or misperception? Hear this very clear definition, and let it sink into your awareness:

> How can you tell when you are seeing wrong, or some- one else is failing to perceive the lesson he should learn? Does pain seem real in the perception? If it does, be sure the lesson is not learned. And there remains an unforgive- ness hiding in the mind that sees the pain through eyes the mind directs. (7:1–4)

"Does pain seem real in the perception?" That is the sure indicator of unforgiveness, as the Course understands it. Remember that difficult Workbook lesson about choosing the joy of God instead of pain (Lesson 190)? Forgiveness is the answer. What is forgiven no longer hurts. In response to the question "How can you tell when you have really forgiven someone?" someone once said, "You know you have forgiven someone when you feel comfortable in their presence." That is saying the same thing; when you have forgiven, there is no more pain. Another way of picturing it is that you are free to laugh with the person. God's Will is that laughter should replace all tears (9:4–5).

Forgiveness is what time was made for (10:4). This is where our attention is best focused. This is what speeds us on the way to Heaven. In our quiet practice times, we can "think about all things we saved to settle by ourselves, and kept apart from healing" (11:4). We do not know how to look on them so that they disappear, but the Holy Spirit knows; give them to Him. We are even advised to stop every hour, review the hour that has passed, and bring each little grievance to Him for healing, so that it does not carry over into the hour that follows. "Let no one hour cast its shadow on the one that follows" (12:4). This is the way we learn to "remain unbound, in peace eternal in the world of time" (12:5).

LESSON 194 ✦ JULY 13
"I place the future in the Hands of God."

Practice instructions

Purpose: To accept today's idea, and so pass countless obstacles and set your foot on the lawns before the gate of Heaven. This is the last of the Workbook's giant strides.

Morning/evening quiet time: At least five minutes; ideally, thirty or more.

Today again there are no specific practice instructions for morning and evening. I would suggest beginning by going through the various situations that are causing you concern (see W-pI.47.4-5) and, with each one, repeating, *"I place the future in the Hands of God."* Then, after about ten minutes of this, spend the rest of your time in meditation, resting untroubled in God's Hands, sure that only good can come to you.

Hourly remembrance: One or two minutes as the hour strikes (reduce if circumstances do not permit).

Review the happenings of the previous hour that are still weighing on you, and with each one, release the pain it appears to thrust on you by repeating, *"I place the future in the Hands of God."*

Response to temptation: Whenever you feel tempted to become upset.

Quickly react by repeating today's idea, realizing that this is an appeal to God to choose for you to abandon temptation. And as you leave temptation behind, the world does as well.

Remarks: If you really see the value in today's idea, you'll give consistent effort to making it part of your thinking, both today and afterward. Do your utmost to make it a rule of thought, "a habit in your problem-solving repertoire" (6:2), a key device in your response-to-temptation toolkit.

Commentary

The block to remembering our Self that is dealt with in today's lesson is the "fear of future pain" (7:6). Again, the holy instant is a major part of the remedy. All the references to "in no one instant" (3:1; 3:2; 3:3) and "the instant in which time escapes the bondage of illusions" (5:2) are indirect references to the holy instant, which is directly referred to in 5:3: "Then is each instant which was slave to time transformed into a holy instant."

The idea is a simple one: placing the future into God's Hands. Yet it is referred to as another "giant stride" toward quick salvation (1:1; the other "giant strides" were in Lessons 61, 66, 94, and 135). This giant stride is said to take us all the way to the lawns that welcome us to Heaven's gate. It is the remedy for anxiety, pits of hell, depression, thoughts of sin, and guilt. How can this simple idea be so powerful?

Think, for a moment, how your life and your mental attitude would change if you deeply and fully knew—not just *believed* but *knew*—that your future was wholly in the Hands of a loving God. Isn't it fairly easy to see how this would remove anxiety, fears of hell, depression, temptation, and even guilt? Simple as it is, this is an extremely powerful idea, and a powerful one to practice.

Once again we are not expected to suddenly shift from a state of near-constant anxiety (Ernest Becker, in his book *The Denial of Death*,[1] refers to man's so-called normal state as one in which there is "the rumble of panic underneath everything") to one of blissful trust in God. We are being asked to practice having *instants* of such trust, free of panic. For a moment, just for a moment, "let the future go, and place it in God's Hands" (4:5). In so doing, we will understand that by doing this we have given past and present to God as well. In that holy instant we will be free of grief and misery, pain and loss. The light within us will be free to shine and bless the world.

In any particular instant, when we take that instant for itself, without past or future, we cannot feel depression, experience pain, or perceive loss; nor can we experience sorrow, or even die (3:1–3). Every such experience depends on our awareness of the past or future to sustain it and give it the illusion of reality, but none of them exist in the present moment.

Take grief, for instance. Grief is so clearly based on the past that it hardly requires explanation to say that if the past were momentarily put out of our minds, grief would vanish. The mind is calling up memories of our loved one, and then insisting that the absence of that loved one now demands emotional pain. Yet when the loved one was part of our life, there were thousands of moments in which they were not physically present with us, and we were still happy; why, then, cannot we be happy now? Grief is really nothing more than a cruel mental trick we are playing on ourselves. The future enters into grief because we envision an endless string of moments that lack the beloved. But those moments are not now; again, it is a mental trick. Grief does not exist when we are wholly in the present moment, in the holy instant.

As we learn to give the future into God's Hands, one instant after another, we are released. "And so each instant given unto God in passing, with the next one given Him already, is a time of your release from sadness, pain and even death itself" (3:4). Note the similarity to yesterday's practice of applying forgiveness at the end of each hour to all that has passed in the hour, freeing the hour that follows. This kind of thing, says the lesson, needs to become "a thought that rules your mind, a habit in your problem-solving repertoire, a way of quick reaction to temptation" (6:2). That is what all this practice is about: developing new *habits* of spirituality that break the pattern of our deranged thinking, freeing us for a new experience. The more we experience, the more we will want it, until eventually it takes over our minds entirely.

---

1. Ernest Becker, *The Denial of Death* (New York: Free Press, 1997).

LESSON 195 ✦ JULY 14
"Love is the way I walk in gratitude."

Practice instructions

Purpose: To "learn to think of gratitude in place of anger, malice and revenge" (9:1). To let true gratitude replace our ungrateful attitude (in which we feel pushed about by the world) and our unloving gratitude (in which we thank God that we're better off than others).

Morning/evening quiet time: At least five minutes; ideally, thirty or more.

Again we are given no specific instructions. We are only told that today is a day for learning gratitude. This means replacing both our ungrateful attitude (see 9:3) and our unloving gratitude with true, *loving* gratitude. Unloving gratitude means being thankful because we are better off than others. This obviously involves comparisons, which are essentially competitive and therefore unloving. "Love makes no comparisons" (4:2). Loving gratitude thanks God for blessings that He has bestowed on everyone, not just on us. It also means being thankful for *all* our brothers, even those "who walk the way of hatred and the path of death" (5:2).

Given this, you may want to spend the longer practice periods trying, in some way, to replace your ungrateful attitude and your unloving gratitude with true gratitude. You may want to thank God for the items on the list below. According to the lesson, we should be grateful:

- "to Him alone Who made all cause of sorrow disappear throughout the world" (1:7)
- "to One Who offers you the certain means whereby all pain is healed" (2:2)
- "to God our Father that in us all things will find their freedom" (4:4)
- for "the sick, the weak, the needy and afraid, and those who mourn a seeming loss or feel apparent pain, who suffer

cold or hunger, or who walk the way of hatred and the path of death" (5:2)

- "that we are separate from no living thing, and therefore one with Him" (6:1)
- for our brothers (7:2) and "for every living thing" (6:3)
- "that everything has earned the right to love by being loving, even as your Self" (8:6)
- that "We have been given everything" (9:2)
- that "God has cared for us, and calls us Son" (9:5)

You can also thank God for specific blessings you have received, but you must choose to view these as windows onto the nonspecific blessings He bestows on everyone.

Hourly remembrance: One or two minutes as the hour strikes (reduce if circumstances do not permit).

Review the happenings of the previous hour that are still weighing on you, and let each one go by repeating, *"Love is the way I walk in gratitude."* Imagine yourself walking the pathway of love, without a care in the world, filled with gratitude toward your Father for the gift of everything.

Response to temptation: Whenever you feel mercilessly pushed about by the world.

Repeat the idea, replacing your exasperation with true gratitude, which is justified, since God has given you everything.

Commentary

Gratitude is viewed in this lesson both from a dark side and a light side. The lesson first considers how, so very often, when our thinking is aligned with our egos, our gratitude is really a kind of attack on others. Then, it goes on to consider sincere gratitude, which can only occur when joined with love (4:3).

The dark side of gratitude comes from an ego perspective. This is the "gratitude" that prays, "Thank God I am not as others; thank God I am better off." It is the kind of gratitude based firmly on comparisons. It is the thankfulness we feel when we have a bigger house than others, a better car, a more attractive spouse. It is a kind of thankfulness that depends on others who have less, who suffer more than we do. It comes from a view that sees our brother as the rival for our peace (3:1), and rejoices when he is in distress. This kind of "gratitude" is really nothing more than a form of vengeance. And if we examine ourselves honestly we will find ourselves indulging in this kind of false gratitude far more often than we realize.

True gratitude is something far different. "We thank our Father for one thing alone; that we are separate from no living thing, and therefore one with Him" (6:1). "We offer thanks to God our Father that in us all things will find their freedom. It will never be that some are loosed while others still are bound" (4:4–5). This gratitude gives "thanks for every living thing, for otherwise we offer thanks for nothing" (6:3).

Today I am joyful that the gifts I have received belong to everyone. I am grateful for every living thing, every person I meet. I rejoice that everyone goes with me, that no one is excluded. I am grateful that each of you who reads this is a part of me, that none of you can ever lose your inheritance and so diminish me. I recognize that if anyone is diminished, I am diminished, and I thank God that "everything has earned the right to love by being loving," for all is part of my Self (8:6).

Today, if I feel badgered by the world, or pushed about without any thought or care for me, I will choose to replace such foolish thoughts with gratitude (9:1–4). "God has cared for us, and calls us Son. Can there be more than this?" (9:5–6).

Another word for gratitude is "appreciation." I offer you these thoughts about appreciation from the Course:

> Only one equal gift can be offered to the equal Sons of God, and that is full appreciation.   (T-6.V(A).4:7)

> Only honor is a fitting gift for those whom God Himself created worthy of honor, and whom He honors. Give them the appreciation God accords them always, because they are His beloved Sons in whom He is well pleased.
> (T-7.VII.6:1–2)

> There are no idolaters in the Kingdom, but there is great appreciation for everything that God created, because of the calm knowledge that each one is part of Him.
> (T-10.III.6:1)

> God knows His Son as wholly blameless as Himself, and He is approached through the appreciation of His Son.

(T-11.IV.7:2)

Only appreciation is an appropriate response to your brother. Gratitude is due him for both his loving thoughts and his appeals for help, for both are capable of bringing love into your awareness if you perceive them truly.

(T-12.I.6:1–2)

In the holy instant we share our faith in God's Son because we recognize, together, that he is wholly worthy of it, and in our appreciation of his worth we cannot doubt his holiness. And so we love him.   (T-15.VI.2:5–6)

LESSON 196 ✦ JULY 15
"It can be but myself I crucify."

Practice instructions

Purpose: To realize the truth of today's idea and thereby take an important step forward, so that you may go ahead from here quickly, taking each future step as it comes to you.

Morning/evening quiet time: At least five minutes; ideally, thirty or more.

As usual with these final lessons of Part I, we are given no specific instructions. We are simply told to take a major step forward in our awakening by practicing today's idea. To do this, we must see the idea not as a statement that we are doomed to continually crucify ourselves, but as a statement of liberation, which contains "the light of resurrection" (3:4) and "salvation's song" (9:1). Our belief in the opposite of today's idea—that we can crucify others yet remain free ourselves—has unconsciously convinced us that God is our "deadly enemy" (5:5), Who has been using the world's injustices to punish us for our unkindness.

Today's idea is the antidote for that. We must devote our practicing, therefore, to doing our utmost to realize the truth of this idea. This may involve applying it to specific examples in our life, or perhaps letting related thoughts come (see Lesson 42), or some other practice. The idea contains the most wonderful news, that we never actually crucify others, and therefore that God is not out to punish us. Instead, there is a murderer within us, who tricks us into attacking others so that it can crucify us from within. We must strive today to realize this. We must pray to enter into an instant of profound inner discovery, in which we look upon the murderer within, and realize that *it*, not God, is the source of all our pain. Only then can we truly, deeply view God as our Friend, and call on Him to save us from the murderer within.

Hourly remembrance: One or two minutes as the hour strikes (reduce if circumstances do not permit).

Search your mind for the happenings of the previous hour in which you felt crucified by the world, or in which you felt tempted to crucify others. In response to each one, repeat the idea.

Commentary

This is a restatement of one of the fundamental lessons of the Course, the first step of forgiveness in another form: taking the problem back from outside ourselves, withdrawing the projection, and seeing that "I am doing this to myself."

The ego likes to misuse this idea to punish us, or to make us think we inevitably punish ourselves. The ego makes us think we are inherently self-destructive. The truth is, we do self-destructive things but we have a choice in the matter. We don't have to do that, and at the core it is not our will to do so. We are not devils; we are the holy Son of God.

The block to awareness this lesson addresses is our belief that we have injured or "crucified" the world. It is the belief that we have made ourselves into monsters who cannot be trusted, ready to lash out without provocation to hurt and to kill.

The Course calls the acceptance of today's idea—that any way in which we crucify another is actually crucifying ourselves—"one step we take in leading us from bondage to the state of perfect freedom" (4:1). It urges us to take "every step in its appointed sequence" (4:2), that is, not to skip steps. Today's idea is a step that is differentiating self from the body and the ego:

> Thus do you also teach your mind that you are not an
> ego…You will not believe you are a body to be crucified.
>
> > (3:1, 3)

Because we believe we made ourselves into egos, we think we are guilty. Because we believe in guilt, we made the body to suffer punishment. Recognizing that we are the ones inflicting punishment upon ourselves is the first step in freeing ourselves from the whole mess. To recognize that we are the ones inflicting punishment we have to step back from the ego and body, and become aware of a greater part of ourselves. We thus realize that the Self is something other than ego or body, something greater than both. This something greater also includes my brothers and sisters. We are all part of that Self. The "others" I thought I injured are really parts of my Self.

If I believe that I can "attack another and be free" myself (6:1), I am really reacting, says the lesson, from a hidden fear of God; from the belief that God is other, an enemy who waits to destroy me. My relationship to those around me always reflects the unconscious belief I have about my relationship to God, to the ultimate Unity and Whole. "The fear of God is real to anyone who thinks this thought [that I can attack another and be free myself] is true" (6:4). If I can attack another and still be free, so can God. Therefore, God is to be feared.

Paragraph 7 seems crucial to me. It is saying that the thought I can attack others and still be free has to be *changed in form* before I can even question the idea, at least to the point where I stop being afraid of retaliation and start to become responsible, start to realize that "it is but your thoughts that bring you fear, and your deliverance depends on you" (7:3). If I begin to realize that I am not attacking others, but attacking myself, I can stop being afraid of retaliation from these "others" I thought I was attacking. Before this thought changes, I am afraid of others; after it changes, I realize my fear is coming from my own thoughts. If that is true, I have the potential for changing those thoughts.

It seems to me from the lesson that the turning point, the point at which the fear begins to abate, is found in 9:2: "If it can but be you you crucify, you did not hurt the world, and need not fear its vengeance and pursuit." Freedom from fear of vengeance from the world is the start of freedom from fear of God, when "God...can be welcomed back within the holy mind He never left" (8:5).

I feared my own strength and freedom because I thought I was dangerous! I thought I was a threat to the world; I thought that I had injured it. No wonder I don't want to be strong and free. If I were, I might destroy the universe. I thought I might attack and damage things to the point where the universe would turn in anger and wipe me from the face of the earth. In fact I have secretly believed, all along, that this describes things exactly as they are, and that is why I have been afraid, both of the world and of God.

The Course seems to be saying here that our unconscious fear of ourselves, hidden by our projection of cause to outside factors, has to become conscious, at least for a brief, terrifying moment. "When you realize, once and for all, that it is you you fear, the mind perceives itself as split" (10:2). "Now, for an instant, is a murderer perceived within you, eager for your death, intent on plotting punishment for you until the time when it can kill at last" (11:1).

This seems like a terrible moment; why would we deliberately seek it? "Yet in this instant is the time as well in which salvation comes" (11:2). Now, seeing the enemy within instead of outside our mind, we no longer have reason to fear God. Recognition of our own terrible responsibility makes us realize that it has not been God punishing us; it has been ourselves. We stop projecting our own dreams of vengeance onto God. "And you can call on Him to save you from illusions by His Love, calling Him Father and yourself His Son" (11:4).

LESSON 197 ✦ JULY 16
"It can be but my gratitude I earn."

Practice instructions

Purpose: To realize the truth of today's idea, to realize that you don't need visible gratitude from others, that your own gratitude for your gifts is sufficient.

Morning/evening quiet time: At least five minutes; ideally, thirty or more.

Once again there are no specific instructions. The focus of the lesson is on being grateful for the gifts that you give others, especially the gift of forgiveness. Often, says the lesson, you will withdraw your gift of love and forgiveness unless it is received with "external gratitude and lavish thanks" (1:3). When you are tempted to withdraw your love, you should realize that "your gratitude is all your gifts require" (3:3). You have the right to be grateful, for your gifts are given to you. Also, remind yourself that somewhere deep in your brother's mind, he is thanking you. And realize that God Himself has received your gift and thankfully acknowledges it. So instead of taking it back, be grateful to this brother of yours. Be grateful for what he is, for the fact that, as part of your Self, he makes your Self complete.

How do you turn these ideas into a practice period? One possibility is to search your mind for times when you felt that another didn't show enough gratitude to you. With each case, repeat the idea, realizing that your own gratitude is all your gift requires, and that by snatching your gift away, you snatch it away from yourself. Then replace your ingratitude with gratitude toward yourself and toward your brother, for being part of your Self.

After spending time practicing gratitude in this way, you may want to spend the rest of the practice period in meditation.

Hourly remembrance: One or two minutes as the hour strikes (reduce if circumstances do not permit).

Search your mind for the happenings of the previous hour that

69

are still burdening your mind. With each one, let it go by repeating the idea. Realize that you can give that situation the gift of love right now, and that the only gratitude you need in return is your own.

Response to temptation: (Suggestion) whenever you feel incensed because another is not sufficiently grateful to you.

Repeat the idea, realizing that your gifts were received by you, and that the only gratitude you require is your own.

Commentary

This lesson identifies itself as "the second step" (1:1) in freeing our minds from the belief in outside forces pitted against us. Yesterday's lesson was the first step (W-pI.196.4:1–2). It taught us that our attacks are always directed at ourselves, and that the attacks we thought were coming from outside of ourselves were really coming from our own minds. In other words, "It is impossible that you be hurt except by your own thoughts" (W-pI.196.8:3). Today's lesson takes the other side of the coin: gratitude. This is definitely a step beyond yesterday's lesson. We may understand that our attack is coming from ourselves, and yet not realize that any gratitude we receive is *also* coming from ourselves, and not from outside forces.

I remember attending a workshop of Ken Wapnick's with a friend, when Ken was talking about how to respond to criticism and even outright attack from people who were close to us. Ken's advice was to remember that such attacks are just the other person's ego reacting to its perception of our ego; "Don't take it personally," Ken advised. The next day my friend went to Ken with a personal issue. He'd begun to lead some groups in healing techniques, and he had received many glowing compliments. He was worried that all the praise (or gratitude) would go to his head. Ken's advice to him was quite memorable, coming on the heels of the earlier advice about criticism: "Don't take it personally!"

While some of us may have problems with *receiving* gratitude, we have a much greater problem with *not* receiving it. Every Course student goes through the experience of expressing love, kindness, and forgiveness to someone, only to have it rejected or thrown back in their face. This lesson directly addresses the way we react to such a situation. What we are being asked to do is to express that kindness and love, to "give our gifts," without any attachment to the response of the other person. All the gratitude we require, the lesson says, is *our own gratitude* for the opportunity of giving and forgiving! (3:3). Gratitude does not come from outside us any more than attack does.

If we fail to understand this, when someone fails to acknowledge our gifts, we will typically react by taking them back. "Well, I tried to forgive you and overlook your error, but if this is how you are going to treat me in response, then to hell with you!" And quite obviously, our attempts at kindness have turned into attack! (see 1:2–3).

The lesson says it quite directly: "It does not matter if another thinks your gifts unworthy" (4:1). In other words, in our giving, let us be completely unconcerned with the response of the person we are giving to, and whether or not they express gratitude. Our giving to them is sufficient gift to ourselves, and our own gratitude for the gift we have given is all that we need. If we take back the gifts we give when they are not received with "external gratitude and lavish thanks" (1:3), then we will always suspect that God's gifts are equally undependable. If we take back our gifts, we are taking them away from ourselves. I am the one who needs to be grateful for the gift I have given, for I am the one who has received it! (3:5).

To help us understand why external gratitude isn't necessary, Jesus explains that there is a part of the other person's mind that *is* grateful, even when that isn't expressed outwardly (4:2). The other person's "right mind" is very grateful to you for the gift, and receives it with thanks. The gift will be held, waiting until the person is consciously ready to receive it. As the Manual puts it:

> No teacher of God should feel disappointed if he has offered healing and it does not appear to have been received. It is not up to him to judge when his gift should be accepted. Let him be certain it has been received, and trust that it will be accepted when it is recognized as a blessing and not a curse. (M-6.2:7–9)

The Manual goes on in a way that very clearly echoes the thought we have been discussing:

> It is not the function of God's teachers to evaluate the outcome of their gifts. It is merely their function to give them. (M-6.3:1–2)

This entire section of the Manual, and the one that follows, might be very interesting reading in light of today's lesson.

If we fail to learn this second step, that gratitude as well as attack comes only from within ourselves, we will forever be uncertain about the gifts of God (5:3).

LESSON 198 ✦ JULY 17
"Only my condemnation injures me."

Practice instructions

Purpose: To go past your argument with forgiveness and truly embrace it. If you accomplish this, it will be cause for great celebration, in Heaven and on earth, for it will mean that today your deliverance has come.

Morning/evening quiet time: At least five minutes; ideally, thirty or more.

Although we have no specific instructions, we are told today to practice forgiveness (9:1; 10:4). The lesson assumes that we are familiar with forgiveness, but that we have been opposing it, arguing with it (4:3), trying to find other ways to happiness. Instead, today, we are supposed to take a major step forward in ending our argument with forgiveness and accepting it as our way home. "Now is the time for your deliverance" (13:4). To take this step forward, we are given extremely powerful lines as the focus of our practice: *"Only my condemnation injures me. Only my own forgiveness sets me free."* One way to use these lines would be to call to mind various people in your life and then apply these lines to each one specifically: *"Only my condemnation of [name] injures me. Only my own forgiveness of [name] sets me free."* Or, you may want to search your mind for situations in your life in which you are experiencing pain or stress. Identify the person who seems to be the source of the stress and say, *"Only my condemnation of [name] injures me. Only my own forgiveness of [name] sets me free."*

After this forgiveness practice, you may want to use the remainder of your practice period for meditation.

Hourly remembrance: One or two minutes as the hour strikes (reduce if circumstances do not permit).

Apply the lines we are given today (*"Only my condemnation injures me. Only my own forgiveness sets me free"*) to the happenings of the previous hour that still have you wrapped in their chains.

Response to temptation: (Suggestion) when tempted to succumb to any form of suffering or injury.

Realize your pain really comes from a condemning thought and say, *"Only my condemnation injures me. Only my own forgiveness sets me free."* You may want to use the more specific form of these lines that I suggested above.

Commentary

When I condemn another, I am offering injury to myself. How is that so?

When I condemn anyone, I am wishing injury on them, some form of punishment for their "wrong." At the very least, my condemnation states that the person is less worthy of love. I am believing, therefore, that I can injure, even that I would be justified in offering injury or withholding love. The principle I have established by this belief, however, can be turned against me. I can be injured, too. If I measure my love to others according to my perception of them, I am affirming that this is how love works. Therefore, I am asserting that God measures His love to me based on my appearance or my current state of character development, for instance. Do I really want that?

In reality, "Injury is impossible" (1:1). Neither God, nor my true Self as His creation, can be injured in any way. Nor have they been. But "illusion makes illusion" (1:2), and the illusion of condemnation makes the illusion of injury. We will continue, therefore, to experience injury until we lay down condemnation as an undesirable tool, "unwanted and unreal" (1:4).

There is a principle that lies underneath the surface of this lesson that is really quite important in understanding the Course. Injury is impossible; so is condemnation (2:5). "What seems to be its influence and its effects have not occurred at all" (2:6). Thus, as the Course says in many places, the separation never happened, there is no sin, there is no death, sickness is illusion, and even our bodies and this world do not really exist. "There is no world!" (W-pI.132.6:2). We are not really here where we think we are; we are asleep in Heaven, dreaming of exile. The apparent problem has already been solved, and indeed, it never happened! This is the truth on the level of what the Course calls knowledge or Heaven.

And yet…what? For there is an "and yet" to the Course's teaching. It does not state the ultimate truth and stop; it has something to say about the apparent illusion. It affirms with meticulous care the unreality of the illusion, *and yet* it deals with it!

> What seems to be its influence and its effects have not occurred at all. Yet must we deal with them a while as if they had. (2:6–7)

What are the influence and effects of condemnation? Every form of "injury" imaginable. The apparent effects of our self-judgment include the making of the world and of bodies as well. These are the things, then, that we must deal with *as if they had really occurred*—for a while. Time itself is an illusion, yet the Course talks a good deal about saving time, and urges us to use time wisely, particularly in the practice instructions that are part of these lessons. It knows time is illusory, and yet it deals with it as if it were something real, using the very illusion to lead us out of illusion; using time to bring us back to eternity.

We meet illusion with illusion; we meet the effects of condemnation with forgiveness. In reality there is nothing to forgive because nothing happened. But to undo the *illusion* of what happened and so become aware of the unchanging reality, we need the illusion of forgiveness.

The Course affirms that this world is illusion, and yet, for a time, it teaches us to deal with it as if it were not an illusion; as if it had really occurred. The only way to thus deal with it is to forgive it, to proclaim to it that "there is no condemnation in God's Son" (10:1). Forgiveness is the bridge that brings illusion to the truth, that provides the escape passage out of illusion entirely.

LESSON 199 ✦ JULY 18
"I am not a body. I am free."

Practice instructions

Purpose: To go past your identification with the body, to experience the freedom of abiding in the boundlessness of God. To free your mind from bodily limits and give it to the Holy Spirit's use, that He may use your body to carry the message of freedom to those who still think they are imprisoned in a body.

Morning/evening quiet time: At least five minutes; ideally, thirty or more.

As is usual by now, we are left on our own to decide how to spend our longer practice periods. Choose some form of practice that reflects today's goal. The goal is to realize that you are not a mind imprisoned within a body, but rather that you are a "mind within the Holy Spirit" (6:6), a mind that "rests in God" (2:3). Your mind, then, is inherently free, "unlimited forever" (2:1), and your body is gone from your self-concept. The body, then, rather than the slave master, becomes "a worthy servant" (6:6) of the Holy Spirit's plan to extend forgiveness to every mind. It will then return to mind whenever it is needed to communicate forgiveness.

I would suggest a meditation in which you try to feel your mind surrounded by the Holy Spirit, resting in God, unbound by any limits whatsoever. Sink into the feeling that this is your home, not the body, so that the body vanishes from your picture of yourself.

Hourly remembrance: One or two minutes as the hour strikes (reduce if circumstances do not permit).

Search your mind for the events of the past hour that are still compromising your peace. Notice how each one has something to do with the body—how your body was treated by another's body, what your body said or did, how it feels, how well it is functioning, how it looks, etc. Then free yourself of these bodily limits by repeating, *"I am not a body. I am free. I hear the Voice*

76

that God has given me, and it is only This my mind obeys." This means that your mind does not obey the body, it only obeys the Voice of freedom.

Response to temptation: (Suggestion) when tempted to engage in any thoughts which reinforce a bodily identity.

Repeat, *"I am not a body. I am free. I hear the Voice that God has given me, and it is only This [rather than the body] my mind obeys."*

Overall comments: This is a hugely important idea. To make progress on this path, we are told, we must accept this idea and even "hold it very dear" (3:1). We are encouraged to use it in all of our practice periods, even beyond today, for it will boost the power of each lesson we combine it with (5:3). Indeed, in a couple of days, we will be instructed to use it precisely in this way for twenty straight days.

Commentary

To the ego, today's idea is "quite insane" (3:2). Yet it is one of the basic principles the Course uses to free us from our bondage. The lesson attaches a great deal of importance to it, more than to most ideas the Course presents. We are told to "cherish" it and "practice it today and every day" (5:1). And evidently Jesus expects us to integrate the idea that "I am not a body" into every practice period from now on! (5:2).

Let's face it: Before we encountered the Course, the body was something we took for granted. If we knew anything, we thought, we knew we were a body. Our bodies held a very different place in our lives from every other physical object. If someone stepped on a CD we owned, we might say, "Hey! You're breaking my CD." But if they stepped on our toe (part of our body), we would say, "Hey! You're stepping on *me*!" It is part of our consciousness. "I" am where my body is. We say, "I am eating. I was asleep. I am in my car. I am sick." And all of those "I's" refer to the body. Even if we have been Course students for ten or fifteen years, we are probably still saying those same things, and still, out of habit, thinking of the body as our self.

The ego has expended millennia of effort at mentally programming into the mind the identity of "me" and the body. It isn't something the mind will let go of easily; it is a habit of thought that will take a great deal of counterprogramming to unlearn. That is why we are urged to make it a part of daily practice. The body-as-self identity will not be broken by a few simple repetitions. We all still believe in it. As Ken Wapnick has said, if you doubt that you still believe in the identity of body and self, just try holding your breath for ten minutes.

What are we to do with our awareness that we hold this false belief about ourselves? The lesson tells us, "Be not concerned" (3:2). Like a runner practicing to break the four-minute mile, we need not be concerned that we haven't done so yet. We just need to keep on practicing, doing what needs to be done to achieve that goal. Our goal is to realize we are a "mind...[that] no longer sees itself as in a body, firmly tied to it and sheltered by its presence" (1:4). That is the state of mind in which total freedom is found. When we have entered that state of mind, we will be right-minded, and in the real world. Our only concern now is to move in that direction.

The holy instant offers us foretastes of that state of mind. The body recedes from awareness in the holy instant, and what we are aware of is oneness, something so vast no body or collection of bodies could ever contain it. As we experience this state more and more it will come to dominate our consciousness. We still have a body, but we realize we are not bound to it. It becomes simply

> [a] useful form for what the mind must do. It thus becomes a vehicle which helps forgiveness be extended to the all-inclusive goal that it must reach, according to God's plan.
>
> (4:4–5)

Ironically, the more we detach our mind from our body, the more perfect the body becomes. "It becomes perfect in the ability to serve an undivided goal" (6:4). If perfecting the body is the goal, we will never achieve it; the body will find wholeness only when our goal becomes unified with the Holy Spirit in seeking to extend forgiveness to everyone and everything, which places the body in its proper place. Trying to hold on to the body destroys it; letting it go brings it health.

The body is not the home of the mind; the Holy Spirit is (6:1). Our aim in practicing, in each holy instant we take, is to free our mind from its connection to the body, and to give our mind to the Holy Spirit for His purposes. Our energy then is not directed at acquiring food or clothing, or housing, or physical well being, but at bringing forgiveness to the world. If we do this, the Holy Spirit promises that He will take care of all the rest. As Jesus put it in the Bible: "Seek ye first the kingdom of God, and his righteousness; and all these things shall be added unto you" (Mt 6:33).

Or, as the Course puts it: "Once you accept His plan as the one function that you would fulfill, there will be nothing else the Holy Spirit will not arrange for you without your effort" (T-20.IV.8:4).

LESSON 200 ✦ JULY 19

"There is no peace except the peace of God."

Practice instructions

Purpose: To no longer seek peace from things of the world, but only from God. To no longer wander off the path seeking worldly satisfactions, but take the straight path to God.

Morning/evening quiet time: At least five minutes; ideally, thirty or more.

Again we are not given specific instructions. The goal today is to cement our determination to seek peace only from God, not from the world. We find God's peace through choosing a new perception of the world, a perception in which "all the world is seen by you as blessed" (5:3). The way to reach this new perception is forgiveness (see paragraph 6). Rather than forcing things to go our way, we forgive them for not going our way. That is how we find the peace of God.

You may want to ask your internal Teacher what kind of practice period will allow you to reach this goal. What form of practice will help you no longer be lured off the path by the siren song of the world but instead take the straight road to God?

Hourly remembrance: One or two minutes as the hour strikes (reduce if circumstances do not permit).

Search your mind for the happenings of the previous hour in which you didn't get what you wanted. Then let each one go by repeating, *"There is no peace except the peace of God, and I am glad and thankful it is so."* Realize you don't want the thing you thought they could give you. All you want is the peace of God.

Response to temptation: (Suggestion) when tempted to seek peace from anything of this world.

Quickly repeat, *"There is no peace except the peace of God, and I am glad and thankful it is so."*

Commentary

The basic message of this lesson is that every means we use to try to find peace *through or from the world* will fail; only the peace that comes from God, a peace that we already have as part of our created being, is real and eternal. (Some good sections to read in conjunction with today's lesson are Section 11 in the Manual, "How is peace possible in this world?" and the Text, Chapter 31, Section IV, "The Real Alternative.")

Everything in this world ends in death. This world is hell, because no matter what course we follow, no matter how hard we strive, we wind up losing everything in the end. What a depressing game it is, when the only outcome is losing! This is the source of "the agony of bitter disappointments, bleak despair, and sense of icy hopelessness and doubt" (1:3). If we are playing the game of the world, seeking for "happiness where there is none" (2:1), we can only be hurt. We are "asking for defeat" (2:3).

We may not be fully conscious of this despair, yet it underlies everything we do. Ernest Becker's book *The Denial of Death*[1] is all about the ways in which we anxiously and firmly push the awareness of death out of our minds, burying it in the trivia of daily life, struggling to find meaning in something to which we can attach ourselves and somehow achieve immortality. Becker reaches the same conclusion as the Course, in some respects: that we are all insane, all bound up in denial and projection. The only difference between us and those called "insane" is that our form of denial is a little more successful than theirs. Yet in some ways the "insane" are more honest than we are. They have admitted the emptiness of the world and have chosen to create their own fantasy world in its place, or have become suicidal in despair. The rest of us still stumble along in naive hope that the world will yet bring us satisfaction.

The lesson asks us to give up the futile search for happiness through our bodies and the world, and to relax into the peace of God. If we can simply accept the fact that we will not find happiness or peace anywhere else, we can save ourselves all this misery. If I look at my own life, my most miserable moments have been those in which someone or something on which I had pinned my hopes for happiness failed me: a marriage, a church, a job, a noble purpose, a hope of romance. The lesson is saying these are not isolated events. They represent the whole.

The search for peace apart from the peace of God is hopeless, and the sooner we realize it, the sooner will we find true happiness.

"This world is not where you belong. You are a stranger here" (4:3–4). So give it up. Let it go. Stop expecting it to make you happy; it never will. "But it is given you to find the means whereby the world no longer seems to be a prison house or jail for anyone" (4:5). *There is a way out!* "You must change your mind about the purpose of the world, if you would find escape" (5:2).

The Text tells us the same things:

> Until you see the healing of the Son as all you wish to be accomplished by the world, by time and all appearances, you will not know the Father nor yourself. For you will use the world for what is not its purpose, and will not escape its laws of violence and death. (T-24.VI.4:3–4)

> To change all this, and open up a road of hope and of release in what appeared to be an endless circle of despair, you need but to decide you do not know the purpose of the world. You give it goals it does not have, and thus do you decide what it is for. You try to see in it a place of idols found outside yourself, with power to make complete what is within by splitting what you are between the two. You choose your dreams, for they are what you wish, perceived as if it had been given you. Your idols do what you would have them do, and have the power you ascribe to them. And you pursue them vainly in the dream, because you want their power as your own. (T-29.VII.8:1–6)

If we can decide that we do not know the purpose of the world, we will be free to receive the purpose the Holy Spirit sees in it. Until we give up our imagined purposes, His purpose will seem dim and indecipherable. It is the letting go of what we think the world is for that allows its only true purpose to dawn upon us. That purpose, in a word, is forgiveness; or as the line in Chapter 24 puts it, "the healing of the Son" (T-24.VII.4:3). Forgiveness is needed in hell, and this world, therefore, must be hell (6:4). Forgiveness offers, to me and to everyone "the escape…from evil dreams he imagines, yet believes are true" (6:5). All the world is good for, we might say, is for us to "learn to look on it another way, and find the peace of God" (7:6).

If the world is such a terrible, depressing place, we might think that logically, the way to find peace is to leave the world. To die. To get out of this body. But that is not what the lesson says. "Peace," we are told, "begins within the world perceived as different" (8:2). Notice: peace begins *within the world*. It begins with a new perception of the world, not as a prison house, but as a classroom. Beginning here, the road of peace will lead us on "to the gate of Heaven and the way beyond" (8:2). But it must begin here.

In poignant images of a road "carpeted with leaves of false desires," we can see ourselves lifting our eyes away from the "trees of hopelessness" to the gate of Heaven (10:3). It is the peace of God we want, and nothing but the peace of God. In the holy instants we enjoy in today's practicing, we recognize the peace we have sought, and "feel its soft embrace surround your heart and mind with comfort and with love" (10:6).

The closing lines, given us for practice, sum up the whole lesson. Most of us, if confronted with the thought that there is no peace but the peace of God, do not yet respond with gladness and thanks. The message that "there is no hope of answer in the world" (T-31.IV.4:3) seems a dour and bitter pill to swallow. Instead of joy, we feel sad, and a bit resentful. We wistfully cling to our vain hopes that the idols of this world will still, somehow, satisfy us. We want them to, so very much. Only when we have learned to release them gladly and thankfully will we be, finally, free of their hold upon us.

Let me, then, in today's practicing, seek to find that gladness and thanks within myself. The Christ in me wants to "come home" (4:1). There is a part of me that breathes a sigh of relief as I begin to realize the world can never satisfy me, and whispers to me, "At last! At last you are beginning to let go of the source of your pain. Thank you!" Let me connect with that part of my mind that is native to Heaven, and knows it does not belong here; it is the only part there is in reality. The more I connect with it, the sooner will I know the peace that is my natural inheritance.

---

1. Ernest Becker, *The Denial of Death* (New York: Free Press, 1997).

II

Review VI: Introduction
and Lessons 201 - 220

INTRODUCTION

This is the final review of the Workbook, the end of Part I. Back in the introduction to the Workbook we were told: "The workbook is divided into two main sections, the first dealing with the undoing of the way you see now, and the second with the acquisition of true perception" (W-In.3:1). The last forty lessons or so have said they were preparing us for Part II of the Workbook. So now we are coming to the end of the first phase of our training. Presumably, if we have been doing the exercises as instructed (and that is the real key, of course), we are now ready to enter a new, higher phase of our practicing.

Two things are clearly different about the second part of the Workbook. First, the written lessons are much, much shorter; none is more than a half page, although we will be asked to read a one-page teaching section ten times, once each day along with the lesson. The emphasis in the second part, as we will see, is much less on learning new ideas (or unlearning old ones), and much more on having new experiences, and on reinforcing the habits we have formed during Part I.

The second major difference is that, from this review which ends Part I and the introduction to Part II forward, the lessons contain *no more practice instructions*. It seems quite clear that the pattern of practice we are meant to follow has been established, and we are expected to know what it is, and to follow it for the remaining 145 lessons of Part II.

That pattern was begun in Lesson 153, which established the longer morning and evening quiet times, and the hourly remembrances. The remaining two elements—frequent reminders between the hours, and response to temptation as needed—remained somewhat optional for the rest of the lessons through 200. It is only here, in the introduction to the final review, that they are added in as something definitely expected of us every day.

"Besides the time you give morning and evening, which should not be less than fifteen minutes, and the hourly remembrances you make throughout the day, use the idea as often as you can between them" (W-pI.rVI.1:2). The word "besides" makes it clear that these frequent reminders are now being given *in addition* to the morning and evening quiet times and the hourly remembrances. The response to temptation is clearly added as well, in paragraph 6:

> When you are tempted, hasten to proclaim your free-dom from temptation, as you say: *This thought I do not want. I choose instead* _____. And then repeat the idea for the day, and let it take the place of what you thought.
>
> (6:1–4)

Those four elements of practice, firmly set in place in this final review, are meant to be the instructions we follow on a daily basis for the rest of the year:

1. Morning and evening quiet time of not less than fifteen minutes each
2. Hourly remembrances of a few minutes, in which we recall the idea for the day and apply it to the hour past and the hour to come
3. Frequent reminders in between the hours, when we simply call the idea to mind
4. Response to temptation, in which we deliberately replace our ego thoughts with the thought for the day

We are told that any one of the ideas we are given is "sufficient for salvation, if it were learned truly. Each would be enough to give release to you and to the world from every form of bondage, and invite the memory of God to come again" (1:3–4). This is true of the ideas to come, and also of the ideas in the last twenty lessons. Notice the conditional phrases that modify this statement, however: "if understood, practiced, accepted, and applied to all the seeming happenings throughout the day" (2:2). Any one idea is enough...*if* we apply that idea without exception (2:4).

If any single idea is enough, why do we need 365 lessons? The answer is simple. The author knows perfectly well that we won't apply any single idea without exception to every happening throughout every day. "And so we need to use them all and let them blend as one, as each contributes to the whole we learn" (2:5).

In this final review, which lasts for twenty days, repeating each day one of the thoughts from the previous twenty days, we are asked to let our practicing center around a unifying theme:

I am not a body. I am free. For I am still as God created me.

(3:3–5)

We are asked to repeat these three short sentences every morning and evening, every hour, and every time in between that we remember our true function here. We repeat it along with the review idea for the day. That simple repetition is the only specific instruction we are given. Beyond that, all that we are asked to do in our practice times is, in a short phrase, to clear our minds of any opposing thoughts (3:8). This is to be a "deep relinquishment" (3:8), not simply a blanking of the mind; a letting go of every thought that stands in the way of sanity and truth.

> We merely close our eyes, and then forget all that we thought we knew and understood. (4:3)

In this final half of the Workbook we are moving "beyond all words" (4:1). We are seeking to experience serenity and the peace of God.

The only exception is something we do when an "idle thought" (5:2) intrudes itself into our quiet. Paragraph 5 gives us clear instructions about how to deal with these intrusive thoughts, which will surely occur. The main point is not to allow such a thought to simply pass by unchallenged. Rather, we instruct our minds, "This is not a thought I want," and replace it with the idea for the day. We follow the same practice all through the day, whenever we are tempted by our egos.

This is a rigorous kind of mind training. It asks a great deal of us. I believe it is what is meant by the phrase in the Text, "Be vigilant only for God and for His Kingdom" (T-6.V(C).2:8). How can we expect our minds to become free of ego thinking if we let the ego's thoughts go unchallenged? Early in the Text, Jesus tells us we are "much too tolerant of mind wandering" (T-2.VI.4:6); this vigilant watchfulness, challenging the ego thoughts and replacing them with thoughts of God, is the Course's remedy.

Jesus, the author, says that he places our practice periods in the hands of the Holy Spirit (6:6; 7:1–2). We are to listen to Him for specifics about what to "do and say and think, each time you turn to Him" (7:2). The primary emphasis seems to be on simple quiet (6:6). Yet the mention of what we do and say and think leaves us a great deal of latitude. Generally speaking, I think, we can use any of the techniques we have practiced earlier in the Workbook, such as forgiveness exercises, offering peace to the world, reviewing situations in our lives and applying the idea for the day, and so on. The major emphasis is on quietly listening to the Voice for God and allowing our minds to come to serenity and peace. The Workbook has ended its specific practice instructions, but now we are to learn to listen to the Holy Spirit instead,

> allowing Him to teach us how to go, and trusting Him completely for the way each practice period can best become a loving gift of freedom to the world.   (7:4)

REVIEW VI PRACTICE INSTRUCTIONS

Purpose: To carefully review the last twenty lessons, each of which contains the whole curriculum. To go with quickened pace along the path to God. To finish our preparation (begun in Lesson 141) for entering a higher phase of learning: Part II.

Morning/evening quiet time: At least fifteen minutes.

For our longer practice periods, we are doing what I call Open Mind Meditation (for more complete instructions on this method, see the cameo essay on page 91).

- Begin by repeating, *"I am not a body. I am free. For I am still as God created me."*

- Then repeat today's idea, perhaps also repeating the italicized lines that follow the idea (which are meant "to aid in practicing"—6:5).

- For the bulk of the time, close your eyes and relinquish all mental clutter and all beliefs you have about yourself and the world. Hold your mind in silent readiness to receive the experience of God. Do not repeat words. Simply wait for that experience to dawn, holding your mind still and expectant without the aid of verbalizing. Rather than relying on words, rely on the Holy Spirit. Offer the practice period to Him, and be open to His guidance, which may take your meditation in unexpected directions.

- If a wandering thought intrudes—which will no doubt happen regularly—immediately respond with, *"This thought I do not want. I choose instead [today's idea]."* This is perhaps the Workbook's most effective way of dispelling distracting thoughts.

- Close by again repeating, *"I am not a body. I am free. For I am still as God created me."*

Hourly remembrance: One or two minutes as the hour strikes (reduce if circumstances do not permit).

Repeat the idea, plus the central thought, *"I am not a body. I am free. For I am still as God created me."* Then spend a quiet moment in Open Mind Meditation, waiting in stillness to feel the peace of God.

Frequent reminder: As often as possible within each hour.

Repeat the idea for the day, plus, *"I am not a body. I am free. For I am still as God created me."*

Response to temptation: (Suggestion) when you are tempted to be upset.

Quickly proclaim your freedom by saying, *"This thought I do not want. I choose instead [today's idea]."*

Overall remarks: The preceding forty-eight lessons have schooled us in a basic framework of practice, which includes morning and evening practice periods and hourly remembrances. What is missing from this framework are the frequent reminders, which were such an important focus earlier in the Workbook. Here, those are finally added back into the mix, so that now, as we prepare to enter Part II, we have in place the entire fourfold structure of practice: Morning and evening quiet time, hourly remembrance, frequent reminders, and response to temptation (the last item has been present throughout the Workbook, as well as in many of the last forty-eight lessons).

In this review, in a continuation of a trend that began in Lesson 124, words and specific instructions are even further withdrawn. We repeat words at the beginning and then pass into a silence that is empty of thoughts and words. This lack of structure, we are told, will help us "reach a quickened pace along a shorter path to the serenity and peace of God" (4:2). It will help prepare us for the formlessness of Part II.

It is implied that God might show up in the form of the Holy Spirit inspiring us to practice in some particular way. He may, as the final lessons say, give us a word to help our practice, or a thought to focus on, or just "stillness and a tranquil, open mind" (W-pII.361-365.1:3). If He directs you to practice in a more specific way, then fine. Otherwise, the instructions are to wait in a mental silence without words or thoughts.

In keeping with this reliance on the Holy Spirit, Jesus asks us to place every practice period in His hands, and, at the outset, to dedicate the entire review to Him.

OPEN MIND MEDITATION

Meditation is a fundamental part of Workbook practice. Training in meditation begins early, in Lesson 41. There, we learn the Workbook's standard "down-and-inward" technique. After that, it becomes a genuine staple of daily practice. However, as the Workbook nears its second part, meditation begins to change in form. Up until this point, we have used words as a focus in our meditations. The words aid us in keeping our focus and help carry us toward our goal. Now, however, we are asked to go beyond words, to practice nonverbally.

This is essentially a new method of meditation—new for the Workbook, at least. Indeed, it is the Workbook's crowning method. It is taught in nearly all of the final sections of the Workbook:

- Review V—Lessons 171-180 (see the introduction, paragraph 12)
- Review VI—Lessons 201-220 (see the introduction, paragraphs 4-6)
- Part II—Lessons 221-360 (see the introduction, paragraphs 3-5)
- Final Lessons—Lessons 361-365 (see the introduction, paragraph 1)

Why is it the crowning method? Because it takes us beyond words to direct experience. Indeed, whenever the Workbook talks about going "beyond all words" (W-pI.rVI.In.4:1), it is almost always talking about Open Mind Meditation. Actually, going beyond words is important for the same reason that words themselves are important. The Course is all about entering a new world of meaning. Words are so central to the Course (which is really just one long string of them) because they point to that new world. They signify meaning, and so they serve as excellent *mediators*. They introduce us to that world; they help us get in touch with it. Yet, like all mediators, they get in the way of direct encounter. When the parties are ready to join, the mediator's job is over. And so, ultimately, we need to set words aside if we are to have the total, *unmediated* experience of meaning.

> We wait for the experience, and recognize that it is only here conviction lies. We use the words, and try and try again to go beyond them to their meaning, which is far beyond their sound. The sound grows dim and disappears, as we approach the Source of meaning. It is Here that we find rest.
> (W-pI.rV.In.12:3-6)

Open Mind Meditation is not just about being ushered into an ecstatic state that words cannot describe; it's about emptying our mind of words in order to *reach* that state. In this meditation, then, we clear away all words and thoughts from our mind. We hold a nonverbal intent, a pure, expectant waiting for the arrival of God. Our mind becomes like the cloudless sky, filled with nothing but "still anticipation" (W-pI.157.4:3), waiting for the sun to peek over the horizon. The nonverbal attitude we hold could be translated into the following poetic words:

> The memory of God is shimmering across the wide horizons
> of our minds. A moment more, and it will rise again. A
> moment more, and we who are God's Sons are safely home,
> where He would have us be.   (W-pII.In.9:5-7)

Unlike other Workbook meditations, we hold this attitude wordlessly; we do not repeat words to maintain it (although, thankfully, we are allowed to use words to draw our mind back when it wanders). As I have said, our mind is supposed to be empty of *all* words, even the words of the Course. Few of us find this easy. Ironically, although we all like to *talk* about going beyond words, when it actually comes to doing without them we tend to find it quite difficult. However, if we can master this technique, we will also find it deeply rewarding. And we need to try to master it. There is a reason why the final half of the Workbook's year is devoted to this method. In the end, the Course is not about looking at a painting of Heaven, it's about going there yourself.

Summary of the technique

1. Repeat the idea for the day as an invitation to God to come to you

Have a sense of placing the practice period in His Hands.

2. In preparation for direct experience, empty your mind of all words, all thoughts, and all that you think you know and understand

You may want to use the following lines as an induction into this state of emptiness:

> *I do not know what I am.*
> *I do not know what my attributes are.*
> *I do not know what God is.*
> *I do not know what the world is.*
> *I do not know what is true and what is false.*
> *I do not know what will make me happy.*

I will forget my body, its comfort and its needs,
I will forget the past and future, and come with wholly empty hands
  unto my God.

3. In the silence, hold your mind in a state like a vacuum

On the negative side, a vacuum is *empty*, yet on the positive side, this emptiness *draws fullness* to itself, it *"desires"* to be filled. The essence of the technique is to wordlessly hold in place both the negative and positive sides of the vacuum: *In a mind that is empty of words, thoughts, and ideas* (negative), *wait expectantly for a fullness to come from God* (positive).

3a. **Negative**: Let your mind be empty of words, thoughts, and ideas

- Empty of *words*. Don't repeat words. Being symbols, they stand in the way of direct, unmediated knowing.
- Empty of *thoughts*.
- Empty of *all you think you know and understand*. Your "knowledge" stands in the way of real knowledge.

3b. **Positive**: Wait for a fullness to come from God

- Wait in silent expectancy for God (or truth, or peace, etc.). Hold your mind still, filled with pure expectancy and anticipation. Wait for God as one would wait for the sunrise.
- Open your mind to a completely different kind of knowing, a knowing beyond words.
- Be sure to *rest*; do not strain. "Open your mind to Him. Be still and rest" (W-pI.128.6-7).

4. Whenever your mind wanders (which will happen regularly), use words again to draw it back to silent, nonverbal waiting

You might repeat a single word, the idea for the day, or *"This thought I do not want. I choose instead [the idea for the day]."*

5. Realize that the practice period is in the Holy Spirit's hands

Be open to Him stepping in and helping your practice in some way, perhaps by giving you a word or thought to focus on (which breaks the rules, but it's okay if *He* breaks the rules), or just giving you a peaceful, open mind. Or He may step in and give you guidance, or a vision, or some other kind of experience. Because His activity may go outside the rules established in the previous points, it is important to distinguish between *His* activity and *your* thoughts and daydreams.

6. Conclude by repeating the idea for the day

LESSON 201 ✦ JULY 20

Central theme:

"I am not a body. I am free. For I am still as God created me."

Review of:

(181) "I trust my brothers, who are one with me."

 Practice instructions
    See instructions on page 89.

Commentary

Today, let us remember, as often as we can, that there is no one who is not our brother. Let us remember that we are all part of the one Self, and that our oneness with All-That-Is is a blessing we can never lose.

Together, we are a whole. Apart, we are nothing.

There is only one of us.

Everyone is linked immutably to God and to each other. Everything that is, is a direct offshoot of the Creator, equally worthy, equally holy, equally loveable.

My brothers and sisters are my joy and my delight. Let me see each one today as the blessing that they are to me.

LESSON 202 ✦ JULY 21

Central theme:

"I am not a body. I am free. For I am still as God created me."

Review of:

(182) "I will be still an instant and go home."

 Practice instructions

See instructions on page 89.

Commentary

Right now, this very instant, and every instant of this day, I have the opportunity simply to be still, to quiet my mind, and to go home to Heaven. Heaven is here. Heaven is now. There is no other time and no other place.

This world of turmoil is not my home; my home is in peace. This world of sorrow is not my home; my home is in joy. This world of hatred is not my home; my home is in love. This body is not my home; my home is in God.

The Voice of God is calling me constantly to come home, and I can do so any time I choose to. How thankful I am today for this inner calling! How grateful I am that, no matter where I go, no matter what I do, this Voice is always with me, always calling me home.

When I hear this Voice, why would I choose to stay an instant more where I am not at home? Every reason I might think to give dissolves into nothing when I become aware of the sweet and gentle calling of His Voice. I will remember right now, and at every opportunity during this day. "I will be still an instant and go home."

LESSON 203 ✦ JULY 22

Central theme:

"I am not a body. I am free. For I am still as God created me."

Review of:

(183) "I call upon God's Name and on my own."

 ### Practice instructions

See instructions on page 89.

Commentary

To "call upon" the Name of God is not simply to repeat a word, but to reach out from within myself, affirming my connection to my Source. To call upon this Name means to remind myself of my union with God. "It is my own [name] as well as His" (1:2). In a sense, it is similar to the way soldiers in battle might cry out the name of their king, or the way a football crowd chants the name of a favorite player. It is a means of identification, an affirmation of a solidarity and unity.

Yet it is more than any such thing that we might compare it with in this world, because God's Name is my name in a much deeper sense than mere emotional identification. I am the extension of God. What He is, I am as well. I am created of the essence of Godhead. "I am still as God created me" (1:5). I affirm this every time I call upon His Name.

To call upon God's Name is to remind myself that the lesser name and the lesser self with which I commonly identify is not who I am. "I am not a body" (1:3). In the midst of the daily crunch of "busy-ness," when I call on this Name, I am delivered "from every thought of evil and of sin" (1:2). When I feel limited or confined, I can rediscover my freedom by calling on His Name. I remember that I am not this body; I am free.

As I sit in quiet today, let me open to the experience of God. Let me become aware of the vast Love without boundary or restriction. Let me sink into His limitless peace. Let me be transported in His joy. And as I

97

do, let me remember that all that I experience of God, *I am*. Let me call, too, on *my own name*. In remembering God, let me remember, "This is me."

LESSON 204 ✦ JULY 23

Central theme:

"I am not a body. I am free. For I am still as God created me."

Review of:

(184) "The Name of God is my inheritance."

 Practice instructions

See instructions on page 89.

Commentary

If I bear the Name of God, I am His Son. I have the heritage of God's family—and what an inheritance that is! I am not the offspring of random molecules of DNA. I am not the product of survival of the fittest in a vicious battle for supremacy in life. I am not the product of my human family, my upbringing, my education, my failures, or my culture. What I am I have inherited from God Himself.

As the Son of God I am "not slave to time" (1:2). I am not limited to the short span of my body's "life" on earth. I do not require long years of development to attain my inheritance; it is mine now. Nor am I the product of my past. I do not need to fear the future. I am free of all limitations time might try to impose on me.

I am "unbound by laws which rule the world of sick illusions" (1:2). Laws of time, of space, of economics, of health and nutrition, or any laws we think are immutable and inevitable here, do not rule me. I am a child of God. I am spirit. I am free. I am "forever and forever one with Him" (1:2).

LESSON 205 ✦ JULY 24

Central theme:

"I am not a body. I am free. For I am still as God created me."

Review of:

(185) "I want the peace of God."

 Practice instructions

See instructions on page 89.

Commentary

The introduction to Review VI says that "each of these ideas alone would be sufficient for salvation, if it were learned truly" (W-pI.rVI.In.1:3). It adds, "Each contains the whole curriculum if understood, practiced, accepted, and applied to all the seeming happenings throughout the day" (W-pI.rVI.In.2:2). I find that easy to believe about today's lesson. If you are into memorization (as I am), this lesson is an excellent one to add to your repertoire.

It's worth noticing the list of four verb forms that are identified as steps in making any of these ideas into "the whole curriculum":

Understood: No matter how strongly the Course advocates experience, and points out that a universal theology is impossible (see C-In.2:5), you cannot get around the fact that it makes understanding very important. How can we enter into the experience of an idea if we do not understand it? Understanding is here presented as the fundamental step. Before we can really utilize the idea "I want the peace of God," we have to understand it. Implied in the idea (and clearly presented in Lesson 185) is the fact that there is a very strong thought in my mind, perhaps unacknowledged, that I do not want the peace of God, and this is demonstrated by the fact that I do not experience it. That contrary thought, however, is a mistaken one, to be dismissed whenever we become aware of it, and replaced with the truth: I *do* want the peace of God.

Practiced: That is what we are doing in these Workbook lessons. Practicing. Repeating frequently. Spending some extended time allowing the thought to soak in and penetrate the recesses of our minds.

Accepted: Notice that acceptance comes after practice. Our minds do not accept the idea at the start, even after we understand the idea. When we begin to practice, we do not truly accept that we want the peace of God. We think we want something else, something more, something besides peace. It takes a good deal of practice to retrain our minds, until we begin to realize that "the peace of God is everything I want" (1:2).

Applied: Having accepted the idea, we can now begin to apply it to each different "seeming happening" during the day. When the car cuts us off in traffic: "I want the peace of God." When we find ourselves wistfully longing for a more fulfilling relationship: "The peace of God is everything I want." When we begin to feel driven to obtain some earthly goal at any cost: "The peace of God is my one goal" (1:3). When we start to think we don't know what to do or where to go: "The peace of God is the aim of all my living here." And when we start to feel impelled to fulfill some need of our bodies: "I am not a body. The peace of God is everything I want. I am free."

Thank You, Father, for today's reminder of Your peace. There is nothing else I need, and nothing else I want. Oh, may today's lesson become the keynote of my life, so that I can say and truly mean: "The peace of God is my *one* goal."

LESSON 206 ✦ JULY 25

Central theme:

"I am not a body. I am free. For I am still as God created me."

Review of:

(186) "Salvation of the world depends on me."

 Practice instructions

See instructions on page 89.

Commentary

I am not a body; I am the Son of God. I am spirit, endowed with the gifts of God. I am not what I appear to be, nor what I have thought I was for most of my life. I am a spiritual being having a human experience, and my mission here (if I will accept it) is to give the gifts of God wherever He asks me to give them. And that is to everyone.

The Course requires a radical revision of my self-concept. I have thought of myself as some sort of poor, lost soul, wandering, alone, afraid. I have thought of myself as needy and lacking. I have felt like an orphan; as though, no matter how hard I tried, no matter how many places I visited, I never quite fit in. I have seen myself at the bottom trying to get up.

Now, this book comes along, a message from God to me, and tells me that the salvation of the world depends on me. I am a key figure in the plan of the ages. Everything depends on me, and that seems frightening. And yet, I have the gifts to give the world that will save it. I can give it my love. I can give it my trust. I can give it my kindness and my mercy. I can give those around me my understanding and my faith in them. Through my forgiveness I can release them from guilt.

This is such a startling idea of what I am that at first it seems ludicrous. I think at first that to see myself this way would be the height of arrogance. And yet...and yet, if this is how God created me, if this is what He created me for, it is arrogant to refuse the task being given to

102

me. He is not asking me to set myself above anyone else. On the contrary, He is asking me to demonstrate to everyone that they have the gifts of God as well, that they are all like me.

God is asking me, "Are you ready yet to help Me save the world?" (C-2.9:1) All Heaven waits breathlessly to hear my decision. Will I say, "Yes"? Will I dare to say, with understanding, meaning every word: "Salvation of the world depends on me"?

LESSON 207 ✦ JULY 26

Central theme:

"I am not a body. I am free. For I am still as God created me."

Review of:

(187) "I bless the world because I bless myself."

 Practice instructions
See instructions on page 89.

Commentary

All that I need is already within me. It is released for me when I release it to others, because in reality, there are no "others," there is only one. We get caught up in questions such as "Do I forgive myself first, and thus release myself to forgive others? Or do I forgive my brother, and thus find forgiveness for myself?" and "Must I love myself before I can love others, or vice versa?" When we ask such questions we are trying to figure out a unified reality on the basis of duality; we can't get a clear answer because the question is framed in the wrong terms.

To "accept His boundless Love for me" (1:3) and to accept that Love for others is the same thing, because all of us are merely fragments of the one mind we all share. There is no such thing as loving myself to the exclusion of loving others; that is not love at all. Nor is it love to "love" someone else and sacrifice myself on their behalf.

"I bless the world because I bless myself." This doesn't mean that meeting the demands of my ego benefits everyone else. Many people, in the wake of what ACIM teachers Hugh and Gayle Prather call "separation psychology" (in their book *I Will Never Leave You*),[1] think that loving yourself means such things as looking out for your own happiness at the expense of marriage partners and children. This is not what the Course is teaching here. The pendulum has swung from sacrificing yourself for the family or your partner (in the 1940s and 1950s) to sacrificing the family and partner for yourself (in the 1980s

104

and 1990s). Both are mistaken approaches based on dualism.

"I bless the world because I bless myself" could be reversed, with equal truth, to read, "I bless myself because I bless the world." Giving and receiving are the same thing; this is one of the major lessons of the Course, and, by its own admission, one of the hardest for us to learn.

"God's blessing shines upon me from within my heart, where He abides" (1:2). The radiant and all-embracing Love of God is within me. When I turn to it, it engulfs me and instantly spills over to embrace everyone through me. Discovering that is what the Course is all about. "I am still as God created me." I am still that love. How can I know that I am love without expressing it? Love, by its nature, extends to others and includes them in its heart. The marvelous discovery of my own nature as love cannot be made without the extension of that love to my brother. To bless myself and to bless the world is a single event. It is when I bless the world that I learn to love myself; and likewise, when I truly love myself, I become a blessing to the world around me. I need my brothers, not to give me what I do not have, but to be the recipients and sharers of What I am.

---

1. Hugh and Gayle Prather, *I Will Never Leave You* (New York: Bantam, 1996).

LESSON 208 ✦ JULY 27

Central theme:

"I am not a body. I am free. For I am still as God created me."

Review of:

(188) "The peace of God is shining in me now."

 Practice instructions

See instructions on page 89.

Commentary

Over and over again, the Course urges us to "be still." It is remarkable how much benefit can be derived from simply pausing, even just for ten seconds, closing the eyes, and remembering the peace of God that is within me. Just the word "peace," repeated silently, can have a soothing, healing effect on the mind. This is not something that will come to us without conscious cooperation. Practice is necessary. "I *will* be still" (1:2, emphasis mine); it is an act of the will, a choice, a decision. The frantic onflow of thoughts and concerns has to be interrupted, and the mind turned towards that "stillness" (1:3) that "is within my heart" (1:4).

Most of our waking hours (and probably most of our sleeping hours as well, although we aren't aware of it) are spent in various concerns that, when stripped down to their basics, are concerns about our bodies, in one way or another. The daily caretaking of bathing, grooming, dressing, feeding, and resting our bodies goes on and on. The time we spend "earning a living" is necessitated by the need for money to purchase food, clothing, and shelter, and to entertain ourselves. But we are not bodies. We need frequent reminders of that fact. We need to pause and say, "Peace, be still" to ourselves. It seems easier not to make the effort, to just let the current of bodily concerns carry us onward from one moment to the next. Yet when we make the effort, when we step out of the flow for a minute to simply be still and find the peace of God,

106

everything begins to go more smoothly. We find ourselves happier than we were before. As an old Christian hymn put it, "Things that once were wild alarms cannot now disturb my rest."

We have a wellspring of peace within our hearts. It waits for us to simply dip into it and drink from its refreshing pool. It is there now, shining within us. Right now, and often today, "I will be still." I will draw on that inner wealth, "which witnesses to God Himself" (1:4).

LESSON 209 ✦ JULY 28

Central theme:

"I am not a body. I am free. For I am still as God created me."

Review of:

(189) "I feel the Love of God within me now."

 Practice instructions

See instructions on page 89.

Commentary

I was created by the Love of God (1:2). Creating and loving are the same (see T-7.I.3:3). Love, by its nature, extends outward and creates more of Itself, creates like Itself. "God created you by extending Himself as you" (T-7.I.5:2). "Think you that you can judge the Self of God? God has created It beyond judgment, out of His need to extend His Love" (T-15.V.11:1–2). Our Self was created out of the need of Love to extend Itself. We are the natural result of Love's extension.

Therefore, we are that Love, extended. What I am is Love; Love is what I am. It is everything I am. There is no part of me that is not Love. I am wholly Love. That in me which seems to be something else— which may seem this morning to feel fearful, or depressed, or dull, or lifeless, or angry, or spiteful—is only illusion, a figment of my imagination. It is not real. It is not me. I am only Love, and therefore I teach only Love.

I am Love's Son, by Love's own proclamation (1:4). I am made in the image and likeness of Love. I cannot be anything other than loving, nor have I ever been anything other than loving. When I have believed I was something else, I was only dreaming. I am not a body, obsessed with self-preservation. I am free to love, and free to love freely. "God will never cease to love His Son, and His Son will never cease to love Him" (T-10.V.10:6).

"The Love of God within me sets me free" (1:5). It is connecting with that Love within myself that liberates me from my self-imposed bondage. It is accepting this Love *as* myself that frees me from guilt. It is allowing that Love to flow through me that frees me from sorrow and fills me with joy. Love is my liberator.

Let me accept today that the Love of God is in me. Let me *feel* Its presence. Let me be glad that Love is what I am. All the little things that seem to trouble me, that seem to tell me I am less than Love, or that anyone is less than Love, fade into nothing as I open my heart to Love.

LESSON 210 ✦ JULY 29

Central theme:

"I am not a body. I am free. For I am still as God created me."

Review of:

(190) "I choose the joy of God instead of pain."

Practice instructions

See instructions on page 89.

Commentary

If we saw, clearly, that this was our choice—*joy* or *pain*—would there be any difficulty in making the choice?

Learning that this *is* the only choice is what takes so much time.

We are so confused about what brings us joy. We are quite convinced that our bodies can bring us joy. We are certain that a good romantic relationship would bring us joy. (Is that an oxymoron, "a good romantic relationship"?) We are very sure that giving up certain things in this world would bring us a great deal of pain. It takes time, and sometimes the illusion of "giving up," to learn that we give up nothing. "It takes great learning both to realize and to accept the fact that the world has nothing to give" (M-13.2:1).

"Pain is my own idea" (1:2). What a stunning statement! Pain is an idea I thought up independently of God. In fact, pain *is* thinking independently of God. Pain is trying to find happiness *in this world*. I have taught myself that the greatest pleasure of all is total autonomy, complete independence, absolute self-sufficiency. I have chosen this, and in doing so, invented pain. Now, I am unlearning what I taught myself. Now, I am learning to choose God's Will instead of what I made, joy instead of pain. "I am teaching you to associate misery with the ego and joy with the spirit" (T-4.VI.5:6).

Let me realize today that in saying, "I am not a body," I am choosing joy instead of pain. In continuing to affirm, "I am a body," I am choosing pain instead of joy.

LESSON 211 ✦ JULY 30

Central theme:

"I am not a body. I am free. For I am still as God created me."

Review of:

(191) "I am the holy Son of God Himself."

 Practice instructions

See instructions on page 89.

Commentary

To seek the glory of God in my Self—that sounds a little pretentious. Yet the lesson says we seek this glory "in true humility" (1:2). Naturally, the Course is speaking of *the* Self, and not *my* self. "This does not refer, however, to the self of which the world speaks" (M-4.VII.2:2). When someone says, "The glory of God is in me," or "I am the Son of God Himself," it makes a very big difference what "me" is being spoken of. If it is the self that we believe exists separate from the billions of other selves in this world, we are not speaking the truth. We *are* being pretentious. If it refers to the Self that is shared by all those billions, the Self of which my little consciousness is just one fragment, it is the truth that sets us free.

The glory of God does not reside in the little self, but it does reside in the Self. And beholding that glory "in the Son whom He created as my Self" (1:2) does not lead to delusions of grandeur, but to true grandeur, a grandeur that is instantly perceived as shared with all living things. There can be no setting of myself above any others, for the glory in them is my own.

These final review lessons, before Part II of the Workbook, refer a lot to things like silence, and beholding the glory of God. In these times of practice, let us seek to open ourselves to that kind of experience, to a seeing that is not of the eyes, to an awareness of the reality of our Self, God's Son. Let my little thoughts be silent, and let me hear the Voice for God speaking within me, speaking to my self of my Self, wooing me

111

back into harmony with that vastness of Being to which I belong, gathering together the seeming fragments of the Sonship into one harmonious whole. I am, indeed, still as God created me. Not just a body, not bound by the body, not characterized by the body, but "free of all limits, safe and healed and whole" (W-pI.97.7:2). I am that which God created, the holy Son of God Himself.

LESSON 212 ✦ JULY 31

Central theme:

"I am not a body. I am free. For I am still as God created me."

Review of:

(192) "I have a function God would have me fill."

Practice instructions
See instructions on page 89.

Commentary

What is the function God has for me? Lesson 192, which this lesson reviews, told me that "forgiveness represents your function here" (W-pI.192:2:3). I need to be reminded of that. My function is not some particular career or occupation. The content is what matters; the form will shape itself to that content, based on the circumstances of my life. Forgiveness is the content. If I am asking myself what my occupation should be, or what direction my life should take, let me ask myself this question: How does forgiveness best take form in my life right now? Or better yet, let me ask the Holy Spirit that question.

An "occupation" is what occupies most of my life. How, in form, can I occupy most of my life with forgiveness? How can I best serve to look upon illusions and see them disappear? How can I best serve to assist myself, and others, to let go of all guilt? How can I best reflect love in this world?

I work as a writer (you may do something quite different—fill in as you please). But that occupation is not my function; it is only one means of *expressing* my function, which is forgiveness—the same function God has given to all of us. The form may change or disappear; my function remains unchanged. A few years ago I was working as a computer consultant because, at that time, I felt that was the best means I had of fulfilling my function. Then, the form changed. But not the content.

Let me not seek any function in terms of form. Let me always seek the content. It is the content of forgiveness, of reflecting love in this world and releasing from guilt, that will set me free from illusions. No form can do that, since every form is itself part of the illusion. So all that I seek, and all that I lay claim to as mine, is the function God gave me (the content) and not any occupation, or job, or situation.

I am not a body (a form). I am free. I am formless, and I am therefore not tied to form of any kind.

LESSON 213 ✦ AUGUST 1

Central theme:

"I am not a body. I am free. For I am still as God created me."

Review of:

(193) "All things are lessons God would have me learn."

 Practice instructions
See instructions on page 89.

Commentary

Every circumstance of life offers me the choice between a miracle and my own ego thoughts, which will hurt me. Or as the Text puts it, "The choice is miracles instead of murder" (T-23.IV.5:6). That is the lesson that all things have to teach me, today and every day. Which voice, ego or Holy Spirit, will I listen to in this moment, and the next, and the next? It's always one or the other, never neither, never both. "You will not make decisions by yourself whatever you decide. For they are made with idols or with God. And you ask help of anti-Christ or Christ, and which you choose will join with you and tell you what to do" (T-30.I.14:7–9).

In each situation I face today, this is what is going on. The ego offers its interpretation, and the Holy Spirit offers His; I choose which to listen to. I can choose the miracle, or murder. My choice determines my perception and my experience of the situation. Which will I choose today?

> When the temptation to attack rises to make your mind darkened and murderous, remember you *can* see the battle from above. Even in forms you do not recognize, the signs you know. There is a stab of pain, a twinge of guilt, and above all, a loss of peace. This you know well. When they occur leave not your place on high, but quickly choose a miracle instead of murder. (T-23.IV.6:1–5)

This choice is what sets me free. The Holy Spirit is always with me to help me make this choice. In each instant I can choose to learn the lessons God wants me to learn, and forget what I have been teaching myself. Let me not evaluate anything without His help.

If we could grasp just this one lesson, this habit of referring everything to the Holy Spirit, rather than trying to figure it out by ourselves (which always means *with the ego's help*), everything else would simply fall into place. This alone is enough to set us free.

One thing the Holy Spirit sees differently from the ego is my body. "The Holy Spirit does not see the body as you do, because He knows the only reality of anything is the service it renders God on behalf of the function He gives it" (T-8.VII.3:6). When I choose to protect the body, to make it the center of what I am doing, mistaking the body for myself, I am choosing murder. I am not a body. I do not exist for my body's sake; its purpose is to render service to God as I carry out the function He has given me in the world, and that is all. If I listen to the Holy Spirit, I have to be willing to see the body as meaningless in itself (W-pI.96.3:7), and useful only as a communication device with which to reach my brothers. Let me remind myself that I am not a body, as in each moment I seek to hear the Voice for God.

LESSON 214 ✦ AUGUST 2

Central theme:

"I am not a body. I am free. For I am still as God created me."

Review of:

(194) "I place the future in the Hands of God."

 Practice instructions

See instructions on page 89.

Commentary

Accepting that the past is gone is simply common sense, because by definition, what is "past" is no longer here; it is gone. Only our mental attachment to things past, our insistence on regurgitating past incidents and chewing them over again, can have any effect on the present. The effects we feel are not of the past, but of our present thinking about the past.

Accepting that the future has not yet arrived is also common sense, because again by definition, what is future is not here now. It cannot have any effect on the present moment. Only our mental imagination of what the future might hold, and our thinking about what has not yet occurred, can have present effect.

In both cases, the effects that we imagine come from past or future come, in fact, from our present thinking. Therefore, only by changing our present thinking can those effects be altered. When I am able to mentally let go of the past and the future, placing the future in God's Hands, I am freed from their apparent effects. I am at liberty, in the now, to open myself to accept what God is giving me *now*.

The present circumstances in which I find myself may appear to be threatening. They may have come about, in my perception, because of past events. They may appear to lead inevitably to some unhappy future. Yet if I can open my mind to believe that "what God gives can only be for good" (1:4), then that good will come to me. We cannot know all the factors involved in the events of our lives and their effect on everyone around us. But God knows. We can safely and confidently take our hands off, and place the future in God's Hands. We can look upon things that seem to bring evil and refuse the evil, accepting only what *God* gives as what truly belongs to us. In everything, there is a gift of God, if we look carefully enough. To place our future in God's Hands we must let go ourselves, and stop trying to orchestrate the events of our lives. Doing so is a constant lesson in trust. Trust is the key, an essential ingredient in placing the future into God's Hands.

In the Manual for Teachers, the fundamental stage in the process of development from "teacher of God" to "advanced teacher of God" is the development of trust. The full flowering of trust is not an overnight process. It goes through several stages, clearly set out in the Manual. Most of those stages involve some discomfort, because until we have truly acquired trust, we keep trying to second-guess God. The pain comes not from the learning, but from what we have not yet learned. What we are learning will bring the removal of the pain, but pain along the way seems almost unavoidable. "Few teachers of God escape this distress entirely" (M-4.I.5:3). Yet when the lesson is learned, the peace will be like nothing we have ever known. We can only imagine what total freedom from all anxiety feels like, and yet, if we have wholly placed our future into God's Hands, what else could be the certain result?

Each effort we make in this direction is beneficial. Each moment we place into His Hands will lessen the burden of care we carry constantly for our lives. Gradually, we are learning to cast all our cares on Him, trusting in His caring for us.

LESSON 215 ✦ AUGUST 3

Central theme:

"I am not a body. I am free. For I am still as God created me."

Review of:

(195) "Love is the way I walk in gratitude."

 Practice instructions

See instructions on page 89.

Commentary

Today's review adds a new note to the lesson. I walk in the way of love. As I walk, the Holy Spirit walks with me (1:3–4), and shows me the way to go.

Walking in the way of love is not always simple. Often, the "loving thing" to do is not obvious. If someone breaks into my home, and is arrested, do I press charges, or do I let them off the hook? Which action is "loving"? Or, to make it much more simple: A friend, prone to misuse of money, asks me for a loan. Do I give them the money, or refuse? Which is the way of love?

I do not know. Even if I think I know, I do not know. I cannot possibly know all the variables. I cannot evaluate the ego motivation of another. How could I possibly do that when I can't even evaluate my own ego motivations? I cannot judge when a person is open to a merciful action, or when the most loving thing would be to let them face the consequences of their mistakes. But the Holy Spirit does know all those things. He is my only Guide. My past experiences, no matter how extensive, are never enough to grant me perfect judgment. The Holy Spirit, however, knows every detail of every situation. He knows the ramifications of every possible outcome, and can guide me in the loving action I should choose.

How do I discern His Voice? Again, there is no guaranteed way. Learning to discern His Voice clearly is a lifelong process. All I need do

119

is to refer the situation to Him, consciously give it into His hands, and then act in whatever way seems best to me. Each day, and in each situation, I renew my resolve to never make a decision by myself. Sometimes I will sense an inner "nudge" in a certain direction, for no reason I can detect. Perhaps circumstances will occur that seem to point me in a particular direction. Serendipitous coincidences may occur that seem to be signs, directing me. Other times I will seemingly be left on my own. The Course promises us that if we make a mistake, He will correct us, if we have given the situation to Him. We will make mistakes, but we have His promise of correction.

One of the most important aspects of hearing His Voice, I have learned, is letting go of any investment in a particular outcome. The only outcome I seek is the outcome of forgiveness, the outcome of love, the outcome of peace of mind in all concerned. I cannot pick what external circumstances are best suited to this kind of outcome; only the Holy Spirit knows. A rebellious teenager threatens to leave home, or drop out of school. As a parent or friend I may believe that the best thing is that she stay at home, or stay in school. I do not know. Perhaps the lessons she needs to learn can only be found if she distances herself for a while from family and friends. So I lay the situation in the hands of the Holy Spirit, and ask that I be guided to say and do whatever best serves the way of love. Then, I keep my hands off. I trust that I *am* being guided, even if things begin to move in a way I, in my shortsightedness, do not like. My primary responsibility is simply not to interfere with Him.

Today, let me walk the way of love in gratitude, trusting the Holy Spirit to guide my every word and action. Let me remind myself that I am here only to be truly helpful, to represent Him Who sent me, knowing that I do not have to worry about what I will say or do, for He will direct me (see T-2.V(A).18:2–6).

LESSON 216 ✦ AUGUST 4

Central theme:

"I am not a body. I am free. For I am still as God created me."

Review of:

(196) "It can be but myself I crucify."

Practice instructions

See instructions on page 89.

Commentary

The heart of the little summary today is the first sentence: "All that I do I do unto myself" (1:2). If we applied that one idea consistently, what a transformation there would be in our part of the world!

My own little personal list (you can make your own):

- How do I greet people on the telephone?
- How do I respond to interruptions?
- How do I regard people serving me in stores and restaurants?
- How do I react to snippets of talk I hear on the evening news?
- How do I treat poor or homeless people I encounter?
- How do I think about the very rich?
- How do I think about other drivers?
- What do I say to others about my friends when they are not present?

"All that I do I do unto myself." Is it any wonder I feel mistreated and misunderstood? All of these "little" examples are expressions of the ego's desire to crucify the Son of God. Each of them betrays the way I am treating myself, when I listen to my ego. This explains that wonderful saying in the Manual, "The teacher of God is generous out of Self interest" (M-4.VII.2:1).

LESSON 217 ✦ AUGUST 5

Central theme:

"I am not a body. I am free. For I am still as God created me."

Review of:

(197) "It can be but my gratitude I earn."

Practice instructions

See instructions on page 89.

Commentary

The salvation described by the Course is unique in the way it combines total responsibility for our own salvation with total dependence on God. My Self is what "saves" me, yet that Self is discovered only by recognizing that what I am is not any result of my own action, but the gift of God in creation.

There is a line in the Text that says, "Give thanks to every part of you that you have taught how to remember you" (T-13.VII.17:8). The gratitude we feel as we begin to awaken to what we are is due to the Self that we are discovering. I am the one who gives thanks; I am also the One to Whom thanks are being given.

It is very hard to understand all of this until you begin to experience it. I vividly recall one particular time in which it seemed to come to crystal clarity for me, for a few moments at least. I became aware of a loving part of myself that was continually moving me and motivating me in the direction of inner peace and Self-acceptance. It was something that had always been there, more than a part of me, the reality of myself. I was simultaneously aware of another part of my mind that had begun to open up to that love, and in that moment, I felt a deep and inexpressible gratitude to myself for being willing to receive that love. I was aware both of being the giver of the love and the receiver of it, and in that moment the little self I had always thought was me felt swallowed up in this much larger, constantly moving, tide of love.

This peculiar gratitude to my Self can find expression in many little ways. Sometimes when I have taken the time for a quiet meditation, one in which I feel strongly renewed, I find the gratitude welling up, and I say, "Thank you." And I am not sure whether I am thanking God or myself. I am grateful to myself for having readied myself to receive this Course. I am thankful to myself for reading it, and continuing to study it and to apply it. When a line from the Course pops into my head at just the right moment, I can thank my Self for it.

The Course teaches that we all are already awake; the truth lives untarnished in our right mind. And it is this right mind, this Self that is the only part of us that has reality in truth, which is teaching us and calling us home. This right mind is the home of the Holy Spirit; He is part of us as well as part of God. His Voice is the Voice for God, yet it is also the Voice of my Self. It is my Self that brought the Course into the world. It is my Self that drew me to it. It is my Self that is bringing me to awareness. Everything that nudges me in the right direction is a gift from my Self.

Let me be grateful to my Self today. Let me recognize that I am deserving of my own gratitude. Instead of being annoyed with myself, impatient with myself, harsh on myself, discouraged with myself, or untrusting of myself, let me offer myself my own gratitude. And let me realize that my own gratitude is all I need and want. Let me understand that when I have learned fully to be completely grateful to my Self for what I am, I will have completed the journey, and will have learned, at the same time, to be fully appreciative and grateful to God for the gift He has given me: my Self.

LESSON 218 ✦ AUGUST 6

Central theme:

"I am not a body. I am free. For I am still as God created me."

Review of:

(198) "Only my condemnation injures me."

 Practice instructions

See instructions on page 89.

Commentary

Condemnation does not injure the body. It reminds me of the old childhood chant, "Sticks and stones may break my bones, but names can never hurt me." I am not a body; what I am cannot be hurt by "sticks and stones." Only my own condemnation, my acceptance of those "names," can hurt me.

Haven't you called yourself names? I know I have. "You idiot!" "You are so stupid, Watson!" These self-mocking name-callings still, after all these years, pop into my head and out of my own mouth. They are only surface symptoms of a much deeper self-condemnation and mistrust of myself that is at the root of all my problems. Marianne Williamson hits the target when she says, "The ego is my self-loathing."

And when I realize that every other form of outward-directed condemnation—anger, prejudice, hatred, resentment, common dislike, even simple discomfort with someone—are all, every one, projections of my own self-attack, then I begin to realize just how deep and how far-reaching this self-condemnation really is. This condemnation injures *me*. I hurl my spears of attack out at the world, and every one returns to stab me in the back. "It can be but myself I crucify" (W-pI.216.1:1).

As long as I keep this war against myself going, my eyes are sightless to see my own glory. I cannot see the Christ in myself because of the dust storm of self-condemnation, whether it is directed inward or projected outward on illusions of myself I think are outside of me. It is the constant stream of judgment that blinds me.

Today, if I only choose to do so, I can see my own glory. All that I need is to accept Atonement for myself. Tune out the Judgment Channel. Tune in the Forgiveness Channel. Let me be quiet now, and sense the Love within: the Love of God for me, His child; my love for Him; my Self's own love for me, and mine for my Self. And often, today, let me stop and remind myself that the only thing that *can* injure me is my own condemnation. And I am free to choose to let that go, assisted by the Holy Spirit, my inner Self, and all the angels of Heaven.

Whenever I feel a rush of judgment within, wherever it is directed, let me bring my case to Heaven's Higher Court, and hear the Holy Spirit dismiss the case against me (see T-5.VI.4, 10).

LESSON 219 ✦ AUGUST 7

Central theme:

"I am not a body. I am free. For I am still as God created me."

Review of:

(199) "I am not a body. I am free."

Practice instructions

See instructions on page 89.

Commentary

Well, we don't get much choice today. We've got to take another look at the fact that we are not bodies.

The belief that I am a body, I think, is what put us here in this world, wearing a body. I may say I believe I am not a body, and that I understand what I am saying, but I'm still wearing a body. That shows that my words and the deep belief of my mind are not entirely in synch. The reason the Course has had us repeating this idea for the last twenty days (it started with Lesson 199) is certainly not because we already believe it and don't need it; obviously, the Course is recognizing that our belief that we are bodies is deeply imbedded in us, and the repetition is necessary to begin counteracting that belief. Remember that in Lesson 199, it suggested we make this idea a part of our practice *every day*. Our identification with our bodies is not an idea that will be easily dislodged.

The juxtaposition of the words "I am not a body" with the words "I am free" is interesting. If I had written the Course I would probably have said, "I am not a body. I am a spirit," or something like that. Why do you suppose Jesus put these two thoughts together?

The body is an enslaving thing. All of us are slaves to our bodies. Think how much time and energy of our so-called life in this world is devoted to caring for the body. We feed it, we work to house it and cloth it, we wash it, we devote entire rooms in our house to taking care of the needs for elimination and cleansing, we buy all sorts of gadgets to groom it. Every week or so we clip our nails. We make appointments for haircuts. Look at the cookbook section in a bookstore some time to get a feel for the thought and care that goes into just the feeding aspect. Look at our supermarkets, our clothing stores, shoe stores. Most stores in a mall have to do with caring for the body. Look at the expense we devote to health care and hospitals.

What if I am not a body? What if this great focus of effort and attention is all misdirected? What if we are majoring in minors? What if the center of gravity in our lives began to shift from caring for the body to caring for the spirit? What would my life and your life be like if that happened? What if I were as consistent in seeking holy instants as I am in feeding my face? What if I began stopping several times a day to feed my spirit as regularly as I do to eat, or go to the bathroom? We find it so easy to say to a friend, "Care for a cup of coffee?" What if it were just as easy to say, "Care to spend a few minutes in meditation with me?"

Just thinking about this makes it evident how unbalanced our lives are and how centered on our bodies. It makes me realize how far we have yet to go. And since change begins in the mind, just reminding myself as often as I can remember to do so, "I am not a body," is a good way to begin the great shift. Perhaps something as simple as letting my meals be a reminder to say a prayer can help, not because praying over food makes it any better, but because it helps me remember that I need my spiritual nourishment as much, or more, than I need physical food. Each time I become aware that I am taking time and effort to care for my body, let it remind me also to care for my spirit.

Think, too, of the freedom that will come to us when we realize that our body is no big deal. What I am is not something that wears out, grows old, and dies. What I am is not something that is a "brief candle," as Shakespeare called it, but an eternal star shining forever in the heavens. The body is deserving of care because it is a useful tool for the situation in which we find ourselves, but no more than that. Like a car it is good for the purpose it serves. But the body is not "me" any more than my car is "me" (auto ads to the contrary). Think of all the anxiety and constant concern that would be lifted from our shoulders if we can think of our bodies in this way. Changing our mind in this respect is worth all the effort it will take.

LESSON 220 ✦ AUGUST 8

Central theme:

"I am not a body. I am free. For I am still as God created me."

Review of:

(200) "There is no peace except the peace of God."

 Practice instructions
See instructions on page 89.

Commentary

To see ourselves as bodies is to be in conflict. Peace can be found only in God. Searching for peace in the realm of the physical is doomed to failure, because the body is an expression of conflict.

The prayer in this review lesson is about not wandering from "the way of peace" (1:2). What might that mean? Obviously, it refers to any unpeaceful state of mind, any thought of antagonism, or anger, or attack, or hatred. The Course calls us to mental vigilance, watching our thoughts for anything that opposes peace, and, as soon as such a thought is detected, bringing it to the presence of the Holy Spirit for healing. We are told to think along these lines: "This is not what I want. I want the peace of God." So when we sense our thoughts moving into conflict mode, we respond. Perhaps we pray, "Let me not wander from the way of peace" (1:2).

Wandering from the way of peace, however, includes more than overt attack. The ego can disguise attack very subtly; indeed, the Course sees even our special love relationships, our false forgiveness, and our ego's attempts at empathy as veiled attacks. If there is no peace except God's peace, then to seek for peace in some other way is really a hidden attachment to attack. If there is only one road to my destination, and I choose not to follow the road, I am choosing my destination's opposite. It is really seeking peace through war, which is impossible. The ego, for instance, often seeks for illusory peace through force, attempting to physically or mentally overpower the situation. We cannot find peace by attempting to browbeat the world into submission. On any such road, we are not moving toward peace; we are lost.

The way to God's peace is through following the Holy Spirit, "Him Who leads me home" (1:3). When we try to solve our problems on our own, we are not following the way to peace:

> The ego always tries to preserve conflict. It is very ingenious in devising ways that seem to diminish conflict, because it does not want you to find conflict so intolerable that you will insist on giving it up.   (T-7.VIII.2:2–3)

Trying to use our own ingenuity to resolve conflict, then, is another way we wander from the true road to peace.

When conflict seems to arise today, let me remember my lesson, that there is no peace except the peace of God. Let me instantly seek peace, but not in my own way. Let me turn to the Holy Spirit within and ask His direction.

> When you feel the holiness of your relationship is threatened by anything, stop instantly and offer the Holy Spirit your willingness, in spite of fear, to let Him exchange this instant for the holy one you would rather have. He will never fail in this.   (T-18.V.6:1–2)

III

The Introduction to Part II

The introduction to Part II of the Workbook is the last set of practice instructions we will receive for the next 140 days. The final instructions will be for the last five lessons, and do not really change much. So, since we will be following this set of instructions every day for the next five months, we need to pay close attention and fix them in our minds.

Remember that the Workbook is designed to train us in practicing, and to help us form a habit of daily practice that will endure until engaging with God in our lives has become a moment-to-moment way of life, with no need for any further practice. For a very few, this happy habit might be formed in a single year of doing the Workbook, although I know of no one for whom this is true. For most people, it seems, the pattern of practice being taught is still poorly formed and sporadically practiced after only one pass through the Workbook. Many find repeating the Workbook very beneficial, and its clear structure a necessary support in continuing to develop the desired habits.

Before we go over what the desired pattern of practice is, though, let me encourage you with a few observations from my own practice and that of several friends. Do not be discouraged if, on reading over the description of the daily practice, you realize that you are still far from "matching up" to the pattern. The form of daily practice described in this introduction is the *goal*; being distressed because you don't match up to it right now is like being upset that you can't play Tchaikovsky's First Piano Concerto after only a few weeks of practice. Forming habits takes a lot of time. Just do the best you can each day, and practice forgiving yourself when you don't measure up to your intentions. Whatever you do, keep at it! Don't allow the ego to kill your motivation to practice by pointing out how poorly you are doing it. Failure to follow the instructions fully is not a reason to stop practicing; it is a reason to return to practice with renewed vigor, as soon as you realize you have slipped.

The goal of our practice is to completely retrain our minds. It is to become so habituated to listening to the Voice for God that it becomes natural, something we do without even thinking about it, the first response to every temptation. The goal is to respond to every ego thought without fear, and instantly bring it into the holy place where we meet with God in our minds. The long-term goal of our practice is to arrive at the place where life becomes one continuous holy instant (W-pI.135.19:1), in which we never cease to think of God (W-pI.153.18:1). The short-term goal of Workbook practice is to form the habit of daily practicing that will take us to that long-term goal (W-pI.rIII.In.11:2; W-pI.194.6:2).

What, then, is the pattern of daily practice that is set forth for the next 140 days?

1. *Spending time with God each morning and night,* "as long as makes us happy" (2:6). The result we desire is "direct experience of truth alone" (1:3), or an experience of "rest" and "calm" (3:1), or experiencing the presence of God (4:1; 4:6). In sum, we desire to enter the holy instant; indeed, this introduction twice refers to our morning and evening practice times as "holy instants" (3:2; 11:4), or "times in which we leave the world of pain, and go to enter peace" (1:4). These experiences of holy instants are called "the goal this course has set" and "the end toward which our practicing was always geared" (1:5).

   So, every morning and evening practice period is meant to bring us to the holy instant, and "we will use as much [time] as we will need for the result that we desire" (2:8). The time is flexible, perhaps even a half hour or longer if we need or want that much time.

2. *Hourly remembrance* (2:9). Once each hour during the day, we will pause to remind ourselves of the lesson for the day, using the thought for the day to "calm our minds at need" (3:1). But the hourly remembrance is not simply a repeating of the words; it is a brief time in which we "expect our Father to reveal Himself, as He has promised" (3:3). Ideally this will be two or three minutes in which we can be quiet, perhaps closing our eyes, to refocus on our goal and regroup our thoughts, bringing any grievance or upset of the past hour to the Holy Spirit for healing (see W-pI.153.17 and W-pI.193.12). When such an extended pause is impossible, briefly turning our thoughts to God and reaffirming our goal is sufficient.

3. *Frequent reminders* in between the hours, although not specifically mentioned in this introduction to Part II, were singled out in the introduction to the review period we have just completed, and we can assume they are meant to be continued.

4. *Response to temptation.* Whenever we are "tempted to forget our goal" (2:9), we need to call to God. That the temptation mentioned is "to forget our goal" implies that all the rest of the time *we are remembering it*! So any time we notice our minds are about to wander from our goal, or have wandered, we call to God to help us return our minds to Him.

This is a rigorous spiritual practice. It demands considerable effort to form such habits. But the results are more than worth it. The goal of the Course, the whole purpose of Workbook practice, has been to bring us to this kind of direct experience of the truth. Without such direct experience, the concepts of the Text will be nothing more than empty concepts.

We are offered a little more detail about how to spend our extended morning and evening times. The specific words of the day's lesson, as it appears in the Workbook, are of diminishing importance. This is reflected in the fact that no more than a half page is given to them. The words of the lesson are not the focus any more (1:1); they are "but...guides on which we do not now depend" (1:2). The primary goal is direct experience of the truth, or the holy instant. Reading the daily lesson and repeating its main thought is only the beginning (2:1); having used the words to focus our minds, we spend our time waiting for God to come to us (3:3; 4:6). These times are called "periods of wordless, deep experience" (11:2). The bulk of our morning and evening times should be spent thus, in silent waiting and receptivity, without verbal thought.

If you look ahead at the lessons in Part II you will see that every one contains a short prayer to God the Father. There is no specific mention of these prayers nor how to use them, but I believe the following words give such instruction:

"We say some simple words of welcome, and expect our Father to reveal Himself, as He has promised" (3:3). "So our times with Him will now be spent. We say *the words of invitation that His Voice suggests*, and then we wait for Him to come to us" (4:5–6, my emphasis). Finally, the introduction itself shifts into prayer with a sort of un-self-conscious naturalness in 6:2–7:8; in 6:5 our prayers are called "little gifts of thanks" from us to God.

Those "words of invitation" suggested to us by God's Voice are, I believe, the prayers given to us in each day's lesson. They are words suggested for our use, to invite God to speak to us, to offer welcome to Him. Actually speaking these prayers, praying them, can be a powerful tool in bringing us the direct experiences with God these lessons intend for us.

> Instead of words, we need but feel His love. Instead of prayers, we need but call His Name. Instead of judging, we need but be still and let all things be healed.　　(10:3–5)

So the morning and evening times are not intended to be spent in thinking about the concepts of the Course, nor in saying prayers for ourselves or for others, nor in making decisions about what to do or making judgments of how to solve our problems. They are meant to be times of *experience* and not thought. Simply feeling God's Love. Simply repeating His Name in our awareness of relationship with Him. Simply being still, letting go, *letting* all things be healed, like a patient lying still as the Healer does His work. "Sit silently and wait upon your Father" (5:5).

There are words of encouragement in this introduction, assuring us that we couldn't have come this far if the goal were not our true will; if, in our hearts, we did not want God to come to us and reveal Himself. This *is* our will, in case we are having any doubts, or looking at what is being asked of us and questioning whether or not we want it deeply enough. We do.

Jesus says, "I am so close to you we cannot fail" (6:1). "For now we cannot fail" (5:4). He reviews the way we have come, from our insane wish that God would fail to have the Son He created, to our recognition that illusions are not true. The end is near, he tells us. I think it is important to realize that he is speaking in the context of eons of time; "near" is a relative term, and probably is not referring to days or weeks or months. He says here that "the need for practice [is] almost done" (10:1). Yet in the Manual (Section 16) he makes it clear that some kind of practice is part of the lifelong habit of the teacher of God. "Almost done," as well, is relative to the billions of years we have spent in separation. We *are* very near the goal, in that context!

One last item about our daily practice for the next five months, which should be carefully noted: we are supposed to read one of the "What Is" sections *every day*, preceding either our morning or evening quiet time. Thus, each section will be read ten times. And each time we read it, we are asked to read it "slowly" and to think about it for a while (11:4).

Going along with this instruction, therefore, in the daily lesson comments that follow I will include my thoughts for that day about the current "What Is" section. I will comment, usually, on just a few sentences from the "What Is" section each day, covering the entire page over the period of ten days.

PART II PRACTICE INSTRUCTIONS

Purpose: The introduction to Part II talks as if, in the remaining part of this year, we are trying to reach the end of our spiritual journey: "This year has brought us to eternity" (10:8). However, the Manual, in Section 16 ("How Should the Teacher of God Spend His Day?") implies a more modest goal: to reach a place where we practice because of our own motivation and inspiration, rather than because a book is telling us to. This would transform our practicing from a special assignment into a way of life. Part II of the Workbook, with its absence of daily practice instructions, is an important step in this direction. If here, in the relatively formless landscape of Part II, your practice can blossom, rather than wither, you are close to graduating from the Workbook.

I think we need to combine these two goals: We should aim for eternity, realizing that by aiming high we will carry ourselves farther than if we didn't, even though we may only get as far as weaning ourselves from the Workbook's support. In other words, we should aim to graduate from time and space, *so that* we can reach the more realistic goal of graduating from the Workbook.

Reading the lesson: The lessons in Part II take a very different form than in Part I. After the day's idea, we find just two paragraphs, both worded in the first person, which expand and comment on the idea. This makes the Part II lessons look much like what we see in most of the reviews, where the idea for the day is followed by a series of "related comments" (W-pI.rI.In.2:3; 3:3) which are worded in the first person and expand on the idea. In the reviews, these related comments become part of the exercises. We read them over several times, we think about them, we repeat them to ourselves, we savor each word. We make them our own, which is why they are worded *as if* they are our own. We so fully engage them that reading them becomes more like a practice than a simple act of reading.

It makes sense that we should use the comments in the Part II lessons in the same way that we used the comments in the reviews, simply because the two are so similar. And the introduction hints at this. For it speaks of our reading of those paragraphs as an "exercise" (2:1) that is meant to induct us (1:4) into "the periods of wordless, deep experience which should come afterwards" (11:2). Let's look at how we can turn the reading of those two paragraphs into a genuine exercise.

First, the *commentary paragraphs* (the nonitalicized paragraphs). I recommend that you read these over slowly, perhaps several times, and imagine that these really are your own thoughts (which is how they are worded). To facilitate this, you may want to emphasize words like "I," "me," "my," and "mine."

Second, the *prayers.* These read as if you yourself are praying them to God, and I recommend doing just that. Fix one sentence at a time in your mind and then close your eyes and say that sentence to God. Try to really mean it and expect Him to hear you. These appear to be designed to carry you into the meditative state, and many of them virtually say that. Lesson 307 says of its prayer, "And with this prayer we enter silently into a state where conflict cannot come" (W-pII.307.2:1). To enhance this effect, you may want to pray the prayer several times.

Morning/evening quiet time: As long as you need for the effect you want.

The longer practice periods are meant to consist of Open Mind Meditation. Begin by repeating the idea for the day, but in a special way: as an invitation to God to come to you. "We say the words of invitation that His Voice suggests, and then we wait for Him to come to us" (4:6). After repeating these words, go into a time of expectant, wordless waiting (the word "wait" here occurs six times). To wait normally means to stay physically still in anticipation of some event. Here it means to stay *mentally* still in anticipation of a wondrous event: the dawning of God on your mind. Wait as if holding your breath for this event. Wait with an attitude that "the memory of God is shimmering across the wide horizons of our minds" (9:5). Your waiting, then, though motionless, should be very much alive. It should be filled with expectancy: "We…expect our Father to reveal Himself, as He has promised" (3:3). The basis for your expectancy, in other words, is your trust that God will keep His promises. He promised to come to you when you asked. You are asking; He will come. Hold this state without the aid of repeating words. However, whenever your mind wanders, you should use words—repeat the idea to draw yourself back to this nonverbal waiting. "We will use that thought…to calm our minds at need" (3:1).

If you find Open Mind Meditation either too challenging or too unrewarding, I would recommend using either of the other two methods the Workbook has taught: Down-and-Inward Meditation or Name of God Meditation. In fact, Lesson 222 clearly instructs you to use Name of God Meditation: *"Father, we have no words except Your Name upon our lips and in our minds, as we come quietly into Your Presence now"* (W-pII.222.2:1).

Hourly remembrance: One or two minutes as the hour strikes (reduce if circumstances do not permit).

Do a miniature version of the morning practice. Repeat the idea as an invitation to God, and then wait in wordless silence for Him to come to you.

Frequent reminder: As often as possible within each hour.

"Repeat [the idea], and allow your mind to rest a little time in silence and in peace" (W-pI.rIII.In.10:5).

Response to temptation: When you are tempted to let upset cause you to forget your goal.

Repeat the idea as a way of calling on God to dispel your upset (see 2:9 and 10:2).

Reading the "What Is" section: Before one of the day's practice periods (not necessarily the morning one), read the relevant "What Is" section. Don't just read it casually. Read it slowly and think about it "a little while" (11:4).

IV

Lessons 221 - 230
What Is Forgiveness?

LESSON 221 ✦ AUGUST 9

"Peace to my mind. Let all my thoughts be still."

Practice instructions

See complete instructions on page 135. A short summary:

- **Read** the commentary paragraph slowly and personally.
- **Pray** the prayer, perhaps several times.
- **Morning and evening:** Repeat the idea and then spend time in Open Mind Meditation.
- **Hourly remembrance:** Repeat the idea and then spend a quiet moment in meditation.
- **Frequent reminders:** Repeat the idea often within each hour.
- **Response to temptation:** Repeat the idea whenever upset, to restore peace.
- **Read the "What Is" section** slowly and thoughtfully once during the day.

Practice comments: Use the beautiful prayer here as an introduction to your meditation. With the prayer, you announce your intention to come to God in wordless silence, waiting for His

139

peace (1:1), waiting for His Voice to speak (1:3-5), waiting for the revelation of His Being (2:6). I suggest praying it several times, to draw you into that deep, silent waiting.

Commentary

As I emphasized in my comments on the introduction to Part II, a large part of our two longer daily practice times is meant to be spent in wordless quiet. Receiving our healing, listening rather than talking. Today's lesson is a great one for inducing that state of mind. We begin by directing our minds to be peaceful, our thoughts to be still.

The opening prayer in the first paragraph speaks of coming in silence, and in the quiet of our hearts, waiting and listening for God's Voice. The words used—"quiet," "silence" (twice), "the deep recesses of my mind," waiting, listening, coming to hear His Voice—all these words are pointing us in the same direction, fostering the same attitude in us. An attitude of receptivity. A passiveness, we the feminine to God's masculine, the receiver to the Giver of Life. We still our own thoughts, and allow God's Thoughts to come to us. We call to Him, and await His answer.

Jesus is with us as we quietly wait. He voices his confidence that God is with us, and that we will hear Him speak if we wait quietly with him. He asks us to accept his own confidence, telling us that his confidence is our own confidence. Often, I have found it helpful to realize that Jesus symbolizes the part of my own mind that is already awake. His confidence really *is* my confidence, a confidence I have denied so that I see it as outside myself.

We wait with only one goal: to hear His Voice speaking to us of what we are, and revealing Himself to us. In these times of quiet, this is what we are listening for: an awareness of the purity and perfection of our own being as He created us, and an awareness of His Love, His tender care for us, and His peace that He shares with us in these peaceful moments.

How can we hear a message without words? What we listen for is the song of love, eternally sung, forever thrumming its harmony throughout the universe. It is a song we hear wisps of in the eyes of our beloved, in the laughter of children, in the loyalty of a pet, in the expanse of a peaceful lake or the stately flowing of a river, and in the wonder of a well-told fairy tale. It is the song to which our hearts resonate, showing their true nature. It is our eternity calling us to dance. It is the Father sharing His Love with His only Son.

WHAT IS FORGIVENESS?

Part 1: W-pII.1.1:1

"Forgiveness recognizes what you thought your brother did to you has not occurred" (1:1).

Forgiveness is a different way of seeing yourself.

I want to emphasize the words "you thought" and "to you" in that description of forgiveness. It does not say, "What your brother did has not occurred," but rather "What *you thought* your brother did *to you* has not occurred." It is not a denial that an event happened, but rather a different way of seeing yourself in relationship to the event. You thought that you were affected by it, hurt by it, damaged by it, whatever "it" was; in fact you were not affected by what your brother did at all! You are affected, so the Course tells us, only by your thoughts.

First and foremost, forgiveness means seeing yourself differently in relation to an event. It does not begin with seeing an event or another person differently. When you forgive, what happens first is that you recognize that you have not lost your peace or your love because of what happened; you lost it because you chose to lose it. You decided, at some point, to let go of the peace of God in your heart. The event then came along to justify your loss of peace. You projected the loss of peace onto the event and said, "That is why I am upset."

Therefore, once your thought in regard to yourself has been corrected, you now can see your brother is innocent in spite of his action. He may indeed have done something despicable. You don't have to approve of what he did, or like it, or put up with it like a doormat. However, his action or words did not hurt you. It was not what he did that took away your peace. He did not affect you, he did not injure you. You now can see that "sin" did not occur, and that he has done nothing that warrants guilt. He has perhaps made a grievous mistake, but that hurts only himself, not you.

So much of what the Course talks about is implied in this simple statement, "What you thought your brother did to you has not occurred." You think he injured you, your self, because you are identified with your ego feelings, with your body, with your possessions, with your family members and their bodies and possessions and feelings. The Course teaches that we have identified incorrectly. We are not our bodies. We are not our possessions. We are not the ego with all its hurt feelings. We are something much grander and vaster than that, something that cannot be touched in any way by external forces.

To fully forgive, our identification with our bodies has to be completely over. None of us has attained that, yet. That is why the Course so confidently implies that not one of us has ever, yet, completely forgiven anyone! That is why it says that if only one person completely forgave one sin, the world would be healed (see M-14.3:7). (That is what Jesus accomplished, and because of it, the world is already healed. We just haven't been ready yet to receive it.)

A large part of my dealing with the Course has been in recognizing that, far from having no one to forgive, I have everyone to forgive.

If, in your picture of any situation, you still see yourself—or someone close to yourself—as having been in some way injured or hurt by the situation, you have not yet completely forgiven it in your mind. The Course teaches that if pain is real in your perception, you have not yet been completely healed (see W-pI.193.7:1–3).

Now, I haven't gotten past the first line on this page and probably I've got us all, including myself, feeling a little guilty about the fact that despite all our study of the Course we haven't yet learned to forgive. So I have to stop here, back off, and say: This is completely normal. Don't be surprised. And don't feel guilty about it! Before we can learn to forgive we have to admit that we are not forgiving! We need to recognize all the ways we still make pain real in our experience and belief, and just recognize that we are doing so. One lesson in forgiveness may be to forgive ourselves for being unforgiving.

"Forgiveness...is still, and quietly does nothing....It merely looks, and waits, and judges not" (W-pII.1.4:1, 3). Treat yourself that way! Get in touch with the part of you that does not want to forgive, that does not want peace. Look at it, and do nothing, just wait without judging. It will disappear (in time) and peace will come of itself.

LET US PRAY

What are we supposed to do with the prayers in Part II of the Workbook for *A Course in Miracles*? There are 140 of them, one for each lesson. This has puzzled many a Course student who, upon reaching Part II, finds himself confronted each day with an italicized prayer directed at God. Is this prayer offered by the author of the Course on our behalf? Do we simply read it? Do we actually pray it? If so, why?

Actually, I am only *assuming* that this issue has puzzled Course students. I have never really heard much discussion about these prayers. They sit there on the page, staring at us every day for five straight months, but we don't seem to talk much about them. The only perspective I recall hearing is that they must be metaphorical because God can't hear our prayers.

Having done the Workbook several times, I too didn't know what to do with these prayers. Yet, to be honest, I hadn't really confronted the question. I would just dutifully open my book and read the prayer attached to that day's lesson. The prayers generally struck me as being a kind of Course word salad: a series of typical Course words—Christ, peace, joy, Heaven, etc.—tossed together as one would toss a salad.

Then one day a few years ago, all that changed for me. I was on a short retreat and, for some reason, the first thing I did was sit down and try to discover what the Course wants us to do with its prayers. Having spent many years studying the Workbook's practice instructions, I had learned that virtually all our questions about practice are answered right in the Workbook, if we pay careful attention. Now, for the first time, it occurred to me that this ought to be true for those prayers; we should expect there to be instructions for what to do with them.

The logical place for those instructions was the introduction to Part II, since that is where we find the practice instructions for the entirety of Part II, where the prayers are found. Within minutes I found two sentences that ended my search and changed my relationship with the Course and with God. Here they are:

> We say some simple words of welcome, and expect our Father to reveal Himself, as He has promised. (W-pII.In.3:3)

> We say the words of invitation that His Voice suggests, and then we wait for Him to come to us.   (W-pII.In.4:6)

From these sentences and the paragraphs around them I obtained the following picture:

The Course has given us words (from the Holy Spirit) which we are to say to God as words of invitation and welcome. Once we invite Him with these words, we sit in a state of silent expectancy, waiting for Him to come and reveal Himself to us in direct wordless experience.

What are these "words"? In this context, they are definitely the thought for the day, the lesson title. But are they confined to that? Don't these "simple words of welcome" also sound like they could be the prayers? After all, like these words, the prayers are words given us by the Course which are written as if we are saying them to God.

So I turned the page and looked at the first prayers in Part II. They resoundingly confirmed what I was thinking. This is how the first prayer begins:

> Father, I come to You today to seek the peace that You alone can give. I come in silence.   (W-pII.221.1:1-2)

Just as the introduction described, in this prayer we state our intention to have an encounter with God in the silence of our minds. The comments that follow this prayer continue along the same lines: "Now [that we have said this prayer] do we wait in quiet....We wait with one intent...[for God] to reveal Himself unto His Son" (W-pII.221.2:1, 6). Here is exactly what the introduction said: Once we say these words of welcome, we wait in silence for God to reveal Himself to us.

The next prayer was very similar. In it we state our intention to silently enter into an experience of God's Presence:

> Father, we have no words except Your Name upon our lips and in our minds, as we come quietly into Your Presence now, and ask to rest with You in peace a while.
> (W-pII.222.2:1)

This was a very intellectual process of detective work, but its results were extremely practical: At last I felt I knew what to do with those prayers! I am to say them directly to God as preparation for a direct wordless encounter with Him.

So I immediately tried this out. I spent the next hour or so going through the first twenty prayers in Part II, praying them as I had just discovered I should. I will never forget that time. It was a pivotal moment in my journey with the Course. Until that moment, I had no idea how much richness was in those prayers. What seemed like word salad when read as information became a wealth of emotional experience when repeated as prayer, when spoken to God.

I was astonished by the sense of loving intimacy with God that shone through these prayers. I had never realized that *this* was how the Course wanted me to think about God. God came across not as a remote metaphysical abstraction, an impersonal essence that is completely unaware of us. Instead, He came across as near and dear, as the most attentive, loving Father one could possibly imagine, always there, always listening, always answering, wanting only to lavish all of His Love upon us. "He covers me with kindness and with care" (W-pII.222.1:4), one of the lessons said. And that is exactly how I felt, blanketed in His kindness and care.

Since that day, these prayers have become a staple in my daily life. There are few things I enjoy doing more than sitting down and spending time with them. They have literally transformed my relationship with God. My sense of God before was somewhat remote and abstract. Yet increasingly these prayers have implanted in me *their* sense of God, so that my feeling for Him has become a deep well of sustenance and comfort that I draw from daily.

As time went on, I fell into the habit of using these prayers before my meditation time, because I found them to be the ideal way to prepare my mind for seeking God in meditation. They gathered the scattered and chaotic threads of my thought into a single desire to be with God. After I had been using them in this way for some time, I remembered something: *This is exactly what they are for.* This is what the instructions in the Workbook say is their purpose. We are to use the words of these prayers to prepare our minds for a direct, wordless encounter with God. I can attest to the fact that they serve their intended purpose very well indeed.

I therefore encourage every student of the Course to avail him- or herself of the great benefit of these prayers. Try them out and see if you are not drawn to return to them. Here are some tips for getting the most out of them:

1. *Focus on one line at a time.* Dwell on each line and let it sink in before going on to the next.
2. *Say it directly to God.* When the prayer says "Father," have a sense of speaking directly to God, and of Him in some sense hearing you.
3. *Make it from you.* When the prayer says "I" or "me," have a sense of you being the one saying the prayer.
4. *Mean it*, as much as you can. Try to make it the prayer of your own heart.
5. *Make it specific.* For instance, when the prayer we will use below

says "a something I have called by many names," list some of the names you have given what you seek.

6. *Feel free to elaborate* on the prayer as it evokes additional thoughts and feelings in you.

To try out this method of using these prayers, I would like to utilize the following prayer from Lesson 231, "Father, I will but to remember You." My suggestion is for you to repeat each line slowly, with concentration and sincerity. Try to see the fullness of meaning contained in each line. Try also to go through the prayer twice or more.

1. *What can I seek for, Father, but Your Love?*
2. *Perhaps I think I seek for something else; a something I have called by many names.*
3. *Yet is Your Love the only thing I seek, or ever sought.*
4. *For there is nothing else that I could ever really want to find.*
5. *Let me remember You.*
6. *What else could I desire but the truth about myself?*

What was your experience in repeating these lines? Was it an experience you want more of? I sincerely hope that the prayers in the Workbook will become the blessing in your life that they continue to be in mine.

LESSON 222 ✦ AUGUST 10
"God is with me. I live and move in Him."

Practice instructions

See complete instructions on page 135. A short summary:

- **Read** the commentary paragraph slowly and personally.
- **Pray** the prayer, perhaps several times.
- **Morning and evening:** Repeat the idea and then spend time in Open Mind Meditation.
- **Hourly remembrance:** Repeat the idea and then spend a quiet moment in meditation.
- **Frequent reminders:** Repeat the idea often within each hour.
- **Response to temptation:** Repeat the idea whenever upset, to restore peace.
- **Read the "What Is" section** slowly and thoughtfully once during the day.

Practice comments: The prayer for this lesson states that we will be doing Name of God Meditation. It speaks of a time when we come to God with no words in our minds except His Name, using the repetition of that Name as a request to enter His Presence and rest with Him in peace. This, of course, is a perfect encapsulation of Name of God Meditation.

Commentary

Again we are brought to the Presence of God, without words, in quiet. Our only awareness is of God, His Name upon our lips.

What does it mean to "live and move" in God? This is the message that the Apostle Paul brought to the Athenians, speaking of the "unknown God," and saying that "in Him we live and move and have our being" (Acts 17:16–28). The lesson speaks of the omnipresence of God—that God is everywhere and "everywhen." In beautiful imagery, the lesson turns our thoughts to the all-pervading Presence, never apart from us, "closer...than breathing, and nearer than hands and feet," as

Tennyson wrote.

This is imagery and not (in my opinion) literal. If the world is illusion, as the Course has so often said, God is not *literally* "the water which renews and cleanses me" (1:2). This is speaking of our spiritual reality, where we *really* are. God is the reality of all things in which we look to the world for sustenance, the true Source of our life. We think we live in the world, but we live in God. We think our body contains our life, but He is our life. We think we breathe air, but we breathe Him. God is our true food and our true drink, our true home. We do not live and move in the world; we live and move in God.

Reading this lesson aloud is an excellent exercise. Or turning the first part into a prayer: "You are the Source of my life...You are my home...." Use these words at the start of your practice period to set your mind into a consciousness of being immersed in and filled with God, kept in His loving care. Then, be still, and let yourself sink into that Presence, to rest with Him in peace a while.

WHAT IS FORGIVENESS?

Part 2: W-pII.1.2–7

"Forgiveness," it says, "does not pardon sins and make them real. It sees there was no sin" (1:2–3). This is the whole distinction between true and false forgiveness, which the *Song of Prayer* calls "forgiveness-to-destroy" (S-2.1:2). There is such a difference between seeing sin in someone and struggling to overlook it or to refrain from the desire to punish, and seeing not sin but a mistake, a call for help from a confused child of God, and naturally responding with love. When the Holy Spirit enables us to see the "sin" of another in this way, suddenly we can see our own "sins" in that same very different light. Instead of trying to justify our own errors, we can admit they are mistakes and simply let them go, without guilt.

Sin is simply "a false idea about God's Son" (1:5). It is a false self-appraisal projected onto everyone around us. It is the belief that we are truly separate, attackers of God's Love in our separation; it sees attackers everywhere.

Forgiveness is seen here (1:6–7) in three steps. *First*, we see the falsity of the idea of sin. We recognize that no sin has occurred; the Son of God (in the other or ourselves) is still the Son of God, and not a devil. He has been mistaken, but he has not sinned. *Second*, closely following on the first step and a natural consequence of it, we let the idea of sin go. We drop it. We relinquish our grievances, abandon our thoughts of attack. Only the first step depends on our choice; the second step follows as its inevitable result. When we no longer see attack, what reason is there to punish with counterattack?

The *third* step is God's part. Something comes to take sin's place; the Will of God is freed to flow through us unhindered by our illusions, and Love follows its natural course. In this we experience our true Self, the extension of God's own Love.

All we need do, then, if it can be called doing, is to be willing to see something other than attack, something other than sin. We need only to be willing to admit that our perception of sin is false. When we do, the Holy Spirit will share His perception with us. He knows how to forgive; we do not. Our part is merely to ask to be taught by Him. He does the rest, and everything flows out of that simple willingness.

LESSON 223 ✦ AUGUST 11
"God is my life. I have no life but His."

Practice instructions

See complete instructions on page 135. A short summary:

- **Read** the commentary paragraph slowly and personally.
- **Pray** the prayer, perhaps several times.
- **Morning and evening:** Repeat the idea and then spend time in Open Mind Meditation.
- **Hourly remembrance:** Repeat the idea and then spend a quiet moment in meditation.
- **Frequent reminders:** Repeat the idea often within each hour.
- **Response to temptation:** Repeat the idea whenever upset, to restore peace.
- **Read the "What Is" section** slowly and thoughtfully once during the day.

Practice comments: In praying this particular prayer, I find it helpful to convert it to first person singular: *"My Father, let me see the face of Christ instead of my mistakes,"* etc.

Commentary

Our only mistake is thinking that we have some sort of life apart from God. We do not. God *is* Life. He is Being. He is Existence. He created all that there is, and there is nothing apart from Him. "Nothing can be apart from Him and live" (W-pI.156.2:9). "I do not exist apart from Him" (1:2).

Most of my time here on earth I have spent thinking of myself as someone or something apart from God. Most of my spiritual seeking has been a striving to "get back to God," as if He were unimaginably distant from me. He is not distant. He is not Something separate from my Self. "I have no life but His." There is a blessing often used in Unity churches which ends with the words "Wherever I am, God is." Yes. My life is God's Life. My thoughts are God's Thoughts. There is nowhere to go.

There is nothing to do to find Him; He is here. He is with me. He is my life. If I live, I am participating in God.

There is a blessed relief that washes over us when we realize our unity with God. All the bitter struggle, all the fruitless longing, all the aching sense of being on the outside looking in—all of it ends. A thought of pure joy fills our minds. At times it bubbles over into laughter, a certain compassionate amusement at the ludicrous idea we have tormented ourselves with, that we could ever, in any remote or tiny way, be separated from Him. Can the sunbeam be separate from the sun? Can an idea be separate from the mind that thinks it?

And so we turn again to the quiet place within, where all this is already known. We ask to "see the face of Christ instead of our mistakes" (2:1). We affirm that we no longer want to be lost in forgetfulness. We state clearly that we want to leave our loneliness and find ourselves, as we have always been, at home. And in the quiet, God speaks to us, and tells us we are His Son.

WHAT IS FORGIVENESS?

Part 3: W-pII.1.2:1–2

The second paragraph is all about *un*forgiveness. The distinguishing characteristic of an unforgiving thought is that it "makes a judgment that it will not raise to doubt, although it is not true" (2:1). The distinguishing characteristic of a forgiving mind, then, is that this mind *will* be willing to cast doubt on its own judgments! The unforgiving mind is saying, "My mind is already made up; don't confuse me with facts." The forgiving mind is saying, "Perhaps there is another way to look at this."

In the section discussing the ten characteristics of *advanced* teachers of God (Section 4 of the Manual for Teachers), the final characteristic is "open-mindedness." It says:

> As judgment shuts the mind against God's Teacher, so open-mindedness invites Him to come in. As condemnation judges the Son of God as evil, so open-mindedness permits him to be judged by the Voice for God on His behalf. (M-4.X.1:3–4)

The willingness to let go of our own judgments and hear the judgment of the Holy Spirit is what makes forgiveness possible. An unforgiving mind "is closed, and will not be released" (2:2). The forgiving mind is open. Over and over the Course asks us simply to be *willing* to see things differently, simply to be willing to question what we think we know, simply to "do this":

> Be still, and lay aside all thoughts of what you are and what God is; all concepts you have learned about the world; all images you hold about yourself. (W-pI.189.7:1)

With judgment set aside, "What then is free to take its place is now the Will of God" (1:7).

LESSON 224 ✦ AUGUST 12

"God is my Father, and He loves His Son."

Practice instructions

See complete instructions on page 135. A short summary:

- **Read** the commentary paragraph slowly and personally.
- **Pray** the prayer, perhaps several times.
- **Morning and evening:** Repeat the idea and then spend time in Open Mind Meditation.
- **Hourly remembrance:** Repeat the idea and then spend a quiet moment in meditation.
- **Frequent reminders:** Repeat the idea often within each hour.
- **Response to temptation:** Repeat the idea whenever upset, to restore peace.
- **Read the "What Is" section** slowly and thoughtfully once during the day.

Commentary

These lessons are helping us remember who we are: God's Son. Who we are is an Identity that is far beyond anything we can imagine, "so lofty...that Heaven looks to It to give it light" (1:1). In Lesson 221 we were silently waiting for God to "speak to us of what we are" (W-pII.221.2:6). In Lesson 222, we learned that what we are exists in an environment of God. In Lesson 223, we recognized that we are not separate, but exist entirely in union with God. And now, we remember our true Identity: His Son. Our Identity "is illusion's end. It is the truth" (1:6–7).

The truth of what we are is the end of all illusions. Or, the flip side, a mistake about what we are is the source of all illusions. We have forgotten it, but in these times of quiet with God, we ask Him to remind us, to reveal that Identity to us. We are "lofty, sinless, glorious and great, wholly beneficent and free from guilt" (1:1). Reading these words, notice how our conscious minds instantly question it, instantly recoil from the audacity of saying such things. It only shows how thoroughly we have deceived ourselves, how well we have learned our own lies. Yet something within, on hearing these words, begins to sing. Something within recognizes the melody of Heaven and starts humming along with it. Listen to that humming. Tune in to it. It is your Self, responding to God's Call. Say it! "God *is* my Father, and He *loves* His Son."

WHAT IS FORGIVENESS?

Part 4: W-pII.1.2:3–4

The unforgiving thought "protects projection" (2:3). Our minds, tormented with their own guilt, have projected the blame for our condition outside ourselves. We have found a scapegoat, as Adam did with Eve: "The woman gave me the fruit to eat. It was her fault." And so we cling to our unforgiveness, we *want* to find blame in the other, because to forgive, to let it go, would be to open the closet door that hides our guilt.

The more we cling to unforgiveness, the more we blind ourselves, the more solid our illusory projections seem to be, until we think it would be impossible to see in any other way. The distortions we impose on reality become "more veiled and more obscure" (2:3). Our self-deceptions become harder and harder to see through, "less easily accessible to doubt" (2:3). All we are being asked to do is to doubt them, to question our projections, to listen to a little reason. Unforgiveness blocks the way to this and tightens our own chains.

We see guilt in others because we *want* to see it there (2:4), and we want to see it there because it keeps us from seeing guilt in our own minds. Yet seeing the guilt in ourselves is the only way we can have it healed. If we deny we are wounded we will not seek the remedy. If we deny our own guilt and project it onto others, we will not bring ourselves into the healing Presence within, which is the only place it can be undone. If our mind is closed, if we are not willing to doubt our version of things, we are shutting the door to our own healing. Only in opening our mind, in loosening our determined grasp on finding others to be wrong, in allowing that "there *must* be a better way" (T-2.III.3:6), can we find our own release.

LESSON 225 ✦ AUGUST 13
"God is my Father, and His Son loves Him."

Practice instructions

See complete instructions on page 135. A short summary:

- **Read** the commentary paragraph slowly and personally.
- **Pray** the prayer, perhaps several times.
- **Morning and evening:** Repeat the idea and then spend time in Open Mind Meditation.
- **Hourly remembrance:** Repeat the idea and then spend a quiet moment in meditation.
- **Frequent reminders:** Repeat the idea often within each hour.
- **Response to temptation:** Repeat the idea whenever upset, to restore peace.
- **Read the "What Is" section** slowly and thoughtfully once during the day.

Practice suggestions: Here are some suggestions for praying this lesson's lovely prayer:

- *blazing in my mind:* Just imagine God's Love for you blazing in your mind.
- *and keeping it [my mind] within its [God's Love's] kindly light:* Imagine your mind kept, held, embraced within the kindly light of God's Love.
- *inviolate:* Held in this kindly light, your mind would be totally *inviolate*—free from violation, injury, and desecration, its sanctity untouched.
- *beloved:* Is there a better feeling in the world than to feel truly, totally beloved?
- *with fear behind:* Imagine feeling so loved that you felt like literally all fear was behind you.
- *and only peace ahead:* Imagine feeling so loved that all you could see ahead of you was *peace*.

● *How still the way Your loving Son is led along to You!* This final sentence speaks of how we will journey home when we love God (when we are His "loving Son") and so receive His Love for us. We will be led home in stillness, with all fear behind us and only peace ahead. Try to imagine this—journeying through life with your heart full of love for God and your mind shining with His Love for you, walking toward Him in pure stillness and peace. This is the end result of loving God—a life at peace because it is infused with the "full awareness" of His Love for you.

Commentary

Love is reciprocal. We receive God's Love for us by returning it to Him; there is no other way to receive it, for "giving and receiving are the same" (1:1). This *exact* phrase occurs six times in the Course, and there are many others very much like it. We may think we understand what it means, but the Course assures us that no concept it teaches is more difficult for us to truly learn.

The way to know God's Love blazing in our minds is to return It to Him. If in our times of quiet yesterday we focused on feeling His Love of us, let us today focus on our awareness of our love for Him. Donna Cary has a beautiful song I was listening to on tape just a day or two ago, which says, "I'll be forever in love with You." I wish I could send you all this song; it expresses so beautifully what I feel this lesson is saying. "I'll dance in the light of Your Love, forever in love with You."

What would it be like to have the Love of God "mine in full awareness, blazing in my mind and keeping it within its kindly light" (1:2)? Is this not what, in our heart of hearts, we all want? Let us cultivate this sense of love in our hearts today. Let simply this be our focus. Nothing complex, nothing even conceptual, just letting our hearts sing with love for God, basking in His Love for us. As the Song of Solomon in the Old Testament put it, "I am my Beloved's, and He is mine" (Song 6:3). To know God as the Beloved is one of the highest of spiritual expressions.

Have you ever sat in stillness with one you deeply love, simply gazing into his or her eyes, without words? That stillness of love is what this lesson is leading us to, a silent communion of love given and received, acknowledged and returned, flowing in an endless current that energizes and transforms our minds and hearts.

WHAT IS FORGIVENESS?

Part 5: W-pII.1.3:1–2

In contrast to the stillness today's lesson speaks of, an unforgiving thought is frantically active. It has to be. It must be frantic because it flies in the face of truth, and attempts to make real an illusion. Frenetic activity is often the sign of unrecognized unforgiveness. Things that seem to oppose what we want to be the truth keep popping up, like gophers in the silly kids' game of "bang the gopher," and we have to keep bashing them down to maintain our version of reality.

Stilling our mind and becoming quiet, in and of itself, is often enough to begin dissolving our unforgiveness. Unforgiveness cannot exist in quiet. You cannot be peaceful and unforgiving at the same time. "Peace to my mind. Let all my thoughts be still" (W-pII.221.Heading). One thing that can foster this peace and stillness is focusing on the very exchange of love that is the center of today's lesson. The power of our affection for God, and His for us, can quell the stormy thoughts and bring, even if only briefly, a moment of quiet peace, in which unforgiveness simply dissipates.

LESSON 226 ✦ AUGUST 14

"My home awaits me. I will hasten there."

Practice instructions

See complete instructions on page 135. A short summary:

- **Read** the commentary paragraph slowly and personally.
- **Pray** the prayer, perhaps several times.
- **Morning and evening:** Repeat the idea and then spend time in Open Mind Meditation.
- **Hourly remembrance:** Repeat the idea and then spend a quiet moment in meditation.
- **Frequent reminders:** Repeat the idea often within each hour.
- **Response to temptation:** Repeat the idea whenever upset, to restore peace.
- **Read the "What Is" section** slowly and thoughtfully once during the day.

Practice comments: In the prayer, notice the image of God as parent waiting for us to return home. Like a mother at dinnertime, His Voice is calling us home. Like a parent who hasn't seen us for a long time, His Arms are open, waiting to embrace us in joyous welcome. As you pray the prayer, you may want to visualize all this. It is true that God has no arms and no audible voice, but such earthly symbols can help carry our minds toward that which cannot be symbolized.

Commentary

Home. What an evocative word that is! "I'm going home." Sometimes just thinking about going home, even in an abstract sense, can cause deep emotions to rise up in us—happy ones, I hope, although for some an unhappy home life has tainted the word. Even then, when our "real" home was unhappy, most of us are still filled with a deep longing for home *as it ought to be.* Our real home is in God. Our longings for home find their roots in our longing for this spiritual home in God.

How can I "go home"? There are songs that convey the common idea that we go home to Heaven when we die: spirituals such as "Goin' Home." But the Course here is extremely clear. It speaks of departing this world, and says, "It is not death which makes this possible, but it is a change of mind about the purpose of the world" (1:2).

As long as we think that the purpose of the world lies within itself, that somehow happiness, freedom, and contentment are to be found here, in the world, we will never leave it. Not even when we "die." The chains that bind us to the world are mental, not physical. Our valuing of the world is what holds us to it. If I value the world "as I see it now" (1:3), it will hold on to me even when my body crumbles. But if I no longer see anything in this world "as I behold it" (1:4) that I want to keep or search for, I am free.

There is a world of meaning—literally!—in those phrases "as I see it now" and "as I behold it." In the ego's perception this world is a place of punishment and imprisonment, and simultaneously a place where I come to seek for what seems to be "lacking" in myself. As long as I somehow value that punishment and imprisonment, perhaps not for myself but almost always for others upon whom I have projected my guilt, I will be bound to the world, and I will not go home. As long as I think there is a lack in myself and continue to search for it outside myself, valuing the world for what I think it can give to me, I will always be bound to the world, and I will not go home.

"My home *awaits* me." Our home is not under construction. It is ready and waiting, the red carpet rolled out, everything is ready, and God's Arms are open and we hear His Voice (2:2). Home is available right now, if I only choose it. Let me be willing to look at what keeps me from choosing it, because those are the hindrances that keep me from finding it. Do I still wistfully long for my prince to come (or my princess)? Do I still have things I want to do before I am ready to go? Do I still find secret pleasure when the "wicked" (in my sight) suffer? If this world could vanish an hour from now, what would I regret? Would I be ready to leave? If a shimmering curtain were to appear in the doorway and a Voice proclaim, "Pass this portal and you will be in Heaven," would I go through? Why not?

This is not a fantasy. The Voice *is* calling us, and Heaven is here and now. We can pass the portal any time we choose to. If we are not experiencing Heaven, we *must* be choosing not to do so, and finding out what holds us back is the work we are assigned to in this classroom. This is what the world is for—to teach us to let it go.

"What need have I to linger in a place of vain desires and of shattered dreams, when Heaven can so easily be mine?" (2:3).

WHAT IS FORGIVENESS?

Part 6: W-pII.1.3:3–4

We do not realize how much our unforgiving thoughts distort the truth (3:3). Unforgiving thoughts twist our perception of things which are not in accord with how unforgiveness wants to see things. They overlook any evidence for love, and find evidence of guilt. In the Text section "The Obstacles to Peace," in the subsection on "The Attraction of Guilt" (T-19.IV(A).i), our unforgiving thoughts are compared to scavenging messengers "harshly ordered to seek out guilt, and cherish every scrap of evil and of sin that they can find, losing none of them on pain of death, and laying them respectfully before their lord and master" (T-19.IV(A).11:2). That is, we find what we are looking for, and the ego is looking for guilt.

But distortion is not only the *method* used by the ego; distortion is also the ego's *purpose*. Thus, the purpose of unforgiveness is to distort reality. Unforgiveness furiously aims "to smash reality, without concern for anything that would appear to pose a contradiction to its point of view" (3:4). Reality is the hated enemy, the intolerable presence, because our reality is still the Son of God, never in the slightest separated from Him. Reality exposes the ego as a lie, and cannot be tolerated. So the way our minds work, when dominated by unforgiving thoughts, is designed from the beginning to distort reality beyond all recognition.

In contrast to this, the Course asks us to dream of our brother's kindnesses instead of his mistakes, and to not brush aside his many gifts just because he isn't perfect (see T-27.VII.15). It asks us to look for love instead of looking for guilt, and rather than finding fault, to try finding love instead. To begin with, we can simply start to question the way we see things, in awareness that our thought processes and our methods of making judgment have been severely impaired and simply are not reliable. It isn't that we *should not* judge, it's that we *cannot* judge (see M-10.2:1). We are operating at diminished capacity; we need a healthy mind to judge on our behalf. And that mind is the Holy Spirit.

LESSON 227 ✦ AUGUST 15

"This is my holy instant of release."

Practice instructions

See complete instructions on page 135. A short summary:

- **Read** the commentary paragraph slowly and personally.
- **Pray** the prayer, perhaps several times.
- **Morning and evening:** Repeat the idea and then spend time in Open Mind Meditation.
- **Hourly remembrance:** Repeat the idea and then spend a quiet moment in meditation.
- **Frequent reminders:** Repeat the idea often within each hour.
- **Response to temptation:** Repeat the idea whenever upset, to restore peace.
- **Read the "What Is" section** slowly and thoughtfully once during the day.

Practice suggestion: To expand on the prayer, you may want to use the following visualization.

You see yourself walking through mist toward a giant pair of feet, the feet of truth.

Visualize these feet however you like.

Maybe they are made of stone.

Maybe they are luminous and semitransparent.

You are carrying a bundle in your hands which you are planning to lay at these feet as an act of tribute to the truth.

It would be traditional to assume that this bundle is your sins, and that you will be laying them before the truth in an act of giving them up for the sake of truth.

Yet the bundle is not your sins; it is your belief in your sinfulness, your belief that you are defined by your separate will that does not will with God.

Visualize the bundle however you want, but let its appearance and weight reflect the fact that this is your belief that you are sinful, your belief that you possess a wayward, destructive will that has corrupted your innocence.

You reach the feet of truth. See yourself kneel before the feet and humbly lay before them this bundle.

Let it be a genuine act of tribute to the truth.

Laying this belief before the feet of truth is your act of giving it up, in tribute to the truth and in acknowledgment of the falsity of this belief.

As you look at the bundle there on the ground, it is shined away in light, and is gone.

Your belief in your sinfulness has been removed forever from your mind.

Feel yourself freed of the heavy burden of feeling like a selfish sinner.

Feel the release as you are lifted into a holy instant.

Feel your right mind restored to you, as if, after a long bout of insanity, you are finally sane again.

You look down at yourself and see that you are clad in robes of holiness; your purity has remained untouched.

You arise, free now to come home, to walk through the door of your Father's house.

Commentary

Today's lesson is another reminder that these practice times are meant to be holy instants for us. Not every one will be a dramatic experience of wordless bliss, of course. Remember that simply being willing to turn your mind to God can be considered a holy instant, whether or not you consciously experience anything special. The seminal holy instant, from which the Course sprang, was simply a time when Bill Thetford said, "There must be another way," and Helen replied that she would help him find it. The mental shift into alignment with God's purpose is what really counts. If we faithfully practice, the direct experience of truth spoken of in the Workbook will come, not by our efforts, but by God's grace, when we are ready to receive it.

Consider the effect it has on our mind to focus on today's idea, "This is my holy instant of release," and then to sit in quiet stillness, open and receptive to whatever is given to us. We should enter each such time expectantly, waiting to hear what God's Voice will speak.

I am already free; now, today. My thought of separation had no effect on my reality, so the imprisonment I have imagined never happened. "Nothing that I thought apart from You exists" (1:3). How wonderful to know that the thoughts I believed were apart from God don't exist! How healing it is to give them up, lay them down at the feet of truth, and to have them "removed forever from my mind" (1:5). This is the healing process of the Course: to take each thought that seems to express a will separate from God's, and bring it into this Presence to be removed from my mind, with God's own assurance that it has affected nothing. I am still His Son.

This is how my mind is restored to me. This is how my awareness of my Identity is returned to my awareness.

WHAT IS FORGIVENESS?

Part 7: W-pII.1.4:1–3

"Forgiveness, on the other hand, is still, and quietly does nothing" (4:1). If we can understand these first few sentences we will have a clear grasp of what forgiveness really is. The words "on the other hand" refer to the preceding two paragraphs which described an unforgiving thought, especially in 3:1, "An unforgiving thought does many things." Forgiveness, on the other hand, does nothing. Unforgiveness is highly active, anxiously trying to make things fit into its picture of reality; forgiveness does nothing. It does not rush to interpret or to attempt to understand. It lets things be as they are.

Notice once again the heavy emphasis on stillness and quiet. The practice of the holy instant, as the practice of forgiveness, is practice at being still, being quiet, doing nothing. Our usual state of mind is the product of the ego's training—habitually active, constantly working. We need *practice* at being still and doing nothing. It takes a lot of practice to break the habit of frantic activity and form a new habit of being still and quiet.

One trick of the ego I notice, frequently, is that it will try to make me guilty about being still and quiet! When I try to take ten minutes to sit in stillness, my ego floods my mind with thoughts of what I ought to be doing instead.

The mental state in which forgiveness occurs is one in which we simply allow all of reality to be as it is, without judging anything. "It offends no aspect of reality, nor seeks to twist it to appearances it likes" (4:2). The appearance my ego usually likes is some form of "I am right and they are wrong." Or "I am good and they are bad." Or simply "I am better than he/she is." Even more simply, "I am not like him/her." All of these thoughts share one theme: I am different from others, and therefore separate from them. Any such thought is twisting reality, because the reality is that we are the same, we are equal, we are one. Forgiveness stills such thoughts and abandons all efforts to mash reality into a "more desirable" shape.

"It merely looks, and waits, and judges not" (4:3). It does not deny what it sees, but it puts no interpretation on it. It waits to be told the meaning by the Holy Spirit. "My mate is having an affair." Forgiveness looks, and waits, and judges not. "My child is sick." Forgiveness looks, and waits, and judges not. "My boss just fired me." Forgiveness looks, and waits, and judges not. We are so quick to think we know what things mean! And we are wrong. We do not know. We leap to an understanding based on separation, and such understandings understand nothing.

The most salutary thing we can do when any such upsetting event occurs in our lives is—nothing. Simply to let our minds become still and quiet, and to open ourselves to the healing light of the Holy Spirit. To seek a holy instant. Let this become the ingrained habit of our lives, and we will see the world in an entirely different way, and Love will flow through us to bring healing instead of hurt to every situation.

LESSON 228 ✦ AUGUST 16

"God has condemned me not. No more do I."

Practice instructions

See complete instructions on page 135. A short summary:

- **Read** the commentary paragraph slowly and personally.
- **Pray** the prayer, perhaps several times.
- **Morning and evening:** Repeat the idea and then spend time in Open Mind Meditation.
- **Hourly remembrance:** Repeat the idea and then spend a quiet moment in meditation.
- **Frequent reminders:** Repeat the idea often within each hour.
- **Response to temptation:** Repeat the idea whenever upset, to restore peace.
- **Read the "What Is" section** slowly and thoughtfully once during the day.

Practice comments: While repeating today's idea, realize it is a subtle reference to the story of the woman caught in adultery. As the crowd is about to stone her for her sin, Jesus utters the famous line, "Let him who is without sin cast the first stone." The crowd, of course, leaves one by one, and then Jesus says (to paraphrase), "They have condemned you not. No more do I." In other words, since literally no one condemns her, she is truly forgiven. Now, in this lesson, *you* are the woman caught in adultery. You unconsciously see yourself ringed about by God's vengeance, in the form of all those hands poised to chuck rocks at you. You see the death penalty staring at you—the payment for your sins. Yet that is all your own projection. God has condemned you not. And now you, your fiercest critic, decide to stop condemning yourself. No one condemns you, and so you are truly free. While repeating the idea today, you might want to think of all this, maybe even picturing yourself as the woman caught in adultery. Try to feel the sense of unexpected liberation that she must have felt.

In the commentary paragraph, try to sincerely ask yourself the

166

series of questions that make up the bulk of that paragraph. Such questions can be powerful tools of mind change.

With the prayer, notice how it builds to a statement of intention in the last two sentences. There, you state your intention to let go of your mistaken idea that you are sinful and then stand ready to receive from God the awareness of Who you really are. Try to really mean these closing sentences. And realize that "I stand ready" means "I wait in silent expectancy." This prayer, then, is meant to introduce your period of Open Mind Meditation.

Commentary

It takes great courage to let go of our self-condemnation. We are so afraid that if we stop condemning ourselves we will go berserk, the evil in us will be unchecked and will break out in some terrible disaster. But what if there is no evil in us? What if God is right? Is it so very likely that He is wrong and we are right? What God knows, the lesson says, makes sin in us impossible. "Shall I deny His knowledge?" (1:2).

The lesson is asking us, quite simply, to "take His Word for what I am" (1:4). Who knows what something or someone is better than its Creator? And what does God know about me? "My Father knows my holiness" (1:1). Every time I read such statements I watch my mind struggle to oppose the idea, cringing in a pseudo-humility that cries out, "Oh, no, I can't accept that about myself." If I dare to ask myself, "Why not?" my mind immediately comes up with a whole list of reasons: my flaws, my lack of total dedication to the truth, my addiction to this or that pleasure of the world. Yet every one of those things, brought into the light of the Holy Spirit, can be seen as nothing more than a misdirected prayer, a cry for help, a veiled longing for God and for Home.

"I was mistaken in myself" (2:1). That is all that has happened. I forgot my Source, and what I must be, coming from that Source. My Source is God, and not my dark illusions. My mistake about myself is not a sin to be judged but a mistake to be corrected; it needs not *condemnation*, but the healing of love. "My mistakes about myself are dreams" (2:4), that is all, and I can let these dreams go. I am not the dream; I am the dreamer, still holy, still a part of God.

Today, as I still my mind in God's Presence, I open myself to receive His Word concerning what I am. I brush aside the dreams, I recognize them for what they are, and let them go. I open my heart to Love.

WHAT IS FORGIVENESS?

Part 8: W-pII.1.4:4–5

In the last two sentences of this paragraph, notice that a contrast is made between judging and welcoming the truth exactly as it is. The opposite of judgment is the truth. Judgment, then, must always be a distortion of the truth. This section has already pointed out that unforgiveness has distortion as its purpose. If I do not want to forgive, I must distort the truth; I must judge. Judgment here clearly carries the meaning of condemnation, of seeing sin, of making something wrong. Forgiveness does not do that; forgiveness makes right instead of wrong, because "right" is the truth about all of us.

None of us is guilty. That is the truth. God does not condemn us. If I do so, I am distorting the truth. Judgment is always a distortion of the truth of our innocence before God. When I judge another, I do so because I am trying to justify my unwillingness to forgive. I have gotten very good at it. I always seem to find some reason that justifies my unforgiveness. But what I do not realize is that every such judgment twists the truth, hides it, obscures it. It "makes real" something that is not real.

Furthermore, in obscuring the truth about my brother or sister, I am hiding the truth about myself. I am substantiating the basis of my own self-condemnation. That is why the last sentence of the paragraph switches from my unforgiveness of another to the forgiveness of myself: "He who would forgive himself" (4:5). If I want to learn to forgive myself, I must abandon my judging of others. If their sin is real, so is mine. Instead I must learn to "welcome truth exactly as it is" (4:5). Only if I welcome the truth about my brother or sister can I see it for myself. We stand or fall together. "In him you will find yourself or lose yourself" (T-8.III.4:5).

To a mind habituated to seeing itself as a separate ego, abandoning all judgment is frightening. It feels like the rug is being swept out from under our feet; we don't know where to stand. How can we live in the world without it? We literally do not know how. Judgment is how we have ordered our lives; without it, we fear chaos. The Course assures us this will not happen:

> You are afraid of this because you believe that without the ego, all would be chaos. Yet I assure you that without the ego, all would be love. (T-15.V.1:6–7)

When we let go of judgment, when we are willing to welcome the truth exactly as it is, love rushes in to fill the vacuum left by the absence of judgment. It has been there all along, but we have blocked it. We don't know how this happens, but it happens because love is the reality, love is the truth we are welcoming. Love will show us exactly what to do when our judgment is gone.

LESSON 229 ✦ AUGUST 17

"Love, Which created me, is what I am."

Practice instructions

See complete instructions on page 135. A short summary:

- **Read** the commentary paragraph slowly and personally.
- **Pray** the prayer, perhaps several times.
- **Morning and evening:** Repeat the idea and then spend time in Open Mind Meditation.
- **Hourly remembrance:** Repeat the idea and then spend a quiet moment in meditation.
- **Frequent reminders:** Repeat the idea often within each hour.
- **Response to temptation:** Repeat the idea whenever upset, to restore peace.
- **Read the "What Is" section** slowly and thoughtfully once during the day.

Practice comments: When you repeat today's idea, you may want to repeat it in the spirit suggested by the first paragraph. Realize this idea represents the end of all your seeking. All along you've been seeking to answer a single, paramount question, "Who am I?" And here, in this idea, you've found that answer. Try to repeat it in that spirit.

Commentary

Many of these lessons in Part II of the Workbook may seem to be expressing a state of mind that is beyond where I am as I read them. In reality, they express my *true* state of mind, the state of my right mind. It is this state of mind we can reach in the holy instant. Right-mindedness is not some future state I am trying to reach. There is an aspect of my mind that already knows these things and already believes them. It is this part of my mind that is leading me home. "Now need I seek no more" (1:2) is the truth right now. It is the part of my mind that doubts this, that denies it, which is unreal.

Love *is* what I am; It is my Identity. Let me look honestly at what I believe I am instead, because it is in discovering what Love is not that I will come to know Love.

> Love is not learned. Its meaning lies within itself. And learning ends when you have recognized all it is *not*. That is the interference; that is what needs to be undone.
>
> (T-18.IX.12:1–4)

Love waited for me, "so still" (1:4). Love is still because that is what forgiveness does; it is "still, and quietly does nothing" (W-pII.1.4:1). My own Love waits to forgive me all I think I have done, all that I have believed I was other than Love. I actually "sought to lose" my Identity (1:5), but God has kept that Identity safe for me, within me, as me. "In the midst of all the thoughts of sin my foolish mind made up" (2:1), my Father kept my Identity untouched and sinless. Let me turn to that Identity now. Let me give thanks, and express my gratitude to God that It has never been lost, even when I was sure It was. I cannot be anything other than what God created me to be. "Love, Which created me, is what I am."

In my heart, in my mind, in the still and tranquil core of my being, lies everything I have ever been seeking for. Let me now remember.

WHAT IS FORGIVENESS?

Part 9: W-pII.1.5:1–2

Faced with this stark contrast between forgiveness and unforgiveness, what then are we to do? "Do nothing, then" (5:1). We are not called upon to *do*, we are called upon to cease doing, because there is nothing that need be done. To the ego, to do means to judge, and it is judgment we must relinquish. If we feel there is something that must be done, it is a judgment that affirms lack within ourselves, and there is no lack. That is what we must remember. To believe that something must be done is a denial of our wholeness, which has never been diminished.

"Let forgiveness show you what to do, through Him" (5:1). To forgive ourselves means to take our hands off the steering wheel of our lives, to stop trying to "make things right," which only affirms that something is wrong. To forgive others means we stop thinking it is our job to correct them. The Holy Spirit is the One Who knows what we should do, if anything, and His guidance will often surprise us. Yes, there may still be something for us to "do," but we will not be the ones to determine what that is. Our doing is so often deadly, quenching the spirit instead of affirming it, imparting guilt instead of lifting it.

The Holy Spirit is my Guide and Savior and Protector. In each situation where I am tempted to do something, let me stop, remember that my judgment is untrustworthy, let go, and give it into His hands. He is "strong in hope, and certain of your ultimate success" (5:1). How often in a time when I am judging, whether myself or another, am I certain of my ultimate success? Let me then give the situation into the care of One Who is certain. He will show me what to do.

"He has forgiven you already, for such is His function" (5:2). Each time I bring Him some terrible thing I think I have done, let me remember: "He has forgiven you already." I do not need to fear entering His Presence. His function, His reason for being, is to forgive me. Not to judge me, nor to punish me, nor to make me feel bad, but to forgive. Why would I stay away an instant more? Let me fall gratefully now into His loving arms, and hear Him say, "What you think is not the truth" (W-pI.134.7:5). He will still the troubled waters of my mind, and bring me peace.

LESSON 230 ✦ AUGUST 18
"Now will I seek and find the peace of God."

Practice instructions

See complete instructions on page 135. A short summary:

- **Read** the commentary paragraph slowly and personally.
- **Pray** the prayer, perhaps several times.
- **Morning and evening:** Repeat the idea and then spend time in Open Mind Meditation.
- **Hourly remembrance:** Repeat the idea and then spend a quiet moment in meditation.
- **Frequent reminders:** Repeat the idea often within each hour.
- **Response to temptation:** Repeat the idea whenever upset, to restore peace.
- **Read the "What Is" section** slowly and thoughtfully once during the day.

Commentary

"In peace I was created. And in peace do I remain" (1:1–2). Jesus, in his Course, never tires of reminding us that we remain as God created us. He repeats it often because we so obviously do not believe it. We may believe that God created us in peace. How, indeed, could we believe otherwise? Would a God of Love have created us in pain and agony, in turmoil and confusion, in conflict and strife? So the first sentence isn't really a problem to us; we can accept that God created us in peace.

The problem arises, in our minds, with the second sentence: "In peace do I remain." Quite simply we don't believe it. In fact, we are firmly convinced that we know otherwise. Perhaps this morning I am distraught by something that happened yesterday, or worried about what may happen today, or next week. I can look back on a lifetime that, in my experience, has had very little, if any, peace. Some days it seems as though life is conspiring against me to rob me of peace. It seems as

173

though, in most of my busy days, I rarely have a moment of peace. So how can I accept this statement: "In peace do I remain"?

It seems incredible to us, unbelievable, when the Course insists that since God created me in peace, I must still be in peace. God's creation of me took place, the lesson says, "apart from time, and still remains beyond all change" (2:2). It tells me, "It is not given me to change my Self" (1:3). My experience of life in this world tells me otherwise.

The question is, which one will I believe? God's Voice, or my experience? One of them must be false. And it is earth-shattering, mind-blowing, even to consider that my entire experience of this world has been a lie, a mistake, and a hallucination. Yet what is the alternative? Shall I believe, instead, that God is a liar? Shall I believe that His creation was flawed, and capable of corruption? Shall I believe that what He willed for me was overcome by my own independent will? Yet this is what I *must* be believing if I insist that I am not at peace, in this very moment.

If God is not a liar and His creation is not flawed, then what must be true is that my own mind has deceived me and has manufactured an entire lifetime of false experience. If I am willing to listen, this is not as far-fetched as it sounds at first. In fact, if I simply watch my mind, I can catch it in the act of doing that very thing. I can watch and observe how I see what I expect to see. I can notice how different people perceive the same events quite differently. I can remember times when I was quite sure I understood things clearly, only to have the whole situation turned on its head by some new fact that I had been unaware of. I need only watch the sun rise, move across the sky, and set, to realize that my perception is faulty. It is not the sun that moves; it is me, as the earth turns. When night comes and the sun is "gone" in my perception, the sun shines on; it is my world that has turned its face from the light.

What if my apparent lack of peace does not mean what I think it means? What if the peace of God has never left me, but shines on, while I have turned my face from it? In the holy instant I can find that this is the truth. Simply by turning my mind away from its mad belief in unrest, I can discover the peace of God shining in me now.

WHAT IS FORGIVENESS?

Part 10: W-pII.1.5:3

There is another part to forgiveness. Since the Holy Spirit has already forgiven me, carrying out His only function, I now "must...share His function, and forgive whom He has saved" (5:3).

Consider what we have said about the way the Holy Spirit interacts with us, how we can come to Him with our darkest thoughts and find them absorbed and dissipated in His Love. The utter lack of judgment. His gentleness with us, His acceptance of us, His knowledge of our sinlessness, His honoring us as the Son of God, unchanged by our foolish thoughts of sin. Now, we are to share His function in relation to the world. Now, we are to be His representatives, His manifestation in the lives of those around us. To them, we offer this same gentle kindness, this same conviction of the inner holiness of each one we deal with, this same quiet disregard for thoughts of self-condemnation in everyone we see, or speak to, or think about. "It is the privilege of the forgiven to forgive" (T-1.I.27:2).

What we reflect to the world is what we believe in for ourselves. When we judge, condemn, and lay guilt on those around us, we are reflecting the way we believe God is towards us. When we experience the sweet forgiveness in the loving Presence of the Holy Spirit, we reflect that same thing to the world. Let me, then, enter into His Presence, allowing Him to look upon me, to find Him quietly doing nothing, but simply looking, and waiting, and judging me not. Let me hear Him tell me of His confidence in my ultimate success. And then, let me turn and share this blessing with the world, giving what I have received. Only as I share it will I know, for sure, that it is mine.

V

Lessons 231 - 240
What Is Salvation?

LESSON 231 ✦ AUGUST 19
"Father, I will but to remember You."

Practice instructions

See complete instructions on page 135. A short summary:

- **Read** the commentary paragraph slowly and personally.
- **Pray** the prayer, perhaps several times.
- **Morning and evening:** Repeat the idea and then spend time in Open Mind Meditation.
- **Hourly remembrance:** Repeat the idea and then spend a quiet moment in meditation.
- **Frequent reminders:** Repeat the idea often within each hour.
- **Response to temptation:** Repeat the idea whenever upset, to restore peace.
- **Read the "What Is" section** slowly and thoughtfully once during the day.

Commentary

This lesson is talking about our will. When the Course uses the word "will" in this way, it is talking about a fundamental, unchanging part of us, the permanently fixed goal of our Self. It isn't talking about our wishes and our whims, but our *will*. Jesus speaks to us directly in the second paragraph and says, "This is your will, my brother" (2:1). It is a will we share with Him, and also with God our Father.

What is our will? To remember God; to know His Love. And that is all. Not many of us, as we began reading this Course, would have answered the question "What do you want out of life?" with the words "To remember God and know His Love." A lot of us probably don't feel those words fit us even now. The lesson recognizes that: "Perhaps I think I seek for something else" (1:2).

What is the "something else" you are seeking? It might be wealth, or fame. It might be some form of worldly security. It might be romance. It might be hot sex. Or a good time. Or a quiet family life, in the tradition of the American dream. We've called it by many names. We *think* these things are what we are seeking for. Yet no matter what we may think, these things are not what we truly will for ourselves. They are all forms, forms that we believe will give us something. It isn't the form we are really seeking, it is the content, it is what we believe these things offer to us.

And what is that? Inner peace. Satisfaction. A sense of completion and wholeness. A sense of worth. An inner knowing that we are essentially good; lovable and loving. A feeling of belonging, of being valuable. Ultimately these things come only from remembering God and knowing His Love. They are something inside of us, not something outside of us. Only when we remember the truth about ourselves, only when we remember our connectedness to Love Itself, will we find what we are seeking. And we will find that we *are* what we have been seeking, and always have been.

"To remember Him is Heaven. This we seek. And only this is what it will be given us to find" (2:3–5). Remembering God is the *only* thing I am really looking for. Let me then, today, spend time, morning and evening, reminding myself of this fact: "Father, I will but to remember You." Let me stop briefly every hour to recall it to my mind. And each time I find myself thinking that I want "something else," let me gently correct myself: Remembering God is all I want.

WHAT IS SALVATION?

Part 1: W-pII.2.1:1–3

To begin with, it will help to realize that the Course does not attach the same meaning to this word as does traditional religion. "Salvation" carries, for most of us, the connotation of some impending disaster from which we are "saved." From hell, for instance. From some terrible punishment. From the consequences of our wrongdoing. The picture often used in traditional Christianity is of a drowning man being thrown a life-preserver; "Throw out the lifeline," the old Gospel hymn says. The Course directly refutes this idea:

> Your Self does not need salvation, but your mind needs to learn what salvation is. You are not saved *from* anything, but you are saved *for* glory. (T-11.IV.1:3–4)

Salvation in the Course *is* a "life preserver," but not in the same sense. It does not save us from death; it preserves us in life. It is a guarantee that death will never touch us: "Salvation is a promise, made by God, that you would find your way to Him at last" (1:1). We are not in danger of destruction, never have been, never will be. The Course's version of salvation does not reverse a disaster; it prevents the disaster from ever happening.

Before time began, God made His promise, a promise that "cannot but be kept" (1:2). That promise guaranteed that time, and all the mess we appear to have made in time, would have an end, and ultimately be without any effect at all. It guaranteed that life cannot end, that holiness cannot become sin, that Heaven cannot become hell. It guaranteed that there could never be more than an *illusion* of separation and a *dream* of suffering and death. It promised that the ego could never become real, that no will independent of God could ever arise. It defined the end from the beginning, and made it perfectly secure. We *will* find our way to God at last, because God has promised that it will be so.

179

LESSON 232 ✦ AUGUST 20

"Be in my mind, my Father, through the day."

Practice instructions

See complete instructions on page 135. A short summary:

- **Read** the commentary paragraph slowly and personally.
- **Pray** the prayer, perhaps several times.
- **Morning and evening:** Repeat the idea and then spend time in Open Mind Meditation.
- **Hourly remembrance:** Repeat the idea and then spend a quiet moment in meditation.
- **Frequent reminders:** Repeat the idea often within each hour.
- **Response to temptation:** Repeat the idea whenever upset, to restore peace.
- **Read the "What Is" section** slowly and thoughtfully once during the day.

Practice suggestion: The prayer for today's lesson is one of my favorites in the Workbook. I have benefited from a practice that you may want to try today: Attempt to have the kind of day the prayer describes by focusing on each part of the prayer at the time of day which that part speaks of. Here is how it might look:

- **From the moment of waking to 9 am**, make this line your frequent reminder: *"Be in my mind, my Father, when I wake, and shine on me throughout the day today."*
- **From 9 am to 5 pm**, make this line your frequent reminder: *"Let every minute be a time in which I dwell with You."*
- **On the hour throughout the day**, repeat: *"And let me not forget my hourly thanksgiving that You have remained with me, and always will be there to hear my call to You and answer me."*
- **From 5 pm to 9 pm**, make this line your frequent reminder: *"As evening comes, let all my thoughts be still of You and of Your Love."*

● **As you begin evening quiet time and while you drop off to sleep**, repeat, *"And let me sleep sure of my safety, certain of Your care, and happily aware I am Your Son."*

Commentary

When I wake, God is in my mind; His Presence is with me and in my awareness. His Love, and the joy and peace of knowing God are with me; they take precedence over any other thoughts. Physical discomfort and concerns about scheduling the day arise, but none of these displace the peace of God; it is my bedrock, my foundation, and my first concern. It is a constant awareness, like the background hum of an air conditioner, always there, often unnoticed, but ready to be noticed any time I turn my attention to it.

"Let every minute be a time in which I dwell with You" (1:2). Here *is* my desire! To dwell with God every minute of the day. It reminds me of John 15 in the New Testament: "Abide in me, and I in you" (John 15:4). Or the Old Testament expression of the same idea: "The eternal God is a dwelling place, and underneath are the everlasting arms" (Deut. 33:27, NASB). Let me remember today, each hour, to say, "Thank You for being with me today. Thank You for *always* being with me."

> *As evening comes, let all my thoughts be still of You and of Your Love. And let me sleep sure of my safety, certain of Your care, and happily aware I am Your Son.* (1:4–5)

Sure of my safety. Thus, free of all fear. For the most part, our lives are run by fears of various kinds; the ego is driven by fear. Peace is the absence of fear. And since fear is only the absence of love, peace and love are interdependent. When I am loving, I am peaceful. When I am peaceful, I am loving. Where I am sure of my safety, knowing the Presence of God in every moment, I am at peace and love flows through me.

"This is as every day should be" (2:1). This is the goal for life in this world: to live every day with God in my mind. To wake in His Presence, to walk in His shining Love, and to sleep in His care and protection. To so live that His Presence becomes my foreground and all else, the hum and bustle of the world, becomes background.

What is a day like for someone who has learned what the Course is teaching? Simply this: To constantly practice the end of fear. To walk with faith in Him Who is my Father, trusting all things to Him, letting Him reveal all things to me, and in everything to be undismayed because I am His Son (2:1–5).

WHAT IS SALVATION?

Part 2: W-pII.2.1:4

How does salvation work? The essence of it is stated here in a single sentence: "God's Word is given every mind which thinks that it has separate thoughts, and will replace these thoughts of conflict with the Thought of peace" (1:4). The instant our mind had a thought of conflict, God's Word was implanted in our mind as well. Before disaster could even begin, the Answer was given.

You and I, who think of ourselves as separate entities, are such minds, which think that they have separate thoughts. But God's Word has been implanted in us; the truth lies beneath all our self-deception. From within, the Thought of God is quietly working, waiting, moving to replace all our thoughts of conflict. The thoughts of conflict are myriad, taking thousands of forms, each in conflict with the universe and most in conflict with each other. The Thought of peace is one. It is the one remedy to every thought of conflict, whether it be hatred, anger, despair, frustration, bitterness, or death. The Thought of God heals them all.

The remedy lies within me, now. This is salvation: To turn within to the Thought of peace, and find it there within myself.

"BE IN MY MIND, MY FATHER"

AN APPRECIATION OF
THE PRAYER FOR LESSON 232

There is tremendous value in really praying the prayers in Part II of the Workbook. I have found this to be one of the most rewarding elements of

Workbook practice. I highly recommend doing this, speaking these prayers (silently or aloud) directly to God as deeply felt personal communications, as a kind of "love speech" between the created and the Creator. For that is exactly how these prayers read.

To encourage this practice I want to focus on the prayer for Lesson 232, which is probably my favorite prayer in the entire Course. I have used this prayer countless times. If I am driving some distance I will sometimes spend the time praying it over and over. Over time each line has come to feel permeated with a beautiful meaning. I would like to share that meaning now, by going through the prayer, line by line, commenting on each line as I go.

I would strongly encourage you to go beyond merely reading the following material and actually pray the prayer with me as I go through it. To do so, I suggest the following form: Preferably do it in the morning, since, as you will see, the prayer assumes that. Read the line from the prayer and then read my commentary on that line. Then go back to the line I am commenting on and spend some time really speaking it to God. If you can, spend a full minute or two with it, dwelling on it, going over and over it, perhaps adding your own elaborations, until it really sinks in and registers in your feelings. Hopefully, my commentary will have enriched this experience, but see what new meanings come out of your time spent with that line. Then go on to the next line and its commentary, repeating the same process.

> *Be in my mind, my Father, when I wake, and shine on me throughout the day today. Let every minute be a time in which I dwell with You. And let me not forget my hourly thanksgiving that You have remained with me, and always will be there to hear my call to You and answer me. As evening comes, let all my thoughts be still of You and of Your Love. And let me sleep sure of my safety, certain of Your care, and happily aware I am Your Son.*

"Be in my mind, my Father, when I wake,"

Notice what a personal communication this opening line is. You are asking someone to be inside of your mind. In a way this is more intimate than asking someone to be in your *bed* when you wake. And you are asking it of "my Father." This is not the same as saying "God." It makes this God *yours*. Being yours, you don't really have to *ask* that He be in your mind. "Be in my mind" is not a question. There is nothing timid about it. There is no "please would you perhaps be in my mind, Your

Greatness?" In saying this line you are assuming you have the right to walk up to God, address Him as your Father, and simply say, "Be in my mind." You can even give Him a time: "when I wake." You are not a servant in the fields, but a son in the household, with every right to his father's presence.

How wonderful it would be to wake up in this state, to open our eyes in the morning feeling God's Presence in our mind. Because we are not so alert when we awake, we usually have only the most basic and immediate things on our mind—making coffee, getting to the bathroom, being ready for an appointment. What if, instead, *God* was the most basic and immediate thing to us? What if, as soon as we came out of sleep, He was the foremost thing on our mind, and we felt Him within us? Perhaps we wouldn't greet the new day with our customary sense of burden, our urge to turn off the alarm clock and pull the sheets over our head. Maybe we wouldn't even be so groggy. Perhaps we would feel something like what the following passage says. It is talking about forgiveness, but we could also apply to God: "[He] sparkles on your eyes as you awake, and gives you joy with which to meet the day" (W-pI.122.2:2).

"and shine on me throughout the day today."

This line calls to mind an image of God as the perfect warm sun that feels just right, not too hot and not too remote. Like the sun, He rises on you in the morning and shines on you all through the day. Also like the sun, His shining is completely impartial. He shines without letup, whether you are peaceful or angry, kind or cruel. He just shines. Yet what He shines is not physical light. For what is shining here is not a physical object like the sun. What does it mean for a *person* to shine on you? It means for that person to radiate on you the warmth of his love and approval. For God to shine on you, then, is for God to *smile* on you, as another one of the Workbook prayers says:

> I am he on whom You smile in love and tenderness so dear
> and deep and still the universe smiles back on You, and
> shares Your Holiness. How pure, how safe, how holy, then,
> are we, abiding in Your Smile, with all Your Love bestowed
> upon us.   (W-pII.341.1:2-3)

So, if you will, just imagine yourself basking in His sun, abiding in His smile, "throughout the day today"—at noon, at three, at five, as you sit at your desk, as you drive in your car. And imagine that happening *today*. As I said above, it helps to fill in the day of the week and the date.

"Let every minute be a time in which I dwell with You."

Who would you say this kind of a thing to? Imagine walking up to a friend and saying, "Let every minute be a time in which I dwell with you." If this person really thought you meant it, you might get slapped with a restraining order. To say this to someone you must not only have an all-consuming desire to be with that person, but you must have an extraordinary permission that removes the normal boundaries of politeness and courtesy.

Not only am I stating my desire to be with God every minute, being with Him seems to be what primarily characterizes each minute. Each one is not a time in which I am mainly doing other things, but am also somewhat cognizant of God. Each minute is entitled "a time in which I dwell with You." That is what defines it; that is what it is, even if other activities occur on its periphery. And what engrossing things am I doing with God as He and I pass the minutes away? Just dwelling. Just being together. Just resting our heads against each other. That's all.

And so I ask you again, who would you say this to? It would have to be someone you wanted to be with so much that it would be completely satisfying to be together every minute, without diversions or other activities, doing nothing else but "dwelling" in each other's presence. And it would have to be someone whom you knew would not reject you, but wanted to dwell with you just as constantly.

"And let me not forget my hourly thanksgiving that You have remained with me,"

Imagine a relationship that was so precious, so irreplaceable, that you wanted to sit down every single hour of every single day and thank that person just for *remaining* with you. Imagine doing this not because it was your duty and not because otherwise he would leave. Of your own free will you wanted to "not forget [your] hourly thanksgiving," simply to experience the sweetness of your gratitude. If we had such a relationship, words could not capture the treasure it would be in our life. Little do we realize that we already do have such a relationship, and always have had it.

When I say this part of the prayer to God, my mind often spontaneously adds, "in spite of it all." God has remained with me in spite of it all. We each have our own versions of what "it all" is. Yet all those versions come down to one thing: We left Him. We dumped Him for other lovers. Even while we drove away, however, He climbed in the back seat. Though we left Him, He remained with us. Therefore, we really didn't succeed in leaving Him at all. And that is cause for endless gratitude. Thanking Him every hour of every day hardly begins to capture it.

"and always will be there to hear my call to You and answer me."

Here are more reasons to thank God every single hour. If you are lucky, there have been certain people in your life who have always been there for you. What greater gift can one have in this world? How can you ever tell these people the depth of your gratitude? This line portrays God as a kind of perfect, omnipresent version of these people. So sure are you of His fidelity that you are thanking Him in advance. You just finished thanking Him for remaining with you up until now. Now you thank Him because you trust He *"always will"* remain with you.

Yet more than just remain, He will always *"be there"* for you. He will hear your every call and answer every one. What are these calls? They are not just confined to your intentional prayers. According to the Course, every thought and feeling, every bit of pain or pleasure, everything you experience or do, is a call to your Father, a call for His Love. This line, then, anticipates that He will truly hear every single call and will answer every one with His Love.

A great example of this is found in Lesson 267: "Each heartbeat calls His Name, and every one is answered by His Voice, assuring me I am at home in Him" (W-pII.267.1:7). What a wonderful image. Each heartbeat, this says, calls on God's Name. You are calling to Him sixty, maybe ninety times a minute. And what is the call of your heart? Is it not to be loved, to belong, to have a home? Thus, for every single heartbeat, God answers you, assuring you that you are loved by Him, that you have a home in Him.

Of course, most of us do not really trust that God is hearing every call, and especially do not trust that He is answering. Yet imagine for a moment that the Course is right, and He has always been there, never leaving, never disapproving, infinitely patient, silently hearing every plea and instantly responding with all His Love? What if this is going on all the time and you have just turned a profoundly deaf ear to Him? Now imagine being in the position He is, being completely attentive to someone who rarely, if ever, noticed you were there. Could you have waited all this time in love, as He has done? Or would you instead have screamed at this person by now, or gotten bored and walked off? The fact that God has done neither is yet more cause to thank Him every hour.

"As evening comes, let all my thoughts be still of You and of Your Love."

It is still going on. This dwelling with God has been going on all day, through every hour and every minute. And, "as evening comes," it still goes on. The coming of evening we often associate with a peaceful time of rest. The day comes to an end and we can simply relax and enjoy that ending in peace, as we watch the sunset and the coming out of the stars. Evening can be a satisfying conclusion to a successful day, or a needed rest after a crazy day.

Here in this line of the prayer, evening is not a resting at home after our frantic activity out in the world. Rather, evening is a *continuing* of a resting, a deepening of an experience of being home that has been going on all day. It is the satisfying conclusion to a day of peace. We have spent all day resting on the porch with our Love. And now, "as evening comes" and we sit with Him still, our rest grows even deeper.

"Let all my thoughts be still of You and of Your Love." Again, what person would you say this to? In our normal experience, is there anything that we could devote all our thoughts to without dying of boredom? Nothing seems interesting enough. That is why our minds flit around so much, sucking tiny droplets from one shriveled flower after another. Think of what kind of love we would need to feel before we could really say, "Let all my thoughts be about you." Think how profoundly *loved* we would have to feel in order to really say, "Let all my thoughts be of your love for me."

Something in us longs to say these words to someone. Yet who in this world could we say them to with sincerity? At least for very long? The impression I get from this line and from the entire prayer is that God can answer a longing in our heart that nothing here can. There is a relationship that our whole being calls out for, but which we cannot find with anything in this world. Yet we can find it with God.

Imagine that this very day you will experience an evening like this. Imagine that after an entire day of basking in the sunshine of God's Love, you will reach the peaceful glow of sunset, and find that all your thoughts are *still* of Him and of His Love. If this really happened, would any evening you have ever had be better?

"And let me sleep sure of my safety, certain of Your care, and happily aware I am Your Son."

It still goes on, even as we reach bedtime and the prayer concludes. We carry our resting with God right into our sleep. I believe these lines speak to a deep need in us, a need for a kind of sleep we always want but perhaps never experience. We all want sleep to be something more than just physical rest. We want our minds to be able to truly drop all cares and drift into a state of pure peace. We want to rest in some thought that is totally certain and endlessly happy. We want to drop off in some glad awareness, with a smile on our face and our arm around our love. That would be rest for the *mind* and not just for the body.

Yet how often do we experience this kind of sleep? We usually haul our cares right into sleep with us. Our mental fists remain clenched even while our body is inert. We have no thought that we can totally rest in, no thought that is happy enough and certain enough to put a smile on our face and keep it there while we drift off. Imagine, then, sleeping in the manner that this last line of the prayer speaks of. Let's take the three final phrases one at a time.

"Sure of my safety." Sleep is a time of physical vulnerability. While we lie there and drool on our pillow, anything could be done to us. And so something in our minds feels insecure about totally letting go. If we were completely sure of our safety in God, if we knew that while we slept our Love had His Arms around us, how could we not let go?

"Certain of Your care." In the same manner, something in our minds is reluctant to completely relinquish our cares. If *we* don't worry about them, who will? Yet imagine going to sleep absolutely certain of *God's* care. If we knew we were enveloped in His care, what need would there be to hang onto our cares?

"Happily aware I am Your Son." Another thing that keeps our minds from true rest is a sense of not belonging, of being alone. We can feel alone even with our arm around a mate. If we truly believed that we were God's Son, the apple of His Eye, the object of all His Love, the heir to all that is His, could there be a happier thought? Imagine dropping off to sleep in that happy awareness. Is that not the kind of rest we have always wanted?

I have been talking about holding these thoughts in mind while we doze off. Yet the prayer says something even stronger. It speaks of abiding in these thoughts while we *sleep*. Although we think of sleep as total unconsciousness, it is not. Sleep researchers have found that even when awakened from deepest sleep, subjects report trains of thought. Of course, the thoughts that pass through our minds during sleep are generally bizarre and incoherent. Yet thoughts *are* passing through. What would it be like, then, to sleep all night filled only with these thoughts: "sure of my safety, certain of Your care, and happily aware I am Your Son"?

Now the prayer has concluded and you have spent the entire day with God. He was the first thing in your mind as you awoke. In every minute of the day you dwelt with Him and basked in the sunshine of His Love. As every hour struck you expressed to Him your undying gratitude. As evening came, your rest went on, as all your thoughts were still of Him. And even while you slept, it still went on, all through the night. Having passed the night in this way, can you guess what would be in your mind as you awoke the next morning? And what the next day would be like? It would still go on.

And that is how it should be, says the line immediately following the prayer: "This is as every day should be."

LESSON 233 ✦ AUGUST 21
"I give my life to God to guide today."

Practice instructions

See complete instructions on page 135. A short summary:

- **Read** the commentary paragraph slowly and personally.
- **Pray** the prayer, perhaps several times.
- **Morning and evening:** Repeat the idea and then spend time in Open Mind Meditation.
- **Hourly remembrance:** Repeat the idea and then spend a quiet moment in meditation.
- **Frequent reminders:** Repeat the idea often within each hour.
- **Response to temptation:** Repeat the idea whenever upset, to restore peace.
- **Read the "What Is" section** slowly and thoughtfully once during the day.

Practice suggestion: I find that it helps to make the idea more specific by saying, *"I give this situation to God to guide today."*

Commentary

One thing I find very interesting about the Course is that it is not persnickety about its theology. There are places in the Course that make it quite clear that God does not hear the specific words of our prayers (although He *does* hear the prayers of our heart, of which words are only symbols, see M-21.1-2), and that, knowing only the truth, He does not know the details of our errors (He simply knows we are asleep [T-6.V.1:5-8]; the content of our nightmares, being false, is unknown to Him because He knows only truth). *Technically*, then, if we wanted to be theologically correct, prayer ought to be addressed to the Holy Spirit or to Jesus, who are specifically spoken of as intermediaries between truth and illusion, or as bridges between us and God. Yet, here in the second half of the Workbook, we have 140 lessons, each of which contains a prayer addressed to "Father."

In today's lesson, the Father is asked to guide us. Yet elsewhere, being Guide is defined as the function of the Holy Spirit. So I get the feeling that Jesus (the author) isn't particularly concerned with strict theological correctness. I think he is a good example for all of us to follow. Would he be teaching us to pray to the Father if it were some sort of substandard spiritual practice?

If we gleaned nothing more from the Course than the practice of daily giving our lives over to God's guidance, we would be quickly taken home. We can ask Him to replace our thoughts with His own, and to direct all our acts during the day, all we do and think and say. To act or think on our own is, literally, a waste of time. His wisdom is infinite, His Love and tenderness are beyond comprehension. Could we ask for a more reliable Guide?

The first step in following God's guidance is a stepping *back*, releasing our tight hold on our lives and deliberately placing them under His control. The guidance will come. Sometimes, perhaps rarely, we will hear an inner Voice. In my personal experience this is very rare. Other times, things will happen around us that make our way plain. Or an inner conviction will build for no apparent reason. We will "just happen to notice" something someone says, or a song on the radio, or a line in a book. If we are *listening* for it, we will hear it.

Another key is giving our day to Him "with no reserve at all" (2:2); that is, holding nothing back. Sometimes we are so fixated on what we think we want or need that we are not willing to hear any guidance to the contrary. And if we aren't willing to hear it, we won't. We're like a broken shopping cart that always wants to steer left or right; we just don't respond well to guidance. We have to be willing to let go of all our preferences, all our investment in the outcome, and become completely malleable, completely open to whatever direction He wants to give to us. An old Christian hymn says:

> Have Thine own way, Lord,
> Have Thine own way.
> Thou are the potter,
> I am the clay.
> Mold me and make me,
> After Thy will,
> While I am waiting,
> Yielded and still.

That is what stepping back means. That is how we give our lives to God to guide. He guides. We follow, without questioning (1:7).

WHAT IS SALVATION?

Part 3: W-pII.2.2:1–3

The Thought of peace that is our salvation "was given to God's Son the instant that his mind had thought of war" (2:1). No time intervened at all between the thought of war and the Thought of peace. Salvation was given instantly when the need arose. In a beautiful image, the Text says that "not one note in Heaven's song was missed" (T-26.V.5:4). The peace of Heaven was completely undisturbed. And having been answered, the problem was resolved for all of time and all eternity, in that timeless instant.

Our discovery of salvation, however, takes time. Or at least seems to. A poor analogy: Imagine that you are suddenly burdened with a ten thousand dollar tax bill for a hitherto unexpected reason, but at that very instant, someone deposits one million dollars into your checking account. You could spend a lot of time trying to raise the needed money if you didn't know about the deposit, but actually all you need to do is nothing, because the problem is already solved. Your only need, then, is to stop trying to solve the problem, and learn that it has already been answered.

Before the thought of separation (or war) arose, there was no need for a "Thought of peace." Peace simply *was*, without an opposite. So in a certain sense we could say that the problem created its own answer. Before the problem, there was no answer because there was no need of one. But when the problem arose, the answer was already there. "When the mind is split there is a need of healing" (2:3). It is the thought of separation that makes the thought of healing needful, but when the healing is accepted, or when the thought of separation is abandoned, healing is no longer needed. Healing is a temporary (or temporal, related to time) measure. There is no need of it in Heaven.

As the Course says of forgiveness, because there is an illusion of need, there is need for an illusion of answer. But that "answer" is really simple acceptance of what has always been true, and always will be. Peace simply is, and salvation lies in our acceptance of that fact.

Salvation, as the Course sees it, is not an active divine response to a real need. It is, instead, an apparent response to a need that, in truth, does not exist.

This is why the Course calls our spiritual path "a journey without distance" (T-8.VI.9:7) and, indeed, "a journey that was not begun" (W-pII.225.2:5). While we are in it, the journey seems very real, and often very long. When it is over, we will know that we never left Heaven, never traveled anywhere, and have always been exactly where we are: at home in God. The journey itself is imaginary. It consists in learning, bit by bit, that the distance we perceive between ourselves and God is simply not there.

LESSON 234 ✦ AUGUST 22
"Father, today I am Your Son again."

Practice instructions

See complete instructions on page 135. A short summary:

- **Read** the commentary paragraph slowly and personally.
- **Pray** the prayer, perhaps several times.
- **Morning and evening:** Repeat the idea and then spend time in Open Mind Meditation.
- **Hourly remembrance:** Repeat the idea and then spend a quiet moment in meditation.
- **Frequent reminders:** Repeat the idea often within each hour.
- **Response to temptation:** Repeat the idea whenever upset, to restore peace.
- **Read the "What Is" section** slowly and thoughtfully once during the day.

Practice suggestion: I see today's lesson as a kind of holy escapism, in which we anticipate that glorious day when we at last awaken to Heaven. So, as you repeat today's idea, imagine that this is the day when you awaken from time and space once and for all and open your eyes in Heaven again. You may want to try repeating it once in this spirit now and see how it feels.

Commentary

This lesson is about anticipating Heaven.

"Today we will anticipate the time when dreams of sin and guilt are gone, and we have reached the holy peace we never left" (1:1).

That is what we do each day as we draw near to God in these times of quiet and stillness. We are giving ourselves a foretaste of Heaven. Just in this moment, just for now, imagine that all your dreams of sin and guilt are gone. Imagine that all fear has ended—all fear! Imagine that every thought of conflict is past. Imagine that there is nothing and can be nothing ever again that will disturb your perfect rest.

What you are imagining is real—the true state of things.

"Nothing has ever happened to disturb the peace of God the Father and the Son" (1:4).

The dreams of sin and guilt, the dream of fear, the dream of conflict, the dream of any disturbance at all is just that. Nothing more than a dream. Let it go, let it float away, meaningless and without significance. Just a bubble in the stream.

> Merely a tiny instant has elapsed between eternity and timelessness. So brief the interval there was no lapse in continuity, nor break in thoughts which are forever unified as one. Nothing has ever happened to disturb the peace of God the Father and the Son. This we accept as wholly true today. (1:2–5)

In these moments of remembrance, these holy instants we set aside each day, we are anticipating the time when our bad dreams are wholly absent. No, I am not there yet, nor are you, not in our experience—although in reality, as the lesson states so clearly, we never left. There has never been a "lapse in continuity," and not one note in Heaven's song was missed. We, however, are still living most of the time in the dream. But we can experience moments of anticipation, direct experiences of the truth. It is that we seek right now. A moment of anticipation. A sense in the core of our beings, something we identify with the word "peace," something that words cannot capture.

These are practice times in which we deliberately stretch ourselves above the level of our normal, mundane experience. We choose to "accept as wholly true" the fact that the peace of God, Father and Son, has *never* been disturbed. Just for the moment, just for now, we allow ourselves to experience believing that. We don't worry that in fifteen minutes we may not believe it. We don't worry about what will happen to our lives if we believe it. We don't consider all the evidence to the contrary our senses have brought us in the past. We just let all that go, and breathe deeply of the rarified atmosphere of Heaven. This is my Home. This is what I really am. This is what is really true. This is all that I want.

If thoughts of sin, or of guilt, or of fear do arise in our minds, we gently dismiss them. "This is not what I want to experience right now. Right now, I want the peace of God. Right now, I have the peace of God."

Jesus, our elder brother, joins us and leads us in prayer, praying with us:

> *We thank you, Father, that we cannot lose the memory of You and of Your Love. We recognize our safety, and give thanks for all the gifts You have bestowed on us, for all the loving help we have received, for Your eternal patience, and the Word which You have given us that we are saved.*
>
> (2:1–2)

WHAT IS SALVATION?

Part 4: W-pII.2.2:4–5

To our mind, the separation is real. "The separation is a system of thought real enough in time, though not in eternity" (T-3.VII.3:2). "The mind can make the belief in separation very real" (T-3.VII.5:1). The mind experiences itself as split, separated from God, and with one fragment of mind separated from other fragments. This is our experience in time, and it is "real enough" in time, although it is not real in eternity. In truth, the mind is not actually split; it is simply failing to recognize its oneness (2:4). But within that one mind, the experience of separation *seems* real.

Think of nearly any dream you have had in which you are interacting with other people. You are yourself in the dream, and there are other characters. Perhaps someone is making love to you. Perhaps you are arguing with someone, or being chased by a monster. Within the dream, every character is distinct and separate. The other people in the dream may say or do things that surprise you, or that you do not understand. And yet, in fact, every one of those "other characters" exists only in your one mind! Your mind is making them up. In the dream there is separation between the characters. In reality, there is only one mind, and different aspects of that mind are interacting with one another as if they were separate entities.

This, according to the Course, is exactly the case with this entire world. It is one mind, experiencing different aspects of itself as if they were separate beings. Within that dream the separation between the different characters seems to be clear and distinct, unbridgeable. And yet the mind is still one. The one mind does not know itself; it believes that "its own Identity was lost" (2:5). But the Identity was not lost in fact, only in a dream.

And so, within each fragment of the mind that is failing to recognize its oneness, God implanted the Thought of peace, "the Thought that has the power to heal the split" (2:4). This "part of every fragment" (2:4) remembers the Identity of mind. It is a part that is shared by every fragment. Like a golden thread running through a piece of fabric, it binds us all together, and draws the seemingly separated fragments constantly toward their true oneness. This Thought within us knows that "nothing has ever happened to disturb the peace of God the Father and the Son" (W-pII.234.1:4).

This Thought, implanted within us by God, is what we seek when we become still within the holy instant. By quieting all the separated thoughts, we listen for this Voice within us, speaking of our oneness, our wholeness, our eternal peace. This Thought has power to heal the split, to dissipate the seeming solidity of our illusions of separation, and to restore to the Sonship the awareness of its unity. "[Salvation] restores to your awareness the wholeness of the fragments you perceive as broken off and separate" (M-19.4:2).

LESSON 235 ✦ AUGUST 23
"God in His mercy wills that I be saved."

Practice instructions

See complete instructions on page 135. A short summary:

- **Read** the commentary paragraph slowly and personally.
- **Pray** the prayer, perhaps several times.
- **Morning and evening:** Repeat the idea and then spend time in Open Mind Meditation.
- **Hourly remembrance:** Repeat the idea and then spend a quiet moment in meditation.
- **Frequent reminders:** Repeat the idea often within each hour.
- **Response to temptation:** Repeat the idea whenever upset, to restore peace.
- **Read the "What Is" section** slowly and thoughtfully once during the day.

Practice comments: Notice the response to temptation instructions. Whenever something seems to hurt you, assure yourself with certainty, *"God wills that I be saved from this,"* and you can watch it disappear. Of course, the physical situation itself may not change, but what will disappear is the power it has over your emotions.

Commentary

If we look at our own thoughts honestly we will be able to see many ways in which we believe the direct opposite of today's lesson. We think, "God in His anger wills that I be punished." Somewhere in each of us is a pathetic voice telling us that we must deserve whatever we get in the way of pain, or that what joy we have may be taken from us because we are undeserving of it.

To those who begin to list their complaints about the world and how it mistreats them, the Course has very abrupt advice: "Give up these foolish thoughts!" (M-15.3:1). It is in my power to reverse these things.

All I need to do is to assure myself, "God wills that I be saved from this" (1:1). God does not will my pain, my sadness, or my loneliness. By changing the way I think of all this, I can change the world.

We think our hurt and sadness is caused by the events of the world; the Course is teaching us that it is the other way around. Our belief in God's anger is what brings us suffering; our belief in His mercy and Love can transform our lives. What needs changing is not out there in the world, but here, in my own mind. Let me today remember, Father, that I am "safe forever in [Your] Arms" (1:3). Let the thought that You will my happiness fill my mind today. If You are Love, if You love me, what else could You want for me?

WHAT IS SALVATION?

Part 5: W-pII.2.3:1–3

> Salvation is undoing in the sense that it does nothing, failing to support the world of dreams and malice. Thus it lets illusions go. (3:1–2)

To participate in salvation is not the addition of a new activity, but the letting go of our ancient drama of dreams and malice. To be saved is to *stop* supporting our illusions, to cease adding fuel to the fire of anger, attack, and guilt that has ravaged our minds for eons. Salvation is not a doing but an undoing. It is to end our resistance to the flow of love, both the flow from God to us, and the flow from us to God and to our brothers. Salvation means we stop inventing excuses not to love. It means we stop inventing reasons why we are not worthy of it.

"The ego has no power to distract you unless you give it the power to do so" (T-8.I.2:1). The only power the ego has is what we give to it; it uses our own power against us. All ego illusions are funded by our investment in them. When we withdraw that power, and stop our support of the ego's illusions, they "quietly go down to dust" (3:3). How is the ego undone? By our choice to no longer support it.

"The secret of salvation is but this: That you are doing this unto yourself" (T-27.VIII.10:1).

LESSON 236 ✦ AUGUST 24

"I rule my mind, which I alone must rule."

Practice instructions

See complete instructions on page 135. A short summary:

- **Read** the commentary paragraph slowly and personally.
- **Pray** the prayer, perhaps several times.
- **Morning and evening:** Repeat the idea and then spend time in Open Mind Meditation.
- **Hourly remembrance:** Repeat the idea and then spend a quiet moment in meditation.
- **Frequent reminders:** Repeat the idea often within each hour.
- **Response to temptation:** Repeat the idea whenever upset, to restore peace.
- **Read the "What Is" section** slowly and thoughtfully once during the day.

Commentary

If the "secret of salvation" is that "I am doing this to myself" (T-27.VIII.10:1), the reason that is "salvation," or good news, is that it means there are no inimical external forces imposing themselves on me. It's just my own mind screwing up. And if that is true, there is hope. Because nobody is running my mind but me! Therefore, I can turn things around. My mind is my kingdom, and I am king of my mind. I rule it; nobody and nothing else does.

Yes, it's true that "at times, it does not seem I am its king at all" (1:2). At times! For most of us it seems more like most of the time. My "kingdom" seems to run me, and not the other way around, telling me "what to think, and what to do and feel" (1:3). *A Course in Miracles* is a course for kings; it trains us how to rule our minds. We've been letting the kingdom run wild instead of ruling it. We've made the problem, projected the image of the problem, and then we've blamed the image for being the problem. As the Text says, we've reversed cause and

200

effect. We are the cause, we made the effect, and now we think the effect is causing us (see T-28.II.8:8). So we need a course in "mind training" that teaches us we are the rulers of our minds.

The mind is a tool, given to serve us (1:4–5). It does nothing except what we want it to do. The problem is that we have not been watching what we've asked the mind to do. We've asked for separation, we've asked for guilt, and being guilty, we've asked for death, and the mind has delivered as asked. We've given it over to the wild insanity of the ego, and the result is the ego's world we live in. So we need to see that, stop doing it, and give the mind's service to the Holy Spirit instead.

That raises a question for me. If I am supposed to rule my mind, how is giving it to the Holy Spirit doing that? To give the mind to the service of the Holy Spirit is said, here, to be the way "I thus direct my mind" (1:7). The answer is actually quite simple. There are only two alternatives: ego or Holy Spirit, fear or love, separation or union. The Holy Spirit is not a foreign power ruling over me, He is the Voice of my own Self, as well as the Voice for God. He is the Voice of both Father and Son because Father and Son are one, with one Will. The call to rule my mind is not a call to total self-reliant independence, the king as me-all-by-myself. That is the *ego* version of ruling the mind. The call to rule my mind is a call to total dependence, to total *Self* reliance; reliance upon the Self that is shared by us all.

I have the choice between the illusion of independence, in which my mind is actually enslaved by its effects, and real freedom, in which my mind is given to its divinely intended purpose, serving the Will of God. Who can deny that our experience of being independent minds is actually an experience of slavery, with our "kingdom" telling us what to think and do and say? Let us today realize there is an alternative, and gladly give our minds to God. Let us enter with willing hearts into the process of retraining our minds to think with God.

WHAT IS SALVATION?

Part 6: W-pII.2.3:4

When we stop supporting the mind's illusions, and they fall down into dust, what is left? "What they hid is now revealed" (3:4). When illusions are gone, what remains is the truth. And the truth is a wonderful reality within ourselves. Instead of the malice, pettiness, and evil we fear to find within us, we find "an altar to the Holy Name of God whereon His Word is written" (3:4). The truth that lies behind all the masks, the misdirection, the subtle deceptions of the ego, is an altar to God within my own heart, a sacred place, an ancient and eternal holiness.

There are treasures lying before this altar. And they are treasures I have put there! They are the gifts of my forgiveness. And it is only a short distance, a moment of time, from this place to the memory of God Himself (3:4).

The discovery of the holy altar to God within my mind is the result of doing nothing; of failing to continue my support of the ego's illusions, of refusing any longer to give my mind to the ego and its purposes. The discovery of what is true about me, and the memory of God that follows from it, all grow out of my willingness to question the illusions and let them go. I do not need to build the altar or rebuild it; it is there, behind the mists of self-deception. The way to truth is through the exposure of the lies that hide it. Deep within me, communion with God continues uninterrupted, waiting only that I turn from the lies that tell me otherwise. I can turn to that altar now. I can brush past the curtains that hide it, and enter God's Presence, and find my Self waiting there.

LESSON 237 ✦ AUGUST 25

"Now would I be as God created me."

Practice instructions

See complete instructions on page 135. A short summary:

- **Read** the commentary paragraph slowly and personally.
- **Pray** the prayer, perhaps several times.
- **Morning and evening:** Repeat the idea and then spend time in Open Mind Meditation.
- **Hourly remembrance:** Repeat the idea and then spend a quiet moment in meditation.
- **Frequent reminders:** Repeat the idea often within each hour.
- **Response to temptation:** Repeat the idea whenever upset, to restore peace.
- **Read the "What Is" section** slowly and thoughtfully once during the day.

Commentary

These lessons in Part II all seem to be about realizing Who or What I really am. As the introduction to the Workbook says:

> The workbook is divided into two main sections, the first dealing with the undoing of the way you see now, and the second with the acquisition of true perception.
>
> (W-In.3:1)

So the emphasis in this entire last section of the Workbook, the last 145 lessons, is on true perception. The assumption is that the reader has at least become aware of the ego thought system in his life, although by no means is it supposed that the ego is entirely undone. If that were the case, additional lessons would not be needed.

What we are doing in these last lessons is putting the positive side of the Course into practice, and attempting to bring it into application. "Now I would be as God created me." The goal is not just to understand the idea and file it away under "Facts: human nature, true," but *to be* the Son of God, by bringing that truth to my awareness throughout the day, and living accordingly.

"I will arise in glory" (1:2). Each day can begin in glory. Radiance, bright outshining. Glory, according to my dictionary, means "majestic beauty and splendor; resplendence." It is not a word we easily associate with ourselves. Today I can make a conscious effort to be aware of my glory. I am a radiant being. The light of love and joy shines out from me to bless the world. Let me sit a moment in silence, just picturing that, being aware of my own shining.

As I go through the day, let me

> allow the light in me to shine upon the world throughout
> the day. I bring the world the tidings of salvation which I
> hear as God my Father speaks to me. (1:2–3)

This has more to do with being than with doing. It has more to do with radiating than with speaking. We teach peace by *being* peaceful, not so much by talking about it. If I am joyful, restful, loving, and accepting of those around me, my attitude will speak louder than my words.

So in this day, as I work and visit with friends, let me be radiant. I am as God created me, so I *am* radiant; I don't need to do anything to become radiant. All that is needed is to notice what my thoughts would do to dim that radiance, and to choose otherwise.

In a certain sense this supersedes the earlier lesson where I ask the Holy Spirit where to go, what to do, and what to say. Now the emphasis is on what I am. It really doesn't matter so much where I go, what I do, or what I say, as long as I am acting as the being whom God created rather than my independent self.

I come to see "the world that Christ would have me see" (1:4), and I see it as "my Father's Call to me" (1:4). Seen through the eyes of Christ the world can become a constant call to be who I am, to shine, to radiate His Love, to be His Answer to the world.

WHAT IS SALVATION?

Part 7: W-pII.2.4:1

If the altar to God is within me, yet remains largely hidden from my habitual awareness, what I need to do is to "come daily to this holy place" (4:1). This is the practice of the holy instant recommended by the Text (see T-15.II.5–6 and T-15.IV), a premeditated turning aside from our routine activities to bring our minds into this holy place, with Jesus at our side ("Let *us* come...and spend a while together" [4:1, emphasis mine]). If you are open to it, it seems to me that Jesus is here asking us to spend some time, daily, with him, in God's presence. If the figure of Jesus is somehow discordant for you, picture an anonymous spiritual guide, perhaps representing your higher Self. With him or her, you enter this temple, stand by the altar, and spend time there in communion with God.

We need to form this habit of bringing our minds into the holy instant, reminding ourselves of the presence of Jesus (or the Holy Spirit), remembering this altar to God within ourselves, with His Word written on it (3:4). That Word, I think, is the Word of salvation, the promise He made that we would find our way to Him (1:1). It is the Thought of peace, which will replace our thoughts of conflict. This meeting place is where we experience the unbroken communication between ourselves and God. This is where we bathe in the flow of love that streams constantly between the Father and the Son.

Chapter 14, Section VIII of the Text describes this holy meeting place, and says:

> All this is safe within you, where the Holy Spirit shines. He shines not in division, but in the meeting place where God, united with His Son, speaks to His Son through Him. Communication between what cannot be divided cannot cease. The holy meeting place of the unseparated Father and His Son lies in the Holy Spirit and in you. All interference in the communication that God Himself wills with His Son is quite impossible here. Unbroken and uninterrupted love flows constantly between the Father and the Son, as Both would have it be. And so it is. (T-14.VIII.2:10–16)

And so it is. This is what I want to know and experience daily, in coming to this place. Here I bring my guilt and fear and lay it down, accepting Atonement for myself. Here my mind renews its contact with its Source. Here I rediscover the unending communion which is mine, my inheritance as God's Son. Here my nightmares are all banished, and I breathe the fragrant air of Heaven and of home.

LESSON 238 ✦ AUGUST 26

"On my decision all salvation rests."

Practice instructions

See complete instructions on page 135. A short summary:

- **Read** the commentary paragraph slowly and personally.
- **Pray** the prayer, perhaps several times.
- **Morning and evening:** Repeat the idea and then spend time in Open Mind Meditation.
- **Hourly remembrance:** Repeat the idea and then spend a quiet moment in meditation.
- **Frequent reminders:** Repeat the idea often within each hour.
- **Response to temptation:** Repeat the idea whenever upset, to restore peace.
- **Read the "What Is" section** slowly and thoughtfully once during the day.

Practice suggestion: I suggest making this line more specific from time to time today. Pick someone you are with, or someone with whom you feel irritated, or someone who needs you, and insert that person's name: *"On my decision [name's] salvation rests."*

Commentary

In Lesson 236 I saw that I alone rule my mind. God has created me free to choose to listen to His Voice, or not to listen. Salvation thus rests entirely on my decision. The message of today's lesson is that if this is true, God must have a great deal of trust in me. As humankind is typically pictured, it is weak, vacillating, or downright rebellious. Sinners at the core, and totally untrustworthy. But if God "placed [His] Son's salvation in my hands, and let it rest on my decision" (1:3), that dark picture cannot be the truth. If I were such an untrustworthy being, if humankind were so unreliable, God would never have put such enormous trust in us. Therefore, "I must be worthy" (1:1). "I must be beloved of You indeed. And I must be steadfast in holiness as well"

(1:4–5). In sum: If God trusts me, I must be worthy of that trust.

It isn't just my own salvation that rests on my decision; "all salvation" rests on it, because the Sonship is one. If one part remains separate and alone, the Sonship is incomplete. Yet God "gave [His] Son to me in certainty that He is safe" (1:5). If God is certain that the Son is safe in my hands, He must know something about me that I have forgotten. He knows me as I am (1:2), and not as I have come to believe I am. The trust He displays is amazing, because the Son is not simply His creation, the Son is "still part of" Him (1:5). God has entrusted part of His very Being to my care, in confidence of what my decision will be: to freely, willingly choose to join with and enter into His Love and His Will. He knows that in the end I will not choose otherwise and cannot choose otherwise, for He formed me as an extension of His own Love.

Let me, then, today, reflect often on how much God loves me, how much He loves His Son, and how God's Love for His Son is demonstrated by entrusting all salvation to my decision. Let me rest assured that the outcome is as inevitable as God. Let me take confidence in God's confidence in me.

WHAT IS SALVATION?

Part 8: W-pII.2.4:2-5

When we come daily to this holy place, we catch glimpses of the real world, our "final dream" (4:2). In the holy instant we see with the vision of Christ, in which there is no sorrow. We are allowed to see "a hint of all the glory given us by God" (4:3). The goal of the Course for us is to come to the place where we carry this vision with us always; where our minds are so transformed that we see nothing but the real world, and live a life that is one continuous holy instant. That time may seem far off to me, but it is much nearer than I believe, and in the holy instant I experience it as *now*. It is by repeatedly coming to the holy instant, repeatedly immersing our minds in the vision of the real world, that this world becomes the only reality to us, the final dream before we waken.

In this happy dream, "earth is being born again in new perspective" (4:5). The images of grass pushing through the soil, trees budding, and birds coming to live in their branches speak to us of springtime, of a rebirth after a long winter. The images stand for the new perception we have of the world, in which our spiritual night is gone, and all living things stand together in the light of God. We look past illusions now, past what has always seemed like solid reality to us, and see something more firm and sure beyond them, a vision of everlasting holiness and peace. We see and hear "the need of every heart, the call of every mind, the hope that lies beyond despair, the love attack would hide, the brotherhood that hate has sought to sever, but which still remains as God created it" (W-pI.185.14:1).

Here, in the vision of the real world, we "hear the call that echoes past each seeming call to death, that sings behind each murderous attack and pleads that love restore the dying world" (T-31.I.10:3). We see that the only purpose of the world is forgiveness. "How lovely is the world whose purpose is forgiveness of God's Son!" (T-29.VI.6:1).

"How beautiful it is to walk, clean and redeemed and happy, through a world in bitter need of redemption that your innocence bestows upon it!" (T-23.In.6:5).

LESSON 239 ✦ AUGUST 27
"The glory of my Father is my own."

Practice instructions

See complete instructions on page 135. A short summary:

- **Read** the commentary paragraph slowly and personally.
- **Pray** the prayer, perhaps several times.
- **Morning and evening:** Repeat the idea and then spend time in Open Mind Meditation.
- **Hourly remembrance:** Repeat the idea and then spend a quiet moment in meditation.
- **Frequent reminders:** Repeat the idea often within each hour.
- **Response to temptation:** Repeat the idea whenever upset, to restore peace.
- **Read the "What Is" section** slowly and thoughtfully once during the day.

Practice suggestions: As you repeat today's idea, be aware that "glory" means "divine radiance." Thus, according to this idea, whatever holy light radiates from God is your light as well. Try to imagine this as you repeat the idea. I have found it helpful to add the following lines (based on paragraphs 1 and 2): *"I claim this glory, setting all false humility aside. I see it in my brothers and realize this glory unites us with each other and unites all of us with God."*

Commentary

"Let not the truth about ourselves today be hidden by a false humility" (1:1).

One thing I am aware of as I have not been before while doing the Workbook is that when it uses the words "we," "us," and "ourselves," it is not referring to just us students of the Course. The "we" includes Jesus. After all, it is Jesus who is speaking throughout the book. This is no ordinary, generic "we" that any author might use. Jesus is identifying himself with us, and us with him, each time a third-person pronoun is used.

The "truth about ourselves" is the truth about you, me, and Jesus. In recognizing that, I get a sense of his joining with me that I've never quite had before. And I see in his use of the terms a purpose, to focus my attention on the sameness of himself, myself, and my brothers.

When I see traces of sin and guilt "in those with whom He shares His glory" (1:3), I am seeing them in myself. That is a false humility! When I see my brother as guilty or sinful it is because I am putting myself in that same class, and thus hiding the truth about myself. Guilt can take a seemingly saintly form: "We are all just poor students of the Course, weak and frail and constantly failing." And that guilt, that false humility, obscures your glory and my own.

It is true that we are all just students, that we are on the lower rung of the ladder and just beginning to be aware of all we really are. It is false spirituality to pretend to what we do not experience. But it is false humility to constantly emphasize our weakness by judging or focusing on failures. We all have egos, but we also all share the same glorious Sonship. We need to spend time, from time to time, giving thanks for "the light that shines forever in us...We are one, united in this light and one with You, at peace with all creation and ourselves" (2:1, 3).

What I dwell on in my brothers is what I am seeing and dwelling on in myself. How I view my brothers only reflects my view of myself.

> Perception seems to teach you what you see. Yet it but witnesses to what you taught. It is the outward picture of a wish; an image that you wanted to be true.
> (T-24 VII.8:8–10)

> "How can you manifest the Christ in you except to look on holiness and see Him there?" (T-25.I.2:1). In other words, you manifest the Christ in you only by looking on your brother and seeing the Christ in him.

> Perception tells you *you* are manifest in what you see.
> (T-25.I.2:2)

> Perception is a choice of what you want yourself to be; the world you want to live in, and the state in which you think your mind will be content and satisfied....It reveals

211

yourself to you as you would have you be. (T-25.I.3:1, 3)

If I would not hide the truth of my own glory, I cannot hide that of my brother. "What is the same can have no different function" (T-23.IV.3:4). If I deny the truth in my brother, I am denying it to myself. I am denying it in him *because* I am denying it about myself. When I mentally separate myself from someone, and make him or her less than myself by judging, I am seeing only what my mind is doing to myself. I am hiding my own glory, and therefore judging another, projecting the guilt outside. My judgment of another can then become a mirror to show me that I have forgotten who I really am. It can remind me, cause me to remember, and cause me to choose again, to remember my status as Son of God, "at peace with all creation and [myself]" (2:3).

WHAT IS SALVATION?

Part 9: W-pII.2.5:1–2

We turn from the world to the holy place within; we enter the holy instant, where our illusions fall because we no longer support them, and we begin to see with the vision of Christ, seeing the real world. And *then we return to the world.* "From here we give salvation to the world, for it is here salvation was received" (5:1). This movement is repeated again and again in both Workbook and Text: Away from the world of dreams—into the holy instant—returning to give salvation to the world. The Course does not plan for us to retreat from the world, but to save it. It does not urge us into a withdrawn, contemplative life, but urges us *from within the state of mind we find in contemplation* to offer what we have found to the world.

"The song of our rejoicing is the call to all the world that freedom is returned" (5:2). Our inner healing bubbles over in a "song of our rejoicing," and that song, that ebullient joy, becomes the very thing that calls the world back to its freedom. Nothing is so healing as a person whose face is radiant with joy. It is not so much that we come to the world preaching a new religion (see W-pI.37.3:1–2), but that we transform it by our joy. We represent a new state of mind. As the Manual puts it, we "stand for the Alternative" (M-5.III.2:6). We save the world by being saved.

LESSON 240 ✦ AUGUST 28
"Fear is not justified in any form."

Practice instructions

See complete instructions on page 135. A short summary:

- **Read** the commentary paragraph slowly and personally.
- **Pray** the prayer, perhaps several times.
- **Morning and evening:** Repeat the idea and then spend time in Open Mind Meditation.
- **Hourly remembrance:** Repeat the idea and then spend a quiet moment in meditation.
- **Frequent reminders:** Repeat the idea often within each hour.
- **Response to temptation:** Repeat the idea whenever upset, to restore peace.
- **Read the "What Is" section** slowly and thoughtfully once during the day.

Practice suggestion: Try to be vigilant all day for any instance of fear, including worry, anxiety, or nervousness. When you notice an instance, repeat the line in this specific way: *"Fear is not justified in this form, because fear is not justified in any form."*

Commentary

"Fear is deception" (1:1). When we are afraid, we have been deceived by some lie, because given what we are (Sons of God, a part of Love Itself) (1:7–8), nothing can ever harm us or cause us loss of any kind. Therefore, when fear arises, we must have seen ourselves as we could never be (1:2). The reality of what we are is never in danger: "Nothing real can be threatened" (T-In.2:2). All the things in the world that appear to threaten us are simply impossible, because we cannot be threatened. "Not one thing in this world is true" (1:3). "Nothing unreal exists" (T-In.2:3).

All the threats of the world, whatever their forms, witness only to one thing: our illusions about ourselves (1:4–5). We are seeing ourselves as something vulnerable; a body, a fragile ego, a physical life form that can be snuffed out in an instant. That is not what we are, and when we fear, that is what we are thinking we are. In order for us to come to believe that we are something else—the eternal Son of God, forever secure in God's Love, beyond the reach of death—we must be willing to learn the unreality of all that the world seems to witness to. Eventually we must come to see that to attempt to hold on to the reality of this world is to hold on to death.

If we insist on making the world real, today's statement, "Fear is not justified," will never seem true to us. *Everything* in this world is vulnerable, changeable, and will ultimately pass away. If we try to hold on to it, fear is inevitable because the end of what we are holding on to is also inevitable. The only way to be truly free from fear is to cease to value anything but the eternal.

This does not mean that we cannot enjoy what is temporary, that we cannot, for instance, pause to appreciate the beauty of a sunset which passes in minutes. But we come to understand that it is not the sunset we value, but the beauty it mirrors for a moment. It is not the touch of a body we value, a body which withers and is gone, but the eternal love it catches and expresses in the moment. Not the form, but the content. Not the symbol, but its meaning. Not the overtones, the harmonics, or the echo, but the eternal song of love (S-1.I.3:4).

Let me practice, then, today, by repeating, "Fear is not justified in any form." And when fears arise, let me remember they are foolish (2:1). Let me recall there is no real reason for them. Let my very fears remind me that the truth of what I value *never* passes away.

WHAT IS SALVATION?

Part 10: W-pII.2.5:2

Salvation results not in a perfect material world, but in a state in which "eternity has shined away the world, and only Heaven now exists at all" (5:2). As we enter more and more fully into the holy instant, and the vision of the "real world" it brings, we are literally hastening the end of time itself. The phrase "the real world" is in actuality an oxymoron, a self-contradictory pair of words, for the world is not real (see T-26.III.3:1–3). The real world is the goal of the Course for us, and yet, when we have attained it fully, we will barely have time to appreciate it before God takes His last step, and the illusion of the world vanishes into the reality of Heaven (see T-17.II.4:4). The nightmare is gradually translated into a happy dream, and when all the nightmares are gone there is no longer any need for dreaming; we will awake. ·

Salvation, then, is the process of translating the nightmare into the happy dream, the process of undoing the illusions, the process of removing the barriers we have built to love, the process, in short, of forgiveness. The experience we are now in is our classroom. The reason we are here is to learn the truth; or rather, to unlearn the errors. The Course urges us to be content with learning, and not to be impatient. We will not be, and cannot be "abruptly lifted up and hurled into reality" (T-16.VI.8:1). It would terrify us, like a child in kindergarten abruptly being made President, or a first-year piano student being forced to do a solo recital in Carnegie Hall. Each of us is exactly where we belong, learning just what we need to learn. Let us, then, enter wholeheartedly and joyously into the process, practicing our holy instants, receiving our little glimpses of the real world, each one assuring us of the reality of our goal, and the certainty of its attainment.

VI

Lessons 241 - 250
What Is the World?

"This holy instant is salvation come."

Practice instructions

See complete instructions on page 135. A short summary:
- **Read** the commentary paragraph slowly and personally.
- **Pray** the prayer, perhaps several times.
- **Morning and evening:** Repeat the idea and then spend time in Open Mind Meditation.
- **Hourly remembrance:** Repeat the idea and then spend a quiet moment in meditation.
- **Frequent reminders:** Repeat the idea often within each hour.
- **Response to temptation:** Repeat the idea whenever upset, to restore peace.
- **Read the "What Is" section** slowly and thoughtfully once during the day.

Practice suggestion: The following visualization may help you more fully experience the meaning of today's lesson:

Imagine a city or town, a place where there are large amounts of people, just before sunrise.

The sun begins to peek over the horizon, but this is not the usual sun.

This is the sunrise of salvation. Now hear these lines: "The day has come when sorrows pass away and pain is gone" (1:4).

Imagine that, wherever the rays of this sun touch, sorrows pass away.

Imagine them touching a hospital, and all pain within it is gone.

"The glory of salvation dawns today upon a world set free" (1:5).

What is dawning is not mere physical light.

It is salvation.

Because of this dawning, the world will be set free today.

"This is the time of hope for countless millions" (1:6).

Imagine countless millions waking up to this sunrise.

Not as they normally do, numb with despair and dreading what the day may bring, but filled with hope.

"Watch fear disappear from every face as hearts rise up and claim the light as theirs" (W-pI.168.4:3).

"They will be united now" (1:7).

Picture people all over joining with one another.

See them joining hands.

See them feeling at one.

See countless millions greeting this sunrise as one family.

Now realize that this sun is not just salvation.

It is something far more specific.

It is your forgiveness of the world.

Your forgiveness has this kind of power.

It has the power to set the world free.

It has the power, once unleashed, to give the world this kind of dawn.

So choose someone you have not forgiven and say to him or her,

"This holy instant is salvation come, because I have
forgiven you, [name]."
Keep repeating it, realizing that each repetition invites
this glorious dawn to illumine the world.

Commentary

When the lesson says that today "is a time of special celebration"
(1:2), I rather suspect it is using the word "special" in the same way it
uses it in one place in the Text, where Jesus says, "All my brothers are
special" (T-1.V.3:6). Today is special because, in the holy instant,
salvation has already come. And yet, "You can claim the holy instant
any time and anywhere you want it" (T-15.IV.4:4). Whenever you claim
the holy instant, it is a special time! A day of joy!

This is just like telling a child that they can have Christmas every day
if they want it. And indeed the Course tells us exactly that, in the section
titled "The Time of Rebirth," written at Christmas. It tells us that
Christmas is the time of Christ, and the time of Christ is the holy instant
(see T-15.X.2:1); then it tells us, "It is in your power to make the time
of Christ be now" (T-15.X.4:1).

And so, why not today? Why not every day? Why not now? Any
time I want to, I can make it a time "when sorrows pass away and pain
is gone" (1:4). The practice of the holy instant offers me this. Within my
mind I can, at any instant, open a window onto the real world, and
breathe its fragrant atmosphere. I can experience a united world, drawn
together by my forgiveness.

I do not yet find that I experience bliss the moment I close my eyes
and say, "This holy instant is salvation come." The reality I have
experienced, from time to time, is always here; I am certain of that. Yet
my awareness of it remains spotty. (*Very* spotty!) But once you have
tasted it, and in that instant *known* that what you are experiencing is
eternal, you can never fully doubt its eternal presence. There are still
many barriers blocking my awareness of it. I am still holding on to quite
a few of those barriers. My grievances are still, most of the time, hiding
the light of the world from me. But it is there. My forgiveness can
release it (1:7–2:1).

Every time I pause to remember, every time I attempt to claim the
holy instant, another barrier falls, another drop of willingness is added
to my reservoir. What better way could I possibly spend my time? As

Lesson 127 said: "There is no better use for time than this" (see paragraphs 7 and 8).

One aside: Notice that in 1:8, Jesus speaks of our forgiving *him*. Let me examine myself today, to see if there is something I still hold against him; something in him I mistrust; some way in which I still fear him, or blame him, or resent him. Even if I respect him as my teacher, it is very easy to feel resentful of one's teachers.

WHAT IS THE WORLD?

Part 1: W-pII.3.1:1-4

The first sentence answers the question: "The world is false perception" (1:1). The rest of the page is the explanation of this summary statement. Some of us, on first reading the Course, think that perhaps the Course is not saying that the world is unreal, but that our perception of it is false. Yet here, quite clearly, Jesus is saying that the world and false perception are the same thing. The world is a hallucination; we are perceiving something that isn't there.

In my perception, "I" am inside my head, looking out at a world that is not me. Separate. And that is simply not the truth. There is no world outside my mind (see T-18.VI.1:1 and T-12.III.6:7). "What is projected out, and seems to be external to the mind, is not outside at all" (T-26.VII.4:9).

The world was "born of error" and it has not left our minds which sourced it (1:2). As the Course so often says, ideas leave not their source. The world is the mistaken idea of separation in our minds (1:4), and it has never left our minds. When our mind (the one mind we all share) no longer cherishes the idea of separation, the world which represents that idea will simply disappear.

Many who were raised in a religious tradition which taught that God created the world have gone through a lot of distress and confusion, wondering how God could ever have created such a mess! If He was responsible for this, we weren't sure we wanted to know Him. What a relief it is to realize that He did *not* create it; it was born of the error of our mind, from our mistakenly entertaining the idea of separation. The misery of this world only reflects the misery brought to our mind by the thought of separation. It is as if we wondered, "What if we were separate?" and were instantly given a virtual reality tour of what would result.

An early lesson said, "I can escape from this world by giving up attack thoughts" (W-pI.55.3:1, reviewing Lesson 23). The thought is the same. Heal the attack thoughts, the thoughts of separation which I still cherish, and I can leave the world behind. The Course is helping us to do just that; to let our attack thoughts go, and solve the problems of the world at their source.

LESSON 242 ✦ AUGUST 30
"This day is God's. It is my gift to Him."

Practice instructions

See complete instructions on page 135. A short summary:

- **Read** the commentary paragraph slowly and personally.
- **Pray** the prayer, perhaps several times.
- **Morning and evening:** Repeat the idea and then spend time in Open Mind Meditation.
- **Hourly remembrance:** Repeat the idea and then spend a quiet moment in meditation.
- **Frequent reminders:** Repeat the idea often within each hour.
- **Response to temptation:** Repeat the idea whenever upset, to restore peace.
- **Read the "What Is" section** slowly and thoughtfully once during the day.

Commentary

"I will not lead my life alone today" (1:1).

In a day that seems rushed and over full with things to do, it is a relief to remember that I need not lead my life alone. I can burden myself with a thousand little decisions, or I can relax into His hands. I may list what needs to be done, but I can let go of all attachment to doing any of them. In each moment, I can trust that I will know what to do next, and that my choice will be perfect.

What is important, however, is not the guidance of the Holy Spirit, but His companionship. I will not be alone today, although I may have no other human presence with me. I can consciously be with God, and God with me. Instead of talking out loud to myself, why not talk out loud to Jesus? He is a much wiser companion than my limited mind.

"I do not understand the world, and so to try to lead my life alone must be but foolishness" (1:2).

There is such resistance in me, in us all, to realizing that we do not and cannot understand the world. I understand nothing. My awareness of what is going on is about one five-billionth of just our physical planet and its people. I know nothing of other planets and galaxies, and I am nearly totally unaware of the numberless realms beyond the physical—spirit beings, angels, ascended Masters, whatever there may be. I don't know that the clerk in the laundry may need a smile, or whatever else is going on in minds apparently separated from me. How can I even think of rationally deciding what to do, where to go, what to say, all on my own?

Some event occurs, such as an appointment being juggled around from one time to another and finally settling on the time I least wanted (by my preferences). If I think I understand what is going on, if I think my preference is all that matters, I could be upset. If I realize I don't understand the world, I let go, I accept, I trust. And I show up at my friend's door minutes after she has heard the news about a friend's sudden death, present to comfort her when she needs it. And, not coincidentally, prepared by an afternoon of discussing death with another friend, when I had no idea why I agreed to take time for that discussion when I had other things I thought important to do. How foolish not to let Him lead me!

So today, again, I resign as my own teacher and settle a bit more deeply into the awareness that I do not know, I do not understand, and knowing that is wisdom. I release this day into God's hands; "It is my gift to Him." This is a really good deal! I let go of my day, and He makes it full of miracles! That's what He wants it for. It takes great effort, at first, to let go of wanting to understand. But when I do, nothing but joy follows.

> But there is One Who knows all that is best for me. And He is glad to make no choices for me but the ones that lead to God. I give this day to Him, for I would not delay my coming home, and it is He Who knows the way to God.
>
> (1:3–5)

"Best for me" doesn't necessarily mean that I will get done all I think I have to do, or that everything will work out perfectly (in my eyes) in form. Often it does mean that, but sometimes not. "Best for me" means the things "that lead to God." It means "coming home" and making progress on "the way to God." Because that is all that life in this world is for. "The healing of God's Son is all the world is for" (T-24.VI.4:1), and nothing else. If I give my day to God, to the Holy Spirit, I will end the day closer to God, nearer home; that is my goal every day of my life. Nothing else. All other events are stage props for this one unfolding drama.

No matter what else may happen, if I spend this day more conscious of Jesus' companionship, a little more often at peace, a little more joyful in every minute or a few more minutes spent joyfully, it is a success.

And so we give today to You. We come with wholly open minds. We do not ask for anything that we may think we want. Give us what You would have received by us. You know all our desires and our wants. And You will give us everything we need in helping us to find the way to You.
(2:1–6)

"Wholly open minds." No preconceptions about what should take place. "Wholly" means totally, completely open. As for what we expect to come, anything can fail to happen and we are not distraught. As for what we do not expect, anything can come, and we are not dismayed. I recognize that my mind does not want to be wholly open. For instance, I think if I did not finish writing my article before lunch I might be upset. If I have that thought, let me see it is only my thought. Not a fact. What other things am I attached to today? Jesus, I want to be wholly open. And it isn't easy.

How can I let go of my wants and needs? By remembering that "You know all our desires and our wants." He knows what I think I need, and I do not need to ask Him for those things. He knows. And if the day does not bring what I think I want, it is not because He did not know, or that He lost my case file, or that He is punishing me for some imaginary guilt. It is because what I thought I wanted was not best for me. The Holy Spirit is not inconsiderate nor forgetful. He "will give us everything we need in helping us to find the way to" God. Let me let down the defenses of my planning mind, and follow this advice: "Let no defenses but your present trust direct the future, and this life becomes a meaningful encounter with the truth that only your defenses would conceal" (W-pI.135.19:2).

WHAT IS THE WORLD?

Part 2: W-pII.3.1:4–5

If the world is simply the effect of the thought of separation in my mind, then obviously it is true that

> when the thought of separation has been changed to one of true forgiveness, will the world be seen in quite another light, and one which leads to truth. (1:4)

The antidote for the thought of separation is true forgiveness. If the Course is a course in changing our thoughts, the thoughts that are being changed are separation thoughts, and they are being changed into thoughts of true forgiveness. The "wall" that keeps us separate is our unforgiveness, our grievances, our judgment upon one another as undeserving of love. The result of changing those thoughts to thoughts of forgiveness is that we see the world very differently. Instead of a world of judgment we see the real world. Instead of enemies we see brothers. And the vision of this real world "leads to truth," beyond perception to knowledge; beyond the real world to Heaven.

This light "leads to truth, where all the world must disappear and all its errors vanish" (1:4). In other words, as we've already seen, the progression is from "the world" (the result of the thought of separation) to "the real world" (the result of the thought of forgiveness) and then to "Heaven" (the truth), where there is no world at all.

The process we are going through in the world is the healing of our thoughts of separation. As those thoughts are healed, we begin to see the real world more and more, a world in which only love is reflected. But when the thought of separation is *entirely* healed in every part of every fragment of the mind, the world will not simply be seen differently; it will disappear. "Now its source [the thought of separation] has gone, and its effects [the world and all its errors] are gone as well" (1:5).

LESSON 243 ✦ AUGUST 31
"Today I will judge nothing that occurs."

Practice instructions

See complete instructions on page 135. A short summary:

- **Read** the commentary paragraph slowly and personally.
- **Pray** the prayer, perhaps several times.
- **Morning and evening:** Repeat the idea and then spend time in Open Mind Meditation.
- **Hourly remembrance:** Repeat the idea and then spend a quiet moment in meditation.
- **Frequent reminders:** Repeat the idea often within each hour.
- **Response to temptation:** Repeat the idea whenever upset, to restore peace.
- **Read the "What Is" section** slowly and thoughtfully once during the day.

Practice suggestion: Think of some situation that has been upsetting you, and repeat the following lines:

I do not know what this means,
Because meaning is supplied by context,
And I do not see the whole context for this.
The whole context for this is the whole—totality, infinity.
Yet I see only bits of my perception.
I do not know what this means.

Commentary

If attempting to practice today's lesson does nothing else, it will show me just how constantly my mind *is* judging. The eventual goal, of course, is to truly relinquish all judgment, and to allow the Holy Spirit to judge everything for us. Letting go of judgment is a key to transcending the ego: "The ego cannot survive without judgment, and is laid aside accordingly" (T-4.II.10:3).

"I will be honest with myself today" (1:1). The Course teaches us that letting go of judgment is simply learning to be honest with ourselves. This lesson is paralleled in the Manual:

> It is necessary for the teacher of God to realize, not that he should not judge, but that he cannot. In giving up judgment, he is merely giving up what he did not have. He gives up an illusion; or better, he has an illusion of giving up. He has actually merely become more honest. Recognizing that judgment was always impossible for him, he no longer attempts it. (M-10.2:1–5)

So giving up judgment is simply being honest about the fact that I *cannot* judge. To judge accurately I would have to know many things that "must remain beyond my present grasp" (1:2). I would have to know "the whole" (1:3) just from what my limited perception is telling me. And I can't do that. So any judgment I make has to be an illusion, no more valid than a wild guess.

Still—just watch yourself doing it! Our minds automatically categorize every person we see. We evaluate their clothes, their grooming, their sexual attractiveness, the appropriateness of their behavior, the way they walk, and on and on. We get up, see the sunshine, and say, "What a nice day!" or we see rain and say, "What miserable weather!" We read a book and tell a friend what a "great book" it is. We take a bite of food and instantly judge it. The ego mind seems to do little else but judge. Just watch yourself.

That isn't going to stop overnight, if ever. What we can do, however, is to become aware of these judgments constantly going on and realize that they are without any real meaning. We can tell the ego, "Thank you for sharing," and choose to realize that we don't really know what anything means or how to react to it, despite what the ego is telling us. We can turn instead to our inner guidance. We can "leave creation free to be itself" (2:1) without our constant interference. We can bring our judgments to the Holy Spirit and ask Him to heal our minds. And, perhaps most important of all, we can simply *desire* that judgment be undone. In the end, that desire is all it takes:

> Vision would not be necessary had judgment not been made. Desire now its whole undoing, and it is done for you.
> (T-20.VIII.1:5–6)

> Undoing is not your task, but it *is* up to you to welcome it
> or not. (T-21.II.8:5)

Don't worry about *how* your judgments can be undone. Don't try to undo them yourself. Just desire that they be undone; just welcome the undoing. That is all, and the Holy Spirit will do it for you.

WHAT IS THE WORLD?

Part 3: W-pII.3.2:1–3

"The world was made as an attack on God" (2:1). That is probably one of the most shocking statements in *A Course in Miracles*. It puts to bed any idea that perhaps the world was, at least partly, created by God; God would not create an attack on Himself. The world is the ego's attempt to replace and displace God, and to provide us with an alternative satisfaction.

In Chapter 23, Section II, the Text speaks of "The Laws of Chaos," the ego's laws. It tells us that these laws are what make the world real; it says, "These *are* the principles which make the ground beneath your feet seem solid" (T-23.II.13:5). The ego's laws are what made the world.

What of the world's beauty? What of the glitter of the stars, the fragile beauty of a flower, the majesty of an eagle in flight? Nothing but glitter, a shiny surface hiding the death-rot underneath. "Kill or be killed" is the law of this world. Beneath the lovely, glittering surface of the ocean lies a world of sharp teeth, cruel deception, and constant warfare, where life consists of eating some things and avoiding being eaten by others.

"Can you paint rosy lips upon a skeleton, dress it in loveliness, pet it and pamper it, and make it live?" (T-23.II.18:8). "There is no life outside of Heaven" (T-23.II.19:1).

The world symbolizes fear, which is the absence of love. "Thus, the world was meant to be a place where God could enter not, and where His Son could be apart from Him" (2:4). The ego made the world as a place to hide out from God, to get away from Him. Yes, we can find symbols of God in nature, and we should; true perception sees nothing but love in all things. But that means we see Him in tornadoes and earthquakes as well as in flowers and birds. It means we see Him in everything because He is in our minds. But at its root, this world is a place where God is not. That is why the ego made it. That is our purpose in coming here, as egos. And we egos did a pretty good job; people have been trying to "prove" the existence of God within the context of this world for millennia, and nobody has ever done so except, perhaps, to the satisfaction of a few who were already inclined to believe. Finding God *in* the world is quite a stretch. The world does a far better job of hiding God than it does of demonstrating Him.

What is the message in all of this for us? Remember, "The world is false perception" (1:1). It is not the truth. The picture of the world, symbolizing fear and attack, is the picture of the ego's thoughts. "It is born of error" (1:2). This world is not what we want. We cannot attempt to cling to its "better" parts and forget about the horror all around us. We take it whole or let it all go. And so, we can learn to look upon the world with love—all of it. Loving it gives it the only value it has (see T-12.VI.3:1–3). With forgiveness, we look past the messages of hate and fear it constantly tries to give us, and see there, as well as in the more "pleasing" aspects, the universal call for love.

> You do not want the world. The only thing of value in it is whatever part of it you look upon with love. This gives it the only reality it will ever have. Its value is not in itself, but yours is in you. As self-value comes from self-exten-sion, so does the perception of self-value come from the extension of loving thoughts outward. Make the world real unto yourself, for the real world is the gift of the Holy Spirit, and so it belongs to you. (T-12.VI.3:1–6)

LESSON 244 ✦ SEPTEMBER 1
"I am in danger nowhere in the world."

Practice instructions

See complete instructions on page 135. A short summary:

- **Read** the commentary paragraph slowly and personally.
- **Pray** the prayer, perhaps several times.
- **Morning and evening:** Repeat the idea and then spend time in Open Mind Meditation.
- **Hourly remembrance:** Repeat the idea and then spend a quiet moment in meditation.
- **Frequent reminders:** Repeat the idea often within each hour.
- **Response to temptation:** Repeat the idea whenever upset, to restore peace.
- **Read the "What Is" section** slowly and thoughtfully once during the day.

Practice suggestion: Whenever you think of it, especially when you are feeling afraid, repeat the lesson in this more specific form: *"I am in danger nowhere in the world, including in this situation."*

Commentary

Who I have believed myself to be is in danger *everywhere* in the world. We are assaulted constantly with signals of danger. Smoking can kill me; even residual smoke is deadly. Our water is unsafe, I need a purifier. Preservatives and coloring in foods cause cancer. Stay well away from your microwave while using it. Don't sit too close to your TV or computer screen (and watch out for carpal tunnel syndrome). Beware of computer viruses; even more, beware of HIV viruses. Don't feed bears when camping. Don't use your telephone in a lightning storm. Don't drink and drive, and watch out for those who do.

In order to even begin to accept today's idea, I have to realize that I am not who I have believed myself to be. This little identity of Allen

Watson, wrapped in a very fragile body, is not the one who is in danger nowhere in the world: "Your Son is safe wherever he may be" (1:1). It is the Son Who is safe; the Son Who is beloved of God, held "in the safety of Your Fatherly embrace" (1:3). In my quiet times today I will recall that this is Who I really am, and, at least in these moments, I will let go of my sense of danger, relax my defensiveness, and enjoy the awareness of the Father's Love and protection (1:2). I will realize that Who I really am "cannot suffer, be endangered, or experience unhappiness" (1:3).

Let me attempt to feel my safety today. What would I feel like if I truly knew, to the depths of my being, that I can never suffer, or be in danger, or experience unhappiness? What effect would that have on the tension in my shoulders, the knot in my stomach, or the rapid beating of my heart? Let me thoughtfully consider this. Let me try to imagine the peace I would feel. Let me experience the softening in every part of my body, and more importantly, the melting of the hardness of my mind. I would feel, I think, like the very young child who, when Mommy or Daddy says, "Everything will be all right now," really believes it. The shuddering stops, the little body relaxes, and the child falls asleep in Mommy's arms.

"And there we are in truth," "in the safety of Your Fatherly embrace" (2:1; 1:3). "In God we are secure" (2:3). Yes.

WHAT IS THE WORLD?

Part 4: W-pII.3.2:4–7

The world is where perception was born (2:5). It was born because *knowledge* could not give birth to thoughts of fear; knowledge knows only the peace of God. Knowledge, in the Course, always speaks of Heaven and its oneness; perception, on the other hand, is the only means of "knowing" in this world. The two are often contrasted in the Text. Perception is inherently unreliable: "Eyes deceive, and ears hear falsely" (2:6). We all know this to be true. One has only to engage in one marital argument about what was seen and said the evening before to demonstrate it to ourselves. (Of course it is always the other person who seems to be perceiving falsely!)

Has it ever occurred to me, in all the times my senses have deceived me, that they were made deliberately to do so? "They were made to look upon a world that is not there; to hear the voices that can make no sound" (T-28.V.5:4; the rest of the paragraph is relevant also).

> The body's eyes see only form. They cannot see beyond what they were made to see. And they were made to look on error and not see past it. (T-22.III.5:3–6)

With our dependence on our eyes and ears, we have made ourselves very vulnerable to error: "Now mistakes become quite possible, for certainty has gone" (2:7).

Unreliable and deceptive perception enables the ego to make this world seem real. Perception shows us the sight of a world full of danger, demanding defensiveness and constant vigilance against attack. "The world *is* false perception" (1:1, my emphasis). Only the vision of Christ, which sees the light of God, can reveal anything different.

> The purpose of the world you see is to obscure your function of forgiveness, and provide you with a justification for forgetting it. It is the temptation to abandon God and His Son by taking on a physical appearance. It is this the body's eyes look upon.
>
> Nothing the body's eyes seem to see can be anything but a form of temptation, since this was the purpose of the body itself. Yet we have learned that the Holy Spirit has another use for all the illusions you have made, and therefore He sees another purpose in them. To the Holy Spirit, the world is a place where you learn to forgive yourself what you think of as your sins. In this perception, the physical appearance of temptation becomes the spiritual recognition of salvation. (W-pI.64.1:2–2:4)

LESSON 245 ✦ SEPTEMBER 2
"Your peace is with me, Father. I am safe."

Practice instructions

See complete instructions on page 135. A short summary:

- **Read** the commentary paragraph slowly and personally.
- **Pray** the prayer, perhaps several times.
- **Morning and evening:** Repeat the idea and then spend time in Open Mind Meditation.
- **Hourly remembrance:** Repeat the idea and then spend a quiet moment in meditation.
- **Frequent reminders:** Repeat the idea often within each hour.
- **Response to temptation:** Repeat the idea whenever upset, to restore peace.
- **Read the "What Is" section** slowly and thoughtfully once during the day.

Commentary

God's peace is *always* with me, and I am always safe. It isn't a sometime thing. God's peace is with me *now* and always. Unrest is always something I am superimposing on the underlying peace, which never leaves me. Unrest is a false perception; peace is reality. If I am willing to stop, to say, "Peace! Be still!" to the storm in my mind, God's peace is always there, waiting to be discovered.

I am surrounded by God's peace (1:1). It goes with me wherever I go (1:2). I bring it with me, and I can "shed its light on everyone I meet" (1:3). I can be, as St. Francis prayed, an instrument of His peace, bringing it "to the desolate and lonely and afraid" (1:4). Oh, I want that to be what I am today! I want to be willing to pray, "Send them to me, my Father" (1:6). Let me hear the lesson of the Holy Spirit, "To have peace, teach peace to learn it" (T-6.V(B)). As I bring peace to those "bereft of hope and happiness" (1:5) I will find it in myself (2:2–3). I will recognize my Self. I will hear the Voice for God. I will recognize

233

Your Love.

Today, if I do not feel Your peace within me, let me bring it to someone else who needs it. In so doing, I will recognize its presence in myself.

WHAT IS THE WORLD?

Part 5: W-pII.3.3:1–2

"The mechanisms of illusion have been born instead" (3:1), instead of certainty (2:7). The mechanisms of illusion include not only our eyes and ears, our physical perceptive organs, but also the mechanisms of the mind that interpret and adjust what is perceived to fit the patterns being looked for. We see what we expect to see, what we want to see. I was discussing, just last night, the very strange "blind spot" in our eyes. All of us have it. There is a place on the retina (where the optic nerve attaches to it) that does not pick up the light shining through the lens. The very strange thing is this: the mind "fills in" the blind spot with what "ought" to be there. None of us see a blank spot at the side of our vision, but it is there; the mind simply makes up what it thinks should be there! This is a "mechanism of illusion" indeed! And our mind "makes up" what "ought" to be there far more often then we realize.

The whole process of perception is a process of illusion. Our mind sends out its information gatherers "to find what has been given them to seek" (3:2). The mind tells them, "Find evidence of guilt," and Lo! They find it. "Find evidence of attack." They bring it back. "Find evidence of separation." They produce it. The ego sees only what it wants to see. And the ego's purpose in perception is to witness and make real the absence of love, to demonstrate that God is not here, and that we *are* here, apart from Him.

LESSON 246 ✦ SEPTEMBER 3
"To love my Father is to love His Son."

Practice instructions

See complete instructions on page 135. A short summary:
- **Read** the commentary paragraph slowly and personally.
- **Pray** the prayer, perhaps several times.
- **Morning and evening:** Repeat the idea and then spend time in Open Mind Meditation.
- **Hourly remembrance:** Repeat the idea and then spend a quiet moment in meditation.
- **Frequent reminders:** Repeat the idea often within each hour.
- **Response to temptation:** Repeat the idea whenever upset, to restore peace.
- **Read the "What Is" section** slowly and thoughtfully once during the day.

Practice suggestion: I suggest applying this idea specifically to people in your life throughout the day. Say, *"To love my Father is to love His Son, [name]."* You might want to add, *"Let me not think that I can attack the Son and still know the Father."*

Commentary

We can't love God without loving what He created. The Apostle John, in his epistles, said very much the same thing as today's lesson:

> If a man say, I love God, and hateth his brother, he is a liar: for he that loveth not his brother whom he hath seen, how can he love God whom he hath not seen? And this commandment have we from him, That he who loveth God love his brother also. (1 John 4:20–21)

The "Son of God" in the Course refers not simply to Jesus, nor just to all our brothers and sisters; it also includes ourselves. The measure of the quality of relationship we have with God is the relationships we have with those around us, and with ourselves. Our love for our brothers and sisters reflects the love we have for God. "Let me not think that I can find the way to God, if I have hatred in my heart" (1:1). If in some way I am wishing harm to my brother, I cannot know God, nor can I even know my Self (1:2). And if I am, in my mind, diminishing *myself*, I who am God's own Son, I will be unable to truly know God's Love for me, or mine for Him (1:3).

The ego is a thought of attack; it believes it has attacked God and succeeded. And yet it sees that battle reflected in everyone around us, and projects its fear and its attack onto everything, often in subtle disguises, some even bearing the name of "love."

Let me be open to discovering the "little" bits of hatred that still lie in my heart—especially those directed at myself. There are far more than I would like to believe. The Text teaches me that uncovering the hatred within myself is "crucial" (T-13.III.1:1). It tells me, "You must realize that your hatred is in your mind and not outside it before you can get rid of it" (T-12.III.7:10). The scraps of hatred I clutch to me must be seen for what they are, and chosen against. With a deliberate act of will I need to say, "I choose to love Your Son" (2:4). The choice for love is the choice for God and the choice for my Self.

WHAT IS THE WORLD?

Part 6: W-pII.3.3:3–5

The "mechanisms of illusion" are what make this world seem so real. They include even our eyes and ears, and all our physical senses:

> The body's eyes see only form. They cannot see beyond
> what they were made to see. And they were made to look
> on error and not see past it.   (T-22.III.5:3–5)

When we view things with the ego's perception, illusions seem solid; the separation of the ego seems to be nothing but the truth (3:4). To see with the vision of Christ, to see the oneness instead of the separation, we need to be willing to discount what our eyes are showing us, because "they were made to look on error." "Everything that they report is but illusion which is kept apart from truth" (3:5). The miracle enables us to see what eyes see not; it lifts our perception into the realm of the spiritual, away from the physical (see T-1.I.22 and T-1.I.32).

We need to be willing to question what our senses seem to make real, and to be willing to perceive, with a different kind of vision, something else entirely. We have been victims of a very clever and very successful propaganda campaign, conducted by the master of disinformation—the ego. We need to realize that nothing we have believed to be true and counted upon as solid reality can be trusted; everything must be called to question. We have been surrounded by a conspiracy of lies, emanating from within our own mind. We have misdirected our senses until we became unconscious of what we were doing, but we can, today, redirect them. We can choose to look for evidence of love, instead of hate; for peace instead of attack. We can say:

Above all else I want to see things differently.

(W-pI.28.Heading)

LESSON 247 ✦ SEPTEMBER 4
"Without forgiveness I will still be blind."

Practice instructions

See complete instructions on page 135. A short summary:

- **Read** the commentary paragraph slowly and personally.
- **Pray** the prayer, perhaps several times.
- **Morning and evening:** Repeat the idea and then spend time in Open Mind Meditation.
- **Hourly remembrance:** Repeat the idea and then spend a quiet moment in meditation.
- **Frequent reminders:** Repeat the idea often within each hour.
- **Response to temptation:** Repeat the idea whenever upset, to restore peace.
- **Read the "What Is" section** slowly and thoughtfully once during the day.

Practice suggestion: Choose someone in your life whom you have been judging or failing to appreciate, and say to this person:

Without forgiving you, [name], I will still be blind.
Brother, come and let me look on you with my now open eyes.
Your loveliness reflects my own.
Your sinlessness is mine.
You stand forgiven, and I stand with you.

Commentary

All unforgiveness is, in reality, of myself. Today I am seeing a more subtle form of unforgiveness. Perhaps I am willing to admit that my unloving or unjoyful feeling in the present is due to my own wanting and choosing *in the past.* If I am truly looking at my ego without judgment, though, I will be able to admit that I am feeling loveless or joyless now because I am choosing those feelings *now,* in the present. If I cannot do that, I am still listening to the voice of guilt.

For a brief instant, sin and Atonement must lie on the altar together.

The guilt must be brought to the present to be healed.

If I avoid seeing my identification with ego in the present, if I avoid seeing my guilt in the present, then I am blinding myself. Avoiding seeing the ego in the present means, very simply—due to the perfect power of my mind—that I *never see it* in the present. I stumble through life blind to my ego in the present moment. I am always caught off guard. Again and again the ego trips me up, and I stumble and fall, saying stupidly, "Oh! That must have been my ego!"

In order to say "yes" to God, I must recognize that I am, right now, saying "no." "'Yes' must mean 'not no'" (T-21.VII.12:4). It isn't so much that I need to say "yes" as I need to notice I'm saying "no." When I notice that fact, I will stop. And when my "no" stops, the peace that was always there becomes conscious. To say "no" to the "no," to deny the denial, is the way we say "yes." But I can't say "no" to the "no" until I admit I'm saying "no" in the first place!

One piece of unerring evidence that I have not owned my guilt is that I will still be projecting it. I will still be making excuses for myself, talking about my weakness, feeling that I'll "never make it." Or I'll be caught up in wanting others to admit their own responsibility for the situation in the relationship. If someone tries to get me to see my responsibility for things, I'll feel attacked, even if it is done in true love. I will be saying things like "I didn't realize what I was doing," or "I wasn't aware of attacking you at the time." I will still feel that, while I may have acted from my ego, so did you—and you'd damn well better admit it.

"I was not aware" or "I didn't realize what I was doing" is not an excuse! If I was not aware, there is only one reason—I was choosing to be not aware. I have formed a habit of refusing to see my guilt in the present, and so, in each present moment, I live in unawareness of my ego thoughts.

The terror of looking at the ego now is so great that the instant I begin to become aware I want to project my ego into the past, to push it away and deny that I am now identified with it. But healing occurs only in the present. The horror of the ego, the desire to separate myself and to murder my brother must be seen *now* in order to be healed. When I can allow that, the healing is instant. Brought into the present, guilt encounters the Holy Spirit and Atonement, for that is the only place Atonement lives, and that is all that lives in the present. The guilt is here and then gone, flashing out of existence. Guilt cannot exist in the presence of Atonement, any more than darkness can exist in the light.

If I am seeing anything but total innocence in my brothers, I am hiding guilt in myself. There is no guilt but my own. And when I see that, there is no guilt at all.

WHAT IS THE WORLD?

Part 7: W-pII.3.4:1–2

Though our sight was made to lead away from truth, "it can be redirected" (4:1). The ego's purpose for perception can be replaced with a new purpose, that of the Holy Spirit. "Yet we have learned that the Holy Spirit has another use for all the illusions you have made, and therefore He sees another purpose in them" (W-pI.64.2:2). "The Holy Spirit teaches you to use what the ego has made, to teach the opposite of what the ego has 'learned'" (T-7.IV.3:3). So the Holy Spirit teaches us to use our eyes and ears not to see separation and the absence of God, but to see oneness and His Presence in everything.

> Sounds become the call for God, and all perception can be
> given a new purpose by the One Whom God appointed
> Savior to the world.   (4:2)

The preceding discussion might make us think that, since our eyes were made to see error, they are now useless. But the Holy Spirit will use everything the ego has made. He uses our bodies as communication devices. He uses our special relationships to teach us forgiveness and love and union. He uses our learning ability (made to learn error) to teach us the truth. He uses the whole world as a classroom of forgiveness and a mirror of Heaven. There is nothing the ego has done that cannot be used by the Holy Spirit. So in the end, there is no loss whatsoever, because all the ego's energies have been "recycled" by the Holy Spirit for His own purposes.

LESSON 248 ✦ SEPTEMBER 5
"Whatever suffers is not part of me."

Practice instructions

See complete instructions on page 135. A short summary:

- **Read** the commentary paragraph slowly and personally.
- **Pray** the prayer, perhaps several times.
- **Morning and evening:** Repeat the idea and then spend time in Open Mind Meditation.
- **Hourly remembrance:** Repeat the idea and then spend a quiet moment in meditation.
- **Frequent reminders:** Repeat the idea often within each hour.
- **Response to temptation:** Repeat the idea whenever upset, to restore peace.
- **Read the "What Is" section** slowly and thoughtfully once during the day.

Practice suggestion: As a response to temptation, notice something that is upsetting you, and repeat the idea, specifying the emotion you are feeling: *"Whatever worries [or grieves, or is afraid, or is angry, etc.] is not part of me."*

Commentary

The title of this lesson is interesting to me because I have just finished writing an article about our mistaken identity, and the need the Course speaks of for us to *separate* from our egos. (No, the Course does not always put a negative spin on the world "separation"; see, for instance, T-22.II.6:1.) The lesson affirms that whatever suffers is not really a part of me at all. This *must* be true if I am the Son of God, and the Son of God "cannot suffer" (W-pII.244.1:3). What I really am cannot suffer; therefore, "whatever suffers is not part of me."

Now, be honest. If we think for only a moment about the suffering, of various kinds, that we have experienced in our lives, one thing is pretty certain: We were quite sure *we* were suffering. Not some thing that isn't even part of ourselves, but *us*. To take a mild example, when I get the flu, *I* feel miserable. It isn't somebody else being miserable; it isn't anything I can even conceive of separating from (although I certainly have wished that I could!). That is how it seems. Is this proof that the Course is wrong? Or is it evidence of how completely we are still identified with our egos and our bodies?

The lesson is asking us to begin to learn to disengage ourselves from our egos and our bodies. "I have disowned the truth. Now let me be as faithful in disowning falsity" (1:1–2).

Then follows a series of statements in which we deliberately distinguish our Self from that which experiences various things the Course sees as illusion: suffering, grief, pain, and death. The statement about death is particularly strong: "What dies was never living in reality, and did but mock the truth about myself" (1:6).

It is especially difficult to practice this kind of lesson when we are "in the frying pan." Yet if we are willing, it can be curiously comforting. For instance, if I am going through grief, and I am able to say, "What grieves is not myself" (1:4) it can be helpful. Notice: this is not denial in the negative sense. I am not saying, "I do not really feel grief." I am saying, "What grieves" (and there is the acknowledgement of the grief) "is not myself." I am not denying the grief; I am denying that grief is me. I am recognizing that the thing that is feeling grief is not really who I am; it is a false image of myself, an illusion of myself I have identified with, but it is not truly myself. When grief feels as if it would swallow me whole, and engulf me so that I disappear into it, the realization that "what grieves is not myself" can be reassuring. And certainly in facing physical death, to know that what dies is not myself can be comforting.

This disowning of falsity, disowning "self-concepts and deceits and lies about the holy Son of God" (1:7), prepares us to welcome back our true Self. As I realize that none of these dark things affects Who I really am, "my ancient love for [God] returns" (2:1). That love is blocked and suppressed when I believe that what suffers *is* me; I blame God for my suffering, consciously or unconsciously, and cannot find it in myself to truly love Him. Down below the level of consciousness, every little bit of suffering, grief, and pain we experience in this world is laid at God's feet, and we point an accusing finger in His direction. We think He wanted this for us. When we begin to disengage ourselves from our bodies and egos, when we begin to realize that our Self is not suffering,

242

we can remember God's Love, and love Him in return. "I am as You created me" (2:2); nothing has been damaged. Nothing has been lost. God has never been angry. And we can reunite our love with God's, and understand that they are one (2:4).

WHAT IS THE WORLD?

Part 8: W-pII.3.4:3–5

So, then, rather than following the evidence of our senses, the "proof" the ego wants us to see that we are alone and separate, we can turn to "Follow His Light, and see the world as He beholds it" (4:3). I find that this is most often, especially at the beginning, a case of first seeing as the ego sees, realizing it is an illusion, and then asking the Holy Spirit to help me see differently. Some event occurs—for instance someone close to me criticizes something I am doing—and at first I see it through the ego's eyes. I see attack. I feel hurt. I feel angry. But God's Voice speaks to me, and reminds me that "I am never upset for the reason I think" (W-pI.5.Heading). And so I turn to Him and say, "Okay, Holy Spirit." And I add:

> *I do not know what anything, including this, means. And so
> I do not know how to respond to it. And I will not use my
> own past learning as the light to guide me now.*
> (T-14.XI.6:7–9)

I ask Him to show me how He sees it. And He always sees everything as either an expression of love or a call for love, both of which can be answered only with love. If I truly open my mind to Him, and *let go* of how I am seeing the situation, His vision will replace my seeing.

"Hear His voice alone in all that speaks to you" (4:4). The Holy Spirit is speaking to us all the time; He is speaking to us through our brothers and sisters, and through the events of our lives. The call for help in our brothers is the Voice of the Holy Spirit calling to us to be ourselves, to be the love that we are. Behind every illusion is the Voice for God, constantly calling us to reclaim our Identity and to respond as the saviors of the world that we are.

He will give us peace and certainty (4:5). We threw them away, but He kept them safe for us and will return them to us whenever we are willing to have them again. Our peace and certainty will not come from the world; they never have come from the world and never will. They will come from His vision of the world, however. "When you want only love, you will see nothing else" (T-12.VII.8:1). If we disregard all the ego's evidence, and let the Holy Spirit interpret all we see, we will see an entirely different world than the one we have been seeing. And this world, the real world, will fill us with peace and certainty.

LESSON 249 ✦ SEPTEMBER 6
"Forgiveness ends all suffering and loss."

Practice instructions

See complete instructions on page 135. A short summary:

- **Read** the commentary paragraph slowly and personally.
- **Pray** the prayer, perhaps several times.
- **Morning and evening:** Repeat the idea and then spend time in Open Mind Meditation.
- **Hourly remembrance:** Repeat the idea and then spend a quiet moment in meditation.
- **Frequent reminders:** Repeat the idea often within each hour.
- **Response to temptation:** Repeat the idea whenever upset, to restore peace.
- **Read the "What Is" section** slowly and thoughtfully once during the day.

Practice suggestion: Again I would recommend applying the idea specifically. Pick a person in your life and say, *"My forgiveness of [name] ends all suffering and loss."*

Commentary

Unforgiveness is painful. There is a tightening, a hardening, an armoring of the heart. It hurts to shut someone out of my heart. Forgiveness ends that suffering, that pain, that loss, that aloneness.

To believe that forgiveness ends *all* suffering and loss is not that easy. It still seems that some of my pain is not related to unforgiveness; yet it is, all of it:

> Certain it is that all distress does not appear to be but unforgiveness. Yet that is the content underneath the form.
> (W-pI.193.4:1–2)

If I do not suffer and have no loss, if I forgive in the sense the Course speaks of so that I see that there was no sin, that I was not hurt, and that

245

I lost nothing, then "anger makes no sense" (1:1). If there is no anger, there is no attack. If forgiveness were accepted by the minds of all of us—forgiveness received as well as given—there would be no more suffering, no more loss.

> The world becomes a place of joy, abundance, charity and
> endless giving.   (1:5)

This is how I will see the world when I look with the eyes of Christ. Jesus, even when he was being crucified, saw the world in this way, and his heart held nothing but "charity and endless giving" for those who condemned him and drove in the nails.

To see the "real world" does not mean that suddenly everyone around us becomes transformed into angelic beings. Jesus saw the real world and he was crucified. But he did not suffer, nor did he lose! He was no longer identified with his body; he knew that the body could not die because it was never alive, so he was not losing his life. Likewise for us, attaining the real world through forgiveness does not mean that all our life becomes a flower-strewn pathway to glory. There may be resistance. There may be those who attempt to harm us. Our bodies may still become sick. Loved ones will still die, cars will still be stolen, houses will still burn down, jobs will still be lost. The healed mind will not see loss, nor experience suffering, knowing that "nothing real can be threatened" (T-In.2:2).

I do believe that as more and more minds embrace forgiveness, the physical reflection of those minds will transform as well, becoming more peaceful, more loving, more abundant, more full of kindness and charity. The transformation of the physical reflection, however, is a side-benefit, not the goal. It is our *minds* that we return to God.

When our minds have reached this height of true perception, Heaven is very near. The world will quickly be "transformed into the light that it reflects" (1:6).

Let me, then, return my mind to God today. Let me release myself from the vise of bitterness, and ease my mind of its fear of violence and death. Let me rest myself in God today. Let me forgive all things that seem to wish me harm, and in so doing, free myself from suffering. May I be free of suffering today. May I be at peace.

WHAT IS THE WORLD?

Part 9: W-pII.3.5:1–2

Although the Course says, "The world is false perception" (1:1), the Course does not disdain the world. On the contrary, Jesus calls to us: "Let us not rest content until the world has joined our changed perception" (5:1). We do not just turn our backs on the world, shake its dust off our feet, and walk away. Indeed, we cannot do that even if we want to, because the world is a part of ourselves, our guilt, the pieces of ourselves we have rejected, projected out and given form. If I am to be saved, the world must be saved, because the world is myself.

Salvation, to be salvation, must be complete. Nothing can be left out. "Let us not be satisfied until forgiveness has been made complete" (5:2). We are asked not to rest content, not to be satisfied with our individual salvation. "Individual salvation" is an oxymoron; an impossibility. Separation is hell; salvation is oneness. How can I, apart from you, be saved, if salvation is the end of separateness?

There is a tendency among Course students, especially with the emphasis on its supposedly being a "self-study course," to become introverted and occupied with one's own spiritual development, and pretty much unconcerned with bringing the rest of the world to join our changed perception. The idea that we are called to save the world, which is a *major emphasis* throughout the Course, seems somehow to get lost in the shuffle. "Oh, isn't that making the illusion real? Isn't saying that our calling is to bring light to the darkness some kind of betrayal of the Course's nondualistic teaching? Don't we bring our darkness to the light?" Jesus doesn't seem to think the one excludes the other. Read these two sentences again. Or hear these words from the Text:

> You who are now the bringer of salvation have the function of bringing light to darkness. The darkness in you has been brought to light. Carry it back to darkness, from the holy instant to which you brought it.   (T-18.III.7:1–3)

Over and over, the Course points out that we cannot become certain, we cannot fully recognize the truth in ourselves, until we share it with others. "To give is how to recognize you have received" (W-pI.159.1:7). To turn our backs on the world is to leave the unforgiveness in our minds unhealed. Our task is not to preach to the world, nor to argue it into agreement with us, nor to "convert" everyone. Our task is to forgive the world, to open our hearts to the world in love. It is to erase guilt from every mind through our forgiveness. It is, in thought, in word, and in deed, to communicate the message which the Course says is central to its aim: "The Son of God is guiltless" (T-13.I.5:1; M-1.3:5; M-27.7:8).

> There is no conflict in this curriculum, which has one aim however it is taught. Each effort made on its behalf is offered for the single purpose of release from guilt, to the eternal glory of God and His creation. And every teaching that points to this points straight to Heaven, and the peace of God.   (T-14.V.6:3–5)

And we are called not to be satisfied, not to rest content, until forgiveness is complete, and guilt has been lifted from every troubled mind.

LESSON 250 ✦ SEPTEMBER 7
"Let me not see myself as limited."

Practice instructions

See complete instructions on page 135. A short summary:

- **Read** the commentary paragraph slowly and personally.
- **Pray** the prayer, perhaps several times.
- **Morning and evening:** Repeat the idea and then spend time in Open Mind Meditation.
- **Hourly remembrance:** Repeat the idea and then spend a quiet moment in meditation.
- **Frequent reminders:** Repeat the idea often within each hour.
- **Response to temptation:** Repeat the idea whenever upset, to restore peace.
- **Read the "What Is" section** slowly and thoughtfully once during the day.

Practice suggestion: You may want to try this active exercise before you enter meditation. Choose someone in your life, and apply the following lines to that person:

Let me behold the Son of God in [name].
Let me witness his glory.
Let me see his holy light and not my darkness.
Let me see his strength and not his frailty.
Let me see his sovereignty and not attack it with lacks that I perceive.
Let me behold his gentleness and not the illusion of harmfulness I laid on him.
For by seeing him as limitless, I will see myself as limitless.

Commentary

There is really nothing to see but myself. If I see those around me as limited, I am seeing myself that way, for "as I see him so I see myself" (2:3). The lesson is not talking so much about the kind of limitlessness

249

that is touted in self-help seminars ("I can do anything I set my mind to—I can achieve all my goals") as it is talking about the limitations we place on holiness, goodness, and love when we view others and ourselves. Do I see my brothers and sisters today as the Son of God in glory? Or do I see them with "strength diminished and reduced to frailty" (1:2)? Do I see the holy light (1:2) shining in all those around me, or is it obscured by the darkness I have projected onto them? Do I behold the sovereignty of God's Son, or do I continue to attack that majesty by perceiving lacks where there are none?

If I am honest with myself, I will be aware of how consistently I perceive lack in everyone, or almost everyone, I meet. Nobody quite lives up to my high standards. My mind is constantly comparing myself to others as well, and perceiving lacks in me. The perception of lack is one: as I see myself I see others; as I see others I see myself. Does the problem perhaps lie in the perceiver, and not in what is being perceived?

Yet I can choose a different perception; I can choose to see with the vision of Christ. I can choose to see light, to see love, to see gentleness. Let this be my choice today, Father. When I become aware that I am perceiving your Son as less than You created him to be (in others or myself), let me recognize those thoughts as illusions born of fear, and bring them to Your Love. I choose today to watch my mind for these scraps of fear, and to ask Your Spirit to step around them to reveal what they have been hiding from my sight (see T-4.III.7:4–5).

> *Today I would see truly, that this day I may at last identify with him.* (2:4)

WHAT IS THE WORLD?

Part 10: W-pII.3.5:3–5

We are not to rest or to be satisfied until forgiveness has been made complete, and all the world has joined our changed perception. And in addition:

> Let us not attempt to change our function. We must save the world. (5:3–4)

Have you noticed how often the Course talks about our function or our purpose? The word "purpose" occurs 666 times in the Course; the word "function," 460 times. Some of those occurrences, of course, refer to other things, such as the function of the Holy Spirit, but a vast majority of them are referring to *our* function:

> *I am the light of the world. That is my only function. That*
> *is why I am here.* (W-pI.61.5:3–5)

There is no other reason for being in this world, except to be its light. There is no other reason to live on earth except to save the world, and to bring forgiveness to every mind. In fulfilling my function I find my happiness: "My happiness and my function are one" (W-pI.66.Heading). In fulfilling my function I discover the light within myself: "It is through accepting my function that I will see the light in me" (W-pI.81.3:2). Fulfilling our function is an integral and key part of the Course's program for our own enlightenment.

Why would we "attempt to change" our function? What are the ways we do that? We attempt to change our function when we try to find some other purpose for living in the world, whether it be career, family, pleasure, power, or anything that is "of" the world. And we do so in an insane attempt to make this world a substitute for God, to make the illusion real and thus substantiate our ego identity. "We must save the world." This is our only function; this is the only purpose for the world itself and for me in it. "The healing of God's Son is all the world is for" (T-24.VI.4:1).

This does not mean that everyone must enter a recognized "healing profession," although some of us may indeed do so. (The Manual says that immediate changes in life situations are asked of only a small minority; see Section 9.) Rather, it means we must learn to translate every profession into a healing profession ("The Atonement…is the natural profession of the children of God," T-1.III.1:10). As Marianne Williamson says, every job can become a front for a church. Our first priority is the healing of our minds and attitudes, especially in our relationships, right where we are.

Our function is to behold the world through the eyes of Christ (5:5). We made the world. We made it to die. It is our responsibility now to restore it to everlasting life (5:5).

VII

Lessons 251 - 260
What Is Sin?

"I am in need of nothing but the truth."

Practice instructions

See complete instructions on page 135. A short summary:
- **Read** the commentary paragraph slowly and personally.
- **Pray** the prayer, perhaps several times.
- **Morning and evening:** Repeat the idea and then spend time in Open Mind Meditation.
- **Hourly remembrance:** Repeat the idea and then spend a quiet moment in meditation.
- **Frequent reminders:** Repeat the idea often within each hour.
- **Response to temptation:** Repeat the idea whenever upset, to restore peace.
- **Read the "What Is" section** slowly and thoughtfully once during the day.

Practice suggestions: The first paragraph of this lesson is one of

253

my favorites in the entire Course. I have memorized it and enjoy repeating it to myself from time to time. You may want to do the same (if memorizing it would be too much, you can write it out on a card and carry it with you).

For response to temptation, I suggest identifying the unmet need that is behind your upset and saying, *"I think I need [specify the need], but I am in need of nothing but the truth."*

Commentary

Any one of us could, if asked, sit down right now and write a fairly long list of things we think we need. Even if we restrict ourselves to things we don't presently have, the list would be fairly extensive. For instance, I need more memory on my computer (what computer owner doesn't?); I need new pajamas; I need some dental work; I need a new bookcase; I need a new mattress and box spring; I need a new pair of jeans; I need a better guitar.

At various times in my life, I've believed that I needed to be married, or needed to be divorced. I needed a better job. I needed a brand new car, one that would not break down all the time. I needed to move. "I sought for many things, and found despair" (1:1). I got most of what I was looking for (never got quite all the money I wanted), but none of it made me happy. And I know, with all the lists I can make of things I now "need," none of them will make me happy, either.

Happiness is a choice I make. Nothing more, nothing less.

I think the reason why the Course appeals to me so much is that I can relate to things like this lesson so well. Oh, I still make the mistake of thinking something I "need" will bring happiness, but when I find myself thinking that way, at least now I know I'm just kidding myself. I can honestly say, when I pause to reflect, "Now do I seek but one, for in that one is all I need, and only what I need" (1:2). I wander from that single direction sometimes, I get suckered into going after something else, but I keep on coming back to this one, central need, which is really the *only* need I have: the truth. The truth about myself, about God, about the universe. That which is real and everlasting.

Some of the things I sought before "I needed not, and did not even want" (1:3). I usually found that out after I had them. I recall one night, several years ago, when I was sitting home, alone, watching TV. I got the munchies, so I got up to get something. I looked at the ice cream in the fridge and thought, "No, that's not what I want." I looked at fruit, at crackers and cheese, at popcorn, and with each one found myself saying, "No, that's not what I want." Finally, literally scratching my head, I stood in the middle of the kitchen and said aloud, "What is it I really want?" And it hit me like a ton of bricks. What I really wanted was God. I was feeling some kind of emptiness inside, and my little mind was translating that into physical craving of some sort, trying to find a way to fill the emptiness by means of my body. I actually laughed out loud! I suddenly realized that all my "needs" and "wants" were substitutes for that one thing I really needed, which was something I always had, only waiting for me to choose to recognize it.

How can we ever be at peace when all our lives are filled with an endless list of cravings? Can we not begin to see that the craving itself is a form of unhappiness? That each thing I think I need that I do not have is a burden, a nagging pain in the back of my mind, keeping me from peace? What I really want is the peace. What I really want is to be at peace within myself, content with Who I am. I want fulfillment. I want completion. And these things are *instantly* available, whenever I choose them. They are granted or withheld not by anything external, but only by my own choice.

> And now at last I find myself at peace.
> *And for that peace, our Father, we give thanks. What we denied ourselves You have restored, and only that is what we really want.* (1:9–2:2)

WHAT IS SIN?

Part 1: W-pII.4.1:1–3

"Sin" is the belief that I am evil, corrupted somehow by the mistakes I have made, and forever disfigured by my misguided thoughts. "Sin" is the belief that the perfect creation of a perfect God can somehow become imperfect, warped and twisted and unworthy of its Creator. "Sin is insanity" (1:1).

Out of this belief comes guilt, which drives us mad, and leads us to seek for illusions to take the place of truth (1:2). This is the source of the world we see: "The world you see is the delusional system of those made mad by guilt" (T-13.In.2:2). This is the cause behind the illusion. Because of guilt we are afraid of the truth, afraid of God, afraid of our Self. We believe we have forfeited Heaven, and so we must make up another place where we can, or at least can hope we can, find satisfaction. Such is this world. Because of sin we believe we cannot have Heaven, so we make a substitute.

Because of the madness induced by sin and guilt, we see "illusions where the truth should be, and where it really is" (1:3). We hallucinate. We see attack in love. We see love in attack. We seek satisfaction in mirages. We seek eternal happiness in things that wither and die.

Our healing begins when we begin to recognize illusions as illusions. This can be a time of great despair, when everything we thought we could trust in turns to dust. Yet it is the beginning of wisdom, the start of a great awakening.

> The thoughts you hold are mighty, and illusions are as strong in their effects as is the truth. A madman thinks the world he sees is real, and does not doubt it. Nor can he be swayed by questioning his thoughts' effects. It is but when their source is raised to question that the hope of freedom comes to him at last.   (W-pI.132.1:4–7)

We are surrounded by illusions, the effects of our thoughts. We do not truly doubt the reality of those effects. Only when their source "is raised to question," only when we begin to question the thought of sin that induces our madness, will "the hope of freedom" begin to arise.

LESSON 252 ✦ SEPTEMBER 9
"The Son of God is my Identity."

Practice instructions

See complete instructions on page 135. A short summary:

- **Read** the commentary paragraph slowly and personally.
- **Pray** the prayer, perhaps several times.
- **Morning and evening:** Repeat the idea and then spend time in Open Mind Meditation.
- **Hourly remembrance:** Repeat the idea and then spend a quiet moment in meditation.
- **Frequent reminders:** Repeat the idea often within each hour.
- **Response to temptation:** Repeat the idea whenever upset, to restore peace.
- **Read the "What Is" section** slowly and thoughtfully once during the day.

Commentary

We don't know Who we are.

"My Self" is so much greater and higher than I can even imagine. The first paragraph extols the holiness, the purity, the love, and the strength of my Self. I am reminded of something I heard in an "est" weekend many years ago. It spoke of becoming aware of the self I present to the world, my "mask" (the Course calls it "the face of innocence" [T-31.V.2:6]); then, discovering the self I am *afraid* that I am (the ego); and finally, discovering who I really am, "which is magnificent" (the Son of God).[1] Think about that, my soul; let yourself hear it with acceptance: "I am magnificent."

I am aware today that, no matter how high my thoughts go, I have only scratched the surface of What and Who I really am. "My Self is holy beyond all the thoughts of holiness of which I now conceive" (1:1). Let me sit and dream thoughts of holiness, let me stretch my mind to its limits to understand what holiness is; the reality of my holiness is

257

"beyond all the thoughts" I can conceive of. The Course says that if we could realize how holy our brothers and sisters are, we could "scarce refrain from kneeling at [their] feet" (W-pI.161.9:3). Yet we will take their hand instead, because we are their equals. "They are all the same; all beautiful and equal in their holiness" (T-13.VIII.6:1).

To realize that I am the holy Son of God entails the parallel realization that you are the same. You are so beautiful, my friends; so ineffably holy! You are the expression of God, the outshining of His Being, the glory of His creation. How can I do anything but love you?

My Self, and yours, has a "shimmering and perfect purity" that is "far more brilliant than any light that I have ever looked upon" (1:2). Have you ever seen that in another being? Have you ever seen it *in yourself*? Ah, that is what we all are seeking! It is what we are praying for: "Reveal It now to me who am Your Son" (2:2). Imagine seeing and knowing such perfect purity in your Self. Imagine it, and ask to have it revealed, for such you are.

And the *love* of this Self! It "is limitless, with an intensity that holds all things within it, in the calm of quiet certainty" (1:3). Oh, to know that this love is my Self! Oh, to know that this is what I am, forever and forever! Can I, dare I, believe this about myself? My love, holding the whole world, floating like a bubble in the ocean of my love. My love, without limits of any kind. My love, the very Love of God Itself. Let me dwell on it, let me consider it, let me give expression to it now, sending my love to the whole world, to every being who longs for it. How intense it is, this love! How perfect, how unquestioning, how overpowering!

The *strength* of my Self "comes not from burning impulses which move the world, but from the boundless Love of God Himself" (1:4). What I am is this Love, God's own Love. It is not a "burning" thing, a violence, an anger; it is a quiet, calm, certain Love. It knows the reality of what It beholds. It has perfect faith in every child of God, because of what they are. It uplifts, it encourages, it believes in all that it beholds. Vast is Its mercy; infinite Its understanding. Softly It embraces, gently It comforts, Its power coming from the calm sureness of the inevitability of Love Itself.

> How far beyond this world my Self must be, and yet how
> near to me and close to God! (1:5)

Father, You know that this is Who I am, for You created me to be It. I long to know this reality of my Self. I feel so much less than this, so unloving at times. Reveal my Self to me. Show me that this is Who I am. Help me to know my Self as Love. To know my Self as Love is Heaven; to know my Self as Love is peace.

WHAT IS SIN?

Part 2: W-pII.4.1:4–9

Our very eyes are the product of sin: "Sin gave the body eyes" (1:4). Or as the next paragraph says, "The body is the instrument the mind made in its efforts to deceive itself" (2:1). Perception itself is the result of sin, "for what is there the sinless would behold?" (1:4). Our true Self is beyond perception entirely. Perception is inherently dualistic; "I" over here perceive some object over there. It implies a separation. The sinless, evidently, would have no desire for anything to perceive because nothing would be separate. The desire to separate, to be apart and "objective" to something else, is part and parcel of the concept of sin and guilt. The sinless being, in the Course's view, would experience all things as part of itself. It would "know" them rather than "perceive" them.

The sinless would have no need of sight or sound or touch because everything would be part of itself; known, but not perceived. Perception is so limited. So incomplete and imperfect. The sinless Self has no need of sense at all, for everything is known to it. "To sense is not to know" (1:8). The purpose of perception is *not to know*. Or better yet, the purpose of perception is *to not know*. Perception is a separating, a standing off, a being apart from. The consciousness of sin is what causes that withdrawal, that contracting inward, away from unity.

Truth, by contrast, "can be but filled with knowledge, and with nothing else" (1:9). Truth does not sense things; truth *knows* things. It knows them by being one with them. I do not know you through perception. Perception deceives me; that is its intent. Perception prevents me from knowing you. I can only know you as I experience that I *am* you. This is what happens in the holy instant, for the holy instant is an experience of minds as one. Such an experience can be truly

259

disorienting for a mind habituated to its aloneness; the seeming identity we have grown used to for all of our lives is suddenly gone, I am no longer certain whether I am me or you. I realize for a moment that the "me" I thought I was may not, in fact, truly exist. As it does not, in fact.

The consciousness of sin and guilt is what stands in the way of this joining of minds. I hold myself apart from you in fear. I constrict my love, I doubt yours. The Course is bringing us to the point where that fear dissolves, and union, always there, is once again known for what it is.

---

1. For a detailed and very inspiring discussion of the several layers of our false self-concept, see *Shrouded Vaults of the Mind*, by Robert Perry. For a less detailed but still illuminating discussion, see Robert's book *Path of Light: Stepping into Peace with 'A Course in Miracles.'* Both books are published by Circle Publishing.

LESSON 253 ✦ SEPTEMBER 10
"My Self is ruler of the universe."

Practice instructions

See complete instructions on page 135. A short summary:

- **Read** the commentary paragraph slowly and personally.
- **Pray** the prayer, perhaps several times.
- **Morning and evening:** Repeat the idea and then spend time in Open Mind Meditation.
- **Hourly remembrance:** Repeat the idea and then spend a quiet moment in meditation.
- **Frequent reminders:** Repeat the idea often within each hour.
- **Response to temptation:** Repeat the idea whenever upset, to restore peace.
- **Read the "What Is" section** slowly and thoughtfully once during the day.

Practice suggestion: Pick an event where you felt powerless. Then say the following lines to yourself:

What happened is what I desired, on some level.
Even in this world, it is I who rule my destiny.
For in Heaven, my Self is ruler of the universe.

Commentary

Today's lesson is perhaps the most "outrageous" in the ego's eyes. There is an odd paradox about the ego. Wanting to be ruler of the universe, it views the actual assertion of that function to be the height of blasphemy. Asserting that I am the ruler of the universe actually cuts the legs out from under the ego, and destroys everything it stands on. The whole idea of projection, or of finding blame for what is wrong outside myself, is done away with.

Nothing comes to me that I have not asked for. "It is impossible" (1:1). That seems a harsh truth. Lest we try to water it down, the lesson immediately adds, "Even in this world, it is I who rule my destiny"

(1:2). Our fear of this truth is that it seems to make us incredibly guilty. The Course is always asking that we take one hundred percent responsibility with zero percent guilt.

> What happens is what I desire. What does not occur is what
> I do not want to happen. (1:3–4)

There is just no way to squirm out of what the Course is saying here. The ego tells us that it makes us very guilty if we do this. In reality, it gives us complete power over our lives. Consider what the alternative is to these statements: "Things can happen no matter what I want. What does not happen is not under my control." This belief system, which we all live by, leaves us powerless, hopeless victims of things beyond our control. It is the belief system of guilt, the attempt to avoid the reality of our Self, which is all-powerful. It is the voice of the ego trying to place the blame elsewhere, anywhere but within our own minds.

"My Self is ruler of the universe." This way lies freedom. "This must I accept" (1:5). Please note that this does not speak of our "individual self," the illusion of ourselves we all have made. It speaks of the "Self" with a capital "S," the Self we share with all creation. It is our collective Mind we speak of, the Mind of all of us. It is the individual responsibility of each one of us to choose differently, to reverse the trend within the Mind of the Sonship. In this view there is no one but Me, the one Son of God. Each of us is responsible for the whole. Each of us *is* the whole, for the whole is in every part.

We *must* accept the truth of today's lesson; it is the only way out of hell. Anything less is the denial of our divinity, the assertion of the reality of separation. Only in accepting this truth can we be "led past this world to [our] creations" (1:6).

In the closing prayer, spoken to God, we say, "You are the Self Whom You created Son, creating like Yourself and one with You" (2:1). God Himself is our Self. We are His extension, more of Him, like Him, one with Him. My true Self is simply my will in perfect union with God's, assenting to God's own extension in me and through me (2:2). If God is my Self, and God is ruler of the universe, so am I.

What does this mean in a practical sense? It means that I have to begin to accept that I am responsible for everything I see, choosing my feelings, asking for what happens to me (see T-21.II.2:3–5). It means that I see, in every moment, it is up to me to choose to either suffer, or to be happy. It means that I begin to deny the power of all things outside of me to affect me. It means I accept my role as ruler of my own mind, first of all. I begin to acknowledge the power of my wanting, and to know that "what is strong enough to make a world can let it go" (see T-21.II.2–4).

WHAT IS SIN?

Part 3: W-pII.4.2:1–4

As we have seen already, "The body is the instrument the mind made in its efforts to deceive itself" (2:1). The purpose of the body, as seen by the ego, is "to strive" (2:2). To be in conflict and competition with other bodies, often for other bodies. The body struggles, it carves out its existence from the world through the sweat of its brow and through attack on other bodies. Its law is the law of the jungle, "Kill or be killed" (M-17.7:11).

Does this mean that the body is a hateful, evil thing, to be despised and subdued? No. The *goal* of the body's striving can change (2:3). Given to the ego, the goal is strife itself, with no real end. Strife keeps the ego going. But given to the Holy Spirit, our striving can take on the goal of truth, instead of lies.

The Holy Spirit can use everything the ego made to undo the purposes of the ego. He can use our special relationships, our words and thoughts, the world itself, and our bodies, all to serve the purposes of the truth. The key lies in the changing of the goal, the purpose which the body, and everything associated with it, serves. A special relationship becomes holy when its purpose is changed from sin to holiness, from trying to find a completion we think is lacking to striving to remember a completion we already have.

In the words of an old Christian hymn by Frances Ridley Havergill, we can pray:

> Take my life, and let it be
> Consecrated, Lord, to Thee.
> Take my moments and my days;
> Let them flow in ceaseless praise.

Take my hands and let them move
At the impulse of Thy love.
Take my feet and let them be
Swift and beautiful for Thee.

Take my lips, and let them be
Filled with messages from Thee.
Take my voice, and let me sing
Ever, only, of my King.

LESSON 254 ✦ SEPTEMBER 11

"Let every voice but God's be still in me."

Practice instructions

See complete instructions on page 135. A short summary:

- **Read** the commentary paragraph slowly and personally.
- **Pray** the prayer, perhaps several times.
- **Morning and evening:** Repeat the idea and then spend time in Open Mind Meditation.
- **Hourly remembrance:** Repeat the idea and then spend a quiet moment in meditation.
- **Frequent reminders:** Repeat the idea often within each hour.
- **Response to temptation:** Repeat the idea whenever upset, to restore peace.
- **Read the "What Is" section** slowly and thoughtfully once during the day.

Practice comments: The prayer for this lesson is simply beautiful. It is one of those prayers which, as in Lesson 221, announces an intention to come in mental silence before God, asking to experience only the truth. I suggest praying it many times as a way of entering into that state of quiet meditation.

Notice the response to temptation instructions in paragraph 2. Throughout the day, whenever you notice an ego thought, quietly step back and look at it. Then let it go by declaring, *"Let every voice but God's be still in me."* You don't want the effects of this thought, and so you choose to let it go. With thoughts like this out of the way, you can then enter into silence, where God speaks to you and tells you what you *really* want.

Commentary

Silence. Inner silence as well as outer silence is something most of us are not used to. When I lived in New Jersey, one of the things I used to notice when I visited a rural area was the silence, particularly in the

265

morning around dawn. I was not aware of how continual the noise was where I lived until it was absent. Trucks passing on a nearby highway, dogs barking, televisions playing, boom boxes, sirens. Even the constant hum of air conditioning or refrigerators. I was used to having a TV or radio or stereo playing most of the time.

Even more difficult to tune out is the constant inner chatter of the mind.

The Course is constantly engaging us in the practice of silence. "In deepest silence I would come to You" (1:2). Mental silence is an acquired habit; it takes a great deal of practice, at least in my experience. Even when I meditate my inclination is to use some words; perhaps to repeat a thought from a lesson; or to invent some kind of mental instruction for myself, such as "Breathing in love, breathing out forgiveness." My mind wants to engage in a running commentary on my "silent" meditation. Lately, however, I have found myself beginning with a simple instruction to myself, such as "Now let me be silent," or "Peace to my mind. Let all my thoughts be still." And then just sitting for fifteen minutes or so, attempting to be completely still and silent.

In silence, the lesson says, we can hear God's Voice and receive His Word. If I seldom seem to receive anything concrete, the odds are that it is because my attempts at silence are not yet terribly successful. But I am practicing.

The lesson contains some specific instructions that seem to me to apply to the question "What do I do with the thoughts that arise while I am meditating?" The instructions are quite simple: "step back and look at them, and then...let them go" (2:2). In mentally "stepping back" from my thoughts, I am holding my awareness still in the silence. I am watching the thoughts rather than engaging with them. This practice of *disengaging* ourselves from our egos is a key practice. The thoughts arise. Rather than identifying with them and playing with them, I step back. Rather than fighting against them and resisting them, I simply step back. I recognize that I

> do not want what they would bring with them. And so [I]
> do not choose to keep them.   (2:3–4)

"They are silent now" (2:5). When you simply disengage from the thoughts, not condemning them or approving them, simply noting them as of no consequence, as something unwanted at the moment, they really do begin to fall silent. I discover that I am really in charge of my own mind (who else would be?). As the thoughts fall away, "in the stillness, hallowed by His Love, God speaks to us and tells us of our will, as we have chosen to remember Him" (2:6).

One final note. As we begin to learn this practice of silence, it starts to spill over into our lives during the day. We discover that we are able, in the throes of some disturbing situation, to "step back" from the reactive thoughts of our minds, note the reactions, and simply choose, with His help, to let them go. The place of silence we have found in our special times of quiet comes with us into our day. "This quiet center, in which you do nothing, will remain with you, giving you rest in the midst of every busy doing on which you are sent" (T-18.VII.8:3).

WHAT IS SIN?

Part 4: W-pII.4.2:4–7

When we have changed the goal of our striving, and set a new purpose for our body with its senses, it begins to "serve a different aim" (2:4). The aim now is holiness rather than sin; forgiveness rather than guilt. Our minds were trying, through the body and the senses, to deceive themselves (2:5; 2:1). Our minds were trying to make their illusions of separation real. Now our aim is to rediscover the truth. When our mind selects a new goal, the body follows. The body serves the mind, and not vice versa (see T-31.III.4). It always does what the mind directs. So when we consciously select a new goal, the body begins to serve that goal (see T-31.III.6:2–3).

"The senses then will seek instead for witnesses to what is true" (2:7). Simply put, we will start to see things differently. The Text explains in some detail how this works (see T-11.VIII.9–14 and T-19.IV(A).10–11). We begin to look for our brothers' loving thoughts instead of their sins. We are seeking to learn of their reality (which is the Christ) instead of trying to discover their guilt. We look past their egos, their "variable perception" of themselves (T-11.VIII.11:1), and past their offenses. We ask the Holy Spirit to help us see their reality, and He shows it to us. "When you want only love, you will see nothing else" (T-12.VII.8:1).

What we see depends on what we *choose*, in our minds, to look for. Choose love, and the body will become the instrument of a new perception.

LESSON 255 ✦ SEPTEMBER 12
"This day I choose to spend in perfect peace."

Practice instructions

See complete instructions on page 135. A short summary:

- **Read** the commentary paragraph slowly and personally.
- **Pray** the prayer, perhaps several times.
- **Morning and evening:** Repeat the idea and then spend time in Open Mind Meditation.
- **Hourly remembrance:** Repeat the idea and then spend a quiet moment in meditation.
- **Frequent reminders:** Repeat the idea often within each hour.
- **Response to temptation:** Repeat the idea whenever upset, to restore peace.
- **Read the "What Is" section** slowly and thoughtfully once during the day.

Practice comments: Today is the first of three days of peace in Part II (the other two are 273 and 286). All are attempts to have a day of undisturbed peace, and all highlight the importance of our ability to have such a day. So really "give today to finding" (1:6) the peace God wills for you. Use your repetition of paragraphs 1 and 2 as a device for dedicating the day to this purpose. Practice frequently, in the faith that this peace really is there, and that your practice can lay hold of it for you.

Commentary

Peace does not seem to be purely a matter of choice: "It does not seem to me that I can choose to have but peace today" (1:1). Our egos would have us believe that peace can be taken from us, or given to us, by things outside our minds. It is not so.

If I am God's Son, and therefore like Himself, I have the power of decision, the power to simply *choose* peace (1:2–3). God says it is so; let me have faith in Him, and let me act upon that faith. Let me give it a try! Let me choose to spend this day in perfect peace. The more I determine to "give today to finding what my Father wills for me," which is the peace of Heaven, and "accepting it as mine" (1:6), the more I will experience that peace. I will probably also find a lot of things that pop up trying to disturb that peace. But I can respond to these things simply by saying, "I would choose peace instead of this," or "This cannot take away the peace my Father has given me." As I do this, the peace I choose and experience will "bear witness to the truth of what He says" (1:4).

Remember, your mental state isn't perfect, nor is it expected to be perfect. You are in training; this is a course in mind training. When I practice guitar chords, especially new ones, at first placing my fingers in the right position takes a lot of concentration and effort. I am forced to break the rhythm of the song, slowing down so I can place my fingers just so. I don't expect to get it right every time. Getting it wrong and correcting myself is part of the training. Eventually, with time, my fingers start forming a habit pattern; they go more and more frequently into the right configuration to strike the chord without any buzzing or dead notes. The training period is a time of doing it wrong, doing it deliberately with conscious concentration, until it becomes a habit I no longer have to think about. That is what we are doing in these lessons: practicing the habit of peace.

Our aim today is to spend the day with God (2:1). We, His Son, have not forgotten Him, and our practice is witness to that fact. The peace of God is in our minds, where He put it. We can find it, we can choose to spend our day there, in peace, with Him. We *can* do this; God assures us we can. So let us practice. Let us begin. Let us accept His peace as our own, and give it to all our Father's Sons, along with ourselves (1:6).

WHAT IS SIN?

Part 5: W-pII.4.3:1–2

Our illusions come from, or issue from, our untrue thoughts. Illusions are not really "things" at all; they are symbols, standing for imaginary things (3:1). They are like a mirage, a picture of something that is not really there at all. Our thoughts of lack, our feelings of unworthiness, our guilt and fear, the appearance of the world attacking us, even our bodies themselves—all of them are illusions, mirages, symbols representing nothing.

Sin is "the home of all illusions" (3:1). The idea of our inner corruption, our bent nature, houses every illusion. The thought of sin and guilt makes an environment that fosters and nourishes every illusion. What needs changing is that thought of the mind. Take away the thought of sin, and our illusions have no place to live. They simply fall down into dust.

These illusions, which come from untrue thoughts and make "sin" their dwelling place, "are the 'proof' that what has no reality is real" (3:2). Our bodies seem to prove to us that sickness and death are real, for instance. Our senses seem to prove that pain is real. Our eyes and ears see all kinds of evidence of guilt, of the reality of loss, and of the weakness of love. The world seems to prove that either God does not exist, or that He is angry with us. These things that our illusions seem to prove have no reality at all, and yet they seem real to us. All of this is housed in our belief in sin, and without that belief, they would simply cease to be.

LESSON 256 ✦ SEPTEMBER 13
"God is the only goal I have today."

Practice instructions

See complete instructions on page 135. A short summary:

- **Read** the commentary paragraph slowly and personally.
- **Pray** the prayer, perhaps several times.
- **Morning and evening:** Repeat the idea and then spend time in Open Mind Meditation.
- **Hourly remembrance:** Repeat the idea and then spend a quiet moment in meditation.
- **Frequent reminders:** Repeat the idea often within each hour.
- **Response to temptation:** Repeat the idea whenever upset, to restore peace.
- **Read the "What Is" section** slowly and thoughtfully once during the day.

Commentary

The title of the lesson talks about our goal. The first two sentences speak of the *means* to the goal:

> The way to God is through forgiveness here. There is no other way. (1:1–2)

We are speaking of means and end. Just the other day I read the Text section on "Consistency of Means and End" (T-20.VII), which reasons how, if we accept the goal, we must accept the means for getting there.

The means is forgiveness, and the Course continually insists that forgiveness is not difficult and cannot be difficult, because all it asks is that we recognize that what has never been has not occurred, and only the truth is true. How can it be difficult to be what you already are? If we experience forgiveness as difficult, there can only be one reason: we do not want the means because we still do not want the goal.

In other words, any difficulty stems not from something inherent in forgiveness, but from my unwillingness. It points me right back to recognizing what I am choosing, back to recognizing that I always have exactly what I want. Forgiveness seems difficult because I want it to seem difficult, and I want the means to appear difficult so I can project my unwillingness out onto the means God provided, blaming that means instead of recognizing myself as the cause of the problem.

"There is no other way" (1:2). If the problem is sin and the whole idea of sin, the only solution must be forgiveness. "If sin had not been cherished by the mind, what need would there have been to find the way to where you are?" (1:3). We are trying to find our way to God and we're already there! There would have been no need for such foolishness if we had not "cherished" sin. We (in listening to our ego thoughts) wanted to find a reason for separation, and sin, guilt, and fear provided the reason. We made it all up, and we must be the ones to let it go.

If we simply woke up, the dream of sin would be over. But we are too terrified to wake up, and the dream of sin and guilt has seemingly become self-sustaining. There seems to be no way out. "Here we can but dream" (1:7). But—and this is a big "but"—"we can dream we have forgiven him in whom all sin remains impossible, and it is this we choose to dream today" (1:8).

So I spend my days, noticing the dream of sin and forgiving it, over and over, more and more, until there is nothing left to forgive. At that point, my fear of God will be gone, and I will awake.

As I notice fear or guilt in myself today, or judging thoughts about those around me, let me look at those thoughts and recognize how insignificant they are, how meaningless. Let me be undisturbed by it all, and know my peace is inviolate. Let me understand that none of it matters, and I am still at rest in God. It is not this I want; I have no goal except to hear God's Voice.

WHAT IS SIN?

Part 6: W-pII.4.3:3–4

If "sin" is something real, the implications are enormous. And quite impossible. What does the reality of sin seem to prove? "Sin 'proves'

God's Son is evil; timelessness must have an end; eternal life must die" (3:3). If the Son created by God has sinned in truth, then God's Son must be evil. Is that possible? If the Son of God is evil, then what was created eternal must now be brought to an end; the eternal Son of God must die. "Justice" would demand it. Is it possible for something timeless to end, for something eternal to die? Of course not; these things are absurd. Therefore, sin also must be absurd. It cannot be.

Sin also "proves" that "God Himself has lost the Son He loves, with but corruption to complete Himself, His Will forever overcome by death, love slain by hate, and peace to be no more" (3:4). The thought that God would lose what He loves always seemed impossible to me; it made the whole idea of hell and eternal damnation seem completely inexplicable. I used to think, "If I go to Heaven, and my father [who did not believe in God] goes to hell, how could I ever be eternally, blissfully happy in Heaven, knowing my father is suffering eternally in hell? If I could not be happy with this, how could I be in Heaven? And if I could not be happy with this, how could God?"

If sin is real, the Son created to be God's own completion is now corrupt; God has only corruption to complete Himself. His Will has been totally thwarted. Evil wins. There can nevermore be peace.

Therefore, sin simply cannot be real. Guilt and fear follow sin into the unreality. If there is no sin, there is no guilt. If there is no guilt, there is no fear. How else could peace exist? "Sin is insanity" (1:1). It simply cannot be, if God is God, if His Will is to be done, if His creation is eternal. This is what forgiveness shows us:

> Sin remains impossible, and it is this we choose to dream today. God is our goal; forgiveness is the means by which our minds return to Him at last.   (W-pII.256.1:8–9)

LESSON 257 ✦ SEPTEMBER 14
"Let me remember what my purpose is."

Practice instructions

See complete instructions on page 135. A short summary:

- **Read** the commentary paragraph slowly and personally.
- **Pray** the prayer, perhaps several times.
- **Morning and evening:** Repeat the idea and then spend time in Open Mind Meditation.
- **Hourly remembrance:** Repeat the idea and then spend a quiet moment in meditation.
- **Frequent reminders:** Repeat the idea often within each hour.
- **Response to temptation:** Repeat the idea whenever upset, to restore peace.
- **Read the "What Is" section** slowly and thoughtfully once during the day.

Practice suggestion: As you begin your day, I suggest spending a moment going through the day you normally have, trying to see how you are usually serving contradictory goals. See yourself reaching after the goals of the world, and then at other times reaching after the goal of God. Try to get in touch with how divided this makes you feel, how it makes you unsure of who you are, and how it makes you feel that you will never reach either set of goals—the earthly or the heavenly—simply because you are giving each set only half of your energy.

Then spend another moment imagining what your day would be like if you only pursued the goal of God today, if you unified your thoughts and actions behind that single goal, and therefore achieved only what God would have you do today. Ask yourself how that day would feel. And then dedicate today to being *that* day.

Commentary

The purpose this lesson is alluding to is forgiveness (2:1). Over and over, the Course tells us that forgiveness is our function, our purpose, our reason for being here. And it is our *only* function:

> *I am the light of the world. That is my only function. That is why I am here.* (W-pI.61.5:3–5)

> Forgiveness is my function as the light of the world.
> (W-pI.62.Heading)

What if, today, I remembered that forgiveness is my only purpose? What if I realized that, whatever else happens, if I forgive everything and everyone I see today, I have fulfilled my function? What if I realized that all the things I think are important are nothing compared to this purpose? When I am behind that slow driver while trying to get someplace on time, forgiving is my purpose, not getting there on time. In any situation of conflict, forgiveness is my goal, not winning. When the person from whom I am seeking signs of love fails to respond, forgiveness is my goal, not getting the response I seek. And so on. What kind of difference would it make if I really made forgiveness my primary goal, my only goal?

If I forget the goal, I will always end up being conflicted, trying to serve contradictory goals (1:1–2). The inevitable result of conflicting goals is "deep distress and great depression" (1:3). Sound familiar? As we begin the spiritual path we are almost always conflicted, because we have adopted a new, higher goal without really letting go of the older ones. We're trying to serve two masters, which reminds me of the time I had a job where I was taking orders from two bosses! What a time of distress and depression that was! The only way to peace of mind in our lives is to firmly settle on a single purpose or goal (2:3), and to continually put that above everything else. We need to "unify our thoughts and actions meaningfully," by recognizing that God's Will for us is forgiveness, and seeking to do only that (1:4; 2:2).

WHAT IS SIN?

Part 7: W-pII.4.4:1–3

The lesson compares our belief in sin, and the projected illusions we have made to support that belief, to "a madman's dreams" (4:1). The dreams of a madman can be truly terrifying; likewise, our outpicturing of sin in this world can also be very frightening. "Sin appears indeed to terrify" (4:1). Sickness, death, and loss of every kind cannot but result in terror in us. The illusion is not gentle.

"Yet what sin perceives is but a childish game" (4:2). None of it really has any lasting consequence. In the light of eternity, our wars and plagues are no more real and no more frightening than a child's imaginary war between superhero action figures. There is no question that this is very hard to accept, particularly when you are in the middle of it all, believing it to be real. Yet it is what the Course is saying. If the body does not really live, it does not really die. "The Son of God may play he has become a body, prey to evil and to guilt, with but a little life that ends in death" (4:3). But that is not really the case. It is just a game we are playing. None of it really means what we think it means.

When we go to a movie, we may weep when a character we have identified with suffers loss or dies. Yet a deeper part of our mind knows we are watching a story; the actor did not really die. And at some level, the Course is asking us to respond to what we call "life" in the same way, with a deeper level of knowledge that knows that any life God created cannot ever die. The character in the movie may die, we may weep, and yet underneath all that, we know it is only an imaginary game, and not the final reality.

LESSON 258 ✦ SEPTEMBER 15
"Let me remember that my goal is God."

Practice instructions

See complete instructions on page 135. A short summary:

- **Read** the commentary paragraph slowly and personally.
- **Pray** the prayer, perhaps several times.
- **Morning and evening:** Repeat the idea and then spend time in Open Mind Meditation.
- **Hourly remembrance:** Repeat the idea and then spend a quiet moment in meditation.
- **Frequent reminders:** Repeat the idea often within each hour.
- **Response to temptation:** Repeat the idea whenever upset, to restore peace.
- **Read the "What Is" section** slowly and thoughtfully once during the day.

Commentary

Have you noticed we are into a series of "let me remember" days? Starting with yesterday's lesson, there are four "let me remembers" in a row: "what my purpose is," "that my goal is God," "that there is no sin," and "God created me." There was one earlier lesson also (Lesson 124): "Let me remember I am one with God."

That is one of the things Workbook practice is all about: remembering. How often during the day does the lesson for the day cross my mind? How often do I pause to reflect on it for a minute or two? How often does my state of mind reflect my only purpose, or God as my goal? And how much of the time does my mind reflect something quite contrary? The purpose of set times—morning, evening, and hourly—is to retrain my mind to think along the lines of the Course. There is no question in my mind that we need such training and such practice.

All that is needful is to train our minds to overlook all

278

little senseless aims, and to remember that our goal is God.
(1:1)

The "little senseless aims," however, loom large in our consciousness, and do not seem little to us; they preoccupy our minds and keep them from their true goal. So training is "needful." The memory of God is in us already (1:2); we don't have to dig for it. "God is in your memory" (T-10.II.2:4). All that we need to do is "overlook" or give up "our pointless little goals which offer nothing, and do not exist" (1:2); they are obscuring the memory of God within us. With them out of the way, the memory of God will come flooding back into our awareness.

The "toys and trinkets of the world" that we so avidly pursue cause "God's grace to shine in unawareness" (1:3). God's sunlight is shining, but we do not see it; we go shopping. Not just in malls for things, but in relationships for specialness, in the marketplace for power and influence and wealth, in the bars for sex, and with our TV remote controls for entertainment. Do I want the memory of God? All that is needful is that I be willing to train my mind to stop blinding me to it.

"Let me remember." Oh, God, let me remember!

God is our only goal, our only Love. We have no aim but
to remember Him. (1:4–5)

What else could I want that compares with this? Each time today that my heart is tugged to "shop" for something else, let it be a signal to my mind to stop, and to remember: "My goal is God."

A poem I learned in my Christian days pops into my mind. Some of those folks knew what they were talking about:

My goal is God Himself, not joy, nor peace,
Nor even blessing, but Himself, my God;
'Tis His to lead me there—not mine, but His—
At any cost, dear Lord, by any road.

One thing I know, I cannot say Him nay;
One thing I do, I press on towards my Lord;
My God my glory here, from day to day,
And in the glory there, my great Reward.
—*Frederick Brook*

A Course friend sent us some baseball-type caps imprinted with the letters "MOGIG." They stand for "My only goal is God." I think I'll wear that hat today as I work; it will be a good reminder.

WHAT IS SIN?

Part 8: W-pII.4.4:4

While we are all deeply involved in the drama of this "childish game" (4:2), reality continues. It has never changed. "But all the while his Father shines on him, and loves him with an everlasting Love which his pretenses cannot change at all" (4:4). Our "pretenses," the childish game, the playing at being bodies that suffer evil and guilt and death, has not changed and cannot change the deep, abiding reality of God's Love; the endless, perfect safety in which we dwell in Him.

> The changelessness of Heaven is in you, so deep within that nothing in this world but passes by, unnoticed and unseen. The still infinity of endless peace surrounds you gently in its soft embrace, so strong and quiet, tranquil in the might of its Creator, nothing can intrude upon the sacred Son of God within. (T-29.V.2:3–4)

In a sense, God's Love guarantees our eternal safety. Because His Love is "everlasting," so are we. While His Love endures, we endure also.

> The Son of Life cannot be killed. He is immortal as His Father. What he is cannot be changed. He is the only thing in all the universe that must be one. What *seems* eternal all will have an end. The stars will disappear, and night and day will be no more. All things that come and go, the tides and seasons and the lives of men; all things that change with time and bloom and fade will not return. Where time has set an end is not where the eternal is. God's Son can never change by what men made of him. He will be as he was and as he is, for time appointed not his destiny, nor set the hour of his birth and death. (T-29.VI.2:3–12)

LESSON 259 ✦ SEPTEMBER 16
"Let me remember that there is no sin."

Practice instructions

See complete instructions on page 135. A short summary:

- **Read** the commentary paragraph slowly and personally.
- **Pray** the prayer, perhaps several times.
- **Morning and evening:** Repeat the idea and then spend time in Open Mind Meditation.
- **Hourly remembrance:** Repeat the idea and then spend a quiet moment in meditation.
- **Frequent reminders:** Repeat the idea often within each hour.
- **Response to temptation:** Repeat the idea whenever upset, to restore peace.
- **Read the "What Is" section** slowly and thoughtfully once during the day.

Commentary

The concept of sin includes the idea that what I have done or thought or said has in some way irretrievably altered what I am. We think of sin not as a smudge of dirt on a clean surface, but as some kind of dry rot that has settled into the fabric of our being.

When Jesus says there is no sin, he is saying that our ideas are wrong. Nothing we have done has altered what we are in any way. The surface is uncorrupted and can be simply wiped clean. We are created with an amazing psychic layer of Scotchgard protectant. Underneath the layers of grime, we are still the holy Son of God.

If we think of sin as we normally do, the goal of God seems unattainable (1:1). If we see it as Jesus does, we can understand that the goal is already attained; it is not something to attain, it is something to celebrate.

When we see sin in another as dry rot, we feel justified in our attacks (1:3). When we see it as surface smudges, our love responds with a desire to wipe the surface of our brother's mind to reveal the beauty hiding in the dirt.

We are all aware of some self-destructive habit patterns. All of them come from the sense that we deserve punishment and suffering because we are guilty (1:4). We are unworthy of health, happiness, and uninterrupted joy. We think the evil is *in* us rather than *on* us.

When we fully accept the truth of our own innocence, we have opened the way to complete abundance and health. The universe is set up to support us, good is continually flowing our way, but we constantly block it off because, unconsciously, we don't think we deserve it. All this comes from the belief in sin.

Sin makes us afraid of love (2:2). To be afraid of love is insane, but then, "sin is insanity" (W-pII.4.1:1). If God is the Source of everything that is, then all there is must be Love; there can be no opposite, no fear, no sin (2:3–5). To remember that there is no sin is to accept our own perfect innocence, and the perfect innocence of all that is. And all the evidence we perceive that seems to prove otherwise is an illusion made up by our own minds.

WHAT IS SIN?

Part 9: W-pII.4.5:1–4

How long, we are asked, will we maintain this childish game of sin? That is all it is, a foolish game. Not an awful, terrible thing; just immature minds playing with "sharp-edged children's toys" (5:2). I think it is no coincidence that in the famous biblical chapter on love, 1 Corinthians 13, the Apostle Paul speaks of how, when we are children, we speak as children and act as children, but when we are grown, we "put away childish things" (1 Cor 13:11). That is what the lesson is asking us to do. It is asking us to grow up. "Sin" is a sharp-edged childish thing we have been playing with for eons. It is time for us to lay it aside, and to assume our "mature" role as extensions of God's Love.

It is time for us to put away these toys. Time to lay aside the whole concept of sin and guilt, the idea that we can do (and have done) something that immutably changes our nature. Something that merits everlasting condemnation and punishment. It is time to look around us and to realize that nothing, absolutely nothing, falls into this class. Sin, as a class or category of human behavior, simply does not exist. There are no sins, only mistakes. Nothing is beyond correction. Nothing bans us from God's Love. Nothing takes away our eternal inheritance. Nothing can separate us from the Love of God.

> How soon will you be ready to come home? Perhaps today? (5:3–4)

We have left home. We have run away because we believed we were evil and had done something unforgivable. But nothing is unforgivable. It is only our own belief in sin and guilt that keeps us here, homeless. Home is still waiting for us. Like the son in the parable of the prodigal, we sit in our pigsty lamenting our loss, while the Father watches at the end of the road, asking, "How soon will you be ready to come home? I'm here; I still love you. I'm waiting for you." Today, now, in this holy instant, let us be still a moment, and go home.

LESSON 260 ✦ SEPTEMBER 17
"Let me remember God created me."

Practice instructions

See complete instructions on page 135. A short summary:

- **Read** the commentary paragraph slowly and personally.
- **Pray** the prayer, perhaps several times.
- **Morning and evening:** Repeat the idea and then spend time in Open Mind Meditation.
- **Hourly remembrance:** Repeat the idea and then spend a quiet moment in meditation.
- **Frequent reminders:** Repeat the idea often within each hour.
- **Response to temptation:** Repeat the idea whenever upset, to restore peace.
- **Read the "What Is" section** slowly and thoughtfully once during the day.

Practice suggestion: Think of something you wish you hadn't done, or wish you had done better. Try to get in touch with how doing that thing seemed to make you into something undesirable. Perhaps it seemed to make you stupid, or selfish, or inconsiderate, or petty. Then repeat these lines:

In my eyes, that action made me _____.
Let me remember God created me.
I cannot make me [the attribute you used in first line], because God created me [choose an attribute that contrasts with the one you assigned yourself].

Commentary

In the Course's reasoning there is an intimate, unbreakable connection between acknowledging our true Source ("I am as God created me") and knowing our true Identity. Once we acknowledge God and only God as our Source, all questions about our identity disappear, because we are whatever God created us to be. "Now is our Source remembered, and Therein we find our true Identity at last" (2:1). If our goal is to remember who we truly are, the only way to that goal involves accepting God as our Author. All our false self-concepts derive from the idea that, somehow, we made ourselves, or at least have played a prominent role in shaping ourselves.

In our "insanity," we thought we made ourselves (1:1). Perhaps we grudgingly acknowledge God as the original creator, and yet we all believe that, since that time, we have been the primary factor in shaping our own lives and destiny. We must believe that, if we believe in sin. Would *God* create sin? Yet if He did not, and sin exists—who made it? So whether or not we consciously admit it, we *do* believe that we made ourselves, if we believe we are anything other than totally innocent and perfect. In sum, we think that "God created us; we screwed things up."

And yet, the Course would argue, we have not left our Source. God is all there is, and everything that is, is in Him. We are still part of Him. Therefore we cannot be what we think we are. We cannot separate ourselves from Him as we think we have. Separation not only never happened; it *cannot* happen.

If we simply remember God created us, we will simultaneously remember our Identity (1:4–5). Just as the nature of a sunbeam is defined by the nature of the sun, so we are defined by our Source. This is what Christ's vision shows us as we look upon our brothers and ourselves. We are sinless and holy "because our Source can know no sin" (2:2). We are, therefore, "like each other, and alike to Him" (2:3).

Let me remember, today, that God created me. My Source defines what I am. I am not defined by my past, by my upbringing, by my unkind words or deeds. Nor are my brothers defined by theirs. We are, all of us, defined by God. And what we are is His perfect Son.

WHAT IS SIN?

Part 10: W-pII.4.5:5–8

There is no sin. Creation is unchanged.   (5:5–6)

This is what remembering our Source tells us. "Sin" is only a childish game we have invented, and it has had no effect whatsoever on

God's creation. It is a game played only in our imagination; it has not changed reality one iota. The "Fall" never happened. There is nothing to atone for, nothing to pay for. The door to Heaven is wide open in welcome.

All that we need do, then, is to stop imagining this childish game. All that we need do is to cease imagining that guilt—our own or that of another—has any value at all, and to let it go. We hold on to guilt and sin only to maintain our illusion of separateness. Is it worth the price we pay? When we let go of sin, separateness is gone, and Heaven is restored to us.

> Would you still hold return to Heaven back? How long, O
> holy Son of God, how long? (5:7–8)

VIll

Lessons 261 - 270
What Is the Body?

LESSON 261 ✦ SEPTEMBER 18
"God is my refuge and security."

Practice instructions

See complete instructions on page 135. A short summary:

- **Read** the commentary paragraph slowly and personally.
- **Pray** the prayer, perhaps several times.
- **Morning and evening:** Repeat the idea and then spend time in Open Mind Meditation.
- **Hourly remembrance:** Repeat the idea and then spend a quiet moment in meditation.
- **Frequent reminders:** Repeat the idea often within each hour.
- **Response to temptation:** Repeat the idea whenever upset, to restore peace.
- **Read the "What Is" section** slowly and thoughtfully once during the day.

Practice suggestion: Search your mind for things in this world that you believe make you safe. Then, with each one, affirm that God is your safety. You may want to use the following form:

I think that my bank account [or job, or spouse, or family, etc.] makes me safe.
I see myself living within the walls of its protection.
But I live within God, not in this world.
In Him I find refuge; in Him I am safe.

Commentary

If you have read over the preceding page in the Workbook on "What Is the Body?" you will have noticed that the last paragraph of that section talks about how we "will identify with what [we] think will make [us] safe" (W-pII.5.5:1). The thought is echoed in the start of this lesson: "I will identify with what I think is refuge and security" (1:1). If we have a home which makes us feel safe and secure, for example, we will identify with that home. The thing which makes us feel safe becomes part of our identity. If the connection is strong enough, it will actually *become* our identity in our minds. We begin to see our "citadel" (1:2) of safety as an essential part of ourselves. "I will behold myself where I perceive my strength" (1:2).

This is what we have done with our own bodies. We mistakenly see our bodies as that which makes us safe ("safe from love," actually—see W-pII.5.1:1–3). The body becomes the thing that protects us from God, or from the conflict between love and fear within our minds: you "interpret the body as yourself in an attempt to escape from the conflict you have induced" (T-3.IV.6:3). Seeing the body as what makes me safe, I identify with it and perceive my "self" as existing within it. I also perceive my individual ego identity in the same way. It protects me from "losing myself" in the unity love encourages. I therefore encourage my sense of "danger" and even engage in "murderous attack" (1:3) because these things seem to protect my individuality from the inroads of other "selves." The same dynamic is reflected in the world in people and even nations who violently attack others, claiming they are only seeking to preserve their own peace. The stance is obviously self-contradictory. How can we "find security in danger" or "peace in murderous attack" (1:3)?

Our true security is in God. "I live in God" (1:4), and not in my body nor my ego self.

> In Him I find my refuge and my strength. In Him is my
> Identity. (1:5–6)

To know this as true, we have to release our hold on the thoughts that identify us with our bodies and our egos, and we have to begin to give up attack as a way of life and self-preservation. Attack does not preserve the Self; it preserves the ego, the false self. It preserves fear, chaos, and conflict. The only way, therefore, to truly find peace and to find "Who I really am" is to put an end to our protection of the false self, and to remember that our true everlasting peace is found only in God (1:7- 8).

May I, Father, come home to You today. May I, in entering into Your Presence in this holy instant, feel that sense of peace and security that is mine in truth, in my Identity in You. May I be able to sigh, "Ah! Home!" and feel the release of tension it brings to be here, in You. May I find my Self, and let go of all false identification with lesser things. Be my refuge, today, Father. "The eternal God [is thy] refuge, and underneath [are] the everlasting arms" (Dt 33:27). May I allow myself to fall back into Your arms today. When the day presses on me, be my refuge, my fortress and my high tower. Let me escape to You in the holy instant, and know the safety of Your Love.

WHAT IS THE BODY?

Part 1: W-pII.5.1:1–3

What is the body? Who, outside the Course, would have answered as does this paragraph? "The body is a fence the Son of God imagines he has built, to separate parts of his Self from other parts" (1:1). The body is a fence. What a strange concept that is! (It is an idea expanded on in the Text section entitled "The Little Garden" [T-18.VIII].) Its purpose (the reason the ego made it) is to keep something out; to separate parts of my Self from other parts. The body is a tool for division and separation; that is why we made it. It is a device intended to protect us from our wholeness. My body separates and distinguishes me from all the other "selves" walking this world in other bodies.

We believe we live "within this fence" (1:2), i.e., in the body. Is there anyone who can deny that this is how they approach life, the fundamental presupposition behind nearly all their actions? We think we live in the body, and we think that when the body decays and crumbles, we die (1:2). Much fear surrounds the death of the body. When our quadriplegic friend, Allan Greene, was still living next door, with only one leg and withered arms, and fingers black and shriveled, dead on his hand, most people found it profoundly disturbing to meet him (although somehow, in his presence, many of us quickly got over that discomfort because of his awareness of not being that body). Why do we generally feel such discomfort around disfigured, maimed, or dying people? One reason is that it triggers our own buried fears of the decay of our own bodies, and behind that, the fear of death itself.

The Course is leading us to a new awareness of a Self that does *not* live in a body, a Self that does *not* die as the body decays and crumbles. It is leading us to disengage ourselves from our identification with this bodily, limited self, and to strengthen our sense of identity with the non-corporeal Self.

Why have our egos made the body as a fence? What is the fence keeping out? Strangely, it is keeping out *love*. "For within this fence he thinks that he is safe from love" (1:3). Why would we want to keep love out? Why would we ever believe we needed something to keep us "safe" from love? Love lets in all the parts of our Self we are trying to keep out. Love destroys our illusion of separateness. Love understands that we are not this limited thing we believe we are, and that our brothers are parts of us; it constantly extends, giving and receiving, like a magnetic force drawing all the fragmented parts of the Self together again.

Have you ever experienced, in a moment of intense love for another person, a surge of fear? Have you ever felt like you were about to lose yourself if you gave in to this love? That feeling gives you some hint of the abject fear the ego has of love. The ego wants you looking for love (because you know you need and want it) in order to keep you satisfied (and trapped), but it never, ever wants you to find it. Love represents the loss of the ego identity. To the ego, it *is* death. And so the body is manufactured to keep love out, as a means of preserving our sense of separateness.

LESSON 262 ✦ SEPTEMBER 19
"Let me perceive no differences today."

Practice instructions

See complete instructions on page 135. A short summary:

- **Read** the commentary paragraph slowly and personally.
- **Pray** the prayer, perhaps several times.
- **Morning and evening:** Repeat the idea and then spend time in Open Mind Meditation.
- **Hourly remembrance:** Repeat the idea and then spend a quiet moment in meditation.
- **Frequent reminders:** Repeat the idea often within each hour.
- **Response to temptation:** Repeat the idea whenever upset, to restore peace.
- **Read the "What Is" section** slowly and thoughtfully once during the day.

Practice suggestion: Throughout the day, when you have a spare moment, pick someone and silently say to him or her:

You are not that one form. You are the Mind behind all forms.

Your name is not [name], for you are not separate. Your name is "Father," for you are part of Him.

You are not a stranger to your Father. You are His beloved Son.

You are not a stranger to me. You are my ancient friend.

Commentary

In order to move toward perceiving no differences, I must begin to let go of identification with the body, both in identifying myself with a body, and in identifying my brothers and sisters as bodies. The body, says the reading for the week, is a fence (W-pII.5.1:1). It establishes difference; it fairly screams, "I am different." Why is it that every body has different fingerprints, different retinal prints, different DNA patterns? How can it be that in all the billions of bodies, no fingerprint is ever duplicated? Our bodies are saying, "I am different. I am unique. I am completely unlike all of you."

Love sings softly, "We are the same. We are one. We share one life, and that with God." It is the one Son that we would look upon today (1:1–2). The "thousand forms" (1:4) are different; the life we share is one. We need not denigrate the body to do this. The body can become a means to heal the separation of our minds. We use the body to express our unity. We touch, we embrace, we care for one another, we assist one another. We *use* the illusion to transcend the illusion.

In each body that comes before us, we see the one Son. "Let me not see him as a stranger to his Father, nor as stranger to myself" (1:7). Each one I see today is part of me, and I of him, and together we are part of God our Source (1:8). Seeing this is what seeing no differences means. Of course, I will still see male and female, tall and short, fat and thin, poor and rich, black and white and brown and yellow and red. But I choose to look beyond these differences today, and to see the sameness, the one Son in whom we are the same, not different.

Separation means differences, and differences breed judgment and attack. The vision of our sameness and our unity brings peace, "and nowhere else can peace be sought and found" (2:3). We choose not to let our sight stop at the differences, but to go beyond them to the oneness. We look and we say, "This is my brother (sister) whom I love, part of me, loved by God and part of God with me. Together we are the holy Son of God."

WHAT IS THE BODY?

Part 2: W-pII.5.1:4–5

When we see our safety in the body, we identify with it. We see ourselves as bodies (1:4). It is this that promotes and supports the ego's ideal of separation, judgment, and attack. To the ego, this is the purpose of bodies, although it tells us that the purpose is our own safety. It seems to me that it is beneficial, then, to recognize the frailty of our bodies, their temporary and ephemeral nature. The sickness and death of the body, then, instead of being a fearful thing, can become a gentle reminder that this is not what we are. Why would we want to identify with such a vulnerable thing? Recognizing the body's impermanence and the brevity of its existence can impel us to seek a more permanent identity elsewhere. Becoming aware of the lunacy of seeking our safety in the body, we can understand that our strong attachment to the body must come from some hitherto unsuspected motive: the ego's desire for separateness.

> How else could he be certain he remains within the body,
> keeping love outside? (1:5)

If we did not have this strong attachment to and identification with the body, if we realized that what we are transcends the body and dwarfs its significance, we could not keep love away from us. This is the ego's purpose in promoting our bodily identity: to keep love out. This is where our seemingly instinctive need to regard ourselves as bodies comes from. It is a deception and trap of our egos, and when we see this clearly, we realize that it is not something we want at all.

The seemingly good reasons for identifying with our bodies, in the Course's eyes, simply do not hold water. Bodies are unsafe vehicles; there is no security in them. Behind the seemingly benign reasons our egos set forth there is a much darker hidden motivation: the ego's blind belief in the value of separateness and difference. The Course is asking us to acknowledge this dark motive within ourselves, and to disavow it, turning instead to the eternal safety of Love Itself, which is our true nature as God's creation.

LESSON 263 ✦ SEPTEMBER 20
"My holy vision sees all things as pure."

Practice instructions

See complete instructions on page 135. A short summary:

- **Read** the commentary paragraph slowly and personally.
- **Pray** the prayer, perhaps several times.
- **Morning and evening:** Repeat the idea and then spend time in Open Mind Meditation.
- **Hourly remembrance:** Repeat the idea and then spend a quiet moment in meditation.
- **Frequent reminders:** Repeat the idea often within each hour.
- **Response to temptation:** Repeat the idea whenever upset, to restore peace.
- **Read the "What Is" section** slowly and thoughtfully once during the day.

Practice suggestion: Look randomly about you for a minute or two. In relation to whatever your eyes alight on, say, *"My holy vision sees this _____ as pure, that I may pass it by in innocence."*

Then close your eyes and think of various people you know. In relation to each one, say, *"My holy vision sees [name] as pure, that we may walk together to our Father's house."*

Commentary

This lesson is about seeing all things as God created them: without sin, innocent, and pure. His Mind created all that is, His Spirit entered into it, and His Love gave life to it (1:1). To see things in this way, at first, has to be a conscious choice, because we have trained our minds to see otherwise. We have learned to judge. We will categorize, evaluate on a scale of one to ten, and attempt to determine whether this is something or someone we want to draw closer to us or to push away. We've trained our minds to do so since birth, and probably in many previous lifetimes. Thus, there has to be a conscious choice to say, "No. I choose to see this as pure." We downgrade our reflexive evaluations and choose instead to accept the Holy Spirit's judgment.

Eventually—a long eventually—our minds will become retrained. The choice to see purity will become more and more automatic. The judgmental thoughts will probably always be there, slowly receding into the background, until we leave this world completely, but the choice to see purity will become less and less a conscious choice, and more and more a habit of thought. Frequent and persistent repetition will speed the process.

WHAT IS THE BODY?

Part 3: W-pII.5.2:1–4

The body, of course, is transient. It will not last (2:1). The biblical psalmist compared man's life to grass, as brief as a flower in the field, and quickly disappearing (Ps 103:15).

Our transient nature is near to the surface of every mind, as I was reminded last night in a restaurant, when someone came in and greeted the host with, "How's life?"

"Too short," he replied.

You might think that the shortness of physical life would instantly alert us to the fallacy of the ego's attempt to have us find safety in the body, but the ego quickly twists the very shortness into a proof of its case. The ego wants to prove separation. And what is more separating than physical death? So the short life of the body "proves" that the fence works; we really are separate from one another and from God (2:3). We made the body to manifest separation, and lo! it does. One body can attack another and kill it. If we were really one, so the ego's logic goes, this would be impossible (2:4). The ego is a master of sophistry.

There is a masterful counterargument in Chapter 13 of the Text. There, it says:

> For you believe that attack is your reality, and that your destruction is the final proof that you were right.
>
> Under the circumstances, would it not be more desirable to have been wrong, even apart from the fact that you were

295

wrong? While it could perhaps be argued that death suggests there *was* life, no one would claim that it proves there
is life. Even the past life that death might indicate, could
only have been futile if it must come to this, and needs this
to prove that it was at all.   (T-13.IV.2:5–3:3)

If you have to die in order to prove you were right (separation does
exist), wouldn't you rather be wrong—and live? "Even though you
know not Heaven, might it not be more desirable than death?"
(T-13.IV.3:6). Much of our fear of letting go of our identification with
the body lies right here; we're afraid of being proven wrong. If we are
wrong in this one thing, so much else of our lives has been wasted effort.
We've been pouring our very souls into something that, in a very short
time, will be only dust. The Course is asking us to realize the futility of
all this, and to look around us and ask, "Is there perhaps something else
more deserving of all this effort?" And there is.

LESSON 264 ✦ SEPTEMBER 21

"I am surrounded by the Love of God."

Practice instructions

See complete instructions on page 135. A short summary:

- **Read** the commentary paragraph slowly and personally.
- **Pray** the prayer, perhaps several times.
- **Morning and evening:** Repeat the idea and then spend time in Open Mind Meditation.
- **Hourly remembrance:** Repeat the idea and then spend a quiet moment in meditation.
- **Frequent reminders:** Repeat the idea often within each hour.
- **Response to temptation:** Repeat the idea whenever upset, to restore peace.
- **Read the "What Is" section** slowly and thoughtfully once during the day.

Practice suggestion: This is one of my favorite prayers. I recommend praying it over and over. Give each line your full awareness. Make it a personal communication from you to God. To aid this process, you might want to insert the specific comments I've indicated in brackets below:

Father, You stand before me [in that _____] and behind [in that _____],

beside me [in that _____ on my right and that _____ on my left],

in the place I see myself [on this chair, couch, floor, street, etc.],

and everywhere I go [such as _____, where I am going later].

You are in all the things I look upon [like this _____ and that _____, which I am seeing right now],

the sounds I hear [like this _____ and this _____, which I am hearing right now],

and every hand that reaches for my own [such as the hand

of _____, who journeys with me].
In You time disappears [because every moment, being
filled with You, is the same],
and place becomes a meaningless belief [because every
place, being filled with You, is the same].
For what surrounds Your Son, [insert your name],
and keeps him safe is Love Itself [not time, not place].
There is no Source but This, and nothing is [including
_____, that difficult person in my life]
that does not share Its Holiness;
that stands beyond Your one creation,
or without the Love which holds all things within Itself.
Father, Your Son is like Yourself [and Your Son is all of us].
We come to You in Your Own Name today [we are not tres-
passers; we come at your invitation],
to be at peace within Your everlasting Love.

Commentary

The bulk of today's lesson is a beautiful prayer, and my suggestion to us all is that we take the time not only to read it, but to read it aloud, with all the expression of which we are capable. Jesus says:

> My brothers, join with me in this today. This is salva-
> tion's prayer. (2:1–2)

Will you do that? Perhaps we might pause at noon, each in our time zone, and as we do, realize that others are joining us in that very moment to pray this same prayer, together. And Jesus joins with us all, every time we repeat it. "Let all the world be blessed with peace through us" (W-pII.360.Heading).

(If you can't pause at noon, pause on another hour. Someone, somewhere, will be joining with you.)

Imagine the effect on yourself if, at least once an hour, and more often if possible, you simply pause for a moment and silently repeat to yourself, with conviction, "I am surrounded by the Love of God."

"Love is your safety," says the "What Is the Body?" section (W-pII.5.5:4). The purpose of these ten lessons is to focus our attention on love, which is "invisible," rather than on the body, which is visible. A passage in the Text I happen to be reading today goes right along:

> When you made visible what is not true, what *is* true
> became invisible to you....It is invisible to you because
> you are looking at something else.   (T-12.VIII.3:1, 3)

What is not seen is not therefore gone. Love is still in my mind
because God placed it there. Love is still in everything, all around me,
and I will see it if I will but stop looking at something else. Jesus says
that if we look at love enough, what is not there will become invisible to
us. That process is the shift the Course is talking about. As we learn to
stop wanting to see something other than love, we will stop seeing anything but love. That outcome is inevitable because love is all there is.

We want to see separation, we want to see bodies, because we think
somehow that keeps us safe. It preserves our individuality. Our real
safety, however, lies in love. Our real safety lies in realizing that we are
part of that ocean of love, never ending. Body, ego, and individual consciousness are not what need to be preserved and adhered to. Rather, we
need to adhere to Universal Consciousness and to playing our part as a
synapse in that Universal Mind, with no purpose that ends in this little
cell of self, but only a purpose that serves the whole.

The way to experience love is to give it. "For if love is sharing, how
can you find it except through itself?" (T-12.VIII.1:5). Let me today
open my heart to love the world. Let me know that this is my function.
As I open to let love out, love will flood in. It always flows both ways.
And what I am loving is myself, not a separate thing or things. I am not
simply a cell; I only exist in relationship to the universe. The whole is
in every part. Everything is related to everything else, and only the
whole has meaning. I am surrounded by the Love of God.

WHAT IS THE BODY?

Part 4: W-pII.5.2:4–9

Our identification with the body seems to protect us from love. The
insanity of the ego believes that death "proves" that we are separate. Yet
in reality there is only our oneness. If we are one, the lesson asks:

> Who could attack and who could be attacked? Who could
> be victor? Who could be his prey?   (2:4–6)

We believe attack is real, that there are really victims and really murderers. If our oneness remains untouched (2:4), this simply cannot be. And therefore all such appearances must be illusory, or else the oneness *has* been destroyed. The horrors of this world are the ego's attempts to demonstrate the destruction of oneness. Death is the ego's demonstration that "God's eternal Son can be destroyed" (2:9). As students of the Holy Spirit, we deny this.

We do not deny that, within the illusion, victims and murderers exist. We do not pretend that children have not been blown up with bombs, that genocide is not practiced, that atrocities do not occur, that wars are not going on, that lives and families and emotional stability are not being shredded all over the world. All this is true *within the illusion.* What we deny is the entirety of the illusion. We deny that this picture represents the truth. We deny that anything real is threatened. We are aware that what we see is only a dream. We see the dream figures come and go, shift and change, suffer and die, but we are not deceived by what we see (see M-12.6:6–8). We bear witness to reality, invisible to the body's eyes, but seen by the vision of Christ.

The truth is: Oneness is. The world, the body, and death, all deny this truth. Our task as miracle workers is to *"deny the denial of truth"* (T-12.II.1:5). We deny separation, the denial of oneness. We stand, with hands outstretched to help, and by our words, our actions, our thoughts, and above all, by our love, we demonstrate the truth of eternal oneness.

SEEING THE MEANING IN THE IDEA FOR THE DAY

Much of doing the Workbook is repeating the idea for the day, the sentence at the top of every lesson. Therefore, if this idea falls flat in our mind, chances are that we will not get much out of that day's practice. We might as well be repeating some phrase in Latin. At least that is how it feels sometimes. The remedy to this is understanding the meaning contained in that brief sentence. This meaning is what makes the practice come alive. The more meaning we see in those words, the more powerful will be the practice of them.

This meaning is supplied in large measure by Text study, but also by careful reading of the lesson. After all, most of the lesson's words are teaching about what that idea for the day means. Therefore, we should ideally read each line of the lesson with an eye for what it says about the meaning of the day's idea. I prefer a kind of mental posture in which I have one eye on the idea for the day while the other eye is reading the lesson's teaching. I will read a sentence or paragraph in the lesson and then go back and ask how this relates to the day's idea. This will often give that idea a different meaning than I would have otherwise assumed, as well as a deeper and more multifaceted meaning. In short, it will make the practice of it more powerful and effective.

Let's see this at work in the case of Lesson 264 and its accompanying prayer, which provides the teaching for that lesson.

I am surrounded by the Love of God

When we first read this idea we would probably assume that it means there is a presence of God that surrounds us, somewhat like an aura, and follows us wherever we go. This in itself is a comforting thought, but let's see what meaning the lesson's teaching puts in this idea.

> 1. Father, You stand before me and behind, beside me, in the place I see myself, and everywhere I go.

This first sentence does not say anything too different from what we would assume about the day's idea. It does, however, make that idea more concrete by specifically mentioning "before," "behind" and "beside." It also makes the idea more absolute. God is not only around me, He is everywhere I go, and even in the place I see myself. This gives us a hint of what is to come.

> 2. You are in all the things I look upon, the sounds I hear, and every hand that reaches for my own.

This sentence expands and deepens the idea considerably. God is not merely a kind of invisible presence that hovers around me in, say, a four-foot radius. He is in everything I look upon. He is not one invisible item among a great many more visible things. He is all-pervasive. What's more, He is even in the *sounds* I hear. Somehow it is much easier to imagine Him being in physical objects than in sounds. Sounds are not things. They are just vibrations in the air, just motion. This means that God is not only in things, but also in processes, in movements. He, of course, is inside those who walk with me. Yet He is also in their hands that reach for mine,

301

and in the movement of the hands as they reach, and in the sound of their footsteps. I am literally surrounded by God, for He dwells in every sight, sound, person, object, and movement—in everything. We have now come a long way from God as aura.

> 3. *In You time disappears, and place becomes a meaningless belief.*

This sentence seems to take off in a new direction, yet it is just the logical outcome of the previous sentences. If God is in everything, then every place contains the same thing: God. And if every place contains the same thing, if all places are the same, then there really is no such thing as place. The very concept of place implies that one place is different from another, distant from another. The same with time. If God is in every moment, then apparently different moments are really the same, which means that there aren't different moments. Without different moments there can't be time. Without different places there can't be space. Therefore, "time disappears, and place becomes a meaningless belief."

This thought is somewhat different than what I have encountered in some spiritual teachings. I have heard many times that God is in everything, but the impression I usually got was that those things were therefore real. By the act of God dwelling in a rock, for instance, He is sanctioning the rock's reality. That rock must be real, or God would not bother to be inside of it. In fact, in these thought systems, God Himself gave birth to the rock and dwells inside the house He created.

The Course is doing something very different with the idea. It is implying that God is the only thing real in that rock. The form of the rock, its physical substance, is not real at all. The form is not a manifestation of God. It is just an illusory picture of the crazy thought that God is absent. Thus, the rock is not really there at all. Only God is.

> 4. *For what surrounds Your Son and keeps him safe is Love Itself.*

This sentence takes things even further. We seem to be surrounded by time and space. Enveloping us is space; behind us is the past; ahead of us, the future. That is what it means to be in this world—being surrounded by time and space. Yet the lesson has told us that what is behind and before us is God, not past and future, not physical space. If that is really true, then *we are not in this world at all.* We are really in God's Love, in Heaven. If we could only see, if the scales could fall off our eyes, we would realize that right now we are standing not in this world but in Heaven, enveloped by His Love. We have now come very far indeed from

God's Love as four-foot aura.

> 5. *There is no Source but This, and nothing is that does not share Its holiness; that stands beyond Your one creation, or without the Love Which holds all things within Itself.*

The scope of God's Love continues to expand. Now we are not only surrounded by God's Love, we *came* from that Love. It is our Source; what gave birth to our being. Further, this total relationship with God's Love is now extended to cover everyone and everything. Not just us but *everything* comes from that Love and is made of It, sharing Its holiness. And *nothing* has been left outside Its eternal embrace. Everything is held within It, not within time and space. How can there be a world of time and space when there is only Love creating more of Itself?

> 6. *Father, Your Son is like Yourself.*

Sentence 5 was a longer, more philosophical statement about the relationship of the Source to everything else. Now we take those ideas and, in sentence 6, compress them into a brief, direct, and intimate statement from a Son to his Father. "This is the only Source and everything shares Its attributes" becomes "Father, we are all like You, because we are all Your Son." This Son is us individually, but (given the context of the previous sentence) it is also everyone and everything.

With this direct, intimate statement, the prayer is beginning to wrap up and lead us into the place it has been talking about. The implied "we" of sentence 6 continues into the prayer's concluding line.

> 7. *We come to You in Your Own Name today, to be at peace within Your everlasting Love.*

The ideas the prayer has described are a kind of red carpet it has laid out before us. Now, with this concluding line, we are meant to walk that carpet straight into the reality of what has been discussed, the reality of God's Love. We know that in doing so we are not just acting on our own. We are not trespassing. We walk up to God's front door holding in our hand an invitation from the Lord of the house Himself. We come to Him in His Own Name. He Himself has rolled out the red carpet. How do we know this? As the rest of the prayer says, He has already placed us forever within Himself. If His Love is what created us and what surrounds us, and indeed is all there is, where else would we go?

The situation we may have initially read into the idea for the day has now been completely reversed. God's Love is not merely an aura that surrounds us, a silent ghost we take with us on our busy tour through the world of separate things. The world is the ghost; God's Love is the only reality there is. It is the all-pervasive realm that beckons us beyond this shadow world and into Itself. And not just us—It beckons everyone and everything; all the countless minds that comprise the one Son of God.

Thus, rather than, "How nice of You, God, to come with me on my errands," we conclude by saying, "*We* (the entire world and all living things) come to *You.*" We come to Him, to rest from our busy doings and nervous plans, to be free of the endless parade of little objects scurrying through frantic days. We come to Him, to leave behind the thousands of shadows that haunt this unreal place and pass forever into the light of Heaven. As one Son, we come to Him to forget all anxious separate identities as together we find eternal rest in His boundless Arms. We come to Him to be at peace within His everlasting Love.

"I am surrounded by the Love of God" means so much more than we ever would have guessed at first. Holding in mind this deeper, broader, expanded meaning, do you think that practicing this lesson would be any different?

LESSON 265 ✦ SEPTEMBER 22
"Creation's gentleness is all I see."

Practice instructions

See complete instructions on page 135. A short summary:

- **Read** the commentary paragraph slowly and personally.
- **Pray** the prayer, perhaps several times.
- **Morning and evening:** Repeat the idea and then spend time in Open Mind Meditation.
- **Hourly remembrance:** Repeat the idea and then spend a quiet moment in meditation.
- **Frequent reminders:** Repeat the idea often within each hour.
- **Response to temptation:** Repeat the idea whenever upset, to restore peace.
- **Read the "What Is" section** slowly and thoughtfully once during the day.

Commentary

This lesson so clearly states how the world comes to be, apparently, attacking us:

> I have indeed misunderstood the world, because I laid my sins on it and saw them looking back at me. How fierce they seemed! And how deceived was I to think that what I feared was in the world, instead of in my mind alone.
>
> (1:1–3)

I feel guilt over some aspect of myself. I project that guilt outward; I lay my sins on the world and then see them looking back at me. "Projection makes perception" (T-21.In.1:1). There is more than one place where the Course says quite clearly that we never see anyone's sins but our own (for instance, T-31.III.1:5). The world I see is the outward reflection of an inward condition (see T-21.In.1:5). *The Song of Prayer* says:

> It is impossible to forgive another, for it is only your own
> sins you see in him. You want to see them there, and not in
> you. That is why the forgiveness of another is an illu-
> sion....Only in someone else can you forgive yourself, for
> you have called him guilty of your sins, and in him must
> your innocence now be found. Who but the sinful need to
> be forgiven? And do not ever think you can see sin in any-
> one except yourself. (S-2.I.4:2–4, 6–8)

"Do not ever think you can see sin in anyone except yourself." Wow!
What a powerful statement. "It is only your own sins you see in him."
A lot of people, including myself, have some trouble with this concept.
I really think our egos fight this, and use every possible way of refusing
to accept it.

A common reaction to statements like this in the Course is, "No way!
I never beat my wife. I never murdered or raped or betrayed the way he
did." Where I think we go off the track is in looking at particular actions
and saying, "They do that. I don't," and thinking we've proved that the
sin we see isn't our own.

The action is not the sin. The guilt is. The principle is much broader
than specific actions. The principle of attack is this: "It is the judgment
of one mind by another as unworthy of love and deserving of punishment" (T-13.In.1:2). The person's action that we are judging isn't relevant; we are seeing another person as "unworthy of love and deserving
of punishment" because we see ourselves that way first. We feel our
own unworthiness, dislike the feeling, and project it onto others. We
find particular actions to associate the unworthiness with that we don't
perceive as being in ourselves (although sometimes they are in us, just
suppressed or buried); that's exactly how we try to get rid of the guilt!

Projection and dissociation go on within our own psyche as well as
externally. When I condemn myself for, say, overeating, and think I feel
guilty because I overate, I am doing the same thing as when I condemn
a brother for lying or whatever. I am putting the guilt outside of myself
in one case; in the other case, I am putting the guilt onto a shadow part
of myself which I then disown. "I don't know why I do that; I know better."

When I feel guilty, I am actually disowning a part of my own mind.
There is some part of me that feels a need to overeat, or to be angry at

my mother, or to sabotage my career, or to abuse my body with some drug. I do these things because I am guilty and think I need punishment. The original guilt comes not from any of these petty things, but from my deep belief that I have really succeeded in separating myself from God. I have actually succeeded at making myself other than a creation of God. I am my own creator. And since God is good, I must be evil. Deep down we think the evil is in us, that we are the evil. We can't stand that idea, and so we push away some part of our mind and our behavior and lay the guilt at its feet.

It is exactly the same mechanism at work when I see sin in a brother. But from the ego's perspective seeing guilt in *someone else* is much more attractive and does a better job of concealing the guilt it wants us to keep; it puts the guilt completely away from myself. In reality, my brother is a part of my mind just as much as the shadow self is a part of my mind. The whole world is in my mind; my mind is all there is.

> How deceived was I to think that what I feared was in the world, instead of in my mind alone. (1:3)

> He [one who identifies with the ego] always perceives this world as outside himself, for this is crucial to his adjustment. He does not realize that he makes this world, for there is no world outside of him. (T-12.III.6:6–7)

> Take off the covers and look at what you are afraid of. (T-12.II.5:2)

We need to look at what we are afraid of until we realize that all of it is in our own mind. When at last we recognize the truth of that, we will be in a place where we can do something about it. Until then, we are helpless victims.

We see sin in others because we think we have a need to see sin in others, to avoid seeing it in ourselves. We believe in the principle that some people are unworthy of love and deserving of punishment. Deep down we know that we are one of the condemned, but the ego tells us that if we can see the guilt out there in others, see them as worse than ourselves, we may escape judgment. So we project the guilt.

What this Workbook lesson is saying is that if we lift the blot of our own guilt off the world, we will see its "celestial gentleness" (1:4). If I can remember that my thoughts and God's thoughts are the same, I will see no sin in the world, because I am not seeing it in myself.

The world around us, therefore, offers us countless opportunities to forgive ourselves. "Only in someone else can you forgive yourself, for you have called him guilty of your sins, and in him must your innocence now be found" (S-2.I.4:6). When someone appears in our life as a sinner, we have a chance to forgive ourselves in him. We have a chance to let go, a bit more deeply, of the fixed perception that what this person did makes him guilty of sin. We have a chance to look past his harmful actions to see the underlying innocence. We lay aside our conditioned judgment and allow the Holy Spirit to show us something different.

It seems as if we are working with forgiving another person. In reality we are always forgiving ourselves. When we find the innocence in that other person, suddenly we know our own innocence more deeply. When we see what they did as a call for love, we can more easily see our own misbehavior as likewise a call for love. We discover a common innocence, a radical innocence. It is absolute innocence, totally unchanged since the instant God created us.

WHAT IS THE BODY?

Part 5: W-pII.5.3:1–3

> The body is a dream.   (3:1)

This whole melodrama of attacking and being attacked, victor and prey, murderer and victim, is a dream, with the body playing the chief role. Think about the implications of my body as a dream. In a dream, everything seems completely real. I've had some really gross and terrifying dreams about my body. Once I dreamed that all my teeth were disintegrating and falling out. But when I woke up, nothing of the kind was happening. It was all in my mind while I slept.

By calling the body "a dream," the Course is saying that what happens to our bodies here is really not happening at all; it is happening only within our minds. It is saying that the body itself is not happening; it is not a real thing. We are not really here, as we think we are; we are dreaming about being here. My son, who is working in computers in the field of virtual reality, was once hooked up to a robot by computer, seeing through its eyes and touching things with its hand.

He had the very weird sensation of experiencing himself on one side of the computer lab while his body was on the other side; he even looked across the lab and "saw" his own body, wearing the VR helmet. Our mind experiences itself as being "here," on earth, in a body; but it is not here. *Here* is not here. All of it is within the mind.

Dreams can picture happiness, and then very suddenly revert to fear; we've all experienced that in dreams, most likely. And we've experienced it in our "lives" here in the body. Dreams are born of fear (3:2), and the body, being a dream, is born of fear also. Love does not create dreams, it "creates in truth" (3:3). And love did not create the body:

> The body was not made by love. Yet love does not condemn it and can use it lovingly, respecting what the Son of God has made and using it to save him from illusions.
>
> (T-18.VI.4:7–8)

The body was made by fear, and the dreams that result will *always* end in fear.

The body was made by fear for fear, yet "love can use it lovingly." When we give our bodies to the Holy Spirit for His use, we change the dream. For now the body has a different purpose, motivated by love.

LESSON 266 ✦ SEPTEMBER 23
"My holy Self abides in you, God's Son."

Practice instructions

See complete instructions on page 135. A short summary:

- **Read** the commentary paragraph slowly and personally.
- **Pray** the prayer, perhaps several times.
- **Morning and evening:** Repeat the idea and then spend time in Open Mind Meditation.
- **Hourly remembrance:** Repeat the idea and then spend a quiet moment in meditation.
- **Frequent reminders:** Repeat the idea often within each hour.
- **Response to temptation:** Repeat the idea whenever upset, to restore peace.
- **Read the "What Is" section** slowly and thoughtfully once during the day.

Practice suggestion: I have found it helpful to make today's idea more specific. Think of someone in your life and say, *"My holy Self abides in you, [name]."*

Commentary

These are not words I speak to Jesus, or to the Christ as some abstract being. These are words I speak to the person who is sitting next to me, to my boss, to my family members, to whomever is in front of me or in my mind. "My holy Self abides in *you*, God's Son."

If my mind is enlightened, everyone is my savior. Everyone points the way to God (2:2–3). Jesus is saying here, "Wake up! You can't miss the way home. The world is filled with people, and *every one* is pointing the way to God. Every one reflects His Son. Your Self is in every one of them. Just let your eyes be opened and I will give you the sight to see it."

God's Will is your salvation. Would He not have given you the means to find it? If He wills you to have it, He must

310

have made it possible and easy to obtain it. Your brothers
are everywhere. You do not have to seek far for salvation.
Every minute and every second gives you a chance to save
yourself.   (T-9.VII.1:1–6)

Nothing shows quite so vividly how skewed our perception is than
our reaction to this lesson. Perhaps right now you are thinking, "Yeah,
sure. They certainly don't seem like saviors and bearers of God's holy
Voice to me!" If we are honest, most of us will admit that we perceive
our brothers as the stumbling blocks and barriers on the way to God, if
not outright antagonists. Let us, then, consider the possibility that the reason we see them that way has nothing to do with them, or with the truth.
Let us consider that perhaps we have laid our sins on them, and see them
looking back at us (W-pII.265.1:1). Let us begin to realize that our perception is truly upside down, and needs to be turned right side up.

May I open my eyes today. May I remind myself with each person I
encounter, or think about, "She (or he) is my savior, my counselor in
sight, the bearer of God's Voice to me." Let me ask, "God, give me the
sight to acknowledge my Self in this person." Let me acknowledge that
seeing anything but this, which God says is their reality, is my own
sickness of mind, my own twisted perception, and let me bring those
perceptions to the Holy Spirit for healing.

WHAT IS THE BODY?

Part 6: W-pII.5.3:4–5

Our minds chose to make the body. We made it from fear, and we
made it to be fearful. Once that purpose is in motion it will continue,
unless the purpose is changed. The body "must serve the purpose given
it" (3:4), and it will continue to serve fear as long as we do not question
the premises on which it was made. It will continue to preserve our separateness, fencing us in, protecting our little self from love.

Our minds have great power, however. Our minds can choose to
change the purpose of the body. Our minds do not serve the body; the
body serves the mind. If, within our minds, we change what we think
the body is for, the body will begin to serve that new purpose. Instead
of using the body to keep love out, we can begin to use the body to

extend love, to express love; to heal rather than to hurt, to communicate rather than to separate, to unite rather than to divide. Instead of being a fence, it can become a medium of communication, the mechanism by which the Love of God can be seen and heard and felt and touched in this world.

This is our function here.

> Fail not in your function of loving in a loveless place made out of darkness and deceit, for thus are darkness and deceit undone. (T-14.IV.4:10)

We are here to express the Love of God, to be the Love of God in this dark and loveless place. God's formless Love takes form in our forgiveness, and in our merciful and grateful acknowledgement of the Christ in all our brothers and sisters (see W-pI.186.14:2), as we reach out our hands to help them on their way (see W-pII.5.4:3).

LESSON 267 ✦ SEPTEMBER 24
"My heart is beating in the peace of God."

Practice instructions

See complete instructions on page 135. A short summary:

- **Read** the commentary paragraph slowly and personally.
- **Pray** the prayer, perhaps several times.
- **Morning and evening:** Repeat the idea and then spend time in Open Mind Meditation.
- **Hourly remembrance:** Repeat the idea and then spend a quiet moment in meditation.
- **Frequent reminders:** Repeat the idea often within each hour.
- **Response to temptation:** Repeat the idea whenever upset, to restore peace.
- **Read the "What Is" section** slowly and thoughtfully once during the day.

Commentary

This is a short Workbook lesson, but very powerful. It is one of those very positive lessons that say wonderful things about us. If most of you are like me—and I am certain you all are to some degree—often when you read a lesson like this, there is a kind of mental filtering going on. The lesson says, "Now is my mind healed" (1:4), and you instantly edit it. "Well, partly." "My mind will be healed some day." "My mind is in the process of being healed." We dilute the meaning. When it says, "Peace fills my heart, and floods my body with the purpose of forgiveness" (1:3), we are tempted to deny that it is so and to think, "Peace is not flooding my heart." The ego is constantly trying to negate the truth about ourselves.

What the Course is saying about us often does not fit the picture of ourselves we have in our mind. The very low opinion of ourselves that we constantly maintain is one of our major problems. When we do a Workbook meditation, we need to practice letting go of that poor self-

313

image for a while. The Course is constantly saying that we actively block from our awareness a true picture of who and what we really are. The Workbook meditations are part of our training in letting go of our self-made picture, and accepting God's picture instead. Somewhere within each of us there is a dim flicker of recognition that this paragraph is about us, and not about some impossibly distant saint. It is that little spark, as the Course calls it, that the Holy Spirit wants to fan into a flame.

That is the whole point of the Course. We are underestimating ourselves, undervaluing ourselves. "I am a messenger of God" (1:6). I really am. I may feel like something much less than that, but I am always that messenger. I always have all I need to save the world.

As you read this lesson today, attempt not to edit the lesson in your mind. When it says, "Now is my mind healed," just let that be true for you right now. Don't worry about how you were all day yesterday. Don't worry about how your mind will be after the meditation is over. Just for that moment, let it be so. Agree with the way the vision of Christ sees you, and say in response, "Yes, now is my mind healed."

Read slowly, to give yourself time to absorb each phrase. We need time, mostly to spot the negative responses that the ego mind will be throwing up and to, quite simply, ignore them. Don't fight or argue with the ego. Just decide, for these few minutes, not to listen. Just decide, for these few minutes, to listen to the Voice for God.

WHAT IS THE BODY?

Part 7: W-pII.5.4:1–2

What a shift there is as paragraph 4 begins! We have been told the body is a fence to separate parts of our Self from other parts (1:1); the body is impermanent (2:1, 3); the "proof" in its death that God's eternal Son can be destroyed (2:9); and a dream, made of fear, made to be fearful (3:1, 4). Now, with a change of purpose, everything suddenly changes: "The body is the means by which God's Son returns to sanity" (4:1).

It's worth stopping and repeating that to myself: "The body is the means by which God's Son returns to sanity." With all the apparently negative things the Course says about the body, this is an astonishing statement. Most of us, certainly myself, could do with a good, solid shot of some positive thoughts about the body like this. I find that making it personal helps to bring it home: "*My* body is the means by which God's Son returns to sanity."

Instead of the negative, almost hateful attitude of some religions towards the body, attitudes that make a person impatient to get out of the body and leave it behind, this statement of the Course gives one an affirmative attitude towards the body. "This body is my way home!" How can the body be our way back to sanity?

It becomes that when we change its purpose. We substitute "the goal of Heaven" in place of "the pursuit of hell" (4:2). We begin to use the body to express and to extend the love that the body was made to shut out, and shut in. Clearly this implies physical activity in the world, since anything involving the body is, by definition, physical. Remember what Jesus said to us back in Review V:

> For this alone I need; that you will hear the words I speak, and give them to the world. You are my voice, my eyes, my feet, my hands through which I save the world.
>
> (W-pI.rV.In.9:2–3)

This is how the body becomes "the means by which God's Son returns to sanity." As we give our bodies to serve God's purposes in this world, using our voices, our eyes, our feet, and our hands to give Jesus' words to the world (perhaps verbally, or by example, or through physical assistance, helping and healing), our minds are healed, along with the minds of those around us. In this physical dream, God needs physical messengers. And you and I are those messengers.

LESSON 268 ✦ SEPTEMBER 25
"Let all things be exactly as they are."

Practice instructions

See complete instructions on page 135. A short summary:

- **Read** the commentary paragraph slowly and personally.
- **Pray** the prayer, perhaps several times.
- **Morning and evening:** Repeat the idea and then spend time in Open Mind Meditation.
- **Hourly remembrance:** Repeat the idea and then spend a quiet moment in meditation.
- **Frequent reminders:** Repeat the idea often within each hour.
- **Response to temptation:** Repeat the idea whenever upset, to restore peace.
- **Read the "What Is" section** slowly and thoughtfully once during the day.

Practice suggestion: When I repeat this idea, I often add an extra word: *"Let all things be exactly as they really are"* (or, making it more specific, *"Let this thing be exactly as it really is"*). The word "really" emphasizes that accepting things as they are does not mean resigning ourselves to the "what is" seen by our eyes. Rather, the world we see is itself our refusal to accept what is, our attempt to be God's critic (1:1), our projection of separation onto Heaven's unity (1:3). Accepting things as they really are means *refusing* to accept the world our eyes see, refusing to accept it as real, and accepting instead only the pristine reality of Heaven as "what is." This is how we "let all things be exactly as they are," and this is how we find our peace.

Commentary

Seen in the light of forgiveness, this lesson teaches us that to criticize what *is* is to judge and condemn God. To let all things be exactly as they are is a form of forgiveness. To insist that things be different is to judge and to be unforgiving. As Paul Ferrini wisely says in his little book *From Ego To Self*,[1] "Only when I resist what is here do I desire what is not."

We are all filled with wishes for how things should be. We are all discontent with things as they are. Is anybody really perfectly content with everything in their life?

Yet this is what this lesson counsels. It could seem to be cruel counsel, both towards myself and towards the world around me. If we are in unpleasant conditions—sick, trapped in a destructive relationship, dying of an illness, financially strapped, miserably unhappy—how can we say in any honesty, "Let all things be exactly as they are"? It seems a horrible thing to affirm.

If we see horrible conditions around us, in family, friends, or the world, with people in some condition like the above, how can we say, "Let it be"?

Our reluctance to say these words under such circumstances testifies to our firm belief that the conditions we see are real. If we believe the suffering is real, of course we do not wish that it continue! We cannot say it if what it means to us is "Let my mother be dying in pain," or "Let my husband continue to drink and beat me." Of course not!

The lesson is really a call to recognize that the conditions of suffering we see are not real. "Only reality is free of pain" (2:2). It is a call to recognize that "nothing real can be threatened [and] nothing unreal exists" (T-In.2:2–3). We cannot say "let it all be" until we first recognize that "all" means only what is real, only what is of God. The rest is illusion.

To say, "Let all things be exactly as they are" is an affirmation of faith that what appears to be pain and suffering is not really there. It is a response to God's call, drawing us up out of the world of conditions and into unconditional truth. It is a phrase that applies not to the world we see with physical eyes, but to the world we can see only with the eyes of Christ. It is an affirmation that we want to see the solid reality behind all the illusion of pain.

It does not mean that we turn our eyes on a brother in suffering and pain, see that, and callously say, "Let that be exactly as it is." That is the old Christian mistake of "It's God's will." It is not God's will that we suffer and die. To think so is to see the error, make it real, and then blame it on God.

This lesson is about not seeing the error at all.

> *Do not see error.* Do not make it real. Select the loving and
> forgive the sin.   (S-2.I.3:3–5)

To say, "Let all things be exactly as they are" is an affirmation that
conditions do not need to change for love to be real. Only the love is
real, no matter what the conditions appear to be; that is what this is proclaiming.

The error, the pain and suffering we see, does not come from God. It
is not, therefore, real. It is only a projection of our collective minds. It
is there because we have allowed ourselves to wish conditions would be
different. Ending the wish for different conditions is the start of dispelling the illusion. Resigning as creator of the universe is what is called
for. We think we can change this, fix that, patch this up, and the world
will be a better place. It is our interference with reality that has made it
what it is! It is our interference that must stop.

While we are in the world of illusion, we must function there sanely. If I cut my finger, I don't let it bleed untended because I know the
body is not real. No, I put a Band-Aid on it. Yet as I do that, let me recognize that what I am doing is "magic." I'm just patching the illusion,
and it isn't really important. It just makes for a more comfortable illusion. Making the illusion more comfortable is fine, but in the end it is
completely irrelevant.

The same therefore applies to extreme conditions. Suppose I am
dying of cancer. Of course I treat it. How I treat it does not really matter. I may use medical therapy. I may try to heal myself through diet. I
may do affirmations and mental conditioning. All of it is magic, all of it
is patching the illusion. In the final evaluation, it does not matter if my
body lives or dies. "Let all things be exactly as they are" in this circumstance means, "What happens to my body is not what counts.
Giving and receiving love counts. I don't need to be free of cancer to be
happy; what happens to my body does not affect who I really am."

If, when ill, I live with a continual insistence that the condition of my
body must change in order for me to be happy, I am merely perpetuat-
ing the error that made me sick in the first place. "Let it be" does not
mean I cease all effort to change conditions, but it does mean I give up
all investment in the outcome. It means that, however the conditions
evolve and manifest, I rest assured that they cannot affect the ultimate

good of all living things.

"I do not perceive my own best interests," says Lesson 24. Saying "let it be" is the natural outcome of realizing our ignorance. Operating from our extremely limited viewpoint, we can still attempt to change conditions, but as we do so, we recognize that there is a lot we don't understand, a lot we haven't taken into consideration because, from the perspective of a separated mind, we simply cannot see it. So we do what we see to do, but we are not attached to the outcome, recognizing that whatever our efforts, the results are in God's Hands, and God's Hands are good Hands.

Jesus praying in the Garden of Gethsemane is an example of this attitude: He said, "Let this cup pass from me: nevertheless not as I will, but as thou [wilt]" (Mt 26:39). From his perspective as a human individual, Jesus did not want to be nailed to a cross. From his trust in God, he could still say, "Let it be unto me as You will."

> It is necessary for the teacher of God to realize, not that
> he should not judge, but that he cannot.　　　(M-10.2:1)

To say "let it be" is to realize this, and to affirm that God's judgment is perfect. We are not to judge anything that happens. "Today I will judge nothing that occurs" (W-pII.243.Heading). That means we don't judge anything bad, and *neither do we judge it good.* We don't judge at all. What is, is. Period. Let it be.

WHAT IS THE BODY?

Part 8: W-pII.5.4:3–4

How does it work out, practically, when we change the purpose of our bodies from murder to miracles, from the pursuit of hell to the goal of Heaven? "The Son of God extends his hand to reach his brother, and to help him walk along the road with him" (4:3). It's that plain and simple. We reach out and help a brother. We put our hand under his elbow when he stumbles and help him walk with us, to God. We allow ourselves to be the first to smile in welcome. We drop our pride and become the first to seek reconciliation in a wounded relationship. We visit a sick friend. We *help* one another.

Some people say that since our only responsibility is accepting the Atonement for ourselves, there is no connection to outward actions. It's all a mental thing. I say, "Bushwa!" Accepting the Atonement for ourselves is the sole responsibility of "miracle workers." This means that if you *do* accept the Atonement, you will work miracles. If you aren't working miracles—bringing healing to those around you— you aren't accepting the Atonement. The two go hand in hand. Read the paragraph in which that "sole responsibility" statement occurs (T-2.V.5), and notice what follows that statement. By accepting the Atonement, your errors are healed and then your mind can only heal. By doing this,

> you place yourself in a position to undo the level confusion of others. The message you then give to them is the truth that their minds are similarly constructive.
> (T-2.V.5:4–5; see entire paragraph)

In order to be a miracle worker, you must accept the Atonement for yourself; to heal the errors of others, you must have your own errors healed first (see M-18.4).

If you are familiar with Christian theology, this confusion about healing myself versus healing others is like the old argument about salvation by grace versus salvation by works. Doing good works will not save you, the Bible says; salvation is only "by grace through faith." And yet, it also says that if you *have* faith you will do good works; the good works are the evidence of the faith. Therefore, "faith without works is dead" (Jas 2:20). Similarly, accepting the Atonement is all that is necessary, but the evidence of doing so, the "proof" you have accepted healing for your own mind, is the extension of miracles of healing to those around you. The Course repeats this over and over, saying that the way you know you are healed is by healing others.

> That is why miracles offer *you* the testimony that you are blessed. If what you offer is complete forgiveness you must have let guilt go, accepting the Atonement for yourself and learning you are guiltless. How could you learn what has been done for you, unknown to you, unless you do what you would have to do if it *had* been done for you?"
> (T-14.I.1:6–8)

So what these sentences are saying (back in "What Is the Body?") is that the body becomes holy as we use it in service to others. By extending our hands to help, we bring healing to our own minds. Reaching out instead of drawing back, seeking to heal rather than to wound, is *how* we accept the Atonement, or better, how we demonstrate to ourselves that we have accepted it. The mind that has accepted Atonement can only heal, and by healing, we know our true Self. Notice here that *the body* "serves to heal the mind" (4:5). Yes; the mind is what needs healing, but the body serves to heal it, by acting in healing love towards our brothers.

---

1. Paul Ferrini, *From Ego to Self* (Greenfield, Mass.: Heartways Press, 1990).

LESSON 269 ✦ SEPTEMBER 26
"My sight goes forth to look upon Christ's face."

Practice instructions

See complete instructions on page 135. A short summary:

- **Read** the commentary paragraph slowly and personally.
- **Pray** the prayer, perhaps several times.
- **Morning and evening:** Repeat the idea and then spend time in Open Mind Meditation.
- **Hourly remembrance:** Repeat the idea and then spend a quiet moment in meditation.
- **Frequent reminders:** Repeat the idea often within each hour.
- **Response to temptation:** Repeat the idea whenever upset, to restore peace.
- **Read the "What Is" section** slowly and thoughtfully once during the day.

Practice suggestion: You may want to apply this idea specifically to people in your life. Say, *"My sight goes forth to look upon Christ's face in [name]."* You might then imagine a giant luminous face of Christ looming behind the body of this person as a symbol of what true perception will show you.

Commentary

Today's lesson is about forgiveness; about choosing in advance to see innocence in others. Let's recall a few things that earlier lessons have taught us about forgiveness.

Lesson 126: *Giving forgiveness is how I receive it.*

How is this lesson on "giving is receiving" related to forgiveness? It discusses how, in the world's understanding of forgiveness, there is no room for us to receive anything from forgiveness. "When you 'forgive' a sin, there is no gain to you directly" (W-pI.126.3:1). If I believe in the reality of someone's sin but "forgive" it, it is just an act of charity to someone unworthy of it. I am giving him a gift he does not deserve. It could easily appear that I in fact am losing something, not gaining anything. There is no release for me in doing something like this.

Only when I have truly received forgiveness for myself can I give it; and only in giving it do I recognize I have received it. I don't even know what it is! How could I recognize it? So in order to know what forgiveness is, and to know that I have it, I have to give it away. I have to see it "out there" to recognize it "in here." When I do I will also begin to understand that there is no difference between out there and in here.

The idea that giving is receiving, that the "giver and receiver are the same" (W-pI.126.8:1), is a necessary preparation for releasing our minds from every bar to what forgiveness really is. Judgment is based on separation and differences: the sin is in someone else and not in me. He is bad, I am better. Forgiveness is based on unity and sameness: there is no "other" to be done to or to do it to me. We are both innocent. There never was any sin. We are all part of the same Heart of Love.

Lesson 134: *True forgiveness forgives illusions, not real sins.*

Here we learn that the major obstacle to learning true forgiveness is the belief that we must forgive something real. We believe that sin really exists, that injury has really been done. It is impossible to forgive a sin that we believe is real. "It is impossible to think of sin as true and not believe forgiveness is a lie" (W-pI.134.4:2). "Guilt cannot be forgiven" (W-pI.134.5:3).

This is really a major obstacle. I can testify that it is possible for something you once thought of as sin to be seen as no more than a mistake, a call for love. I've experienced that. I didn't make the shift myself. We can't do it ourselves. But we do need to be willing to have the shift occur. I know there are many things that, consciously or unconsciously, I still judge and condemn as sin, as evil. Every time I encounter judgment in my mind, I need do nothing but recognize that it is there and believe that there is another way to perceive it. I affirm I am willing to see it differently. I ask for help in understanding forgiveness through this experience. And I wait.

I allow myself to look at the anger, the fear, the resentment I may be feeling. I don't hide it; that just perpetuates the wrong-mindedness. I am willing to see my own feelings differently as well. I recognize that perhaps I am judging myself for feeling them. So, as I did with the external judgment, I do with the internal: I affirm I am willing to see it differently and ask for help. And I wait.

What happens then is of God. A shift occurs in my mind. It may occur first in regard to the other, the "sinner"; it may occur first in regard to myself. Since the other and myself are one and the same it doesn't matter how it is experienced, or in what order. In the shift, I come to see something I am judging, in the other or in myself, as a call for love. I come to see that regardless of the appearance it takes, innocence lay behind the act. I may see that I was angry because I wanted to be close to the other person and they pushed me away; I wanted joining, oneness. There is nothing to be guilty of there. I thought I saw attack and attacked back. Now I see there was no attack; we both want the same thing, so I let go of my attack and respond with love. Or I may see how the other person was fearful, felt threatened by me somehow (and I know I am not a threat), and so flipped out. My return attack was just the same mistake. I see there was no sin in what happened, and the whole thing can simply be dropped from my mind.

Today's lesson: *We see innocence when we choose to see it.*

"My sight goes forth to look upon Christ's face." "Today I choose to see a world forgiven" (1:5). Seeing the "face of Christ" is a symbolic way of saying we see innocence, we see a world forgiven.

In this lesson we see that forgiveness is a choice. When we decide that what we want to see is innocence, we will see innocence. The Holy Spirit will give us the gift of that sight. "What I look on belongs to me" (1:5). If I see mistakes out there, they are my mistakes. If I see innocence, it too is my own. If I can see innocence—and I will if I choose to, I will if I ask to—it is the proof of my own innocence. Only the innocent can perceive innocence. Only those who perceive innocence in others know their own innocence. The guilty will always perceive guilt. Perceiving innocence in others is the means God has given us to discover our own innocence. We can't find it if we look directly. It's like trying to see your own face; you must have a mirror. The world is my mirror; it shows me the state of my own mind. The image in the glass is only an image, only an illusion, but in this world it is a necessary illusion, and will be until there is a knowing that exists without perception.

WHAT IS THE BODY?

Part 9: W-pII.5.5:1–3

What was pointed out in Lesson 261 is echoed here: "You will identify with what you think will make you safe" (5:1; see W-pII.261.1). If we think our physicality and individual identity are what make us safe, we will identify with them; if we understand that being the love that we are is what gives us safety, we will identify with that, rather than the body and ego. If we identify with the body, our life becomes a cramped, futile attempt to preserve and protect it. If we identify with love, the body becomes simply a tool used to express our own loving being, which is God expressed through us.

"Your safety lies in truth, and not in lies" (5:3). The body is a lie about us; it is not what we are. The truth about us is that we are love: "Teach only love, for that is what you are" (T-6.I.13:2). That is where our true safety lies, and that is what we must learn to identify with.

What seems "more real" to me today? My body, or my loving Self? Where does my emphasis lie? On what do I center most of my time and attention? What takes most of my care and concern? The practice of the Workbook lessons can be very revealing in this regard, as I begin to realize that rarely, if ever, do I fail to take care of my body, giving it food, clothing, cleansing, and sleep. How well do I care for my spirit? When my attention to my spiritual needs and to the expression of my inner nature has become paramount, when I would rather miss breakfast than miss my quiet time with God, I will know that I have begun to shift my identity from lies to truth.

If in observing myself I realize that this is not yet the case, let me not make myself guilty about it. Guilt accomplishes nothing positive. My identification with the body is not a sin. It is simply a mistake, and an indication that I need to practice unlearning that identification, and learning to identify with love instead. When I practice guitar and notice that I am missing a certain chord, I do not feel guilty about it; I just intensify my practice of that particular song until I learn it.

I can even use my habit of identifying with the body to help me form a new focus. When I shower or wash my face I can use the time to mentally repeat the day's lesson and think about its meaning to me. (What other more valuable thing is occupying your mind at those times, anyhow?) When I eat, I can remember to give thanks, and let it be a trigger to remember God. If I am alone, perhaps I can read a page from the Course, or a lesson card, while I eat. I can make the body into a tool to help me walk the road to God.

LESSON 270 ✦ SEPTEMBER 27
"I will not use the body's eyes today."

Practice instructions

See complete instructions on page 135. A short summary:

- **Read** the commentary paragraph slowly and personally.
- **Pray** the prayer, perhaps several times.
- **Morning and evening:** Repeat the idea and then spend time in Open Mind Meditation.
- **Hourly remembrance:** Repeat the idea and then spend a quiet moment in meditation.
- **Frequent reminders:** Repeat the idea often within each hour.
- **Response to temptation:** Repeat the idea whenever upset, to restore peace.
- **Read the "What Is" section** slowly and thoughtfully once during the day.

Commentary

Of course this does not mean I will walk around with a blindfold on, crashing into things. I will not, however, let my sight stop at the physical. I won't "use" the information of the eyes, I won't depend on that.

> Christ's vision...has the power to translate all that the body's eyes behold into the sight of a forgiven world.
>
> (1:1)

There's that word "translate" again. What I want to see, today, my Teacher, is a forgiven world. I want to see the truth behind all appearances. My function, the function of every Son of God, is that of a translator. We are here to heal the world by seeing it differently, and thus we also heal ourselves.

One of the chief components of that different vision is *lack of judgment*. No condemnation. No making wrong. No demand for outward changes. Seeing that everyone and everything is worthy of love, exactly as they are. No comparisons or evaluations, no making of differences, but seeing everything as part of one whole.

> To forgive is to overlook. Look, then, beyond error and do not let your perception rest upon it, for you will believe what your perception holds. Accept as true only what your brother is, if you would know yourself. Perceive what he is not, and you cannot know what you are, because you see him falsely. (T-9.IV.1:2–5)

> You do not understand how to overlook errors, or you would not make them. (T-9.IV.2:2)

We are told to overlook error. Then we are told we don't know how to do it. Instead, we are to turn to the Holy Spirit. It seems to me a fundamental lesson of the Course is "Don't trust your perceptions." Don't use the body's eyes. Don't think that seeing begins and ends with physical sight and our own mental interpretations.

What we do as we go through the world is something like this: We perceive something. Our mind may interpret it, almost certainly will, and nearly always with some evaluation, some judgment. At that point, what we need to do is recognize that judgment is impossible for us, and just let it go. We abandon our perception. We don't think of it as dangerous, or fearful, or sinful; we just recognize that it is meaningless (see M-16.10:8). That giving up of our own perceptions is the crucial step. "And for this 'sacrifice' is Heaven restored to his awareness" (M-16.10:10).

We step back and take what appears to be a very inferior position. We say, "I do not understand what this means." This is the *very first lesson* in the Workbook, "Nothing I see…means anything" (W-pI.1.Heading).

And then we open ourselves to the Holy Spirit. "I am willing to see things differently." That's it. If you get this far, you will become hooked, because God will answer that prayer. You *will* see things differently. Maybe not at once, not in that instant, but it happens. How? I don't know! Understanding the *how* of the Atonement is not our job, not our function, but His.

WHAT IS THE BODY?

Part 10: W-pII.5.5:4–8

> Love is your safety. Fear does not exist.　　　(5:4–5)

When I do not use the body's eyes, this is what I will see. When I let go of my unquestioning trust in my perception of things, I will see love. My body's eyes were made out of fear and made to see fear. I need to end my reliance on this mechanism of perception, and ask for a new one: Christ's vision.

The statement "Fear does not exist" may seem incredible to me, particularly as I advance in my practice of the Course, because one of the consequences of practicing the Course is that all kinds of buried fears bubble up in my mind. The Course teaches me, however, that what has happened is this: In order to hide my own true nature of love from me, my ego invented all kinds of fear; then I found them so terrifying that I repressed or denied them and covered them over with deceptive disguises, supported by my perception of the world. Now, as I let go of my confidence in my perception, the disguises are dissolving, and the fears I have buried are surfacing. This simple message, then, is an antidote to those surfacing fears: "Fear does not exist." In other words, what I am seeing is not real; it is an illusion I have made.

How can I escape from my fears?

> Identify with love, and you are safe. Identify with love, and you are home. Identify with love, and find your Self.
> 　　　　　　　　　　　　　　　　(5:6–8)

As I begin to look within, I see all these different forms of fear. Rather than fighting the fear, or running from it, or burying it again, I need to learn to see past it to the love it is hiding. We have to go through what the Course calls "the ring of fear" in order to reach our Self, our home (see T-18.IX, especially paragraphs 3 and 4). This is where most of us get stuck. The fear seems too real.

Let me, today, allow the Holy Spirit to show me that this seemingly impenetrable wall of fear is really nothing. It is made of clouds that cannot stop a feather. Let me take His hand and allow Him to lead me past it to the truth, to my Self, and to my home. Let me choose to identify with love, and find my safety.

IX

Lessons 271 - 280
What Is the Christ?

"Christ's is the vision I will use today."

Practice instructions

See complete instructions on page 135. A short summary:

- **Read** the commentary paragraph slowly and personally.
- **Pray** the prayer, perhaps several times.
- **Morning and evening:** Repeat the idea and then spend time in Open Mind Meditation.
- **Hourly remembrance:** Repeat the idea and then spend a quiet moment in meditation.
- **Frequent reminders:** Repeat the idea often within each hour.
- **Response to temptation:** Repeat the idea whenever upset, to restore peace.
- **Read the "What Is" section** slowly and thoughtfully once during the day.

Commentary

Once again the Workbook faces us with the fact that we *choose* what we want to see, and see it. It tells us this process is going on continuously, constantly: "Each day, each hour, every instant, I am choosing what I want to look upon, the sounds I want to hear, the witnesses to what I want to be the truth for me" (1:1). The latter part of that sentence is significant because it gives us the *reason* for our choice: we choose to see what we want to be the truth for ourselves. For instance, if I am constantly seeing people who are victims, it is because there is a part of me that wants to be a victim. I may think that I do not want to be a victim, but if the alternative is to be responsible for everything that happens to me—it sounds pretty good! Every time I see a victim, I am secretly wanting to be able to blame someone else for my faults.

The main point of this lesson is not our negative choices, however. The point is that there is a choice. There is an alternative. If I listen to the ego my choice will be to see sin, guilt, fear, and death. If I listen to the Holy Spirit, however, I will want something different to be the truth about myself, and therefore I will want to see something else in the world—and I will see it. Seeing it in the world is how I will know it is the truth about myself. Instead of wanting to see witnesses to sin, I will want to see witnesses to the truth, and what I look for I will find.

As my perception merges more and more with Christ's vision, I will approach the point where perception will entirely disappear (1:3). The changed perception will show me what the Course calls the real world; the disappearance of perception refers to the end of the world and our awakening to Heaven.

How do I want to see myself? If I want to see myself as love, let me seek today to see love in my brothers and sisters. If I want to see myself as innocent, let me look for innocence in others. If I want to see myself as without guilt, let me seek to see others without guilt. Today, let me remember:

> When you meet anyone, remember it is a holy encounter. As you see him you will see yourself. As you treat him you will treat yourself. As you think of him you will think of yourself. (T-8.III.4:1–4)

> Each one you see in light brings your light closer to your awareness. (T-13.VI.10:3)

Teach no one that he is what you would not want to be.

(T-7.VII.3:8)

WHAT IS THE CHRIST?

Part 1: W-pII.6.1:1–2

Christ is God's Son as He created Him. (1:1)

This is what we are learning to see in one another, so that we can remember to see Him in ourselves. Christ is the original creation of God, before we "remade" him, and painted another image over God's masterpiece. We wanted to be something else, and so we have perceived something else in everyone around us. Now, we are learning to look past the images we have made to rediscover the hidden masterpiece beneath the forgery.

He is the Self we share, uniting us with one another, and with God as well. (1:2)

Christ is *the* Son of God. We all are aspects of that one Son. (I believe that part of the reason the Course uses "Son" rather than "sons and daughters" is because the latter phrase denotes a separation which does not exist in God's creation.) Our original Self, our only real Self, is a Self we share with everyone. One reason we resist knowing this Self is that it is not "my" self alone; it is *our* Self. To claim Christ as my Self, I cannot exclude anyone, because the Self I am claiming is a universal Self, of which everyone is a part.

Not only are we united with one another in this Self, we are also united with God as well (1:2). Without God this Self would not exist; He sources It and sustains It. It cannot *be* apart from Him. It cannot be independent of Him. Nor can It oppose Him in any way; all of the characteristics of this Self arise and emerge out of God's own Being.

LESSON 272 ✦ SEPTEMBER 29
"How can illusions satisfy God's Son?"

Practice instructions

See complete instructions on page 135. A short summary:

- **Read** the commentary paragraph slowly and personally.
- **Pray** the prayer, perhaps several times.
- **Morning and evening:** Repeat the idea and then spend time in Open Mind Meditation.
- **Hourly remembrance:** Repeat the idea and then spend a quiet moment in meditation.
- **Frequent reminders:** Repeat the idea often within each hour.
- **Response to temptation:** Repeat the idea whenever upset, to restore peace.
- **Read the "What Is" section** slowly and thoughtfully once during the day.

Practice comments: Notice the response to temptation instructions in paragraph 2. They ask us to watch our minds today for any instance in which we hear some earthly thing "call to us to stay and linger in a dream" (2:2). Instead of answering this call, "we turn aside and ask ourselves" (2:2), *"How can illusions satisfy God's Son?"* I recommend trying this practice now. Think of an earthly thing that is calling to you. See your mind going toward it, but then turn aside and ask yourself, *"How can illusions satisfy me, when I am God's Son?"*

Commentary

The Course, like some TV commercials, is telling us to accept no substitutes. We want "the real thing" (Classic version, of course). The irony of it is that most of the time we allow ourselves to be satisfied with illusions: illusions of love (special love relationships), illusions of safety (financial security), illusions of meaning (fame, worldly rewards and recognition). We allow ourselves to be content with dreams, and sometimes even dreams within the dream, such as drugs and fantasies.

We do need lessons like these. We need to ask ourselves, "Can illusions bring me happiness?" (1:4). We know the answer if we are willing to ask the question. A Christian writer and missionary, Jim Elliot, once wrote, "He is no fool who gives what he cannot keep to gain what he cannot lose."[1] Another missionary, Amy Carmichael, wrote, "It is the life that has no time for trifling that tells."[2] When the glitter of the world attracts us, when a special relationship seems to promise us meaning and fulfillment here, in the world, let me remind myself: "I will accept no less than what You have given me" (1:6).

We may find temporary pleasure and satisfaction in some of our illusions. Ultimately, however, nothing can satisfy us but the memory of God (1:5). Nothing can bring complete contentment except the knowledge that "I am surrounded by Your Love, forever still, forever gentle and forever safe" (1:7). Today, will I pursue yet another illusion? Or will I use my time wisely, and choose Heaven and the peace of God?

WHAT IS THE CHRIST?

Part 2: W-pII.6.1:3–5

Christ is "the Thought Which still abides within the Mind that is His Source" (1:3). The Course teaches us that our reality is a Thought within the Mind of God. Over and over the Course insists that ideas do not leave their source. They remain within the mind that is thinking them. An idea cannot be separate from a mind; it is a part of the mind, a function of the mind that thinks it. And we are just like that in relation to God. Separation between our Self and the Mind of God is no more possible than separation between an idea and the mind that thinks it.

My true Self, your true Self, our true Self, is the Christ. Our Self has never left our holy home (1:4) in God's Mind. That is fact. Based on that fact, anything that appears to be contrary to it must be a lie, an illusion. We are not wandering, lost, in this world, we are "at home in God, dreaming of exile" (T-10.I.2:1). Our separation is only a dream, not a reality; this is why the Course is so certain of the final outcome.

We have not left God, and because we have not, we have not lost our innocence (1:4, also W-pI.182.12:1). All the awful things we may think we have done or said have no reality in truth; they are part of the dream of exile. We are still at home. Have you ever had a dream in which you did something terrible or embarrassing, and then wakened, terrified, horrified, only to experience a sudden relief? "It was only a dream!" All of us, one day, will have that experience on a grand scale; we will awaken to realize that this whole world was a dream that never happened. Despite all that we have imagined, we will awaken and find ourselves "unchanged forever in the Mind of God" (1:5).

---

1. Quoted in Elizabeth Elliot, *Shadow of the Almighty: The Life and Testament of Jim Elliot* (San Francisco: HarperSanFranciso, 1989).
2. Amy Carmichael, *God's Missionary* (Fort Washington, Penn.: CLC Publications, 2002).

LESSON 273 ✦ SEPTEMBER 30
"The stillness of the peace of God is mine."

Practice instructions

See complete instructions on page 135. A short summary:

- **Read** the commentary paragraph slowly and personally.
- **Pray** the prayer, perhaps several times.
- **Morning and evening:** Repeat the idea and then spend time in Open Mind Meditation.
- **Hourly remembrance:** Repeat the idea and then spend a quiet moment in meditation.
- **Frequent reminders:** Repeat the idea often within each hour.
- **Response to temptation:** Repeat the idea whenever upset, to restore peace.
- **Read the "What Is" section** slowly and thoughtfully once during the day.

Practice comments: Today's lesson again provides instructions for response to temptation. Whenever you give way to a disturbance today, tell your mind with certainty, *"The stillness of the peace of God is mine."* You then might add some related thoughts based on this lesson's teaching, such as *"Nothing can intrude upon the peace God gave His Son,"* or *"Nothing can rob me of what He would have me keep."*

Commentary

I love the way the Course makes room for all of us, whatever our level of attainment. Some of us, it says, may be "ready for a day of undisturbed tranquility" (1:1). And for some of us, this may not yet be "feasible" (1:2). If we have done the Workbook lessons from the beginning, we have already done 272 lessons. Yet a day of undisturbed tranquility may not yet be feasible. "Feasible" means "possible" or "doable." There is no sense of putdown in this, no tone of saying, "Some of you haven't been doing your work." It simply says it isn't possible for you—yet. Even the "yet" has meaning, because it clearly states that it *will* be possible for us eventually.

The author of the Course has total confidence in every one of us. Not just those of us doing the Course, but every one of us. One day, it will be possible for me, for you, and for everyone to spend a day in "undisturbed tranquility." Isn't that wonderful to think about, if you aren't at that place yet?

> Do you want a quietness that cannot be disturbed, a gentleness that never can be hurt, a deep, abiding comfort, and a rest so perfect it can never be upset?
> All this forgiveness offers you, and more.
> (W-pI.122.1:6–2:1)

The lesson suggests to us that if we are not yet ready to spend a day in perfect peace, we can still be "content and even more than satisfied" (1:2). The way *to* peace is also a way *of* peace. There is no need to be upset because we cannot yet be perfectly peaceful! To lose what peace we have because we are not *perfectly* at peace is not a productive state of mind to be in. We can be at peace about not being at peace. That is where we begin. We are content and satisfied to learn how a day of undisturbed tranquility is possible.

We need to be happy learners, happy to be learning how to be peaceful, even while we are not yet peaceful. And how do we learn that?

> If we give way to a disturbance, let us learn how to dismiss it and return to peace. We need but tell our minds, with certainty, "The stillness of the peace of God is mine," and nothing can intrude upon the peace that God Himself has given to His Son. (1:3–4)

In other words, we simply instruct our minds that peace has been given us by God. When disturbance arises, we "dismiss it." This is the practice of mental vigilance so often taught in the Text. We do not allow the disturbance to remain undisturbed; we recognize it as something we do not want, and instruct our minds to return to peace.

It says we do this "with certainty." This is not a striving, trying to shout down the ego. It is gentle but firm, calm and not anxious. We are telling our minds, "Peace, be still." There is no stressed-out way to peace. The words "The stillness of the peace of God is mine" come from a place within us that is always at peace. In speaking them to ourselves with quiet certainty, we have already connected with that place of peace within us.

> *And so the peace You gave Your Son is with me still, in*
> *quietness and in my own eternal love for You.* (2:4)

WHAT IS THE CHRIST?

Part 3: W-pII.6.2:1–3

Christ is the link that keeps us one with God (2:1). If we have any awareness at all of the Christ within us, it seems as if He is only a part of us, perhaps a small part or an obscure part. That is not the reality (3:2), but that is how it seems. And yet every one of us is aware of *some-thing* in us that is more than what we appear to be, something that links us to God. We probably would not be reading this Course if we did not have that awareness. And this part, small and obscure as it may seem, links us to God. Somehow we know that.

If that link is real, then the separation is not real. It is "no more than an illusion of despair" (2:1). If we are linked with God, one with Him, then we are not separate, and everything that seems to tell us we are must be illusion. In every one of us, in the Christ within us, "hope for-ever will abide" (2:1). Something in us knows that this is true. The link with God has not been broken. Each of us has this hidden ally in our hearts. Within me, within you, there is the Christ. The Course relies on this fact totally because Jesus, who remembered his Christ Self fully, *knows* that it is so.

> Your mind is part of His, and His of yours. (2:2)

He is there, in you. And you are in Him. All we are doing is, as the Bible says, to let the mind of Christ be in us. We are recognizing this part of our minds we have denied and doubted. His mind is in us, and this is our salvation. It is part of us; we cannot be rid of it, even if we want to.

In this part of our mind, "God's Answer lies" (2:3). The Answer to separation. The Answer to pain and suffering. The Answer to despair.

The Answer to every problem. The Answer is in you. The Answer is *part of you*. It is not outside, not to be found in something in this world, nor in someone else. You already have it. You already *are* it. The Answer is *in you*.

In this part of your mind, "all decisions are already made, and dreams are over" (2:3). What this is saying is so wonderful we can scarcely believe it. There is a part of our minds in which we all, every one of us, have *already decided for God*. We have already chosen peace. We have already relinquished all attack and judgment. And all of our dreams are already over. Armed with this knowledge we can be absolutely certain that we will "make it." Because the Christ in us has already made it.

All that remains to be done is to recognize that this "part" of us is really all there is. All that remains is to let go of everything else but this. We do not need to attain enlightenment; we need only accept that it is already accomplished. This is the truth, and all we are doing in this world is learning to "*deny the denial of truth*" (T-12.II.1:5), to let go of all the "blocks to the awareness of love's presence, which is your natural inheritance" (T-In.1:7).

LESSON 274 ✦ OCTOBER 1

"Today belongs to Love. Let me not fear."

Practice instructions

See complete instructions on page 135. A short summary:

- **Read** the commentary paragraph slowly and personally.
- **Pray** the prayer, perhaps several times.
- **Morning and evening:** Repeat the idea and then spend time in Open Mind Meditation.
- **Hourly remembrance:** Repeat the idea and then spend a quiet moment in meditation.
- **Frequent reminders:** Repeat the idea often within each hour.
- **Response to temptation:** Repeat the idea whenever upset, to restore peace.
- **Read the "What Is" section** slowly and thoughtfully once during the day.

Practice suggestion: Pick someone whom you expect to deal with today, but whom you'd rather avoid. Say to him or her:

I let you be as God created you.
I give you the honor due your sinlessness.
I love you like a brother and like a friend.

Commentary

Give this day to Him, and there will be no fear today, because the day is given unto Love.   (2:2)

Fear is what happens when we shut off our awareness to Love. It is nothing but the illusory absence of Love—"illusory" because Love is never absent. Nothing but Love exists. Like the physical sun, Love is always shining. We say sometimes that "the sun isn't out today." In fact, of course, the sun is out, but there is interference, clouds, something in between which is blocking our awareness of the sun. We then experience darkness, which is no more than the absence of light. Darkness is nothing in itself. When the interference is removed, light is there, just as it always was.

So too, when we remove the interference to our awareness of Love, Love is there and fear is gone. If we give this day to Love, there will be no fear.

It is easy to see how we can understand any form of fear as no more than a call for Love. "Fear is a symptom of your own deep sense of loss" (T-12.I.9:1). Fear is how we feel when Love appears to be absent; therefore, it is simply an automatic cry for Love's presence. It is a call for Love, and nothing more. Fear can take many forms—anger, worry, sadness, jealousy, sickness, or an addictive desire for a thing or for a person—but all of these are just forms of fear. When I am aware of them in myself, let me bring them to the Holy Spirit so that He can reinterpret them (see T-12.I.8:8–9), so that I can understand that all forms of fear are nothing but an unconscious call for Love (see T-12.I.8:13), and therefore they are nothing to be guilty about.

When I was a child I believed that all sickness was caused by germs. I had a pretty clear understanding that some kind of invader bugs got into my body and messed things up; I could understand that. Even if metaphysically this is not a true picture, nor even wholly true scientifically, it was what I believed to be the truth. That was what real sickness was for me.

One day I was riding in the back seat of the car on a long drive, reading a comic book. I started to feel sick. I guess I had never experienced motion sickness before, so I must have been quite young. I thought I was "getting sick," and told my parents to stop the car because I was going to be sick. I went into a service station restroom. As I walked in I felt less sick. I used the toilet, and after a few minutes, I felt fine. I was utterly baffled; what had happened to the sickness?

When I returned to the car and told my parents, they said, "Oh! You must have been feeling carsick." They explained to me that sometimes motion can make you feel sick, but that it isn't the same as having the flu. I remember clearly saying something like, "You mean I'm not really sick? I just feel sick?" They more or less agreed with my interpretation. They told me it had to do with the mind being confused because my eyes were looking at something motionless while the rest of my body felt motion. In effect, they told me the sickness was caused by false perception in my mind!

In my young mind, something clicked. I wanted to read that comic book! Even though my parents advised against it, I went back to reading it. I started to feel sick again. But I now knew the truth that I wasn't really sick! This was a false sickness. There was no real reason (i.e., germs) to be sick. My mind was doing it to me, so my mind could undo it. So, despite the nausea and pain in my stomach, I went on reading. "I'm not really sick," I told myself. And the nausea went away, and I never had motion sickness again in my life, except one time on an ocean liner in a very heavy storm, after all eleven hundred people on the ship had thrown up except for me and another dozen or so—I guess the "evidence" was just too overwhelming.

Just as that day I convinced myself that my sickness was not real— a very clear lesson in my life of the power of the mind—the Holy Spirit wants to convince us that our fears are not real. Just as I realized that day that nothing was truly wrong with my body, He wants us to know that when we are feeling fear, nothing is really wrong with our minds. Despite what we perceive in the world, the Holy Spirit wants us to know that the fear is being manufactured by our own minds; it is not real, because Love is never absent and therefore there is no real reason for fear. You may feel fear in one of its many forms—He never asks us to deny that, instead He asks us to look at it and recognize it very clearly— but He does ask us to realize that what we are feeling is false. It has no cause. It is just something manufactured by a mind that has blinded itself to the truth. We don't even need to cure our fear, because the sickness isn't real!

We will either love our brothers or fear them; those are the only two emotions in this world, according to the Course (see T-12.I.9:5). To give the day to Love means, then, that we will not react with fear to our brothers. We will "let all things be as You created them" (1:1), and therefore we will honor our brothers in their sinlessness. We will give each of them, as the Son of God, "the love of brother to his brother and his Friend" (1:1).

The path of the Course lies here, in learning to let go of our fears and to respond to one another with love instead, honoring what we all are in truth, instead of fearing what our brothers or sisters appear to be. This is how we are redeemed (1:2); this is how light replaces all the darkness in the world (1:3).

Today belongs to Love. Let me not fear.

WHAT IS THE CHRIST?

Part 4: W-pII.6.2:4,5

The Christ is the part of our mind in which God's Answer lies (2:3). This part of our mind "remains untouched by anything the body's eyes perceive" (2:4). Our mind, as we are aware of it, is more than merely touched by what our eyes perceive; it is dominated by it, controlled by it, and tossed about like a leaf in the wind (as advertisers well know!). But there is something in us, somewhere in us, according to this statement, that is untouched and unmoved by our physical perceptions. It remains perfectly calm no matter what seems to be happening around us. It remains perfectly loving, no matter what assault is made upon our love. This is the Christ, our true Self.

It is this part of ourselves we are practicing to become aware of. This is the quiet center of our being that we are seeking to connect with in the holy instants we spend, quietly listening. This is the Voice that we attempt to hear, a Voice of majestic stillness and complete tranquility. The Christ is not some alien being, something apart from us that we must learn, somehow, to emulate. He *is* our Self. He is like the eye of the hurricane. When our minds are agitated and seemingly out of control, we can, if we are willing to leave the objects of our turmoil behind, enter that eye of the storm and find the peace within ourselves that is always, always there. The moment we do, the change is so startling it is unmistakable. The howling of the wind ceases. The blast of the elements suddenly stops. There is nothing but peace. In this still center of our being, all of the events of our lives that have driven us to and fro, helpless in their grip, have absolutely no effect whatsoever. And in that moment we know, "This is Who I am."

Because of our confusion of mind, because we have made a seeming problem where there is none, the Father has placed in Christ the "means for your salvation" (2:5), the Answer to our illusions. And yet this Christ remains untouched by the "problems" themselves, pristinely pure; He "knows no sin" (2:5). The Answer to sin is incorporated within Him, and yet in Him the problem being answered does not even exist. Christ's perfection has not been sullied by our madness. He is still as perfect as the day he was created. And *He* is *me*. "I am the holy Son of God Himself" (W-pI.191.Heading). Here, in the stillness of Christ's being, I know that all my "sins" are nothing, and without effect of any kind. Here I am more than guiltless; I am holy. All things are holy. And nothing unreal exists.

LESSON 275 ✦ OCTOBER 2
"God's healing Voice protects all things today."

Practice instructions

See complete instructions on page 135. A short summary:

- **Read** the commentary paragraph slowly and personally.
- **Pray** the prayer, perhaps several times.
- **Morning and evening:** Repeat the idea and then spend time in Open Mind Meditation.
- **Hourly remembrance:** Repeat the idea and then spend a quiet moment in meditation.
- **Frequent reminders:** Repeat the idea often within each hour.
- **Response to temptation:** Repeat the idea whenever upset, to restore peace.
- **Read the "What Is" section** slowly and thoughtfully once during the day.

Commentary

Jesus tells us in this lesson that we need to join him in hearing the Voice for God (1:3). "For the Voice for God tells us of things we cannot understand alone, nor learn apart" (1:4). Notice that the joining Jesus urges on us here is not primarily with one another, with other people, although that is certainly implied; it is joining with him that is called for.

If the problem is a belief in the reality of separation, that problem cannot be healed alone and apart. Being alone and apart is the problem! Any healing, any salvation, any enlightenment that the Voice for God brings to us will be something that is shared.

I can join with Jesus in hearing the Voice for God; that is something I can do now, in the privacy of my home, with no other people around. What I hear—which is always some form of the message "God's Son is innocent"—is something that applies to Jesus as well as to me, and to me as well as to Jesus. I share it with him. Peace, safety, and protection come in letting go of any mental defenses I have against Jesus and allowing his presence to be with me. I own and acknowledge that Jesus and I share a common goal and common interests. I see that he has no attack in his heart toward me, and I have none toward him. "It is in this [joining] that all things are protected" (1:5).

As I move out into the world, to meet with other people, I can extend what I have found in Jesus' presence to everyone I meet. What he and I have heard together is shared, not only between the two of us, but also with the Son of God in everyone. I hear the Father's healing Voice, and it protects all things, so that "I need be anxious over nothing" (2:2). All beings share this common interest and common goal. We are all in the world for this one purpose. Any perception of competition or attack on my part, or on the part of another, is merely a mistake in perception, and is not anything to be afraid of.

"The safety that I bring is given me" (2:4). I bring safety from my companionship with Jesus to the world, and as I give it, it is given to me. "Everyone I meet is safe with me today," I can say. "And I am safe with everyone I meet." Each encounter is holy because I am holy. When the purpose of the day is thus set as it begins, I can be sure of full direction. We will be given very specific directions for our activity here within this world, even if the world is only an illusion: "For Your Voice will tell me what to do and where to go; to whom to speak and what to say to him, what thoughts to think, what words to give the world" (2:3).

It is a healing Voice I hear, a healing that consists in sharing, in joining, in having no separate interests. The joining is the healing. "The healing of God's Son is what the world is for" (T-24.VI.4:1), and the healing of God's Son in myself and everyone I meet is what this day is for. Nothing else. Let today be a day when I especially listen for the Voice. Let me "seek and hear and learn and understand" (1:2).

Alan Watts wrote a book called *The Wisdom of Insecurity*.[1] As I remember, it speaks about how seeking security is unwise because security for the ego and the body simply is not possible. If you are constantly seeking security you will drive yourself nuts. It is much better and wiser to accept the fact of insecurity and to simply go with the flow of the universe.

When this lesson speaks of how listening to the Voice protects all things, it is really saying the same thing. We recognize that we don't know the answers, we can't figure everything out. We don't know "what to do and where to go; to whom to speak and what to say to him, what thoughts to think, what words to give the world," but He does. Instead of constantly trying to acquire the answers for ourselves, we stay in relationship with the Answer Himself, the One who does know. Instead of having millions of our own in the bank, we trust that what we need will be given as we need it, and don't worry about it. We leave the running of the universe in God's Hands.

Our safety and protection is not something that resides in us, alone and apart. It comes only from listening to the Voice moment to moment. We don't know the road to heaven, but we walk with One who does.

WHAT IS THE CHRIST?

Part 5: W-pII.6.3:1–3

Christ, our Self, is "Home of the Holy Spirit" (3:1). The Course often refers to the Holy Spirit as "the Voice for God"; this Voice emanates from our Self, the Christ. This is His Home, where the Holy Spirit "resides," so to speak. When we sense an inner prodding in a certain direction, or, as was the case with Helen Schucman (who wrote down the Course), we seem to hear actual words spoken within our minds, it is the presence within us of this "part" of our mind that makes this possible. Christ is "the link that keeps you one with God" (2:1). If the Christ did not exist within us, we would not be hearing these messages, because the link with God would be nonexistent. (To go a bit further, if there were no link with God we would not exist at all!) Therefore, the fact that we *do* sense these inner messages moving us in the direction of God and of love proves that a link to God must still exist within us. That, in turn, validates what the Course is saying: we are not separated from God.

Secondly, Christ is "at home in God alone" (3:1). Again this is borne out in our experience. The feeling of not being at home in this world is almost universally acknowledged; at one time or another, it seems that everyone has felt this way, some more strongly than others, perhaps, though we have all felt this to some degree. Where does that feeling come from? Is it not possible that we *are not* at home in this world? Given the widespread nature of this experience, is it not likely that there is some part of us, at least, which actually is not at home here at all, but only in God? The Course advises us to listen to this inner voice that seems to be calling us to come home to a home we cannot clearly remember, but which, somehow, we know to be real (see especially "The Forgotten Song" in the Text [T-21.I], or "I will be still an instant and go home" [Lesson 182]).

Christ remains "at peace within the Heaven of your holy mind" (3:1), as we have already discussed in the last day or two. Whatever may be happening externally, the Christ part of our minds stays eternally peaceful.

> This is the only part of you that has reality in truth. The rest
> is dreams. (3:2–3)

This is really a key statement. For most of us, this eternally peaceful part of our minds seems very distant and hidden, something which, perhaps, we connect with in times of deep meditation. The "real" part of our consciousness seems to be the agitated and confused part. The Christ within we may acknowledge to be real, but it seems to be only a small part of what we are. In reality, this lesson says, that deeply tranquil and holy "part" is the *only* real thing about what we think we are; the rest is only dreams.

I think this is often the source of fear for many of us. The idea that most of what we think of as ourselves is not real at all, but only a dream, is rather terrifying. We have so identified with these aspects of ourselves, and have become so convinced of their reality, that the idea that they might dissolve and disappear if we really got in touch with the Christ within ourselves is frightening. It seems like some kind of death, or personal annihilation, as if the bulk of our person were simply going to be erased in some kind of cosmic lobotomy. The Text speaks often, and strongly, about our fear of finding our Self (see, for instance, T-13.II-III). One such statement is:

> You have built your whole insane belief system because
> you think you would be helpless in God's Presence, and
> you would save yourself from His Love because you think
> it would crush you into nothingness. You are afraid it
> would sweep you away from yourself and make you little,
> because you believe that magnitude lies in defiance, and
> that attack is grandeur. (T-13.III.4:1–2)

Consider this from the other side of the question for a moment. What if the bulk of what we believe ourselves to be *is* only a dream? What would we lose if we lost it? Nothing. Nothing but dreams of pain and suffering, nothing but our profound sense of loneliness.

Enlightenment does not destroy individual personality. It does not destroy anything at all; it only removes dreams and illusions. It takes away what is not and never has been true in the first place. The Christ is the only "part" of ourselves that has any reality at all, and the only loss we will ever experience is the loss of things that have never been.

1. Alan Watts, *The Wisdom of Insecurity* (New York: Vintage, 1968).

LESSON 276 ✦ OCTOBER 3

"The Word of God is given me to speak."

Practice instructions

See complete instructions on page 135. A short summary:

- **Read** the commentary paragraph slowly and personally.
- **Pray** the prayer, perhaps several times.
- **Morning and evening:** Repeat the idea and then spend time in Open Mind Meditation.
- **Hourly remembrance:** Repeat the idea and then spend a quiet moment in meditation.
- **Frequent reminders:** Repeat the idea often within each hour.
- **Response to temptation:** Repeat the idea whenever upset, to restore peace.
- **Read the "What Is" section** slowly and thoughtfully once during the day.

Practice suggestion: The following is a visualization inspired by this lesson.

Imagine that you have traveled to the Middle East, far out into the desert.

You have come all this way to visit an ancient temple, which contains a holy relic.

See yourself standing before it. Perhaps it is one of those temples carved from the rock of a cliff.

You walk through the entrance and into a massive room, with lofty ceilings and shafts of sunlight shining through high apertures.

You walk down the central aisle and reach a flight of stairs on the other side of this room.

As you walk up the stairs you are filled with anticipation for what you are about to see, the artifact you have journeyed all this way to look upon.

At the top of the stairs is a corridor. You walk down this and reach a heavy, ancient curtain, on the other side of which is the

351

inner sanctum of this temple, the holy of holies.

You pause, thinking about what lies on the other side of the curtain, in this room.

For in this room is the very stone tablet on which God wrote His Word in the time of Moses.

What artifact could be holier?

You walk through the curtain and there, in the middle of a room filled with candles, is the stone tablet.

Hardly breathing, you walk up to it and read the words carved into it so long ago by the Hand of God.

It says, "My Son, known as..." and here, to your astonishment, you see your own name, "is pure and holy as Myself."

Your eyes are rooted. You can scarce believe what you read. What can it mean that this was God's Word to humanity, that this was God's message for the ages?

While you are looking at the tablet and seeing its words—"My Son, known as [name], is pure and holy as Myself"—try to take it in. Try to let the magnitude of this truth sink all the way in. Let it wash over you like a wave of realization.

Now look around and see that the perimeter of the room is lined with other stone tablets.

As you walk over to these you see that they have the same line carved on them, only with a different name on each one. Each one has the name of someone you know.

Spend a minute or two now, going around the room, looking at each tablet and seeing there the name of a different person in your life: "My Son, known as [name], is pure and holy as Myself."

After you have spent time looking at each tablet, and have had one last sacred look at the one in the middle with your name on it, you are ready to leave the room.

Being here and seeing what you've seen has been a holy experience, one that will leave you forever changed.

You realize now, as you stand before the curtain, ready to exit, that your life has changed. Your job now is to bring this message to the world, not just by talking about the truth you've discovered, but mainly by conveying this stupendous truth with the way you behave towards people.

Say, *"The Word of God is given me to speak, with my lips, my hands, my eyes, my deeds, my life, my love."*

Commentary

The phrase "the Word of God" in *A Course in Miracles* is defined here as "My Son is pure and holy as Myself" (1:2). In another place it is said to be "I am as God created me" (W-pI.110.11:4–6). We were created by this Word; as in the Bible, He spoke, and it was so. "God said, 'Let there be light,' and there was light" (Gn 1:3). Even so, God spoke, "My Son is pure and holy as Myself," and the Son, pure and holy as God, came into being. God's Thought of us was His creative act of Fatherhood; it stands unaltered and unalterable. I cannot make my Self other than God created me.

> Let us accept His Fatherhood, and all is given us. (1:5)

Hearing His Word is accepting His Fatherhood, accepting that we were created in His Love and can be no other than what He created us to be. It is to accept the Atonement (see M-22.1:6), the unassailable fact that I—that is, my true Self and not my ego image of myself—am as pure and as holy as God Himself.

> *And it is this that I would speak to all my brothers, who are given me to cherish as my own.* (2:2)

What I want to communicate to my brothers and sisters is that they all share this innocence with me. My grievances, my judgments, or my criticisms communicate guilt. My forgiveness communicates their innocence. Father, show me how to communicate the Atonement today; show me how, in word and deed, to speak the Word of God: "You are as pure and holy as God."

This clearly relates to the lead-in page on the Christ:

> Christ is God's Son as He created him. He is the Self we share. (W-pII.6.1:1–2)

> This is the only part of you that has reality in truth. The rest is dreams. (W-pII.6.3:2–3)

WHAT IS THE CHRIST?

Part 6: W-pII.6.3:4

> The rest is dreams. Yet will these dreams be given unto
> Christ, to fade before His glory and reveal your holy Self,
> the Christ, to you at last. (3:3–4)

I may think, "Okay. Christ is the only real part of me. All the rest, the stuff I think is really me most of the time, is just dreams. But these dreams seem very, very real to me. What the heck do I do about all these dreams?" The answer is in three words: the dreams are "given unto Christ." The Course often asks us to do this in varying forms; it speaks of bringing our darkness to the light, of bringing our fantasies to reality, our illusions to the truth. We, in our confusion, cannot see the truth about ourselves or others, because we are blinded by our illusions. The Holy Spirit was created for us to see the truth on our behalf until we can see it for ourselves (see T-17.II.1:6–8). He represents Christ for us, in us. We bring our dreams to Him, and He translates them into truth (4:1).

In practical terms this means that when I become aware that I am seeing from the ego's standpoint of separation and attack, I need to become quiet, and gently expose these beliefs to the Holy Spirit within my mind. I need to tell Him, "This is how I am seeing things. Show me how You see them. I am willing to see them differently."

Our natural (read "egoic") response when we discover dark thoughts in our minds, thoughts like anger, jealousy, self-pity, and despair, is to hide them, unless we are so blind as to totally identify with them and justify them. Embarrassed at our misthoughts, we attempt to sweep them under the rug and pretend they are not there. This does not dispel them, it merely causes them to go underground. For instance, in speaking of the ego's hatred, the Course teaches that we seek special love relationships to offset our hatred. It says:

> You cannot limit hate. The special love relationship will
> not offset it, but will merely drive it underground and out
> of sight. It is essential to bring it [the hate] into sight, and
> to make no attempt to hide it. (T-16.IV.1:5–7)

Hiding our unpleasant thoughts is denial. It leads straight to projection—we see our hidden thoughts played out by others. We think we gain ego points by condemning the other people. When we are upset by the mistakes of others, this is what is happening (see T-17.I.6:5).

When, instead, we make no attempt to hide our own ego, but willingly bring it to the light within us to be dispelled, it *is* dispelled. We don't have to understand how this happens, because we do not do it; the Holy Spirit does (see T-17.I.6:3–4). All we need be concerned about is being willing to have it happen. When the illusions which are hiding the truth are dispelled, our holy Self, the Christ, is revealed to us at last (3:4).

LESSON 277 ✦ OCTOBER 4

"Let me not bind Your Son with laws I made."

Practice instructions

See complete instructions on page 135. A short summary:

- **Read** the commentary paragraph slowly and personally.
- **Pray** the prayer, perhaps several times.
- **Morning and evening:** Repeat the idea and then spend time in Open Mind Meditation.
- **Hourly remembrance:** Repeat the idea and then spend a quiet moment in meditation.
- **Frequent reminders:** Repeat the idea often within each hour.
- **Response to temptation:** Repeat the idea whenever upset, to restore peace.
- **Read the "What Is" section** slowly and thoughtfully once during the day.

Commentary

When the Course uses the term "Son" in this context, with me addressing God concerning His Son, the term usually refers to the whole Sonship, which includes all of my sisters and brothers as well as myself. "Your Son," in other words, can be anybody on whom my mind focuses. So when I pray, "Let me not bind Your Son," I am referring to my boss, my spouse, my friends, my family, or whomever I might encounter today. It's a good prayer to repeat often as we interact with people today.

In our local study group the other night, one woman shared an insight she had. She said that she had realized that whenever she placed a limit on anyone else within her mind, if that person already was accepting such a limit within their own mind, she was reinforcing it. And as well, she was placing the same limit on herself. We can see this dynamic very strikingly in a situation involving parents or teachers and young children. It manifests quite vividly. The child will often manifest the limits that the adult "sees" in them, whether those limits are real or not. The fact that we do not see it so plainly with adults, however, does not mean that it is not happening all the time. When we limit someone in our minds, we can be literally binding them with laws that we made up.

"Your Son is free, my Father" (1:1). And each person we encounter today is that Son, equally free. We have all read stories of how the refusal of a parent, partner, or friend to accept the "normal" limits on someone else has enabled them to transcend those limits—stories of "impossible" healings, and so on. These are but elementary demonstrations of the power of today's idea. The limits the Course has in mind are not so much physical ones, or even intellectual ones, but limits such as guilt and sin. When we believe a person is beyond help or beyond hope, we bind them with laws we have made. We imagine an order of difficulty in miracles and impose it on those around us. "There is no order of difficulty in miracles" (T-1.I.1:1) is the first principle of miracles.

> *He [whoever he or she may be] is not changed by what is changeable.* (1:4)

He is still the perfect Son of God, as God created him. He has not been marred or scarred by anything in this world because everything in this world is changeable. The Son of God has not been changed by anything that has happened to his body, which is changeable. A feather cannot scratch a diamond, not even a pile of feathers, not even an ostrich plume. We are being asked to remember this about all our brothers; they have not been changed by what appears to be their sins or mistakes. Nor are they slaves "to any laws of time" (1:5); this covers our persistent belief that a healing may take a very long time, for instance. They are subject only to one law: the law of love (1:6).

Our brothers are not bound by anything except their own beliefs (2:2). And what they really are is "far beyond [their] faith in slavery or freedom" (2:3). Their bound appearance is a flimsy thing, barely covering the solid reality of holiness and love that lies beneath it. They cannot be bound "unless God's truth can lie, and God can will that He deceive Himself" (2:5). What kind of God would that be?

What if, today, I looked upon everyone around me from this frame of reference? What miracles might happen? What chains might fall away? What blind person might see again? What long-standing wound of the heart might be healed? Exactly that is our function here as workers of miracles.

WHAT IS THE CHRIST?

Part 7: W-pII.6.4:1

From within our innermost being, from the Christ in us, the Holy Spirit reaches forth "to all your dreams, and bids them come to Him, to be translated into truth" (4:1). Let me not, therefore, hide any of my dreams from Him today. Let me not let a sense of shame keep me from bringing them to Him. He will not condemn me. He is not shocked by anything He sees in us; He is unshockable. On the contrary, "He loves what He sees within you" (T-13.V.9:6), for He sees past the illusion of sin to the reality of love it has been hiding.

In every thought of attack He sees our call for love. In every shudder of fear He hears a call for help. In all our lust for the things of this world He beholds our longing for completion. Whatever we bring to Him, He translates into truth. Nothing is beyond redemption, nothing is outside the reach of the Atonement. The task of the Holy Spirit is to "reinterpret [us] on behalf of God" (T-5.III.7:7). All that we bring to Him, he will translate into truth. But only if we bring it. If we hide it He cannot help us.

> Bring, therefore, all your dark and secret thoughts to Him, and look upon them with Him.　　　　(T-14.VII.6:8)

> Open every door to Him, and bid Him enter the darkness and lighten it away.
> 　　　　(T-14.VII.6:2; the whole paragraph should be read)

LESSON 278 ✦ OCTOBER 5

"If I am bound, my Father is not free."

Practice instructions

See complete instructions on page 135. A short summary:

- **Read** the commentary paragraph slowly and personally.
- **Pray** the prayer, perhaps several times.
- **Morning and evening:** Repeat the idea and then spend time in Open Mind Meditation.
- **Hourly remembrance:** Repeat the idea and then spend a quiet moment in meditation.
- **Frequent reminders:** Repeat the idea often within each hour.
- **Response to temptation:** Repeat the idea whenever upset, to restore peace.
- **Read the "What Is" section** slowly and thoughtfully once during the day.

Commentary

The Course often sets forth a set of what, for us, seem to be rather confusing interrelationships. It says that how I treat my brother is a reflection of how I treat myself. It says how I treat myself is a reflection of how I treat God. It says how I treat my brother is a reflection of how I treat God. For all three you could substitute the phrase "how I see" for "how I treat."

This set of connections seems confusing to us only because we persist in conceiving of our Self, our brother, and God as separate beings. We are not separate. It is not simply that how I see myself *reflects* how I see God; it *is* how I see God, because I am part of God, an extension of Him, an extrusion of His nature. God is all that is. There is no other.

Therefore:

> If I accept that I am prisoner within a body, in a world in which all things that seem to live appear to die, then is my Father prisoner with me. And this do I believe. (1:1–2)

The Course is constantly telling me that I believe things I don't think I believe. It says I believe I have crucified God's Son (T-13.II.5:1). And here it tells me that I believe God is a prisoner.

I certainly don't go around *saying* that God is a prisoner. The idea that God is a prisoner seems shocking to me; my mental concept of God is that He is omnipotent. How can I believe something without being aware I believe it? Actually it is quite easy; I do it all the time. And sometimes I've even caught myself doing it.

For instance, sometimes I have noticed that when another person approaches me in a very open and loving way, my first reaction is not welcome but suspicion. I think that behind the appearance of love there is probably some ulterior motive, something that I need to be on guard against. "What does this person want from me?" might be my thought. Or perhaps I suspect them of trying to manipulate me in some way. What that kind of response is indicating is that I believe love itself is suspect. I don't trust love. I don't trust my own, I don't trust the love of others, and above all, I don't trust God's Love.

Another way I see that same suspicion of love in myself is when *I* feel loving feelings for another person. *I suspect my own motives*, particularly if the person is an attractive female. Again, there is the underlying belief, a belief I have not consciously admitted to myself, that *love cannot be trusted*.

What this lesson is saying is that when I accept *myself* as a prisoner, I am betraying a hidden belief that *God* is a prisoner, too. This is so because the facts of reality are that God and I are one, part of the same Being, or rather, I am part of His Being. Since reality is one, what I believe about any part I am believing about the whole, whether or not I realize it.

> If I am bound in any way, I do not know my Father nor my
> Self. And I am lost to all reality. (1:3–4)

We could easily use this line to condemn ourselves and get into a guilt trip. There isn't one of us who doesn't see himself or herself as bound in some way. We *all* feel we are limited by the laws of the world—laws of nutrition, laws of finance, laws of health, laws of marriage. We *all* believe that we will die. We all believe that certain of our weaknesses are real and can't be overcome; if we did not believe that we would have already overcome them! We all believe that we are limited by time and space; for instance, that if a friend moves a thousand miles away we can no longer relate to them as closely as we have before. So am I then "lost to reality"? Is my situation hopeless?

No, it isn't hopeless. All we need to do is recognize these beliefs in ourselves and admit that we *do* hold them. We need to see that every belief in our own limits is a belief that God is limited; every belief that I am imprisoned or trapped in some way is a belief that God is imprisoned and trapped. Notice what we are doing. Acknowledge we are doing it. And simply tell God, for instance, "I'm seeing You as limited and blocked, and You are not limited and blocked. Help me to see that." And that is all.

> *Father, I ask for nothing but the truth. I have had many foolish thoughts about myself and my creation, and have brought a dream of fear into my mind. Today, I would not dream. I choose the way to You instead of madness and instead of fear. For truth is safe, and only love is sure.*
>
> (2:1–5)

That is all. Acknowledge that you have had "foolish thoughts" (not "sinful thoughts"), and ask for the truth. That's all.

WHAT IS THE CHRIST?

Part 8: W-pII.6.4:2–3

What does the Holy Spirit do with our dreams of sin and guilt when we bring them to Him, and He translates them into truth? "He will exchange them for the final dream which God appointed as the end of dreams" (4:2). This is speaking of what the Course calls "the happy dream," otherwise known as "the real world" or "true perception." He takes our nightmares from us and translates them into the happy dream. In the happy dream, we are still dreaming; we are still here in the world, still operating in the realm of perception. But what we see is something completely different from the nightmares of a mind made mad with guilt. "The real world is attained simply by complete forgiveness of the old, the world you see without forgiveness" (T-17.II.5:1).

This happy dream is appointed by God to be "the end of dreams."

"Forgiveness is illusion that is answer to the rest" (W-pI.198.2:10). The world ends, the Course says, through the illusion of forgiveness: "The illusion of forgiveness, complete, excluding no one, limitless in gentleness, will cover it, hiding all evil, concealing all sin and ending guilt forever" (M-14.1:4). Our dark, guilty thoughts, brought to the Holy Spirit, are met and dispelled with forgiveness, and replaced with the vision of a world of total innocence.

The "illusion of forgiveness" will end all dreams because it will end separation:

> For when forgiveness rests upon the world and peace has come to every Son of God, what could there be to keep things separate, for what remains to see except Christ's face? (4:3)

The "face of Christ" does not mean (of course) that we will see a bearded Semitic man everywhere we look; the phrase is a symbol of the innocence of God's Son. If forgiveness rests upon the entire world, and every mind has come to peace, free from guilt, what is there to see except innocence? The Course has said that the world is a symbol of guilt. When guilt is gone, its symbol will also vanish. The dream, made by guilt, will end when its cause has disappeared.

Clearly this is speaking of a final end, "when peace has come to *every* Son of God." It is the goal toward which the Holy Spirit is leading us, the final consummation, when guilt has been removed from every mind. Each of us plays our part in this, for as long as there is guilt within *my* mind, the end of guilt has not occurred. The whole cannot be complete without all its parts. Being the Christ is not something we have to attain; we already are the Christ. But we do need to learn to remove all the blocks of guilt that are hiding our true Self from us.

> The state of guiltlessness is only the condition in which what is not there has been removed from the disordered mind that thought it was. This state, and only this, must you attain, with God beside you. (T-14.IV.2:2–3)

Once we have removed "what is not there," and have attained the state of guiltlessness, what we are—the Christ—will be revealed.

LESSON 279 ✦ OCTOBER 6

"Creation's freedom promises my own."

Practice instructions

See complete instructions on page 135. A short summary:

- **Read** the commentary paragraph slowly and personally.
- **Pray** the prayer, perhaps several times.
- **Morning and evening:** Repeat the idea and then spend time in Open Mind Meditation.
- **Hourly remembrance:** Repeat the idea and then spend a quiet moment in meditation.
- **Frequent reminders:** Repeat the idea often within each hour.
- **Response to temptation:** Repeat the idea whenever upset, to restore peace.
- **Read the "What Is" section** slowly and thoughtfully once during the day.

Commentary

Because creation is free, I am free. Because no one is bound, I am not bound. "Now is freedom his already" (1:4). It is here and now. Freedom is not future.

As I recognize the freedom that belongs to everyone, I find my own. In giving, I receive. In loving, I am loved. In healing, I am healed. In recognizing the existence of absolute perfection I experience my participation in that perfection, and I am most aware of it when I am recognizing Christ in my brothers.

Yesterday's lesson was the inverse of this: "If I am bound, my Father is not free." When we accept the apparent prison we are in we are saying God is imprisoned. If I see no way out, then God must be stymied too. Here again it becomes plain that:

As I see my brother, so I see myself.
As I see myself, so I see God.

The simplicity of this lesson is staggering. Everything keeps coming back to this.

Why do some people fear God? Why does the concept, the very word, scare them away? It is because they see God in their own image; we always do. If I see myself as threatening, I see God that way. If I see myself as weak and ineffective, I see God that way. I am running from my own idols, not from the truth.

> Only in dreams is there a time when he appears to be in
> prison, and awaits a future freedom, if it be at all.   (1:2)

We can understand how we can be perfectly free, safe at home in bed, and in our sleep, dream of imprisonment. That exactly describes our experience in this world. We are already free, but dreaming we are imprisoned. Salvation, to the Course, is simply becoming aware that we are dreaming, and that the freedom we think we lack is already ours. We become aware of it through recognizing it in others.

What are we seemingly imprisoned by? Of what do our chains consist? Are they not chains of guilt? "The Holy Spirit knows that all salvation is escape from guilt" (T-14.III.13:4). To see my brother as free is to see him without guilt; in other words, forgiveness. That is how escape from guilt happens: when I realize that creation itself is free from guilt, that everyone is guiltless, I recognize that I must be included. It works this way because what I perceive as the world is a projection of my own self-judgment: "The world you see is but a judgment on yourself" (T-20.III.5:2). In lifting judgment and guilt from the world I am lifting it from myself because what I see is only a reflection of how I see myself.

Creation's freedom promises my own.

WHAT IS THE CHRIST?

Part 9: W-pII.6.5:1–2

When we see "this holy face" (5:1), the face of Christ, in everyone and everywhere, we are seeing all creation as completely innocent, free from guilt. This "true perception" will not last long, according to the Course, because it is merely "the symbol that the time for learning now

364

is over, and the goal of the Atonement has been reached at last" (5:1). The face of Christ symbolizes the end of the time for learning because what we are learning is that we are without guilt, and that God's creation, His Son, is without guilt. So when we see only the face of Christ, learning has achieved its objective. It's graduation time!

If we believe we have a purpose in this world at all, we tend to think of it as some great thing within time. We think, as a Southern Baptist friend of mine used to say, that we are here to "do great wonders and eat cucumbers." (I never did figure out exactly what he meant by the last part, but it makes the silliness of our other goals apparent.) But our only function here, the Course tells us, is to learn forgiveness. We are not here to fix the world but to forgive it. We are not here to become a great, world-renowned healer. We are not here to establish a great spiritual teaching center. Our goal and our function is not defined in terms of this world at all. "Your only calling here is to devote yourself, with active willingness, to the denial of guilt in all its forms" (T-14.V.3:5). That is the sole objective of our learning. In the symbolism given here, it is to see the face of Christ.

> So therefore let us seek to find Christ's face and look on
> nothing else. (5:2)

In all our seeking, seek only this. If I am starting a new job, what is my purpose? To seek Christ's face, to deny guilt in all its forms. If I am entering a new relationship, what is my purpose? To seek Christ's face; to escape from guilt by seeing no guilt in my brother. If I am beginning some new project under the guidance of the Holy Spirit, what is it for? To seek Christ's face, to remove guilt from every mind I encounter. This is my sole purpose in *anything* that I do. And only in accepting this as "the one function that I would fulfill" (T-20.IV.8:4) will I find my happiness.

LESSON 280 ✦ OCTOBER 7
"What limits can I lay upon God's Son?"

Practice instructions

See complete instructions on page 135. A short summary:

- **Read** the commentary paragraph slowly and personally.
- **Pray** the prayer, perhaps several times.
- **Morning and evening:** Repeat the idea and then spend time in Open Mind Meditation.
- **Hourly remembrance:** Repeat the idea and then spend a quiet moment in meditation.
- **Frequent reminders:** Repeat the idea often within each hour.
- **Response to temptation:** Repeat the idea whenever upset, to restore peace.
- **Read the "What Is" section** slowly and thoughtfully once during the day.

Practice suggestion: Think of someone in your life, and apply these lines to that person:

Being a Thought of God, [name] has not left his Father's Mind.
Being a Thought of God, [name] is not limited at all.
Being a Thought of God, [name] is forever pure.
Being God's Son, what limits can I lay upon him?

Commentary

The Course is calling on me to not deny to anyone—my brothers or myself—the limitless freedom in which God created us. I find in myself what seems like a natural tendency to compare myself to others, and to find myself, in some way, superior to them. I am more intelligent. My opinions are more correct. Or my relationships are superior. Or I am more ethical, more compassionate, more understanding, more honest with myself. I have greater integrity. All of these are ways in which I have, at times, felt superior to others. Others have other standards of comparison. But in general, I think, we all have this tendency to feel somehow superior to most of the rest of the human race.

This is what the Course calls specialness. It is a way of seeing others with limits that, we believe, do not exist for ourselves. The Course's call to see our brothers as equally free as ourselves contradicts this pattern of thinking we have taught ourselves. The lesson says, "I can invent imprisonment for him [he whom God created free], but only in illusions, not in truth" (1:2). We are all equal Thoughts of God; none of us has left the Father's Mind; none of us is limited at all—except in illusions.

As students of *A Course in Miracles* we are called to "give honor" (2:1) to the Son of God wherever we meet Him. We are called to recognize the Christ in every one who is sent to meet us. Let me recognize today that the limits I see are my own illusions; they are, in fact, my own belief in my own limits, dressed up, disguised, perhaps, in another form, and projected onto my brother. I find my own freedom by honoring it in others. Let me remind myself today, "This is the holy Son of God, my brother, a part of my Self." Only in so doing will I find my Self, and recognize the Christ as God created Him.

At one point the Course makes a very strong statement. It says that if I really recognized who my brother or sister is, I could "scarce refrain from kneeling at his feet" (W-pI.161.9:3). Yet, it goes on to say that I will take his hand instead, because in the kind of sight that sees my brother or sister in this way, I am equally glorious. We are the Christ. Who we are is magnificent, so far beyond our normal conception of ourselves that on seeing it our inclination would be to worship, except that in that same instant we recognize that same magnificence in ourselves. May God grant us all such vision!

WHAT IS THE CHRIST?

Part 10: W-pII.6.5:3

This sentence speaks of the vision of God's Son, the awareness of the "glory" of what we truly are. In seeking and seeing Christ's face in one another, we find that same glory in ourselves. In the recognition of our true nature as God's creation, all need of "learning or perception or of time" ceases. The removal of the veils of guilt, accomplished by forgiveness, reveals the Christ to us, and there is no longer need of anything "except the holy Self, the Christ Who God created as His Son."

We already are what we are looking for. Only our dreams of guilt have hidden it from our sight. What is the Christ? You are. I am. Learning to undo the blocks to this sight is our only purpose in time. When that has been accomplished, there is nothing left to do except to *be* what we always have been.

X

Lessons 281 - 290
What Is the Holy Spirit?

"I can be hurt by nothing but my thoughts."

Practice instructions

See complete instructions on page 135. A short summary:

- **Read** the commentary paragraph slowly and personally.
- **Pray** the prayer, perhaps several times.
- **Morning and evening:** Repeat the idea and then spend time in Open Mind Meditation.
- **Hourly remembrance:** Repeat the idea and then spend a quiet moment in meditation.
- **Frequent reminders:** Repeat the idea often within each hour.
- **Response to temptation:** Repeat the idea whenever upset, to restore peace.
- **Read the "What Is" section** slowly and thoughtfully once during the day.

Practice suggestion: Think of something that seems to be hurting you, and say:

This outer thing cannot hurt me.
Only my thoughts about it hurt me.
Let me see it through God's Thoughts, for they can only bring me
*   happiness.*

Commentary

If I am perfect I cannot be hurt; it would make me less than perfect. Our reasoning tells us our life would be perfect if it were free from pain, but we are not free from pain, and therefore we must not be perfect. The Course's reason works in the opposite direction: we are perfect; pain would mean imperfection; therefore the pain must be some kind of illusion. "When I think that I am hurt in any way, it is because I have forgotten who I am, and that I am as You created me" (1:2). In other words, we only *think* we are hurt. If we remembered who we really are, we could not be hurt.

Another way of thinking about this is to say that my true Self cannot be hurt; only my illusory self can be hurt, and that, only by my own thoughts. Granted, we make some pretty darn good illusions! But that is all they are: illusions.

Pain comes when we put our own thoughts in place of the Thought of God (1:4). The cause is always in my thinking and nowhere else; nothing outside my mind can hurt me. When I feel attacked, it is always me attacking me. Not even the unloving thoughts of my brothers can hurt me if my mind is thinking God's Thoughts with Him. Early in the Text we are told:

> In reality you are perfectly unaffected by all expressions of lack of love. These can be from yourself and others, from yourself to others, or from others to you. Peace is an attribute *in* you. You cannot find it outside.   (T-2.I.5:6–9)

What I am in truth is "far beyond all pain" (2:2). The Holy Spirit is our Teacher to help us remember that this is who we are. As Lesson 248 tells us:

> Whatever suffers is not part of me. What grieves is not myself. What is in pain is but illusion in my mind.
>   (W-pII.248.1:3–5)

Not only is pain an illusion; the illusion of pain is experienced by an illusion of myself. It is my thoughts, specifically my thoughts about myself, that cause this illusion. When I think I am what God created not, I experience pain.

Let the words "I will not hurt myself today" be much in my mind today, my Father.

WHAT IS THE HOLY SPIRIT?

Part 1: W-pII.7.1:1–2

"The Holy Spirit mediates between illusions and the truth" (1:1). He bridges "the gap between reality and dreams" (1:2). Illusions and truth are mutually exclusive; reality and dreams can never meet. Our minds are caught in illusions, and in order to restore them to truth, something or Someone is needed who can act as a bridge, somehow connecting the unconnectable. This is the purpose served by the Holy Spirit. He bridges the gap because He is able to operate in both arenas; He touches on illusion without losing contact with the truth. He is the One Who "mediates," bringing illusion back to truth.

Because He is what He is, "those who turn to Him for truth" (1:2) can be led to truth by means of the very perception which is part of their illusion. Without Him, perception would lead only to more perception, the illusion continually reinforcing itself. Because the Holy Spirit, Who is within us and part of our minds (as well as part of God's), is linked eternally to truth, He can guide our perception in such a way as to undo our illusions and restore us to knowledge. This ability is "the grace that God has given Him" (1:2).

Our part in the equation, then, is simply to "turn to Him for truth." We bring our perceptions to Him, and He translates them into true perception, which leads straight to knowledge. He plays a very clear and crucial role in the Course's prescription for healing our minds. If He were not there, within us, there would be no bridge between reality and illusion. The more actively we cooperate with Him, consciously and willingly bringing our perceptions to Him, asking for the truth instead of our illusions, the more He can help us.

The word "turn" is an interesting one. It is a mental turning, a mental change of direction that can be almost physically felt when it occurs. Sometimes it feels as though we must literally tear our minds away from their focus on fear, and impel our thoughts towards the light like a flower turning to the sun. When I am distraught, I have found great power in simply closing my eyes and saying, "I turn to You." Almost at once, if these words are heartfelt, there comes a great sense of peace, a great widening of the horizons of my mind. I sense the Presence of infinite Help and Wisdom, waiting to assist. I feel the nearness of the Great Mediator, filled with the grace God has given Him, ready to purify my perception and lead me towards the truth. May we learn, more and more often, to turn to Him for truth.

LESSON 282 ✦ OCTOBER 9
"I will not be afraid of love today."

Practice instructions

See complete instructions on page 135. A short summary:

- **Read** the commentary paragraph slowly and personally.
- **Pray** the prayer, perhaps several times.
- **Morning and evening:** Repeat the idea and then spend time in Open Mind Meditation.
- **Hourly remembrance:** Repeat the idea and then spend a quiet moment in meditation.
- **Frequent reminders:** Repeat the idea often within each hour.
- **Response to temptation:** Repeat the idea whenever upset, to restore peace.
- **Read the "What Is" section** slowly and thoughtfully once during the day.

Practice suggestion: Lesson 282 says, in essence, that our true Name is love, as is God's. We have given ourselves the name of fear, but this is simply a mistake—we have not *become* fear. We are still love.

First, sign your name as you usually do, on the line below (or grab an extra piece of paper for this), and date it:

Signed, _____

(Dated: _____)

Look at your signature, and try to get in touch with your sense of whose name that is. What concept of that person are you holding as you sign the signature? Is it not a separate person? A person with a particular history? And a special station or place in the world? With special attributes?

Isn't this self trying to make its way through a perilous world? Isn't that why you sign your name to things? To protect yourself from something? Or to procure some needed thing for this endangered self? If, for instance, you sign a legal document, are you not often afraid of what it may bring into your life, even while you are hoping it will protect you in other ways? In short, isn't the identity signified by your name filled with fear? What else would a separate self trying to make its way through a perilous world be filled with?

Therefore, sign your name again, and this time sign it simply as "Fear."

Signed, _____

(Dated: _____)

Once you sign it, try to see this signature and the first one as the same. Look back and forth between the first and second signatures and try to let them blend into one. Try to realize that when you sign your name in everyday life, you *are* signing "Fear." You are saying, "This self who is separate, vulnerable, and beset by the dangers of a perilous world." Regardless of the specific words you write, the content of what you are writing is fear.

Now sign your name one more time. This time sign it as "Love."

Signed, _____

(Dated: _____)

As you sign it, try to really mean it. Don't think of it as a given name like "Joy," which doesn't mean much. Think of it as a statement that you really are love. Love is your nature. You are not a being who *can* love, who can love at times and hate at other times, whose love is partial, selective, and intermittent. You *are* love. Love is your nature. You are a segment of Love Itself. In your true nature, you are incapable of any anger, any hatred, even any neutrality. Being love, all you can do is love.

Realize that this is not an aspiration of what you want to be. This is who you are now, beneath all appearances. You are love, a segment of God's Love, merely dreaming that you are a separate being filled with fear. You are love masquerading as something else.

Look at this final signature and try to identify with it. Think to yourself, "That's me. That's who I am." Does that make you see yourself differently? What feelings does it evoke?

Commentary

Here is another of the dozens of statements which the Course says, if accepted without reservation, can constitute the entirety of salvation. "If I could realize but this today, salvation would be reached for all the world" (1:1). A few of the others that fall into this category are "I am as God created me" (W-pI.94.1), "Ideas leave not their source" (W-pI.167.3:6–11), "There is no world" (W-pI.132.6:2–3), "Nothing real can be threatened. Nothing unreal exists" (T-In.2:2–3), and "Forgive the world, and you will understand that everything that God created cannot have an end, and nothing He did not create is real" (M-20.5:7–10).

How often do I realize that I am afraid of love? We are afraid of love far more frequently than we realize. Ken Wapnick has used a variation of this thought as a suggested mental response whenever we notice our egos acting up: "I must be afraid of love again." There is a sense in which we could say that the ego *is* the fear of love. It is a mental stance that rejects Love as our Source, that rejects Love as our Self, and that refuses to recognize Love in everyone and everything around us. When we look at it in this way, it begins to be more understandable that if we could simply realize this one thing—not to be afraid of love—the salvation of the world would be accomplished.

Fear of love is insane on the face of it. Of all the things we might be reasonably afraid of, love is not one of them. A famous old-time Christian evangelist, Charles Grandison Finney (famous in the 1800s), once wrote that "Love is the eternal will to all goodness." To be afraid of that which eternally wills only our good is truly insane. So to accept today's idea is "the decision not to be insane" (1:2).

Fear of love is a fear of our own Self, which is Love. Therefore, to realize today's idea is "to accept myself as God Himself, my Father and my Source, created me" (1:2). We are indeed afraid to recognize ourselves as Love; it seems a very dangerous thing to do, to our egos.

Fear of love is to fall asleep and dream of death, because in rejecting love we are rejecting that which guards us, protects us, and brings us joy. In fearing love we are imagining ourselves to be something other than loving, or in other words, evil and sinful. In such a picture of ourselves we imagine we deserve death. To forget what we are and to believe we are something else, the mind *must* fall asleep. Therefore, to realize today's idea is a determination not to be asleep in dreams of death (1:3).

To will not to be afraid of love is a choice to recognize my Self because my Self is Love.

No matter what names we may have called ourselves in our madness, names cannot change what we are in truth (2:1–3). To choose not to fear love is to remember this. What we have done in calling ourselves unloving is not a sin:

> The name of fear is simply a mistake. Let me not be afraid
> of truth today.   (2:4–5)

WHAT IS THE HOLY SPIRIT?

Part 2: W-pII.7.1:3–5

The Holy Spirit is the Mediator or bridge between illusion and truth, dreams and reality, perception and knowledge. He becomes the means by which we can carry all of our dreams to the truth "to be dispelled before the light of knowledge" (1:3). His purpose within our minds is to effect this transformation of our mistaken perception into true perception. Our only task is to bring Him everything we do not want, so that He can dispel it. The Course refers to its curriculum as

> an organized, well-structured and carefully planned pro-
> gram aimed at learning how to offer the Holy Spirit every-
> thing you do not want. He knows what to do with it. You
> do not understand how to use what He knows. Whatever is
> given Him that is not of God is gone.   (T-12.II.10:1–4)

Across the bridge, in the light of knowledge, "sights and sounds" are "forever laid aside" (1:4). "Sights and sounds" represent the whole realm of perception. We bring our perceptions to the Holy Spirit to be "cleansed and purified, and finally removed forever" (T-18.IX.14:2). The Holy Spirit's purpose is to perform this task; He is the Mediator between perception and knowledge (see W-pI.43.1:3):

> Without this link with God, perception would have
> replaced knowledge forever in your mind. With this link
> with God, perception will become so changed and purified

that it will lead to knowledge. (W-pI.43.1:4–5)

This transformation of perception is identical to forgiveness; it is forgiveness that "has made possible perception's tranquil end" (1:5). "Forgiveness, salvation, Atonement, true perception, all are one" (C-4.3:6). Perception as managed by the ego always sees sin, and manifests in judgment and attack. Perception as managed by the Holy Spirit always sees the face of Christ, and manifests in love and joining. The ego's perception sees differences; the Holy Spirit's perception sees sameness and identity.

> This is the shift that true perception brings: What was projected out is seen within, and there forgiveness lets it disappear. (C-4.6:1)

The Holy Spirit is, therefore, central to the process of forgiveness. He is the means by which the transformation of perception from false to true is possible, and without Him, we would forever be lost in our dream of judgment. With Him, we can learn to forgive.

LESSON 283 ✦ OCTOBER 10
"My true Identity abides in You."

Practice instructions

See complete instructions on page 135. A short summary:

- **Read** the commentary paragraph slowly and personally.
- **Pray** the prayer, perhaps several times.
- **Morning and evening:** Repeat the idea and then spend time in Open Mind Meditation.
- **Hourly remembrance:** Repeat the idea and then spend a quiet moment in meditation.
- **Frequent reminders:** Repeat the idea often within each hour.
- **Response to temptation:** Repeat the idea whenever upset, to restore peace.
- **Read the "What Is" section** slowly and thoughtfully once during the day.

Commentary

"Abides" means "lives or dwells," but it also means "remains unchanged." I think that is the sense it has in this lesson: "My true Identity remains unchanged in You." (At least that is how I'm hearing it today.) "I made an image of myself" (1:1). I made a false picture of what I am, an idol, and I have imagined that this image is what I am: "it is this I call the Son of God" (1:1). This is the Course's understanding of what has, traditionally, been called "the Fall." In traditional Judeo-Christian understanding, man was created innocent and sinless, but he fell into sin, and thus corrupted his nature forever ("original sin"). In the Course's understanding, all that really happened is that we *imagined* we had changed; we made a false picture of ourselves and thought, "This is me." But what we really are never changed at all! Our true Identity remains unchanged, despite our making of idols. Creation is still, now, as it always was, because God's creation cannot be changed (1:2).

There is a vast difference between having actually corrupted our nature and only *thinking* that we did. In the old view, we had a real problem, resolvable only by the supernatural intervention of God. Real sin had been done, and had to be met with real punishment. Sin against an infinite God required a payment equally infinite, and so God's infinite Son had to die in our place, and then a "new nature" had to be created by God and somehow injected into humanity (being "born again"). Those who did not receive this new life were doomed to hell.

In the view presented by the Course, no real sin has been done, and the original perfection of God's creation remains unchanged. All that is necessary is for us to recognize our mistaken self-identification and to change our minds about it. When we let go of the idols or false images ("Let me not worship idols" [1:3]), the nature of Christ within us is uncovered and revealed as untouched by our insanity.

I am still the one my Father loves; that has not changed (1:4). My holiness still "remains the light of Heaven and the Love of God" (1:5). How could what God created as the light of Heaven be destroyed and become darkness? (1:6–7). If God created everything that is, how could I possibly be something else? (1:8). There is nothing else for me to be.

Each time today I find myself judging something about myself, disliking myself, berating myself, or feeling guilty about what and who I am, let me remind myself that none of what I am seeing is my true Identity. My true Identity remains in God and part of Him. The seeming other identity is an idol; let me not worship it, bow down to it and attribute some great power to it or fear it. This is not who I am. Let me be still an instant and go home.

As I recognize this true Identity, I must realize that by the nature of what It is, It must be shared with all creation. Everything is part of me, and I of it, all coming from the same Source (2:1). When I recognize everything as part of this shared Identity, other aspects of my one Self, I will naturally "offer blessing to all things, uniting lovingly with all the world" (2:2).

WHAT IS THE HOLY SPIRIT?

Part 3: W-pII.7.2:1–2

The ending of our dreams is the goal of the Holy Spirit's teaching (2:1). The dreams (our current perception), as we have seen, are brought to an end by translating our false perception of fear into the perception of love. The learning process we are engaged in here, and the subject of the Course's curriculum, is this very transformation of perception that will lead, in its final outcome, to the end of all perception—the end of dreams. Sometimes we get over-anxious, and we want the dream to end *now*. We want a direct infusion of knowledge. But that is not possible; we can't skip the process of transforming our perceptions.

> We have been emphasizing perception, and have said very little about knowledge as yet. This is because perception must be straightened out before you can know anything. (T-3.III.1:1–2)

Before we can "know" anything, our perceptions must be transformed by our interaction with the Holy Spirit, by our bringing our darkness to Him so that He can dispel it with the light. "For sights and sounds [perception] must be translated from the witnesses of fear to those of love" (2:2). There are so many things in our lives that seem to be witnesses to fear. They "testify" to the reality of fear; they seem to justify fear and even to demand fear. The translation that the Holy Spirit is seeking to effect within our minds is to so change our perception of things that everything (literally everything) that now seems to justify and demand fear becomes instead, in our transformed perception, something that justifies and demands love.

That is what "forgiveness" means in the Course; it is far more than merely seeing someone's actions differently. It means seeing everything differently. It means looking at every horror in this world, every atrocity, every betrayal, every bit of sickness and death, and somehow seeing all of it as something that justifies love and demands love. Something that, instead of proving the reality of fear, proves the reality of love. And that, folks, takes a miracle! But this is "a course in miracles." That is exactly what it is all about.

How can our perception of things be changed so radically? We do not know. We do not *need* to know. That is the job of the Holy Spirit within our minds. He knows how to do it. All we need to do is bring our fearful perceptions to Him with willingness to have them replaced by His perception. If we will bring them, and if we are thus willing to have them taken from us and replaced, He knows exactly how to do that, and He will do it. He *already* sees everything we see as a justification for love. He already sees everything in you and me as justifying His love. He sees it that way *for* us until we learn to share His perception with Him. "He was created to see this for you, until you learned to see it for yourself" (T-17.II.1:8). This is what the Holy Spirit is; this is what He does.

LESSON 284 ✦ OCTOBER 11
"I can elect to change all thoughts that hurt."

Practice instructions

See complete instructions on page 135. A short summary:

- **Read** the commentary paragraph slowly and personally.
- **Pray** the prayer, perhaps several times.
- **Morning and evening:** Repeat the idea and then spend time in Open Mind Meditation.
- **Hourly remembrance:** Repeat the idea and then spend a quiet moment in meditation.
- **Frequent reminders:** Repeat the idea often within each hour.
- **Response to temptation:** Repeat the idea whenever upset, to restore peace.
- **Read the "What Is" section** slowly and thoughtfully once during the day.

Practice suggestion: When you repeat today's lesson, you may want to make it more specific: *"I can elect to change this thought about _____."*

Commentary

This is one of the very good capsule statements of the practical teaching of the Course. What is seen as outside must be seen, first, as originating inside, in my thoughts. Then this lesson applies. If the origin of the problem is my thoughts, I can affect the problem. I can change all thoughts that hurt. Nothing outside me can affect me. The cause of problems, and therefore the solution to them, is entirely within my mind and entirely within my control.

"Loss is not loss when properly perceived" (1:1). Wham! Zap! That really hits a lot of buttons. Perhaps recently there was something I wanted to do, or someplace I wanted to go, and I could not do it. I could perceive that as a loss, and be upset. Yet, properly perceived, that loss can be seen as not a loss at all. The perception of an event, any event, as a loss is purely within my mind; the "hurt" comes not from the external event but from my thoughts about it, and "I can elect to change all thoughts that hurt."

But we have a mental scale of lesser and greater losses, and as we go up our scale this gets harder and harder to accept. Not getting to a meeting or a concert is one thing. But a few years ago I lost my computer hard disk, totally. I lost several years of personal journals and a mailing list with hundreds of names on it, no backups, no way to retrieve them. Gone. It took me a long time to work through to not seeing that as a loss. But the principle is the same. The perception of loss was purely in my mind, and all perception of loss and pain is always there and nowhere else. And it is always possible for me to change those thoughts if I really want to.

Up the scale still further: What about when someone we love dies, especially unexpectedly, "tragically," from sickness or violence or accident? How is it possible to apply "Loss is not loss when properly perceived" to such an event? It is evident the lesson means for us to do just that, because it continues:

> Pain is impossible. There is no grief with any cause at all.
> And suffering of any kind is nothing but a dream. (1:2–4)

The lesson is saying that, properly perceived, even death is not a cause for grief. All of it is just a more extreme form of the same case; the cause for our hurt, our pain, and our grief is not external to us. It is in the way we are thinking about things. And we can change the way we think about them and eliminate the pain. The major issue of life is not in the externals; it is in our thinking.

You would not go up to someone who had just lost a loved one and say, bluntly, "There is no cause for grief here." It very likely would be perceived as cruel and cold, as if you were saying, "He's no loss. Look at the bright side; now you won't have to put up with his/her faults any more, and you can find another who will make you really happy." People who try to tell a grieving person, "There is no cause for grief" are often choosing to be "spiritually correct" at the expense of kindness.

I think, however, that the lesson is asking us to say something like that—that there is no cause for grief—to *ourselves*, even in cases of what seems like extreme loss. It is suggesting, in the lines that follow, a process we can follow to change our thoughts even in such seemingly impossible cases [see the essay after this commentary for more on the process]. It is not an instant process, and it may take considerable time to turn the tide of our thoughts. But it is possible, it is within our power to change all thoughts that hurt. Our aim should be, eventually, to see that "grief and pain must be impossible" (2:1). Why? Because our Father would not give us anything that hurts us, and there is no other Source. He gives only the joyous, so only the joyous is the truth (2:2).

WHAT IS THE HOLY SPIRIT?

Part 4: W-pII.7.2:3–4

The process of translating our perceptions being discussed here is exactly the same as the process of changing our thoughts described in Lesson 284: "I can elect to change all thoughts that hurt." "Sights and sounds must be translated from the witnesses of fear to those of love" (2:2). This process of "changing thoughts that hurt" is all that learning is for, and when it has been accomplished, the game is over (2:3). This is the goal, the end of all spiritual process.

Lesson 193 put it well:

> How can you tell when you are seeing wrong, or some-
> one else is failing to perceive the lesson he should learn?
> Does pain seem real in the perception? If it does, be sure
> the lesson is not learned.   (W-pI.193.7:1–3)

A perception of pain is an unforgiveness. It indicates a need for a shift in perception. It is not sinful or bad to feel pain or grief; it is simply a mistaken perception that needs to be corrected. Nor is there shame if we find it hard to make such a shift. This is what the Holy Spirit is for, to help us through this process of translating our thoughts and changing our perceptions. This is what life is all about; this is the only lesson in the classroom. We do it through frequent repetition of the truth, and through persistently bringing our perceptions of pain to Him for healing. The complete absence of such perceptions comes only at the end of the entire process. The Manual puts it well: "It is your function to escape from them [perceptions of pain, for example], but not to be without them" (M-26.4:2). It is our own personal experience with pain and grief, and our experience of escape from them, that enables us to be of help to others who are caught in their grasp.

Learning from the Holy Spirit, then, involves openly acknowledging our false perceptions and not being guilty about them, but simply bringing them to Him for healing. This kind of learning "becomes the means to go beyond itself, to be replaced by the eternal truth" (2:4). If we gripe and complain about the learning process we will only delay the desired outcome. We are not expected to be without experiences of pain and grief, nor should we expect to be without them. But we should engage ourselves in the work of escaping from them when they occur, bringing them to the gentle kindness of the Holy Spirit's presence, asking Him to translate our perceptions so that what we see as witnesses to fear become, instead, witnesses to love.

The Process of Changing Thoughts
Extra Comments on Lesson 284

Frequent repetition of an idea is necessary to our learning that idea, particularly if the idea is directly contrary to something we have previously accepted as true. From the Course's perspective, all of us have accepted the ego's thought system, which is demonstrated by our very presence in this world of separation. Since the thought system of the Holy Spirit is diametrically opposite to the ego's thought system, frequent repetition of the ideas of the Course is basic to our learning the Course.

All through the Text and Workbook, the same ideas are repeated and restated, over and over. In the lessons of the Workbook we are urged to repeat the idea for the day every hour, and in Part I each idea is reviewed so that we spend two days with it, at the least. Jesus recognizes that replacing the ego's thoughts with God's thoughts is a slow, gradual process, and there is no guilt in recognizing that while I may conceptually understand some idea from the Course (such as "Loss is not loss when properly perceived"—W-pII.284.1:1) I am still far from total acceptance of it. If I recognize my imperfect acceptance of the ideas of the Course, continued repetition of the idea and continued application of it in varied situations is the prescribed remedy.

Five Stages in the Process of Thought Change

Lesson 284 in the Workbook speaks directly of this process by which our thoughts are changed. Its title is "I can elect to change all thoughts that hurt." This is how it describes the process of thought change (W-pII.284.1:5–6):

> This is the truth:
> 1. at first to be but said
> 2. and then repeated many times;
> 3. and next to be accepted as but partly true, with many reservations.
> 4. Then to be considered seriously more and more,
> 5. and finally accepted as the truth.

There are clearly five stages in the process of thought change. Preceding all these stages is a state in which we believe the exact opposite, or have no opinion on the subject. For most of us, this Zero State is our condition when we first begin to read the Course.

Take, for instance, the simple statement given in this lesson: "Loss is not loss when properly perceived." Most of us open the Course firmly convinced that loss is loss, and it is very real; our belief in the reality of loss is unquestioned. In the Course we encounter very clear statements that tell us we are wrong, that loss does not really exist except as a mistaken belief in our minds. In working with that idea, we will slowly move through these five stages of thought change.

1. Verbal Belief - "at first to be but said"

Change of thought begins with what is really no more than lip service to an idea. At this beginning stage we are really saying no more than, "I think this idea is true and I would like to believe it." With many ideas in the Course, the Verbal Belief stage is even less than that: it is coming to the place of saying, "This *may* be true and I am willing to believe it." If we are honest with ourselves we will realize that with many of the Course's ideas, we have progressed no further than this. With some of the ideas of the Course, such as the teaching that God did not create the world, it took me nearly three years to even reach this stage of being willing to consider the idea as true.

2. Mental Belief - "and then repeated many times;"

Having decided to admit the new idea into our thought system (Stage 1) does not do much; it isn't any more than cracking open the door to let it in. The next stage is where frequent repetition comes in. We repeat the idea over and over, perhaps aloud, perhaps silently. We buy cassette tapes of readings from the Course and listen to them over and over. We actually do the Workbook lessons. (I am convinced that the reason most of us "fail" in our practice of the Workbook lessons, "forgetting" to do the frequent repetitions, is that in truth we have not even reached Stage 1 with the idea in question; we are not willing to let it in.) We read the Text over and over. During this stage we still don't actually believe the idea; we are trying to convince our minds it is true. With most of the ideas of the Course, most students are still working in this second stage. I am sure that is true of myself.

3. Partial Belief - "next to be accepted as but partly true, with many reservations."

The frequent repetition of the idea brings us into situations where we find specific experiences that validate the truth of the idea for us. We have a holy instant, or a moment of forgiveness in one relationship, and we recognize the truth of something the Course has been telling us. This is the "Aha!" experience, the realization of "Now I know what the Course means by this!" Perhaps we experience a shift in perception with one person and see their innocence, see that there was no sin and therefore nothing to forgive. We now can see the truth of the Course in this situation. But we still have difficulty applying it to someone who deeply abused us, or to someone like Hitler, or to other mass murderers. We are still perceiving orders of difficulty in miracles. We accept the idea but "with many reservations." Some of us, with some of the ideas of the Course, have reached Stage 3.

4. Increasing Belief - "Then to be considered seriously more and more,"

Stage 4 is what the Course refers to as generalization. Once we have seen the truth of one of the Course's ideas in one situation, we begin to experience it more and more, in situation after situation. Here, in this stage, is where serious Course students will spend most of their lives. If

Stage 1 was mental acceptance and Stage 2 was mental repetition of the idea, then Stage 3 is experiential acceptance and Stage 4 is experiential repetition of the idea. We realize that if the idea was proved to be true in this situation, then perhaps we can apply it to that situation, and another, and another. Over and over, again and again, we must validate the idea in one experience after another.

Even in this late stage, we have not arrived at total acceptance of what the Course is saying. I believe that is what Helen Schucman meant in her frequently quoted statement to the effect that she knew the Course was true, but she didn't believe it. She was perfectly aware that she still had many reservations, and was in the process of considering the ideas seriously, more and more, but she had not yet arrived at final accept-ance. We find her statement a little shocking or disturbing only because Helen was more honest than the rest of us. Very few have moved beyond this stage.

5. Total Belief - "and finally accepted as the truth."

This final stage is our goal in this world; it is the end of the journey. Here, the idea which started out as a mental concept, won a fuller place in our minds through frequent repetition, began to be applied in experi-ence and gradually grew to encompass more and more of our lives, has finally been completely generalized. We now see the idea as complete-ly true, applying to everything equally. There is no more order of diffi-culty in miracles, and there are no more reservations and no more excep-tions. As I said above, few, if any, have reached this stage with more than a few of the Course's concepts.

It is like learning a foreign language. At the start the sounds of the foreign language are incomprehensible (we all have probably had that experience with the Course!). You choose to take in the language. You apply yourself through frequent repetition. You begin to be comfortable with the language in limited situations, gradually extending your expe-rience with the new language to more and more aspects of your life until one day, if you are diligent, what you take, takes you. The language becomes your own; it becomes part of you and you part of it. It now seems to come naturally to you, without effort. But it took a great deal of effort to reach the state of effortlessness.

Learning to play a musical instrument proceeds through exactly the same stages: struggling with the strings of a guitar, feeling unnatural and uncomfortable; learning chord after chord, song after song; playing scales, repeating things over and over and over. Then, one day, you find that you don't even have to think about it; it just happens. What you take, takes you.

This stage is the final goal, the end result. If you expect simply to leap into effortlessness without any effort, you will never get there. With the ideas of the Course, we are in the learning process, somewhere in those first four stages. That is the purpose of our being in the world—learning, healing, changing our thoughts.

Being a Happy Learner

The Course advises us, "Be you content with healing" (T-13.VIII.7.1). While we are in the world, we are healing, learning, going through these stages with one aspect of truth after another. When learning is over there will be no more need to be here, so we should expect no more than this learning process as long as we stay here. We need not be guilty because we have not yet arrived at the goal.

In "The Happy Learner" (T-14.II) and the section that follows, Jesus offers us some advice about the process we are in:

1. Learn to be a happy learner.

"The happy learner cannot feel guilty about learning. This is so essential to learning that it should never be forgotten" (T-14.III.1:1–2).

2. "Learning is living here" (T-14.III.3:2).

And living here is learning. That is all that living here is: being in the process and not being guilty about it. "Be you content with healing" (T-13.VIII.7:1).

In other words, the world's purpose, for us, is to be a school. What we do here is to learn. That's what we are here for. So settle down, don't be stressed out that you haven't learned it all yet. Learning will get you where you are going, so be content with it, be happy to be in the learning process, and be patient with yourself for not yet being complete.

If you are confronted with a hard truth, something difficult to accept, and you realize that you are still in the first stage of thought change, mere verbal belief, don't be upset that you can't immediately make your mind accept the truth completely. Just get on with the learning process.

Repeat the idea as often as possible to yourself. Use every situation to teach it to yourself. Be at peace with the apparent slowness of your progress. Learning is what you are here for, and you have all the time in the world.

LESSON 285 ✦ OCTOBER 12
"My holiness shines bright and clear today."

Practice instructions

See complete instructions on page 135. A short summary:

- **Read** the commentary paragraph slowly and personally.
- **Pray** the prayer, perhaps several times.
- **Morning and evening:** Repeat the idea and then spend time in Open Mind Meditation.
- **Hourly remembrance:** Repeat the idea and then spend a quiet moment in meditation.
- **Frequent reminders:** Repeat the idea often within each hour.
- **Response to temptation:** Repeat the idea whenever upset, to restore peace.
- **Read the "What Is" section** slowly and thoughtfully once during the day.

Practice suggestion: In the spirit of the teaching in this lesson's opening paragraph, try repeating the following:

I normally wake expecting painful things to come to me.
They seem to fit me because I think I am unholy.
Today I wake expecting only happy things.
They are what really fit me, because I am holy.

Commentary

Today I ask only for joyful things to come my way. "I will ask for only joyous things the instant I accept my holiness" (1:3). The only reason I experience pain and grief and suffering and loss is because somewhere in my mind I think I deserve it. In some way I think suffering is good for me. I judge myself unholy, in conflict with God and His love, and so I need to be taught a lesson. I need to be rehabilitated. I think suffering and hardship will teach me a lesson. So I send forth an invitation to those kind of thoughts, and by golly they come!

When I accept my holiness, "what would be the use of pain to me?" (1:4). The idea that suffering is necessary is poppycock. We think we learn through our trials. And we do. But what we are learning is not how to become holy; we are learning that we *are* holy. Once we get ahold of that fact, we don't need suffering any more. Once we get rid of the idea that we are sinful and guilty, that somehow we need to be whipped into line, we understand that we deserve joy because we are already holy.

We think that if we were to become totally happy too quickly we'd miss something. We are absolutely convinced that our past actions prove that we don't deserve happiness and are not ready for it. We think some critical element is missing from our personality that only suffering and pain can teach us. Nothing is missing. Nothing is lacking. If the pain, grief, and loss all ended this instant, you would be just fine; you'd be perfect, in fact, because you already are!

It's as if we have a transmitter in our heads. We have a picture of ourselves as guilty and incomplete. We think suffering is needed to correct that condition. So we broadcast an invitation to pain, suffering, grief, and loss: "Come to me! Help me out. I need to suffer some more." Because our mind has all the creative power of God, we succeed in our attempt. We make all the suffering happen, at least in appearance.

When we learn to see ourselves as innocent and complete, the perfect creation of the Father, we have no further reason to broadcast such thoughts. Instead we sing, "Send joy only! Send happy things of God. Today I am accepting only the joyous; no suffering allowed." I am the ruler of the universe (Lesson 253). My mind has complete power to create the experience of life I want. Today, I choose to create joy.

WHAT IS THE HOLY SPIRIT?

Part 5: W-pII.7.3:1

> If you but knew how much your Father yearns to have you recognize your sinlessness, you would not let His Voice appeal in vain, nor turn away from His replacement for the fearful images and dreams you made.   (3:1)

This sentence is here because we *are* letting His Voice appeal in vain, not listening to it, and we *are* turning away from His Thoughts with which He would replace our terrifying dreams and images. Our own egos, in their scramble for self-survival, have convinced us that God is doing *anything but* yearning for us to recognize our sinlessness. We're more likely to think (if we think about it at all) that God is sitting up in Heaven with his big book of records carefully tracking all our mistakes and tallying them up against us. We are afraid that we have really screwed it up and are too far gone to be recovered. We are more afraid of God than we are believers in His Love. We cannot imagine that He still sees us as sinless. But He does.

When something bad seems to happen to us, we still think along the lines of "Now what did I do to deserve this?" We still think of the world as some kind of system in which the universe makes us pay dearly for every slip-up. The Course says over and over that God is not in the vengeance game. We are the only players in that game, and we bring on our own punishments. God, on the other hand, is yearning for us to stop thinking we are guilty and to recognize our sinlessness.

We turn away from the transformation of our thoughts being offered to us because, somehow, we've convinced ourselves that if we bring any of this dark and dirty stuff into God's Light, a lightning bolt will come out of heaven and zap us. We think that hiding it is safer than exposing it. We don't want to admit that we have gone off searching for idols, for things to replace God in our lives, because we think that has forever marred us and made us unacceptable to God. It has not. All God wants is for us to stop this silly game and come home to Him. He has given us the Holy Spirit to help us do exactly that, but we avoid turning within to Him because we think we will lose, or even die, in the process.

Read the Text section on "Justice Returned to Love" (T-25.VIII). It describes our fear of the Holy Spirit quite clearly. It says that we fear Him and think He represents God's wrath, rather than God's Love. We become suspicious when His Voice tries to tell us we have never sinned (T-25.VIII.6:8). It says we "flee the Holy Spirit as if He were a messenger from hell, sent from above, in treachery and guile, to work God's vengeance on [us] in the guise of a deliverer and friend" (T-25.VIII.7:2).

If I look honestly at how often I actually turn to the Holy Spirit for the healing of my thoughts, as opposed to how often I *do not* do so, it seems to bear out what is being said here. Something in me is keeping me from doing this very simple action; something is motivating me to stay away from the Holy Spirit. If I really knew how much my Father yearns for me to recognize my sinlessness, I would not behave like this.

So what can I do? I can start where I am. When I realize that I've been shunning the Holy Spirit again, I can begin by bringing that realization to Him: "Well, Holy Spirit, it looks as if I've been afraid of You again. Sorry about that." And that simple turning is exactly what He asks of us; to bring our darkness to Him for healing. In opening up about my fear, I've neatly sidestepped it. I'm in communication again.

LESSON 286 ✦ OCTOBER 13

"The hush of Heaven holds my heart today."

Practice instructions

See complete instructions on page 135. A short summary:

- **Read** the commentary paragraph slowly and personally.
- **Pray** the prayer, perhaps several times.
- **Morning and evening:** Repeat the idea and then spend time in Open Mind Meditation.
- **Hourly remembrance:** Repeat the idea and then spend a quiet moment in meditation.
- **Frequent reminders:** Repeat the idea often within each hour.
- **Response to temptation:** Repeat the idea whenever upset, to restore peace.
- **Read the "What Is" section** slowly and thoughtfully once during the day.

Practice suggestion: The prayer for this lesson is without doubt one of the most beautiful prayers in the Course. I call it the "I Need Do Nothing Prayer." It induces a wonderful state of rest and peace. I recommend taking a chunk of time today—fifteen to thirty minutes—and praying this prayer over and over again, slowly and meaningfully, sinking more deeply into it each time. Don't close your eyes and zone out after the first time; you'll be grateful for the experience if you stay with it. To aid in this process, I've broken the prayer into three parts and have put some extra lines after each line of the prayer, to draw out its meaning.

A Day of Doing Nothing

1. Father, how still today!
Let me imagine a day of perfect stillness,
in which everything is resting, everything is at peace,
  glowing with a soft radiance.

395

2. How quietly do all things fall in place!

Normally, life seems to be a chaotic jumble of conflicting
   elements.
But today, all things have quietly fallen into their proper place.
As I look out on the world, everything is exactly where it
   belongs.

3. This is the day
that has been chosen as the time
in which I come to understand the lesson
that there is no need that I do anything.

This is the day You have appointed for me to finally realize,
   "I need do nothing."

Rest from Doing

4. In You is every choice already made.

This is why I need do nothing.
In You all those hard choices that face me have already
   been made.
Let me feel myself resting in You, no more difficult decisions
   to make.

5. In You has every conflict been resolved.

I feel constantly surrounded by conflict,
   trying to resolve one while hoping that the others will not
   spring out of control.
But in You, all my conflicts are forever behind me.

6. In You is everything I hope to find already given me.

I am always seeking, striving to find the happiness and safety
   that I lack.
But in You, I can rest from seeking, for I have found.
   In You I have everything.

The Peace that Is Mine

7. *Your peace is mine.*
You are totally free from choice, conflict, and seeking.
Your peace must be limitless, unfathomable!
Yet because I am in You, Your peace is mine.

8. *My heart is quiet, and my mind at rest.*
In Your peace, with no need to do anything, I am totally at rest,
*   completely filled.*

9. *Your Love is Heaven, and Your Love is mine.*
What could be more heavenly than being loved by You?
And I am loved by You; You love me with all that You are.
I need only accept Your Love, and Heaven is mine.

Commentary

"How quietly do all things fall in place!" (1:2). I love that line! That is what realization is like; things just quietly fall into place, and there is nothing to do.

"This is the day that has been chosen as the time in which I come to understand the lesson that there is no need that I do anything" (1:3).

Several years ago in a study group, we read a section that described the state of *knowledge*. Someone asked if it is possible for an individual to attain this, or do we all have to do it together? "Is everybody waiting for me? Am I waiting for everybody else?" The leader (I'll call him Ted) began to discuss Jesus and how we are all in this together.

"Then Jesus isn't in this state of knowledge yet either, is he?" said the questioner.

I injected myself into the discussion: "Yes, he is. Jesus has passed from perception to knowledge. *And so have you.*"

We are "at home in God, dreaming of exile" (T-10.I.2:1). We are all already in Heaven. (Actually we never left.) The story is already over! We're at the end, looking back and remembering. "We're living a rerun," someone said. "The fact that Jesus has already done it is the guarantee that we all will do it, we all will experience what he has experienced because we are really all one mind," Ted said.

This is the reason that "I need do nothing." We all continue to make the error that we have to accomplish something. We think that there is this great mountain to climb, the mountain of enlightenment or perfection. We may believe Jesus has climbed it, along with others like Buddha, but we think we're still at the bottom looking up. We are intimidated by how hard it is going to be, awed by all the work that has to be done, discouraged by the thought of how far we have to go to get there.

These thoughts are simply the way the ego tries to handle the situation when you finally get a glimpse of the promised land, of the realm of knowledge that God intends for you to live in.

> The ego can accept the idea that return is necessary because it can so easily make the idea seem difficult. Yet the Holy Spirit tells you that even return is unnecessary, because what never happened cannot be difficult. However, you can *make* the idea of return both necessary and difficult. Yet it is surely clear that the perfect need nothing, and you cannot experience perfection as a difficult accomplishment, because that is what you are. (T-6.II.11:1–4)

The ego tries to convince you that what you have seen is something you *lack* instead of something you *already have*. "In You is everything I hope to find already given me" (1:6). *You are what you have been looking for.*

The Christ-nature is not something you have to develop. You don't have to slave over the ego trying to change it into a Christ! That simply isn't possible. If you think you have to *become* the Christ, you have put yourself in a situation where "You can't get there from here." And that is exactly where the ego wants you to be.

The Christ-nature is Who you really are! You just don't remember. It is already inside you. It is you. You think you are something else, but you aren't. That is the illusion the ego has cast. You think the ego is you! You think that all this awful stuff, all this miserable little worm nature, this weakling, this sniveling coward, is what you are. That is not you. The ego is not you. The ego is not anything, and not anywhere; it is just a thought you have about yourself, a thought that is wholly false. Christ "is the only part of you that has reality in truth" (W-pII.6.3:2).

When you feel as if you have to struggle, when you feel as if you have to make all kinds of difficult choices, then you are seeing yourself as an ego, at the bottom of the mountain looking up. When you see yourself as the Christ, there is nothing to do.

Our only problem is thinking we have a problem. The thought that "I don't have it yet" *is the problem*. We need to be enlightened from thinking we need to be enlightened. All that has to change is that thought, and the thought changes nothing, does nothing, because we are always already enlightened, always already happy, always already perfect. God created us that way and we can't change it; all we can do is forget it and pretend we are something else.

In today's moment of quiet we can taste the flavor of that stillness in which there is nothing to do and nowhere to go. "The stillness of today will give us hope that we have found the way, and travelled far along it to a wholly certain goal" (2:1). We can taste the reality of the end, even in the midst of our traveling; we can know the goal is "wholly certain," and even inevitable.

> Today we will not doubt the end which God Himself has promised us. We trust in Him, and in our Self, Who still is one with Him. (2:2–3)

WHAT IS THE HOLY SPIRIT?

Part 6: W-pII.7.3:2–3

What are "the means you made, by which you would attain what is forever unattainable" (3:2)? The unattainable is, of course, separation, or life that is separate from God. The means we made to attain this goal include our bodies, the illusions of choices (alternatives to God and to love), fear, attack, conflict, denial, special relationships, sights and sounds, and the whole phenomenal world of perception. The Holy Spirit understands all of these things perfectly. He knows exactly what they are, how they work, and why we made them.

"And if you offer them to Him, He will employ the means you made for exile to restore your mind to where it truly is at home" (3:3).

This is the miracle. Everything we made to exile ourselves from God can be used to restore our minds to their real home. But for that to happen we must "offer them to Him." He is the bridge between what we made and what we are. He is "the Great Transformer of perception"

(T-17.II.5:2). He can completely reverse the purpose of everything we made in madness, and use it to restore us to sanity. If we give those things to Him.

And so we need to bring all these things to Him, asking Him to use them for His purposes, rather than the purpose for which we made them. Give Him our bodies. Give Him our special relationships. Give Him our power of decision. Give Him our attack thoughts, our defenses, our very denial. (He can use even denial to "deny the denial of truth" [T-12.II.1:5].) Give Him our perceptions, our eyes and ears. Give Him our whole world and everything in it. He will not take them *away* from us. He will take them and use them to restore us to Heaven.

LESSON 287 ✦ OCTOBER 14
"You are my goal, my Father. Only you."

Practice instructions

See complete instructions on page 135. A short summary:

- **Read** the commentary paragraph slowly and personally.
- **Pray** the prayer, perhaps several times.
- **Morning and evening:** Repeat the idea and then spend time in Open Mind Meditation.
- **Hourly remembrance:** Repeat the idea and then spend a quiet moment in meditation.
- **Frequent reminders:** Repeat the idea often within each hour.
- **Response to temptation:** Repeat the idea whenever upset, to restore peace.
- **Read the "What Is" section** slowly and thoughtfully once during the day.

Commentary

This lesson comes from a very high place. It is something that would be spoken by a person ready to live in the real world, a prayer from the heart of Christ within me. It *is* the heartfelt thoughts of Christ, expressed in words; it is the mindset that I seek to listen to all the time. And so it is true of me; I can speak these words with honesty, even though I know that often I listen to the ego, which has every other goal *but* God.

If I feel today that I cannot say with simple honesty, "You are my goal, my Father. Only You," then let me look with honesty, and without fear, on what other goals I still cherish. Let me ask myself, "What could be a substitute for happiness? What gift could I prefer before the peace of God?" (1:2–3). Any such other goal is obviously a foolish one. Any goal that distracts me from the peace of God is unworthy of me.

If I have another goal, if I cannot say "Only You," then I am desiring to go someplace other than Heaven; I am looking for a substitute for happiness; I am seeking something which I think is preferable to the peace of God; I am looking to find and keep something which I think is better than my own Identity; I am choosing to live with fear rather than with love.

It really is that simple.

In the Course, Jesus assures me that it is not shameful to recognize these things about myself. Recognizing my false goals is the beginning of wisdom. All that is needful is for me to recognize what I am doing, what other goals I am choosing, and the power of those things will simply fall away. *Pretending* to love only God while secretly holding on to other goals is a sure guarantee of failure and unhappiness. Honest recognition of those other goals, and of my responsibility in choosing them, is the sure way of release.

WHAT IS THE HOLY SPIRIT?

Part 7: W-pII.7.4:1

> From knowledge, where He has been placed by God,
> the Holy Spirit calls to you, to let forgiveness rest upon
> your dreams, and be restored to sanity and peace of mind.
>
> (4:1)

The Holy Spirit has been placed in knowledge, by God. Knowledge is not a place but a condition, a state of knowingness. The Holy Spirit knows the truth; He knows reality. He knows our real being, what and who we really are. On the one side He is firmly linked with God, knowledge, and reality. From that place of knowingness, He calls to us within our dreams. On the other side He is linked firmly with us. He is aware of our dreams, aware of what and who we think we are, as well as knowing what and who we really are. He is perfectly equipped to lead us out from those dreams and into the truth of full sanity.

If we listen, we can hear Him calling. We can become aware of something within ourselves moving us to "let forgiveness rest upon [our] dreams." The discipline of Workbook practice is teaching us, if we are doing the exercises, to listen to that Voice, to respond to that inner urging. Gradually we are becoming more and more aware of the times we are dreaming; gradually we become aware we are dreaming most of the time. We can let forgiveness rest on our dreams by bringing them to the Holy Spirit and asking for His perception to replace our dreams. This is the way to sanity; this is the way to peace of mind.

In Chapter 5, the first chapter in the Text which strongly presents the Holy Spirit and His place in our return to God, He is often referred to as "the Call." He is called "the Call to Atonement" (T-5.I.5:4), "the Call to return" (T-5.I.5:5), "the Call to joy" (T-5.II.3:2), "the Call to awaken and be glad" (T-5.II.10:5), and "the Call for God" (T-5.II.10:7). This Call is something within our own minds. Something is drawing us home; if you are reading this Course, you have felt that Call and responded to It. We can dissociate that Call and block it from our awareness, or we can deliberately turn our attention to It, and listen. He always calls us to forgiveness, both to forgive and to be forgiven. His goal is the end of guilt. He speaks to us, always, of innocence. He seeks to turn us from the way of fear to the way of love. If we give Him our full attention, He will safely guide us home. He knows the way.

LESSON 288 ✦ OCTOBER 15
"Let me forget my brother's past today."

Practice instructions

See complete instructions on page 135. A short summary:

- **Read** the commentary paragraph slowly and personally.
- **Pray** the prayer, perhaps several times.
- **Morning and evening:** Repeat the idea and then spend time in Open Mind Meditation.
- **Hourly remembrance:** Repeat the idea and then spend a quiet moment in meditation.
- **Frequent reminders:** Repeat the idea often within each hour.
- **Response to temptation:** Repeat the idea whenever upset, to restore peace.
- **Read the "What Is" section** slowly and thoughtfully once during the day.

Practice suggestion: For a longer version of today's idea, try thinking of a particular person you are carrying a grievance toward, and then repeating the following:

Let me forget my brother [name's] past today.

Because if I see that his sins are in the past, I will see that mine are, too.

Because if I believe that he bears God's Name, I will believe that I do, too.

Because if I see that he is God's creation, I will see that I am, too.

Commentary

"I cannot come to You without my brother" (1:2). The decision for God *is* the decision to share. What we recognize, in recognizing our Identity, is an Identity that is *shared* with all living things. Because my salvation lies in awaking to this shared Identity, it is impossible to come to God *alone*. The problem is separation; therefore the solution is unity.

"[My brother's] sins are in the past along with mine, and I am saved because the past is gone" (1:5). If the past is gone for me, it is gone for everyone. If I hold on to the past in regard to my brother, therefore, and hold grievances against him in any way, I am denying my own salvation. "Let me not cherish [the past] within my heart, or I will lose the way to walk to You" (1:6).

The lesson teaches that "to know my Source, I first must recognize what You created one with me" (1:3). In other words, to fully appreciate my own origins in God, to know my own holiness and perfection, I need to see that "that awful person" and everyone else was created by God in just the same way. "I cannot come to You without my brother" (1:2).

We all have certain people we just can't see as being in Heaven. Let's say one of mine is named George. I can't see George as being worthy of Heaven. Maybe, for me, if George were there it wouldn't *be* Heaven. Do you know the kind of person I mean?

Well, "I cannot come to You without my brother" does not mean that I can't get to Heaven until George does. It means that I can't get to Heaven until I see George as already there. It is still something in my control; I'm not made dependent on the other person's seeing. In my mind George must be seen as the same as myself. In my mind, I must see his holiness, I must forget his past. When I can forget his past, I can forget my own.

If I hold the past against my brother I am holding it against myself. We cannot see ourselves as any higher than we see our brother. I can't be any holier than he is. Yet I cannot be any less holy than Jesus.

The bottom line is, I can't see myself as having any gift of God that I am not willing for everyone to have.

When I honor my brother as my savior, I am recognizing Who he really is, and thereby I recognize my own Identity, shared with him. My brothers and sisters are my saviors, not in the sense that they provide me with something I do not have or do something for me I cannot do, but in the sense that by forgiving them, by forgetting their past, I remind myself of the truth about myself which I share with them. They show me my own judgment on myself, and give me opportunities to let it go. When I see my brother, I *am* seeing myself, and my gentleness and kindness toward them, in forgiveness, is the way I can give these gifts to myself.

In the closing paragraph, Jesus speaks to us. It is important to recognize him as the speaker:

Forgive me, then, today. And you will know you have forgiven me if you behold your brother in the light of holiness. He cannot be less holy than can I, and you can not be holier than he. (2:1–3)

I have said that how I see my brother is how I see myself. In this paragraph, Jesus makes it plain that how I see my brother is also a reflection of how I see him, and how I see God. And thus my forgiveness of a brother is identical to forgiving Jesus, and to forgiving God.

"You can not be holier than he [your brother]" (2:3). The limit I mentally place on my brother, by how I perceive him, is a limit I am placing on myself. If I hold *him* to the past, then *I* am held to the past. If I see him as incapable of understanding, incapable of learning, incapable of perfection, then I am seeing myself that way. No one is beyond redemption. If I see a brother as if I believe "he will never find God in this lifetime," I am placing that limit on myself. And in every case, the limit is false. "There is no order of difficulty in miracles" (T-1.I.1:1).

WHAT IS THE HOLY SPIRIT?

Part 8: W-pII.7.4:2–3

Without forgiveness will your dreams remain to terrify you. (4:2)

Our dreams disappear when we forgive them, which means that we see that what we *think* was done *to us* never occurred (see W-pII.1.1:1). Not that the events did not happen, but that our interpretation of them (what we thought was being done to us, the perception of attack) was incorrect. If we do not forgive, the dreams will remain terrifying to us. Forgiveness means seeing that there is nothing to forgive. It means reinterpreting the past and remembering only the love that was there, or the call for love, and denying any reality to our perception of attack.

We may resist doing this. We may think that, for some reason, it is important to hold on to our perception of injury. But if we do, we will continue to experience terror. The past will continue to perpetuate itself in our present and in our future. Eventually all of us will come to realize that this isn't what we want, and we will let the past go. "Let me forget my brother's past today" (W-pII.288.Heading).

Until we forgive the past and let it go, "the memory of all your Father's Love will not return to signify the end of dreams has come" (4:3). How can we remember God's Love when we continue to see ourselves as injured? "Would a loving God have allowed this?" we ask ourselves. Do I want to believe in the reality of sin, or in the Love of God? The Holy Spirit is calling to us, from within ourselves, to let forgiveness rest on *all* of our dreams. That is the only way we can be restored to sanity and peace of mind.

LESSON 289 ✦ OCTOBER 16

"The past is over. It can touch me not."

Practice instructions

See complete instructions on page 135. A short summary:

- **Read** the commentary paragraph slowly and personally.
- **Pray** the prayer, perhaps several times.
- **Morning and evening:** Repeat the idea and then spend time in Open Mind Meditation.
- **Hourly remembrance:** Repeat the idea and then spend a quiet moment in meditation.
- **Frequent reminders:** Repeat the idea often within each hour.
- **Response to temptation:** Repeat the idea whenever upset, to restore peace.
- **Read the "What Is" section** slowly and thoughtfully once during the day.

Commentary

We are learning in the Course that mind is the cause of the world we see. Say I find myself angry at someone. Instead of assuming, as I have done all my life, that what I have seen is real, I recognize that it is an illusion of some kind. I don't try to figure it out, I just give it to the Holy Spirit. I recognize that my angry thoughts are not caused by what I see, but rather, my thoughts of anger caused my perception of what I see.

My thoughts are prior to any sight and sound. Many people see this in what to me is a partial way. They see that our present feelings are not caused by what is presently happening, but they assume that there must be something in the past that caused these feelings. "Can you recall another time you felt like this?" is their key question. The idea is that you can remember some past event that aroused this feeling, and by realizing that the feeling is an unresolved feeling from the earlier event, you can detach the feeling from the present one. "I'm not really angry at you; I am angry because you represent my mother to me." That sort of thing. The Course does talk about this kind of "shadow figure" from the past, but it points out that such shadow figures "are not real, and have no hold over you unless you bring them with you" (T-13.IV.6:2). (Sections IV through VI in Chapter 13 all deal with releasing the past.) In other words, our present distress or anger is not caused by the past, but by a present decision to bring its pain into the present. A decision being made in the present can be undone in the present.

The past "can touch me not." Past events are not the cause of my feelings, either. The mistake in that kind of connecting of present emotions to past events, which certainly can be useful to a limited degree, is that it still makes the false connection of some event or person as the cause of my feeling, with my feeling as the effect. The key the Course gives is that "the past is over." If I am seeing the past I am "seeing but what is not there" (1:2). The one true thought that can be had about the past, says the Course, is that it is not here (W-pI.8.2:1). It does not (any longer) exist. All that exists is a thought in my mind which I call a memory, and that memory is imperfect, slanted to my perceptions and with no awareness of the inner reality of other people who were also present. All I remember is what I saw, what I heard, what I thought, what I felt. So my picture of the past is totally inadequate and cannot be the basis for any kind of rational judgment.

When I do recognize that my present feeling is caused by viewing present events through the filter of a memory of the past, that is good because it can serve to help me detach my feelings from the things happening in the now. But I need to go one step further. I need to see that my feelings are not caused by the past, either. The past has no power over me. The past doesn't exist. The past I remember is my own thoughts about the past.

If my feelings are not caused by the present and not caused by the past, then what are they caused by? Certainly not by the future, which has not happened yet. Then what?

"I am affected only by my thoughts" (W-pII.338.Heading). Only by my thoughts. That is the bottom line. The Course says that eventually we must learn that there is nothing outside of our mind to affect us; thought is all there is. Everything else is the effect of thought, not the cause of anything (T-26.VII.4:9; T-10.In.1:1).

> There is nothing outside you. That is what you must
> ultimately learn.   (T-18.VI.1:1–2)

Why do we have thoughts that cause bad feelings? It all goes back to the original thought of separation. We think we have stolen our being from God, we think we succeeded in creating a separate self, and we think that God must be angry. We believe in the wrath of God. In less theological terms, we are guilty because we see ourselves existing in a world that demands selfishness for survival. We are guilty because (we think that) we are separate and it is our own fault.

We have this profound sense of guilt, so profound it terrifies us. We cannot even bear to look at it. We are afraid of oblivion, afraid of death, more afraid of hell. Fear transmutes into many forms: anger, depression, jealousy, apathy. We open our eyes and immediately we are looking for a scapegoat, something we can blame as the cause of these terrible feelings. Inevitably we find a culprit. "You! You are the one who has stolen away my peace!" We made the world to serve this purpose.

The Holy Spirit comes into our lives to "employ the means you made for exile to restore your mind to where it truly is at home" (W-pII.7.3:3). *We* look on each event as a possible scapegoat for our awful feelings. The *Holy Spirit* looks on each event as a possible means of showing us love. We learn to see everything as either love or a call for love. To the ego, everything witnesses to separation and guilt. To the Spirit, everything witnesses to the reality of love.

To perceive the world forgiveness offers we must be willing to let the past go, to see that it cannot touch us *now*. The forgiven world can only be seen *now*. We have to choose to stop looking at "a past that is not there" (2:1).

WHAT IS THE HOLY SPIRIT?

Part 9: W-pII.7.5:1–2

The Holy Spirit is the "Father's gift…a call from Love to Love, that It be but Itself" (5:1–2). That is what the calling within us is all about. It is Love calling to Itself to *be* Itself. Whenever I start feeling as though God is calling me to some kind of "surrender" that makes it appear as though I am submitting my will to another, superior will, I recall that what is happening is simply that I am surrendering to Love. I am surrendering *to myself*, to what I am in truth. God is not calling me to give up myself and become something I do not want to be; God is calling me to *be my Self*. To be what I was created to be and still am.

I have confused myself and convinced myself that I am something else, and now, in hearing the call to return to myself, to "return to love," as Marianne Williamson puts it, I feel fear. It seems as though I am being asked to give up myself, to "surrender" to God at the expense of my own being. Exactly the opposite is true. I am being called to surrender only to what I am in truth. I am called to be Love, because Love is what I am.

LESSON 290 ✦ OCTOBER 17

"My present happiness is all I see."

Practice instructions

See complete instructions on page 135. A short summary:

- **Read** the commentary paragraph slowly and personally.
- **Pray** the prayer, perhaps several times.
- **Morning and evening:** Repeat the idea and then spend time in Open Mind Meditation.
- **Hourly remembrance:** Repeat the idea and then spend a quiet moment in meditation.
- **Frequent reminders:** Repeat the idea often within each hour.
- **Response to temptation:** Repeat the idea whenever upset, to restore peace.
- **Read the "What Is" section** slowly and thoughtfully once during the day.

Commentary

"Unless I look upon what is not there, my present happiness is all I see" (1:1). That is the real key: not looking at what isn't here. So often we are looking at the past, or as I was doing as I lay in bed this morning, the future. Neither past nor future is here. By definition they are "not now."

What Jesus is saying here is that if we can stop for a moment looking at past or future, what we will see is present happiness. As one guru says, "You are always already happy."

What does this have to do with the leading lesson on the Holy Spirit? "What I perceive without God's Own Correction [the Holy Spirit] for the sight I made is frightening and painful to behold" (1:4). The future is frightening; the past is painful. I need the corrective spectacles of the Holy Spirit to see the truth.

The world I see is painful because the ego made it to support itself. If I just go on looking at it through the eyes the ego made, I am going to see witnesses to evil, sin, danger, and guilt. I need to see it a different way.

I'm not being asked to blind myself, to bury my head in the sand and pretend the world is not there. I'm being asked to willingly put on corrective lenses and see the world differently, as a witness to love, joy, and peace. First of all, in this lesson, I am being asked to look within and notice that without reference to the past or the future, I am naturally happy. I am being asked to stop looking at what *isn't* there. Seeing what *is* there in a different way is the next stage, and there will be little effort to it because I will start from a place of happiness.

If I am already happy, nothing in the present can change that because I don't approach it from a sense of lack. I don't approach it at all, I am already in it.

This is a great technique for meditation: as thoughts arise, if they concern the past in any way, just let them float by. If they concern the future in any way, just let them float by. If you can do that, what you will discover, always, is your present happiness. You don't have to manufacture it because it always exists.

WHAT IS THE HOLY SPIRIT?

Part 10: W-pII.7.5:3–4

> The Holy Spirit is His gift, by which the quietness of
> Heaven is restored to God's beloved Son.   (5:3)

I am so grateful today for this gift, without which the quietness of Heaven would be forever beyond my reach. If I were to try to summarize this page's answer to the question it poses, "What is the Holy Spirit?" I would put it something like this:

The Holy Spirit is God's gift to us to restore our minds, caught in illusion, back to peace and sanity. He is a changeless link between our minds and God's. Through His awareness of both the eternal truth of God and our insanity, He is able to utilize the very illusions we have made to lead us back to reality. We bring our illusions to Him. He translates our illusions from witnesses to fear into witnesses to love, giving us a completely new perception of everything we see. This new perception is so aligned with truth that it enables the end of perception, and the final transfer of our minds to their original state of knowledge.

> Would you refuse to take the function of completing God,
> when all He wills is that you be complete?   (5:4)

Once again the Course appeals to us to actively take our part in this process, and to accept our function as given by God: to complete Him. That is a startling phrase, isn't it? Elsewhere the Course tells us that whenever we question our own value, we should say, "God Himself is incomplete without me" (T-9.VII.8:2). A little later it explains, "God is incomplete without you because His grandeur is total, and you cannot be missing from it" (T-9.VIII.9:8). It tells us, "Without you there would be a lack in God, a Heaven incomplete, a son without a Father" (T-24.VI.2:1).

Of course it is impossible that God should be incomplete: "God is not incomplete, and He is not childless" (T-11.I.5:6). The point is that if we are part of God, then God would be incomplete if we were not forever united with Him. We cannot be missing from God; therefore, let us take the part in Him given to us, and end our *refusal* to do so. Our part in completing God is to be complete: "All that He wills is that you be complete" (5:4). We are being asked only to bring our illusions of incompletion to the Holy Spirit, that He can dispel them and restore to us the awareness of our eternal completion.

The process of bringing our illusions to the Holy Spirit often seems fearful because, from our perspective, it seems to entail loss. We *are* being asked to give up something. But the something we are asked to give up is only our illusion of separation, our illusion of incompletion. We give up our lack, and remember our wholeness. This is, as Lesson 98 puts it, a bargain in which we cannot lose:

> You are being asked for nothing in return for everything.
> Here is a bargain that you cannot lose. And what you gain
> is limitless indeed!   (W-pI.98.6:3–5)

XI

Lessons 291 - 300
What Is the Real World?

"This is a day of stillness and of peace."

Practice instructions

See complete instructions on page 135. A short summary:

- **Read** the commentary paragraph slowly and personally.
- **Pray** the prayer, perhaps several times.
- **Morning and evening:** Repeat the idea and then spend time in Open Mind Meditation.
- **Hourly remembrance:** Repeat the idea and then spend a quiet moment in meditation.
- **Frequent reminders:** Repeat the idea often within each hour.
- **Response to temptation:** Repeat the idea whenever upset, to restore peace.
- **Read the "What Is" section** slowly and thoughtfully once during the day.

Commentary

I write my comments on this lesson at the end of the day (so that it is awaiting you in your morning e-mail).[1] My day today seemed to be anything but a day of stillness and peace, more like a day of staggering pace. I was rushing about meeting my body's needs, stocking up on groceries I'd let run down to nothing, buying some vitamins, razor blades, and so on. In the back of my mind was a booklet waiting its finishing touches (and already behind schedule), a flyer for an upcoming workshop, phone calls to make, a stack of correspondence-school papers to read and respond to. I had lunch at 3:45 PM and supper at 8:15. My details are different from yours, but I'm sure lots of your days are similar in tone, if not in content.

We all have the demands of time and circumstance upon us. How do we find inner peace in the midst of it? This lesson speaks of "Christ's vision," which "looks through me today" (1:1). "His sight shows me all things forgiven and at peace, and offers this same vision to the world" (1:2). The peace being spoken of here is the peace that comes from a different perspective, an *inner* peace. Elsewhere the Course acknowledges that when we live in this world we are involved in "busy doing" (T-18.VII.8:3). It isn't that the busy doing ceases. It's that our mind can be at peace even in the midst of busy doing, a "quiet center" from which we operate (same reference).

I was not doing so well at maintaining that quiet center today, or rather, at remembering it was there and making use of it; I was operating more on the surface of my mind. As a result, I felt a little frantic. This lesson calls me back to home base. The vision Christ offers me is one of loveliness and holiness (1:4–5). It is the sight of a forgiven world, whose forgiveness includes my own. It is the peace of knowing that, although I may forget the toilet paper or fail to write the needed letter, my Self is unchanged, God is my Father, and I share the holiness of God Himself.

In my hyper-activity today there was a certain sense that, somehow, my salvation depended on remembering everything I had to buy or finishing all the tasks I hoped to accomplish. What a relief to know I was wrong! Even in my study of the Course, sometimes, an anxiety creeps in, thinking I have to understand everything perfectly in order to find my way home. Instead, as I read this lesson, I can relax:

I do not know the way to You. But You are wholly certain.
Father, guide Your Son along the quiet path that leads to
You. Let my forgiveness be complete, and let the memory of
You return to me. (2:3–6)

WHAT IS THE REAL WORLD?

Part 1: W-pII.8.1:1–2

The Course's discussion of the term "real world" is somewhat paradoxical. We've read its statement, earlier in the Workbook, that "There is no world!" (W-pI.132.6:2). How, then, can there be a *real* world? It even admits there is a contradiction in the term (see T-26.III.3:3). And here we are told, in the opening statement on the topic, "The real world is a symbol" (1:1). A symbol is not the thing it represents; it only stands for something else, as the word "tree" stands for the object we call by that name. The real world is only a symbol, "like the rest of what perception offers" (1:1).

The word "tree" is not a tree. Likewise, the real world is not the thing it represents or stands for. It only symbolizes it. What does the real world symbolize or stand for? "Yet it stands for what is opposite to what you made" (1:2). We made separation; the real world symbolizes unity (but is not itself that unity). We made fear; the real world symbolizes love (but is not itself that love). We made error; the real world symbolizes truth (but is not itself that truth).

The world itself is nothing but a symbol of a thought. It can symbolize the thought of fear, or it can symbolize the thought of love. It can, in our perception, consist of "witnesses to fear" or witnesses to love (W-pII.7.2:2). The world itself is not the reality of anything; it merely stands for something that exists in the mind, as all perception does. It is "the outside picture of an inward condition" (T-21.In.1:5). What changes in the transformation effected by the Holy Spirit is not the world itself, but how we see it; what it symbolizes for us. This is why the message of the Course to us is this: "Seek not to change the world, but choose to change your mind about the world" (T-21.In.1:7).

The real world that we seek, and which is the goal of the Course for us, is not, then, a changed world, but a changed perception of the world.

1. I have left this sentence almost exactly as it first appeared when the lesson commentaries were first mailed out by electronic mail on the Internet, in order to preserve the original feel of immediacy in the whole paragraph.

LESSON 292 ✦ OCTOBER 19

"A happy outcome to all things is sure."

Practice instructions

See complete instructions on page 135. A short summary:

- **Read** the commentary paragraph slowly and personally.
- **Pray** the prayer, perhaps several times.
- **Morning and evening:** Repeat the idea and then spend time in Open Mind Meditation.
- **Hourly remembrance:** Repeat the idea and then spend a quiet moment in meditation.
- **Frequent reminders:** Repeat the idea often within each hour.
- **Response to temptation:** Repeat the idea whenever upset, to restore peace.
- **Read the "What Is" section** slowly and thoughtfully once during the day.

Practice suggestion: As I often do, I suggest that you make today's idea more specific in your practicing of it. Think of a situation that is weighing on you or worrying you. Then say, *"A happy outcome to this situation is sure."* Realize there is no time limit on when that happy ending might come, yet also realize that "it is up to us when this [outcome] is reached" (1:3).

Commentary

God's promises make no exceptions. And He guarantees that only joy can be the final outcome found for everything. Yet it is up to us when this is reached; how long we let an alien will appear to be opposing His.   (1:1–3)

"It is up to us when this is reached." We keep coming back to that: *When* we experience the outcome of joy in all things is *up to us*. My experience of anything less than total joy is due to my own choice to "let an alien will appear to be opposing His." It seems to me as if *my own will* is at times opposing God's. It seems as if I don't want to let go of the little creature comforts, the physical, mental, and emotional indulgences I continually grant myself in the illusion that I need them.

The law of perception states, "You see what you believe is there, and you believe it there because you want it there" (T-25.III.1:3). If I see in myself a will that differs from God's, I see it because I believe it is there. I believe my will *is* different from God's will. And I believe that because I *want* to believe that. If I am alike to God in every way, God and I have only one Will, and the alien will I perceive has no meaning. That is the exact truth! The alien will *has* no meaning! It does not exist. That is why I want to see "my" will as opposed to God's, and why I do. The apparent conflict in my life is just the ego's vain attempts to hold on to its identity, which is wholly illusory.

The truth of the matter is that what I see—my resistance to the will of God, which is my perfect happiness—does not exist. I am projecting that from my mind. What I see is an illusion of myself. It is not real, and therefore carries no taint of guilt.

> And while we think this will is real, we will not find the end He has appointed as the outcome of all problems we perceive, all trials we see, and every situation that we meet.
>
> (1:4)

All of us go around most of the time consciously or unconsciously disturbed by the undercurrent of resistance to God we believe exists within our selves. We think it is *real*. We read *A Course in Miracles* and determine to be more loving, more forgiving, and then we encounter a deep resistance to the entire idea, a seemingly immovable wall that will not allow us to change. We have an addiction we can't break. We find one relationship in which forgiveness seems impossible despite all of our efforts. We determine that "today I will judge nothing that occurs" (W-pII.243.Heading) and then, minutes later, flare up in anger over some small unfairness. And we feel despair, we feel we cannot do it. Somehow we are incorrigible. Some part of us is beyond redemption. Some part of our will is implacably opposed to God.

As long as we believe that this part of us which seems opposed to God is *real*, Jesus is saying, we won't find the real world. We won't find our escape. We won't find the "happy outcome to all things."

We have to come to the point where we are simultaneously fully aware of that stubborn knot within us, and aware that it is not real. We have to get to the place where we *see* it, *own* it, and *take responsibility* for it, and yet do so entirely without guilt. To look on the ego's darkness without guilt is possible only if, as we look, we have abandoned all belief in its reality. That is what the Holy Spirit will enable us to do. Through His enabling, we will come to see that the ego is an illusion of ourselves projected from our minds, nothing more than an illusion, and therefore nothing to be upset about. "Yes, I see the knot of resistance in me, but what I see is not really there. I am seeing it, but it isn't real. It doesn't change anything about reality. I am the beloved Son of God, even if I can't see that now."

We want the ego knot to change. We want it to go away. And while we believe in its reality, it won't. The ego *is* incorrigible. Self-forgiveness involves accepting that about ourselves. The ego will always be the ego, that's the bad news. But the ego is not who we are, and that's the good news.

When we catch ourselves listening to the ego, believing in the reality of an alien will, we can come to the point of learning not to take it seriously. It's as if we say, "I was dreaming again. Now, I choose to be awake." And if we find we are not ready yet for full wakefulness, if the appearance of resistance in ourselves still seems real, we can say, "Yes, I see that, I'm not awake yet, and it still *seems* real, but at least I am *aware* that I am dreaming." The ego is of no consequence. It's "no big deal," as Ken Wapnick says. Even if we seem to be caught in the dream, we don't have to accept guilt about it.

> Yet is the ending certain. For God's Will is done in earth
> and Heaven. We will seek and we will find according to
> His Will, which guarantees that our will is done.   (1:5–7)

All the raging of the ego, all the apparent struggle: it's all a dream. The ending is certain, and is totally unaffected by the ego's madness. There *is* no will opposing God's, and therefore, His Will and ours *will* be done. My will and God's are in fact the same, which *guarantees* the outcome. The craziness of the ego dream has no effects, just as a dream has no effect on the physical world. The craziness of the ego is just a play of images in the mind, and nothing more than that. In the end there will be nothing but joy.

We thank You, Father, for Your guarantee of only happy
outcomes in the end. Help us not interfere, and so delay the
happy endings You have promised us for every problem that
we can perceive; for every trial we think we still must meet.

(2:1–2)

"Help us not interfere." That is our prayer. Resisting the ego, being guilty about it in ourselves, striving to change it, or demeaning ourselves because of it, are all forms of interference. They all make the mistake of believing the ego is real, believing there really is an alien will in us that opposes God. To not interfere is to recognize that the ego is just a dream about ourselves, and that nothing need be done about it. The most potent force "against" the ego is the simple thought: "It doesn't matter. It doesn't mean anything." Just bring it to the Holy Spirit and let Him handle it. Just say, "Look, I'm dreaming again." And let it go.

WHAT IS THE REAL WORLD?

Part 2: W-pII.8.1:3–4

The world is a symbol, either of fear or of love. "Your world is seen through eyes of fear, and brings the witnesses of terror to your mind" (1:3). The voice we choose to listen to, within our minds, determines what we see. If we listen to fear, the world we see symbolizes fear, and is filled with "witnesses of terror." The world thus tells us what we tell it to tell us.

When we listen to fear, we see things in the world that justify our fear. We see hatred, attack, selfishness, anger, conflict, and murder. All of these things are *interpretations* of what we are seeing. There is another interpretation possible in every case. We can join our perception to that of the Holy Spirit, and He will enable us to see the world differently.

"The real world cannot be perceived except through eyes forgiveness blesses, so they see a world where terror is impossible, and witnesses to fear cannot be found" (1:4). When we listen to love or forgiveness, we see things in the world that justify love. Nothing we see witnesses to terror. Imagine a world in which "terror is impossible," where nothing you see is saying to you, "Be afraid!" That is the real world as the Course defines it. Everything is seen "through eyes forgiveness blesses." The

422

interpretation of everything we see becomes entirely different from the one we are used to.

The mind determines which world we see. With the help of the Holy Spirit we can choose what we want to see, and we will see it. The world we are looking at may or may not have changed, but the interpretation we put upon it will have done a 180. No longer will we see any of the vast variety of forms of fear the ego has invented; in their place we will see nothing but love, or the call for love. Nothing we see will call for condemnation and punishment. Everything we see will call only for love.

LESSON 293 ✦ OCTOBER 20
"All fear is past and only love is here."

Practice instructions

See complete instructions on page 135. A short summary:

- **Read** the commentary paragraph slowly and personally.
- **Pray** the prayer, perhaps several times.
- **Morning and evening:** Repeat the idea and then spend time in Open Mind Meditation.
- **Hourly remembrance:** Repeat the idea and then spend a quiet moment in meditation.
- **Frequent reminders:** Repeat the idea often within each hour.
- **Response to temptation:** Repeat the idea whenever upset, to restore peace.
- **Read the "What Is" section** slowly and thoughtfully once during the day.

Practice suggestion: The following exercise is based on this lesson's teaching that your fear is caused by your past mistakes. Their presence in your memory tells you that punishment is on the way, that you better be afraid because you've got it coming to you. But these past mistakes are gone. If you could open your eyes and see the present, you would see that only love is really here.

Now for the exercise. Look ahead into your day and identify anything you are afraid of, any event that's causing you worry or anxiety, or that you would simply like to avoid. Try to identify several such fears. With each one you find, say:

This fear is past
  because my past mistakes are gone.
And only love is here,
  because God is here.

Commentary

I think of fear as related to the future, yet here it says "all fear is past." This means more, I think, than that my experiences of fear are all over. Understood that way it is almost wishful thinking. What it seems to actually mean is that fear itself is in the past. Fear comes from the past, it exists in the past only. When the past is real to me, with "all my past mistakes oppressing it" (1:3), then I have fear (and only then). What I fear is that the past determines the future. If my past is filled with mistakes and things of guilt, and I consider it to be real, this generates my present fear of the future.

The source of fear is making the past real in the present.

The Course teaches us that "the past that you remember never was" (T-14.IX.1:10). At first it seems difficult to say to myself, "The things I think happened in the past did not ever happen; they are not real." Perhaps it is easier to say, "The past never existed in the way I think it did." That seems more conceivable, more acceptable. To say that is only a step toward the truth, but I think it can be a helpful step. We begin by admitting that our memories of the past are, to say the least, distorted.

> Each one peoples his world with figures from his individual past, and it is because of this that private worlds do differ. Yet the figures that he sees were never real, for they are made up only of his reactions to his brothers, and do not include their reactions to him. (T-13.V.2:1–2)

More than that, the past we imagine we know is filled with reasons for guilt and attack. We remember wrongs done to us, and wrongs we have done. That perception must shift. If we accept the judgment of the Holy Spirit, the perception of guilt must go. Forgiveness is a kind of selective remembering. We can begin to see the past and everything in it as either the expression of love or a call for help.

This is a kind of intermediate position. In a way we are still believing that the past is (or was) real, but we are deciding to see it differently. The ultimate truth is that time itself does not exist, the world does not exist, bodies do not exist. They are nothing but the play of thoughts in our mind.

A physical analogy helps me. Does an ocean wave exist? Is a wave real? In one sense, yes; in another, no. There is no such thing as a wave apart from the ocean. What we call a wave is no more than the play of physical energy on water. The water, the ocean, is (in this physical plan) what is real; the wave is here one moment, gone the next; in this moment comprised of one set of water molecules, in the next comprised of a wholly different set of molecules. A wave does not exist *in itself,* independent of all else.

The entire physical universe is nothing more than a wave in Eternal Mind. Mind is all that is real.

In this sense, then, nothing of the past is real. All of the past of a wave no longer exists. The past wave is totally and completely gone. Where it passed now lies placid and calm, unaffected by the wave. Waves do not change the ocean.

Some may be able to see it this way, to understand at least in concept that the past simply does not exist. Some of us may need the simpler form, "It never happened the way I think it did. Guilt was never real." The simpler form will eventually lead to the fuller form, so it simply doesn't matter.

When I experience fear, then, one thing to look for is the belief in the past that is behind it, perhaps hidden, but surely there. Only the past makes me fearful of the future. That is why young children are so often lacking in fear: they have no memory of past disasters to give rise to the fear. When I feel fear, let me remember that it depends on my perception of the past, and affirm: "What I remember never happened as I think it did. There is nothing to fear."

When I deliberately choose to exclude the past from my consideration of the present, "in the present love is obvious, and its effects apparent" (1:4). The constant burden of the past, dredging up remembered horrors, totally blocks this awareness of love's presence from my perception. All our *learning* is nothing but an accumulation of ideas about the past. Therefore all of it is nothing. We begin to *unlearn,* to deliberately forget what we think the past has taught us, and in that we find true perception and eventually true knowledge.

The world that we see, when we see without the fear carried over from the past, is the real world. This is the world we are asking to see today in this lesson. Underneath all the sounds of fear, the world is singing "hymns of gratitude" (2:2). The perception of the Holy Spirit is able to penetrate through the veneer of fear we have placed over reality. When we share His perception, we realize the past is gone, and we see and hear what is here *now,* when "love is obvious." Let me, then, join in the prayer: "I would see only this world before my eyes today" (2:4).

WHAT IS THE REAL WORLD?

Part 3: W-pII.8.2:1–2

"The real world holds a counterpart for each unhappy thought reflected in your world; a sure correction for the sights of fear and sounds of battle which your world contains" (2:1). If the real world contains counterparts for each unhappy thought, then it must consist of happy thoughts. The difference is in the thoughts about what is seen, and not in the objects of perception. In this sentence it seems almost as though the real world is like a library of videos, each consisting of a different interpretation of some person or event in our lives. We can choose to watch the videos of the Holy Spirit or those of the ego. Same scenes, but different Director, with a different meaning given to everything.

"The real world shows a world seen differently, through quiet eyes and with a mind at peace" (2:2). The difference lies in the peacefulness of the mind doing the perceiving. This is the first of three references to the state of the mind that is doing the seeing. Others are "the mind that has forgiven itself" (2:6) and "a mind at peace within itself" (3:4).

We all assume that our perceptions of the world are telling us something real about the world. In fact, they are telling us something about our own state of mind. The sights of fear and sounds of battle we perceive are only reflections of the fear and battle within our own minds. When our minds have been brought to peace, the world takes on a different appearance because our minds are projecting their own state upon the world. Let me, then, seek the healing of my own mind, and the healing of the world will take care of itself.

LESSON 294 ✦ OCTOBER 21
"My body is a wholly neutral thing."

Practice instructions

See complete instructions on page 135. A short summary:

- **Read** the commentary paragraph slowly and personally.
- **Pray** the prayer, perhaps several times.
- **Morning and evening:** Repeat the idea and then spend time in Open Mind Meditation.
- **Hourly remembrance:** Repeat the idea and then spend a quiet moment in meditation.
- **Frequent reminders:** Repeat the idea often within each hour.
- **Response to temptation:** Repeat the idea whenever upset, to restore peace.
- **Read the "What Is" section** slowly and thoughtfully once during the day.

Practice suggestion: Think of a number of features of your body that you either like or dislike. With each one, say:

I see this [name the bodily feature] as [good, bad].
It is neither good nor bad.
It is a wholly neutral thing.

Commentary

This statement sums up the Course's attitude towards the body. It is "neither good nor bad" (2:2); it is *neutral*. It derives its value or its harm from the use to which we put it, the purpose that it serves.

There is a view of the body that sees it as inherently good, always deserving that we respect its wishes. If I am sexually aroused by someone I should indulge that urge. If I am hungry I should eat; if I am tired I should sleep. All repression of physical desires is wrong. This view is incorrectly identifying the body with my self. It deifies the body and makes it not only good, it makes it God.

There is another view that sees the body as inherently evil. Therefore

I must master and repress all my bodily urges. This approach denies that the body is in any way an expression of my self. It makes a devil of the body. It produces endless guilt over every physical desire.

The body, says the Course, is not good and not bad. It is neutral. Not sinful, nor sinless. Its only usefulness is in awakening from the dream, or in communicating salvation. Such an approach does not make the mistake of identifying myself with my body. It does not make me wrong for having urges, nor does it make me wrong for ignoring some of those urges. It neither exalts nor condemns the body. It accepts the body as a tool, useful for the purpose of truth and nothing else. It sees no purpose in purely bodily ends.

The lesson states, "I am a Son of God" (1:1). And I am not "another thing," "mortal and corruptible" (1:2–3). God did not create the mortal and corruptible body, and a Son of God has no use for what must die (1:4). Yet if the body is seen as a neutral thing it "does not see death" (1:5). Why? Because "thoughts of fear are not invested there, nor is a mockery of love bestowed upon it" (1:5). We (apparently) experience death when we see the body as evil ("thoughts of fear") or as good ("a mockery of love"). Holding the body as neutral "protects it while it has a use" (1:6). In other words, to the mind that is healed, the body is immortal until its work is done. It lasts as long as it is needed for the mind's purposes of healing in this world, and then it is simply "laid aside" because it no longer has a purpose (1:7). This is not *death* but simply the end of the body. As *The Song of Prayer* puts it, "We call it death, but it is liberty" (S-3.II.3:1).

When a mind that is healed no longer needs the body, the body is simply laid aside. "It is not sick nor old nor hurt. It is but functionless, unneeded and cast off" (1:8–9). There have been a few who have experienced this kind of bodily end that is not death. Robert tells me of reading of a Tibetan monk who, one day, announced to his followers that his work in the body was almost finished and that he would be leaving the body in a few months. He named the exact date. And on that day, he sat in meditation in full lotus, and simply left. He was "not sick nor old nor hurt." His body was simply "unneeded" any more.

How can we attain to such a high state, and such a gentle death (if it can even be called "death")? The lesson indicates that our path lies in the direction of gradually coming to see our bodies as "of service for a while and fit to serve, to keep its usefulness while it can serve, and then to be replaced for greater good" (1:10). It is neither a burden nor an end in itself. It is simply a tool. We use it, in this dream, "to help Your plan that we awaken from all dreams we made" (2:3), and for nothing more than that. Seeing the body as neutral is what protects it while it has a use in this plan. As we align our minds with God's plan, we value the body for its usefulness in fulfilling the plan, and not for itself. We neither exalt it nor abuse it. We do not strive either to keep the body or to leave it. We simply use it to fulfill our function.

WHAT IS THE REAL WORLD?

Part 4: W-pII.8.2:3–6

When we see the real world, "Nothing but rest is there" (2:3). No conflict, no "battle." I think that when I truly see the real world, there will be very little or no sense of urgency. There is a kind of attitude towards spirituality that instills what is almost a mode of panic: "We have to fix things, we have to get it right, and right away!" This is not rest. The sight of the real world is a restful sight, one that fills us with assurance that "nothing real can be threatened" (T-In.2:2) and therefore there is no need for panic.

"There are no cries of pain and sorrow heard, for nothing there remains outside forgiveness" (2:4). I do not think this means that we become indifferent to the world's suffering. In the Text, the Course tells us: "Love always answers, being unable to deny a call for help, or not to hear the cries of pain that rise to it from every part of this strange world you made but do not want" (T-13.VII.4:3). What I think this line means is that the cries of pain and sorrow are not heard as witnesses to fear, but as calls for help, as something requiring a response of love rather than a response of terror. The healed mind that sees the real world is not distraught by the cries of pain and sorrow because it knows that "nothing...remains outside forgiveness." Nothing is beyond hope or help.

> And the sights are gentle. Only happy sights and sounds
> can reach the mind that has forgiven itself.   (2:5–6)

Underneath the sounds of fear, the mind that has forgiven itself hears the hymns of gratitude (see W-pII.293.2:2). The song of love is louder than the dirge of fear. Everything that is seen carries in it the note of redemption.

> There is a way to look on everything that lets it be to you another step to Him, and to salvation of the world.
> (W-pI.193.13:1)

LESSON 295 ✦ OCTOBER 22
"The Holy Spirit looks through me today."

Practice instructions

See complete instructions on page 135. A short summary:

- **Read** the commentary paragraph slowly and personally.
- **Pray** the prayer, perhaps several times.
- **Morning and evening:** Repeat the idea and then spend time in Open Mind Meditation.
- **Hourly remembrance:** Repeat the idea and then spend a quiet moment in meditation.
- **Frequent reminders:** Repeat the idea often within each hour.
- **Response to temptation:** Repeat the idea whenever upset, to restore peace.
- **Read the "What Is" section** slowly and thoughtfully once during the day.

Commentary

My eyes are Christ's. "Christ asks that He may use my eyes today" (1:1). And in the prayer at the end, Christ's eyes are mine. "Help me to use the eyes of Christ today" (2:2). Two ways of saying the same thing: to ask that Christ look through my eyes, or to ask that I see through His eyes, is to ask that His vision, His eyes, replace my own limited vision.

Christ asks for my eyes to "offer peace of mind to me, and take away all terror and all pain" (1:2). He is not asking me for sacrifice, but asking so that He can give a gift to me. He offers to take my perception from me because my perception shows me terror and pain; He offers to replace it with His own vision, showing me peace, joy, and love.

As we give our lives to God we begin to experience that rather than living we are being "lived." The Holy Spirit is looking through our eyes. He is speaking through our lips. He is thinking with our minds. It is an experience of being taken up and carried through life by a limitless energy of love that is far greater than we can contain because it includes everything.

Sometimes I seem so far from that, and yet I know that it is as near to me as breathing. Nearer. This morning I ask, Father, for grace to surrender to that flow of love, to surrender to the Holy Spirit, now, in this moment, and over and over through the day, that I may share His vision of the world.

In a way this lesson is the entire Course: to let the Holy Spirit look through me, to bathe the world with eyes of love. To walk through the day with no purpose in its outward things, yet to live with a hidden agenda, a secret mission: *I will be love in this situation*. That is all it is about, and nothing else matters, nothing else is real. I am the light of the world. I am here to "allow the Holy Spirit's Love to bless all things which I may look upon, that His forgiving Love may rest on me" (2:2). That is what my life is about, that is all it is about. I am here only to be what I am, to be my Self, which is Love.

WHAT IS THE REAL WORLD?

Part 5: W-pII.8.3:1–3

> What need has such a mind for thoughts of death, attack
> and murder?   (3:1)

"Such a mind" as what? "A mind at peace" (2:2). A "mind that has forgiven itself" (2:6). "A mind at peace within itself" (3:4). Can I imagine what it would be like for my mind to be at peace within itself? Can I imagine what it would feel like to have completely forgiven myself, to have no lingering regrets over the past, no fear of future, no hidden guilt, and not one shred of a sense of failure? To be at peace, and to have totally forgiven myself, are the same thing. They must be. How can I be at peace if I have not forgiven myself for something? How can I forgive myself for something if I am not at peace about it?

Let me look at myself and be willing to face the self-condemnation that is hidden in the dark closets of my mind. I know it is there. It is the source of the constant vague uneasiness that haunts me, the tendency to look over my shoulder, the seemingly slight anxiety that comes with an unexpected letter or telephone call. Something in me is expecting to be "found out." But this self-judgment is the source of more than just my personal feelings of uneasiness. It is also the source of all of my thoughts of "death, attack and murder" (3:1). My fear of death comes from my buried guilt. My instinctive attacks on those around me are a defense mechanism I have developed to fend off judgment for my "sins." My desires to take life from others for myself (in the extreme, murder) come from the sense that something is lacking in myself.

And all of these contribute to my perception of the world; they are the reason why I see "sights of fear and sounds of battle" (2:1) everywhere. If my mind were at peace, if I had forgiven myself, I would see the world differently. I would see without these filters that distort my vision. I would see the real world. All "such a mind" would see is "safety, love and joy" (3:2).

Without guilt in my mind, "What is there it would choose to be condemned, and what is there that it would judge against?" (3:3). Guilt in my mind has driven me insane, and the insane world I see is the result of that guilt. That is why the Holy Spirit "knows that all salvation is escape from guilt" (T-14.III.13:4). If my mind had no guilt, it would see no guilt in the world, because all the guilt I see is nothing but the projection of my own. When I see someone as guilty today, when I would judge, let me remind myself: "You never hate your brother for his sins, but only for your own" (T-31.III.1:5). The problem I am seeing is not out there, in the world, but within my own mind. Let me then turn to the Holy Spirit and ask His help in removing guilt from my mind, that it may no longer block my perception of the real world. Let my goal, today and every day, be to have "a mind at peace within itself." From such a mind, free of guilt, the sight of the real world will arise quite naturally, with no effort at all, for I will be seeing clearly for the first time.

LESSON 296 ✦ OCTOBER 23

"The Holy Spirit speaks through me today."

Practice instructions

See complete instructions on page 135. A short summary:

- **Read** the commentary paragraph slowly and personally.
- **Pray** the prayer, perhaps several times.
- **Morning and evening:** Repeat the idea and then spend time in Open Mind Meditation.
- **Hourly remembrance:** Repeat the idea and then spend a quiet moment in meditation.
- **Frequent reminders:** Repeat the idea often within each hour.
- **Response to temptation:** Repeat the idea whenever upset, to restore peace.
- **Read the "What Is" section** slowly and thoughtfully once during the day.

Practice suggestion: You may want to think of the people you expect to interact with today, and with each one ask the Holy Spirit the following questions:

What would You say through me to [name]?
How would You have me tell [name] that he/she is pure and holy as God Himself?"

Quiet your mind. Try to clear it of any preconceptions. Listen deeply. Repeat your questions if nothing comes at first. You may want to have pen and paper in hand, and write down anything that comes to mind.

Commentary

When I allow the Holy Spirit to *look through me* (yesterday's lesson), sharing His perception, then He also *speaks through me.*

Not that I become God's gift to the world in the egoic sense, the oracle who has the answer for all mankind. No, not that. But He does speak through me. He speaks the word of welcome, of acknowledgment, of appreciation, and of gratitude. Through me, the Holy Spirit communicates to my sisters and brothers, "You are safe. You are whole. You are loved."

Having damned the world, now I would set it free. Having plastered everyone with guilt, layering it on with a heavy hand, now I would lift that guilt from everyone. Why grant this escape to all and sundry? Because I want it for myself, and this is the only way to get it. If my brother dies guilty, I die with him. What a tremendous privilege I have, to lift the guilt from those around me, to let them know they are free!

Through me (and you) the Holy Spirit persuades the world to seek and find the path to God. I am His representative on earth, an ambassador for the Kingdom of God. To those who have not learned as yet to listen to His Voice on their own, I represent Him, speaking His words, portraying His attitude and His Love to every person I encounter. That is my function. That is my only purpose. That is my life.

I would be savior to the world I made. For having damned
it I would set it free. (1:3–4)

Am I willing to become savior to my world? Some of the time I find myself wanting to escape it, to just let it fall into ruins and be done with it. The Course is clear on this point: I cannot fly off to Heaven myself and leave the world behind. I cannot reach heaven without my brothers.

The weary feeling toward the world, the sense that "I am so bone-tired of all of this mess," hides my own judgment on myself. Deeply guilty of my own continued separation from the Father, I want to lay the blame on the world. I want to be able to feel, "It is this tiresome place that keeps me from my peace." Peace is here; peace is now. Peace, and Heaven itself, are in me, with me wherever I go. I do not need to fly off, and nothing needs to change.

"The Holy Spirit needs my voice today" (1:1). We live in a conspiracy of silence. There are many, far more than we know, who have caught sight of Heaven. We are among them. Yet we fear to speak because we fear people will mock us, people will think we are crazy.

How often have we hungered, craved with a deep yearning, for someone who would dare to say, in the midst of fear, suffering, loss, and terror, "I am at peace. The peace of God is very real to me." Today, be the one to answer another's yearning. "We teach…what we would learn" (2:1).

WHAT IS THE REAL WORLD?

Part 6: W-pII.8.3:4–5

When our mind has forgiven itself, it is "at peace within itself" (3:4), and the world such a mind sees arises from that inner peace. As we have already seen, inner peace without self-forgiveness is not possible. Likewise, seeing a world of peace comes as we extend the peace within ourselves outward. We had this stated clearly way back in Lesson 34:

> Peace of mind is clearly an internal matter. It must begin with your own thoughts, and then extend outward. It is from your peace of mind that a peaceful perception of the world arises. (W-pI.34.1:2–4)

A mind that has learned to forgive itself and be at peace "is kind, and only kindness does it look upon" (3:5). I have heard several spiritual sages remark that, if spirituality were to be boiled down to only two words, they might be, "Be kind." I have encountered a number of people in my life who set themselves up as very spiritual, perhaps as spiritual authorities, and in the end the thing that led me to mistrust their claims was simply this: They were not kind. I have detected this same tendency in myself as well! It is far too easy to be caught up in being "spiritually correct" or being right, and to lose sight of kindness.

When I have encountered the murderous ego in myself, and have learned to forgive it; when I have discovered my own belief in my weakness and frailty, and learned to forgive it; when I have foundered in doubt for years, and learned to forgive it; when I have discovered how often I do not live up to my own high standards, and learned to forgive it; when I have struggled with my own stubborn unbelief, and learned to forgive it—then, I will be kind. I have learned to be kind by being kind to myself. Let me engrave this lesson on my heart: *The mind that has forgiven itself is kind, and only kindness does it look upon.*

If I am quick to see danger lurking in those around me, and to question another's kind intentions, it is most likely because I am quick to question my own, and have not learned as yet to forgive myself.

LESSON 297 ✦ OCTOBER 24
"Forgiveness is the only gift I give."

Practice instructions

See complete instructions on page 135. A short summary:

- **Read** the commentary paragraph slowly and personally.
- **Pray** the prayer, perhaps several times.
- **Morning and evening:** Repeat the idea and then spend time in Open Mind Meditation.
- **Hourly remembrance:** Repeat the idea and then spend a quiet moment in meditation.
- **Frequent reminders:** Repeat the idea often within each hour.
- **Response to temptation:** Repeat the idea whenever upset, to restore peace.
- **Read the "What Is" section** slowly and thoughtfully once during the day.

Practice suggestion: The opening lines of this lesson are pure gold. I find them very powerful if used as a kind of practice. Here is how I have done that. Pick a particular person in your life, especially someone important to you, and apply the following to him/her:

Forgiveness is the only gift I give,
(Think of seeing past that person's flawed body and personality and seeing the pure Son of God in him/her.)
Because it is the only gift I want.
(Think about the guilt you feel in this relationship, about how much you want to feel forgiven for all your mistakes in the relationship.)
And everything I give I give myself.
(Feel your gift of forgiveness returning to you. Let yourself feel absolved from all your own mistakes in the relationship. See past your own flaws to the pure Son of God in you.)

I highly recommend doing this practice every hour today. It will bring wonderful benefits.

Commentary

What do I want to have? Whatever it is, to give it is the way to have it. And the more I grow, the more I realize that "Forgiveness...is the only gift I want" (1:1).

What can I possibly want more than absolute freedom from the burden of self-judgment? What can I possibly want besides this? To be free of self-condemnation is to acknowledge my perfection and completion as God created me. It is to recognize that nothing I have ever done, ever thought, or ever said has ever diminished, even in the slightest, my value and loveliness in God's sight.

If this is what I want, let me give it today, because "everything I give I give to myself" (1:2). Let me extend this recognition to everyone I meet today, that nothing they have ever done, ever thought, or ever said has ever diminished, even in the slightest, their worth and value in my sight.

Every step in my salvation is already set (2:1). Nothing has been overlooked. There is no need to be restless or anxious, concerned about whether I will make it or when I will make it. I will. That is all I need to know. It is accomplished already, and I can travel this illusory journey in peace knowing that in reality it is already over.

WHAT IS THE REAL WORLD?

Part 7: W-pII.8.4:1

> The real world is the symbol that the dream of sin and
> guilt is over, and God's Son no longer sleeps. (4:1)

The world that is seen by a mind that is at peace, having forgiven itself, is a symbol. A symbol represents something, or stands for something; it is not the thing itself, but something that indicates it or pictures it. What does the real world symbolize? "That the dream of sin and guilt is over, and God's Son no longer sleeps."

The real world is a symbol telling us that our dream of sin and guilt is already over, and in reality, we are already awake. The sight of the real world is a sign to us that what perception sees is only a dream, and there is a higher reality beyond it. When we see nothing to condemn, that sight is telling us of a higher order of reality. When we perceive only safety, love, and joy surrounding us, with no danger lurking anywhere, that perception is communicating to us that we are not these bodies, nor does life have an end. It is telling us that only love is real, and fear does not exist. Within the illusion of perception, we are seeing something that speaks of an eternal reality. What we see reminds us that we are not the dream. Our mind is already awake, because:

> God creates only mind awake. He does not sleep, and
> His creations cannot share what He gives not, nor make
> conditions which He does not share with them.
>
> (W-pI.167.8:1–2)

Mind exists only awake, because God created it awake. What He creates can't be asleep if He did not give us that sleep. Nor can we make ourselves be asleep. Therefore we must be already awake. That is what the real world symbolizes to us. Within the illusion it speaks to us of our eternal reality. Within the world, the perception of this symbol is our only goal. Anything more than this takes us beyond the world of perception entirely. Our ultimate destination *is* beyond this world. But although it is our ultimate destination, what lies beyond perception is not our concern *now*. Our work lies in the realm of perception: "Perception must be straightened out before you can know anything" (T-3.III.1:2). "Instruction in perception is your great need" (T-11.VIII.3:5).

We are engaged in the process of letting our perception be straightened out, which is what forgiveness does. As we do this, we will see the real world more clearly and more frequently, until it is all we see. And then our work will be done, and God will reach down and take us home.

> Forgiveness is the means by which I will recognize my
> innocence. It is the reflection of God's Love on earth. It
> will bring me near enough to Heaven that the Love of God
> can reach down to me and raise me up to Him.
>
> (W-pI.60.1:4–6)

LESSON 298 ✦ OCTOBER 25
"I love You, Father, and I love Your Son."

Practice instructions

See complete instructions on page 135. A short summary:
- **Read** the commentary paragraph slowly and personally.
- **Pray** the prayer, perhaps several times.
- **Morning and evening:** Repeat the idea and then spend time in Open Mind Meditation.
- **Hourly remembrance:** Repeat the idea and then spend a quiet moment in meditation.
- **Frequent reminders:** Repeat the idea often within each hour.
- **Response to temptation:** Repeat the idea whenever upset, to restore peace.
- **Read the "What Is" section** slowly and thoughtfully once during the day.

Commentary

"My gratitude permits my love to be accepted without fear" (1:1). It is speaking here of my love for the Father and His Son. As the Course often points out, in my wrong mind I am afraid of my own love for God and His Son, because it seems that if I give in to it, I will lose myself in the infinity of God. I *will* lose my "little self" in Him, but not my true Identity. It is the false identity I am afraid of losing, and clinging to it, attempting to preserve ego identification, makes me terrified of my own love of God.

"Gratitude" is what "permits my love to be accepted without fear." Gratitude is simply the acceptance of and thankfulness for God's gifts: "I accept instead what God establishes as mine" (1:5). When I let go of what I think I made—the ego identity—and accept instead God's gift of my true Self, with thanks, suddenly my love for God and for His Son is no longer terrifying. All that makes it seem frightening are my vain attempts to make real what never was real and to hold on to my separateness.

Deep in my heart, I love You, Father. I let go, even if only for an instant, of what I have been trying to protect. I liberate my love, freeing it to flow unhindered. I allow myself to feel its depth. So often it seems to me that I do not love You; now, it is refreshing and cleansing to simply allow that love free course, to acknowledge its presence within me. I have the gift of my secure Identity in You; there is no need to protect a nonexistent "something else."

Deep in my heart, Father, I also love Your Son, the Christ Who is my true Self, and the shared Self of every living thing. I accept the Son as my Self, and I accept my sisters and brothers as parts, with me, of that one Self. Your Son is Your gift to me, and is me. So often it seems to me that I do not love some aspects of the Son, some of those who seem to differ from me, or who seem antagonistic to me. Now, in this moment, I acknowledge them all with gratitude as parts of my Self. I am no longer, for this instant at least, protecting this little fenced-off aspect I have known as "me." I embrace them all with love.

I am so glad You describe the journey as going "through fear to meet my Love" (1:5). Because there is fear. I feel frightened to let go of me. Who will I be? What will be left? How wonderful to know that what I fear to lose is not lost at all; it is expanded and uplifted into something far greater than I have ever believed possible. When I have gone through fear, what I meet is my Love. This, truly, is no sacrifice!

"I am grateful for…escape from everything that would obscure my love for God my Father and His holy Son" (2:4).

WHAT IS THE REAL WORLD?

Part 8: W-pII.8.4:2–3

As we begin to perceive the real world, we are beginning to wake up. Perhaps we have had some tiny glimpses of the real world. The Text refers to "a little flicker of your eyelids, closed so long" (T-18.III.3:4); perhaps we have known that much, at least. Each glimpse of the real world we experience is a bit like the misty images of our bedroom as we hover between sleep and wakefulness. Sometimes those images, flashed upon us as our eyes briefly flick open, become integrated into a dream that is still going on. That is what we are like. We are in that odd state halfway between sleeping and waking. The Course refers to a border-land between the worlds, in which "you are like to one who still hallu-cinates, but lacks conviction in what he sees" (T-26.V.11:7).

"His waking eyes perceive the sure reflection of his Father's Love; the certain promise that he is redeemed" (4:2). We are not yet wholly awake, but we are waking. The sights of the real world reflect the Father's Love to us. The new perceptions, given us by the Holy Spirit, bolster our confidence that we are, indeed, redeemed.

The more we see the real world, the more we realize that the need for time is over. "The real world signifies the end of time, for its perception makes time purposeless" (4:3). The purpose of time for us is nothing more than to perceive the real world. When we perceive it, there is no more need for time because it has accomplished its purpose. In Review IV of the Workbook, we are told that each time we pause to practice the lesson for the day, we are "using time for its intended purpose" (W-pI.rIV.In.7:3). Each time we stop and try to overcome an obstacle to peace, each time we let the mercy of God come to us in forgiveness, we are using time for the only purpose it has. "Time was made for this" (W-pI.193.10:4; see all of W-pI.193.10:1–5).

Let me, then, today, use time for its intended purpose. Let me remember the lesson, morning and evening, and every hour in between, and often between the hours. Let me cooperate willingly in the trans-formation of my perceptions. Each time I sense a disturbance in my peace, let me turn within, and seek the healing light of God. Let me real-ize that this is the only thing time is for, and that there is no better way to spend it. Let me seek to hasten the day when I will have no more need of time, when all my perceptions have become united with the vision of Christ, and the real world stands sparkling in beauty before my eyes.

LESSON 299 ✦ OCTOBER 26
"Eternal holiness abides in me."

Practice instructions

See complete instructions on page 135. A short summary:

- **Read** the commentary paragraph slowly and personally.
- **Pray** the prayer, perhaps several times.
- **Morning and evening:** Repeat the idea and then spend time in Open Mind Meditation.
- **Hourly remembrance:** Repeat the idea and then spend a quiet moment in meditation.
- **Frequent reminders:** Repeat the idea often within each hour.
- **Response to temptation:** Repeat the idea whenever upset, to restore peace.
- **Read the "What Is" section** slowly and thoughtfully once during the day.

Practice suggestion: This is another favorite prayer of mine. I recommend praying it very slowly and intentionally, making it a genuine communication from you to God. Expect Him to hear you. Let the prayer draw you into a state of rest and quiet, in which you relax in the happy awareness that nothing you can do can change your original holiness. Let it draw you into a deep meditation, which will be far richer for having been introduced by this lovely prayer.

Commentary

This is the sort of lesson that always brings awareness of my split mind to me. One part is sighing, blissfully, "Ah! How wonderful to know that God's creation rests intact in me." The other part is looking around and over my shoulder while saying, "You talkin' to me?"

Sometimes, Father, I can accept the idea that there is holiness in me. I want to accept it more often, and more deeply. I want to know that holiness is all that I am. I can relate to the first line, that "my holiness is far beyond my own ability to understand or know" (1:1). At least the "beyond my ability" part. Yet there is some part of me that knows the holiness is there; perhaps unknown, perhaps not yet understood, but still…there.

When I am aware of my union with God; when I allow that realization to leak through into my consciousness; then, together with Him, I know that it is so, that holiness abides in me.

The Course belabors this point, repeating it so frequently that I have to realize that there is enormous resistance in me to getting it:

> My holiness…is not mine to be destroyed by sin. It is not
> mine to suffer from attack. Illusions can obscure it, but can
> not put out its radiance, nor dim its light.   (2:1–4)

I can alter my behavior, I can hallucinate and believe I have changed my essential nature, but I cannot in reality change what I am, I cannot change what God created as me. My attack on myself didn't work, and never will. I remain as God created me: the holy Son of God Himself. Anything which seems to say otherwise is an illusion, a fabrication of my mind, desperately striving to hold on to its ego identification. Guilt is such a fabrication. No one who is holy could be guilty; therefore, if I am guilty I must not be holy. This is how the ego mind tries to prove its reality to me.

This day, I affirm that my holiness is not of me (2:1). I'm not responsible for creating it, nor can anything I do, think, or say affect it. God wills that I know it and so it will be known. I lay my cynicism aside. I allow the thought to lodge in my mind:

Eternal holiness abides in me.

WHAT IS THE REAL WORLD?

Part 9: W-pII.8.5:1–2

Once time has served the purpose of the Holy Spirit, He has no more need for it. But it is up to us whose purpose time serves. Two sections in the Text discuss the two uses of time: Chapter 13, section IV, "The Function of Time," and Chapter 15, section I, "The Two Uses of Time." These sections tell us, in sum, that we can use time for the ego or for the

Holy Spirit. The ego uses time to perpetuate itself through seeking our death. It sees the purpose of time as destruction. The Holy Spirit sees time's purpose as healing.

> The ego, like the Holy Spirit, uses time to convince you of the inevitability of the goal and end of teaching. To the ego the end is death, which *is* its end. But to the Holy Spirit the goal is life, which *has* no end.   (T-15.I.2:7–9)

We are asked to "begin to practice the Holy Spirit's use of time as a teaching aid to happiness and peace" (T-15.I.9:4), and we do this by practicing the holy instant. "Time is your friend, if you leave it to the Holy Spirit to use" (T-15.I.15:1). There is a need for time while we are still learning to use it only for His purposes, to take the present moment, letting past and future go, and seek peace within the holy instant.

> Each day should be devoted to miracles. The purpose of time is to enable you to learn how to use time constructively. It is thus a teaching device and a means to an end. Time will cease when it is no longer useful in facilitating learning.   (T-1.I.15:1–4)

Sentence 2 starts with the word "now." That "now" refers to the point at which time has served its purpose. There is nothing more to be done, nothing for Him to teach us, nothing for us to learn or to do, except to wait "for God to take His final step." Time continues briefly, allowing us a short while to appreciate the real world, and then time and perception disappear. This "last step" is something referred to quite often in the Course; the phrase "last step" or "final step" occurs twenty-nine times (see, for instance, T-6.V(C).5 and T-7.I). It represents the transition out of perception (duality) and into knowledge (unity), out of the world and into Heaven, out of the body and into spirit. Every time it is very clear that this is something accomplished by God alone; we have nothing to do with it. Our only part is preparing ourselves for it, cleaning up our perception until all of it is "true perception," free from fear. Or as it was put in the longer quotation above, "Each day should be devoted to miracles." That is all that time is for.

LESSON 300 ✦ OCTOBER 27

"Only an instant does this world endure."

Practice instructions

See complete instructions on page 135. A short summary:

- **Read** the commentary paragraph slowly and personally.
- **Pray** the prayer, perhaps several times.
- **Morning and evening:** Repeat the idea and then spend time in Open Mind Meditation.
- **Hourly remembrance:** Repeat the idea and then spend a quiet moment in meditation.
- **Frequent reminders:** Repeat the idea often within each hour.
- **Response to temptation:** Repeat the idea whenever upset, to restore peace.
- **Read the "What Is" section** slowly and thoughtfully once during the day.

Practice suggestion: As an additional exercise, think of some inner pattern of yours which you wish was gone, or some outer difficulty which you would like to see vanish. Imagine the thing you choose appearing as a cloud in the sky. Note how the cloud looks, what its shape, size, and color are. Then repeat:

Only an instant does this _____ endure.
Let me see beyond that tiny instant to eternity.

Then imagine the cloud vanishing.

Commentary

What a great lesson with which to end a series of ten days in which we have been thinking on the section "What Is the Real World?" The thought here is the flip side of the holy instant. This world is nothing but the unholy instant. Only two instants exist, and we are in one or the other all the time.

The idea for today could be taken negatively, with a focus on the transitory nature of life, "a brief candle," as Shakespeare called it, where

447

our "joys are gone before they are possessed" (1:1). On the other hand, the brevity of this world's existence can be a very encouraging thought! "Yet this is also the idea that lets no false perception keep us in its hold, nor represent more than a passing cloud upon a sky eternally serene" (1:2).

The hallucination that is this world is nothing more than a passing cloud that is crossing the serenity of our right mind. Our false perceptions will endure no more than an instant, and then they will be gone. Like a child on a long automobile trip, "soon" can seem to us to be forever, but our Father knows the end is certain. The clouds of false perception will dissipate, the sun will come out again, having been hidden only for an instant. Our minds will recognize their own serenity once more.

> It is this serenity we seek, unclouded, obvious and sure, today. (1:3)

Let me, then, seek that serenity. Let me seek it now, and every time today I can remember to do so. Let me open myself to that holy instant, and remember that beyond the clouds that seem to darken my mind, the sun shines uninterrupted. Let me be glad and grateful that "the world endures but for an instant" (2:4). Let me "go beyond that tiny instant to eternity" (2:5). Let me do so *now*. Let me reach to that other state of mind often today.

WHAT IS THE REAL WORLD?

Part 10: W-pII.8.5:3–4

"That instant," the instant in which God takes His final step (5:2), "is our goal, for it contains the memory of God" (5:3). An analogy that comes to my mind is that of a football team trying to win the Super Bowl. The "final step" is the awarding of the trophy, so to speak. That is the team's ultimate goal. But they actually have nothing to do with the trophy; their part is to win games and arrive at that moment in victory. The trophy then is given to them by the officials of the NFL. Although the image of striving for a victory over opponents does not really fit our attaining the real world, the general idea does. Our part is only getting to the place (the real world) in which the awarding of the trophy (the memory of God) is possible, but that last step is taken by God Himself. We are not learning to remember God. We are learning to forget everything that makes that memory impossible, to remove all the false learning we have interposed between our minds and the truth. When we have removed the barriers, with the help of the Holy Spirit, the memory of God will return to us of itself.

"And as we look upon a world forgiven" (that is the outcome of the work we have done with the Holy Spirit, learning to forgive), "it is He Who calls to us and comes to take us home" (God is the One Who takes us on this final step beyond the real world), "reminding us of our Identity Which our forgiveness has restored to us" (5:4). When we have forgiven the world, the memory of God is restored to us, and also the memory of our own Identity in Him. This latter part is not something we do; "it is He Who...comes to take us home."

This is not just an interesting theological point. It has practical implications. Sometimes, once we have entered on a spiritual quest, the ego can distract us by getting us to try to go directly to God. We can get caught up in a struggle to try to remember God, to try to recall our Identity as the Son of God. Although this is our ultimate goal (like the trophy in the Super Bowl game), if we make it the object of our direct efforts, we will never get there. That would be like setting out to steal the trophy instead of winning it legitimately. Our attention needs to be focused on doing that which, if done, will prepare us to receive the memory of God from His own hand. Namely, forgiveness. If we make remembering God, or our Identity, our immediate goal, we are really trying to bypass the steps that are necessary to reach that goal. We cannot skip those steps:

> *I will forgive, and this will disappear.*

> To every apprehension, every care and every form of suffering, repeat these selfsame words. And then you hold the key that opens Heaven's gate, and brings the Love of God the Father down to earth at last, to raise it up to Heaven. God will take this final step Himself. Do not deny the little steps He asks you take to Him. (W-pI.193.13:3–7)

Xll

Lessons 301 - 310
What Is the Second Coming?

LESSON 301 ✦ OCTOBER 28
"And God Himself shall wipe away all tears."

Practice instructions

See complete instructions on page 135. A short summary:

- **Read** the commentary paragraph slowly and personally.
- **Pray** the prayer, perhaps several times.
- **Morning and evening:** Repeat the idea and then spend time in Open Mind Meditation.
- **Hourly remembrance:** Repeat the idea and then spend a quiet moment in meditation.
- **Frequent reminders:** Repeat the idea often within each hour.
- **Response to temptation:** Repeat the idea whenever upset, to restore peace.
- **Read the "What Is" section** slowly and thoughtfully once during the day.

> *Practice suggestion:* To make this lesson more personally mean-
> ingful, I have used it in a more specific form. First, pick someone
> whom you are judging. Then repeat:
>
> *And God Himself shall wipe away all tears*
>   *by giving me His world,*
>   *which I will see when I cease to judge [name].*

Commentary

The title of this lesson is a quote from the Book of Revelation in the
Bible, verses 7:17 and 21:4. We've all shed tears in our lives, some more
than others. Back in the days when I believed in hell I used to wonder
how God could wipe away my tears when people I knew and loved were
in eternal torment. I used to wonder how *God* could be happy if most of
His creatures got snatched by the devil. I guess wondering about that is
part of why I don't believe in that stuff any more.

But how *can* God wipe away all our tears? When we look around
with our "normal" (i.e., distorted by the ego) perception, it seems
impossible not to shed at least some tears over the suffering and unfairness of life and death. The Course's answer is that we will not be looking around with that kind of perception at all; we will be looking with a
new kind of vision.

"Unless I judge I cannot weep" (1:1). How will He wipe away our
tears? By removing all judgment from our minds.

We look on the world and we judge it. We judge it to be unfair,
unjust, and unfriendly. We judge some to be victimizers and others the
victims. Most of all, we judge it all to be *real*. If sin and suffering are
real in the final analysis, then tears are inevitable. "But we have learned
the world we saw was false" (2:4). Not real, but false. It is an illusion I
have projected; it exists only in my mind. I cannot blame my suffering
on it because the only one who has attacked myself is me. The only one
who has been unjust is me. I am seeing in the world a reflection of what
I believe I have done in relation to God and my brothers, and nothing
more than that. When I learn to forgive the world, and to accept
Atonement for myself, I will no longer see the world this way.

Jesus is speaking, it seems to me, from a high place, and he is including me in that place. I'm not aware of having learned the unreality of the
world yet; the world still seems pretty real to me, and I still weep. The
Course assures us that a part of our mind—the only part that has reality

in truth—is already awake, and already wholly knows that the world we see is false. Jesus symbolizes that part of our minds that is awake.

This, however, I do know, based on the promises of the Course: I will see the world this way. There will come a time when

> *I cannot weep. Nor can I suffer pain, or feel I am aban-*
> *doned and unneeded in the world.* (1:1–2)

I can see it that way at any time I choose, in the holy instant, and I am learning to allow my perception to be transformed in accord with that vision, more and more each day.

If it seems hypocritical to repeat the prayer in today's lesson, saying, "We have learned the world we saw was false" (2:4), reconsider that opinion. You may say, "But I don't believe it, I haven't really learned that; how can I say it?" *Of course* you don't believe it! That is exactly why you are doing the lesson. If you believed it you wouldn't need the lesson. Just for an instant, suspend your disbelief. Let yourself imagine how it would feel to know that all the ugliness of the world simply isn't real, that it was nothing but a bad dream, an ugly acid trip, and that nothing really happened, nothing really was lost, and nobody was really hurt. Only the projected images died; the reality of life was totally unaffected by the dream. Let yourself slip, just for a moment, into that state of mind. Those little instants will be enough to take you all the way home.

WHAT IS THE SECOND COMING?

Part 1: W-pII.9.1:1–2

The Course's understanding of the Second Coming differs drastically from the teaching of most orthodox Christian churches. Typically, the term refers to a second physical appearance by Jesus, returning (usually in a supernatural way, "in clouds of glory") to be judge and ruler of the world. This section of the Workbook redefines the term completely. (The Course is notable for the way it redefines and gives new content to nearly every major Christian term it uses.) Here, the Second Coming is:

1. The correction of mistakes

Instead of being a cataclysmic event that overthrows the devil in the battle of Armageddon, the Second Coming is a gentle correction of our mistaken beliefs in the reality of sin and separation. The old view of the Second Coming saw evil as a real force with a terrible energy of its own, a will in opposition to God, a will which had to be combated and overcome. The Course, in seeing the Second Coming as the correction of mistakes, does not see evil as a real force. Darkness is not a *thing*, a substance, it is merely the absence of light. So evil, in the thought of the Course, is not an opposite to God, but merely a mistake, merely the incorrect idea that an opposite to God could exist. The Second Coming, then, is simply the correction of that mistaken idea. Nothing needs to be overcome or overthrown. The Second Coming simply "restores the never lost, and re-establishes what is forever and forever true" (1:2).

2. *The return of sanity*

All minds that have harbored the insane notion of separation from God will be healed of their delusions. The Second Coming, in the terminology of the Course, is a corporate event at the end of time. It is the moment when each aspect of the mind of God's Son, which has, in insanity, believed itself to be a separate being, is fully restored to its awareness of oneness with all the other aspects of the one mind. This corporate aspect is shown by phrases later in this section: "the time in which *all* minds are given to the hands of Christ" (3:2); "the Sons of God acknowledge that they *all* are one" (4:3; my emphasis in both quotes). As long as any part of the one mind is not healed, Christ's wholeness is not manifest. The "return to sanity" speaks of the entire Sonship being restored to the awareness of its oneness.

This "wholeness" aspect of the message of the Course is the motivation for each of us to reach out in healing to the world. Without our brothers we cannot fully know our Identity, for they all are part of It. My brother's healing is my own. No one can be excluded from the circle of Atonement. No one is excluded.

> You are God's Son, one Self, with one Creator and one goal; to bring awareness of this oneness to all minds, that true creation may extend the Allness and the Unity of God.
> (W-pI.95.12:2)

LESSON 302 ✦ OCTOBER 29
"Where darkness was I look upon the light."

Practice instructions

See complete instructions on page 135. A short summary:

- **Read** the commentary paragraph slowly and personally.
- **Pray** the prayer, perhaps several times.
- **Morning and evening:** Repeat the idea and then spend time in Open Mind Meditation.
- **Hourly remembrance:** Repeat the idea and then spend a quiet moment in meditation.
- **Frequent reminders:** Repeat the idea often within each hour.
- **Response to temptation:** Repeat the idea whenever upset, to restore peace.
- **Read the "What Is" section** slowly and thoughtfully once during the day.

Commentary

This is the change that a shift in perception brings. Where we saw darkness we now see light. What appeared as attack becomes a call for love. Insanity in a brother becomes an opportunity to bless. Stones we stumbled over become stepping stones. All things become lessons God would have us learn. The light is always there, but we saw darkness. "Now we see that darkness is our own imagining, and light is there for us to look upon" (1:5).

Perhaps today I can find one thing that seems dark and remember to say, "Where I see darkness, I choose to see the light." Perhaps I can remember to look for love instead of condemnation and judgment. Perhaps I can look on something that seems like a curse and learn to count it as a blessing. Let me begin in small increments, and in lessons close to home. It may be beyond me now to look on global disasters and see light in them, but I can begin with things closer to home: my disturbed plans, the intrusive friend, the withdrawing spouse. "Let me forgive Your holy world today, that I may look upon its holiness and understand it but reflects my own" (1:7).

We are not alone as we travel this road.

> Our Love awaits us as we go to Him, and walks beside us showing us the way. He fails in nothing. He is the end we seek, and He the means by which we go to Him.
>
> (2:1–3)

"Our Love," to me, means the Christ. To me, and perhaps to others of you, He is symbolized by Jesus. Perhaps you think of Him as your higher Self. He is both the means and the end of our journey. He waits at the end, calling us toward Him, and yet He also walks alongside of us, instructing us, guiding us, and empowering us as we travel. Let us be grateful today for His help, and aware of it as we go through the day.

WHAT IS THE SECOND COMING?

Part 2: W-pII.9.1:3

> It is the invitation to God's Word to take illusion's place; the willingness to let forgiveness rest upon all things without exception and without reserve. (1:3)

We are continuing from Part 1 the list of descriptions of the Second Coming:

3. The invitation to God's Word to take illusion's place.

This is the Course's vision of how the world and time end. The real world precedes the Second Coming. Individually and collectively our perception is purified, so that we see Heaven's reflection. When all our minds have come into agreement on this perception, that is the Second Coming. This is "part of the condition that restores the never lost" (1:2). The purification of our perception, and the joining of our minds in that perception, "is the invitation to God's Word to take illusion's place" (1:3). Our mistaken perceptions have been corrected; our minds have united in sanity. Now the way is open for God to take His last step.

4. Willingness for total forgiveness

Of what does this united perception consist? "The willingness to let forgiveness rest upon all things without exception and without reserve" (1:3). In other words, a willingness to not see sin, but to see the perfect creation of God everywhere. Note that all four of these definitions refer to the undoing of mistakes our minds have made, not to outward change. If the mind is healed, of course the world will change, since it is only the mirror of our state of mind.

The forgiveness spoken of here is the final state of mind in which we have forgiven:

- *all things*; every person, every condition, God, ourselves
- *without exception*; nothing and no one whatsoever excluded
- *and without reserve*; wholeheartedly, exuberantly, joyously

The Second Coming is the event in time when forgiveness becomes total. No condemnation and no judgment remains in any mind.

LESSON 303 ✦ OCTOBER 30
"The holy Christ is born in me today."

Practice instructions

See complete instructions on page 135. A short summary:

- **Read** the commentary paragraph slowly and personally.
- **Pray** the prayer, perhaps several times.
- **Morning and evening:** Repeat the idea and then spend time in Open Mind Meditation.
- **Hourly remembrance:** Repeat the idea and then spend a quiet moment in meditation.
- **Frequent reminders:** Repeat the idea often within each hour.
- **Response to temptation:** Repeat the idea whenever upset, to restore peace.
- **Read the "What Is" section** slowly and thoughtfully once during the day.

Commentary

This is what it is all about: the birth of Christ in me. As I become still this morning, Heaven's Son is being born in me. The evil self I made is passing away, and Christ is being born. What I have believed I am is not the truth; Christ is "what I really am in truth" (2:4). "He is my Self as You created me" (2:6). Let me feel the wonder of it. Let me hear the rustle of angelic wings, watching with joy as I become aware of what is happening in me.

Why does it seem so hard for us to connect with the truth of all this? As you try to sense the reality of this Christ Self as yourself, notice the thoughts that arise in opposition to it. Thoughts of guilt and unworthiness. Mocking thoughts. Thoughts of feeling foolish. Thoughts of futility. These thoughts comprise the ego; they are thoughts that form the "evil self" (2:2) you made for yourself. They mean nothing. Let them go, dancing in the wind, and allow the awareness of your true grandeur as God's creation take their place. This noble, wondrous Self you sometimes sense, and perhaps sense now; this Self of endless love; this universal beneficence, gentleness, and kindness—this is you.

"Safe in Your Arms let me receive Your Son" (2:8). As our minds turn to the light in us and look for Christ, he is reborn in us (see W-pI.rV.In.7:3). What we are doing in each and every moment that we allow the Holy Spirit to overshadow our minds is bringing Christ into this world, giving birth to the holy Son of God in our midst. We are like Mary, saying, "Be it done to me according to your will."

WHAT IS THE SECOND COMING?

Part 3: W-pII.9.2:1–2

We are continuing point 4 in the list, "Willingness for total forgiveness."

The Second Coming of Christ is "all-inclusive" (2:1). All minds are healed together. This is what "permits" or allows it to "embrace the world and hold you safe within its gentle advent, which encompasses all living things with you" (2:1). If someone or something were excluded from forgiveness, how could there be perfect peace? Conflict would still exist. Because the Second Coming "encompasses all living things," we are all, together, safe. Forgiveness is total and universal, from all things to all things.

"There is no end to the release the Second Coming brings, as God's creation must be limitless" (2:2). No end; it does not stop short of including anything. All bondage, all sense of enslavement, all sense of limits is gone. How else could it be, if God's creation must be without limitation? This is the end we hold in our sight as we do our little part, forgiving those brought to us in our daily relationships. The day will come when my mind and yours will no longer hold a single grievance against anyone or anything, and when no one or nothing holds any grievance against us. All guilt will be gone; all anger will be gone. "God Himself shall wipe away all tears" (Lesson 301). Where we once saw darkness, we will see only light (Lesson 302). What pure and unadulterated joy that day will bring! Then will the Will of God for us, our perfect happiness, be realized and known, and our hearts will overflow with eternal thanksgiving and gratitude, as we join our voices once again in the forgotten song of Love that fills the universe.

LESSON 304 ✦ OCTOBER 31
"Let not my world obscure the sight of Christ."

Practice instructions

See complete instructions on page 135. A short summary:

- **Read** the commentary paragraph slowly and personally.
- **Pray** the prayer, perhaps several times.
- **Morning and evening:** Repeat the idea and then spend time in Open Mind Meditation.
- **Hourly remembrance:** Repeat the idea and then spend a quiet moment in meditation.
- **Frequent reminders:** Repeat the idea often within each hour.
- **Response to temptation:** Repeat the idea whenever upset, to restore peace.
- **Read the "What Is" section** slowly and thoughtfully once during the day.

Commentary

"My world" is, of course, the world I made to support my ego; the illusory world of attack and separation. The sight of Christ, or the vision of Christ as it is mostly called in the Text, is a faculty that is native to all of us, part of our created Being. Christ's vision shows us reality and oneness, not the fragmented chaos we usually see with our eyes. This sight is always available to us, but the world we made "can obscure [our] holy sight" (1:1). So today's thought is a prayer, or a resolution, not to allow that to happen, not to let what our eyes show us prevent our seeing what the vision of Christ can show us all the time and any time—namely, the real world.

> Perception is a mirror, not a fact. And what I look on is my state of mind, reflected outward. (1:3–4)

The same thought is repeated throughout the Course:

> Perception can make whatever picture the mind desires to

see. Remember this.   (M-19.5:2–3)

The world you see is what you gave it, nothing more than
that....It is the witness to your state of mind, the outside
picture of an inward condition.   (T-21.In.1:2, 5)

The world, then, is only showing us our own minds. Nothing more
nor less than our own projections obscure the sight of Christ. Christ is
the only reality, the creation of God, and without our superimposed projections this reality is all we would see. But we cannot use our perception to see it; instead, we must use the vision of Christ, a wholly separate faculty or sense (1:2). We need to let the sight of the world fade
from our minds; this is why closing our eyes can be helpful at first,
when what our eyes show us seems so solid and real.

What we see is determined by what we want to see. Therefore, we
are given these words to say: "I would [i.e., I will to] bless the world by
looking on it through the eyes of Christ" (1:5). Our perception can
become true perception, which sees the world as a reflection of the truth
instead of being a mirror of our projections, if truth is what we want to
see. "When you want only love you will see nothing else" (T-12.VII.
8:1).

Today I want to tune in to my natural, God-given desire to bless the
world. I want to draw upon that will to bless, which is always in me, and
use it to transform my perception of the world around me. I want to see
the world as a mirror reflecting the fact that "all my sins have been forgiven me" (1:6). I will see that when I see all the world as forgiven. "Let
me forgive, and thus receive salvation for the world" (2:2). This is a gift
given me by God that I can offer to His holy Son, of which every person I meet or even think of today is a part. As I forgive those around me,
which is my mission today, they will be helped to once again find the
memory of God, and of the Christ as their own Self (2:3).

WHAT IS THE SECOND COMING?

Part 4: W-pII.9.2:3–4

*We are continuing from Part 2 the list of descriptions of the Second
Coming:*

5. *The recognition of perfect oneness*

The Second Coming is the recognition of our perfect oneness:

> Forgiveness lights the Second Coming's way, because it
> shines on everything as one. And thus is oneness recog-
> nized at last.   (2:3–4)

With perfect forgiveness all barriers, all apparent reasons for separation, vanish, and our oneness can be "recognized at last."

Every unforgiveness is a reason for separation, a justification for
holding ourselves apart. Conversely, every reason for holding ourselves
apart is an unforgiveness, a judgment against another. In order to prepare the way for the Second Coming of Christ, which is the recognition
of oneness, forgiveness must first become complete. Many of us may
remember the song from the musical *Godspell*, "Prepare ye the way of
the Lord," if we don't remember it from the Bible as the message of
John the Baptist prior to the commencement of Jesus' ministry. Well,
forgiveness is how we prepare the way of the Lord, in regard to the
Second Coming of Christ. Forgiveness "lights the Second Coming's
way." It removes the barriers to our awareness of oneness.

Seeing Beyond the Good Illusions
Extra Thoughts on Lesson 304

*This is an "extra" for Lesson 304, some thoughts I wrote some time ago
when reading this lesson. They branch off from the lesson itself to comment on related portions of the Text. As with all my commentaries, some
parts are purely my own opinion, reflections on the Course rather than
an interpretation of it; if you do not agree with all I say, just disregard
the parts you don't like!*

"Let not my world obscure the sight of Christ."

"Perception is a mirror, not a fact" (1:3). We never see the truth, we
always perceive symbols of the truth, and it is our mind that gives those
symbols meaning. The signals reach our brain and a mental filter is
applied, based on fear or based on love, and whatever is in my mind,
that is what I perceive. This is why "what I look upon is my state of

mind, reflected outward" (1:4).

The function of a teacher of God is just to go around reminding everyone, in every way possible, of who they really are. He reminds them of God, and of their Self as God created it. When his brother is deceived and operating from an illusion of himself, he does not attack the illusion or seek to change the behavior, but rather he acts in whatever way he can to deny his brother's denial of his Self, and to remind him of who he really is.

Seeing the real world is not difficult. We already have the vision of Christ. The problem is, we obscure it, overlaying it with our own ego interpretations. We superimpose our filter of fear on perception and block out the vision of Christ, replacing it with our view of the world. To see the real world, what we need to do is to withdraw our support from the ego's perceptions. We need to stop thinking that perception is a fact, and realize it is only the projection of our own thoughts. The world is not really the way we think it is.

This is why, in the Text, we are told this:

> Sit quietly and look upon the world you see, and tell yourself: "The real world is not like this. It has no buildings and there are no streets where people walk alone and separate. There are no stores where people buy an endless list of things they do not need. It is not lit with artificial light, and night comes not upon it. There is no day that brightens and grows dim. There is no loss. Nothing is there but shines, and shines forever.
>
> The world you see must be denied, for sight of it is costing you a different kind of vision. *You cannot see both worlds*, for each of them involves a different kind of seeing, and depends on what you cherish. The sight of one is possible because you have denied the other.
>
> (T-13.VII.1:1–2:3)

This is more than just a different way of looking at the physical world. It is looking beyond the physical world entirely. It is literally denying that the physical world exists at all! No buildings. No streets. No stores. No day. No night. This is pretty far-reaching denial!

The Course is saying that the entire physical world is like a vast hologram that we have superimposed over what is really there. We see the physical world because we have denied the real world. Therefore, to see the real world, we must deny the physical. "The sight of it is costing you a different kind of vision."

A woman in our study group in New Jersey said she had trouble with the idea of not seeing the physical world. "There are wonderful things in it that I value: the fall foliage, the mountains, the music of Bach. I don't want to lose those."

I would say that, yes, indeed, you have to let those go as well, and deny their reality. The thing to see is that it is not the colored leaves you value, nor the sound of music. The real value is in the experience you have when you see or hear them, the sense of oneness, the peacefulness, the joy, the appreciation of beauty. That value lies not in the things, but in you. We have learned to associate our experiences of love and joy with certain things and certain people. The association is wholly within our own mind. In the real world, everything is associated with that experience! "Nothing is there but shines, and shines forever" (T-13.VII.1:7).

We don't really want more fall foliage, more good music, more trips to the mountains. We want God, we want the experience of Him that we have associated with those things. We want the feeling of wholeness, of well-being, of self-completion that we have falsely learned to associate with certain things in our lives. That is always what we really want, and the only thing we truly want.

On the way to fully understanding that, it becomes necessary to deny the reality of even the good things of life. As the phrase from earlier in the Workbook has it, "This is not a part of what I want" (W-pI.130.11:5). The fall foliage is not a part of what I want. This romantic special relationship is not a part of what I want. It is a breaking of the mental associations that we have made, undoing the linking of the experience of God to the physical context in which we had the experience. The physical did not give us that experience; it came about wholly in our mind.

I am not saying that while we are in the world we should deny ourselves these physical pleasures. What I am saying is that we can learn that the experiences of God we have had are not limited to those things! Everything and everyone offers us the same experience. By saying that certain things have the power to give us that experience, and others do not, we are forming a special relationship with those things, with those people.

Even as we settle back to listen to a good symphony, we can remind ourselves that what we are doing is a form of magic thought. The symphony has no power to give us the experience; it has no more power than anything else. It is our thoughts that give us the experience as we listen. What we experience is not limited to the music; it is something inherent in our being. "God is in everything I see because God is in my mind" (W-pI.30.Heading). We are the source of the beauty, not the physical thing we have chosen as a doorway to that experience of beauty. The beauty I think I see in the world is really something in my Self, "my state of mind, reflected outward" (1:4).

LESSON 305 ✦ NOVEMBER 1
"There is a peace that Christ bestows on us."

Practice instructions

See complete instructions on page 135. A short summary:

- **Read** the commentary paragraph slowly and personally.
- **Pray** the prayer, perhaps several times.
- **Morning and evening:** Repeat the idea and then spend time in Open Mind Meditation.
- **Hourly remembrance:** Repeat the idea and then spend a quiet moment in meditation.
- **Frequent reminders:** Repeat the idea often within each hour.
- **Response to temptation:** Repeat the idea whenever upset, to restore peace.
- **Read the "What Is" section** slowly and thoughtfully once during the day.

Commentary

I find myself a little resistant to the lesson today. I judge it; it isn't "inspiring enough," or it doesn't tell me anything new. It asserts this wonderful peace, "a peace so deep and quiet, undisturbable and wholly changeless, that the world contains no counterpart" (1:1). I'm not experiencing that this morning. I'm not fraught with anxiety or anything, but I have only a limited peace; it doesn't feel changeless; I think I could be disturbed. So I feel a bit frustrated. I know that aloneness, for instance, is there, gnawing away at the peace. It seems that it would not take much to upset the boat, and my peace would disappear. I think this is something most of us feel at times while reading the Course.

I recall one morning when I was doing a lesson, perhaps this very lesson, and all it took to "destroy" my seeming peace was to have someone walk through the room I was in—twice!

The lesson says that God's peace is a gift, "come to us to save us from our judgment on ourselves" (2:3). It offers a prayer: "Help us today…[to] judge it not" (2:2). How do we *judge* the peace of God?

I judge peace as *inappropriate* due to my circumstances. The peace of God is here, now, and part of my mind believes that, but I refuse to let myself accept it and *feel* it because my mind judges that peace would be inappropriate because of some external circumstance. "I can't be peaceful until *this* changes, until *that* changes, or until *this* happens." It is an assertion of a belief that something other than the will of God exists, something which has power to take away my peace. God gives the peace; something else, something apparently more powerful, removes it. There *is* no other will, nothing more powerful than God, but my refusal of peace is asserting a belief that there is.

> You see what you believe is there, and you believe it there
> because you want it there.   (T-25.III.1:3)

The Course teaches that in reality I do not have peace because I don't *want* peace. The first obstacle to peace is my desire to get rid of it (T-19.IV(A))! That is the only reason. Since nothing really exists that can take away the peace of God, my insistence that there is such a thing is a delusion chosen to excuse my refusal of God's gift. "It isn't my fault!" I can cry. "This person, this circumstance, did it to me. I want Your peace but they took it away." I am projecting my refusal of peace onto something else.

There is another way I judge God's peace. I judge it as weak and vulnerable, easily disturbed.

Why would I want to get rid of peace? Why would I refuse God's gift? In T-19.IV(A).2, the Text asks the same question:

> Why would you want peace homeless? What do you
> think that it must dispossess to dwell with you? What
> seems to be the cost you are so unwilling to pay?
>   (T-19.IV(A).2:1–3)

There is something, Jesus is saying, that I think I will *lose* if I accept peace. What is it?

It is the ability to justify attack against my brothers; the reasonableness of finding guilt in them (see T-19.IV(B).1:1–2:3). I want to be able to place the blame somewhere else. If I simply accepted peace I would have to give up, forever, the idea that anyone else can be blamed for my unhappiness. I would have to give up all attack, and behind that is the fact that in order to give up attack, I need to give up guilt, I need to give up feeling separate and alone, I need to give up separation. I need to give up the belief in my own incompletion, which is the foundation of my belief in my separate identity.

The peace of God "has come to save us from our judgment on ourselves" (2:3). I judge myself as sinful, as unworthy, as incomplete. That judgment is behind my need to hold on to attack as a defense mechanism, my need to have someone or something else to blame for the inadequacy I see in myself.

If I accept the peace of God as *unconditional* peace it feels to me as if I am giving up all hope of ever having things, and other people, the way I want them. It feels as if I am saying, "It is okay if you don't love me and leave me alone. It is okay if you take my money. It is okay if you ignore me or mistreat me. None of this disturbs my peace." *Unconditional* means it does not matter what the conditions are. And I don't want that! I want the conditions the way I want them!

Unconditional peace! The very idea scares the living daylights out of my ego. Everyone is seeking peace; of course they are. But we want to achieve peace by adjusting the conditions according to our own idea of what will bring peace. Jesus is offering to give us peace regardless of the conditions. "Forget the conditions," he is saying. "I can give you peace in *any* circumstance." We *don't want* unconditional peace; we want peace our own way. "Peace?" we ask. "What about the conditions?" We don't want to hear that they don't matter.

The truth of the matter is that our world reflects our mind. We see an unpeaceful world because our minds are not at peace. We think the world is the cause, and our peace—or lack of it—is the effect. Jesus is saying that our mind is the cause, and the world is the effect. He approaches us on the level of cause, not effect. He isn't going to change the conditions to give us peace; he is going to give us peace, and *that* will change the conditions. The peace of God must come *first*. We have to get to the point of saying, "The peace of God is *all* I want." We have to give up all other goals, goals related to conditions. Accept the peace, and the world projected from our mind will change accordingly—but that is not the goal. That is not the healing we seek; it is only the effect of the healing in our minds.

Father, help me today to accept the gift of peace, and not to judge it. Let me see behind my refusal of peace my judgment on myself as unworthy of it, and my desire to attack something outside myself and place the blame on it. In the eternal sanity of the Holy Spirit in my mind, I *do* want peace. Enable me today to identify with that part of my mind. Let me see the insanity of holding on to grievances against anyone or anything. Speak to me of my wholeness. Let me understand that what I see that contradicts peace is not real and does not matter. It is only my self-judgment (which is not real) projected on the world (which is not real). Heal my mind, my Father. "Peace to my mind. Let all my thoughts be still" (W-pII.221.Heading). I am home. I am loved. I am safe.

WHAT IS THE SECOND COMING?

Part 5: W-pII.9.3:1

> The Second Coming ends the lessons that the Holy Spirit teaches, making way for the Last Judgment, in which learning ends in one last summary that will extend beyond itself, and reaches up to God. (3:1)

The sequence the Course sees as ending the world, then, starts with our individual minds going through the process of perception correction, or forgiveness, until forgiveness has embraced the entire world. Each of us comes, more and more, to see the real world, until all minds have been restored to sanity, which is the Second Coming. This re-establishes the condition in which reality can again be recognized. The lessons are over. The Second Coming makes way for the Last Judgment (which is the subject of the next "What Is" section, starting with Lesson 311).

The Text has already discussed the Last Judgment at some length (see T-2.VIII and T-3.VI); we'll touch on those passages with that next "What Is" section. This single sentence, however, gives a couple of interesting previews. The Last Judgment is called "one last summary" that is the capstone of all learning. To the Course, the Last Judgment is something the Sonship does, not God. Perhaps the best description of it is in a passage in which the phrase "Last Judgment" does not even occur. It comes in the section "The Forgiven World" (T-17.II), which speaks of how the real world will appear to us, and then talks of the last evaluation of the world that the united Sonship will undertake, guided by the Holy Spirit:

> The real world is attained simply by complete forgive-
> ness of the old, the world you see without forgiveness. The
> Great Transformer of perception will undertake with you
> the careful searching of the mind that made this world, and
> uncover to you the seeming reasons for your making it. In
> the light of the real reason that He brings, as you follow
> Him, He will show you that there is no reason here at all.
> Each spot His reason touches grows alive with beauty, and
> what seemed ugly in the darkness of your lack of reason is
> suddenly released to loveliness.   (T-17.II.5:1–4)

This is the time when, at last, the nagging question we all ask—
"Why did we make this world in the first place?"—will be fully
answered, and we will see "there is no reason here at all." Under His
gentle tutelage, we will carefully search out "the seeming reasons for
your making it." We will at last be ready to look at that "terrible"
moment of the original thought of separation. What seemed irre-
deemably ugly to us in our fear, will grow alive with beauty, and the
loveliness of our united mind will be restored and released to our awareness. The primal guilt will finally be undone, and we will once again
know our innocence.

The Last Judgment, which follows the Second Coming, will be one
last, great summary lesson of forgiveness. This lesson will "extend
beyond itself" for it will finally and decisively remove the last barrier of
guilt, our collective guilt at having tried to usurp the throne of God. It
will reach "up to God," for it will completely restore the memory of God
to our united mind. The way will be fully open for God to reach down
and once again to gather us into His Arms, home at last.

LESSON 306 ✦ NOVEMBER 2

"The gift of Christ is all I seek today."

Practice instructions

See complete instructions on page 135. A short summary:

- **Read** the commentary paragraph slowly and personally.
- **Pray** the prayer, perhaps several times.
- **Morning and evening:** Repeat the idea and then spend time in Open Mind Meditation.
- **Hourly remembrance:** Repeat the idea and then spend a quiet moment in meditation.
- **Frequent reminders:** Repeat the idea often within each hour.
- **Response to temptation:** Repeat the idea whenever upset, to restore peace.
- **Read the "What Is" section** slowly and thoughtfully once during the day.

Practice suggestion: Try to read the first paragraph of this lesson as if it were a diary entry of your own, as if it were a series of your own spontaneous thoughts. See if that doesn't change your experience of this paragraph.

For an additional exercise, think of a series of situations in your life right now. With each one, note the main thing(s) you are currently seeking in that situation. Then say to yourself:

The gift of Christ is all I seek in this situation.
The goal of [specify the goal you are currently seeking] is either secondary or irrelevant.

Commentary

Often these closing lessons of the Workbook tell me that I can enter the real world today.

Today I can forget the world I made. Today I can go past all fear, and be restored to love and holiness and peace.

(1:2–3)

471

And it is true. If the "world so like to Heaven" (1:1) is truly real, then it exists now, and can be entered at any instant I am willing to do so.

Yet these lessons, to me and to many others, seem to be speaking from a vantage point that is beyond our current reach. Most of the time, I don't feel that I am on the verge of reaching the end of the journey; do you? I may think that I would like to go past all fear, but that hasn't been my general experience to date. Only, perhaps, in a few holy instants. So the lessons, perhaps, seem a little above my head. But really, they aren't.

The lesson for today itself implies a less than exalted state; it says that the gift of Christ is all I "seek" today. If I am seeking it, I don't possess it yet in full awareness. Strongly, then, the lesson reminds me that today I can forget the world; today I can go past all fear and be restored to love. It reminds me that, in the core of my being, this is what I want. Aware I am not there, I need to be reminded that the goal I seek is truly possible and not simply an idle dream.

More than that, though. One of the means for our salvation the Course propounds is the holy instant. The holy instant is, in simple terms, a brief interval in which I allow my mind to enter the real world, to reach to another state of mind (see T-27.IV.2:1–4) which is, in fact, my natural condition as God created me. I may still have too much fear to let go entirely, but I can come for a few minutes at least and, just for now, forget the world and go past my fear to experience a taste of Heaven's peace, a glimpse of Heaven's light. I can do this repeatedly during the day. Today, then, I really can forget the world and go past fear, even if just for a second or two.

I may not be able to sustain that state of mind. Yet I can taste it. I can bring back the vision of what I see there. The Course says that only in rare cases can this state be maintained; even Jesus, early in the Course, says that listening only to the Voice for God was the last lesson he learned, and *that* only with "effort and great willingness" (T-5.II.3:9–11). We need not despair at this, and should not. The brief instants are all we need to guarantee that eventually, when we are fully prepared, we will make that final decision and choose at last not to draw back from Love. That end is sure. For now we can be content with the fact that we are healing, we are learning, we are nurturing our attraction to God, and that eventually it will carry us all the way home.

WHAT IS THE SECOND COMING?

Part 6: W-pII.9.3:2

> The Second Coming is the time in which all minds are given to the hands of Christ, to be returned to spirit in the name of true creation and the Will of God. (3:2)

We are continuing from Part 4 the list of descriptions of the Second Coming:

6. The Second Coming is the giving of all minds to Christ

The Second Coming is a corporate event, in which every mind participates. One by one, in an accelerating profusion, minds enter the realm of true perception and perceive the real world, shown by forgiveness. Each newly restored mind draws all those around it to join in the circle of Atonement until every last fragment of mind has been rejoined to the whole (or more correctly, each fragment recognizes its place as part of the whole). "Salvation…restores to your awareness the wholeness of the fragments you perceive as broken off and separate" (M-19.4:1–2). The Second Coming is the culmination of this process.

LESSON 307 ✦ NOVEMBER 3
"Conflicting wishes cannot be my will."

Practice instructions

See complete instructions on page 135. A short summary:

- **Read** the commentary paragraph slowly and personally.
- **Pray** the prayer, perhaps several times.
- **Morning and evening:** Repeat the idea and then spend time in Open Mind Meditation.
- **Hourly remembrance:** Repeat the idea and then spend a quiet moment in meditation.
- **Frequent reminders:** Repeat the idea often within each hour.
- **Response to temptation:** Repeat the idea whenever upset, to restore peace.
- **Read the "What Is" section** slowly and thoughtfully once during the day.

Practice suggestion: This exercise requires writing, so if you would like to do it, please get out paper and pen. Choose a situation in which you are feeling some degree of unloving feelings toward someone.

1. Put a #1 towards the upper left of your paper, as if starting a list. Label #1 "My will to attack." Under this heading, list all the unloving things you feel an impulse to do in this situation. Be as honest and as uncensored as you can be.

2. After finishing that, put a #2 on the page, and label it "My will to love." Under that heading, list all the loving things you want to do (either mentally or physically), the loving impulses that are somewhere inside you, perhaps obscured by your attacking impulses.

3. Then put a #3 below this, and label it "My feelings of conflict." Under this list the feelings of conflict that are engendered by having both sets of impulses in you. Look back and forth between #1 and #2 and try to get a sense of how you feel about being so divided inside, about both love and attack contending within you.

4. Then put a #4 on the paper and label it "My separation from God." Here, list the sense of conflict with or distance from God that arises in you from the inner conflict between #1 and #2.

5. Then write a #5 and label it "My feelings of peace." Here, imagine that #2 is your only will, the only thing you truly want. #1 is not what you really want, because once you get it you don't feel genuinely happy. You discover that you don't want it as much as you thought. While imagining that #2 represents your one true will, feel the lack of inner conflict, the wholeness, and the peace with yourself implied in that idea. Note what feelings arise in you and write these under #5.

Commentary

"There is no other will for me to have" (1:2) except the Will of God. No other will exists. The idea that there could be something—the devil, myself, even a part of myself—that is opposed to God is the root idea of separation. Trying to "make another will" (1:3) is futile; nothing exists outside of God, the Ground of all being. Trying to make a will other than God's is the source of pain (1:3); pain is the false witness to the attempt.

If no will but God's exists, then "conflicting wishes cannot be my will." The apparent experience of mental conflict I feel, the mental war between the Jekyll and Hyde within myself, must be an illusion and cannot be what I want. I must learn to accept that the desires in me that seem to be in conflict with my true Self are not real, and do not contain any truth about me. They do not mean I am depraved or hopeless. They mean nothing at all.

I have no alternative.

> *If I would have what only You can give, I must accept Your Will for me, and enter into peace where conflict is impossible, Your Son is one with You in being and in will, and nothing contradicts the holy truth that I remain as You created me.* (1:5)

In simple terms, God created me; I did not. What I am is not the result of my independent choice. I am as God created me. I have no choice in the matter. Total peace is impossible until I accept this as the truth, and let myself fall back into what is so, putting an end to my fight with reality. Let me end the war; let me surrender to my Self.

WHAT IS THE SECOND COMING?

Part 7: W-pII.9.4:1–2

"The Second Coming is the one event in time which time itself can not affect" (4:1). This is true because the Second Coming is merely the remembrance of what is eternal, and can never change. It is an "event in time," that is, it still takes place within the context of time, although it brings an end to time itself. The Second Coming affects time, but time cannot affect it.

"For every one who ever came to die, or yet will come or who is present now, is equally released from what he made" (4:2). When we say that in the Second Coming *all minds* are "given to the hands of Christ" (3:2), the "all" has to include not only the people alive now, but those who lived before and those still yet to come. The Second Coming therefore, although it occurs within time, transcends time. It reaches back into the past to release those who lived before, as well as including those "alive" in bodies at the time. It is a trans-temporal event. No one is excluded. The Text says that miracles "undo the past in the present, and thus release the future" (T-1.I.13:3). The idea that we can literally "undo" the past is astounding, and very reassuring. We are told that the Holy Spirit can "undo all the consequences of [our] wrong decision if [we] will let Him" (T-5.VII.6:10). The Second Coming is the ultimate expression of that, in which everyone, even those in the past, are "released from what [they] made," or freed from the illusions they set up.

I don't know how this will happen. When the Course tells us that the Holy Spirit is not limited by time (see T-15.I.2:3–5), I can't say that I understand how He can reach back in time and heal things that have already happened from our perspective. Yet the Course is quite clear that He can do so. In the Second Coming, every false perception from the beginning of time to the end of it will be healed. No condemnation, and no guilt, will remain in any mind, any where, any when.

LESSON 308 ✦ NOVEMBER 4
"This instant is the only time there is."

Practice instructions

See complete instructions on page 135. A short summary:

- **Read** the commentary paragraph slowly and personally.
- **Pray** the prayer, perhaps several times.
- **Morning and evening:** Repeat the idea and then spend time in Open Mind Meditation.
- **Hourly remembrance:** Repeat the idea and then spend a quiet moment in meditation.
- **Frequent reminders:** Repeat the idea often within each hour.
- **Response to temptation:** Repeat the idea whenever upset, to restore peace.
- **Read the "What Is" section** slowly and thoughtfully once during the day.

Commentary

The Course's way of looking at time goes counter to our normal way of thinking. Time is an illusion. It does not really flow from the past, through the present, to the future. All there is, is now. Past and future do not exist in reality, but only in our minds. One of the keys to reaching "past time to timelessness" (1:2) is in learning to experience now as the only time there is. This is one way of describing what the Course refers to as the "holy instant." (The teaching underlying this short lesson can be found in reading "The Two Uses of Time" [T-15.I]. Read especially paragraphs 8 and 9 in regard to practicing the holy instant.)

"The only interval in which I can be saved from time is now" (1:4). Think about it. What other time have you ever experienced except now? You can't be saved from time yesterday, and you never experience tomorrow. Right now is the only time you can have this experience of being saved from time; this experience of forgiveness. Forgiveness lets the past go and focuses on the present blessing. So right now, this instant, you can enter the holy instant. It can be any instant, and it can be this very instant if you will receive it. Just for this instant, forget the past. Respond to only now. Forget even five seconds ago, what somebody said, what you were feeling. Just be in the moment.

The Course advises us to practice this. I think it means practice in two senses of the word: first, that the holy instant is to be applied, or put into use. Second, the holy instant is to be rehearsed. We are even told to "practice the mechanics of the holy instant" (T-15.II.5:4). The author seems quite aware that we won't get it right the first time, or perhaps not for a long time. So he advises us to practice the mechanics of it, to go through the motions, as it were, until one day our experience will catch up. In other words, rehearse it. The best instructions for rehearsing it are in Section I of Chapter 15, the ninth paragraph.

Taking a short time each morning and evening, at least, to think of this moment as all there is of time is a marvelous exercise. It produces a deep sense of peace when I let myself recognize that nothing can reach me here from the past; that I am absolved of any guilt I may feel about the past, along with my brothers and sisters. And nothing can reach me from the future, either. I can simply be in this instant, free of guilt, and free of fear. There is no past. There is no future. There is only now, and in this instant love is ever-present, here and now.

Thanks for this instant, Father. It is now I am redeemed.
This instant is the time You have appointed for Your Son's
release, and for salvation of the world in him.   (2:1–3)

WHAT IS THE SECOND COMING?

Part 8: W-pII.9.4:3–4

Everyone—past, present, and future—is "equally released from what he made" (4:2) in the Second Coming, which is "the willingness to let forgiveness rest upon all things without exception and without reserve" (1:3). The words "In this equality..." (4:3) refer to that equality of forgiveness, that equality of release from guilt and condemnation.

"In this equality is Christ restored as one Identity, in Which the Sons of God acknowledge that they all are one" (4:3). We may say we want oneness, but do we want the *means* for oneness? Forgiveness is the means that restores oneness. There is a section of the Text that talks about the fact that we pretend to want a certain goal, and yet we reject the means for reaching that goal. It says that if we hesitate over the means, it really proves we are afraid of the goal. We may say we want oneness, and yet hesitate to offer complete forgiveness; we may complain that total forgiveness is too difficult, too much to ask. The real problem, according to this passage, is that we are afraid of the oneness that forgiveness would bring:

> To obtain the goal the Holy Spirit indeed asks little. He asks no more to give the means as well. The means are second to the goal. And when you hesitate, it is because the purpose frightens you, and not the means. Remember this, for otherwise you will make the error of believing the means are difficult. (T-20.VII.3:1–5)

Am I willing to acknowledge that I am one with "that person" in my life? If I have a problem with forgiveness it is not because forgiveness is too difficult; it is because I do not want the oneness it would bring.

> Ask only, "Do I really wish to see him sinless?" And as you ask, forget not that his sinlessness is *your* escape from fear. (T-20.VII.9:2–3)

Each time I reach that willingness, the Second Coming grows closer. "And God the Father smiles upon His Son, His one creation and His only joy" (4:4). When we are willing to see one another as sinless, and to recognize our oneness, God the Father once again sees His Son and smiles. We are His one creation and His only joy, and only as we lay down the barriers of "sin" and guilt, and forgive one another, is that oneness seen, and the Father's joy expressed in and through us.

LESSON 309 ✦ NOVEMBER 5
"I will not fear to look within today."

Practice instructions

See complete instructions on page 135. A short summary:

- **Read** the commentary paragraph slowly and personally.
- **Pray** the prayer, perhaps several times.
- **Morning and evening:** Repeat the idea and then spend time in Open Mind Meditation.
- **Hourly remembrance:** Repeat the idea and then spend a quiet moment in meditation.
- **Frequent reminders:** Repeat the idea often within each hour.
- **Response to temptation:** Repeat the idea whenever upset, to restore peace.
- **Read the "What Is" section** slowly and thoughtfully once during the day.

Practice suggestion: The following exercise may help you apply the essence of today's lesson.

First, get in touch with the part of you that feels you're more or less always right, that you're always justified, always doing your best, that the problem always lies in external forces putting too much pressure on you.

Then go the next level down. Try to get in touch with how much you mistrust your own will, how you wish it would naturally and consistently reach for the highest, the most loving, but how instead it often drags you down into the mud.

Now try to get in touch with how defiled you believe this wayward will of yours has made you. It has defined you in your eyes as a petty, self-centered, superficial, and ultimately self-destructive person. A medieval mystic spoke of the "foul, stinking lump" of self. Try to get in touch with that kind of self-loathing within you.

Then realize that all of the above is the voice of your ego, telling you who you are when it doesn't even know. Accept that

God's Voice tells you otherwise. He tells you that you are His holy Son, forever and forever. Place your trust in His Voice, recognizing that He knows who you are even if you don't. Let His view of you sink in. Let it draw you down to that deep place in your mind where God's holiness dwells, and where His holiness is yours.

Spend the rest of the time in quiet meditation, abiding in that place of holiness, where you can look on yourself with love, not with fear.

Commentary

I find that often I am very suspicious of my own motives. I am so aware that in the past I have done a masterful job of hiding my own thoughts and feelings from myself that even when I am not knowingly aware of anything being "off," when my motives on the surface seem pure, I find myself wondering what lurks underneath the rock, and hesitating to look.

For example, I have, in the past, distanced myself from a close friend while convinced the whole time that she was distancing herself from me. It took three hours of intense argument—I can't call it anything better than that—before I finally got in touch with my own fear and anger that was causing me to push her away. I denied vehemently that I was doing so; I claimed that I had been longing for more closeness and that she was not responding.

When you are conversant with the ego's deceptions it seems hard to trust yourself. It always seems to me as if there might be something sneaky going on in my mind that somehow I have been hiding with denial and dissociation.

So, how can I not fear to look within? What ugly, grungy thing will I uncover this time, if I do?

"I fear to look within because I think I made another will that is not true, and made it real" (1:5). If I do look within, often the first things I will see are these ugly, grungy things— "another will that is not true." I will see them, but the good news is that they are not true. I did not succeed in making this other will real. All I succeeded in making were illusions. The ugliness is a smoke screen, a mask, a facade the ego has erected over the eternal innocence of my mind. If I will look at those thoughts with the Holy Spirit, I will find that they are not as terrible as

I have feared. He will translate them into truth for me; He will help me see in them the call for love, the unconscious affirmation of the love which lies buried beneath them, the distorted reflection of the innocence I have never lost.

For instance, in the case I mentioned above, I was pushing my friend away, distancing myself from her. Why? Because I was afraid of losing her love. Because I felt terrified that she did not find me worthy of her time and company, and I was not going to give her the chance to prove my fears correct. I would withdraw before she could push me out. I would punish her for her (imagined) betrayal by taking myself away from her. I was mistaken, both in my own self-evaluation and in my assessment of her evaluation of me. And the Course was demonstrated to me so very clearly that night. She got angry at me. She got furious, and once got up to walk out of the restaurant, saying she would never want anything to do with me again because I was so massively in denial that she couldn't deal with it.

It wasn't until a miracle happened that the impasse was resolved. Suddenly my perception of her shifted. I saw her anger as what it actually was—a call for love. She was furious with me because I was withholding my love, and she was in pain over the thought of losing it. Her anger was no longer attack in my perception; it was a cry for help. It was her love for me, mistakenly trying to find what it wanted through anger and attack. And as I forgave her, I saw the same dynamic in myself. In that moment, I was no longer afraid to look within. I saw the twisted motives that had been running me. I saw my fear. I saw my icy distancing. And behind it all I discovered my love and my innocence, waiting to meet hers.

We need never fear to look within. All that is there is "my will as God created it, and as it is" (1:4). What I made, all those ugly ego thoughts, had no effects at all. There is no reason to fear them; they are meaningless. I can look at them, with the Holy Spirit beside me, and laugh; I can say, "How foolish! These thoughts do not mean anything." Beneath that is the frightened mind, in pain over what it thinks it has done. And past that, far deeper, is the holiness of God, the memory of God. This beneficent mind, this kind and gentle mind, so spacious and open and magnanimous, so all-encompassing—this is my true Identity. This is Who I am.

WHAT IS THE SECOND COMING?

Part 9: W-pII.9.5:1–4

What are we to do about the Second Coming?

1. Pray for it

Ask that it be soon. Desire it, yearn for it, be quietly impatient for its coming.

2. Give ourselves to it wholly

It needs your eyes and ears and hands and feet. It needs your voice. And most of all it needs your willingness.

(5:2–4)

We are the means by which the Second Coming will happen. Let us give our eyes to see love everywhere, and give them no longer to find fault or to see guilt. Let us give our ears to hear only the Voice for God and to hear and answer every call for love around us. Let us give our hands to take the hands of those beside us and lead them home. Let us give our feet to go to those in need, and give our voice to speak the words of healing, of forgiveness, and of release. Most of all, let us give our willingness to join in the great crusade to correct the mad error of sin and guilt wherever we encounter it.

In other words, we are those who will bring Him back. He has never left, in reality; the return is a return to our consciousness, the return of the memory of our Identity. The work I do on myself is the most potent way to invite the Second Coming. The way in which I affirm my brothers' identity with me and with the Christ, through forgiveness, through true perception, is how the Second Coming comes.

Each of us has a vital part in this. "My part is essential to God's plan for salvation" (W-pI.100.Heading). The little shift that occurs in your mind as you practice the Course each day, the seemingly insignificant change of mind that lets you forgive the person who cuts you off in traffic or the friend or relative who acts unlovingly, each little act of kindness, each moment in which you choose to see a call for love rather than an attack, is contributing to the awakening of this Great Mind, the One Being that we are. It is not just *you* that is awakening, it is *the Christ*.

483

He *is* coming again. He is coming again *in you*.

And as you let yourself be healed, you see all those around you, or who cross your mind, or whom you touch or those who seem to have no contact with you, healed along with you. Perhaps you will not recognize them all, nor realize how great your offering to all the world, when you let healing come to you. But you are never healed alone. And legions upon legions will receive the gift that you receive when you are healed.   (W-pI.137.10:1–4)

Each time you practice, awareness is brought a little nearer at least; sometimes a thousand years or more are saved....

The Holy Spirit will be glad to take five minutes of each hour from your hands, and carry them around this aching world where pain and misery appear to rule. He will not overlook one open mind that will accept the healing gifts they bring, and He will lay them everywhere He knows they will be welcome. And they will increase in healing power each time someone accepts them as his thoughts, and uses them to heal.

Thus will each gift to Him be multiplied a thousandfold and tens of thousands more. And when it is returned to you, it will surpass in might the little gift you gave as much as does the radiance of the sun outshine the tiny gleam a firefly makes an uncertain moment and goes out. The steady brilliance of this light remains and leads you out of darkness, nor will you be able to forget the way again.

(W-pI.97.3:2; 5:1–6:3)

That is what is happening today. Down through the centuries a few people have remembered. Their light has shone, and apparently, in many cases, gone out. But it has never really gone out. Each flash of light impacted every mind in the world, shifted it that little bit closer to truth, until today, in our lifetimes, we can see the beginnings of a "steady brilliance," a light that is too bright to ever again become obscured. We are seeing the snowball effect of enlightenment. The snowball has become far too big to be ignored. Victor Hugo said, "Nothing is so powerful as an idea whose time has come," and the time for this idea has come. It is here, and we are part of it.

LESSON 310 ✦ NOVEMBER 6

"In fearlessness and love I spend today."

Practice instructions

See complete instructions on page 135. A short summary:

- **Read** the commentary paragraph slowly and personally.
- **Pray** the prayer, perhaps several times.
- **Morning and evening:** Repeat the idea and then spend time in Open Mind Meditation.
- **Hourly remembrance:** Repeat the idea and then spend a quiet moment in meditation.
- **Frequent reminders:** Repeat the idea often within each hour.
- **Response to temptation:** Repeat the idea whenever upset, to restore peace.
- **Read the "What Is" section** slowly and thoughtfully once during the day.

Practice suggestion: Today's prayer is another of my absolute favorites. We all have a longing for a day that is not of this world, a day spent in quiet communion with God. This prayer captures and kindles that desire. It can be the springboard for a different kind of day. I recommend praying it repeatedly today. You may want to sit down every hour and go through it yet again. To pray these Workbook prayers, I find it helpful to lay out each sentence or phrase on a separate line, as I have done below. And then I will read a line, fix it in my mind, close my eyes, and say it to God with as much sincerity as I can, and then open my eyes and repeat this procedure with the next line.

This day, my Father, would I spend with You,
as You have chosen all my days should be.
And what I will experience is not of time at all.
The joy that comes to me is not of days nor hours,
for it comes from Heaven to Your Son.
This day will be Your sweet reminder to remember You,
Your gracious calling to Your holy Son,

*the sign Your grace has come to me,
and that it is Your Will I be set free today.*

Commentary

All my days are meant to be spent with You, Father, in fearlessness and love (1:1). All of them. I seldom spend my day this way, but today, Father, I would do so. I open my heart to give this day to You. Let it be so, as You will. Let me know the joy that comes from Heaven, not from time (1:2–3). Let the interfering voice in my mind be still, and let me hear Heaven's music (2:2). I ask not for ecstatic visions that transport me out of this world forever, but I do ask that today be something new, something higher, a foretaste of what is in store for me at the end of time.

Let this day be "Your sweet reminder to remember You" (1:4). Gift me with Your grace, Father. Let me experience something that will serve as a continuing reminder to turn my mind to You again and again.

Let this day be "Your gracious calling to Your holy Son" (1:4). Open my ears, and teach me to listen. Let me hear Your calling today. Let me feel the drawing power of Your eternal Love.

Let this day be "the sign Your grace has come to me, and that it is Your Will I be set free today" (1:4). May there be a fresh and poignant awareness of Your working in my life, Your touch upon me. May I see signs that my freedom is Your Will. May I find renewed confidence in the certainty of the outcome that awaits me in Your plan.

Today let a song of thankfulness rise up within me. Increase my awareness that I am joining an eternal song, sung by every part of Your creation. Let me, as the psalmist said, "Sing unto the Lord a new song." Let me recognize the rejoicing that is life itself, given by God, as all the world joins with us in the song.

There is no room in us for fear today, for we have welcomed love into our hearts. (2:4)

WHAT IS THE SECOND COMING?

Part 10: W-pII.9.5:5–6

The third thing we can do in the light of what the Second Coming is, is to become part of the Atonement ourselves, having received it.

> Let us rejoice that we can do God's Will, and join together in its holy light. Behold, the Son of God is one in us, and we can reach our Father's Love through Him.   (5:5–6)

God's Will is Love. God's Will for us is perfect happiness. God's Will is never-ending extension of the radiance of His Being. We can "do" that because He created us to *be* that. We can reach our Father's Love *through* His Son. It is our choice to join together in that oneness of the Son that is the fulfillment of God's Will. Here, in our relationships within time, we are beginning the process that culminates in the Second Coming, the restoration of the single Identity of Christ. As we join in common purpose, to forgive and to be forgiven, to love and to be loved, we shorten the time until the Sonship is fully one in expression. As we give our relationships to the Holy Spirit, to be used only for His purpose, to be transformed into holy relationships through forgiveness, we are joining together in the fulfillment of God's Will.

It is through one another that we reach God's Love. It is in one another that we find God. "The whole reality of your relationship with Him lies in our relationship to one another" (T-17.IV.16:7).

XlII

Lessons 311 - 320
What Is the Last Judgment?

LESSON 311 ✦ NOVEMBER 7
"I judge all things as I would have them be."

Practice instructions

See complete instructions on page 135. A short summary:

- **Read** the commentary paragraph slowly and personally.
- **Pray** the prayer, perhaps several times.
- **Morning and evening:** Repeat the idea and then spend time in Open Mind Meditation.
- **Hourly remembrance:** Repeat the idea and then spend a quiet moment in meditation.
- **Frequent reminders:** Repeat the idea often within each hour.
- **Response to temptation:** Repeat the idea whenever upset, to restore peace.
- **Read the "What Is" section** slowly and thoughtfully once during the day.

Practice suggestion: Choose a person you are currently judging, and repeat the following lines:

I will accept Your judgment of [name].
I cannot understand [name] apart from his oneness with totality.
I do not know [name] and I cannot judge.
And so I let Your love decide who [name] is.

Commentary

The basic lesson of the Course about judgment is that we can't really do it. We simply don't have the equipment. We don't know enough; as this lesson says, our judgment "cannot see totality and therefore judges falsely" (1:4). What our judgment does, then, is to make things into what we want them to be, rather than what they really are. Unfortunately, it does so based upon "the agony of all the judgments we have made against ourselves" (1:6). We project our self-condemnation onto the world, and what we see, as it said back in Lesson 304, is "my state of mind, reflected outward" (W-pII.304.1:4).

Instead of attempting to judge anything, we are asked to take judgment and "make a gift of it to Him Who has a different use for it" (1:5). In other words, we let the Holy Spirit judge for us. He always judges according to the truth, the reality of God's creation. "We let Your Love decide what he whom You created as Your Son must be" (2:3). He gives us "God's Judgment of His Son" (1:6).

Another way of looking at it is that we allow the Holy Spirit to tell us what we truly want: to see the perfection of God's creation everywhere and in everyone. And then, because that is what we want to see, we "judge all things as [we] would have them be," but now we judge differently because we want something different. Given to the ego, our minds always want to find fault because we are trying to deny and project what we think are our own faults; given to the Holy Spirit, our minds always find love or a call for love.

Today, then, Father, I would see Your Son as You created him. I would judge him truly. I would suspend my warped judgment and accept Yours in every way. Today I want to see the truth in everyone. Teach me to relinquish judgment on my own, and to accept the eternal judgment You have made: "You are still My holy Son, forever innocent, forever loving and forever loved, as limitless as your Creator, and completely changeless and forever pure" (W-pII.10.5:1).

WHAT IS THE LAST JUDGMENT?

Part 1: W-pII.10.1:1–2

> Christ's Second Coming gives the Son of God this gift:
> To hear the Voice for God proclaim that what is false is
> false, and what is true has never changed.   (1:1)

This is one of the great statements of the ultimate message of *A Course in Miracles*: "what is false is false, and what is true has never changed." Put into these deceptively simple words, the message almost seems to be trite or tautological, like "Red is red." Of course "what is false is false, and what is true is true." It's obvious.

What gives the statement its profundity is the fact that *we do not believe it*. As we are told in the Text:

> This is a very simple course. Perhaps you do not feel
> you need a course which, in the end, teaches that only real-
> ity is true. But do you believe it? When you perceive the
> real world, you will recognize that you did not believe it.
> (T-11.VIII.1:1–4)

All our problems can be summed up in this: We have taught ourselves to believe that what is false is true, and what is true is false. We believe that the body, sin, guilt, fear, suffering, and death are all real. And we do not believe (or at least strongly doubt) that spirit, holiness, innocence, love, and eternal life are real. The perception of the real world shows us that the latter list—what is real—is really real, and the former list—what is false—is really false. And *that* is the Last Judgment.

All the learning process we appear to be going through is really teaching us nothing except that one lesson, over and over, in one example after another. Something we thought of as real—our own sin, or sin in a brother, or death, or attack, or separation—is shown to be false, and the love we thought was absent is seen to be present. Where we thought we saw sin we now see innocence. Where we thought we saw an attacker we now see our savior (T-22.VI.8:1).

Then will he see each situation that he thought before was

means to justify his anger turned to an event which justifies his love. He will hear plainly that the calls to war he heard before are really calls to peace.   (T-25.III.6:5–6)

Try to imagine what it would be like to have some situation which, right now, seems to justify your anger turned into something that, instead, justifies your love. That is what the miracle does. That is what "what is false is false, and what is true has never changed," really means. The real world is a kind of perception in which *everything* you see justifies your love, because nothing exists which does *not* justify love. That is what is "real" about the real world. What is false is that anger is ever justified: "Anger is *never* justified" (T-30.VI.1:1). What is true is that love is *always* justified. God's Love for you, for instance, is always justified. God's Love for your brother is always justified. And therefore, your love for your brother is also always justified.

"This the judgment is in which perception ends" (1:2). When we have achieved this final judgment about everything, the purpose of perception is over. There is nothing more to perceive, because all reason for separation is gone, and oneness is once again knowable and known. We no longer perceive one another, which requires separation, subject and object; instead, we *know* each other as parts of ourselves, "wholly lovable and wholly loving" (T-1.III.2:3).

LESSON 312 ✦ NOVEMBER 8
"I see all things as I would have them be."

Practice instructions

See complete instructions on page 135. A short summary:

- **Read** the commentary paragraph slowly and personally.
- **Pray** the prayer, perhaps several times.
- **Morning and evening:** Repeat the idea and then spend time in Open Mind Meditation.
- **Hourly remembrance:** Repeat the idea and then spend a quiet moment in meditation.
- **Frequent reminders:** Repeat the idea often within each hour.
- **Response to temptation:** Repeat the idea whenever upset, to restore peace.
- **Read the "What Is" section** slowly and thoughtfully once during the day.

Commentary

This lesson is the second in a pair. The previous lesson told us that we judge all things as we would have them be. This lesson continues: "Perception follows judgment" (1:1). Judgment is, in this context, nearly synonymous with interpretation. We first want a certain thing to be true; we therefore judge or interpret what is around us according to that desire; and having judged (interpreted), we perceive what we wanted. "For sight can merely serve to offer us what we would have" (1:3). The Course's presentation of perception and how it works is consistent and insistent:

> You see what you believe is there, and you believe it there because you want it there. Perception has no other law than this.   (T-25.III.1:3–4)

If we want to see the real world, we will see it. If we join with the Holy Spirit in His goal, we "cannot fail to look upon what Christ would have him see, and share Christ's Love for what he looks upon" (1:6). The key is in what we want.

It's hard to admit that what we are seeing we must have wanted to see, at some level of our minds. The ego has a sick mind, quite literally; the unrecognized ego thoughts and wishes manifest in the world even though we are not conscious of them. But the world is our mind's mirror; what we see is what we have chosen to see. The world does not change because we are afraid to look within our minds and see the thoughts that caused it. If we will look, He will heal.

I recall someone standing during an ACIM workshop, when Ken Wapnick was sharing along these lines, and telling how, during the television reports on a California earthquake, he became aware that there was a part of his mind that was disappointed that the death toll was so low. Something in him wanted it to be more dramatic, wanted to see more death. I remember once realizing quite clearly that I wanted someone dead—someone quite close to me. It was a shock, but when I let myself be aware of it I was also aware that the thought was not new!

We need to be willing to find the cause of the world we see within our own minds, so that we can change our minds about the world. With changed thoughts, we will see a changed world.

If we will, we can look upon "a liberated world, set free from all the judgments I have made" (2:1). Today we can choose to see the world differently—if we want to. There is no guilt in choosing not to see it differently, but think of how unhappy your perception of the world has made you up till now and ask yourself if you don't want to see it differently. Seeing the real world is your will. It is up to you, and to me, to choose to see it today.

> *Father, this is Your Will for me today, and therefore it must*
> *be my goal as well.*   (2:2)

WHAT IS THE LAST JUDGMENT?

Part 2: W-pII.10.1:3–4

In two sentences we have the Second Coming, the Last Judgment, and the final step:

> At first you see a world that has accepted this as true [the
> Second Coming], projected from a now corrected mind.
> And with this holy sight, perception gives a silent blessing
> [the Last Judgment] and then disappears [the final step], its
> goal accomplished and its mission done.   (1:3–4)

The "this" which we see the world as having accepted is the statement from the previous sentence: "what is false is false, and what is true
has never changed." If the *world* has accepted this statement, it indicates
to me that this is not simply the real world (the world seen through forgiving eyes) but the Second Coming, in which all minds have been
given to Christ. The unified, healed mind of the Sonship is still projecting, but "from a now corrected mind," and therefore what is being projected is a healed world. When we see this "holy sight," we pronounce
the Last Judgment, which is a silent blessing, for as the Course says
elsewhere, the Last Judgment is not a meting out of punishment but a
final healing (T-2.VIII.3:3).

With the "final healing," then, the goal and mission of perception
itself (as the Holy Spirit sees its purpose) is over, and so perception
itself vanishes, no longer needed. Here, perception vanishes; in the next
paragraph (2:3) the world itself, which is the object of all our perception, "slips away to nothingness."

What's the point of understanding these eschatological events?
(Eschatology is "The branch of theology that is concerned with the end
of the world or of humankind" [American Heritage Dictionary].) They
represent the goal towards which the Course is leading us. As the Course
itself says, in "Setting the Goal" (T-17.VI), when you accept a certain
goal you begin to overlook or discount everything that stands in its way,
and start to focus on the things that will bring the goal about. It says:

> The value of deciding in advance what you want to hap-
> pen is simply that you will perceive the situation as a
> means to *make* it happen. You will therefore make every
> effort to overlook what interferes with the accomplishment
> of your objective, and concentrate on everything that helps
> you meet it.   (T-17.VI.4:1–2)

If we have even some small understanding that the final goal is a
silent blessing, a final healing, an overlooking of all error and a recog-

nition of the innocence of all of God's creation, and of all of our own creations, we will begin to perceive our day-to-day situations as "a means to make it happen." We will make every effort to overlook attack thoughts and condemning judgments, whether in our own minds or in others, because we will see them as something that interferes with the goal we are seeking.

Another value of this understanding of the Last Judgment is that it eliminates one of the sources of our fear. We'll see more about this further on in this section, but for now, just realizing that God will *not* be running an inquisition and punishing us for every minuscule transgression of His laws will come as a great relief to many of us, influenced by our immersion in a culture where religion is often filled with fear of God's wrath. The idea of a wrathful, vengeful God is something the Course goes out of its way to counteract.

LESSON 313 ✦ NOVEMBER 9

"Now let a new perception come to me."

Practice instructions

See complete instructions on page 135. A short summary:

- **Read** the commentary paragraph slowly and personally.
- **Pray** the prayer, perhaps several times.
- **Morning and evening:** Repeat the idea and then spend time in Open Mind Meditation.
- **Hourly remembrance:** Repeat the idea and then spend a quiet moment in meditation.
- **Frequent reminders:** Repeat the idea often within each hour.
- **Response to temptation:** Repeat the idea whenever upset, to restore peace.
- **Read the "What Is" section** slowly and thoughtfully once during the day.

Practice suggestion: I find that this lesson is more effective if you make it specific: *"Now let a new perception of this person (or situation, or event) come to me."*

Commentary

The vision of Christ "beholds all things as sinless" (1:1). This is a new perception that *comes* to me. I don't go after it; I receive it. I open to it, and it is given to me: "This vision is Your gift" (1:3). To see all things as sinless is not something that I must strive to do; it is a gift, given to me by God. When I perceive sin, what I can learn to do is to ask for a different perception: "Now let a new perception come to me." I can want this new perception, and wanting is all that is required. The rest is given. "Love will come wherever it is asked" (1:2).

Christ—Who is my true Self, eternal, changeless—already "sees no sin in anything He looks upon" (1:5). This is not a vision that my Self has to achieve; it is mine already, in Christ. All I need to do is to allow that new perception to come to me. As I do, as I look out upon the world and see it as forgiven, I will "waken from the dream of sin and look within upon my sinlessness" (1:6). There is the message of the Course in a nutshell: See your own innocence by seeing the world's innocence. Find your forgiveness through forgiving others.

Like vision, which has always been a part of my Christ Self, so too sinlessness: it has been kept by God, "completely undefiled upon the altar to Your holy Son, the Self with which I would identify" (1:6). That is all we are doing: identifying with the Christ, with something that already is. "Enlightenment is but a recognition, not a change at all" (W-pI.188.1:4). There is nothing to achieve, nowhere to go; we are already there, and all that is required is the recognition of what is already so, the identification with what has existed forever. We let the new perception come to us, that is all.

So, my brothers and sisters,

> Let us today behold each other in the sight of Christ.
> How beautiful we are! (2:1–2)

WHAT IS THE LAST JUDGMENT?

Part 3: W-pII.10.2:1–2

> The final judgment on the world contains no condemnation. (2:1)

No condemnation! It seems to be very hard for us to get beyond the idea of condemnation. We've been taught for generations that in the Last Judgment, God will separate the "sheep" from the "goats," the "wheat" from the "tares," the good guys from the bad guys, and will send the bad guys into everlasting punishment. We rather like the idea of vengeance; it seems like justice to us. We go to movies and we cheer when the bad guys finally get blown away. Of course, when it comes to picturing ourselves standing before God's Final Judgment, we get a little nervous—very nervous, in fact. Because we know we aren't perfect.

How can there be no condemnation in the Final Judgment? There can only be one explanation. There is no condemnation because "it sees the world as totally forgiven, without sin and wholly purposeless" (2:2).

The only way there can be no condemnation is if there is no sin. *Everything* and *everyone* is forgiven, totally. And that bugs us. "You mean the bad guys *don't* get blown away at the end of the story?" It doesn't seem fair to us, because we believe that sin is real, and deserves punishment.

The old-time evangelists of the eighteenth century, like Jonathan Edwards (the author of the famous sermon "Sinners in the hands of an angry God"), had some things right. They taught that sin is sin. There is no order of sin—every sin is infinitely sinful and demands eternal punishment because *any* sin is an attack on an infinite God. As C. S. Lewis put it, the idea of a "little" sin is like a "little" pregnancy. Edwards had people so terrified when he delivered his sermon that people in church were holding on to the pillars of the church in fear that the ground would open and swallow them up into hell. If sin were real at all, he was right. All of us would be infinitely guilty, and all of us would deserve eternal punishment. In this picture, there *are* no "good guys."

Therefore, if sin is real at all, and vengeance on *anyone* is justified, then vengeance is justified on all of us. If the bad guys get blown away at the end of the story, we *all* get blown away. In holding on to the idea of condemnation and punishment, we are condemning ourselves to hell. And somewhere inside we know it—that's why we feel so nervous!

The only alternative is *no* condemnation. Total forgiveness. No sin in anyone. And that is the message of the Course: "*God's Son is guiltless*" (T-14.V.2:1). That will be God's Final Judgment, and that will be *our* judgment when we reach the end of our journey.

> For it sees the world as totally forgiven, without sin and
> wholly purposeless. (2:2)

The final judgment sees the world, not only as without sin, but without a purpose. This notion cannot be squared with the idea that God created the world; would God create anything without a purpose? The purposelessness of the world, though, goes quite well with the idea that our ego minds have made the world up.

Have you ever looked at the world and suspected that it was basically without any purpose or meaning? That the endless progression of birth and death doesn't seem to be going anywhere? We all grow up (some with more difficulty than others, some with more success than others), we struggle through life, we attain what we can, and then—so it seems—it all comes to an end, and everything we have accomplished, and everything we have become, is lost (see T-13.In.2). What is the point? Many, particularly among the younger people today, have accepted this point of view, and have succumbed to despair and apathy.

And yet, there is validity to this point of view. In fact, the final judgment will ultimately confirm it! The world *has* no purpose. It is the misbegotten offspring of a mind made mad by guilt (see T-13.In.2:2). The realization, however, need not lead to despair; it can become the springboard to eternal joy. Seen as without purpose, we can at last let it go, and remember that our true home is in God.

LESSON 314 ✦ NOVEMBER 10
"I seek a future different from the past."

Practice instructions

See complete instructions on page 135. A short summary:

- **Read** the commentary paragraph slowly and personally.
- **Pray** the prayer, perhaps several times.
- **Morning and evening:** Repeat the idea and then spend time in Open Mind Meditation.
- **Hourly remembrance:** Repeat the idea and then spend a quiet moment in meditation.
- **Frequent reminders:** Repeat the idea often within each hour.
- **Response to temptation:** Repeat the idea whenever upset, to restore peace.
- **Read the "What Is" section** slowly and thoughtfully once during the day.

Practice suggestion: Think of a past mistake, especially a major one such as long-term lovelessness in a relationship. Then repeat the following lines to God, trying to mean them as much as you can:

I leave this past mistake behind.
I leave the future in Your Hands.
I trust Your present promises to guide my future in their holy light.

Try to feel the freedom from past and future contained in these words. Let your sense of care drop away.

Commentary

In the ego's perception, the future is only the result of the past; it is little more than the past itself extended beyond the present. To the ego, the past determines the future. In the perception of the Holy Spirit, "The future now is recognized as but extension of the present" (1:2). What we choose to perceive and to believe in the now determines what the future

501

will be like; the future is not determined by the past. "Past mistakes can cast no shadows on it, so that fear has lost its idols and its images, and being formless, it has no effects" (1:3).

By letting go of the past and realizing that it cannot touch me now, I bring into being a future different from the past. My present choice for salvation, my present willingness to accept the Atonement for myself, deprives the past of all its fear. The "idols and images" (1:3) of fear are things such as all the guilt of the past and all the false perceptions of the past. They are no longer available to fear when I have released the past into God's Hands and have accepted forgiveness for myself. I am beginning from this present moment with a clean slate. Without the forms of past idols and images, fear can have no effects.

Based on the guilt of the past my future was certain death. But with the past released from "sin," and life now my present goal, death has no claim on me (1:4). My physical body will still "die" most likely (barring some rare miracle of being caught up into heaven in a whirlwind, like Elijah in the Bible, II Kings 2), although the body does not truly die because it never lives; but since I am not my body, I will not die, and I will not fear death. "All the needed means are happily provided" (1:4). When my mind is straightened out and my goal is life, everything I need to reach my goal is provided by the Holy Spirit. "When the present has been freed" from all guilt and all fear, that present will simply extend "its security and peace into a quiet future filled with joy" (1:5).

The key is in allowing my mind to be freed from guilt and fear right now. I can practice doing this in the holy instant. I can take a moment and allow the peace and security this lesson speaks of to flood my mind. I can bring my guilt and hurt and pain and anger to the Holy Spirit and allow Him to heal my mind. As I do this more and more the peace will extend itself outward into my day. Perhaps the most common testimony of people who have been studying the Course for some time is, "I am much more peaceful than I ever was before." It works. And as that peace grows in the present, as more and more of our present moments are spent in that peace of mind, the future will more and more be filled with joy.

Let me, then, "choose to use the present to be free" (2:1). How many of my present moments are spent grieving or sorrowing about the past, lamenting things lost? How many present moments are spent in fear of something future? Let me choose to use the present differently. Let me choose, every time I am aware of the present, to use that moment for peace and for nothing else. To do so is the way out of hell. Leave the future in God's Hands. Leave past mistakes behind (2:2). Let me lay my life in God's Hands, "sure that You will keep Your present promises, and guide the future in their holy light" (2:2).

WHAT IS THE LAST JUDGMENT?

Part 4: W-pII.10.2:3–6

When all of creation, every mind, has at last accepted the new perception of the world as without sin and without purpose, the world will end. "Without a cause" (2:3), I think, refers to the world's being seen without sin, for sin and its companion, guilt, in the Course's view, caused the world. "Without a function" (2:3) then would mean the same thing as "purposeless" (2:2). To the ego, the purpose of the world is destruction, or punishment. Once the cause and the function of the world have been removed from all minds, the world "merely slips away to nothingness" (2:3).

As the Manual for Teachers puts it, "The world will end when its thought system has been completely reversed" (M-14.4:1). (You may want to read this entire beautiful section, entitled "How Will the World End?"—particularly its moving final paragraph.) In the vision of the Course, the end of the world is not a cataclysm, nor is it some great triumph by heavenly hosts, but a quiet melting away, merely the disappearance of an illusion whose apparent necessity has ended.

"There [in nothingness] it was born, and there it ends as well" (2:4). In other words, the world was made up out of nothing, and nothing will be left when it disappears. Only the thoughts of love expressed are real and eternal. Everything else goes, including "the figures in the dream" (2:5), that is, our bodies, which—with sin gone as cause and death gone as their purpose—will simply "fade away" (2:6). As we have read often before, in earlier "What Is" sections and in the Text, the body was made by the ego for its purposes. The Holy Spirit can, and does, co-opt the body for His purposes as long as we are in the dream. He is leading us to realize that "what is false is false, and what is true has never changed" (1:1), and once that purpose has been achieved by us all, the body no longer has any purpose. It simply fades away.

One last phrase is added: "because the Son of God is limitless" (2:6). The body fades away because the Son is limitless, and the body is a limit. When our minds have been returned to Christ, fully, we will no longer have any need of limitation. What we are is limitless, and a limited body would be useless to us.

This is the "end of all things" as the Course sees it. How, then, should we live now, still within the dream, but knowing this is its ending? We "need merely learn how to approach it [the ending]; to be willing to go in its direction" (M-14.4:5). We cooperate with the Holy Spirit, today and every day, in learning to look upon the world without condemnation, to see it as totally forgiven. We allow Him to teach us that there is no purpose in the world, and to gradually wean us of our attachment to it. We open ourselves more and more to the vision, growing within us, of the limitless Son of God.

LESSON 315 ✦ NOVEMBER 11
"All gifts my brothers give belong to me."

Practice instructions

See complete instructions on page 135. A short summary:

- **Read** the commentary paragraph slowly and personally.
- **Pray** the prayer, perhaps several times.
- **Morning and evening:** Repeat the idea and then spend time in Open Mind Meditation.
- **Hourly remembrance:** Repeat the idea and then spend a quiet moment in meditation.
- **Frequent reminders:** Repeat the idea often within each hour.
- **Response to temptation:** Repeat the idea whenever upset, to restore peace.
- **Read the "What Is" section** slowly and thoughtfully once during the day.

Commentary

In Lesson 97 we are told that if we practice with the lesson's idea ("I am spirit") and thus bring reality a little closer to our minds, the Holy Spirit will take the minutes we give to Him in those holy instants "and carry them around this aching world" (W-pI.97.5:1). It says, "He will not overlook one open mind that will accept the healing gifts they [the minutes you give] bring, and He will lay them [the gifts] everywhere He knows they will be welcome" (W-pI.97.5:2). He talks about how "each gift to Him [will] be multiplied a thousandfold and tens of thousands more" (W-pI.97.6:1). Now, one thousand times ten thousand is ten million. So He will multiply our gifts at least ten million times, except it says "tens of thousands," plural tens, so that means as much as ninety million times. Perhaps the numbers are simply symbolic of "an extremely large number," but I'm sure Jesus means, quite literally, that an unimaginably large number of minds will be affected by our choice. Every mind that is open to receive will receive our gift; millions of minds.

Now in this lesson we see the opposite side of the coin. For all those millions who are open, and who, like us, give the gift of their mind to God for a moment, we, in turn, receive their gifts. Thus, every moment, thousands of my brothers and sisters find the way to God for a moment and give a gift, which I receive because all minds are joined, as the first paragraph tells us. A smile between brothers or a word of gratitude or mercy, anywhere in the world, offers a gift to my mind. I can receive the certainty of anyone who finds the way to God.

All minds are joined. Every moment, a thousand gifts arrive at the portal of my mind, given by other minds. If I am open, I can receive every one of them! In a study group where this concept was discussed, a student remarked, "That sounds like a full-time job!" Indeed. Sounds like my kind of job, too.

Ever wonder where some of those blessed thoughts come from? Ever wonder why suddenly, in the midst of a rather blah day, something comes into your mind and gladdens your heart? We usually think, if we think of it at all, that it must be the Holy Spirit. But it could equally well have been your sister whose mind found the way to God at just that moment and smiled at someone, and in so doing sent her gift to you. The Holy Spirit was just the postman. Someone you never knew, halfway around the world, just gave you a blessing!

This cosmic exchange of gifts within the greatest "Internet" in the universe is going on all the time. Everyone is wired in; you just have to read your mail.

So let us lift our hearts in gratitude and thanks to every Son of God. Let us this morning and this evening spend some time in thanks to our brothers, who are one with us, for all their multitude of gifts, most of which have gone unacknowledged for most of our lives.

Let me say to all of you who read this: "Thank you for remembering, my sister or my brother!" Thank you for loving instead of fearing. Thank you for being aware, for being alive. Thank you for smiling, for letting joy through. Thank you for showing mercy. Thank you for forgiving. Thank you for joining with another. Let my meditation today be on all the ways I am constantly being blessed by my brothers and sisters, and on the reality that I gain from each and every one.

I thank You, Father, for the many gifts that come to me today and every day from every Son of God. (2:1)

WHAT IS THE LAST JUDGMENT?

Part 5: W-pII.10.3:1

> You who believed that God's Last Judgment would con-
> demn the world to hell along with you, accept this holy
> truth: God's Judgment is the gift of the Correction He
> bestowed on all your errors, freeing you from them, and all
> effects they ever seemed to have. (3:1)

Most of us, at least in Western society, have grown up believing in
some kind of hell. We say, "God will get you for that." We curse one
another with the words, "Go to hell!" Intellectually we may have rejected the idea of a literal hell, with flames and demons with pitchforks, but
the notion is woven into our thoughts nevertheless. There is a sort of vis-
ceral fear of what may lie after death that gnaws at our guts, denied,
repressed, but still…there. If we do believe in God, as many do, the
worry about how He will judge us, how He will evaluate our lives in the
end, eats at us constantly.

To us, then, the Course appeals: "Accept this holy truth!" Judgment
is not condemnation but a gift, a gift of Correction. Not a punishment,
but a cure. Not "no exit," but a way out. The Last Judgment does not
enumerate our every fault and then lock us into their consequences for
all eternity. No, it corrects our errors and frees us from them, and not
only from the errors themselves but from "all effects they ever seemed
to have."

Think about it. How would it feel to know beyond any shadow of
doubt that you were free from all your errors, and from all their effects?
That would be total jubilation! The "Hallelujah Chorus" in spades. But
that, the Course is telling us, is the *truth*, and it is this truth that "has
never changed" (1:1). We are free from our errors and their effects, we
always have been, and we always will be. That is what we will all, collectively, come to accept in that moment of Last Judgment. And that is
what we are now learning to accept for ourselves, and to teach to all our
brothers and sisters. We release each other from our sins, that those we
release may in turn release us.

507

LESSON 316 ✦ NOVEMBER 12

"All gifts I give my brothers are my own."

Practice instructions

See complete instructions on page 135. A short summary:

- **Read** the commentary paragraph slowly and personally.
- **Pray** the prayer, perhaps several times.
- **Morning and evening:** Repeat the idea and then spend time in Open Mind Meditation.
- **Hourly remembrance:** Repeat the idea and then spend a quiet moment in meditation.
- **Frequent reminders:** Repeat the idea often within each hour.
- **Response to temptation:** Repeat the idea whenever upset, to restore peace.
- **Read the "What Is" section** slowly and thoughtfully once during the day.

Practice suggestion: You may want to try the following visualization. It will probably work better if someone reads it to you, or if you read it onto a tape and play the tape back to guide you through it.

Begin by repeating this line from the Urtext: *"Help me to perform whatever miracles you want of me today."*

Then ask the Holy Spirit to whom he wants you to give a miracle today. For this exercise, we'll focus on just one person.

Once you have a person in mind, then ask the Holy Spirit what form this miracle should take. It might be sitting down and forgiving this person. It might be a kind word or some outer gesture.

Ask Him, *"What form should this miracle take?"* Now visualize actually giving this miracle to this person, at whatever time of day you expect this to occur. See the scene unfold in your mind.

Now, in your mind's eye, look off in the distance a bit. There you see a temple-like structure. Its two magnificent doors are open wide, and on either side of the massive doorway an angel is standing. You see people from all directions walking towards this building, carrying treasures into it. These treasures are the gifts that these people have been given by others. One person has been given the precious gift of forgiveness and is carrying that into the building. Another has been healed by a miracle worker, and is carrying in this gift of healing. Another has received unconditional love from a friend and is carrying that in.

As you look, you begin to see specific people that *you* have given to, carrying into the building the treasures you have given them. See one person after another that you have given gifts to, walking inside to deposit their gifts. You see recent people you've given to, and those you gave to a long time ago. You see people you gave some particular thing to, and people you gave to continually over years. Note each person specifically.

Seeing these people, you realize that this is *your* treasure house. Even though you experience yourself as being outside the building, everything on the inside belongs to you. It's all yours. And after seeing so many people carrying inside the gifts you have given them, you begin to get a sense of just how many treasures you have stored up.

The person you are giving to today is beside you. This person looks at you and says, "Come with me." See this person take you by the hand and walk you towards your treasure house. He or she is your escort into the building. You see the treasure house looming closer. You see the doors open wide in welcome. As you approach, the angels greet you and say, "Welcome. Your house has been waiting for you. Enter in where you are truly welcome and at home, among the gifts that God has given you."

Walk in through the doors and see the dazzling splendor that awaits you. Feel the holiness that pervades the place. Feel the peace and the sense of home. As you look at the treasures, feel a sense of ownership. Feel the abundance that comes from all these treasures being yours. This is your new home, the home in which your mind will live from now on. Sit down in this home and spend some time just soaking in the holiness, peace, and abundance.

Commentary

This lesson is obviously a companion to yesterday's, "All gifts my brothers give belong to me." We receive all the gifts our brothers give, and we also receive all the gifts we give. Of course the reverse is true as well: Everything any brother or sister gives, they also receive, and they receive all the gifts we give as well. Everyone receives everything. It must be so because we are all one.

"Each one allows a past mistake to go, and leave no shadow on the holy mind my Father loves" (1:2). The gifts we are speaking of are gifts of forgiveness in which we let a past mistake go, instead of holding on in unforgiving grievance about it. When I give such a gift, I am blessed because the shadows of that past mistake are removed from my mind. The shadows no longer obscure the truth about my brother; my forgiveness shows me Christ in him.

Therefore, we not only receive a gift every time one is given by someone else—a smile, a word of mercy, an act of love—but also, we receive a gift each time anyone else receives a gift! "His grace is given me in every gift a brother has received throughout all time, and past all time as well" (1:3). When Jesus looked at the woman caught in adultery and said, "Neither do I condemn you, go and sin no more," and she received his gift of forgiveness, I received a gift as well as she.

Our treasure house is full, says the lesson (1:4). "Angels watch its open doors that not one gift is lost, and only more are added" (1:4). The fact that we may not be aware of these gifts makes no difference; they can't be lost. Every loving thought is treasured up and kept for us; not one is lost. The treasure of love just keeps growing, just as God keeps eternally expanding and extending.

You know, if we could really get a grasp on these thoughts our lives would be transformed. We are being showered, deluged, with gifts of love in every moment. We have the rich inheritance of all the love for all of time, "and past all time as well" (1:3), to draw upon. Our perspective is so horribly constrained by our self-inflicted isolation! We have no idea how rich we are.

But I can come now, today, this moment, into my treasure house. I can "come to where my treasures are, and enter in where I am truly welcome and at home, among the gifts that God has given me" (1:5). I can remember all the gifts I have and guarantee them to myself by giving them away, as Lesson 159 instructs us:

> There is no miracle you cannot give, for all are given you.
> Receive them now by opening the storehouse of your mind
> where they are laid, and giving them away. (W-159.2:4–5)

The treasure house is in my mind; the gifts are all there. I can recognize I have them by giving them away. It's like keeping the circulation going. And since all the gifts I give my brothers are my own, giving them is how I know I have them, and how I keep them. That's another way to understand the lesson theme: *The only gifts I have are the ones I give away.* So let me today give love to my brothers, give joy to my brothers. Let me offer peace of mind to everyone. As I do, the gifts will be mine.

If we feel uncertain how to go about claiming and recognizing all these treasures, this deluge of blessing, we can join in the prayer that closes this lesson, phrased to recognize the fact that we do not, as yet, recognize all these gifts, and asking for instruction in doing so:

> *Father, I would accept Your gifts today. I do not recognize them. Yet I trust that You Who gave them will provide the means by which I can behold them, see their worth, and cherish only them as what I want.* (2:1–3)

WHAT IS THE LAST JUDGMENT?

Part 6: W-pII.10.3:2

> To fear God's saving grace is but to fear complete release
> from suffering, return to peace, security and happiness, and
> union with your own Identity. (3:2)

If the Last Judgment contains no condemnation, if we are, all of us, free from our errors and every effect they ever seemed to have, how foolish to fear it! Street evangelists with their placards proclaiming, "Prepare to meet thy God!" are offering a message of fear: "Look out! Soon you will stand before the judgment seat of Christ, and if you are not ready, you will be damned." Jesus, in the Course, is telling us that there is no reason to fear. Fearing God's judgment is fearing the very thing we all want: complete release from suffering. The judgment of

God does not damn, it redeems.

We suffer because of our guilt; forgiveness releases us. We are in distress because of our fear; forgiveness returns us to peace, security, and happiness. We are estranged from our own Identity by our belief in sin, but forgiveness brings back union with our Self.

Our fear of God is deeply ingrained. When God approaches we react like a trapped wild animal, feral, vicious and terrified. Oh, my soul! He comes only with healing! He comes only to bring us everything we have ever truly wanted, and more. "Fear not!" the angels announced at Jesus' birth, "For behold! I bring you good tidings of great joy, which shall be to all people" (Lk 2:10). That is what we are being asked to believe, that underneath all the appearance of terror, death and vengeance we have overlaid on it, God's creation consists of pure joy, pure love, pure peace, pure safety. God waits for us, not to punish, but to fold us forever in His everlasting Arms.

LESSON 317 ✦ NOVEMBER 13
"I follow in the way appointed me."

Practice instructions

See complete instructions on page 135. A short summary:

- **Read** the commentary paragraph slowly and personally.
- **Pray** the prayer, perhaps several times.
- **Morning and evening:** Repeat the idea and then spend time in Open Mind Meditation.
- **Hourly remembrance:** Repeat the idea and then spend a quiet moment in meditation.
- **Frequent reminders:** Repeat the idea often within each hour.
- **Response to temptation:** Repeat the idea whenever upset, to restore peace.
- **Read the "What Is" section** slowly and thoughtfully once during the day.

Commentary

"I have a special place to fill; a role for me alone" (1:1).

There is a place for me in the plan of Atonement. There is something that is meant specially for me to do, and until I find and fulfill my part, "salvation waits" (1:2). My particular twist on the insanity of separation needs to be healed before healing is complete.

I do believe we each have a particular part to play in the drama of salvation. We each have a "special function" to fulfill, and part of following the Holy Spirit is learning to discover what that role is. It may not be anything grand or large in the public eye. It may be the healing of one particular relationship. It might be, as it was with Helen Schucman, bringing some message from God into this world. It might be raising children and bringing them up from the perspective of a healed mind. It might be tending bar and listening to the patrons with forgiveness. But we do have a function, and we need to find and fill it.

Whatever it is, it will be some aspect of healing, some aspect of alleviating guilt, some way of recognizing the Christ in those around us. It will be a function which, in some way, gives and brings grace into the world, for all functions within the plan of God fall into this general category. Healing is our function here.

When I find my function I will find my happiness, for happiness is my function. This is what I choose today. Today, Father, I pray:

"I'll go where You would have me go; I'll do what You would have me do. I'll be forever in love with You."[1]

All my sorrows end in Your embrace.   (2:5)

WHAT IS THE LAST JUDGMENT?

Part 7: W-pII.10.4:1

> God's Final Judgment is as merciful as every step in His appointed plan to bless His Son, and call him to return to the eternal peace He shares with him.   (4:1)

The plan of God and its ending are characterized by one thing: mercy. The final outcome will be mercy, and every step along the way to our learning that will be merciful. God has a plan, and that plan is to call us "to return to the eternal peace He shares" with us. No part of that plan is anything but merciful.

Sometimes, even though we may believe that the ending will be merciful, we think that harshness, pain, and suffering are necessary along the way. I don't think so. I believe that the merciful nature of the outcome permeates the entire pathway. Every bit of it is aimed at release from suffering. "There is no need to learn through pain" (T-21.I.3:1). When we have already, in our blindness, chosen pain, it can be used to teach us; but there is no need for it to be that way. God's only desire is to release us from our suffering.

And in the end, He will. In the end, we will know the fullness of His mercy, the consistency of His Love, and the shining radiance of His joy. At the heart of the universe, God is an infinite expanse of welcome.

ALL MY SORROWS END IN YOUR EMBRACE

In a couple of articles for *A Better Way,* I have shared my love for the prayers in Part II of the Workbook. They are a wonderful way to prepare one's mind to enter into quiet communion with God, which is exactly what the Workbook says they are for (I make this claim based on a careful examination of the introduction to Part II, especially 3:3 and 4:6). To encourage their actual use for this purpose, I would like to comment on the prayer for Lesson 317, "I follow in the way appointed me":

> *Father, Your way is what I choose today. Where it would lead me do I choose to go; what it would have me do I choose to do. Your way is certain, and the end secure. The memory of You awaits me there. And all my sorrows end in Your embrace, which You have promised to Your Son, who thought mistakenly that he had wandered from the sure protection of Your loving Arms.*

My comments take the form of suggestions for how one might pray this prayer, and so I suggest that you may want to do just that. One way to do this is to read a line from the prayer and my commentary on it, and then pause and spend a minute or two focusing on that line, actually praying it, before going on to reading the next part.

"Father, Your way is what I choose today."

This prayer opens (as do more than half of the prayers in Part II of the Workbook) by having you address God as "Father." Rather than speaking into empty space, or beseeching some remote and fearful deity, you begin this prayer by speaking directly to your Father. The word "Father" here is meant to call upon our image of the ideal father, the perfect dad. What is the perfect dad like? He is near, available, accessible. He is a source of safety and protection, a place of refuge. He provides for all your needs, making sure you are not lacking. All he wants is your happiness. He regards you as a part of himself, a continuation of his line, an extension of his very identity. And so he gives you all of his love and plans to pass on to you all that he has, including his name, his station in life, and his fortune. In addressing God as "Father," try to hold this image of fatherhood in mind. And try to make it a personal address, so that you are really speaking directly to your Father. Expect Him to hear you.

This first sentence makes a powerful declaration. You are telling God that His way is what you are choosing today. What is His way? You might try filling in things you associate with God's way. You might say, "Your way of forgiveness (or peace, or love, or salvation) is what I choose today." You might even have specific things that choosing God's way today will entail. It may come to your mind that choosing His way means forgiving your coworker or giving up some fear you are hanging onto.

But to make this prayer meaningful, you have to mean it. As much as you can, endeavor to genuinely view today as a day in which you choose God's way. This may mean reflecting on some questions: How much have you chosen His way as yours? How much are you still holding out, so that His way is only one option among many for you? How much do you still see your happiness as coming from your ability to control external events and situations and people? Based on your experience thus far, which way seems to promise you more: yours or His? To the extent that you can honestly answer "His," then put that feeling into the saying of this line. See this day as one you will look back on and say to yourself, "That was the day when I chose God's way." To make this more real, when you come to the word "today," you might even want to fill in the day of the week and the date.

"Where it would lead me do I choose to go;"

When you enlist in God's way you are agreeing to all that goes with it, which includes going wherever He sends you. You are placing no limits on this agreement. It is a blanket commitment, covering all possibilities. This not because you have some sense of blind allegiance or slavish duty, but because you trust that God knows better than you what will make you happy. So as you speak this line try to evoke a feeling of trust, knowing that your Father would not lead you to your doom. You might even add, "because I trust You."

You might also want to think of some of the places where His way might lead you. "Where" in this line specifically refers to places in this world you would go as part of fulfilling your special function; this lesson begins by saying, "I have a special place to fill; a role for me alone." Yet it can also refer to more abstract "places" like peace or salvation or Heaven. Try taking whatever places come to mind in terms of where His way might lead you and then add them onto the end of the above line: "to my in-laws' house, to move to Maine, to peace, to Heaven."

"what it would have me do I choose to do."

This line is, of course, very much like the previous one. Again, you may want to remind yourself that you can trust your Father's way to lead you to peace, not death. You also might want to listen for things He specifically wants you to do today. Perhaps you can sense that He wants you to call someone, do a favor for someone, or take care of something you have been putting off.

You have now said three times in different ways that you are choosing His way. This is no trivial statement. Remember the power your choosing has. What the Course says about your learning power also applies to your power of choice: "There is no greater power in the world. The world was made by it, and even now depends on nothing else" (T-31.I.3:2-3). If you say, "Your way is what I choose today" and *mean* it, your whole life could change.

"Your way is certain, and the end secure."

Once again the word "way" is used. In addition to being the focus of every line of the prayer so far, it also crops up in the lesson's title ("I follow in the way appointed me") and in the paragraph before the prayer ("when I willingly and gladly go the way my Father's plan appointed me to go"). These two references tell us something about this way. This is a way we can "follow in" and a way we can "go." Clearly, this way is a sort of roadway, pathway, or highway. It is a path that one travels on.

What does it mean, then, to say that this "way is certain"? For this, we can turn to clues in nearby lessons. Lesson 321 tells us that God's way is the certain way to finding our *freedom*. Lesson 331 tells us that it is the certain way to our *release*. So, "Your way is certain" means "Your way will work. It will take me where it promises. It will lead me to freedom, to release, to my home." Try to say this with real conviction. To gather this conviction, you may want to reflect on where *your* way has led you. Has it worked? A recurrent theme in the Course is that our roads, though they promise to lead us to freedom, end up leading us nowhere. Only God's road brings us to the destination we truly desire.

This leads right into the second part of the above line, for it too refers to the destination of this way or path. We now affirm that the end, the goal, the destination of God's way is secure. This means that we will get there for sure. We will reach the destination, for God has guaranteed it.

So when you say this line, "Your way is certain, and the end secure," try to envision your own journey home. You have walked down many dead-end roads in the past, roads which started with high hopes, yet got increasingly bumpy and futile the further you traveled. Yet when you truly set your feet on God's way, you will be walking on a smooth road straight to your destination. It may seem thorny and twisted at first, but this is only because you will frequently leave His road in search of your old pathways. Yet the further you travel on God's way, the more committed to it you will be, and so the easier it will become, until the day comes when you reach its very end. And that day *will* come for you.

"The memory of You awaits me there."

Now the prayer directly speaks of the end of the road. We have been journeying since time immemorial, through countless experiences and untold difficulties. What has it all been for? What wondrous destination awaits us at the end of the journey? "The memory of You"—the memory of God. To appreciate what this memory is, we must first discuss the pre-separation state. Before the separation, we lived in a state of knowledge. We knew God face to face. This knowing was so immediate, so total, that there was no separation between our knowing of God and God Himself. The two were one and the same. God was directly present in our minds, and this Presence *was* our knowing of Him. He was our Love, and knowing Him was our whole existence and unending joy.

This is the knowledge we forgot in the separation, leaving us in a state of chronic lack and loneliness. This is what we have been blindly searching for through all our wandering. This is what we head straight toward as we follow in God's way. This is the sweet reward that awaits us at the end of the road. Our Love Himself awaits us with Open Arms. There, we will remember Him, the One Who was everything to us, the One we loved with our whole being, the One we have searched for through all the ages.

Choosing God's way means that you see this one event as what your journey is for. You see your entire passage through time as an arrow shot at this one event. You see every day, every hour, every situation, every relationship, every event, every lifetime as having a single purpose—to bring you to the event which infinitely dwarfs the entire journey and everything in it: the memory of your Love.

"And all my sorrows end in Your embrace,"

What a beautiful line! Our Love has been waiting for us with Open Arms, and now that we reach the end of the road, now that we remember Him, He wraps us in His embrace. In the total love of this embrace, nothing else matters. All the pain of the journey vanishes. All the sorrows of the human condition, the sorrows we have carried since the world began, are gone. The sorrows were *of* the journey, and both they *and* the journey end together, here in His embrace. Why? Because at the root of each sorrow was the feeling of being separated from Him. Now that we are with Him, as the Course says, "where is sorrow now?" (M-15.1:12).

This poignant line reminds me of two other lines from the Course that express the exact same sentiment:

> The graciousness of God will take them gently in, and cover all their sense of pain and loss with the immortal assurance of their Father's Love. (T-14.IX.4:3)

> *I need but turn to Him, and every sorrow melts away, as I accept His boundless Love for me.* (W-pl.207.1:3)

I suggest that you really spend some time with the above line. To help make it more meaningful to you, you may think of a particular person's embrace that was so loving it made your sorrows melt away. Then imagine that embrace being multiplied an infinite number of times. And you also might want to detail some of your sorrows. List all of the sorrows you can think of, all those sorrows that will one day end in His embrace.

"which You have promised to Your Son,"

Can you ascertain exactly what God has promised to His Son, according to this line? It is His embrace. God's promise to you is that, after all your journeying, you will end up in His embrace forever. How sure do you think a promise from God is? You might even imagine that you have an actual promissory note from Him, for is this not what *A Course in Miracles* is? In fact, you might try this: Take the Course in your hands and while looking at it, think of its origins, how it says it comes from God's Own Voice through Jesus to you. Then dwell on this line: "This is the promissory note You sent to me, Your Son, promising that I will end up in Your embrace forever."

"who thought mistakenly that he had wandered from the sure protection of Your loving Arms."

Up until now the prayer has said that God's embrace waits for us at the end of the journey and that God has promised us this embrace. Now the conclusion of the prayer puts a whole new spin on things. Do you see what that spin is? It is that we never left His embrace. We are still there. That is why the end is so secure. That is why He can promise that we will end up in His Arms. We are there right now and always have been.

Imagine the following scenario: You are within the sure protection of God's loving Arms. In these Arms, you fall asleep and start to dream. And in this dream you "wake up" and leave His embrace. You wander off, and as you wander, a growing sense of lack and loneliness opens up within you. Yet this just provokes more wandering, for now you must find the special thing out there that will fill this gnawing hole in you. By the time you suspect that only God can fill this hole, it is too late; He is out of sight and you are not sure that you can ever get back. And this brings us more or less to where you are right now in the dream of your life, as you read this sentence of this essay. For this story is no metaphor. It is the literal story of your existence. But remember: You never woke up. You are still dreaming. And so you are still lying asleep in the sure protection of His loving Arms. You are still in the safety of His fatherly embrace, merely dreaming that you are on a journey that is soaked with the sorrow of being separate from Him.

Let this idea into your mind as deeply as you can while praying this line. You might want to use this version: "I, Your Son, thought that I had wandered from the sure protection of Your Loving Arms. But I am still there. I am still there. I am still there."

---

1. If you have not heard the wonderful tape album (or CD) by Donna Marie Carey, *Real Love*, which contains a song with the words I have just quoted, all songs based on ACIM, I highly recommend it.

LESSON 318 ✦ NOVEMBER 14
"In me salvation's means and end are one."

Practice instructions

See complete instructions on page 135. A short summary:

- **Read** the commentary paragraph slowly and personally.
- **Pray** the prayer, perhaps several times.
- **Morning and evening:** Repeat the idea and then spend time in Open Mind Meditation.
- **Hourly remembrance:** Repeat the idea and then spend a quiet moment in meditation.
- **Frequent reminders:** Repeat the idea often within each hour.
- **Response to temptation:** Repeat the idea whenever upset, to restore peace.
- **Read the "What Is" section** slowly and thoughtfully once during the day.

Practice suggestion: In repeating today's idea, I have found it helpful to reword it slightly: *"I am the means of salvation and I am the end."*

Commentary

In other words, putting it very simply, the goal of salvation is what I already am, and the vehicle for bringing about salvation is also what I am. I am what salvation is, and I am the way to get there.

Salvation is the recognition of oneness; how, then, could there be any single part that stands alone, or that is more or less important than the rest? (1:2–3). The means of salvation is not in some other part of creation, upon which I am dependent. The wholeness is what it is all about; therefore the means of getting there and the "there" we are getting to must be all the same thing, and therefore must be within me.

"I am the means by which God's Son is saved, because salvation's purpose is to find the sinlessness that God has placed in me" (1:4). The sinlessness is already there, in me, placed there by God. So since the purpose of salvation is finding that sinlessness, I must be the means by which salvation happens. I carry the Answer within myself.

I absolutely love these next few sentences. To me, if I can allow my disbelief to be suspended just for a moment, just long enough to feel the import of these words, I will "get" what they are saying:

> I was created as the thing I seek. I am the goal the world is searching for. I am God's Son, His one eternal Love. I am salvation's means and end as well. (1:5–8)

I am the thing I seek because I have been It since I was created. I am seeking only for my Self, and where can my Self be but in me? This is a search that is guaranteed to succeed because I already am what I am seeking for. The only reason there appears to be a journey of seeking is because I have forgotten what I already am. There is really nowhere to go.

Try repeating to yourself, several times, "I am the goal the world is searching for." Just try it and see how it feels. Notice the thoughts that come up in denial of what you are saying, and take a good look at them. Notice what it is you are believing about yourself that keeps you from saying these words and meaning them with all your heart, and without reservation.

We think we have a disease of sin that we are seeking to cure. A disease of guilt and of separation. But the seeking is part of the disease! In fact, there is no disease, and only the seeking makes it seem as if there is. If we can, for a moment, stop presupposing that we are separate, we will simply realize that we are not. Truth will dawn upon us of itself. Relax; you're okay. We have no need but to accept the Atonement, to accept our oneness with God, to realize that enlightenment is only a recognition, and not a change at all. We don't need to change; we need to accept what we have always been.

> Let me today, my Father, take the role You offer me in Your request that I accept Atonement for myself. For thus does what is thereby reconciled in me become as surely reconciled to You. (2:1–2)

WHAT IS THE LAST JUDGMENT?

Part 8: W-pII.10.4:2–6

In the final evaluation, the Last Judgment is really just love. It is God, acknowledging His Son as His Son (4:3). God's Love for us, in the last analysis, is the *only* thing that will "heal all sorrow, wipe away all tears, and gently waken" us from our dream of pain (4:3). We may think—and indeed, we *do* think—that something other than God's Love will be able to do that for us. We must think so, or else why would we spend so much time looking for it? Yet love stands, waiting for us to receive it. We keep looking elsewhere because, in our insanity, we are afraid of the love being offered to us.

Our egos have taught us to be afraid of God, and afraid of His Love. We are afraid it will somehow swallow us up and make us disappear. But would love do that, and still be love? Twice (4:2; 4:4) we are told not to be afraid of love. That is one way of looking at the whole of what we are learning: to not be afraid of love. Instead, we are asked to "give it welcome" (4:5). And it is your acceptance of love, and mine, that will save the world and set it free.

We are so afraid that, by really opening to love, we will be hurt. Taking the path of love so often seems to us to be taking the path of weakness. There is so much emphasis on watching out for Number One, on setting our boundaries, on keeping our distance, on avoiding being victimized. Those things have their place, to be sure, and yet sometimes I think they are excuses for separation, excuses for remaining isolated, excuses for avoiding love. Giving love seems difficult, and receiving it even more difficult. Yet in the end, opening to both giving and receiving love, which are the same in reality, is all that is needed. We *are* love, and only in opening to love fully will we discover that truth of our own Being.

LESSON 319 ✦ NOVEMBER 15
"I came for the salvation of the world."

Practice instructions

See complete instructions on page 135. A short summary:
- **Read** the commentary paragraph slowly and personally.
- **Pray** the prayer, perhaps several times.
- **Morning and evening:** Repeat the idea and then spend time in Open Mind Meditation.
- **Hourly remembrance:** Repeat the idea and then spend a quiet moment in meditation.
- **Frequent reminders:** Repeat the idea often within each hour.
- **Response to temptation:** Repeat the idea whenever upset, to restore peace.
- **Read the "What Is" section** slowly and thoughtfully once during the day.

Commentary

The Course is quite clear that our purpose here, every one of us, is the salvation of the world. This is quite different from the purpose for which the ego came to the world, which was to find a place where God could not enter; to hide from God, so to speak, and eventually, to die. But the Holy Spirit has a different purpose for everything the ego made for its nefarious purposes. Our purpose here is to bring the world back to light by allowing ourselves to be transformed, becoming God's extensions in the dream to awaken all our brothers along with ourselves.

To say, "I am here to save the world," which is just a slight paraphrase of the lesson title, sounds very arrogant to us. But "here is a thought from which all arrogance has been removed" (1:1). It is not arrogant because it is the truth; this is what God created us for, and the function He has assigned to us. To say otherwise is arrogance because it opposes the truth and tries to make for ourselves a role we do not have.

When our arrogance is removed, "truth will come immediately"

(1:3) to fill up the empty spot left by it. Our self-appointed roles are blocking and interfering with the function given to us by God. The reason thinking that we are here to save the world is not arrogant is that "what one gains is given unto all" (1:6). So accepting our function as saviors means that we accept it for all; our brothers become our saviors just as we become theirs. If the Will of God is total (2:1), then the goal of God must be total; it must be the salvation of the entire world (2:3), not just of me and you and our sister Sue.

To bring the world home to oneness is God's Will, and therefore it is "the Will my Self has shared with" Him (2:4). It is my will as well. We are here for the healing of all minds. Our will is that everyone awaken to love, and that is our only purpose in being here.

"I came for the salvation of the world." Repeating this to myself, reminding myself of this, is an interesting exercise. Another way of saying it is, "I am here only to be truly helpful" (T-2.V(A).18:2). Let me remind myself of this today. I am not here to make a name for myself, to make money, or to achieve the temporal and temporary things I think of as my goals. I am here to help. I am here to heal. I am here to bless. I am here to save the world.

WHAT IS THE LAST JUDGMENT?

Part 9: W-pII.10.5:1

> This is God's Final Judgment: "You are still My holy Son, forever innocent, forever loving and forever loved, as limitless as your Creator, and completely changeless and forever pure."
> (5:1)

I find myself reading this sentence over and over; I feel that I need to hear it often, because I am aware of the part of my mind that does not believe it.

I am forever innocent. And yet I still feel guilty at times. I have done things, in my life, that I am certainly not proud of. I have let others down. I've failed to be there for them when they expected me to be there. I've given up on love. I have said things calculated to hurt. I have been deceitful. Like everyone, I carry a certain amount of regret for some things in my past. But God sees me as forever innocent. To me, one of the most poignant lines in the Course is, "You have not lost your innocence" (W-pI.182.12:1). Sometimes I think that the best definition of "miracle" is the shift in perception that allows us to see ourselves as completely innocent. It is extremely difficult for us to see this about ourselves; to me, that is one of the prime values of a holy relationship. The Course tells us we cannot, alone, see ourselves as totally innocent; we need another with whom we can learn this together.

I am forever loving. Again, there seems to be evidence in my past to contradict this. The Course would say the evidence is false, that we are not seeing the whole picture, and that what appeared to be unloving was really our own fear and call for love. We are in pain over what we think we have done, but the Final Judgment will free us of that pain forever, and we will be able to see that we have always been loving, and are forever. Nothing we have done has changed this.

I am forever loved. Ah! This one is often hard to believe, and for all the same reasons; we do not feel loveable, and we sometimes do not love ourselves. I recall taking part in a guided meditation in which I was directed to extend love, blessing, and compassionate understanding to everyone else in the room, and then to the neighborhood, and finally to the world. And then, imagining myself looking down on the world from above, to see myself, sitting there, and to extend that same love, blessing, and compassionate understanding to myself. I felt a deep melting inside of me, the hardness of self-judgment giving way to compassion, and I wept. How hard we are on ourselves! And how seldom we realize just how tightly we hold ourselves in the vise of judgment.

I am as limitless as my Creator. That stretches my credibility and my comprehension. The place to which the Course is taking us, where this is understood and known as true, is far beyond what we even imagine.

I am completely changeless. The experience of constant change, of mood swings, of up and down, of high and low, is not who I really am. The Course tells me, "It is not *you* who is so vulnerable and open to attack that just a word, a little whisper that you do not like, a circumstance that suits you not, or an event that you did not anticipate upsets your world, and hurls it into chaos" (T-24.III.3:1). That may be who I *think* I am, but that is not me, not my Self.

I am forever pure. Pure means unmixed, unadulterated. I often experience myself as an unwholesome mixture of good, bad, and indifferent.

That is not who I am. I am pure; without mixture.

And in God's Final Judgment, I will know all of this. I can know it now. I can hear His Word to me today, in the holy instant. This message is what is communicated to me, wordlessly, each time I enter His Presence. This message is what is given to me, and to you, to share with the world.

LESSON 320 ✦ NOVEMBER 16
"My Father gives all power unto me."

Practice instructions

See complete instructions on page 135. A short summary:

- **Read** the commentary paragraph slowly and personally.
- **Pray** the prayer, perhaps several times.
- **Morning and evening:** Repeat the idea and then spend time in Open Mind Meditation.
- **Hourly remembrance:** Repeat the idea and then spend a quiet moment in meditation.
- **Frequent reminders:** Repeat the idea often within each hour.
- **Response to temptation:** Repeat the idea whenever upset, to restore peace.
- **Read the "What Is" section** slowly and thoughtfully once during the day.

Practice suggestion: Take a few moments and reflect on the following three questions, one at a time, using the questions beneath each one to guide your reflection. You may even want to write down your reflections.

Can His Will do all things in me?
If not, doesn't that mean that I am not His creation?
If I am not His creation, where did I come from?
Did I spring out of nowhere?

Can His Will reach through me to all the world?
If not, doesn't that mean there are some places He cannot go?
Does that make sense?

Is there any limit on His Will?
Could God's Will possibly be limited?
Just one more limited will among many?

Reflecting on these questions has prepared you to fully accept today's idea. Now repeat that idea in a special way: Imagine that you are the risen Jesus speaking those words. As Allen points out

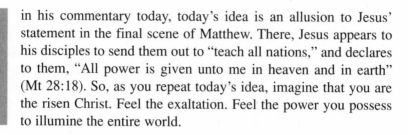

in his commentary today, today's idea is an allusion to Jesus' statement in the final scene of Matthew. There, Jesus appears to his disciples to send them out to "teach all nations," and declares to them, "All power is given unto me in heaven and in earth" (Mt 28:18). So, as you repeat today's idea, imagine that you are the risen Christ. Feel the exaltation. Feel the power you possess to illumine the entire world.

Commentary

Those of us who have not studied the Bible, or the Gospels in particular, may not recognize these words as a paraphrase of words spoken by Jesus shortly after the resurrection: "All power is given unto me" (Mt 28:18). I find it significant that the Course puts these words into *our* mouths. It is an indication of the equal plane on which the Course places us, with Jesus. He was not anything we are not; all of us, along with him, are equal sons of God. He's just a little further along in time (or perhaps out of time), but with the same raw material. We are all the Son of God, together, as God created us.

This lesson expands on the idea of the limitlessness of the Son of God that is mentioned in "What Is the Last Judgment?" There, God says, "You are still My holy Son...as limitless as your Creator" (W-pII.10.5:1). Here we are told we (as the Son of God) are "limitless" (1:1); without limit on any of our attributes, whether strength, peace, joy, or whatever. Limitless strength, limitless peace, limitless joy. To be honest, I can't even conceive of what joy *without limits* is like, and yet this lesson says it is mine. I know joy. I know a great deal of joy. Sometimes, I am so joyful I can scarcely contain it. But joy with no limit at all? What must that be like?

I think we all put mental limits on our strength, our peace, and our joy. And our happiness, for that matter. Haven't you ever had the feeling that it is somehow dangerous to get *too* happy? (What a strange juxtaposition of words is that phrase, "too happy!") "Watch out!" we think. "We don't want to become 'bliss ninnies.'" Yet the characteristic of the Son of God is limitless joy. How will we ever come to know that as our own while we place limits on our joy? Our egos act like governors on the inner engine of happiness and joy; we can get just so happy, and then the power seems to cut out. We need to cut loose from the governor.

Do I really believe that what I will with my Creator "must be done"

(1:3)? Do I believe that my holy will cannot be denied (1:4)? There are those who catch a glimpse of this, and they are those who seem to accomplish so much in their lives, refusing to believe that what they envision cannot come to pass. Instead they realize it *must* come to pass.

Of course, we are not speaking here in earthly terms alone. This isn't the message of mastery of will, of the dominance of our environment by sheer force of will. This speaks of our "holy" will, joined with God's Will, which is expressed in the extension of His Being. Here, we have unlimited power. In this, "Your Will can do all things in me, and then extend to all the world as well through me" (2:1). Each of us can be an unlimited force for good and for God in this world if we transcend our beliefs in limitations. The power of love, for instance, is without limit, because there is nothing *real* to oppose it.

Let me examine my thoughts today, my Father, for the beliefs in limits that hold back Your power working in me and through me. Let me recognize them as false, and open myself to Your great power, working through me, to extend into all the world.

WHAT IS THE LAST JUDGMENT?

Part 10: W-pII.10.5:2–3

"Therefore awaken and return to Me. I am Your Father and
you are My Son." (5:2–3)

The Final Judgment of God ends with this, completing the statement we covered yesterday. All of the things God is here quoted as saying of us are things we have difficulty accepting about ourselves. We need to awaken from the dream in which their opposite seems true, and return to the Father Who has never ceased loving us with an everlasting love. "You are My Son." That is what we all long to hear, and all of us, like the prodigal son in the Bible, fear that we have lost the right to hear them. The prodigal was so filled with guilt that he went back to his father hoping, at best, to be taken in and treated as the hired help. Instead, he was welcomed with a banquet. His father met him on the road.

Do we fear to approach God? Do we hesitate to turn to Him? Do we feel ashamed of how we have lived, and of what we have done with the gifts He has given us? He is not angry. He is not ashamed of us. He only knows that we are His children, His beloved. And He is forever calling to us to return to Him, out of the nightmare in which we have lost ourselves, waiting to welcome us once again into His loving arms.

XIV

Lessons 321 - 330
What Is Creation?

LESSON 321 ✦ NOVEMBER 17
"Father, my freedom is in You alone."

Practice instructions

See complete instructions on page 135. A short summary:

- **Read** the commentary paragraph slowly and personally.
- **Pray** the prayer, perhaps several times.
- **Morning and evening:** Repeat the idea and then spend time in Open Mind Meditation.
- **Hourly remembrance:** Repeat the idea and then spend a quiet moment in meditation.
- **Frequent reminders:** Repeat the idea often within each hour.
- **Response to temptation:** Repeat the idea whenever upset, to restore peace.
- **Read the "What Is" section** slowly and thoughtfully once during the day.

Commentary

This lesson, like many in this last part of the Workbook, is written from the perspective of a person who is entering the last stages of the journey home. Here is the song of one whose uncertainty has ended, whose decision for the Kingdom of God is strong and clear. In the words of "Development of Trust" in the Manual for Teachers:

> The teacher of God is now at the point in his progress at which he sees in it his whole way out. "Give up what you do not want, and keep what you do." How simple is the obvious! And how easy to do! (M-4(A).6:5–8)

These are the words of someone who has realized that the peace of God is all that he wants.

"I did not understand what made me free, nor what my freedom was" (1:1). Our freedom is in God alone. At the start we believed the opposite. Being free seems to mean being independent. How could freedom be found in acceptance of God's Will? Isn't that enslavement? Only as we realize that our will is God's Will, that our will and His are one and the same, can we realize that to do the Will of God is perfect freedom because it is what we truly want, and what we were created for. "Father, it is my will that I return" (1:9).

Not knowing what freedom was we have looked for it where it could not be found: in the exercise of our independent will in this world. Until we hear the Voice for God directing us, and respond, we cannot find freedom. "Now I would guide myself no more" (1:3). Our freedom is found in accepting a new Guide. It is found in resigning as our own teacher (see T-12.V.8:3) and accepting another Teacher. It is found in letting go of our independent goals and accepting the one goal we all share together.

Freedom is the liberty to be all that I am. Freedom is the liberty to express my nature without any hindrance. My nature is love; my nature is the holiness of God Himself. My only freedom is in being that which I am because God created me. To attempt to be something else is to enslave myself, to constrict my soul into a shape not its own. Freedom is to teach and offer only love, because that is what I am.

Let me, then, today, gladly surrender my opinions about what I am, and accept what God tells me I am. Let me readily relinquish the false and illusory freedom I have thought to pursue, and accept the only freedom that is real, in glad capitulation to my own nature. There is no surrender but to my Self. There is no sacrifice but of illusion. When I have reached the point of being willing to hear only the Voice for God, I will be able to say:

The way to You is opening and clear to me at last. (1:7)

WHAT IS CREATION?

Part 1: W-pII.11.1:1–2

The question itself is one that often comes up for Course students. The Course speaks often of "your creations," and yet never seems to clearly say exactly what those creations are. It tells us that our creation process continues unabated despite our unawareness of our creations, and that they are all saved for us by the Holy Spirit. There is an image of us entering Heaven and being greeted by all our creations, as if they were living beings.

We have a fundamental misconception that makes it difficult for us to understand what creations are. For instance, we think God created this world. When we think of creation, therefore, we think of something physical and material. We think our creations must be something in this world. Yet the Course clearly tells us this entire world is an illusion, a miscreation of our mind. How could our creations be here?

My creations, then, cannot be something like a book I write, a relationship I form, a family, or a business. My creations are not objects at all. They must be thoughts.

> Creation is the sum of all God's Thoughts, in number
> infinite, and everywhere without all limit. (1:1)

"Thoughts" is capitalized, so we know this refers to God's Son. The Christ. Again, we are not used to equating thoughts and living beings. We do not think of thoughts as beings who are alive; we do not think of living beings as "only" thoughts. The Course teaches us that we are only Thoughts in God's Mind. We automatically assume some kind of material existence when we think of a living being. The Course, all through, is trying to teach us that living beings are indeed thoughts, or spirits, and not material at all. "You are not a body" (W-pI.91.5:2), means more than just an admonition not to be limited by our body; it means that we are something wholly other than material. The essential part of us is not material at all. We are spirit. We are thought.

> Only Love creates, and only like itself. (1:2)

From just this much it should be clear that "creations" are "thoughts of love." If only Love creates, creations must be the effects of Love. If creations are thoughts, then they must be thoughts of love.

"Only Love creates, and only like itself." Love always creates more love. Creation, it seems to me, is a circular thing, like a self-sustaining energy field, each part of which is upholding the other part, an endless cycle of creation.

The Text teaches us that God, being Love, has no need except to extend Himself. Since we are extensions of His Being, we have a similar unique need: "With love in you, you have no need except to extend it" (T-15.V.11:3).

> Like your Father, you are an idea. And like Him, you can give yourself completely, wholly without loss and only with gain. (T-15.VI.4:5–6)

This is what we learn through the experience of a holy instant. We are Thoughts of Love, with no need except to extend love. In our relationships, we are learning to let go of our imagined "personal" needs, and to dedicate our relationships to "the only need the Sons of God share equally" (T-15.VI.6:10)—the extension of love. Through this reflection of love here on earth, we learn to take our place again in the eternal creation of Heaven.

LESSON 322 ✦ NOVEMBER 18
"I can give up but what was never real."

Practice instructions

See complete instructions on page 135. A short summary:

- **Read** the commentary paragraph slowly and personally.
- **Pray** the prayer, perhaps several times.
- **Morning and evening:** Repeat the idea and then spend time in Open Mind Meditation.
- **Hourly remembrance:** Repeat the idea and then spend a quiet moment in meditation.
- **Frequent reminders:** Repeat the idea often within each hour.
- **Response to temptation:** Repeat the idea whenever upset, to restore peace.
- **Read the "What Is" section** slowly and thoughtfully once during the day.

Practice suggestion:

Spend a moment imagining that you give your life, whole and complete, to God today, holding nothing back.

As you imagine this, ask yourself what you fear you will have to give up, either outer or inner.

With each thing, ask yourself, *"Is this truly real?"*

Then repeat the idea.

Commentary

I cannot give up anything real: "As You created me, I can give up nothing You gave me" (2:3). The whole idea of sacrifice is alien to God and to the thought system of the Course. Oh, we are asked to give up things! The Course even asks us to give up the entire world—but "not to sacrifice" (T-30.V.9:5). The whole point of this lesson is quite simple. It is that nothing that I can give up was ever real in the first place. "I sacrifice illusions; nothing more" (1:1).

I remember once in a relationship in which I wanted marriage, and the lady in question did not, that I felt as if I were losing and sacrificing something by letting go of my dream. Then I realized that I was only giving up something I never had in the first place. It brought home with vivid force the familiar "wall plaque" saying that runs something like this: "If you love something, let it go. If it returns to you then it was truly yours, and if it does not, it was never yours at all." In that circumstance I was able to give up the illusion, and in so doing, retain the reality of a profoundly loving relationship that was not meant to end in marriage, a relationship that lasted for years and brought me more true satisfaction than any marriage relationship I ever saw among my friends.

The illusions we hold on to are hiding the true gifts of God. The idea that we can find our happiness in a romantic relationship, for instance, is one of the ego's substitutes for the reality of our relationship with God and with all living things. A close, loving relationship is a wonderful thing, but it can be an obstacle to our peace if we make an idol of it, expecting it to give us everything, or insisting that we know the form it must take to please us.

"And as illusions go I find the gifts illusions tried to hide, awaiting me in shining welcome, and in readiness to give God's ancient messages to me" (1:2). We not only lose nothing in giving up illusions; we actually gain the reality of what the illusions were substituting for. This is a win-win situation!

The fear of sacrifice and loss is one of the greatest obstacles to our spiritual progress. And as long as we think we are losing something real, we will drag our feet.

> If this [relinquishment] is interpreted as giving up the desirable, it will engender enormous conflict. Few teachers of God escape this distress entirely. (M-4.I(A).5:2–3)

The idea of sacrifice makes it impossible for us to make sensible judgments about what we do and do not want. That is why it is so important for us to refer all our decisions to the Holy Spirit. And when we do, often it will seem to us as if we are being asked to sacrifice something we value. What we do not realize is that the Holy Spirit is only teaching us that we do not really want what we think we want; He is only clarifying the intentions of our own right mind, which already knows there is no value in what we have been holding on to.

"And every dream serves only to conceal the Self Which is God's only Son" (1:4). The gift behind every dream is the memory of Who I really am. Attachment to the ego's "gifts" only serves to diminish my awareness of that Self. I am asking, not for too much, but for far too little. These gifts are not worthy of my Self. What God did not give has no reality (2:4). And so, today, let us give up every thought that anticipates any kind of loss, and recognize that, as God's Sons, we cannot lose.

What loss can I anticipate except the loss of fear, and the return of love into my mind? (2:5)

WHAT IS CREATION?

Part 2: W-pII.11.1:3–5

There was no time when all that [love] created was not there. Nor will there be a time when anything that It created suffers any loss.   (1:3–4)

It is very difficult, if not impossible, for our minds to comprehend something that is *outside of time*. We can conceive of the idea, but to actually conceptualize it or to feel it is beyond minds that think solely in terms of time. The creations of Love are beyond time; they have always been, and they always will be. There is no before or after with Love and Its creations; it is an eternal *now*.

We think of creation as bringing into existence something that never was. But the Course's conception of creation is something that is always complete, and that always exists *now*. All of creation has always been there, and always will be, and yet creation is continuous. Creation is a constant upsurge of beingness, never less, never more, never old, and always fresh. "Forever and forever are God's Thoughts exactly as they were and as they are, unchanged through time and after time is done" (1:5).

God's creations are unaffected by time. Time is part of our illusion, a way of making lack seem real by having things be "in the future," and not now; or to make loss real by seeing them as "past." When the lesson speaks of "God's Thoughts" it is speaking of *us*. "We are creation; we the Sons of God" (4:1). It is saying, in other words, "I am as God created me" (Lessons 94, 110, 162). You and I are those creations, "unchanged through time and after time is done." We are not beings under construction, with our reality still in the future, nor are we beings of corruption, with our purity past and gone. What we are is now, was before time, and will be when time is done. What changes is not me. To see ourselves as God's creations is thus to free ourselves from the tyranny of time.

> *Father, I seek the peace You gave as mine in my creation. What was given then must be here now, for my creation was apart from time, and still remains beyond all change. The peace in which Your Son was born into Your Mind is shining there unchanged. I am as You created me.*
> (W-pII.230.2:1–4)

LESSON 323 • NOVEMBER 19
"I gladly make the 'sacrifice' of fear."

Practice instructions

See complete instructions on page 135. A short summary:

- **Read** the commentary paragraph slowly and personally.
- **Pray** the prayer, perhaps several times.
- **Morning and evening:** Repeat the idea and then spend time in Open Mind Meditation.
- **Hourly remembrance:** Repeat the idea and then spend a quiet moment in meditation.
- **Frequent reminders:** Repeat the idea often within each hour.
- **Response to temptation:** Repeat the idea whenever upset, to restore peace.
- **Read the "What Is" section** slowly and thoughtfully once during the day.

Practice suggestion: Think of some resentment you are holding about someone. Because you find it hard to let go of this resentment, there must be some perceived payoff in it. Perhaps you think it buys you a sense of righteousness or a sense of entitlement, but if you didn't see some sort of payoff in it, you'd easily and quickly let it go. Now realize that the real result of this resentment is fear. That is its real "payoff." As you consider letting your resentment go, repeat these lines:

I gladly make the "sacrifice" of fear.
I freely let Your Love come streaming in.

Commentary

Yesterday's lesson ended with the thought "What loss can I anticipate except the loss of fear?" and today's lesson picks up on that idea. So I'm going to lose, but all I will lose is fear? I can live with that! Losing fear is no sacrifice. I will lose my fear with pleasure.

It may seem as if I am being asked to give up some pleasant and valuable things. All I am really being asked to give up is "all suffering, all sense of loss and sadness, all anxiety and doubt" (1:1). Attachment to things in this world, things that are fragile and that will not last, always brings with it suffering, loss, and anxiety. I may not realize it but the ego's secret attraction to all such things is not the pleasure they bring me, but the pain. When I recognize that ego motivation, surely I will wisely and sanely let my attachment go.

And when I let go, God's Love comes "streaming in to [my] awareness" (1:1). Do I want that today? God's Love streaming in to my awareness? Do I perhaps, this morning, long for such an experience? Then let me gladly sacrifice my fear. Let me simply give it up. Let me recognize that in clinging to anything besides the goal of God I am clinging to fear, and let it go. Yes, my Father: today I am willing to make this "sacrifice." Today I am willing to stop being afraid of Love.

I feel as though I need to remind myself that in letting go of these things I am not letting go of anything real. I am not really letting go at all. I am having an illusion of giving something up, but I never had anything real in the first place. All I am doing is "letting go of self-deceptions and of images [I] worshipped falsely" (2:1). This is just "a debt we owe to truth" (2:1). It is just being honest! And as I acquiesce to truth, truth returns to me "in wholeness and in joy" (2:1). The deception has ended and Love returns to my awareness. The fullness of the gift that is eternally mine—love—resurfaces in my memory. It makes a kind of natural sense that when I pay my debt to truth, truth returns to me.

When "fear has gone...only love remains" (2:4). "I gladly make the 'sacrifice' of fear."

WHAT IS CREATION?

Part 3: W-pII.11.2:1–3

"God's Thoughts" refers to us, the Thoughts of God. Creation is "the sum of all God's Thoughts" (1:1), the sum total of all beings of all time.

The Course makes an amazing assertion here: "God's Thoughts are given all the power that their own Creator has" (2:1). In the Bible it is recorded that Jesus said, toward the end of his life, "All power is given to me in heaven and in earth" (Mt 28:18). The Course says all power is given to us as the Sonship, not just to Jesus. What this is saying is that what God can do, we can do. We are simply His extensions. Therefore, as He creates, we create also.

The reason God shares His power with us is that "He would add to Love by its extension" (2:2). In other words, we have power in order to extend love. One short definition of creation might be the extension of love. But the form of love we share in this world is not Love's reality; it is only a reflection of Heaven's love. Our earthly experience of love is always in the context of separate beings exchanging love; in Heaven is only the awareness of perfect oneness. We can only imagine what love is like in that context. We can have glimpses of it in a holy instant, when the barriers between minds seem to disappear. In that moment, there is an awareness that the other person is you and you are the other person. You are the love in "you" extending to them; you are the love in "the other person" extending towards "you"; and you are the love in yourself loving yourself. It can be a disorienting experience because you literally start to lose track of who you are, in the context of individuals, while simultaneously you become aware of something much larger and more all-inclusive that is what you really are.

Those experiences are wonderful, and asking for them is not discouraged in the Course. But the main thing to realize here is that creation, as the Course talks about it, is not an experience on earth; it is an experience in Heaven. It is something that is always going on, and our dream of separation has not interrupted creation at all. Nothing has been lost or stopped by our illusion of separation. That is why the Course can tell us, as in last week's topic (the Last Judgment), that the final judgment on this world is:

> It is wholly purposeless. Without a cause, and now without
> a function in Christ's sight, it merely slips away to noth-
> ingness.   (W-pII.10.2:2–3)

If creation in Heaven means the extension of love, what is its parallel in our earthly experience? The Course says that the parallel to the extension of love is forgiveness. I think of forgiveness as recognizing creation, rather than actually creating.

LESSON 324 ✦ NOVEMBER 20

"I merely follow, for I would not lead."

Practice instructions

See complete instructions on page 135. A short summary:

- **Read** the commentary paragraph slowly and personally.
- **Pray** the prayer, perhaps several times.
- **Morning and evening:** Repeat the idea and then spend time in Open Mind Meditation.
- **Hourly remembrance:** Repeat the idea and then spend a quiet moment in meditation.
- **Frequent reminders:** Repeat the idea often within each hour.
- **Response to temptation:** Repeat the idea whenever upset, to restore peace.
- **Read the "What Is" section** slowly and thoughtfully once during the day.

Commentary

Learning to follow my inner guidance is a big part of doing the Course. That guidance is the Voice for God, the Holy Spirit. It is part of me and part of God. In the end all is one, but while I think of myself as separate I will experience that Voice as a separate voice, calling me back home: "Your loving Voice will always call me back, and guide my feet aright" (1:5).

Father, I need to learn that I am not on my own, and that Something or Someone has planned "the way I am to go, the role to take, and every step in my appointed path" (1:2). As Lesson 321 reminded me: "I have neither made nor understood the way to find my freedom" (W-pII.321.1:4). In fact, You have set the way, and the Holy Spirit is simply the Voice that speaks for You. So, then, let me follow "One Who knows the way" (2:1). What a relief it is to have this One to trust! When walking through a dark jungle with twisted and confusing pathways, what a comfort to know I have a Guide Who knows every detail of the path. Because of Him, "I cannot lose the way" (1:3).

Today let me remember that every step of my journey has been set by You. As I look back with You, I know that this is true: nothing I have ever done has ever been anything but for my own good; it has all worked together perfectly to get me exactly where I am now. Even my wanderings were perfectly designed to teach me the falsity of the illusions I was following. What I thought were detours away from You were really lessons bringing me closer to home, and I am grateful for them all. Let me now look to the future with the confidence imparted by that knowledge: I cannot lose the way. Every person, every event, and every circumstance of my life today can be, if seen with vision, a step towards home, a means of finding my way back to You.

If I wander today, Father, bring me back. I thank You for the blessed relief of knowing that I do not have to figure it all out. It's been figured out for me. I can let the day unroll in whatever way it does, trusting that it is all perfectly planned by You to bring the memory of You most rapidly to my mind.

"I would not lead." I don't want to be known as a leader of others. I don't know the way for myself; how can I know for anyone else? Some of my brothers may follow me; in fact You will bring them to me for that purpose. But all I am doing is following Your Voice; if anyone follows me in this path they are not following me, but You. Let me always remind them of that and never make anyone dependent upon me.

"We cannot stray except an instant from His loving Hand" (2:2). To Jesus, six billion years is "a tiny tick of time" (T-26.V.3:5) that is nothing in comparison to eternity, so small that "not one note in Heaven's song was missed" (T-26.V.5:4). To us it seems we stray much longer than an instant. A mathematical example that comes to mind is this: When we divide one number by another, we are, in a sense, comparing them. One hundred divided by ten is ten; that means that compared to ten, one hundred is ten times bigger. The interesting thing about the number zero is that any number, compared to it mathematically, is infinite. If you imagine being able to divide a line into points with zero width, there are an infinite number of such points in the line, whether it is an inch long or a mile long.

The "tiny tick of time" is like zero. Eternity is infinite, and compared to it, all of time is literally *nothing*. There is no comparison. The time we spend in wandering, which seems so long to us, is nothing more than an instant, an infinitesimal piece of nothing, a fragment of a dream.

We've all experienced dreams that seemed to last for hours or days, yet happened in a few seconds of "real" time. And that is all this time is:

> Time is a trick, a sleight of hand, a vast illusion in which figures come and go as if by magic. Yet there is a plan behind appearances that does not change. The script is written. (W-pI.158.4:1–3)

There is a plan behind the appearances, and that is what I can rely upon today. Following the Holy Spirit, I know that the ending is sure. He "guarantees a safe returning home" (2:4). I may feel really messed up and confused, but I just can't really blow it! I've got a perfect Guide, and He is going to stick with me until I reach the end and fall once again into my Father's Arms.

I merely follow, for I would not lead.

WHAT IS CREATION?

Part 4: W-pII.11.2:4

> What God has willed to be forever One will still be One when time is over; and will not be changed throughout the course of time, remaining as it was before the thought of time began. (2:4)

God has willed all Creation to be One. Therefore it is One. Time cannot change what God created in any way. Time and change seem inextricably related: change is what signifies the passage of time, and it seems impossible that time should pass without change. It is impossible that God's creation should change. God's creation is outside of the realm of time entirely, and time is simply an illusion, a dream in which change is possible.

What we are, together, as the one Son of God, existed before time was thought of, still exists during the apparent course of time, and will exist, still One, when time is over. The Son of God is as unaffected by what seems to occur during time as the sun is unaffected by my passing a few of its rays through a magnifying glass, and deflecting their path, or as the ocean is unaffected by a child who throws a stick into the water. In other words, not at all. That is the power of creation. It is immutable. Therefore, *I am immutable* when I recognize my Creator.

Your Self is radiant in this holy joy, unchanged, unchanging and unchangeable, forever and forever. (W-pI.190.6:5)

LESSON 325 ✦ NOVEMBER 21
"All things I think I see reflect ideas."

Practice instructions

See complete instructions on page 135. A short summary:

- **Read** the commentary paragraph slowly and personally.
- **Pray** the prayer, perhaps several times.
- **Morning and evening:** Repeat the idea and then spend time in Open Mind Meditation.
- **Hourly remembrance:** Repeat the idea and then spend a quiet moment in meditation.
- **Frequent reminders:** Repeat the idea often within each hour.
- **Response to temptation:** Repeat the idea whenever upset, to restore peace.
- **Read the "What Is" section** slowly and thoughtfully once during the day.

Practice suggestion: I find it helpful to make this idea more specific. Think of a situation you are seeing that is causing you discomfort. Then say:

This thing I think I see reflects ideas.
I am seeing only the projection of my judgmental thoughts.
Father, let me see the reflection of Your Thoughts.

Commentary

This lesson is probably the best single summary of the Course's theory of perception:

> What I see reflects a process in my mind, which starts with my idea of what I want. From there, the mind makes up an image of the thing the mind desires, judges valuable, and therefore seeks to find. These images are then projected outward, looked upon, esteemed as real and guarded as one's own.
>
> (1:1–3)

Everything I see is a projection. By this analysis of perception, we see absolutely nothing real with our physical eyes. All of it "reflects a process in my mind" and nothing more than that. What we see are all projected images. As an early lesson in the Workbook says, "I have given everything I see...all the meaning that it has for me" (W-pI.2.Heading).

As we choose what we want to see, the world arises in our sight. If we choose judgment we see a world condemned; if we choose forgiveness we see "a gentle world" (1:5–6). This is why the Course focuses entirely on healing the mind and not on changing the world. To change the world is not necessary; it will change with our thoughts. As Ken Wapnick points out, trying to fix things in the world is like trying to fix things in a movie by doing things to the screen. The only way you can change the movie is to change what is in the projector (or to fix the projector). The mind is the projector of the world.

When we accept forgiving thoughts in our minds, the world becomes "a kindly home where [we] can rest a while before [we journey] on" (1:6). It becomes a place where we can "help [our] brothers walk ahead with [us], and find the way to Heaven and to God" (1:6). That is what we do in this world when we have had our minds healed: help others do the same.

What we want is the ideas of God reflected in the world, rather than our own ideas. Apart from God's ideas, our ideas only "make up dreams" (2:1).

Today I do not want dreams; I want reality reflected in my world. It all starts from my idea of what I want. Therefore, Father, I ask help in wanting only the truth, only peace, and only what is loving. I want union, not separation. I want healing, not conflict. I want peace, not war. Help me to recognize it whenever I think I want anything else, or anything besides the truth; to recognize it, bring it into Your light for healing, and let it go.

WHAT IS CREATION?

Part 5: W-pII.11.3:1–2

Creation is the opposite of all illusions, for creation is the truth. (3:1)

The Course's general theory about creation holds certain facts as fundamental: only what is created by God is real or true; all that God creates is real, true, and eternal. Therefore, anything that is not eternal and changeless is not real, and not true. Based on these assumptions, the Course concludes that all things of this world—the earth itself, the entire physical universe, and especially our bodies and our apparent "life" here on earth, cannot be God's creations because they are not eternal and changeless. Everything we can see with our eyes, even the seemingly ageless stars, has an end. What ends is simply not real, in the Course's sense of the word. All of it, every bit of it, falls into the category of "illusions."

Furthermore, God's creation is holographic: "every part container of the Whole" (3:2). This is a concept that defies matter-based logic. The nearest analog I know of is the hologram. Once a holographic image has been captured on a photographic plate, light shined on the plate will produce a three-dimensional image of the hologram. If it is a picture of an apple, it will be a 3-D apple, and you can view different angles of the apple by moving the angle of light shining into the image. Now, if that holographic plate is broken into four pieces, you do not end up with four images of *parts* of an apple; instead, you have four *smaller* images of the entire apple. The whole is in every part.

That is what God's creation is like. Fragment it as you will, and the Whole of creation is still reflected in every tiny part. All of creation is in you, and in me. The "wholly whole" creation is what the Course refers to as "the holy Son of God" (3:2). God's Will is complete in every aspect (another word for "part"; the Course will often use different words for "part" such as "aspect" or "fragment," but the unspoken assumption is always that every aspect contains the Whole. The word refers to what we think of as "individuals" or "persons"). You are an *aspect* or *part* of the Son of God, and yet somehow, at the same time, you are also the Whole.

One symptom of our mistaken belief in separation is that we have over-identified with our "partness," and have lost touch with our Wholeness. For instance, I tend to think of myself primarily as Allen Watson. You tend to think of yourself as your individuality. In fact, our primary reality is a shared Self, a Wholeness. Much of the learning process through which the Course is leading us is to change that primary sense of identification from "partness" to Wholeness. The learning environment of the holy relationship is designed to break down our sense of isolation, or "partness," and to strengthen our identification with the Whole by demonstrating to us that what we think of as "the other person" in the relationship is, in fact, a part of our shared Self. We experience the same thoughts. What affects one affects the other. What I think affects you, and vice versa. What I give to you is given to myself. When I forgive you, I am released. As this breakdown of "partness" and realization of Wholeness is learned in the holy relationship, it begins to be generalized and transferred to all the other "aspects" of creation, all that we have thought of as "not me."

LESSON 326 ✦ NOVEMBER 22
"I am forever an Effect of God."

Practice instructions

See complete instructions on page 135. A short summary:

- **Read** the commentary paragraph slowly and personally.
- **Pray** the prayer, perhaps several times.
- **Morning and evening:** Repeat the idea and then spend time in Open Mind Meditation.
- **Hourly remembrance:** Repeat the idea and then spend a quiet moment in meditation.
- **Frequent reminders:** Repeat the idea often within each hour.
- **Response to temptation:** Repeat the idea whenever upset, to restore peace.
- **Read the "What Is" section** slowly and thoughtfully once during the day.

Practice suggestion: Today's prayer is another favorite of mine. Do yourself a favor and spend some time with it today.

Commentary

Any effect is made what it is by its cause. The cause *determines* what the effect is. If I strike a billiard ball with my cue stick, the ball has no say in where it goes. The effect of the ball's motion is entirely determined by the stroke of the cue (plus other causative things like the state of the table surface, etc.). So if I am "an Effect of God" I don't really have any say in determining what I am; that is determined by my Cause, God. This is why it must be true that "as You created me I have remained" (1:3). I cannot change what I am; God "forever and forever [is] my Cause" (1:2). Does this seem to preclude free will? Yes, it does, insofar as actually determining what my nature is. And *thank God* it does! Otherwise, we would have irretrievably damaged ourselves and made sin and hell into realities. Free will, as the Course says in its introduction, does not grant us the right to "establish the curriculum" (T-In.1:4), that is, to decide *what* we must learn; it only grants us the freedom to choose *when* we learn it. And what we are learning is what we are, as God created us. That cannot change.

God's Will is "to have a Son so like his Cause that Cause and Its Effect are indistinguishable" (1:5). What an amazing statement! Indistinguishable from God! Wow! That borders on heresy or incredible hubris, doesn't it? And yet that is what the Course is telling us about ourselves; that what we are is the same stuff of which God is made. If God is Love, so is His Son. "God is but Love, and therefore, so am I" (Lessons 171 to 180).

WHAT IS CREATION?

Part 6: W-pII.11.3:3

> Its [creation's] oneness is forever guaranteed inviolate; forever held within His holy Will, beyond all possibility of harm, of separation, imperfection and of any spot upon its sinlessness. (3:3)

To put this in a short, simple sentence: Separation is impossible. What God created One cannot ever become separate parts; only in mad illusions can this seem to occur. The Wholeness or Oneness is the expression of God's Will, and that cannot be opposed because there is nothing to oppose it. Everything that exists is part of this Oneness, part of this single expression of God's Will. There is no other, no opponent, no enemy, no contrary will. God would not and did not create something opposite to Himself. How could God will something opposite to His own will? All that is truly real, therefore, must be an expression of His Will.

The Wholeness is "beyond all possibility of harm" because nothing outside it exists to oppose it. This is one of the characteristics of what is referred to as "nondual" cosmology. "Nondual" means, simply, not two; only one. There is no opposite to God, and no opposite to God's one creation.

The Course often says that if an opposite to God exists, if sin (opposing God's Will) is truly possible, then God must have created His own opposite, which makes Him insane. If we think that, we must be insane. Either God is insane, or we are. And of the two, which is more likely?

LESSON 327 ✦ NOVEMBER 23

"I need but call and You will answer me."

Practice instructions

See complete instructions on page 135. A short summary:

- **Read** the commentary paragraph slowly and personally.
- **Pray** the prayer, perhaps several times.
- **Morning and evening:** Repeat the idea and then spend time in Open Mind Meditation.
- **Hourly remembrance:** Repeat the idea and then spend a quiet moment in meditation.
- **Frequent reminders:** Repeat the idea often within each hour.
- **Response to temptation:** Repeat the idea whenever upset, to restore peace.
- **Read the "What Is" section** slowly and thoughtfully once during the day.

Practice suggestion: Today's lesson urges us to test out God's promises; specifically, the promise that He will answer our calls. This is an invitation we should not refuse. Think of some question or request for which you really need a response. Put your question or request to God, with all the desire you can muster, and expect a response. Try to open your mind about what the response ought to be. Realize that it may come now, and it may need to work its way past some obstacles in you before it comes. It may even show up initially in a form which does not look like a response to your question, but which makes way for a more direct response later on.

Commentary

This reminds me of a Bible verse in the Old Testament book of Jeremiah (33:3): "Call unto me, and I will answer thee."

The basic thought of the lesson seems to be: "Here are God's promises; try them, and prove to yourself that He means what He says." It tells us we can "learn from...experience that this is true" (1:3). It suggests that we take God's promises and "test them out" (2:1).

I know that my confidence in the Course has increased over the years and continues to increase as I continue to test out its promises. It gives us pretty explicit instructions for Workbook practice, and promises that it will change the way we think about everyone and everything in the world. It promises peace of mind. It promises release from guilt. And what I am finding is that as I make a sincere effort to *do* what it tells me to do, I experience what it says I will experience. In short: it works.

We can sit around judging the propositions of the Course until we are blue in the face, discussing whether or not the Course will work as it says, and we will learn nothing. But if we try it, if we test it out, if we practice what it says to practice, we will inevitably find out that it *does* work, and our conviction of its truth will grow unshakable.

WHAT IS CREATION?

Part 7: W-pII.11.4:1–3

> We are creation; we the Sons of God. (4:1)

We exist. Therefore, since all that exists is God's creation, and creation is the Son of God (3:2), we must be creation. We must be aspects of the Whole, "Sons" who are aspects of the Son.

"We seem to be discrete, and unaware of our eternal unity with Him" (4:2). All of our experience in this world has taught us that we are "discrete," separate beings, distinct from and unconnected to one another. We are aware of our partness to the exclusion of our Wholeness, "our eternal unity with Him." Yet we only "seem" to be separate beings; in reality we are not. Our struggle with the Course, our struggle with all true spirituality, is the struggle of insanely trying to preserve this wholly illusory sense of separateness. We are trying to make "partness" the only truth about ourselves, by excluding the awareness of Wholeness. And in so doing we have cut ourselves off from our Self.

"Yet back of all our doubts, past all our fears, there still is certainty" (4:3). We doubt the Wholeness because we have made up circumstances (this whole world) in which "partness" seems to be the only reality. We fear the Wholeness because it seems to threaten our partness. (It does not, really, because in the Wholeness there is some kind of partness, but it is a partness in which every part *contains* the Whole, rather than *excludes* it.) Despite this insanity of identification only with partness, we are still the Whole. The Whole is "inviolate." It cannot be divided nor damaged in any way. So the Wholeness still exists, and still calls to us.

In every part, no matter how strong the illusion of separation, the Whole is still there. And the Whole, our true Self, is still certain of Itself. It is only the part, falsely imagined to be separate from the Whole, that doubts and fears. The Whole has no doubts, and no fears. What I am and what you are (which is the same) knows Itself with unshakable knowledge. That certainty which lies in our Wholeness is what we are trying to reconnect with. The memory of God and of what we are lies within us, in the Wholeness we have denied and excluded in our mad attempt to be completely separate parts. Through reconnecting with one another, we reconnect with that Wholeness, and in so doing, we remember God.

LESSON 328 ✦ NOVEMBER 24
"I choose the second place to gain the first."

Practice instructions

See complete instructions on page 135. A short summary:

- **Read** the commentary paragraph slowly and personally.
- **Pray** the prayer, perhaps several times.
- **Morning and evening:** Repeat the idea and then spend time in Open Mind Meditation.
- **Hourly remembrance:** Repeat the idea and then spend a quiet moment in meditation.
- **Frequent reminders:** Repeat the idea often within each hour.
- **Response to temptation:** Repeat the idea whenever upset, to restore peace.
- **Read the "What Is" section** slowly and thoughtfully once during the day.

Practice suggestion: Ask for guidance about some situation facing you today. Listen with a quiet, receptive, open mind. You may find that what you hear feels different from your will, from what you want in this situation. If so, try to consider that perhaps what you heard *is* your will. Consider that this is your true will, which you have lost touch with, coming to you in a particular form.

Commentary

The lesson is saying that when we consider choosing to join our will to God's Will (1:5), it seems like some kind of loss, a submission to something outside of ourselves. It seems like taking "second place." It seems subservient, or submissive. And in our mistaken identity as egos, we feel that the only way to have autonomy is to make ourselves independent from God and from the rest of His creation.

We are seeing things upside down (1:1). All that we find by asserting our independence is "sickness, suffering and loss and death" (1:3). We are like a branch trying to become independent of the vine. If we are cut off from the vine, we die. Our identity is not lost by joining with the vine; it is found, because we are not something separate. We are part of God and part of His creation, and only in joining with that willingly can we discover our true Identity. "Our will is His" (1:6).

We choose to "submit" to God's Will (which seems like taking second place) because, in joining with Him, we arrive in first place: one with the Will of the Creator of all things.

WHAT IS CREATION?

Part 8: W-pII.4:4–6

Love created us like Itself. As parts, each of which contains the Whole, we are Thoughts of Love. And "Love remains with all Its Thoughts, Its sureness being theirs" (4:4). The certainty of God is our certainty. It was given us in creation and is still there within us; it has never left us, although we have obscured it. God's memory is in our minds (4:5). Although we seem to be separate parts we are not; we are parts, but not separate, like droplets of water in the ocean. So we still contain all that was in the original creation. What belongs to the ocean belongs to each drop. Each of us still retains our oneness and our unity with our Creator (4:5).

> Let our function be only to let this memory return, only to let God's Will be done on earth, only to be restored to sanity, and to be but as God created us. (4:6)

Our whole purpose in life is to be nothing but this, nothing but the restoration to our awareness of our Wholeness, and our partness-in-Wholeness. This is why we are here. This is the purpose behind every direction taken by the Holy Spirit's guidance in our lives. We are not here to bolster our partness, to meet goals belonging only to the part. We are here to let the memory of God return to our conscious minds, and to fulfill our purpose as the extensions of the Will of Love.

LESSON 329 ✦ NOVEMBER 25

"I have already chosen what You will."

Commentary

It is difficult for us to realize that we have already chosen God's Will. Not only is choosing His Will the only way to find our true autonomy (yesterday's lesson), *we have already made that choice.* We may *think* we have wandered away from God's Will, defied it, and broken its laws (1:1), but we have not. We cannot. Because *we are* the Will of God, "extended and extending" (1:2).

When did we make this choice that we seem so unaware of? In the very instant of our creation (1:5). God created us by extending His Will; when we came into being we were the extension of His Will. Our choice was already made, and "made for all eternity" (1:6). We cannot change that. We can make up an illusion in which we appear to have a separate will from God's, but we cannot make it real. Illusion is all we can make if what we make contradicts God's Will.

This fact is our safety. It is our salvation as well, for it means that we have not done what we thought we did; we have not defied God's Will, we have only *imagined* it, only dreamed about it. The oneness of God and His creation is unbroken, and it is this we can celebrate today.

WHAT IS CREATION?

Part 9: W-pII.11.5:1

Our Father calls to us. (5:1)

"Father" is a personal synonym for "Creator," the One Who gave us being. Perhaps, after this time thinking about what creation is, the word "Father" may have a little more meaning for us. Our Father is the One Who thought us into existence. "Only Love creates" (1:2), and so our Father is Love Itself, Which has created us like Itself. This One desired to add to Love by Its extension, and so, out of that desire, we were created, to be held forever in His holy Will.

That immortal desire of God still stands! With all that infinite desire of His Will, He calls to us to be what He created us to be: the extension of His Love, creating as He does through extending love, forever one with His holy Will, sharing in it, glorying in it, exuding it from every pore of our being. God's Love remains with us. Our minds remember Him, remember our function. From within our minds He calls to us, drawing us with His Love to be the very Love that draws us.

He is our Father, our Creator. We cannot escape that fact, nor can we escape the fact of what we are. "I am as God created me" (W-pI.110.Heading). He calls to us constantly, continually, patiently, unceasingly, and until we end our mad attempt to be "something else," something other than Love, and respond to His call, we can only delay our happiness and postpone our joy.

Father, let me hear Your call today, and answer.

LESSON 330 ✦ NOVEMBER 26
"I will not hurt myself again today."

Practice instructions

See complete instructions on page 135. A short summary:

- **Read** the commentary paragraph slowly and personally.
- **Pray** the prayer, perhaps several times.
- **Morning and evening:** Repeat the idea and then spend time in Open Mind Meditation.
- **Hourly remembrance:** Repeat the idea and then spend a quiet moment in meditation.
- **Frequent reminders:** Repeat the idea often within each hour.
- **Response to temptation:** Repeat the idea whenever upset, to restore peace.
- **Read the "What Is" section** slowly and thoughtfully once during the day.

Practice suggestion: Think of your judgments toward another person. Realize that these judgments hurt *you*. Then say:

I will not hurt myself again today.
I will not teach myself that I am a sinner.
Let my forgiveness teach me that I am God's Son.

Commentary

Whenever I think I am less than what God created, I hurt myself. And only myself. I do no real damage, but I have the entirely realistic illusion of pain, sacrifice, and suffering. All my physical and emotional senses confirm its reality; only the vision of Christ sees past the illusion.

There is a strong passage in the Text that tells how important it is not to depend on what our eyes and ears tell us, to know that it is only the projection of our own thoughts:

> The secret of salvation is but this: That you are doing this unto yourself. No matter what the form of the attack, this still is true. Whoever takes the role of enemy and of

attacker, still is this the truth. Whatever seems to be the cause of any pain and suffering you feel, this is still true...Let them be as hateful and as vicious as they may, they could have no effect on you unless you failed to recognize it is your dream. (T-27.VIII.10:1–6)

The evil dream results from a false picture of myself as something less than the Self which God created. I still believe myself to be capable of sin and capable of suffering. Because I believe that of myself, I believe it of others, and I project my belief onto them. I project my sin and my guilt onto them. Every time I see sin or weakness in a brother, it is only a reflection of my own thoughts about myself. "It is your dream" that you are seeing. You are not seeing something real, but a masterful, near-perfect illusion, projected from your incredibly powerful mind. It is the projected image of your own thoughts about yourself that is "hurting" you.

If I think I am weak, if I think my life is in a mess, I am not seeing my true Identity. None of this is really happening. I am living a bad dream, a dream about myself. From a metaphysical standpoint, nothing happening in my life really matters at all. It is just a bad dream. (It *does* matter as a reflection of my state of mind, however.)

We are being "saved from what we thought we were" (2:3), and the way toward that deliverance is to understand that "life is but a dream," as the old round says. The way of deliverance is to forgive. To understand when I think I see something worthy of my judgment and condemnation that somehow, in some twisted way, all I am seeing is my own thoughts projected outward. And to choose, in that moment, to think differently. To see the situation which I thought justified my anger turned into a situation that justifies my love. "Here is a poor, confused brother, just like me, who has lost track of his true Identity with God. I am seeing him as guilty only because I am projecting my own guilt. I choose not to add to his illusion by broadcasting guilt onto him. I choose instead to direct my love to him that he may begin to awaken, as I have begun." And I know, in so doing, that I am giving that love to myself, I am contributing to my own awakening.

More to the point for me personally are these lines:

Why should we attack our minds, and give them images of pain? Why should we teach them they are powerless?

(1:2–3)

What am I teaching my mind by the thoughts I am thinking? What am I teaching my mind by feeling guilty? I'm a man under reconstruction, I'm not finished yet. If I didn't need rehabilitation I wouldn't be here! Let me observe my thoughts today and see how they attack me if I choose to listen to the ego, and how they build me up when I listen to the Holy Spirit.

WHAT IS CREATION?

Part 10: W-pII.11.5:2

> We hear His Voice, and we forgive creation in the Name of its Creator, Holiness Itself, Whose holiness His Own creation shares; Whose holiness is still a part of us. (5:2)

His Voice is calling us to "forgive creation." We have looked on God's creation—ourselves, our brothers and sisters, and all the rest that makes up creation—and we have pronounced judgment on it. We have seen guilt and ugliness where God created only beauty and holiness. In this world, we cannot truly create nor extend love in the purity that belongs only to Heaven, but we can forgive. We can end our fault-finding, and lift our judgment and condemnation from everything we see. Every moment offers us an opportunity to do this; every encounter is a chance to practice forgiveness.

Whatever we look upon without seeing the holiness of God in it, we need to forgive. To see anything other than God's holiness reflected everywhere is an act of unforgiveness, a condemnation of God's creation. When something appears unholy, we need to ask the help of the Holy Spirit to see past appearances to the truth of God's holiness those appearances are hiding. Sin is an illusion, and only holiness is true.

In a sense, then, all that the Course is teaching us is to acknowledge God's creation everywhere, in everything, and above all, in ourselves. Our Creator's "holiness is still a part of us." Let us say to everyone we meet (in our thoughts, our words, and our actions):

> *I would behold you with the eyes of Christ, and see my perfect sinlessness in you.* (W-pI.161.11:8)

XV

Lessons 331 - 340
What Is the Ego?

LESSON 331 ✦ NOVEMBER 27
"There is no conflict, for my will is Yours."

Practice instructions

See complete instructions on page 135. A short summary:

- **Read** the commentary paragraph slowly and personally.
- **Pray** the prayer, perhaps several times.
- **Morning and evening:** Repeat the idea and then spend time in Open Mind Meditation.
- **Hourly remembrance:** Repeat the idea and then spend a quiet moment in meditation.
- **Frequent reminders:** Repeat the idea often within each hour.
- **Response to temptation:** Repeat the idea whenever upset, to restore peace.
- **Read the "What Is" section** slowly and thoughtfully once during the day.

Commentary

In a study group recently, I said that our fundamental problem is that we really believe that we are terrible people. We don't trust our own love. A fellow was expressing his concern that the material of the Course could be used to justify just about any behavior. "I could go rob a liquor store because the world is just illusion and nobody would really be hurt except in the illusion. Nothing I do affects my relationship to God negatively."

The direct answer to that question is that you only do such things in the world when you believe the world is real. If you *truly* believed that the world is an illusion, you could not be doing such things and would have no desire to do them.

The fear that he would do terrible things if he believed no one would really be hurt belied a belief that he could not be trusted with the truth. The Course is saying that we don't believe that what we truly want is good. The truth is, we can trust ourselves. Even if we are still confused and bemused by illusion, we are not going to make terrible mistakes. It is safe to let go of the constraints of guilt because we truly are extensions of God. We think we need the guilt to restrain the monster within us; *A Course in Miracles* is saying guilt serves no useful function (see T-14.III.1:4), and in fact keeps us locked into the illusion of our sinfulness. That illusion about ourselves is the fundamental error. And it goes on to say that thinking the self has usurped the throne of God is nothing to be guilty about:

> Seek not to appraise the worth of God's Son whom He created holy, for to do so is to evaluate his Father and judge against Him. And you *will* feel guilty for this imagined crime, which no one in this world or Heaven could possibly commit. The Holy Spirit teaches only that the "sin" of self-replacement on the throne of God is not a source of guilt. (T-14.III.15:1–3)

It is just a "trivial mistake" (W-pI.138.11:5). Love has not left Itself. I share God's nature as Love. I could not leave Him, nor He me (1:5).

It is "foolish" (1:1) to believe that I could *in reality* oppose the Will of God, and corrupt myself. Any apparent corruption or conflict between me and God must be an illusion, evidence of nothing except that I am asleep and dreaming of the impossible (1:7–8).

"To know reality is not to see the ego" (W-pII.12.4:1). Yet paradoxically we must see the ego first in order to overlook it. It operates in a hidden fashion, secretly, stealthily. It hides behind all kinds of cover. We must unmask it, see it for what it is, and then overlook it, ignore it. As long as we don't know what our imagined enemy is we will be run by fear. We have to get to the place where we can see clearly, "Oh! It's just the ego, it's just me thinking I'm separate." Then we can let it go.

> When you have at last looked at the ego's foundation without shrinking, you will have also looked upon ours.
>
> (T-11.In.4:2)

Let us look at our ego, then, without shrinking, without being afraid of it, able to see that it is just a "trivial mistake."

WHAT IS THE EGO?

Part 1: W-pII.12.1:1–2

"The ego is idolatry" (1:1). Idolatry is the worship of an idol, a false god. That is what the ego is; the insane attempt to make real an identity that is apart from God, and intended to replace Him in our awareness. The ego is "the sign of limited and separated self, born in a body, doomed to suffer and to end its life in death" (1:1).

Let's pay attention here. The ego is not some "thing" inside of us, some sort of evil twin, the dark side of our soul. The ego *is* the whole concept of a separated self that is set apart from "other selves." Isn't that exactly what we think we are? A distinct soul, born in a body, struggling through this life and sure to end this life in death? Doesn't that describe what we think we are? In other words, the "me" that I think I am, a thing separate from and different from you, *that* is the ego! Changing our self-concept from ego to spirit doesn't just mean that this separate self, which was black, becomes white. It means that this separated self is completely replaced by something far more inclusive, in fact, by something all-inclusive. I cease to be "I" in the way I thought I was.

The ego "is the 'will' that sees the Will of God as enemy, and takes a form in which it is denied" (1:2). If what I think of as "I" is to be separate and independent, it cannot be united with the Will of God. The ego *must* see God's Will as enemy because, to the ego, God is "other," something different from and separate from itself. Since God is a very powerful "other," His Will represents a threat, a challenge to the ego's "will." Therefore, the form the "will" of the ego takes will always be some form of denial of God's Will. For instance, you know that a child is beginning to develop a psychological ego when he or she begins to say "no" every time you say "yes" (otherwise known as "the terrible two's"). The ego is a big "no" to God and His Will.

This ego is precisely what we are *not*. "You are not an ego" (T-14.X.5:5). As we look at what the ego is (or appears to be), let us not be discouraged or depressed by the picture. What we are looking at is not what we are; in fact, it is what we are *not*. This imagined self is the source of all our guilt—and it is unreal, and does not exist.

LESSON 332 ✦ NOVEMBER 28

"Fear binds the world. Forgiveness sets it free."

Practice instructions

See complete instructions on page 135. A short summary:

- **Read** the commentary paragraph slowly and personally.
- **Pray** the prayer, perhaps several times.
- **Morning and evening:** Repeat the idea and then spend time in Open Mind Meditation.
- **Hourly remembrance:** Repeat the idea and then spend a quiet moment in meditation.
- **Frequent reminders:** Repeat the idea often within each hour.
- **Response to temptation:** Repeat the idea whenever upset, to restore peace.
- **Read the "What Is" section** slowly and thoughtfully once during the day.

Practice suggestion: Choose a situation in which you are experiencing fear. Then say:

My fears about [person, situation, or event] bind
  [people involved].
My forgiveness of [people doing the screwing up] will set
  [people involved] free,
  and will set me free, too.

Commentary

Fear and unforgiveness are very closely related. Our fear, in the Course's understanding, is rooted in our guilt. Our primal fear is of punishment for what we believe we have done wrong. Our belief in our sin produces guilt, and that guilt produces fear. The fear "binds" us. It is a restrictive emotion. Forgiveness, which undoes guilt, thus sets us free.

The belief in sin is the ego's foundational illusion. All that the ego makes is illusion (1:1), and not reality. Truth, by its mere presence, evaporates the illusions of the ego (1:2–5). If there is an illusion of a wall in front of us, knowing the truth (in this case, there is no wall) enables us to "walk through" the wall. There is no need to attack the wall to tear it down; we just shine it away with the truth.

The truth about us is that we are guiltless. Forgiveness does not attack sin and guilt. It doesn't have to. It just shines them away. Forgiveness invites truth to enter the mind "and take its rightful place within the mind" (1:6).

"Without forgiveness is the mind in chains, believing in its own futility" (1:7). When I am entrenched in my own guilt my mind seems impotent, unable to accomplish anything at all. I cannot believe in my own power because I am believing in my own weakness. The power of God, given to me in creation, seems non-existent. I seem to be frail, blown about by circumstances beyond my control. But when I am forgiven, I once again realize the power of my own mind. By owning my guilt and taking responsibility for it (realizing that I made the illusion of guilt and sin), I reawaken to the inherent power of my mind to choose, and I realize that I can choose again. And choose differently, if I wish.

When I *exercise* forgiveness, the realization of my mind's freedom and power comes even more quickly. When I realize that the picture of sin I am seeing in my brother is of my own making, and that I can choose to see him differently—that this is entirely within my power, and not at all dependent on anything outside of me—I am reclaiming my inheritance as God's Son. By my forgiveness I release the world from guilt. I have the power to forgive sins! I have the power to free the world from its chains, and that power is the power of forgiveness.

WHAT IS THE EGO?

Part 2: W-pII.12.1:3

> The ego is the "proof" that strength is weak and love is fearful, life is really death, and what opposes God alone is true.   (1:3)

To find its illusory independence, the ego simply negates God and everything about God. The strength of innocence, gentleness, and love is seen as "weak" and is shunned. Attack is seen instead as strong.

"Standing on your own feet" and being "independent" is seen as maturity and strength, and union with others and dependence on God is seen as weakness. The ultimate image of a mighty ego is a lone individual screaming defiance at the entire universe. The ego cannot see nor understand that this lone, limited, and separated self is the very symbol of weakness.

In speaking of this choice we have made to become egos (a choice we can realize only in dreams, never in reality), the Course says:

> Here does the Son of God ask not too much, but far too little. He would sacrifice his own identity with everything, to find a little treasure of his own. (T-26.VII.11:7–8)

To learn to listen to the Voice for God instead of the ego means far more than just listening to the little angel on our right shoulder instead of the devil on our left. That concept of things leaves the "me" who listens unchanged, still the same identity, a separated self. To listen to God instead of the ego means letting go entirely of that "little treasure of [my] own," which is my entire conception of what I am as something apart from God, and instead affirming my "identity with everything" (T-26.VII.11:8).

> I was mistaken when I thought I lived apart from God, a separate entity that moved in isolation, unattached, and housed within a body. Now I know my life is God's, I have no other home, and I do not exist apart from Him. He has no Thoughts that are not part of me, and I have none but those which are of Him. (W-pII.223.1:1–3)

LESSON 333 ✦ NOVEMBER 29
"Forgiveness ends the dream of conflict here."

Practice instructions

See complete instructions on page 135. A short summary:

- **Read** the commentary paragraph slowly and personally.
- **Pray** the prayer, perhaps several times.
- **Morning and evening:** Repeat the idea and then spend time in Open Mind Meditation.
- **Hourly remembrance:** Repeat the idea and then spend a quiet moment in meditation.
- **Frequent reminders:** Repeat the idea often within each hour.
- **Response to temptation:** Repeat the idea whenever upset, to restore peace.
- **Read the "What Is" section** slowly and thoughtfully once during the day.

Practice suggestion: Pick a situation in which you are experiencing conflict. Say:

I perceive conflict in this situation.
This is my *dream of conflict.*
Forgiveness ends the dream of conflict here.

Commentary

This is a magnificent lesson! It states unmistakably, in very certain terms, that we cannot dodge correcting our mistaken thoughts of conflict. Each one must be faced squarely and forgiveness applied. Our thoughts of conflict "must be resolved" (1:1). They will not simply go away. We cannot bury our heads in the sand. Consider the list of defensive tactics that our egos persuade us to use. Conflict is (1:2):

Evaded: We sidestep the issue. When we sense a loss of peace, we watch TV or go shopping. When we become aware of a wall between us and a brother or sister, we walk away, or make ourselves very busy. We avoid facing the conflict in our minds.

Set aside: We shelve the issue "for later consideration," a later that never seems to come.

Denied: We pretend it isn't there. "Me, angry? No, I'm fine; no problem."

Disguised: We blame our upset on a bad mood, hormones, a headache, or a bad day at the office. We paint over our inner rage with "pink paint," as Marianne Williamson so colorfully puts it (pun intended). We smile and choke down the anger or pain. Whatever we are feeling, it cannot be a thought of murder.

Seen somewhere else: "It's not my problem! It's all her fault." "I wouldn't be feeling these awful feelings if he wasn't being so damned selfish."

Called by another name: We deny that what we are feeling is attack or hatred; perhaps we call it "righteous indignation" or "setting my boundaries" or "standing for the truth."

If the conflict in our minds is to be resolved, it cannot be "hidden by deceit of any kind" (1:2). That is the summation of all these tactics. We are trying to *hide* the fact that thoughts of hatred, rage, or murder have actually entered our minds. This ingrained habit of hiding our egos, pushing them into the closet when company comes, has to end if the conflict is to be escaped.

This doesn't mean that, instead of hiding our egos, we should flaunt them and indulge them. The purpose is not to express the ego but to expel it. But we cannot do that if we continue to hide it, and sometimes the process of ripping the mask off the ego will mean that, for a short time at least, we will give vent to the ego instead of covering it up. Sometimes the rage must be expressed before we realize how deep-seated it really is. Yet this is only a transitional phase; there is a healing that we seek.

By contrast with the cover-up, our intent should be:

To see the ego conflict exactly as it is: In other words, to recognize hatred, attack, self-isolation, grandiosity, anger, and the desire to kill for exactly what they are. To stop playing innocent.

Where it is thought to be: This means getting in touch with the situation as your ego sees it. Admitting, for instance, that you really believe your spouse is sadistic, or that you actually do see yourself as unlovable.

In the reality which has been given it: Here we recognize just exactly what we think the situation is, as egos. We understand that we see ourselves as alone in the universe, clawing our way through life and barely surviving. We admit that the conflict seems *really real* to us. If we are not perfectly peaceful and constantly joyful, there *is* a reason, and the reason is always some aspect of ego we are clinging to, but simultaneously denying. We have to see the reality we have given to it.

With the purpose that the mind accorded it: This one takes real discernment. The conflicts we experience exist for a purpose, a purpose given to them by our minds. The purpose is always to support our own egos, always some form of ego autonomy, some illusion of independent, separate existence. Whatever the conflict, *we* give it its reality, and we do so for some hidden, insane reason of the ego. Here is where we uncover our fear of love, our fear of joining, our addiction to separation. Here is where we discover our hidden belief in guilt and the desire to punish ourselves.

Only when we are willing to go through this kind of ruthless self-examination, taking total responsibility for our own thoughts, will the defenses of the ego be lifted, and the truth be free to shine away the ego. The truth is forgiveness (1:4 and 2:1); it is forgiveness that shines away all conflict and all doubt. When I have uncovered my own ego in this way, forgiving others is the most natural and the easiest thing in the world, because I have admitted that my ego is self-generated, and the other person had nothing to do with it. I have been acting for insane reasons which I no longer accept nor want. But if this is true of me, it must be true of everyone. The conflict has been unreal, illusion fighting illusion, fear reacting to fear. And with that realization, my own guilt melts, and the way of return to God is open.

WHAT IS THE EGO?

Part 3: W-pII.12.2:1–3

"The ego is insane" (2:1). To the degree we identify with our egos, we are insane as well, as the Course so often tells us. And we all identify with our egos far more than we realize; indeed, identification with the ego is almost total. The ego is our fundamental assumption, the basis from which we operate all the time. We all see ourselves as limited, separate selves, living in a body, doomed to die with it. This insanity is not our reality, however; our true, shared Self remains sane, and that is our salvation and the ego's doom.

The ego "stands [in fear] beyond the Everywhere" (2:2). God, and His creation, is all there is. But the ego thinks it is somehow beyond all of that; it rejects God as Creator and tries to imagine itself as something outside of God and His creation. The ego "stands...apart from All" (2:2). How can you be apart from All? All is All. It includes everything. And the ego stands "in separation from the Infinite" (2:2). Same idea. All of these stances are, obviously, wholly imaginary. It is not possible to be separate from the Infinite. But the ego defiantly, and insanely, believes that this is its condition. That is the very definition of the ego. In this light, to believe that one is damned is the height of egoity.

"In its insanity it thinks it has become a victor over God Himself" (2:3). That is what damnation is: it is the assertion, "I have succeeded in thwarting the Will of God." Guilt is an egoic denial of the power of God's Love. The thought "I will never learn this Course, I will never become enlightened" is an assertion that your will is more powerful than God's. If God's Will is your happiness, then sadness is a proclamation of victory over God.

The Course is telling us that it is insane to think such things are possible. It does not condemn us for thinking them. Rather, it tells us to stop listening to such thoughts. The ego is an impossibility: "The whole purpose of this course is to teach you that the ego is unbelievable and will forever be unbelievable" (T-7.VIII.7:1). God is infinite; He is Everywhere; He is All. If the ego is a thought that stands beyond God, separate and apart, then the ego is unbelievable. Such a thing cannot be.

LESSON 334 ✦ NOVEMBER 30
"Today I claim the gifts forgiveness gives."

Practice instructions

See complete instructions on page 135. A short summary:

- **Read** the commentary paragraph slowly and personally.
- **Pray** the prayer, perhaps several times.
- **Morning and evening:** Repeat the idea and then spend time in Open Mind Meditation.
- **Hourly remembrance:** Repeat the idea and then spend a quiet moment in meditation.
- **Frequent reminders:** Repeat the idea often within each hour.
- **Response to temptation:** Repeat the idea whenever upset, to restore peace.
- **Read the "What Is" section** slowly and thoughtfully once during the day.

Commentary

"I seek but the eternal" (2:1). This lesson is about deciding not to waste any more time going after the supposed gifts of the ego. "I will not wait another day to find the treasures that my Father offers me" (1:1). The primary use we are making of our free will is to delay our acceptance of our divine inheritance. We are holding on like crazy to our illusion of independence, and denying ourselves the only thing that will ever content us (2:2), like a homeless person stupidly clinging to his rags while being offered brand new clothing.

Let me keep in mind today that nothing in this world is of lasting value. "Illusions are all vain, and dreams are gone even while they are woven out of thoughts that rest on false perceptions" (1:2). This reminds me of the verse in Ecclesiastes that says all our seeking is like trying to hold on to the wind. The illusions of the ego are so evanescent; they can never satisfy a Son of God. Only that which is eternal can satisfy me. A Christian hero of mine, Jim Elliot, once said, "He is no fool who gives what he cannot keep to gain what he cannot lose."

Let me remember that what I truly want is God and His peace in my heart. When I think I want something else, Holy Spirit, please help me to translate that desire into what it truly is, a symbol of my longing for the Father and for Home. God's Voice is offering peace; let that be my only aim, and let everything else fall by the wayside.

"The gifts forgiveness gives": What has all this got to do with forgiveness? Simply this: Every goal other than peace generates unforgiveness, putting me in competition with someone or something for that thing, whatever it is. Peace comes through forgiveness. If peace is my only goal, I will not judge my brothers because a mind in judgment is not a mind at peace. Only a mind free of lesser goals, free of desire for ephemeral things, can see his brothers as sinless.

Every encounter today offers me a chance at Heaven. There does not need to be any great crisis. All the world is my classroom, and every instant is a moment of choice. Today, let me choose peace.

WHAT IS THE EGO?

Part 4: W-pII.12.2:4–5

> And in its [the ego's] terrible autonomy it "sees" the Will
> of God has been destroyed.   (2:5)

This illusion of separation we call the ego, this "terrible autonomy," seems to show us that we have triumphed over God's Will for union. What a terrible thing it would be if this were reality! The ego's very being, if it were real, would be evidence of the most awful guilt imaginable. If I am the ego, then what I am, my very being, is an accusation of murder most foul, for I have wrested my very existence from the destruction of God's Will. And this is just what we believe in identifying with the ego. This is the primal guilt beneath all our vague, uneasy feelings, all our sense of unworthiness.

> It dreams of punishment, and trembles at the figures in its
> dreams; its enemies, who seek to murder it before it can
> ensure its safety by attacking them.   (2:4)

In the "terrible autonomy" of our identification with the ego, we have placed ourselves at odds with God and the universe. Everyone and everything else is a threat to our autonomy. Our dreams are filled with nightmarish punishment for our "crime." The ego state is one of acute paranoia; we are afraid of everything. We expect the executioner's axe to fall at any moment. No one can be trusted. Every figure in our dream is an enemy, and the only option for survival is to kill them before they kill us. The only safety is in attack.

This paranoid frame of mind is inevitable, given the ego's premise of autonomy. We all experience it to greater or lesser degree; some of us merely hide it better than others. When we get down to it, each of us feels unbearably alone, an outsider, crouched in the shadows of the woods while the rest of the world holds hands and sings around the campfire. That is the inescapable result of the premise of ego autonomy. It is the outcome of what we mistakenly presume ourselves to be.

The good news is that this is not what we are; the aloneness is an illusion, an outrageous impossibility. The ego is forever unbelievable. We are no more apart from God and His creation than a cell in my body is apart from the body itself. We live in God; we move and have our being in God. We are, all of us, making this incredible transition from ego autonomy to a transpersonal unity, the recognition of a higher Whole to which we all belong, intrinsically, a Whole which exists in every part— in you, in me. Nothing can stop this transition, because it is simply the recognition of what has always been so.

LESSON 335 ✦ DECEMBER 1
"I choose to see my brother's sinlessness."

Practice instructions

See complete instructions on page 135. A short summary:

- **Read** the commentary paragraph slowly and personally.
- **Pray** the prayer, perhaps several times.
- **Morning and evening:** Repeat the idea and then spend time in Open Mind Meditation.
- **Hourly remembrance:** Repeat the idea and then spend a quiet moment in meditation.
- **Frequent reminders:** Repeat the idea often within each hour.
- **Response to temptation:** Repeat the idea whenever upset, to restore peace.
- **Read the "What Is" section** slowly and thoughtfully once during the day.

Practice suggestion: The practice I will suggest now is a very powerful one, which I have used many times. I recommend using it with a number of people who come to mind. The idea behind it is that we see sinfulness in another *because* that will make us see sinfulness in ourselves, and that, crazily enough, is what we are after, what our ego wants. Just let one person after another come to mind, and apply the following lines to each one:

I chose to see [name's] sinfulness
 because I wanted to see my own.
I choose to see [name's] sinlessness
 because I want to see my own.

Commentary

This continues the thought from yesterday's lesson about decision and choice. Yesterday we read about choosing to follow God's Voice, and beholding our brother as sinless. Today we read:

Forgiveness is a choice. I never see my brother as he is,

for this is far beyond perception. What I see in him is merely what I wish to see, because it stands for what I want to
be the truth.   (1:1–3)

In other words, what we see results from choices we have made
about what we want to see. The Text speaks about "the decision for
guiltlessness" (T-14.III). It says (see the fourth paragraph in that section) that we need to make the choice to see innocence and not to see
guilt. If we make that decision, that is what we will see.

It is startling to be told that we *never* see our brothers as they are
(1:2). Seeing, or perception (which is a dualistic form of knowing,
requiring a seer separate from what is being seen), simply cannot apprehend the reality of what we are. What we are seeing is always a symbol,
an imperfect representation. No wonder it is so easy for perception to be
*mis*perception.

Misperception in terms of guilt and innocence happens like this: I see
guilt in myself. I want to get rid of it, so I project it onto a brother. I see
him as guilty because I want to, I have chosen to. I think this will get rid
of my guilt.

Correction of perception happens in reverse: I realize that I am not at
peace and therefore I must have decided wrongly. I decide to see my
brother as innocent. When I have truly made that choice, I will see his
innocence. That is a law: "You see what you believe is there, and you
believe it there because you want it there" (T-25.III.1:3). When you
want only love, love is all you will see (T-12.VII.8:1).

What we are seeing is always what we *choose* to see because we
want to see it. "It is to this alone that I respond, however much I seem
to be impelled by outside happenings" (1:4). The Course is obviously
aware that the way it describes perception is definitely not how it seems
to us. We are utterly convinced that we are seeing what we are seeing
because *that's the way it is*. We believe it is the happenings outside of us
that are forcing this perception upon us. When we see someone as guilty,
it isn't because we are choosing to see them that way—they *are* guilty!
We think we are just seeing what is the truth. The Course hears our
objections and replies, "No matter how much it seems that way to you,
I am telling you, you are wrong; you are responding *only* to what you
want to see, not what is really there."

"Forgiveness is a choice" (1:1). We can see our brother as guilty, or
as innocent, and the choice is one hundred percent up to us; it has noth-

ing to do with what he did or did not do.

My willingness to see my brother as innocent is the harbinger of my willingness to see myself as innocent (1:6–7). When I am ready to choose to see my brother as innocent, it shows that I have begun to let go of the guilt in my mind that caused me to desire to see him as guilty.

Seeing one another as innocent, seeing one another as sinless, restores the memory of God to us (2:1). There is a formula that runs through the Course: First, we see the face of Christ in one another; then we remember God. "In him I find my Self, and in Your Son I find the memory of You as well" (2:3). So if I want to remember God, what can I do? *Make a choice* to see my brother as innocent instead of guilty. We find our way to God through our brothers.

WHAT IS THE EGO?

Part 5: W-pII.12.3:1–3

> The Son of God is egoless. (3:1)

This begins a contrast between the ego and the Son of God, our true Identity. The Son of God, which is what I really am, has no ego! The ego is the sign of a limited and separated self. The Son of God is not limited or separated from God. The Son is unlimited, and coextensive with the Father; wherever God is, the Son is. They are One. There is no ego; no self that is apart from, and held distinct from, God.

Our true Self does not know the madness of the ego; the concept of the death of God (or victory over Him) is inconceivable because the Son lives (abides) in God (3:2). He lives in eternal joy, and does not know sorrow or suffering.

Insanity, God as enemy, sorrow, and suffering are all consequences of the ego delusion. They are as delusional, and as unreal, as the ego itself. Having been locked in this delusion of a separate self for so long, we can barely begin to imagine a state of mind in which these things simply do not exist. Yet that is where the Course is taking us: beyond the ego, beyond the madness, back into the oneness that has always been and will always be. This is our true state of mind, and it calls to us in our isolation, drawing us to return.

LESSON 336 ✦ DECEMBER 2
"Forgiveness lets me know that minds are joined."

Practice instructions

See complete instructions on page 135. A short summary:
- **Read** the commentary paragraph slowly and personally.
- **Pray** the prayer, perhaps several times.
- **Morning and evening:** Repeat the idea and then spend time in Open Mind Meditation.
- **Hourly remembrance:** Repeat the idea and then spend a quiet moment in meditation.
- **Frequent reminders:** Repeat the idea often within each hour.
- **Response to temptation:** Repeat the idea whenever upset, to restore peace.
- **Read the "What Is" section** slowly and thoughtfully once during the day.

Commentary

In the Text, the Course speaks of the idea that minds are joined as something that is experienced in a holy relationship, where two people have joined together in common purpose, what is called in one place "a common state of mind" (T-22.III.9:7). In a healthy holy relationship, the members of that relationship regularly practice forgiveness with one another. The result is stated as follows:

> This is the function of your holy relationship. For what one thinks, the other will experience with him. What can this mean except your mind and your brother's are one? Look not with fear upon this happy fact, and think not that it lays a heavy burden on you. For when you have accepted it with gladness, you will realize that your relationship is a reflection of the union of the Creator and His Son.
>
> (T-22.VI.14:1–5)

The idea that forgiveness is somehow connected to the experience of

582

linked minds is not intuitively obvious. Yet a little reflection seems to make it clearer for me. If I am unforgiving toward someone, there is certainly a barrier between our minds. I am mentally rejecting that other person and have no desire whatever to find myself mentally linked to them. My judgment is a strong "no" to that person's thoughts. When I forgive, my mind opens to them. "Forgiveness *lets me know* that minds are joined" (my emphasis). It opens the way for me to realize that this is true.

Our perceptions tell us, in a myriad of ways, that we are separate beings. Forgiveness opens the way to an experience that takes us beyond perception and shows us the underlying unity that perception cannot see. Forgiveness "opens the hidden altar to the truth" (1:4). Within our minds we find "the dwelling place of God Himself" (1:6). Forgiveness wipes "away my dreams of separation and of sin" (2:1). In the experience of union with another human being, we begin to remember our union with God and all creation.

WHAT IS THE EGO?

Part 6: W-pII.12.3:4

In contrast to the ego, our true Self, the Son of God, is surrounded by everlasting peace. Where the ego sees itself at war with the universe, and trembles constantly in fear of attack from every figure in its dreams, the Son of God is "forever conflict-free." The Son rests forever "undisturbed, in deepest silence and tranquility" (3:4).

When we begin to get in touch with our Self, we experience a taste of that deep, silent tranquility. That is one of the characteristics of the holy instant. There is a peace in the holy instant that beggars description.

> There is a silence into which the world can not intrude.
> There is an ancient peace you carry in your heart and have
> not lost. There is a sense of holiness in you the thought of
> sin has never touched.   (W-pI.164.4:1–3)

The ego, in isolation from the universe, can never know this peace. It comes only from within our Self, being an attribute of Who we are. It has nothing to do with external circumstance, and is unaffected by any such circumstance. It is part of what we are, together.

LESSON 337 ✦ DECEMBER 3
"My sinlessness protects me from all harm."

Practice instructions

See complete instructions on page 135. A short summary:

- **Read** the commentary paragraph slowly and personally.
- **Pray** the prayer, perhaps several times.
- **Morning and evening:** Repeat the idea and then spend time in Open Mind Meditation.
- **Hourly remembrance:** Repeat the idea and then spend a quiet moment in meditation.
- **Frequent reminders:** Repeat the idea often within each hour.
- **Response to temptation:** Repeat the idea whenever upset, to restore peace.
- **Read the "What Is" section** slowly and thoughtfully once during the day.

Practice suggestion: Think of your day yesterday, and in relation to each thing you did, ask yourself, *"Was there an element of 'If I do this thing right, I'll redeem myself'?"*

Then, with each "yes" you get, ask yourself, *"What was I trying to redeem myself for?"*

Then focus on simply accepting the awareness from God that you are sinless, that you need do nothing to be redeemed, because "God has already done all things that need be done" (1:5).

Commentary

This is a lesson about simply accepting the Atonement and nothing more. It states that there are really only two steps to the full knowledge of complete happiness (1:4–6):

1. Realize that I need do nothing of myself.
2. Accept what God has already done.

All of the turmoil and discomfort we experience as we begin a spiritual path comes from thinking that we lack something (which is not seeing step 2) and therefore we have to do something to get it (which is not seeing step 1).

We feel unhappy, and therefore we think we lack happiness and set out to seek it. Unhappiness is not a condition of lack. It is a condition of denial. We are actively negating happiness, which is our natural state. We are blocking out the awareness of love's presence. We are covering over the joy of our created nature, of simply being, with a filthy patina of unfulfillment. We think the solution is to do something; actually the solution is to stop doing something, to put an end to the activity that is obscuring our happiness.

That is one of the values of meditation. When we deliberately bring a stop to our mental activity we often suddenly feel happy. That is because we are always happy, but we are constantly generating unhappiness by our thoughts. Stop the thoughts and the happiness shines through. Clear away the clouds and the sun is always there.

We have taught ourselves that we *are* this constant mental activity. Letting go of that activity is an extreme threat to the ego. If we let it go nothing is left, or so we fear; so the ego tells us. The ego lies!

All we need to do is to stop doing. What we are, without any activity at all, is enough to support perfect, constant happiness.

WHAT IS THE EGO?

Part 7: W-pII.12.4:1

> To know reality is not to see the ego and its thoughts, its works, its acts, its laws and its beliefs, its dreams, its hopes, its plans for its salvation, and the cost belief in it entails.
>
> (4:1)

Knowing reality consists simply of *not* seeing illusions. Without illusions to conceal it, reality is self-evident. That is why we "need do nothing." We don't have to make reality. We don't have to make ourselves sinless, or happy, or peaceful. We simply have to stop seeing the thing that obscures reality from our sight: the ego, and everything to do with it.

The list of all the aspects of the ego that we are "not to see" is needful for us, because if the lesson simply said that "to know reality is not to see the ego" we would not be sure what was meant. By listing all the things related to the ego—thoughts, works, acts, laws, beliefs, dreams, hopes, plans for salvation, and the cost it demands of us—we are more likely to understand the full import of what not seeing the ego means. Not just the acts of the ego need to be banished from our sight, but all the things that drive those acts.

I am especially struck with "its plans for salvation." The ego has many plans for getting us out of the mess we think we are in. But we aren't really in a mess; we have simply covered over reality with illusions, and the reality is still there. We don't have to do anything to find it. We don't need to make plans for our salvation. Indeed, making plans for our salvation just digs the ego rut deeper. We need, as Lesson 337 points out, to understand that "I need do nothing of myself, for I need but accept my Self, my sinlessness, created for me, now already mine, to feel God's Love protecting me from harm" (W-pII.337.1:6).

LESSON 338 ✦ DECEMBER 4

"I am affected only by my thoughts."

Practice instructions

See complete instructions on page 135. A short summary:

- **Read** the commentary paragraph slowly and personally.
- **Pray** the prayer, perhaps several times.
- **Morning and evening:** Repeat the idea and then spend time in Open Mind Meditation.
- **Hourly remembrance:** Repeat the idea and then spend a quiet moment in meditation.
- **Frequent reminders:** Repeat the idea often within each hour.
- **Response to temptation:** Repeat the idea whenever upset, to restore peace.
- **Read the "What Is" section** slowly and thoughtfully once during the day.

Commentary

This is a key Course concept, repeated many times in different words:

I am responsible for what I see. I choose the feelings I experience, and I decide upon the goal I would achieve.
(T-21.II.2:3–4)

I am never upset for the reason I think. (W-pI.5.Heading)

It is impossible the Son of God be merely driven by events outside of him. It is impossible that happenings that come to him were not his choice. His power of decision is the determiner of every situation in which he seems to find himself by chance or accident. (T-21.II.3:1–3)

Nothing beyond yourself can make you fearful or loving, because nothing *is* beyond you. (T-10.In.1:1)

587

> It is your thoughts alone that cause you pain. Nothing external to your mind can hurt or injure you in any way. There is no cause beyond yourself that can reach down and bring oppression. No one but yourself affects you. There is nothing in the world that has the power to make you ill or sad, or weak or frail. But it is you who have the power to dominate all things you see by merely recognizing what you are. (W-190.5:1–6)

The Course says that accepting this is foundational to our release from our suffering. As long as we think something outside of us is affecting us and causing our pain, we will not look within for the thoughts that are truly at the root of the pain. We will believe ourselves to be innocent victims of forces beyond our control. There are no forces beyond our control; that is the whole point.

> It needs but this to let salvation come to all the world. For in this single thought is everyone released at last from fear. (1:1–2)

The realization that there is nothing outside me threatening me in any way is sure to release us from fear. At first it may seem to induce guilt—because if no one else is doing it to me, I must be doing it, and that seems to be a horrendously difficult admission to make. In fact, however, the realization that I am affected only by my own thoughts brings an expansive freedom from fear.

> Now has he learned that no one frightens him, and nothing can endanger him. He has no enemies, and he is safe from all external things. (1:3–4)

Let me remind myself of this today. Nothing can endanger me. I have no enemies, and nothing external can threaten me. I do not need to live in anxiety and defensiveness; I am safe.

Yet what about the fact that my own thoughts can hurt me? Isn't that something to be afraid of? It seems especially frightening that I can be affected by thoughts I have but of which I am not conscious. The eerie message of psychology that I am driven by subconscious motives that never surface in my conscious mind has always been frightening, and the Course is very much in line with those psychological theories. It is constantly telling us that we do believe certain things we are not aware of believing, and that we are driven by a subterranean guilt about separation so deeply buried that we perhaps will never, in this world, become aware of it. How can we be free from fear when these hidden enemies lurk beneath the surface of our minds, ready to explode like land mines when we unsuspectingly step on them?

> His thoughts can frighten him, but since these thoughts belong to him alone, he has the power to change them and exchange each fear thought for a happy thought of love. He crucified himself. Yet God has planned that His beloved Son will be redeemed. (1:5–7)

The good news is that since our thoughts are our thoughts, we can change them. Even the subconscious ones. That is what the Course is all about. Yes, we have crucified ourselves, but God has planned a way out for us. He has planned that we be redeemed: that is, liberated or released from our self-imposed prison. It is a way of changing our minds, and nothing more than that is needed.

> *All other plans will fail.* (2:2)

They will fail because they are based on an untruth, namely, that the problem is something external, something other than my thoughts. I can try to solve my problems with more money, with medicines or drugs, or by surrounding myself by people who seem to supply what I seem to lack. Being external solutions they will all fail, because the real problem is my own thoughts. No matter how ingenious they are, my plans will fail, because I am solving the wrong problems.

> *And I will have thoughts that will frighten me, until I learn that You have given me the only Thought that leads me to salvation. Mine alone will fail, and lead me nowhere. But the Thought You gave me promises to lead me home, because it holds Your promise to Your Son.* (2:3–5)

Even though I know the truth of this lesson, I will still have frightening thoughts, thoughts that seem to hurt me. That is not anything to be concerned about. When such thoughts surface I can learn to shrug and tell myself, "So I still have an ego. What else is new?" I can bring thoughts that frighten into the presence of the Thought given by God, the Holy Spirit. He is the "Thought that leads me to salvation," the Thought of forgiveness and love. He is a Thought full of promise and certainty, a Thought that tells me I am God's beloved Son, with nothing to fear (as we saw in yesterday's lesson, "My sinlessness protects me from all harm").

Let me today be willing to recognize my fear thoughts when they arise, rather than denying I have them, so that with the help of the Holy Spirit I can change them and exchange them for a happy thought of love.

WHAT IS THE EGO?

Part 8: W-pII.12.4:2

> In suffering, the price for faith in it [the ego] is so immense that crucifixion of the Son of God is offered daily at its darkened shrine, and blood must flow before the altar where its sickly followers prepare to die. (4:2)

This is one of the Course's darkest assessments of our ego. It evokes a picture of a primitive, blood-sacrifice religion such as we read about having existed in Central America, where human beings had their hearts ripped from their bodies still beating, and altars had channels cut into them to drain away the flowing blood. It says that our faith in the ego is the cause of suffering as immense and terrifying as that.

For our faith in the ego's illusion of autonomy, of separated identity, we pay an immense price in suffering. Each day we persist in this insane faith, we crucify the Son of God. For the existence of a separated identity demands the death of our unified Identity. As "sickly followers" of this religion (for religion it is), we are all preparing to die as we watch the sacrifice of the holy Son of God. (Of course, the Son of God cannot die; the sacrifice is illusion. But to our minds it is terribly, terribly real.) Our own death will vindicate our faith; it will prove our separation from God.

Although this suffering is not real in the final sense, it is real to us. And one of the things the Course asks of us, in order to bring about our deliverance from the ego, is that we honestly assess the cost of our belief in it. What does it cost me to hold a grievance? What does it cost me to hate? What does it cost me to insist on being right in an argument? What does it cost me to hold on to my view of myself as a victim? What does it cost me to hold on to my guilt? What does it cost me to hold on to my perception of sin in my brothers and sisters?

We need to count the cost of our belief in the ego. The Course says:

> You will not accept the cost of fear if you recognize it.
> (T-11.V.10:3)

> The ego is trying to teach you how to gain the whole world and lose your own soul. The Holy Spirit teaches that you cannot lose your soul and there is no gain in the world, for of itself it profits nothing. To invest without profit is surely to impoverish yourself, and the overhead is high. Not only is there no profit in the investment, but the cost to you is enormous. For this investment costs you the world's reality by denying yours, and gives you nothing in return.
> (T-12.VI.1:1–5)

> You must learn the cost of sleeping, and refuse to pay it.
> (T-12.VI.5:2)

> Belief in sin needs great defense, and at enormous cost. All that the Holy Spirit offers must be defended against and sacrificed. For sin is carved into a block out of your peace, and laid between you and its return.   (T-22.V.2:6–8)

We pay an immense price in suffering in order to hold on to our tattered, treasured ego. We lose awareness of our real Identity to hold on to an imagined one that we can never make real. Once we see this, once we recognize the insanity of it, we will no longer be willing to accept it. Once we see what the ego demands of us, we will refuse to pay the price, because we will realize that the ego is not what we really want. But first, very often, we must confront the horror of what we have done. We must look at that altar dripping with blood and realize we have been choosing this.

> It is not difficult to relinquish judgment. But it is difficult indeed to try to keep it. The teacher of God lays it

down happily the instant he recognizes its cost. All of the ugliness he sees about him is its outcome. All of the pain he looks upon is its result. All of the loneliness and sense of loss; of passing time and growing hopelessness; of sickening despair and fear of death; all these have come of it. And now he knows that these things need not be. Not one is true. For he has given up their cause, and they, which never were but the effects of his mistaken choice, have fallen from him. Teacher of God, this step will bring you peace. Can it be difficult to want but this? (M-10.6:1–11)

LESSON 339 ✦ DECEMBER 5
"I will receive whatever I request."

Practice instructions

See complete instructions on page 135. A short summary:

• **Read** the commentary paragraph slowly and personally.
• **Pray** the prayer, perhaps several times.
• **Morning and evening:** Repeat the idea and then spend time in Open Mind Meditation.
• **Hourly remembrance:** Repeat the idea and then spend a quiet moment in meditation.
• **Frequent reminders:** Repeat the idea often within each hour.
• **Response to temptation:** Repeat the idea whenever upset, to restore peace.
• **Read the "What Is" section** slowly and thoughtfully once during the day.

Practice suggestion: To get the real thrust of today's idea, you might want to try the following exercise. First, think of three things: a plan you have for today, something you want today, and a thought you have been thinking today. Then repeat the following lines to God:

I plan to do _____, yet I would do nothing by myself, but hear Your Voice in everything I do.

Today I want _____, but I request only what You offer me.

Today I might think _____, but I accept only Thoughts You share with me.

Commentary

This can be an upsetting idea! It means that whatever I have received, I requested. We don't like to hear that, and it can seem harsh. "You've got cancer? You asked for it." Used that way it is harsh, a weapon for separation instead of a tool for union. How could anyone desire sickness and pain? The thought seems absurd.

No one desires pain. But he can think that pain is pleasure. No one would avoid his happiness. But he can think that joy is painful, threatening and dangerous. Everyone will receive what he requests. But he can be confused indeed about the things he wants; the state he would attain.

(1:1–6)

Of course nobody wants pain; nobody consciously refuses happiness. If that is so, and everyone receives what he requests, then how is it that pain and unhappiness arise? We might think of it as a syllogism, which seems to make sense:

Nobody wants pain.
Nobody, therefore, would request pain.
Everyone receives what he requests or wants.
Therefore, we cannot receive pain.

That seems logical, doesn't it? If the first three are true, the fourth must be true. So how come I hurt? We must be missing something; our logic must be flawed. The flaw lies between the first two premises. Nobody wants pain, but nevertheless, we *do* request it; that is why we receive it.

The lesson explains that I can be confused about what I want; that I can think pain is pleasure, or that joy is threatening. The latter is perhaps a little easier to understand since it is a common experience. Haven't you ever had the thought "This is too good to last"? Or perhaps you've found yourself very happy in a relationship and suddenly getting afraid of it because some part of you is nearly certain that if you keep your guard down you're going to get smacked good. I had a friend who somehow entered a very high and totally joyful state of mind and was there for nearly three weeks until she started thinking, "This is wonderful. I love everybody, I have no fear of anything, but if I live like this in the world I'm going to get crucified. Maybe I'm not enlightened; maybe I'm just insane." So she lost the joy, and it never came back in quite the same way.

We really do think that too much joy is threatening and dangerous. We value our suspicions. We cherish our defenses. We're afraid of simply opening up to joy. So, quite unconsciously most of the time, we request unhappiness. We choose not to be peaceful.

The confusion of pain and joy is much more deeply buried, but the Course teaches that pain validates our separateness and justifies our barriers against one another. We choose it to strengthen our ego identity. It is perhaps difficult to believe that all of our pain and unhappiness is chosen, but the Course is insistent on this point.

> What can he then request that he would want when he receives it? He has asked for what will frighten him, and bring him suffering. (1:7–8)

We actually do ask for things that frighten us and bring us suffering. Much of the Text is dedicated to bringing this to conscious awareness; making us aware of what we are choosing so that we can realize how insane it is and make another choice.

> Let us resolve today to ask for what we really want, and only this, that we may spend this day in fearlessness, without confusing pain with joy, or fear with love. (1:9)

We can change our minds. We can begin, consciously, to choose the joy of God instead of pain. When a moment of pain arises we can accept the fact that we are choosing it, and choose again. We can say, "This is not what I want; I choose the joy of God." We can choose peace instead of upset. One thought I repeat so often that it is practically a mantra is "Oops! I'm doing it to myself again." It is remarkable what a change this fundamental realization can make in one's life.

Read now the short prayer that closes this lesson, and start your day with these thoughts. If you've already started the day, start it over right now. Stop a moment and adopt this mindset. Setting the tone of your mind right now will carry over into the day and bring changes you can't begin to foresee now.

> *Father, this is Your day. It is a day in which I would do nothing by myself, but hear Your Voice in everything I do; requesting only what You offer me, accepting only Thoughts You share with me.* (2:1–2)

WHAT IS THE EGO?

Part 9: W-pII.12.5:1

> Yet will one lily of forgiveness change the darkness into
> light; the altar to illusions to the shrine of Life Itself. (5:1)

The "darkened shrine" of the ego is flooded with light; the bloody altar to death is transformed into "the shrine to Life Itself." How? By "one lily of forgiveness." I think of a magical, fantasy tale, where the heroine or hero enters the black, forbidding temple of the evil god, carrying only a single flower. With great trepidation she approaches the altar and lays the pure, white lily upon it, and in a flash, the entire scene is transformed.

Forgiveness is that "magical." It isn't magic, though, it's a miracle. "The holiest of all the spots on earth is where an ancient hatred has become a present love" (T-26.IX.6:1). That is the miracle forgiveness works. I have seen it with my own eyes. I have watched a relationship filled with blood and bitterness transformed into sweet, mutual devotion—through forgiveness. This is no idle theory, no idealistic fantasy; this works.

Forgiveness undoes the ego. The blackest of blackness that the ego has manifested becomes flooded with light when touched by forgiveness. We need not fear to look at our ego's darkness; there is nothing forgiveness cannot heal.

LESSON 340 ✦ DECEMBER 6
"I can be free of suffering today."

Practice instructions

See complete instructions on page 135. A short summary:

- **Read** the commentary paragraph slowly and personally.
- **Pray** the prayer, perhaps several times.
- **Morning and evening:** Repeat the idea and then spend time in Open Mind Meditation.
- **Hourly remembrance:** Repeat the idea and then spend a quiet moment in meditation.
- **Frequent reminders:** Repeat the idea often within each hour.
- **Response to temptation:** Repeat the idea whenever upset, to restore peace.
- **Read the "What Is" section** slowly and thoughtfully once during the day.

Commentary

The Workbook lessons from 221 on are meant to be used as brief introductions to holy instants of direct experience of the truth. As the introduction to Part II of the Workbook says:

> Now we attempt to let the exercise be merely a beginning. For we wait in quiet expectation for our God and Father. (W-pII.In.2:1–2)

> We say some simple words of welcome, and expect our Father to reveal Himself, as He has promised. (W-pII.In.3:3)

> We say the words of invitation that His Voice suggests, and then we wait for Him to come to us. (W-pII.In.4:6)

The "words of invitation" seem to refer to the prayers in each lesson. The idea is that we read the lesson over and perhaps think on it a minute or two. Then, we repeat the prayer that invites God to join us. More and more, as I have worked with these lessons, I have found increasing benefit from really focusing on these prayers, and making them very personal. Then we wait, quietly, until we are aware of God's presence with us. That is the whole purpose of the exercises.

I can be free of suffering today.

So let me remind myself of this. Freedom from suffering is my choice. I have the option, today, to be free. As I listen to God's Voice directing me to find Christ's vision through forgiveness, I will be free forever from all suffering (1:4). Let me think on that a moment, pray the prayer given here, and then sit quietly and wait, listening, opening my mind to that vision.

I do not live in that vision yet, or only sporadically. To me it seems I have some way to go. So I wait. I make my mind empty, available to Him, and ask Him to fill me with this vision and to enlarge it in my mind.

I was born into this world but to achieve this day, and what it holds in joy and freedom for Your holy Son and for the world he made. (1:6)

Achieving Christ's vision fully is all that I am here for; I was born for this. Perhaps today! I open myself to it, I loose my mind from all lesser thoughts and offer it to You. In this holy instant I can find that release. Perhaps it won't last more than a few minutes, a few seconds. Perhaps it will lodge in my mind and stay with me all through the day. Salvation is already accomplished, and I can tap into that awareness right now. Even if I forget in ten minutes, even if I "lose" the awareness, the memory will remain and will sustain me, transforming my day from what it would have been had I not spent these moments with You. So I give myself to this time, this remembering.

We all will remember. God will gather us all to Himself, and together we shall all awake in Heaven in the Heart of Love (2:5–6). Take heart, my soul! The outcome is as inevitable as God. The way may seem long at times, but the ending is sure, and no anxiety need touch my heart. I am content in this moment simply to be with You. There is nothing more that I need. "There is no room for anything but joy and thanks today" (2:3), and only these will I welcome into my holy mind.

WHAT IS THE EGO?

Part 10: W-pII.12.5:2

> And peace will be restored forever to the holy minds which God created as His Son, His dwelling place, His joy, His love, completely His, completely one with Him.　(5:2)

How is it that simple forgiveness can do this? The guilt and fear induced by our belief in the ego's reality is the cause of all our suffering. It is our mad wish to be a separated self that has caused us to see God, and all the universe, as our enemies, and filled us with nightmares of punishment. Forgiveness shows us that what we think we did to ourselves has not occurred. There is no cause for our guilt. Forgiveness releases us from the dread of punishment, and brings us to realize that our oneness with God is undisturbed. We are still "His dwelling place, His joy, His love, completely His, completely one with Him." And in that knowledge, peace is restored forever.

When forgiveness washes over us, we realize that "I can be free of suffering today" (W-pII.340.Heading). It is the ego thought in our mind that paints unrest over the eternal calm of our mind as God created it. Letting go of that thought, even for an instant, brings immediate peace. The thought of separation, of an independent identity, was the original mistake:

> That one error, which brought truth to illusion, infinity to time, and life to death, was all you ever made. Your whole world rests upon it. Everything you see reflects it...
> ....You do not realize the magnitude of that one error. It was so vast and so completely incredible that from it a world of total unreality *had* to emerge.
> (T-18.I.4:4–6; 5:2–3)

Forgiveness shows us that what we think we have done has no real consequence. It removes the barriers to our awareness of God. That terrible mistake, upon which our whole world rests, was inconsequential; our union with God remains forever uninterrupted. We rest, now and ever, in His peace.

XVI

Lessons 341 - 350
What Is a Miracle?

**"I can attack but my own sinlessness,
And it is only that which keeps me safe."**

Practice instructions

See complete instructions on page 135. A short summary:

- **Read** the commentary paragraph slowly and personally.
- **Pray** the prayer, perhaps several times.
- **Morning and evening:** Repeat the idea and then spend time in Open Mind Meditation.
- **Hourly remembrance:** Repeat the idea and then spend a quiet moment in meditation.
- **Frequent reminders:** Repeat the idea often within each hour.
- **Response to temptation:** Repeat the idea whenever upset, to restore peace.
- **Read the "What Is" section** slowly and thoughtfully once during the day.

Practice suggestion: This is yet another favorite prayer of mine. I've laid it out on separate lines to aid in praying it, and added some extra thoughts to each line.

1. Father, Your Son is holy.
And Your Son is me.
You are my Father, Who loves me more than any earthly father could imagine.
Your Love created me holy, and that is how I remain, no matter what I think of myself.

2. I am he on whom You smile
Your Smile is everything to me.
It is my sun, my Source of life, in which I abide.
What could be more joyous than feeling Your Smile shining on me?

in love and tenderness so dear and deep and still
Let me know the love of Your Smile, the tenderness of it.
Let me feel how dear is Your Love, how deep, how still.

the universe smiles back on You, and shares Your Holiness.
Your Holiness lies in Your loving Smile.
In smiling back on you, we share Your Holiness.

3. How pure, how safe, how holy, then, are we,
How pure are we. How safe are we. How holy are we.
Let me feel this purity, rest in this safety, shine in this holiness.

abiding in Your Smile,
Basking in Your Smile.
Living in Your Smile like flowers live in the sunlight and turn their faces toward its warmth.

with all Your Love bestowed upon us,
All of Your Love. How could that be?
Let me know the joy of feeling all of Your Love bestowed on me.

602

living one with You,
With no distance between Us, no space for hate or discord to
   arise.
Living inside the warmth of Your Smile.

in brotherhood and Fatherhood complete;
The experience of brotherhood I long for is there, in Your Smile.
The perfect Father I long for is there, in Your Smile.

in sinlessness so perfect that the Lord of Sinlessness conceives
us as His Son,
Only the perfectly sinless could be the Son of the Lord of
   Sinlessness.
And in my perfect sinlessness, I am Your Son.

a universe of Thought completing Him.
I and my brothers are a universe of thought.
So pure, so sinless, so vast, that we actually complete You.
What more hallowed honor could there be?

Commentary

Whenever I attack anyone I attack myself. When I see sin in another, my own sinlessness is being attacked, and only that keeps me safe. God says I am sinless; who am I to disagree? And why would I do that?

> *I am he on whom You smile in love and tenderness so dear*
> *and deep and still the universe smiles back on You, and*
> *shares Your holiness.*   (1:2)

How foolish, then, to attack at all, when any attack is an attack on what I am! How foolish to so attack the wonder of what I am in a vain quest for some other, lesser identity! Why would I jeopardize my experience of God's deep tenderness?

> *...abiding in Your Smile...*   (1:3)

What a wonderful thought! Sometimes I have met a person whose smile was so radiant I felt as if I could sunbathe in it. Imagine basking in God's Smile! What a warmth of love beams from such a smile! Let me spend a little time now just luxuriating in its compassionate glow.

We live one with Him, "in brotherhood and Fatherhood complete" (1:3). The oneness we enjoy is not just with the Father, but with all our brothers as well. This is the state we are meant to abide in forever. It is the state we *are* in forever, if we are only willing to enjoy it and set aside every thought of attack. "The Lord of Sinlessness conceives us as His Son, a universe of Thought completing Him" (1:3). As such we can be only sinlessness itself. My attack threatens nothing but my awareness of this perfect sinlessness.

> Let us not, then, attack our sinlessness, for it contains the Word of God to us. And in its kind reflection we are saved. (2:1–2)

WHAT IS A MIRACLE?

Part 1: W-pII.13.1:1–3

> A miracle is a correction. It does not create, nor really change at all. (1:1–2)

The miracle *corrects*; it does not *create*. It does not make anything new; it merely adjusts a mistaken assessment of what already is. As Lesson 341 says, we already are sinless. We do not need to become sinless. All that we need to do is to end our attack on our own sinlessness.

We think of a miracle as some amazing change in the way things are. But a miracle, as the Course sees it, changes nothing. It simply takes away a false perception. It removes the veneer of sin and guilt we have laid over our innocence, and reveals the unchanging innocence we have attempted to hide.

A miracle often has external effects, although not always:

> Miracles are expressions of love, but they may not always have observable effects. (T-1.I.35:1)

When there are such effects, something in the illusion seems to change, often drastically. Someone who was sick gets well. Two people who were at war suddenly make peace. Yet that is the *effect* of the miracle, not the miracle itself. The effect simply reveals in form what has always been true in reality—the "sick" person was always whole, the "warring" friends were always joined as one mind. The observable effect shows us that the form was never real in the first place; but the miracle is the perception that *saw* that before it was an observable effect, and by realizing the falsity of the illusion, changed the illusion.

> It [a miracle] merely looks on devastation, and reminds the
> mind that what it sees is false.   (1:3)

The miracle looks on the illusion, and reminds the mind that it *is* illusion. We do see "devastation" in this world, but the miracle reminds us that what we see is false. We see a person's mind twisted with guilt; the miracle reminds us that the guilt is as unreal as its apparent effects, and enables us to see the person's wholeness and innocence behind the illusion they present to the world.

LESSON 342 ✦ DECEMBER 8

**"I let forgiveness rest upon all things,
For thus forgiveness will be given me."**

Practice instructions

See complete instructions on page 135. A short summary:

- **Read** the commentary paragraph slowly and personally.
- **Pray** the prayer, perhaps several times.
- **Morning and evening:** Repeat the idea and then spend time in Open Mind Meditation.
- **Hourly remembrance:** Repeat the idea and then spend a quiet moment in meditation.
- **Frequent reminders:** Repeat the idea often within each hour.
- **Response to temptation:** Repeat the idea whenever upset, to restore peace.
- **Read the "What Is" section** slowly and thoughtfully once during the day.

Practice suggestion: The following is a visualization based on today's lesson. It is long, so it may help if someone reads it to you, or if you read it onto tape and play it back for yourself.

Close your eyes.

Think of your current life as if it's taking place inside of hell.

Think of various problem areas in your life and see actual flames popping up in those places.

Maybe you have a problematic relationship right now. See flames dancing there.

Maybe you are having financial difficulties. See flames coming out of your wallet or purse.

Maybe you feel alone and isolated. You might imagine a ring of flames around you, separating you from others.

Just think of various problem areas and see flames dancing in each of those areas.

Then, a little distance away, you see a massive, glorious door, the gate of Heaven.

Imagine it however you like.

Maybe it's made of gold. Perhaps there are diamonds in it. Perhaps it is shining with an otherworldly light.

You walk toward it, and as you come nearer, you see it has a large keyhole, like you might see in a castle door.

A ray of bright light is streaming out of the keyhole, a hint of the glory that lies on the other side.

You find in your hand a large, old-fashioned key.

Look at the key, feel it in your hand.

As you look, you see that on it is engraved in beautiful writing the word "Forgiveness."

Then you turn the key over, and on the other side it says, "of [name]."

The name is someone you deeply need to forgive, but you have been putting it off.

See whose name is there.

Realize that you have been refusing to use this key for a long time.

If going through the gate means using this key, you are not sure it's worth it.

Maybe the flames are preferable.

How long have you been loitering there, in front of the gate, wondering if you should enter in and be at home?

You finally decide to forgive this person.

Say to yourself, *"I let forgiveness rest upon [name],*
For thus forgiveness will be given me."

Do your best to mean these lines.

"I let forgiveness rest upon [name],
For thus forgiveness will be given me."

One more time: *"I let forgiveness rest upon [name],*
For thus forgiveness will be given me."

Find that you have placed the key in the keyhole

And are already turning it.

You are forgiving this person at last.

The key turns all the way and you pull the door open; it takes virtually no effort.

As it swings open you find yourself face to face with a blazing light.

The light of Heaven.
The light of God.
The light of your true Self.
You are transfixed by this light,
Caught up in the ecstasy of it.
All questions are answered; all longings are satisfied.
You are home at last.
Say to God, *"I forget all things except Your changeless Love.
I forget all things except that You are here."* (based on *The Gifts of God*, p. 126)
Spend a few moments basking in this light,
And then open your eyes when you are ready.

Commentary

As the fourth sentence says, "The key is in my hand" (1:4). Forgiveness is the key. As I forgive, I receive forgiveness—not from God as a reward for my good deed (God has no need to forgive, never having condemned), but—from myself. Forgiveness really means no more than that I "let creation be as You would have it be and as it is" (1:7). In my ego mind, I am the only one who has overlaid an illusion of "sin" onto the world around me. When I look with condemnation on the world, I am not seeing reality as it is. There is nothing to condemn, and that fact is my own salvation. If the sin I think I see in the world is really there, then I am damned with the world. Only when I let creation be as God would have it be—innocent—can I be free of condemnation.

This is God's plan "to save me from the hell I made" (1:1). I made the hell; God gives me forgiveness as the way out. The hell I made is not real, thank God. In this Course I have come right up to the door to the end of dreams (1:4). I hold forgiveness, the key, in my hand. "I stand before the gate of Heaven, wondering if I should enter in and be at home" (1:5). In every instant today when I face the choice between judgment and forgiveness, between murder and a miracle, I am standing at that gate, holding the key in my hand, wondering if I should go in.

Let me not wait again today. Let me forgive all things, and let creation be as You would have it be and as it is. Let me remember that I am Your Son, and opening the door at last, forget illusions in the blazing light of truth, as memory of You returns to me. (1:6–8)

608

Forgiveness is the key; the choice to open the door is mine. To open it I must be willing to forget all illusions. I must be willing to let go of my investment in seeing my own sins in my brother and to release him.

> Brother, forgive me now. I come to you to take you home with me. And as we go, the world goes with us on our way to God.　　　　　　　　　　　　　　(2:1–3)

Let me think of these lines with every person I meet today. "Forgive me now. I come to take you home with me." Oh, let that be the way I greet everyone in my mind! Let us all go home together!

WHAT IS A MIRACLE?

Part 2: W-pII.13.1:4–6

> It [a miracle] undoes error, but does not attempt to go beyond perception, nor exceed the function of forgiveness.
> 　　　　　　　　　　　　　　　　　　　　　　　　(1:4)

A miracle relates to perception, and not to direct revelation. It causes a change in my perception, undoing my perceptual errors.

> Wholeness is the perceptual content of miracles. They thus correct, or atone for, the faulty perception of lack.
> 　　　　　　　　　　　　　　　　　　　(T-1.I.41:1–2)

When my mind experiences a miracle, I see wholeness instead of lack. In regard to "sin," which is a perception of lack of love in someone, the miracle causes me to see their love instead of their "sin." I see them as whole, rather than as lacking. The miracle undoes my error, but it does not attempt to go beyond that. Miracles occur within the context of perception and of time; they do not try to carry me to the realm of knowledge and of eternity. They correct my perception but they do not give knowledge. "Thus it stays within time's limits" (1:5).

The Course makes this point repeatedly; it must be important. What makes it so important to us? This: When we turn to a spiritual path, we can become overanxious. We want a miracle to translate us immediately into the realm of pure spirit. We want a quick fix. But we cannot make a transition directly from false perception to pure knowledge. We have to go through the stage of corrected perception. We can't skip steps. The Text says it clearly: "Perception must be straightened out before you can know anything" (T-3.III.1:2). That is what miracles are for: correcting our perception. Once our perception is corrected, God can take us the rest of the way, from perception to knowledge.

> Redeemed perception is easily translated into knowledge, for only perception is capable of error and perception has never been. Being corrected it gives place to knowledge, which is forever the only reality.   (T-12.VIII.8:6–7)

> Yet it [the miracle] paves the way for the return of time-lessness and love's awakening, for fear must slip away under the gentle remedy it brings.   (1:6)

The "gentle remedy" of the miracle, in correcting our perception, "paves the way" for a return to full knowledge. Without the undoing of our false perception, we will resist knowledge and reject love; we will be afraid of it. Our twisted perception of love, for instance, believes that love means sacrifice, and that total love would mean total sacrifice. We therefore run away from it; we fear it. Such perceptions need to be changed before we would even be willing to let real love awaken within us. Because the miracle removes our fear, it opens the way for love. It ends our resistance; it removes the interference.

LESSON 343 ✦ DECEMBER 9

**"I am not asked to make a sacrifice
To find the mercy and the peace of God."**

Practice instructions

See complete instructions on page 135. A short summary:

- **Read** the commentary paragraph slowly and personally.
- **Pray** the prayer, perhaps several times.
- **Morning and evening:** Repeat the idea and then spend time in Open Mind Meditation.
- **Hourly remembrance:** Repeat the idea and then spend a quiet moment in meditation.
- **Frequent reminders:** Repeat the idea often within each hour.
- **Response to temptation:** Repeat the idea whenever upset, to restore peace.
- **Read the "What Is" section** slowly and thoughtfully once during the day.

Commentary

The whole idea of loss or sacrifice is foreign to the Course. It tells us, "Sacrifice is a notion totally unknown to God" (T-3.I.4:1). As the first line of the lesson points out, how could ending suffering be a loss? How can happiness be gained by sacrificing? It's ridiculous when you look at it, and yet for centuries many religions have believed that in order to find God's mercy you have to give up something, usually something really valuable. You have to suffer to attain Heaven. You have to pay for your mistakes.

Heaven, or salvation, must be only gain. How could it be a loss and still be Heaven? Let me affirm to my Father:

> *You only give. You never take away. And You created me to be like You, so sacrifice becomes impossible for me as well as You. I, too, must give.* (1:3–6)

611

Someone just today was telling me how they got trapped in a mental loop of feeling as though God had given them a dirty deal by creating them capable of experiencing this dream of suffering; it was as if God was putting us through all this for selfish reasons, or at least allowing us to go through this for selfish reasons, for what *He* can get out of it. But God only gives; He does not take away. Let me not think otherwise.

And what God gives is given forever:

> *As I was created I remain. Your Son can make no sacrifice,*
> *for he must be complete, having the function of completing*
> *You.*   (1:8–9)

I can't lose what I am; I can't sacrifice something of value and become incomplete, because that would be contrary to my function of completing God. For God to be complete (which of course He must be, being God), I must be complete, for He created me to complete Himself! Therefore, I cannot sacrifice; I must remain complete.

We are beset with the notion that somehow we have to earn the mercy and the peace of God. Especially when I've been off on some ego detour, I always feel as if I have to "go through" something to find my way back. I need to have a proper period of remorse and feeling guilty. At least I have to sleep it off! It just doesn't seem right to snap instantly from ego madness to a state of peace and joy without paying some kind of penalty first. Yet:

> The mercy and the peace of God are free. Salvation has
> no cost. It is a gift that must be freely given and received.
> And it is this that we would learn today.   (2:1–4)

Because they have no cost, mercy and peace are immediately available in every instant. I need only to be willing to freely give them and receive them.

In this instant, right now, let me give mercy to myself. Let me see my childish heart in pain over what it thinks it has done, and let me spread mercy across it like a warm blanket. Let me embrace myself with love and affirm my own innocence again. Have I forgotten who I am? That's okay. Have I been angry at a brother? I still merit mercy and peace. Have I betrayed a friend? God still counts me as His own. No sacrifice is asked; no penance; no "decent" period of mourning. I can simply, trustingly open my mind to my Friend and find welcome. I can come home to God. What am I waiting for? Let me come to Him now.

WHAT IS A MIRACLE?

Part 3: W-pII.13.2:1–2

One of the most frequently repeated lessons of the entire Course is that giving and receiving are the same: "To give and to receive are one in truth" (W-pII.108.Heading). This lesson, one of the most basic the Holy Spirit wants to teach us (it is the first lesson of the Holy Spirit in Chapter 6: "To have, give all to all"—T-6.V(A).5:13), is also one of the hardest for us to learn because it is the antithesis of our normal way of thinking.

> A miracle contains the gift of grace, for it is given and
> received as one.   (2:1)

To receive a miracle, we must give it; to give it, we must receive it. Receiving a miracle and giving a miracle are one thing, not two. Many of us get wrapped up in trying to figure out whether I must forgive myself first to forgive someone else, or whether I have to forgive the other person before I can forgive myself. The answer is, neither and both. To forgive yourself you must forgive the other person, but to forgive the other person, you must forgive yourself. They are one. They seem to be two distinct actions but they are not; they are one action because my brother and I are one Self. It may often seem, within time, that one precedes the other, but in reality, both happen simultaneously.

"And thus it illustrates the law of truth the world does not obey, because it fails entirely to understand its ways" (2:2). The "law of truth" is, I think, the same as the "law of love" mentioned in the title of Lesson 344: "What I give my brother is my gift to me." Were we to completely appropriate this one thought, we would be out of here, done with the curriculum. A miracle illustrates this law; it gives a pictorial representation of it, a demonstration of it. When I give a miracle to a brother, I am looking on his devastation and realizing that what I see is false (1:3). I am seeing his wholeness rather than the illusion of his lack. My seeing that for someone else reminds them to see it for themselves, if they wish to. And when they receive the miracle, *I* am blessed. I am reminded of who I am.

The world does not obey this law, nor understand it. Unlearning the world's way of thinking about this is what the Course calls "undoing the getting concept" (T-6.V(B).3:1). It calls this the first step in the reversal of our ego's thinking. Miracles are important to us because they illustrate this law; they help us know, by experience, that giving is receiving; that I keep what I want by giving it away.

LESSON 344 ✦ DECEMBER 10

**"Today I learn the law of love; that what
I give my brother is my gift to me."**

Practice instructions

See complete instructions on page 135. A short summary:

- **Read** the commentary paragraph slowly and personally.
- **Pray** the prayer, perhaps several times.
- **Morning and evening:** Repeat the idea and then spend time in Open Mind Meditation.
- **Hourly remembrance:** Repeat the idea and then spend a quiet moment in meditation.
- **Frequent reminders:** Repeat the idea often within each hour.
- **Response to temptation:** Repeat the idea whenever upset, to restore peace.
- **Read the "What Is" section** slowly and thoughtfully once during the day.

Commentary

What if we realized that only what we give away to others will be left to us in the end? What if we recognized that everything we try to hold onto for ourselves alone will be lost? How would that change the way we live?

The lesson is referring to our gifts of love and forgiveness more than to anything physical, although the physical often symbolizes that love. "Yet he whom I forgive will give me gifts beyond the worth of anything on earth" (1:6). The Course teaches us that everything is an idea, and ideas, when given away, only increase; we lose nothing in the giving. On the other hand, when we try to save our affection for ourselves alone, we wind up empty-handed: "And as I looked upon the treasure that I thought I had, I found an empty place where nothing ever was or is or will be" (1:3). Only what is shared is real because only oneness is reality, and separateness is illusory. We can't have something for ourselves

615

alone because we are not alone.

How do we arise and return to God (1:9)? Through forgiving our brothers (1:6–8). Each one we welcome "fills my store with Heaven's treasures, which alone are real" (1:7). There was a short poem I learned back in my fundamentalist Christian days that seems applicable here:

> Only one life, 'twill soon be past;
> Only what's done for Christ will last.

> Only the love is real; only the love is eternal.

> How near we are to one another, as we go to God. How near is He to us. How close the ending of the dream of sin, and the redemption of the Son of God. (2:1–3)

I don't think that as yet we have any idea how inextricably we are all linked to one another, or how near we really are to one another. Each time you choose to listen to God's Voice instead of your ego, in however little a way, you help me on my way to God. Each time I open my eyes to Christ's vision, you see a little better. You and I and all of us are really one. "I am not alone in experiencing the effects of my thoughts," says Lesson 19. If, through my willingness to see another as whole today, I help her or him on the way to God by reminding them of who they really are, I have literally helped myself equally, because our minds are joined. How many opportunities await each of us today! How eager I should be to spread forgiveness over all the world!

WHAT IS A MIRACLE?

Part 4: W-pII.13.2:3–5

> A miracle inverts perception which was upside down before, and thus it ends the strange distortions that were manifest. (2:3)

So the perceptions we have learned from the ego are upside down; a miracle inverts those perceptions and makes them right-side up again. Perhaps this is a reference to the way that physical sight works. In physical sight, the image projected by the lens of our eyes upon the retina is actually upside down. The mind literally learns to see the upside down image as right-side up. In an experiment in which people were given glasses to wear that inverted the image, so that it was right-side up on the retina, the mind saw everything as upside down. After a number of days, however, the mind adjusted and saw everything again as the right way. When the glasses were removed, people now saw things as being upside down!

The perception that what I give, I lose, for instance, is entirely upside down; true perception shows me that what I give I keep. We perceive what is false, but our minds have learned to interpret it as truth. We see illusions and think them real; we believe that reality is the illusion. We fear love, and love fear. We think guilt is good, and innocence is guilty. A miracle inverts all this; it corrects our perception, inverting our understanding. The change in perception is what ends the distortion in what is being manifested (that is, showing up in form).

"Now is perception open to the truth" (2:4). When the miracle inverts my perception, and ends the distortion, I am again capable of perceiving the truth (or its accurate reflection). Until perception is corrected, truth cannot enter.

"Now is forgiveness seen as justified" (2:5). This is perhaps the most dramatic reversal of all. One of the most radical ideas in the Course is that forgiveness is *justified*. If we think of forgiveness at all from the ego perspective, we think of it as someone's being let off the hook for no reason, "out of the goodness of our hearts." The Course says that there is every reason to forgive. It is fully justified (see T-30.VI.2:1). What is unjustifiable is judgment, condemnation, and anger (see T-30.VI.1:1). This is simply not something that can be learned or arrived at through logic (although it is entirely logical). When we see our condemnation of someone as just, that is just how we see it. Trying to reason ourselves into seeing it differently doesn't work. Nor can we "should" ourselves into it. If we try to force ourselves to "forgive" while still seeing guilt, we feel as though we are being untrue to ourselves.

When you give your perception to the Holy Spirit and ask to see as He sees, He gives you His perception. It simply springs into the mind. Suddenly you literally no longer see any reason to condemn, and every reason to give love. Your anger, perfectly justified a moment ago, now seems unthinkable. It is like the shift that occurs in looking at a Magic

Eye illustration (where a 3-D picture is hidden in a two-dimensional one) or a figure-ground optical illusion (such as the one that can be seen either as a wine goblet or as two faces looking at one another). You are seeing it one way; suddenly you are seeing it another way. And when you see it one way you cannot see the other way. Just so is the miracle. It inverts your perception. You were seeing one way; now you see the other. You can't "make" it happen, but when it happens, you know it.

LESSON 345 ✦ DECEMBER 11

"I offer only miracles today,
For I would have them be returned to me."

Practice instructions

See complete instructions on page 135. A short summary:

- **Read** the commentary paragraph slowly and personally.
- **Pray** the prayer, perhaps several times.
- **Morning and evening:** Repeat the idea and then spend time in Open Mind Meditation.
- **Hourly remembrance:** Repeat the idea and then spend a quiet moment in meditation.
- **Frequent reminders:** Repeat the idea often within each hour.
- **Response to temptation:** Repeat the idea whenever upset, to restore peace.
- **Read the "What Is" section** slowly and thoughtfully once during the day.

Commentary

The basic thought is similar to yesterday's: what I give is returned to me. Realizing this is so, let me decide as this day starts, and as every day starts, to offer only what I want. Miracles. To give a miracle means to see past the illusions of my brothers, and to see them as they really are, as God's creations. It means not to accept and support the image my brother has of himself as a limited ego, a tiny fragment of mind trapped in a body. Instead, I see him as an unlimited being of spirit, magnificent in glory. In Chapter 8 of the Text we are told:

> But when you look upon a brother as a physical entity, his power and glory are "lost" to you and so are yours....Do not see him this way for your own salvation, which must bring him his. Do not allow him to belittle himself in your mind, but give him freedom from his belief in littleness, and thus escape from yours.   (T-8.VII.5:3, 5–6)

619

That is giving a miracle. Refusing to see my brother in the limited way he sees himself; seeing the Christ in him, for him. The miracle thus blesses both me and my brother, for as my mind is healed of illusions, it reflects on him as well and brings light to his mind. I give him the opportunity to see himself as God sees him.

> *The law of love is universal. Even here, it takes a form*
> *which can be recognized and seen to work.*   (1:2–3)

The "law of love" was stated yesterday: "that what I give my brother is my gift to me." The form this law takes here is something I can recognize. It isn't merely abstract; it takes form, it becomes concrete. When I offer miracles to those around me, they return to me, not in exactly the form in which I offered them, but in just the form I need to meet my needs as I perceive them (1:4). In Heaven there are no needs (1:5); here on earth, I do perceive needs, and the law of love adapts to my perception (1:6).

I can offer a miracle with a profound act of forgiveness, or I can offer a miracle with a smile to a passerby that tells him, "You are loveable." I offer a miracle with every gesture of kindness, every token of courtesy, every expression of respect, and every act of caring. Whatever the form, if the content of the message is "You are loveable. You are worthy. You are innocent," I have offered the miracle, and it will return to me.

Let me choose, Father, to enter into my day determined to offer nothing but miracles to those around me. May I say, from the depth of my heart:

> Peace to all seeking hearts today. The light has come to
> offer miracles to bless the tired world.   (2:1–2)

And before I step out into the bustle of today, let me pause for a few minutes and spend them simply offering peace to every seeking heart that comes to mind. No such effort is ever wasted, and I will receive as much as I am willing to give.

WHAT IS A MIRACLE?

Part 5: W-pII.13.3:1–3

> Forgiveness is the home of miracles. The eyes of Christ deliver them to all they look upon in mercy and in love. Perception stands corrected in His sight, and what was meant to curse has come to bless. (3:1–3)

A miracle corrects perception, and miracles live in forgiveness. When we look with the eyes of Christ, we see with mercy and in love; we see with forgiveness. And we then "deliver" miracles to everyone we see with that corrected perception. It is not just that something changes within our minds, not just that our perception is altered; something gets communicated or "delivered" from us to those we look upon. A miracle here, and in many places in the Course, seems to include an aspect in which something passes from my forgiving mind to the minds of others. Miracles are said to be "interpersonal" (T-1.II.1:4). When I accept forgiveness within my mind, for myself or another, it extends to others. Indeed it is by extending it that I accept it:

> Miracles are natural signs of forgiveness. Through miracles you accept God's forgiveness by extending it to others. (T-1.I.21:1–2)

The phrase "and what was meant to curse has come to bless" reminds me of the Bible story of Joseph and his brothers. Because Joseph was the favorite of his father, his brothers, jealous of him, sold him into slavery in Egypt. But Joseph, because of his ability to interpret the Pharaoh's dreams, rose to great power in Egypt. Years later, in a famine, his family came to Egypt seeking food, and Joseph was the man in control of the food supply. Instead of taking vengeance on them, Joseph told them:

> God sent me before you to preserve life….it was not you who sent me here, but God….You meant evil against me, but God meant it for good. (Gn 45:5, 8; 50:20)

When we have truly received forgiveness into our hearts, we will be able to see the blessing even in actions that others intend for our harm. "What was meant to curse has come to bless." We find that, as the Text says:

> Gratitude is due him for both his loving thoughts and his appeals for help [that is, what we normally see as his attacks], for both are capable of bringing love into your awareness if you perceive them truly. (T-12.I.6:2)

And *that* kind of perception is, indeed, a miracle.

LESSON 346 ✦ DECEMBER 12

**"Today the peace of God envelops me,
And I forget all things except His Love."**

Practice instructions

See complete instructions on page 135. A short summary:

- **Read** the commentary paragraph slowly and personally.
- **Pray** the prayer, perhaps several times.
- **Morning and evening:** Repeat the idea and then spend time in Open Mind Meditation.
- **Hourly remembrance:** Repeat the idea and then spend a quiet moment in meditation.
- **Frequent reminders:** Repeat the idea often within each hour.
- **Response to temptation:** Repeat the idea whenever upset, to restore peace.
- **Read the "What Is" section** slowly and thoughtfully once during the day.

Practice suggestion: This is one of the most beautiful prayers in the Workbook. It speaks of a day in which I am so caught up in the experience of God's Love that I forget everything else. The things of time fade away and the laws of time no longer bind me. This prayer is very similar to the prayers for Lesson 232 ("Be in my mind, my Father, through the day") and Lesson 310 ("In fearlessness and love I spend today"). All three speak of spending our day with God rather than with all our earthly tasks and happenings. I highly recommend taking some time this morning and praying this prayer over and over. Let it usher you into the joyous day of which it speaks. Fix a line in your mind, close your eyes, and say that line to God, as sincerely as you can. Then open your eyes and do the same with the next line. You may want to write the prayer down on a card so you can use it each hour. You may even want to memorize it. The beauty of memorization is that it enables you to use the prayer anytime, anywhere, and do so without opening your eyes to read each line, thus allowing you to absorb yourself in the prayer more fully.

Commentary

Before I begin to comment on the lesson, let me share a few thoughts in preparation.

Many of the lessons in the latter part of the Workbook, particularly this one, are coming to us from a state of right-mindedness. That state is the goal of the Course's curriculum. Therefore, for most of us, probably all of us, it represents a state of mind we do not normally live in. I know there is a part of me that resonates in perfect harmony with this lesson, but there is also another part that stands off cynically and says to me, "Forget all things except His Love? Hah! More likely you will remember everything except His Love. How long will this high-falutin' attitude last after you walk out the door?" And if this is so, why bother with the lesson at all?

Why bother? Because there is a part of my mind that sings in harmony with the lesson, and it is the only "part" that is real. Each time I seek to align myself with thoughts like these, and to let the significance of them wash over me and draw me with them, something happens. Even if after reading and quietly meditating on them I feel as though nothing has happened, something *has* happened. And if, even for an instant, I can harmonize my mind with them so that, just for that instant, I mean the words as I say them, I may have saved as much as a thousand years in my spiritual development. Truly, truly, it is worth the effort. *We* are worth the effort.

So as we read this lesson now, let us simply attempt to suspend our disbelief for just an instant, and let these words be true for us. Let us believe that what we say represents our true Self, for it does. Let us be in the spirit of these words.

It all seems so simple sometimes. All there is to do is to be happy. Sometimes I feel as if I could simply "be there" right now, with no more effort or struggle. All the strain and struggle comes from resistance, not from any effort to be enlightened or holy. Simply forget all things except His Love. Simply remember nothing but the peace of God.

When those thoughts come to me, I notice, still, a fear of loss. It feels as if I am giving up something valuable when I give up struggle. Yet all

I am giving up is pain.

What if I simply started being happy all the time? What if I let go of all insistence that anything be different?

> *Father, I wake today with miracles correcting my perception of all things. And so begins the day I share with You as I will share eternity, for time has stepped aside today.*
> (1:1–2)

I can share this day with God just as I will share eternity with Him. There is nothing to do, nothing to achieve. Salvation asks nothing of me that I cannot give *right now.*

> *I do not seek the things of time, and so I will not look upon them. What I seek today transcends all laws of time and things perceived in time. I would forget all things except Your Love.*
> (1:3–5)

In all my seeking, Father, what I seek is really Your Love. The things of time will never satisfy me; in this moment I gladly forget them all. I come to You, needing only Your Smile to fill my heart to overflowing.

> *I would abide in You, and know no laws except Your law of love. And I would find the peace which You created for Your Son, forgetting all the foolish toys I made as I behold Your glory and my own.*
> (1:6–7)

Only my belief that I am not worthy of Your Love keeps me from enjoying it in every moment. Your Love is not lacking. I let myself relax in It and lean back on It. I am sustained by Your Love. There is nothing else. In Your Love, I behold not only Your glory, but my own glory as well, for Love is what I am.

> And when the evening comes today, we will remember nothing but the peace of God. For we will learn today what peace is ours, when we forget all things except God's Love.
> (2:1–2)

What is there to prevent me from having a day like this? Nothing. I open my heart to Love. The Love of God rolls over me like a mighty ocean, and I am carried in Its current, surrounded by It, afloat in It.

WHAT IS A MIRACLE?

Part 6: W-pII.13.3:4–5

Each lily of forgiveness offers all the world the silent miracle of love. (3:4)

Love is the real miracle.

Miracles occur naturally as expressions of love. The real miracle is the love that inspires them. In this sense everything that comes from love is a miracle. (T-1.I.3:1–3)

The symbol of the lily represents a gift of forgiveness I give to a brother or sister. Each time I offer this gift, I am offering God's Love to the entire world. I am opening a floodgate and allowing that Love to flow into the world through me. Wherever that river of Love comes, life springs up; and that is the miracle.

And each [lily] is laid before the Word of God, upon the universal altar to Creator and creation in the light of perfect purity and endless joy. (3:5)

My gift of forgiveness given to my brother is also a gift to God. My gratitude to my brothers is my gift to God. In acknowledging His creation, I acknowledge Him. Opening to this current of Love is the source of perfect purity and endless joy. There is nothing so joyful as a loving heart.

LESSON 347 ✦ DECEMBER 13

**"Anger must come from judgment. Judgment is
The weapon I would use against myself,
To keep the miracle away from me."**

Practice instructions

See complete instructions on page 135. A short summary:

- **Read** the commentary paragraph slowly and personally.
- **Pray** the prayer, perhaps several times.
- **Morning and evening:** Repeat the idea and then spend time in Open Mind Meditation.
- **Hourly remembrance:** Repeat the idea and then spend a quiet moment in meditation.
- **Frequent reminders:** Repeat the idea often within each hour.
- **Response to temptation:** Repeat the idea whenever upset, to restore peace.
- **Read the "What Is" section** slowly and thoughtfully once during the day.

Practice suggestion: Today the ideas for the day go from two lines to three lines, which means they have tripled in length since just seven lessons ago. I confess that I find it harder to repeat these longer ideas throughout the day. If you're the same, here are some suggestions that might make it easier:

- Write the idea down on a notecard and pull the card out for practice periods.
- Find a part of the idea that speaks the most to you, and focus on repeating that part.
- Spend time in the morning memorizing the idea so fully that it just rolls off your tongue the rest of the day.
- Reword the idea in a way that captures the gist of it but is shorter and speaks to you personally.

On that last point, don't be afraid to reword the idea, as long as you stay reasonably faithful to the meaning. The Course reminds us of this more than once, saying, "You need not use these exact words" (W-pI.65.6:5) and "It is not the particular words you use that matter" (W-pI.rI.In.6:4).

Commentary

From the sublime heights of yesterday's lesson ("I would forget all things except Your Love"), we return to the level of our split mind, in which we attack ourselves, keeping away the miracle with judgment and attack. The previous lesson was miracle-mindedness; here we see why we do not always experience that state of mind: We actively keep it away from ourselves with judgment and attack. The process of the Course involves learning complete honesty with ourselves. We learn to recognize and admit the duplicity of our own minds:

> *Father, I want what goes against my will, and do not want what is my will to have.* (1:1)

"My will" is my right-mindedness, forgetting everything except God's Love. And yet we seem to want something else, and to actively resist having the Love of God flooding our minds.

I love the next couple of lines:

> *Straighten my mind, my Father. It is sick.* (1:2–3)

I love those lines because of their stark simplicity, and because of the contrast they offer to the frothy denial of our inner darkness that is prevalent in so many circles. The Course does not pull any punches. It does not whitewash our problems. There are times when no other assessment fits: Our minds are sick! It is sick to want what goes against my true will, and to actively resist my own well-being. Self-destruction is always pathological. When we look honestly at the fact that we are literally pushing away our own peace of mind, by active choices we make, it ought to be repugnant. When we see what we have been doing, our saner self will say, "This is sick!"

And so we ask the Father to "straighten my mind." That always reminds me of a science fiction book by Zenna Henderson that I read as a young man, called *The People: No Different Flesh.*[1] In it there were certain persons who could telepathically enter into another person's mind and "sort" their thoughts, soothing their inner turmoil and pain. The idea appealed to me so much that I used to pray, "Sort me, Father," when I felt my thoughts in chaos and confusion. And it seemed to work! I was pleasantly surprised to see this similar phrase here, validating my early experience. "Straighten my mind."

We enable the straightening of our minds by giving all our judgment to the Holy Spirit and asking Him to judge for us (1:5). He sees what we see, "and yet He knows the truth" (1:6). He is looking at the same evidence I am looking at, but He knows the pain is not real; the evidence means something entirely different to Him. To me, the evidence of my eyes seems to prove that separation, pain, loss, and death are real. When I bring all this to Him and ask Him to straighten my mind, He will show me that what I see does not mean what I think it means; He will use what I thought proved my guilt to reveal my innocence.

> *He gives the miracles my dreams would hide from my awareness.* (1:8)

> Listen today. Be very still, and hear the gentle Voice for God assuring you that He has judged you as the Son He loves. (2:1–2)

WHAT IS A MIRACLE?

Part 7: W-pII.13.4:1

> The miracle is taken first on faith, because to ask for it implies the mind has been made ready to conceive of what it cannot see and does not understand. (4:1)

Faith. Yes, *A Course in Miracles* asks for faith, at least at the beginning. "The miracle is taken *first* on faith." This is a fairly traditional meaning for the word "faith." The American Heritage Dictionary defines faith as "Belief that does not rest on logical proof or material evidence." And that is what is being asked of us. We are being asked to receive the miracle (the change of perception, the vision of our brother's innocence) without any "proof or material evidence." We are being asked to look on devastation (such as sickness, or the harm done by someone's unloving actions) and to believe that what we see is false—without "material evidence."

This is not an easy thing to do, to believe in something we cannot see. And yet, if our false perception has blinded us to reality, and we are now perceiving the projections of our own minds in place of truth, then obviously the truth is now something we do not see. And since what our mind chooses to see is what we see, the mind *must* change before we can perceive truly. We have to choose to change our mind *before we see the evidence*, because, in order for the miracle to manifest, our minds must first be "made ready to conceive of what [they] cannot see and [do] not understand." In other words, we must make a choice on faith; we must decide that we desire to see something we cannot now see and something we do not understand.

This reminds me very much of those very early lessons in the Workbook, Lessons 27 and 28: "Above all else I want to see" and "Above all else I want to see things differently." That choice has to be made before we can see anything. We must *want* to see in order to see. That is the faith being talked about here. It is a choice, a decision we must make. We must *want* to see our brother innocent. We must *want* only love. We must be willing to see things differently. Only then will we see miracles.

---

1. This is the title of one of the two original collections of stories about the People. All of Henderson's wonderful stories have been recently republished in a single volume, titled *Ingathering: The Complete People Stories of Zenna Henderson* (Framingham, Mass.: Nesfa Press, 1995).

LESSON 348 ✦ DECEMBER 14

"I have no cause for anger or for fear,
For You surround me. And in every need
That I perceive, Your grace suffices me."

Practice instructions

See complete instructions on page 135. A short summary:

* **Read** the commentary paragraph slowly and personally.
* **Pray** the prayer, perhaps several times.
* **Morning and evening:** Repeat the idea and then spend time in Open Mind Meditation.
* **Hourly remembrance:** Repeat the idea and then spend a quiet moment in meditation.
* **Frequent reminders:** Repeat the idea often within each hour.
* **Response to temptation:** Repeat the idea whenever upset, to restore peace.
* **Read the "What Is" section** slowly and thoughtfully once during the day.

Commentary

"You surround me." Close your eyes and be quiet, and think of the Love or Presence of God as a golden light. Imagine that light shining on the front of you. Feel its warmth, its golden glow, like the radiance of the sun on a bright, summer day.

Now, become aware of that same light behind you. The Love of God is shining on you, front and back. Let yourself feel the safety of it.

The Presence of God is also on your right, and on your left. It is all around you, above you and below you. You are surrounded by this golden light, immersed in it. You are surrounded by perfect safety (1:5), perfect benevolence. Allow yourself to feel what that is like.

In this Love there is no cause for anger or for fear. There is no cause for anything except the perfect peace and joy you share with God.

> God's grace suffices us in everything that He would
> have us do. And only that we choose to be our will as well
> as His. (2:1–2)

Whenever you can today, stop for a moment or two and visualize yourself surrounded by the Love of God.

WHAT IS A MIRACLE?

Part 8: W-pII.13.4:2–3

There must be faith before a miracle: the desire to see it, the choice to ask for what we cannot now see, and to believe that what our ego-generated perception shows us is false. But when that faith arises, when we become miracle-minded, that faith will produce its own vindication:

> Yet faith will bring its witnesses to show that what it rest-
> ed on is really there. (4:2)

When I place my faith in a miracle, there will be evidence—witnesses—to prove that what I put my faith in truly exists. When, for instance, I am willing to look past my brother's ego and to see the call for God in him, something will happen that will witness to me that the call for God in him is really there. Perhaps my forgiveness will be met with gratitude. Perhaps my response of love will be met with love returning. Perhaps, in someone of whom I never believed it possible, I will see a spark of light. Faith *will* bring its witnesses.

> And thus the miracle will justify your faith in it, and show
> it rested on a world more real than what you saw before; a
> world redeemed from what you thought was there. (4:3)

My willingness to believe in love's presence will show me love's presence. I will see what I choose to see. I will see that the world of spirit is more real than the world of mere matter. Sickness will give way to health. Sadness will be replaced with joy. Fear will be transformed to love. And where I thought I saw sin and evil, I will see holiness and good.

It is the transformation of my mind that brings about a different world. It is my readiness to invite the miracle that opens the way for it. The changes in the world I see are not the miracle; they are its results. The miracle *brings* witnesses; it reveals a world different from what I thought it was. First, though, the change of mind, the faith. Then the witness to faith, justifying it, validating it.

LESSON 349 ✦ DECEMBER 15

**"Today I let Christ's vision look upon
All things for me and judge them not, but give
Each one a miracle of love instead."**

Practice instructions

See complete instructions on page 135. A short summary:

- **Read** the commentary paragraph slowly and personally.
- **Pray** the prayer, perhaps several times.
- **Morning and evening:** Repeat the idea and then spend time in Open Mind Meditation.
- **Hourly remembrance:** Repeat the idea and then spend a quiet moment in meditation.
- **Frequent reminders:** Repeat the idea often within each hour.
- **Response to temptation:** Repeat the idea whenever upset, to restore peace.
- **Read the "What Is" section** slowly and thoughtfully once during the day.

Practice suggestion:

- Think of a person you know.
- Once you have chosen someone, imagine your mind stepping back and withdrawing all judgment of this person, all evaluation of any kind.
- Then imagine Christ looking through you at this person. As He looks, He does not judge, He simply loves. He does not strain this person through your filters of suspicion. His only concern is to give him or her a miracle. Try to let Christ actually look through you, so that it's more than just your imagination.

Commentary

"The law of love," mentioned in the second sentence, has been referred to in lessons 344, 345, and 346. We are likely to forget how

Lesson 344 defines it: "Today I learn the law of love; that what I give my brother is my gift to me." The law of love is the law that giving and receiving are the same, that generosity and loving extension is a practical way of life because what I give, I receive. Understanding what the law of love is, the words of this lesson make perfect sense:

> So [by not judging, but giving a miracle of love instead]
> would I liberate all things I see, and give to them the free-
> dom that I seek. For thus do I obey the law of love, and give
> what I would find and make my own.   (1:1–2)

Do I want others to refrain from judging me, forgive my mistakes, and offer me miracles of love? Let me give what I seek; let me give what I want to find for myself.

Each time I accept a gift of God, I have added to my repertoire of miracles I can give (1:4–5). Each time I give that miracle to another, I have solidified my learning that the miracle belongs to me (1:6). And thus I remember God.

Let me not judge today, but offer miracles of love instead. Let me give what I want to receive.

WHAT IS A MIRACLE?

Part 9: W-pII.13.5:1–3

In stark imagery, this section refers to our world as "a dry and dusty world, where starved and thirsty creatures come to die" (5:1). The Course says, more than once, that we came to this world in order to die; we sought death by coming to a place where everything dies. For instance, "You came to die, and what would you expect but to perceive the signs of death you seek?" (T-29.VII.5:2). "It is not will for life but wish for death that is the motivation for this world" (T-27.I.6:3). We came out of guilt, believing in our own sin and seeking our own punishment. We came because somehow, in the twisted logic of the ego, death is the ultimate proof of our success at separating from God. We made this world as a place to die in, and then we came to die in it.

But "miracles fall like drops of healing rain from Heaven" on this parched land we have made, and the miracles turn it into a paradise.

Now they [the starved and thirsty creatures, which are our-selves] have water. Now the world is green.   (5:2–3)

Miracles, then, transform the world of death we made into a place of life. Chapter 26 of the Text, in Section IX ("For They Have Come") extends the same images:

> The blood of hatred fades to let the grass grow green again, and let the flowers be all white and sparkling in the summer sun What was a place of death has now become a living temple in a world of light. Because of Them. It is Their Presence which has lifted holiness again to take its ancient place upon an ancient throne. Because of Them have miracles sprung up as grass and flowers on the barren ground that hate had scorched and rendered desolate. What hate has wrought have They undone. And now you stand on ground so holy Heaven leans to join with it, and make it like itself. The shadow of an ancient hate has gone, and all the blight and withering have passed forever from the land where They have come.   (T-26.IX.3:1–8)

We open to miracles when we open to forgiveness and love, when we open to God. "They" and "Them" in this Text section refer to the face of Christ (the sight of our brothers' innocence) and the memory of God. When we allow ourselves to see the face of Christ in our brothers, the memory of God returns to us. When that happens, the "scorched and...desolate" ground of this world becomes a garden, a reflection of Heaven.

LESSON 350 ✦ DECEMBER 16

"Miracles mirror God's eternal Love.
To offer them is to remember Him,
And through His memory to save the world."

Practice instructions

See complete instructions on page 135. A short summary:

- **Read** the commentary paragraph slowly and personally.
- **Pray** the prayer, perhaps several times.
- **Morning and evening:** Repeat the idea and then spend time in Open Mind Meditation.
- **Hourly remembrance:** Repeat the idea and then spend a quiet moment in meditation.
- **Frequent reminders:** Repeat the idea often within each hour.
- **Response to temptation:** Repeat the idea whenever upset, to restore peace.
- **Read the "What Is" section** slowly and thoughtfully once during the day.

Commentary

To offer a miracle is to remember God, and through offering miracles we literally save the world. We reincorporate the Son of God as God created him (1:2). The theme of miracles has run through these last ten lessons, and the page of teaching that preceded them.

> A miracle is a correction. It does not create, nor really change at all. It merely looks on devastation, and reminds the mind that what it sees is false. It undoes error, but does not attempt to go beyond perception, nor exceed the function of forgiveness. (W-pII.13.1:1–4)

In other words, a miracle and forgiveness are alike; both simply remind "the mind that what it sees is false." To offer a miracle is to look beyond the illusions and to see the truth. It is a refusal to share the lit-

637

tleness in which others see themselves. I offer a miracle when I refuse to believe that my brother is identified with and limited to his body and his ego. I refuse to believe that anyone is defined by their behavior, and offer everyone the opportunity to see themselves as more than they think they are, more loveable and more loving than they think they are. That is a miracle, and that also is forgiveness.

> *What we forgive becomes a part of us, as we perceive ourselves. The Son of God incorporates all things within himself as You created him.* (1:1–2)

That is an amazing statement! When we forgive something or someone, it or she "becomes a part of us." It is almost as if by forgiving things and people, we are regathering the fragmented parts of the Sonship back into our Self. We are acknowledging that they are not separate, as they appear to be, but actually part of our being. Each miracle we offer helps reconstitute the Son of God.

In reality of course, the Son is eternally one; there is no need to reconstitute what is already whole. What we are is not affected by our thoughts. The reality of our being remains inviolate (1:4). But what we "look upon," what we perceive, is the direct result of our thoughts (1:5).

> *Therefore, my Father, I would turn to You. Only Your memory will set me free.* (1:6–7)

Today, Father, heal my thoughts. "Straighten my mind" (W-pII.347.1:2). I want the memory of God to return to my mind, and "only my forgiveness teaches me to let Your memory return to me, and give it to the world in thankfulness" (1:8). To have the memory of God return, I must forgive. I must offer miracles to everyone and everything.

As I remember God (through my forgiveness), "His Son will be restored to us in the reality of Love" (2:2). There is the thought again that forgiveness "restores" the Son, rejoining the separated fragments by an acknowledgment of love and unity.

May we watch today for opportunities to offer miracles.

WHAT IS A MIRACLE?

Part 10: W-pII.13.5:4

As we open our lives to miracles, the world is transformed.

> And everywhere the signs of life spring up, to show that what is born can never die, for what has life has immortality. (5:4)

Miracles demonstrate immortality. Not immortality of the body, but immortality of love, which is what we are ("Teach only love, for that is what you are" [T-6.I.13:2]; "Only the eternal can be loved, for love does not die" [T-10.V.9:1]). It is the immortality of thought, and the Course also teaches that we are the eternal Thought of God, unchangeable. The Course asserts boldly that there is no death, that life and immortality are synonymous ("what has life has immortality"). By that logic, then, the body must not have life, because it is not immortal, and so the Course teaches: "It [the body] is not born and does not die" (T-28.VI.2:4). "The body neither lives nor dies, because it cannot contain you who are life" (T-6.V(A)1:4).

Miracles show us that we are not bodies, that mind is stronger than or primary to the body:

> If the mind can heal the body, but the body cannot heal the mind, then the mind must be stronger than the body. Every miracle demonstrates this. (T-6.V(A).2:6–7)

It shows us that what we are—mind, thought, idea, love—has life and is immortal.

XVII

Lessons 351 - 360
What Am I?

LESSON 351 ✦ DECEMBER 17

**"My sinless brother is my guide to peace.
My sinful brother is my guide to pain.
And which I choose to see I will behold."**

Practice instructions

See complete instructions on page 135. A short summary:

- **Read** the commentary paragraph slowly and personally.
- **Pray** the prayer, perhaps several times.
- **Morning and evening:** Repeat the idea and then spend time in Open Mind Meditation.
- **Hourly remembrance:** Repeat the idea and then spend a quiet moment in meditation.
- **Frequent reminders:** Repeat the idea often within each hour.
- **Response to temptation:** Repeat the idea whenever upset, to restore peace.
- **Read the "What Is" section** slowly and thoughtfully once during the day.

Practice suggestion: Here is a longer, more specific form of to-day's idea. Choose someone to focus on and then repeat:

My sinless brother [name] is my guide to peace,
  He shows me that I am sinless,
    that my Comforter and Friend walks beside me,
    that I walk home along a way that is secure and clear.
My sinful brother [name] is my guide to pain.
He proclaims that I am a sinner,
    that I am alone and friendless,
    that I wander in danger in a fearful world.
Which I choose to see determines my whole journey.
Father, choose for me which I will see.

Commentary

I once read an article by Jon Mundy in *On Course* magazine about Bill Thetford (the man who transcribed the Course from Helen's Schucman's shorthand notes). Bill once said that the entire Course could be summed up in a single sentence: Are you willing to see your brother sinless? Jon relates the following story:

> Judy Skutch Whitson tells an interesting story about Bill. There was one occasion on which Judy experienced a monumental ego attack which was focused on her friend, Dr. Gerry Jampolsky. In an effort to find some peace of mind she called Bill Thetford and proceeded to describe for him all of what she perceived to be Gerry's faults. Bill listened till Judy ran out of breath and then he said quietly, "You know, Judy, the Course can be summed up in just eight words. Are you willing to see your brother sinless?" "No!" Judy screamed. "Well, dear," he replied, "when you are, you will feel much better." And he hung up.

The perception of my brother as sinful is a choice I am making. It is not based on fact. It is not caused by something in my brother; it is purely my chosen perception. Choosing to see my brother as sinful will always lead to inner pain. And truly, when we are willing to see our brother, or sister, as sinless, we really will feel much better. The power of the question Bill asked (and which the Course asks us all) lies in the fact that it reveals the often hidden fact that we are choosing this perception, and that we are not willing to let it go. Until we are, there is nothing the Holy Spirit can do for us. He will not oppose our will. Love does not oppose. We can stay in the pain of unforgiveness as long as we wish.

But when we are willing, when we have recognized that we are choosing how to see our brother, when we have realized that we do not like how we feel when we are choosing to see his sin, and we are willing, at least, to change that perception, then we can pray:

> *Choose, then, for me, my Father, through Your Voice. For He alone gives judgment in Your Name.* (1:6–7)

WHAT AM I?

Part 1: W-pII.14.1:1–3

This section is one of the most powerful statements in the Course of its vision of our true nature, of how it can be realized within this world of time and space, and of the function that follows naturally from the fact of what we are. The opening paragraph is an extremely potent declaration, in the first person, of our real Identity. Often I find that reading something like this aloud, by myself, helps me to focus on it and to *feel* what it is saying. An interesting side effect is that making these statements firmly, saying them as if I truly believed them (even if I do not yet), arouses opposing thoughts in my mind. Noting those opposing thoughts and writing them down can be a very useful exercise in uncovering the hidden beliefs of the ego that have lodged in my mind, so that I can recognize their presence and decide that I do not want them.

For instance, in the first sentence we read, "I am...complete and healed and whole." I find opposing thoughts that arise, such as: "I am far from complete; I have a long way to go." "I am fragmented, not whole." "I wish I were healed but I'm not." These are lessons the ego has taught me, and they are not true. I can recognize that these thoughts are blocking my acceptance of the Course's message, and I can choose against them. For example, I might say, "I feel incomplete and I believe in my incompleteness, but in reality I am already complete. I want to know my own completion."

I am God's Son...shining in the reflection of His Love.
(1:1)

The light in me is the reflection of God's Light and God's Love. I shine, but my glory is a reflected glory, as the moon's light is completely dependent on that of the sun. It is something that emanates from God and radiates *through* me but not *from* me, and unless I acknowledge my connection with my Creator, I mask that shining.

In me is His creation sanctified and guaranteed eternal life.
(1:2)

This sounds like something that, in traditional Christianity, Jesus might say, similar to "I am the way, the truth, and the life." And indeed, Jesus might say this. But so can we! We are all what he was and is; that is what he is telling us in this Course. Creation is "sanctified" (made holy) in me. What I am, my very being, is what makes creation holy. I do not need to be made holy or to become holy; I am the source (a reflected source, but still a source) of holiness. And what I am guarantees eternal life for all creation, because all creation is what I am. I am *God's Son*, the radiance of His Love which has shined out and become me; that is also what all creation is, the extension of His Love. The fact that I am God's Son, an emanation of His Being, like a sunbeam to the sun, guarantees eternal life because what God is, is eternal, and if I am simply an effect of God, Who is eternal, then I, too, must be eternal, "forever and forever" His effect.

In me is love perfected, fear impossible, and joy established without opposite.
(1:3)

We find it very difficult to believe that perfect love is in us. "You have so little faith in yourself because you are unwilling to accept the fact that perfect love is in you" (T-15.VI.2:1). So it isn't really that believing this is *difficult*; it is that we are unwilling to accept it! Our ego identity depends on its not being true. If perfect love from God is in us, then what we are derives from God and not from ourselves alone, which is what the ego wants to believe. We would rather be fear than be love, because we made fear. The truth is still the truth; perfect love *is* in us, whether or not we believe it, whether or not we think we want it. What we believe cannot change God's creation.

Fear is impossible in me. Now that generates a lot of negative feedback, doesn't it? "If fear is impossible, then what the hell is this thing I am feeling?" What is it? The Course would reply that what we feel is an illusion, a nonexistent nothing, a figment of our imagination. What it is is meaningless. What if, when I felt afraid, I told myself, "I think I am feeling fear, but fear in me is impossible"? What if I realized that what I think I am feeling *is not in me*, but in a delusional concept of myself I have mistaken for myself?

"And joy established without opposite." That is my reality. I don't experience it that way now, probably. Even when I do feel joy, there is always an opposite lurking in the shadows. But that opposite, that fear, that dark presence, is unreal. It is nothing to be afraid of and does not, in reality, exist.

LESSON 352 ✦ DECEMBER 18

**"Judgment and love are opposites. From one
Come all the sorrows of the world. But from
The other comes the peace of God Himself."**

Practice instructions

See complete instructions on page 135. A short summary:

- **Read** the commentary paragraph slowly and personally.
- **Pray** the prayer, perhaps several times.
- **Morning and evening:** Repeat the idea and then spend time in Open Mind Meditation.
- **Hourly remembrance:** Repeat the idea and then spend a quiet moment in meditation.
- **Frequent reminders:** Repeat the idea often within each hour.
- **Response to temptation:** Repeat the idea whenever upset, to restore peace.
- **Read the "What Is" section** slowly and thoughtfully once during the day.

Commentary

In the introduction to the Text, Jesus says, "The opposite of love is fear, but what is all-encompassing can have no opposite" (T-In.1:8). Here, he says that love's opposite is judgment. If you relax your mind and let your thinking go loosely associative, it is fairly easy to see that judgment and fear are the same thing. If I judge something as bad, dangerous, or evil, I will fear it. If I fear something I will judge it as bad. In "The Two Emotions" (T-13.V), it is clear that both love and fear are "a way of seeing," and that "different worlds arise from their different sights" (T-13.V.10:2). The same thought is expressed here about judgment and love. And in the surrounding sections of Chapter 13 it is very clear that in giving up the past, we are being asked to give up judgment. The same network of thoughts is there that is found here.

I think in this lesson, the Holy Spirit is viewing two *attitudes* or two *activities* rather than two *emotions*. It is the attitude I have towards others that is in focus, and how I extend myself towards them. Do I love, or do I judge? Rather than how the other person impacts on me, which is the focus in the "Two Emotions" section, the focus here is on how I impact on the other person. The difference is in the direction of the flow of energy; here, the flow being considered is from me to the other person.

All the sorrows of the world come from judgment; no wonder the Course asks us to relinquish it. To love is not to judge; to judge is not to love. Loving brings us peace; judging only sorrow. How to find peace? Give love.

> *Forgiveness looks on sinlessness alone, and judges not.*
> *Through this I come to You.* (1:1–2)

Forgiveness means not judging; how can you judge and forgive at the same time? Forgiveness sees only sinlessness, because only sinlessness is what we are (see W-pII.14.1:6). And through such forgiveness we approach God.

> *Judgment will bind my eyes and make me blind. Yet love,*
> *reflected in forgiveness here, reminds me You have given*
> *me a way to find Your peace again.* (1:3–4)

The Course makes a point, several times, of what is implied here by the phrase "love, reflected in forgiveness here." Love in purity is impossible in this world. "No love in this world is without...ambivalence" (T-4.III.4:6). The closest reflection of love in this world is forgiveness. So the contrast here is really between judgment and forgiveness. By choosing to forgive my brothers rather than to judge them, I find my own peace again, the peace of God.

Peace is lost to us through judgment; it blindfolds us to the truth. Love, which is perfect only in Heaven, is still reflected perfectly here in forgiveness. There is a way to find our way out of blindness, and the way is forgiveness. It is affirming the unreality of our perception of sin in anyone and everyone.

> *I am redeemed when I elect to follow in this way. You have*
> *not left me comfortless. I have within both the memory of*

You, and One Who leads me to it. (1:5–7)

We were lost, "sold" into slavery by our own hand. But God did not abandon us. He gave us two things. It's interesting to notice the distinction here. He gave us 1) the memory of God in our minds, and 2) the Holy Spirit Who leads us to discover that memory. Many times I've heard people say that the Holy Spirit is the memory of God within us; that isn't how it appears here. The memory of God is something that is truly my own, part of me; my own right mind remembers God. The Holy Spirit is the Guide Who leads me back to rediscover the hidden treasure within my Self.

Father, I would hear Your Voice and find Your peace today.
For I would love my own Identity, and find in It the memo-
ry of You. (1:8–9)

The memory of God lies in my own Identity. In remembering my Self I remember God. Let His Voice lead me to that remembrance as I sit, quietly, with Him today. I have very powerful help. And where that help leads me is to the point of loving my own Identity. I cannot love what I am unless I love—in the form of forgiveness—everyone else. That is so because what I am is identical to what everyone is; we are all the Son of God, the Christ. If I judge others I am judging myself, because I am what they are.

WHAT AM I?

Part 2: W-pII.14.1:4–6

I am the holy Home of God Himself. (1:4)

Wow! That makes more of an impact on us, put that way, than simply saying, "God is in me." I am God's Home. Home is not just some place God happens to be; it is where He resides, where He chooses to be, where He can make Himself comfortable, so to speak. In Psalm 132:14, God is said to have proclaimed about Zion, or Jerusalem, "This [is] my rest for ever: here will I dwell; for I have desired it." Now, *we* are His home. Now, He speaks to you, and to me, saying that we are His rest forever, that He will dwell in us because He has desired it. That was His intention all along when He created us.

> *I am the Heaven where His Love resides.*   (1:5)

We may have naively believed that God lives in Heaven and not in us. Here, we see that, yes, God lives or resides in Heaven, but *we are Heaven*. What a mind-blower that is! I'll bet you have thought, for most of your life, that if you were good enough, or if you were holy enough, or if you had enough faith, you'd get to go to Heaven. Sorry, no go. You can't *go* to Heaven because you *are* Heaven, where God's Love resides.

> *I am His holy Sinlessness Itself, for in my purity abides His own.*   (1:6)

Did you notice that all three of these sentences use words about God's place of residence? "...the holy Home...where His Love resides...in my purity abides His own." God isn't just passing through! He isn't just visiting. He *lives* here, in me, in you; this is His home. He *abides* [stays, remains] here, in us.

I have to confess that I can't quite yet wrap my mind around the idea that *I am* God's holy Sinlessness. "Sinlessness" seems like a rather abstract concept; I have a little trouble understanding how I can *be* sinlessness. The second half of the sentence helps me out a little: "for in my purity abides His own."

I can sort of grasp it by an analogy. A parent who gives his or her time and energy to raising a child, teaching it all they know, finds their own success and happiness in that child's success and happiness. "My child's happiness is my own. My child's success is my own." I think it is similar to that. God extended Himself as us. What we are is His extension. Our purity *is* His; if we are not sinless, no more is He. We are what He is, extended outward. If I am not pure, He is not, for our nature is His. If we are what He is, then it is true in reverse; He is what we are. Therefore, "I am His holy Sinlessness Itself."

LESSON 353 ✦ DECEMBER 19

**"My eyes, my tongue, my hands, my feet today
Have but one purpose; to be given Christ
To use to bless the world with miracles."**

Practice instructions

See complete instructions on page 135. A short summary:

- **Read** the commentary paragraph slowly and personally.
- **Pray** the prayer, perhaps several times.
- **Morning and evening:** Repeat the idea and then spend time in Open Mind Meditation.
- **Hourly remembrance:** Repeat the idea and then spend a quiet moment in meditation.
- **Frequent reminders:** Repeat the idea often within each hour.
- **Response to temptation:** Repeat the idea whenever upset, to restore peace.
- **Read the "What Is" section** slowly and thoughtfully once during the day.

Practice suggestion: I enjoy going through the body parts listed in the lesson one at a time, and then adding on some other things at the end:

I give my eyes to Christ today, to use to bless the world with miracles.

I give my tongue to Christ today, to use to bless the world with miracles.

I give my hands to Christ today, to use to bless the world with miracles.

I give my feet to Christ today, to use to bless the world with miracles.

I give my time to Christ today, to use to bless the world with miracles.

I give my money to Christ today, to use to bless the world with miracles.

I give my car to Christ today, to use to bless the world with miracles.

Commentary

These last ten lessons (not counting the final one) represent the state of mind to which the Course seeks to bring us. In this lesson we see the final outworking of the Course's thoughts about the body. Not that the body becomes ignored, despised, or neglected, but rather that its every part be used to bless the world with miracles. The body is not attacked or belittled; rather, it is given a new purpose, shared with Christ.

> *Father, I give all that is mine today to Christ, to use in any way that best will serve the purpose that I share with Him. Nothing is mine alone, for He and I have joined in purpose.* (1:1–2)

In Heaven our function is creation, something that apparently we can't quite fully understand until our mind awakens to Heaven, but here our function is the pure reflection of creation: the giving of miracles, the extension of forgiveness. We might say our function here is recognizing creation, since to forgive is to acknowledge our brother as God created him, and not as we have made him through the projection of our own guilt.

Let me, then, with all the determination I can muster, this day join myself with Christ's purpose. Let me give my hands, my eyes, my tongue, my feet to Him. Why not silently pray and, very specifically, do exactly that? "Father, I give my hands to Christ today to be used only for the purpose I share with Him: to bless the world with miracles." Then repeating the same thing for other parts of my body. Remember this thought through the day and renew your gift to Christ, calling your mind back to its true purpose every time you can remember.

> *Thus has learning come almost to its appointed end. A while I work with Him to serve His purpose. Then I lose myself in my Identity, and recognize that Christ is but my Self.* (1:3–5)

When we have reached the point where we truly have given everything we have to Him to be used for His purpose, we have almost completed the curriculum. All that is left is to stay a little while longer, serving His purpose, sharing the light with minds that still are clouded. This is almost descriptive of an avatar, an enlightened master who is on earth only to serve those not so far along.

When that time of service is over, I will "lose myself in my Identity, and recognize that Christ is but my Self." The ego self will dissolve and disappear; the individual will cease as a separate thing—which it never was in reality—and expand into the One Self of Christ. Nothing will be lost in this process except our separateness.

My heart, do not despair if this seems far beyond you now. It is much nearer than you dare believe. You are much more than you think you are. Simply, in gladness, give yourself to this purpose. The Holy Spirit will provide the means. Be willing simply to move in this direction, and do not judge how near or far you are, how easy or how difficult you think the way. Simply be willing for it to be. Be not anxious or restless if it seems to elude you; restlessness is only a delaying tactic. Rest, my heart. Trust. Angels watch with you, awaiting the birth of the Christ in you. Have no fear. Rejoice!

WHAT AM I?

Part 3: W-pII.14.2:1–3

Our use for words is almost over now.   (2:1)

Throughout the Workbook, words have been used to instruct and inspire us, and we have used the words given to us in our practicing. When we are truly ready to "graduate" from the Workbook and its level of training, we will be ready to leave specific words behind. We will be ready to spend our days in constant communication with the Holy Spirit, with no need for any special saying to act as a trigger, to entrain our minds along the lines of the Course, because, at that point, our minds will be fully trained. We will habitually practice holy instants and spend time often each day renewing our minds in God's Presence.

Few, if any, of us are truly at that point. I know, regretfully, that I am not. I have not followed the training program given to us faithfully, and so I still need more training, in which the use of words is still essential.

I still need the crutch of words; or a better analogy than "crutch"—training wheels. I will be repeating the Workbook again next year.[1] Not with reluctance or with a sense of defeat, oh no! I have made a great deal of progress in this last year, I think. The lessons stick with me during the day much more than ever before, and my mind does remember to apply them in response to "temptation." Not always, but more frequently.

> Yet in the final days of this one year we gave to God together, you and I, we found a single purpose that we shared. (2:2)

Surely this is one of the goals of the Workbook, that we would come to realize that we share a common purpose with Jesus; we are saviors (see paragraph 3). We have begun to remember, not only our own guiltlessness, but our purpose, what we were created for: to extend love to others, as God created us by extending His Love.

> And this, our gift, is therefore given us. (2:3)

Because we have learned that we are here to give blessing to the world, blessing is given to us. Because we have learned to forgive, we receive our own forgiveness. This is the law of love. This is the way love works.

When the training goal of the Workbook is fully achieved in us, we have not only found our own individual salvation, we have found that our salvation lies in bringing release to others. We are saved by saving others, forgiven by forgiving others, healed by healing others. "I will be healed as I let Him teach me to heal" (T-2.V(A).18:6).

---

1. This refers to 1996, since the commentary was written in 1995.

LESSON 354 ✦ DECEMBER 20

**"We stand together, Christ and I, in peace
And certainty of purpose. And in Him
Is His Creator, as He is in me."**

Practice instructions

See complete instructions on page 135. A short summary:

- **Read** the commentary paragraph slowly and personally.
- **Pray** the prayer, perhaps several times.
- **Morning and evening:** Repeat the idea and then spend time in Open Mind Meditation.
- **Hourly remembrance:** Repeat the idea and then spend a quiet moment in meditation.
- **Frequent reminders:** Repeat the idea often within each hour.
- **Response to temptation:** Repeat the idea whenever upset, to restore peace.
- **Read the "What Is" section** slowly and thoughtfully once during the day.

Practice suggestion: I have found it helpful to make this lesson more specific: *"In this situation, we stand together, Christ and I...."* I have also found it helpful to reword it: *"I take my stand with Christ today, united with Him in purpose. And God is in both of us."*

Commentary

This lesson expresses the awareness of my identity with Christ. The Creator is in Christ and also in me; God is in me as He is in Christ. Identical. "I have no self except the Christ in me" (1:2). This awareness of identity is where the Course is leading us. All our study of the Text, our practice of the Workbook, and our application of forgiveness in all our relationships is bringing us to this final awareness: "I have no self except the Christ in me." "And what am I except the Christ in me?" (1:7).

As we arrive at these final lessons, we may feel as though some-where along the line the Course has passed us by. Somewhere we missed the boat, or more likely, got off the boat and stayed behind. I know that I have often felt that way; I also know that, if I continue to practice what the Course has taught me, that will not always be true. One day the realization that I have no self except the Christ in me will resonate in my mind without any resistance or doubt.

I believe deeply that these words I've just quoted are true, yet I am aware there is a part of my mind that, as yet, does not believe them. My experience has not caught up to my understanding. My mind still believes that I am not identical to the Christ, and so my experience fol-lows my belief, and I experience myself, or at the very least parts of myself, that seem to be other than this perfect Self, Who is wholly like His Father.

Does this mean the Course has failed, or that I have failed the Course? No, I don't think so. In the epilogue, which follows Lesson 365, Jesus speaks of how the Holy Spirit will be our "Guide through every difficulty and all pain that you may think is real" (W-Ep.4:1). So he expects that everyone, having finished the Workbook, will still expe-rience difficulties, and, sometimes, still mistakenly think that pain is real. He says there, "Whatever troubles you, be certain that He has the answer, and will gladly give it to you, if you simply turn to Him and ask it of Him" (W-Ep.1:5). Even after all this, we will still experience trou-bles. "This course is a beginning, not an end" (W-Ep.1:1). The Text and Workbook are meant not to bring us to the end of our journey, but to train us in the proper way to travel, to develop proper habits of spiritu-al practice. They introduce us to our Teacher and instill the habit of lis-tening to Him. That is all, and that is enough.

And yet these latter lessons put words in our mouths and have us speak as if we have already arrived. Think of them as foretastes of what your mind will be like when you have finished your journey. Immerse your mind in them and let them soak in, transforming you as they do. Whatever you may feel like today, whatever you may think about your-self, these words are still the truth.

Who we are is beyond the reach of time and free of every law but God's (1:1). We have no purpose but Christ's purpose (1:3). We are one with God, just as Jesus was and is (1:5). And all our learning is designed to help us unlearn everything that tells us anything different.

WHAT AM I?

Part 4: W-pII.14.2:4–5

> The truth of what we are is not for words to speak of nor
> describe. (2:4)

Words can only take us so far. They can bring us to the door of
Heaven, but cannot bring us in. All the words of the Course itself, as
wondrous as they are, can do no more than that. That is not a deficiency in the Course, nor a deficiency in words as such. Words are merely
symbols. They can do no more than symbols can do, and that is quite a
lot, and all that is necessary. The truth of what we are will, itself, do the
rest.

That truth, and the complete knowing of it, is beyond the reach of
words, and therefore, beyond our reach within this world, which is a
world of symbols and not of realities. Still, there is no reason for despair
at that. What we are cannot be here, any more than a "real," physical
person can exist within a dream, any more than a three-dimensional figure could enter a two-dimensional world. (Another example: An actual
cube, with three dimensions, cannot exist on a sheet of paper; the best
that can be done is a perspective drawing that *suggests* three dimensions.)

> Yet we can realize our function here, and words can speak
> of this and teach it, too, if we exemplify the words in us.
> (2:5)

Even though we cannot fully *know* the truth of what we are, here in
this world, we can express it; we can, as it were, create a perspective
drawing that suggests that truth. How? By fulfilling the function God
has given us, the function which the Course has repeatedly stated in various ways: forgiveness; to be happy; extension; to fulfill the Will of
God; giving of ourselves; filling our part in God's plan; adding to God's
treasure by creating our own; giving and receiving healing; using the
Atonement. This is something words *can* speak of, and words can also
teach forgiveness, if (at the same time) "we exemplify the words in us."

If the words we speak run through our very beings like watermarks through a banknote, the words can convey what forgiveness is. If our lives are examples of what we are talking about, our words have power. In other words, if we fulfill our function of forgiveness, we can teach forgiveness. And that is our "perspective drawing" of the truth of our being. That is the reflection, in this world, of the Love that we are.

Consider the Course as an example of the very thing it is telling us here. Why are its words so powerful? I think that the reason is that they are spoken by one who exemplifies the words he speaks. Even in the way Jesus (the author) speaks to us, and deals with our flaws, our stubbornness and thick-headedness, our doubts and our vacillation, we can sense the reality behind the words he is giving us. Never once does he seem to become impatient with us. Never once does he belittle us or verbally snort in disgust at our stupidity. When he speaks of forgiveness, there is a spirit of forgiveness that runs through the very words themselves and conveys itself to us. When he tells us to look on everyone as our equal, we get the sense that *he* is looking on *us* as his equal. When he says we can see everyone without seeing any sin, we can tell that this is how *he* sees *us*.

That is where he is leading us, each and every one of us. It is what the Manual for Teachers, in the section on the characteristics of God's teachers, calls *honesty*.

> Honesty does not apply only to what you say. The term actually means consistency. There is nothing you say that contradicts what you think or do; no thought opposes any other thought; no act belies your word; and no word lacks agreement with another. (M-4.II.1:4–6)

Only in fulfilling our function, only in making ourselves into an incarnation of the Course, can we come to realize and recognize its message for ourselves. Only in giving it to others, in word and in deed, can we come to receive it fully for ourselves.

LESSON 355 ✦ DECEMBER 21

"There is no end to all the peace and joy,
And all the miracles that I will give,
When I accept God's Word. Why not today?"

Practice instructions

See complete instructions on page 135. A short summary:

- **Read** the commentary paragraph slowly and personally.
- **Pray** the prayer, perhaps several times.
- **Morning and evening:** Repeat the idea and then spend time in Open Mind Meditation.
- **Hourly remembrance:** Repeat the idea and then spend a quiet moment in meditation.
- **Frequent reminders:** Repeat the idea often within each hour.
- **Response to temptation:** Repeat the idea whenever upset, to restore peace.
- **Read the "What Is" section** slowly and thoughtfully once during the day.

Commentary

"God's Word," to me, is speaking here of what Jesus, in the Course, is telling me about my own Identity. It is the truth about what I am.

It is You I choose, and my Identity along with You. Your Son would be Himself, and know You as his Father and Creator, and his Love.   (1:7–8)

A Christian lecturer who inspired me years ago, Major Ian Thomas, used to say that man's purpose, my purpose as an individual, is to be "the human vehicle of the divine content." That is what I am here for. Christ wants to be Himself in me, in the form of me. I have no other reason for being here, although the ego thinks I am here to forget God.

The Course teaches that the ego made the world and the body as an attack against God. It wants to use the world to forget God. The Holy

658

Spirit wants to use it as a vehicle to remember God. There is no real purpose to anything except one of those two.

I am here, today as always, to reflect God's Love. I am here to see innocence. I am here to "look on everyone as brother, and perceive all things as kindly and as good." (W-pII.14.3:4). I am here to bless my brothers and to ask them to share my peace and joy.

"Why not today?" Why should I wait? These are the questions the lesson asks.

> *I am sure my treasure waits for me, and I need but reach out my hand to find it. Even now my fingers touch it. It is very close. I need not wait an instant more to be at peace forever.* (1:3–6)

There is no answer to why we wait, because there are no reasons to wait. Nor has there ever been a reason. All there is to do in response is to let the constriction in our hearts unknot, to quell the resistance to the flow of love, and to open our hearts fully to every living thing. To let ourselves be love; to let love be us. To desist from the belief that we are anything else but love.

The resistance that feels so great, like a stone wall, is nothing more than a cloud, unable to stop a feather. Only my belief in its impenetrability makes it a barrier, like an elephant staked to a tiny peg in the ground, believing it cannot move because it has been trained to think it is chained to a tree. We think we are without love; we believe we are unloving. We think the ego stands like a granite battlement between us and God, keeping Him out.

The ego is a cloud. It could not stop a ping-pong ball. It is totally without strength to resist the Love of God, and it cannot and will not resist. God's Love stands at the end of time, having already won. Oh, my heart! Open to that Love today! Receive it; give it. Receive it by giving it, and give it by receiving it. See it everywhere for it is everywhere, in everyone.

WHAT AM I?

Part 5: W-pII.14.3:1–4

What is "our function," spoken of at the end of paragraph 2? "We are the bringers of salvation" (3:1). Have I really considered that this is *my* function? Have I begun to realize that, each day as I live my life, this is what I am really living for—to bring salvation to the world? We are not talking here about rescuing people; we are talking about seeing them as God created them, and seeing them that way so clearly and so strongly that our vision of them begins to open *their* eyes to the same thing. We are talking about holding such an unambiguous picture of their innocence that they can see their own innocence reflected from us.

> We accept our part as saviors of the world, which through
> our joint forgiveness is redeemed. (3:2)

We save the world by forgiving it. And we exercise this forgiveness as *joint* forgiveness, along with Jesus. We join with him in lifting guilt and blame from each person we interact with. This is how the world is "redeemed," bought back from its slavery to guilt and fear.

> And this, our gift, is therefore given us. (3:3)

Once again the oft-repeated theme: We receive forgiveness as we give it.

> We look on everyone as brother, and perceive all things as
> kindly and as good. (1:4)

This is the vision of a savior. This is how a savior sees things. To see everyone as brother is to see them as our equal, sharing in the guiltlessness of God's creation. To see all things as kindly is to realize that even what appears to be attack does not make the "attacker" unkind; behind the fear that drives the apparent attack is still a kind and gentle heart. Some of us, perhaps, have begun to realize this about ourselves and about others. We acknowledge that we have made mistakes, and that we have acted unlovingly, and yet we know that underneath that mask of anger and selfishness our hearts are kind. We do not want to hurt but we feel driven to it by circumstance; it seems the only way we can survive. That is the ego's lie to us, that attack is necessary for survival. The Course asks us:

> Do you not think the world needs peace as much as you do? Do you not want to give it to the world as much as you want to receive it? For unless you do, you will not receive it. If you want to have it of me, you must give it. Healing does not come from anyone else. (T-8.IV.4:1–5)

> There is no living thing that does not share the universal Will that it be whole. (T-31.I.9:1)

Our path to salvation lies in coming to realize that all living things share the universal Will to be whole, that everyone wants peace just as we do, and that, beneath all the masks we wear so faithfully, what we are, all of us, is love.

LESSON 356 ✦ DECEMBER 22

"Sickness is but another name for sin.
Healing is but another name for God.
The miracle is thus a call to Him."

Practice instructions

See complete instructions on page 135. A short summary:

- **Read** the commentary paragraph slowly and personally.
- **Pray** the prayer, perhaps several times.
- **Morning and evening:** Repeat the idea and then spend time in Open Mind Meditation.
- **Hourly remembrance:** Repeat the idea and then spend a quiet moment in meditation.
- **Frequent reminders:** Repeat the idea often within each hour.
- **Response to temptation:** Repeat the idea whenever upset, to restore peace.
- **Read the "What Is" section** slowly and thoughtfully once during the day.

Practice suggestion: I have found it helpful to reword the final line. Instead of *"The miracle is thus a call to Him,"* I say, *"To heal is thus to speak His Name."*

Commentary

It seems to me the Course is always equating things you don't expect to be equated, like it does here: Sickness is another name for sin; healing is another name for God. And toward the end of the lesson, "To call Your Name is but to call his own" (1:6), that is, the Son's own name, or my own name. The Course suggests that when we find God we will have found our Self, and when we find our Self, we will have found God; we and God share the same Name. It seems to be constantly saying that things we believe are quite different are in reality the same. Its advice for a new year is "Make this year different by making it all the same" (T-15.XI.10:11). The Course is constantly boiling everything down to just one problem, the separation, and one solution, the Atonement. And it tells us that complexity is of the ego; therefore, simplicity is of God.

How are sickness and sin the same thing? First, dispense with what this does *not* mean: that being sick is a sin. Anyone who has gone through the entire Workbook and studied the Text cannot possibly hold that mistaken understanding; that is most definitely not the meaning here. There is no such thing as sin; we only imagine there is. This lesson is most emphatically not saying that if you are sick it is because you are a sinful person, or that being sick makes you a sinner. Being sick is nothing to be guilty about! If you are sick, and anyone even suggests to you that "you must be doing something wrong because spiritual people don't get sick," stop listening to that person. The thoughts of our minds do indeed cause sickness. "All sickness is mental illness" (P-2.IV.8:1), according to the *Psychotherapy* supplement. But mistaken thoughts are not "sin"; they are simply mistaken.

When the lesson says that sickness is another name for sin, it means that the sickness of the body is a reflection or manifestation of the mind's belief in the reality of sin. Sickness, says the Course, can be a kind of self-punishment, in which we attack ourselves because of our guilt, hoping thereby to avert the punishment of God we are expecting. "Sickness is anger taken out upon the body, so that it will suffer pain" (T-28.VI.5:1).

I believe that when the Course uses the word sickness it is usually referring to the thought of sickness and not to the physical symptoms. ("Sickness is of the mind, and has nothing to do with the body" [M-5.II.3:2].) A crippled limb, for instance, can be used by the ego to further thoughts of inadequacy, guilt, and separation, or it can be used by the Holy Spirit to break a person's identification with the body and to turn them to God. It is the thought, and only the thought, which is important.

Sickness is "a defense against the truth" (W-pI.136.Heading). We have to remember that in the thought system of the Course everything, including sickness, is a choice we have made, and that choices must have some purpose behind them. The important thing is not the physical symptom. The important thing is the choice, and the purpose behind it.

When we choose to be sick, at some level we are choosing to identify ourselves as a body rather than a spirit or mind. The "truth" we are defending against is that we are a spirit or mind. We are defending against the realization that we are one with God and with everyone else, in God. "The strange, haunting thought that [we] might be something beyond this little pile of dust [is] silenced and stilled" (W-pI.136.8:4) when we are sick. Sickness makes the body seem very real, the only real thing. It seeks to let the illusion of the bodily identity take the place of the truth of our mind, our spiritual identity.

How is that like sin? According to the Workbook, sin "is the means by which the mind...seeks to let illusions take the place of truth" (W-pII.4.1:2). That is exactly what sickness does! When I see "sin" in myself or in a brother, it proves the "sinner" is evil, and therefore separate from God. When I see "sickness" in myself or in another, it proves the body is real and therefore separate from God.

Sin and sickness are the same in that both are means that the mind uses to try to prove that the separation is real. They are not the same in form, but they are identical in purpose. They are both the ego's attempt to prove that I am what I am not. It is the thought of separation which the Course aims to heal, not the physical symptom of sickness, and not the specific behavior of a person. The Course is concerned with the cause and not the effect.

I do believe that if the mind is healed—if the person is healed on the level of thought (which is the level of cause)—it will often result in changes in the form of the person's life. Behavior will often change when thoughts change; physical health will often improve when thoughts change. The change on the level of the body, however, is never the concern of the Course. The body is insignificant (M-5.II.3:12), which means it is without meaning. If the body is insignificant, it means that the body signifies nothing. If our thoughts align with God's Thought, the body will serve the purpose of the Holy Spirit whatever its form. Even if the body dies. The Course is concerned only with healing the mind because the body does not matter.

"Healing is but another name for God." To heal the mind, therefore, means to recognize the identity of my mind and God's mind. To be healed is to recognize that I share God's nature. When the Course talks of healing, it is not talking about getting over the flu! It is talking about letting go of my identification with this body that appears to be suffering chills and fever, recognizing that the body is not my Self, but that I am the eternal Son of God. It is speaking, as always, of a change of mind. When the identity of myself and my body is broken, I will know that what happens to the body does not affect who I really am; therefore, what happens to the body does not matter to me. It may get well and it may not; if I am no longer identified with it, I don't care which it is.

Sin and sickness are the same thing in the sense that both are manifestations of our belief in separation and our resulting (but mistaken) guilt. They are both healed through the miracle of forgiveness. Healing is a return to wholeness, a return to our true Self, and since our Self is one with God, all healing is a return to God. To offer a miracle of forgiveness or healing is "thus a call to Him."

Another way of putting this is that all healing leads to God in the end, even if we are not thinking of or believing in God as we experience it. If it is healing, it is of God. The *Psychotherapy* supplement says, "The patient need not think of truth as God in order to make progress in salvation" (P-1.5:1). If there is healing, and if there is forgiveness instead of condemnation, God is there, even if He is not named or acknowledged. Everyone who learns to forgive will remember God.

> *It does not matter where he is, what seems to be his problem, nor what he believes he has become.* (1:2)

God answers when we call, even when we don't realize we are calling Him. He answers even when we think we do not deserve an answer. I believe there are hundreds of times we have called on God, and He has answered, and we never made the connection. We failed to recognize Him even as we received His help. Our very pain and fear, the Course says, is a call for help. Do you imagine that if the Holy Spirit recognizes all calls for help as what they are, that He does not answer every one of them?

> *He is Your Son, and You will answer him.* (1:3)

He answers us with His Name, which is a shorthand way of saying His Being or His Nature. We are answered by what God is, because what He is is what we as His Son are. God is without sin, and so are we; without sin we cannot be sick, because sickness comes from belief in sin. When I realize my total innocence I "cannot suffer pain" (1:5). God's Name is what speaks to me of that innocence and tells me it must be so. How could God's offspring be unholy?

Let me learn, then, to call on God (whether I use that word or not). Let me open my heart to innocence, gentleness, and mercy. Let me make healing my aim, for myself and for others. In every encounter today let me remember: I am here to heal; I am here to offer miracles; I am here to release from guilt.

WHAT AM I?

Part 6: W-pII.14.3:5–7

Our function, then, is to bring salvation to the world. "We do not seek a function that is past the gate of Heaven" (3:5). In other words, we do not disdain this "lowly" calling of bringing healing to this world of form; we do not try to claim that we are fulfilling our function of creating (which is our function in Heaven), and cannot be bothered with the base forms within the illusion. Doing that is what one of my old Christian teachers used to call "being too heavenly minded to be of any earthly use."

Knowledge will return when we have done our part. (3:6)

"Knowledge" refers to the perfection of Heaven, to direct knowing of the truth, rather than the lower avenue of perception of forms. "Our part" is to purify our perception of forms. Our part is to work within the illusion, to turn the nightmare into a happy dream; only when we have done this will knowledge return.

We are concerned only with giving welcome to the truth.
(3:7)

We are not trying to directly apprehend the truth. We are not focused on having mystical experiences of God, on bypassing the world of form and leaving it behind, although, to be sure, we *do* seek to enter the holy instant frequently to renew our vision of Heaven. Our primary concern, however, is on "giving welcome to the truth"; that is, preparing ourselves for it, making things ready for it, educating ourselves to accept it. And that is something that goes on within this world, within this illusion we call physical life. Here, the many holy instants we experience (and which we desire to experience above all things) lead to a result: the Holy Spirit sends us out in "busy doing" here within the world, carrying with us the quiet center we have found in the holy instant, and sharing it with the world (see T-18.VII.8:1–5).

LESSON 357 ✦ DECEMBER 23

"Truth answers every call we make to God, Responding first with miracles, and then Returning unto us to be itself."

Practice instructions

See complete instructions on page 135. A short summary:

- **Read** the commentary paragraph slowly and personally.
- **Pray** the prayer, perhaps several times.
- **Morning and evening:** Repeat the idea and then spend time in Open Mind Meditation.
- **Hourly remembrance:** Repeat the idea and then spend a quiet moment in meditation.
- **Frequent reminders:** Repeat the idea often within each hour.
- **Response to temptation:** Repeat the idea whenever upset, to restore peace.
- **Read the "What Is" section** slowly and thoughtfully once during the day.

Commentary

An idea is conveyed here, one that is a running theme through the Course, that we find our way to God through others; we see Christ first in our brothers, and then in ourselves (1:2). When we call to God, truth always responds. The first response is "miracles," which we offer to others through our forgiveness. Then, truth returns to us "to be itself."

Your holy Son is pointed out to me, first in my brother; then in me. (1:2)

This is the way of *A Course in Miracles.* "As I look upon Your Son today," that is, as I see the Christ in those around me, "I hear Your Voice instructing me to find the way to You, as You appointed that the way shall be" (1:4). We hear the Voice that directs us to God as we look on Christ in others. Another way of stating this theme is that we see the face of Christ, and then remember God.

The two stages of the answer are 1) miracles, and 2) the apprehension of truth as itself.

Miracles, in the form of forgiveness offered to my brothers, are only a symbol of the truth. Forgiveness is only "truth's reflection" (1:1). In the miracle I see the Son of God, first in my brother and then in myself.

As miracles accumulate and our mind is trained, truth itself begins to dawn, which is the realization of our Identity with God. That isn't our worry, says the Course. We don't need to work to make that happen. Concentrate on the first step, and the second will come of itself. It is God's gift to us.

Many spiritual paths, I think, make a mistake in focusing on God-realization directly. The effort may eventually work because the purpose is right, but it takes a long time, and enormous effort (see T-18.VII.4:9–11). The effort to do what is not doable, to make happen what has already happened, to find what we have never lost, can become a struggle of endless frustration, a perfect vehicle for the continuation of the ego. This kind of spiritual seeking results in the type of person who is "too heavenly minded to be of any earthly use." Here we find the Pharisee who passes by the injured traveler because he does not want to be tainted. The religious bigot. The self-righteous fundamentalist. His prayers are so important that he ignores his family and its needs.

The Course is saying that the path to heaven is "through forgiveness here" (W-pII.256.1:1). Don't get lost in the search for an abstract experience of union with God. Rather, practice forgiveness. Pay attention to the practical. Concentrate on union with your brother, and union with God will be given you. Work with the material given you, the relationships that are at hand. Don't try to run away in some spiritual retreat; it will fail. You will be attempting to grasp at something you are not capable of grasping now. You can't skip over this process. The way to God is through your brother; he is your savior. There is no other way.

The path of the Course is anything but narcissistic or solitary. It teaches us clearly that we cannot find God alone, or in ourselves alone; and we cannot find God anywhere unless we find Him everywhere. "He is approached through the appreciation of His Son" (T-11.IV.7:2). By learning to see those around us as the Son of God, as God's perfect creation, we learn that we are part of that creation as well. This leads us to the memory of God Himself. The way to God lies through the person next to us:

"Behold his sinlessness, and be you healed." (1:5)

WHAT AM I?

Part 7: W-pII.14.4:1–3

This passage is reminiscent of the paragraph in the introduction to Review V:

> Let this review be then your gift to me. For this alone I
> need; that you will hear the words I speak, and give them
> to the world. You are my voice, my eyes, my feet, my hands
> through which I save the world. The Self from which I call
> to you is but your own. To Him we go together. Take your
> brother's hand, for this is not a way we walk alone. In him
> I walk with you, and you with me. Our Father wills His Son
> be one with Him. What lives but must not then be one with
> you?   (W-pI.rV.In.9:1–9)

Christ sees through our eyes. Our ears are those that hear the Voice
for God. Our minds are the minds that join together. As bringers of salvation, we have only one single function: to hear the words Jesus
speaks, and give them to the world. And what is the kernel of those
words? Seeing the world with no thought of sin; hearing the message
that the world is sinless; joining in union to bless the world.

Am I a blessing to those around me, or a burden? Do I lift guilt from
them, or do I lay it on them? I have not really grasped the message of
the Course until I have realized that I am here to be a channel of God's
grace to the world and to release everyone I come in contact with from
their guilt, most especially from the guilt that I have laid upon them.

LESSON 358 ✦ DECEMBER 24

**"No call to God can be unheard nor left
Unanswered. And of this I can be sure;
His answer is the one I really want."**

Practice instructions

See complete instructions on page 135. A short summary:

- **Read** the commentary paragraph slowly and personally.
- **Pray** the prayer, perhaps several times.
- **Morning and evening:** Repeat the idea and then spend time in Open Mind Meditation.
- **Hourly remembrance:** Repeat the idea and then spend a quiet moment in meditation.
- **Frequent reminders:** Repeat the idea often within each hour.
- **Response to temptation:** Repeat the idea whenever upset, to restore peace.
- **Read the "What Is" section** slowly and thoughtfully once during the day.

Practice suggestion: I have had difficulty relating to the wording of today's lesson, so I have used this rewording:

*God loves me so much that He always hears
And always answers
And gives me the answer I really want.*

Commentary

The ego is constantly working to convince us that we want many different things, things that often compete with one another. We have listened to our egos for so long that we are quite confused about what we want. An early Workbook lesson tells us, "I do not perceive my own best interests" (W-pI.24.Heading).

Since I am so confused about what I really want, it is far better to leave that choice in the hands of the Voice for God.

*You Who remember what I really am alone remember
what I really want.*   (1:1)

I need to remind myself of this fairly often—usually any time I get
caught up in thinking that I want something very much. "I want that new
computer." "I want a loving, intimate, and committed sexual relationship." "I want a better job." I need to remind myself, "Wait a minute,
Allen. Remember! You don't clearly remember who you really are, so
how can you know what you really want?"

Part of the learning the Course is taking us through is learning to listen to the Holy Spirit. And part of that lesson is realizing that He speaks
for us, and not just for God. I may think that what I want conflicts with
what He seems to be wanting for me, and I need to realize that what He
wants for me is what I really want, even if my ego is telling me differently.

*Your Voice, my Father, then is mine as well, and all I want
is what You offer me, in just the form You choose that it be
mine.*   (1:4)

So often I am inclined to think that I want what God wants to give,
but then I dictate the form in which that must come to me. I hear that
God's Will for me is perfect happiness, and then I decide the form that
happiness must take. I need to take it a step further, as this lesson does:
I want what God wants, and whether I can see it or not at the moment,
I want it in just the form He chooses to give it, and not the form I think
it must take.

I am reminded of many times, as a parent, when I tried to convince
one of my sons that he didn't really want what he thought he wanted.
Perhaps he was saying, "I want the red gumball!" And I would say, "No,
Ben, the red one isn't sweet; it's hot cinnamon and you won't like it."
And he would say, "I want the red one!!" We do exactly the same sort
of thing with God, far more often than we care to admit.

*Let me remember all I do not know, and let my voice be
still, remembering.*   (1:5)

Let me realize, when I think I know what I want, that I don't really
know. And let me simply shut up and stop throwing a tantrum; let me be

quiet, and listen to my Father's Voice. He speaks for me as well as for God; He knows what I really want, and wisdom is taking His advice. He loves us; He cares for us; He has promised always to be with us. Let me trust Him even when I don't understand, knowing that (Oh! It seems awful sometimes to say these words; so belittling!) Father knows best.

Let me not forget myself is nothing, but my Self is all.(1:7)

The little, individual ego "I" is nothing; Who I really am is everything. The Holy Spirit always speaks from the perspective of that larger Self. He does not seek to benefit and coddle the little "I." He is always working with us to bring us to full awareness of Self. At times what He gives may go contrary to the little "I," while leading us on to full realization of the Self. That is why our picture of what we want is so often distorted, and what He wants for us seems at times to be something we do not want. We are confused about who we are. He is not. So let us trust His wisdom, be still, and know that He is God.

WHAT AM I?

Part 8: W-pII.14.4:4

> And from the oneness that we have attained we call to all our brothers, asking them to share our peace and consummate our joy. (4:4)

We attain oneness gradually. In reality we don't strictly "attain" oneness; we remember it, we become aware of what has always been. But, in time, it *seems* as though we attain it bit by bit. We begin with very brief holy instants, flashes of remembrance, like a forgotten dream we are struggling to recall. Those moments of memory come more and more frequently, more and more clearly, and last longer and longer, until one day we remember fully and forever. Each instant we are in that oneness, we recognize that we are not there alone, and cannot be there alone. We experience peace and joy, and yet our joy cannot be *consummated* until everyone shares it with us, and wakes up to the reality of who and what they are. So we call to them, we reach out to them.

The state of mind we are seeking, which we might call the enlightened state of mind, is one which perceives its connection to all of God's creations, and is moved irresistibly to re-establish the full communication of that perfect oneness in all its parts. As the "bodhisattva" of Buddhist tradition foregoes Nirvana to save others, being unwilling to pass into that state of perfect bliss until "every blade of grass is enlightened," so the right-minded continually call out to all their brothers, asking them to share their peace. Jesus exemplifies this attitude as he speaks in the "Circle of Atonement" section in the Text:

> I stand within the circle, calling you to peace. Teach peace with me, and stand with me on holy ground. Remember for everyone your Father's power that He has given him. Believe not that you cannot teach His perfect peace. Stand not outside, but join with me within. Fail not the only purpose to which my teaching calls you. Restore to God His Son as He created him, by teaching him his innocence.
> (T-14.V.9:4–10)

> Stand quietly within this circle, and attract all tortured minds to join with you in the safety of its peace and holiness. (T-14.V.8:6)

LESSON 359 ✦ DECEMBER 25

**"God's answer is some form of peace. All pain
Is healed; all misery replaced with joy.
All prison doors are opened. And all sin
Is understood as merely a mistake."**

Practice instructions

See complete instructions on page 135. A short summary:

- **Read** the commentary paragraph slowly and personally.
- **Pray** the prayer, perhaps several times.
- **Morning and evening:** Repeat the idea and then spend time in Open Mind Meditation.
- **Hourly remembrance:** Repeat the idea and then spend a quiet moment in meditation.
- **Frequent reminders:** Repeat the idea often within each hour.
- **Response to temptation:** Repeat the idea whenever upset, to restore peace.
- **Read the "What Is" section** slowly and thoughtfully once during the day.

Commentary

Today I want to share some thoughts just on the first line of this lesson. Yesterday we were reminded that "no call to God can be unheard nor left unanswered" and that "His answer is the one I really want" (W-pII.358.Heading). Today we are told that when God answers, the answer "is some form of peace." So the answer that I want is peace. Every call to God is answered with some form of peace, and that is what I really want, despite what I may think to the contrary.

I think that when we begin to grasp that what we really want is peace—in every situation—things start to fall into proper perspective. Say it looks like I may lose my job, or a relationship that I believe I need. Say it looks as if I don't have enough money. I find myself, more or less, praying for that job, or that relationship, or that money. Or perhaps I'm not up to prayer so I just obsess about the situation. I'm thinking this is what I want.

If, when that happens, I can begin to recognize that what I really want is some form of peace, I've made a giant step. It isn't the job I want; it's the form of peace I think it brings. It isn't the relationship I really want; it's the peace I think lies in it. It isn't the money I need; it is the peace of mind I think it buys me.

> The prayer of the heart does not really ask for concrete things. It always requests some kind of experience, the specific things asked for being the bringers of the desired experience in the opinion of the asker.   (M-21.2:4–5)

When I begin to realize that I am not really asking for things but for the experience of peace I think they bring me, I can start to ask for peace directly, bypassing my (perhaps) mistaken opinion that a certain "thing" will bring me that experience. I can open my mind to the possibility that God will bring me the peace of mind I seek through another avenue than the one I see.

Once I can begin to let go of my insistence that the answer must come in a certain form, I will much more quickly be aware of God's answer. I may find I can experience the peace of God completely independent of form. I may find that the peace comes to me in a form I could never have anticipated. I will lose my anxiety over whether or not the form I first envisioned as what I needed ever comes to me at all. If peace of mind comes, I am satisfied because this is all I really ever want.

To tie this in with the rest of the lesson, just briefly, "Help us forgive, for we would be at peace" (1:9). Peace is impossible if my mind is blinded by unforgiveness. Peace is incompatible with anger. A lack of peace is always some kind of unforgiveness, although often it is difficult to see how that could be. When I ask for peace I am asking to be taught to forgive, whether I recognize it or not. If I make peace my goal above all else, I will learn forgiveness.

WHAT AM I?

Part 9: W-pII.14.5:1–2

Whether we really know it or not, "We are the holy messengers of God" (5:1). That is our function; it is what we were created to do—express God. This is our job here, and we won't be completely happy until we are carrying it out. The way this is worded here seems significant; we are "carrying His Word to everyone whom He has sent to us" (5:1); it does not say, "to whom we are sent." It is not so much that we go out looking for people to give the message to; rather, they come looking for us. That is a different attitude than the one which says, "Let us go out and convert the world." This is simply a passing along of the message of peace and the fact of forgiveness to everyone who comes into our lives. People don't just "happen" to show up in our lives; they are sent. And they are sent because we have something to give to them.

Let me begin to learn to ask myself, when someone shows up in my life, in my time, or perhaps in my face: "What do I have to give to this person? What is the Word of God I can communicate to her? What does God want to say to this person through me?" Or, in much simpler terms, "How can I be truly helpful to this person?"

Doing this—actually doing it, not just thinking about it—is how I learn that the Word of God is written on my heart (5:1). And doing this is *how my mind is changed* about what I am and what I am doing here. My mind won't be changed just by trying to change my mind; it is changed by carrying God's Word to everyone He sends to me. When I engage in that kind of active serving and forgiving of my brothers and sisters, I begin to form a new opinion of myself. I begin to see myself in a different light. That is the Holy Spirit's plan of salvation.

LESSON 360 ✦ DECEMBER 26

**"Peace be to me, the holy Son of God.
Peace to my brother, who is one with me.
Let all the world be blessed with peace through us."**

Practice instructions

See complete instructions on page 135. A short summary:

- **Read** the commentary paragraph slowly and personally.
- **Pray** the prayer, perhaps several times.
- **Morning and evening:** Repeat the idea and then spend time in Open Mind Meditation.
- **Hourly remembrance:** Repeat the idea and then spend a quiet moment in meditation.
- **Frequent reminders:** Repeat the idea often within each hour.
- **Response to temptation:** Repeat the idea whenever upset, to restore peace.
- **Read the "What Is" section** slowly and thoughtfully once during the day.

Commentary

This is for all practical purposes the last "regular" lesson of the Workbook. The last five days of the year will be spent on a single lesson, which gives us an idea of how every day can be spent by a Course "graduate," if we can use that term. This final lesson, then, sums up and concludes the practice of the Workbook.

Peace be to me; peace be to my brother; peace be to all the world through us. That is one way of summarizing what the Course is all about: finding peace within ourselves, sharing that peace with another, and together sharing it with all the world. Finding it within ourselves is the basis. Sharing it with another confirms it within us, and the relationship gives us a microcosm in which to learn to extend that peace. Having learned to share together, we then extend the peace to all the world.

*Father, it is Your peace that I would give, receiving it of
you.*   (1:1)

The peace we receive and give is God's peace. It is the peace that
comes of knowing we are God's creation: "In holiness were we created,
and in holiness do we remain" (1:5). "I am Your Son, forever just as You
created me, for the Great Rays remain forever still and undisturbed
within me" (1:2). Nothing God placed in me in creation has been lost.
God, eternally at peace, extended Himself to create me, and His peace
extended into me and included me in its stillness. That stillness always
exists. There is a place in you, and in me, that is at perfect peace always.
We can find that peace at any instant we choose to do so. To find it all
we need do is to be still, to stop our interference. The peace is always
there.

*I would reach to them [the Great Rays] in silence and in
certainty, for nowhere else can certainty be found. Peace
be to me, and peace to all the world.*   (1:3–4)

This morning, close your eyes for a time—for as long as it takes. Let
the thoughts that have been occupying your mind just float away,
detached. Do not push them away; do not hold on to them. Just let them
go, and try to become aware of that place within yourself that is always
at peace. Do not strive to find it; let it find you. Simply be still. Simply
make yourself receptive to the peace and it will appear, because it is
always there. Sit in silence. If a noise comes to your attention, don't let
your mind "stick" to it. You have no other purpose than to be still. You
have no other goal right now but to say, "Peace be to me."

And when you touch that peace, or when it touches you, however
briefly, let yourself add, "and peace to all the world." Gently wish that
peace for all your brothers and sisters. That is all we are here for. That
is all that really needs to be done. It will be enough.

*Your Son is like to You in perfect sinlessness. And with this
thought we gladly say "Amen."*   (1:6–7)

The thought of perfect sinlessness brings the Course to its conclusion; that is its goal.

But the content of the course never changes. Its central theme is always, "God's Son is guiltless, and in his innocence is his salvation." (M-1.3:4–5)

When I have accepted my own perfect sinlessness, and have extended that thought to include the entire world, salvation is accomplished. To do so is to perfectly forgive all things. Sinlessness and peace go together. Only the sinless can be at peace; only the peaceful are sinless. The message of the Course is one of radical innocence. All are innocent, and no one must be condemned for others to be free.

WHAT AM I?

Part 10: W-pII.14.5:3–5

Our function here is to "bring glad tidings to the Son of God, who thought he suffered" (5:3). The Son of God who thought he suffered is you, me, and everyone who comes into our life. What a wonderful calling! To announce, as the prophet Isaiah said in the Old Testament:

> ...to preach good tidings unto the meek; ...to bind up the brokenhearted, to proclaim liberty to the captives, and the opening of the prison to [them that are] bound;...to comfort all that mourn; ...to give unto them beauty for ashes, the oil of joy for mourning, the garment of praise for the spirit of heaviness. (Is 61:1–3)

This season of Christmas is said in the Gospels to be a time of "great joy...to all people" (Lk 2:10). In the Course we have a continuation of that message, and we are its heralds. We can announce, "Now is [the Son of God] redeemed" (5:4). The way is open for every one of us to find our way home, and to know first our perfect forgiveness, and then the immensity of God's Love.

> And as he sees the gate of Heaven stand open before him, he will enter in and disappear into the Heart of God. (5:5)

As these "glad tidings" are received, we will all, in the end, enter in through the heavenly gates, symbolic of entering into the awareness of perfect Oneness. In that Oneness we will disappear into the Heart of God. That word "disappear" does not, in any sense, mean that we shall cease to exist, or that we will be absorbed and somehow blotted out by the absorption. It is just that all sense of difference and separateness will be gone, along with all desire for it. We will disappear in the Oneness, but we will be *in* that Oneness, profoundly a part of it, radiantly fulfilling our function, shining forever in the eternal glory of God.

XVIII

Final Lessons
Lessons 361 - 365

PRACTICE INSTRUCTIONS FOR
LESSONS 361-365

Purpose: To place your practice and your life in the hands of the Holy Spirit, so that from here on, He becomes for you what the book has been. He becomes the Guide for your practice and for your entire walk through life. From now on, you follow in His way, and lead your brothers along that same way. The keynote of this way is extending forgiveness to others and thereby learning that you are forgiven.

Morning/evening quiet time: As long as you need for the effect you want.

Repeat the words of the lesson at the beginning. As you do, realize that these words are an acknowledgment that you have not understood (W-pII.fl.6:1), that your belief in a sinful world has been mistaken (W-pII.fl.1:5). So now you come before God's Voice with empty hands and ask to be shown, to be taught how to love (W-pII.fl.6:1).

The words	The meaning
This holy instant would I give to You.	I set my past beliefs aside and give this practice period to You, so that it may become a holy instant.
Be You in charge.	I set my thoughts and words aside and place You in full charge of this practice period.
For I would follow You, certain that Your direction gives me peace.	I do this because then You can come in and lead me along Your way, Your way of love. And only on that way will I find peace.

After repeating the words, enter into Open Mind Meditation. Simply open your mind to the presence of the Holy Spirit, and hold that openness without the aid of words. For this purpose, I find it helpful to imagine that your mind is His holy temple. Normally, it is your bedroom, to fill with clutter as you please. But during this practice period, it is His temple, to be filled only with His presence. He is in charge. This means that you leave the shoes of your thoughts and words at the door. Whenever you forget and bring your dirty shoes into His temple, repeat *"Be You in charge."* Aside from those times, hold the awareness that your mind is His temple *wordlessly.* Be filled with confidence that He will hear and will come into this holy place.

When He comes, He may give you a word to repeat. He may give you a thought to dwell on. He may speak to you. You may hear God's Voice tell you, "You are My Son, and all I have is yours" (see W-pII.fl.6:3). Or He may simply grant you "stillness and a tranquil, open mind" (W-pII.361-365.1:3). However He shows up, He has come to lead you into a life based on following Him along His pathway of forgiveness.

Hourly remembrance: One or two minutes as the hour strikes (reduce if circumstances do not permit).

Do a miniature version of the morning practice. Repeat the idea as an invitation to the Holy Spirit, and then wait in wordless silence for Him to come to you.

Frequent reminder: As often as possible within each hour.

"Repeat [the idea], and allow your mind to rest a little time in silence and in peace" (W-pI.rIII.In.10:5).

Response to temptation: Whenever you feel upset.

Repeat the idea as a way of calling on the Holy Spirit to dispel your upset.

LESSON 361 ✦ DECEMBER 27

**"This holy instant would I give to You.
Be You in charge. For I would follow You,
Certain that Your direction gives me peace."**

Practice instructions

See instructions on page 683.

Commentary

I will be doing commentary on the "Final Lessons" and "Epilogue" sections intermingled with the daily commentary for the next five days, since the actual lesson is the same for all five days.

So we come to the final lessons of the year. Today and for the next four days we have the same lesson, which gives us the very simple directions by which we are to live the rest of our lives. The intent of the Workbook is to aid us in forming the very habit portrayed by this lesson: to give each instant to the Holy Spirit, asking Him to be in charge, committing ourselves to follow His direction in everything, knowing that He always leads us towards peace.

The introduction to this simple lesson ("Final Lessons") is one that we would do well to read each day for these five days. Each day as we read this over, along with the lesson, we follow the reading with a time of quiet in which we seek a holy instant of communion with our Father and His Voice.

We are not seeking for words:

> Our final lessons will be left as free of words as possible. We use them but at the beginning of our practicing, and only to remind us that we seek to go beyond them. Let us turn to Him Who leads the way and makes our footsteps sure. (W-pII.fl.1:1–3).[1]

What we are seeking is that communion with Him. We open ourselves to the experience of peace. We give our lives to Him, asking to be directed in "all our thoughts to serve the function of salvation"

686

(W-pII.fl.3:1). We are here to remember God through forgiving our brothers, through sharing His reality with everyone.

We are as free of words as possible in these times of practice, and yet "if I need a word to help me, He will give it to me. If I need a thought, that will He also give" (W-pII.361-365.1:1–2). He will give whatever I need. Sometimes there will be words; sometimes, thoughts. And sometimes, nothing but "stillness and a tranquil, open mind" (W-pII.361-365.1:3). We present ourselves to Him and wait for Him to give whatever we need. We do not tell Him what we need; we leave that to Him.

Each day we can begin like this. And during the day, often, whenever we can, we stop and once again renew the set of our minds, our determination to make no decision by ourselves, without Him. These lessons have been, as the Workbook's epilogue says, "a beginning, not an end" (W-Ep.1:1). They have trained us in a practice that is meant to continue for the rest of our lives until our entire life has become a holy instant.

Whenever you can today, remember these words and repeat them: "This holy instant would I give to You." He will never fail to hear you.

---

1. The reference translates as Workbook, Part II, Final Lessons (introduction), paragraph 1, sentences 1 to 3.

LESSON 362 ✦ DECEMBER 28

**"This holy instant would I give to You.
Be You in charge. For I would follow You,
Certain that Your direction gives me peace."**

 Practice instructions

See instructions on page 683.

Commentary

The Workbook leads us to this point: "to Him we give our lives henceforth" (W-pII.fl.1:4). If the idea of giving our lives to God seems unappealing, consider the alternative: "For we would not return again to the belief in sin that made the world seem ugly and unsafe, attacking and destroying, dangerous in all its ways, and treacherous beyond the hope of trust and the escape from pain" (W-pII.fl.1:5).

The idea that we want something other than God is what made all this mess. There is nothing other than God. "The belief in sin" referred to is nothing more than our belief that we succeeded in making something separate from Him. We don't really want this, although we have believed we did. This belief is the source of all our pain, so let us return our lives to the Source of all joy instead. Let us give our lives to be directed by His Voice, the Holy Spirit.

Let us give this holy instant and every instant into His hands.

> His is the only way to find the peace that God has given us. It is His way that everyone must travel in the end, because it is this ending God Himself appointed.
> (W-pII.fl.2:1–2)

Don't let those words "the only way" scare you off. This isn't saying *A Course in Miracles* is the only way to God; it is saying that the route of forgiveness, the truth that we are all innocent before God, is the only way, whatever the form it may take. God created us all to be His expression, and His Will will be done in the end. As it says in the Text introduction, we don't have any choice about the content of the curriculum, just about when we learn it.

> In the dream of time it seems to be far off. And yet, in truth,
> it is already here; already serving us as gracious guidance
> in the way to go. (W-pII.fl.2:3–4)

Robert wrote an article for our newsletter on the topic "How Long Until We Are Out of Here?" or in other words, "How long until we reach the end of the journey?" The Course is full of the paradox stated baldly in this sentence: The truth is already here, and yet—in time—it seems to be far off. Both are true, each in its proper context. A dream that lasts only a few seconds can seem, within the dream, to last for years. Isn't it possible that a dream that lasts only for a "tiny tick of time" (T-26.V.3:5) can seem to last billions of years? Within the dream of time, our journey home seems to be taking a very long time. In reality it is already over, and the power of its ending is present now, guiding us through the dream.

So what should we do? How, then, should we live? Should we proclaim, "It's all over!" and just kick back and relax? No; to us the dream is still real. Therefore:

> Let us together follow in the way that truth points out to us.
> And let us be the leaders of our many brothers who are
> seeking for the way, but find it not. (W-pII.fl.2:5–6)

In his article, Robert reaches the conclusion that "how long" is an irrelevant question, and that we should be equally content whether we go home tomorrow or in 10,000 AD. Our function in the meantime is to be the light of the world as long as we are in it. We are to lead home all our brothers who are still lost, still floundering. We are to forgive the world; to bring the message of guiltlessness to everyone; to extend the peace and love we have found to all the world.

This is what we do when we say, "For I would follow You, certain that Your direction gives me peace." What direction? The direction of forgiveness, the direction of forgiving the world. That is the direction which "gives me peace." Working out our forgiveness of the world becomes the content of our days. It is when we have accepted this as the one function that we want to fulfill that the Holy Spirit will arrange everything for us, providing everything we need as we go.

LESSON 363 ✦ DECEMBER 29

**"This holy instant would I give to You.
Be You in charge. For I would follow You,
Certain that Your direction gives me peace."**

Practice instructions

See instructions on page 683.

Commentary

Once again we repeat this "holy instant" lesson. It seems as if the author is telling us, "Having received all the thoughts we have given you, there is really nothing left for you to do except to put your life into the hands of the Holy Spirit." Helen Schucman, who wrote the first parts of the preface to the Course some time after completing the Course itself (the final section of the preface, "What It Says," was taken down from the same inner dictation as the rest of the books), said there:

> The Course makes no claim to finality, nor are the Workbook lessons intended to bring the student's learning to completion. At the end, the reader is left in the hands of his or her own Internal Teacher, Who will direct all subsequent learning as He sees fit. (preface, pp. ix-x)

That is exactly what these final five days are reinforcing, leaving us in the hands of the Holy Spirit for our further instruction.

The Workbook is a primer, one that is intended to ready us for the ongoing instruction of the Holy Spirit. It serves as a kind of crutch while we are too weak to stand on our own. I sometimes like to think of the Workbook as training wheels on our spiritual bicycle. The training wheels are there to keep the child who is learning to ride from falling over. Once he learns to keep his balance, the wheels become unnecessary, while the rider continues to learn to ride his bike better and better, perhaps learning to do wheelies, ride with no hands, or even do off-road dirt bike maneuvers. The learning isn't over when we are done with the Workbook; there is much yet to learn.

The training of the Course is a mind training. The Workbook offers mental "training wheels," the structure of daily thoughts and suggested practice exercises. Its purpose is to initiate us into the Course's form of spiritual practice, which consists of mentally engaging with God, morning, evening, and moment to moment throughout the day. Its words give us something to grasp while we try to form this new habit. In the beginning it is very structured, and the structure gets fairly demanding. Over time it eases off, in the assumption that we have begun to form the habits it is attempting to impart. Here, in the final lessons, the structure is about to fall completely away; the training wheels are being removed. We are left in the hands of the Holy Spirit alone, with no book to guide us.

Some, perhaps, may be motivated enough to apply themselves diligently throughout the entire first year they do the Workbook, following its instructions (or trying to) every day. If indeed one were to do this, a single year would be enough to form the habits of spiritually engaging with God. For most of us, however, once is not enough.

I have to confess at this writing, this next year (1997) will be, I think, my ninth pass through the Workbook. My first took me most of three years. Since then I've done it once a year except for one year I decided I wanted to do something different for a while. I'm a slow learner; as this year ends, I still haven't formed the daily habits the Workbook is trying to teach us. I'm doing much better each year, but it is still a rare day I remember to practice my lesson every hour, much less recall it briefly five or six times in between the hours—and that is what the practice instructions consist of once we are several months into the book. So I am doing it again, not just so that I can share daily comments with you folks, but because I still have much to learn myself.

Yet even though I don't feel I can take this lesson as fully as it is meant, letting go of the Workbook to go on in my private instruction with the Holy Spirit, I can still take it for each time of practice and remembrance through the day. "This holy instant would I give to You." Every instant can be a holy one. Let's try to remember, today, as often as we can. Each time we do, let's give the instant to Him to be made holy. Or rather, let's give it to Him for His purposes in recognition that it is holy.

As the introduction to this lesson stressed:

Unto us the aim is given to forgive the world. It is the goal that God has given us. (W-pII.fl.3:2–3)

That is the purpose the Holy Spirit has, and each instant given to Him is used for that purpose: forgiving the world. "It is our function to remember Him on earth" (W-pII.fl.4:1). We remember Him by forgiving: "For all that we forgive we will not fail to recognize as part of God Himself" (W-pII.fl.3:5). Our brothers are our saviors; through our forgiveness of them, we remember God.

LESSON 364 ✦ DECEMBER 30

**"This holy instant would I give to You.
Be You in charge. For I would follow You,
Certain that Your direction gives me peace."**

 Practice instructions

See instructions on page 683.

Commentary

I'm going to suggest that for the last two days of this year you read through the epilogue following the last lesson, as well as the lesson. I will share a few comments based on the epilogue over the next two days (all of the Course quotes that follow are from the epilogue unless otherwise indicated); however, your practice should still be of the final lesson.

The epilogue echoes two of the themes of this final lesson: *following* the Holy Spirit as our Teacher and Friend on the path, and the *certainty* of our reaching the end of the path successfully.

Your Friend goes with you. You are not alone.   (1:2–3)

You are as certain of arriving home as is the pathway of the sun laid down before it rises...Indeed, your pathway is more certain still.   (2:1–2)

Today I will discuss the theme of following, and tomorrow, the certainty of arriving home.

The epilogue makes it clear that even when we complete the Workbook and have achieved the purpose it sets for us, having developed a daily habit of giving our lives over to the direction of the Holy Spirit, we have only begun our journey, and there is more to go. The path ahead may yet be long. There will yet be difficulties along the way. Why else would Jesus emphasize the certainty of the ending unless we believed we still have reason to doubt?

We are told this course is a beginning, not an end (1:1). We can expect troubles (1:5) and problems (1:7). We will still be going through lessons, although not the "specific" ones of the Workbook (3:1). "Efforts" will still be required (3:3). We will experience "difficulty" and will still have times in which we think that pain is real (4:1). We are still on the way to Heaven, but not there yet (5:4). We need guidance (5:5), so there must be obstacles or a path that at times seems unclear. We are still on the road towards home (5:7). "We will continue in His way" (6:2). Jesus says he will never leave us without comfort, so comfort will still be needed (6:8).

I am pointing out all the indications that a major portion of our journey is still ahead, because we are so easily inclined to think otherwise; we get impatient and want the journey to be over. The positive themes of this epilogue are designed to counteract the discouragement that may come over us when we realize that there is a long way yet to go.

First, we have a Friend Who goes with us. A "Friend!" Has my experience with the Workbook taught me that? The Holy Spirit is my Friend. (Perhaps, for some of us, that Friend has personalized as Jesus.) Has my interaction with Him been enough that He has earned my trust, "by speaking daily to you of your Father and your brother and your Self" (4:4)? There are such wonderful promises given to us here of His helpfulness. We cannot call on Him in vain. He has the answers for everything we might ask, and He won't withhold them. All we need to do is ask. He speaks to us of what we "really want and really need" (2:4).

> He will direct your efforts, telling you exactly what to do,
> how to direct your mind, and when to come to Him in
> silence, asking for His sure direction and His certain Word.
>
> (3:3)

We do not need to worry about the length or complexity of our journey. We have a Guide. The Workbook is not the journey; it is a training camp that prepares us for it, introduces us to our Guide, and teaches us to trust Him. By doing the Workbook we have learned how reliable and knowledgeable He is; now, we are ready to set out on the journey itself, walking with Him in confidence that He knows how to bring us home.

LESSON 365 ✦ DECEMBER 31

**"This holy instant would I give to You.
Be You in charge. For I would follow You,
Certain that Your direction gives me peace."**

Practice instructions

See instructions on page 683.

Commentary

The last lesson of the year! But certainly not, I hope, our last holy instant. I find myself, as the New Year approaches, thinking of this lesson in terms of "This holy *year* would I give to You." Ah, I really feel that resonating within, finding a common tone echoing from a deep, perpetual longing.

The epilogue, as I was saying yesterday, talks about how our journey continues after the formal study of the Workbook with a continuing walk with the Holy Spirit as Guide through what may yet be a very long journey. The second point that the epilogue makes strongly is that the end of the journey is certain:

> You are as certain of arriving home as is the pathway of the sun laid down before it rises, after it has set, and in the half-lit hours in between. Indeed, your pathway is more certain still. (2:1–2)

We can "walk with Him, as certain as is He of where you go; as sure as He of how you should proceed; as confident as He is of the goal, and of your safe arrival in the end" (4:6). I think that often my feelings of "How much longer is this going to take?" really translate into suppressed fears of "Am I ever going to arrive home?" We convert the length of time into a witness to the idea that we'll never make it. If I *really knew* that my pathway is as certain as the sun, and more, I could "travel light and journey lightly" (T-13.VII.13:4) no matter how long it takes.

I think the attitude the Course encourages in us is:

1. To hold on to this certainty that arriving home is guaranteed,

2. While at the same time being completely unconcerned with how long it may take.

The Text tells us that how long is only a matter of time, and time is just an illusion. It asks us not to be restless, and points out that being restless on a journey to peace is rather inconsistent.

> The end is certain, and the means as well. To this we say "Amen." (5:1–2)

Let *me* say "Amen" as well. "Yes, so be it, and so it is." Why is the end so sure? We have the Holy Spirit with us. "And He will speak for God and for your Self, thus making sure that hell will claim you not, and that each choice you make brings Heaven nearer to your reach" (5:4). He is the guarantee. His presence makes the ending sure. And He is certain because He knows the end depends on us, and nothing is more certain than a Son of God.

> We go homeward to an open door which God has held unclosed to welcome us. (5:7)

Ah, what a beautiful picture! I could have called my booklet *The Journey Home* by that title: *Homeward to an Open Door*. Thank You, God, for the open door.

> God's angels hover near and all about. His Love surrounds you, and of this be sure; that I will never leave you comfortless. (6:7–8)

What more do we need? The Holy Spirit is in us. Angels hover near and all about. God's Love surrounds us, and Jesus promises: I will never leave you comfortless.

Can you get a sense of that as this year comes to a close? Can you close your eyes for a moment and feel Them all around you? Can you realize the holiness of this moment, the birth of Christ in you now moving out into the world to transform it with light? They are here, and They are watching, and as Jesus often says in the Course, They give you thanks for your willingness to open to the light. Let us, then, as the year ends, give Them thanks for giving this light to us.

XIX

Where Do I Go From Here?

Congratulations! You have finished the entire Workbook. If you are new to the Course in this last year, you may not realize how many students begin the Workbook and don't finish it, so finishing is no minor accomplishment. It really deserves congratulations.

Having completed a pass through the Workbook, there are two questions that might occur to you now:

- Should I repeat the Workbook lessons, or is one time through enough?
- If I feel I am done with the lessons, what should I do now to continue my work with *A Course in Miracles*?

Should I repeat the Workbook?

I believe the answer to this question is very much up to you. Yet, in a general way, I can give you an answer. This answer is my opinion, but it is based on some objective observations about the Workbook and its training goal, and some common sense.

The common sense portion is this: How do you determine whether or not to repeat *any* class, in any subject? You ask yourself, "Have I learned what the course was intended to teach?" If you have, you don't need to repeat it. If you haven't, you could very likely profit from repeating the class.

When I was in high school I took three years of French. The last two of those years were from an absolutely *awful* teacher. When I entered college, I took a placement test in French to answer the question "How much French did the high school classes teach me?" The answer turned out to be "Almost none." I placed in French 1 at the college level; I started all over. There was no shame in that. It did not mean I was an incompetent French student. In fact, I ended up majoring in French, spending a year living in France, and being mistaken for French by a French student at the university!

We don't happen to have a simple, written test you can take to determine if you have learned what the Workbook set out to teach you. There is no shame if you haven't learned it yet. I would say, to be perfectly honest, that I do not know one single person who has ever really gotten all there is to get out of the Workbook in just one year. My personal opinion—and there is absolutely no support for this in the words of the Course itself—is that everyone could benefit from doing the Workbook two, three, four, or even more times.

The key piece of information you need to answer the question "Have I learned what the Workbook was intended to teach me?" is: What does the Workbook try to teach us? What is its main goal for us? If you know the answer to that question, it is fairly easy to determine whether or not you have learned it, whether or not the purpose of the Workbook has been achieved in your case.

If you have been reading these commentaries and Robert's practice instructions with understanding, you already know the answers. Whereas the ultimate goal of the spiritual practice given to us by the Workbook is to train our minds to look on everyone and everything in the world differently, to always think with God, to listen always to the Voice for God, and to forgive the entire world, the immediate goal of the Workbook is much more attainable and practical.

That immediate goal is to train us in daily spiritual practice, to establish in our lives the *habit* of spending time every morning and evening to meet with God and to set our minds on His truth, the *habit* of turning our minds within to God every hour or so for a minute or two, the *habit* of thinking frequently of God or of spiritual thoughts in between those hourly remembrances, and the *habit* of responding immediately to temptation with some thought of God, some tool from the problem-solving repertoire that we have developed over the year of our Workbook practice.

So the answer to "Should I repeat the Workbook?" is: If you have established these habits of daily spiritual practice to the degree that you can and will carry them on, daily, without the continuing support of the Workbook, then you do not need to repeat the Workbook. You may still *choose* to repeat it, but you do not need to. If, however, you *have not* established these daily habits of spiritual practice, then you should re-enroll yourself in the program that is designed to help you form such habits—the Workbook!

You probably can fairly easily answer the question for yourself about how strongly you have formed the habits of spiritual practice. If you are still missing your quiet time lots of mornings or evenings; if you rarely remember the lesson every hour, and even more rarely remember it between the hours; if your ego often rises up and seizes control of your mind without being challenged by your right mind, refusing to listen to the ego; then you surely can benefit from doing the Workbook again.

If, on the other hand, you *have* formed strong habits of spiritual practice—not necessarily perfect habits, but real habits, fairly consistent— then you may be ready to set the Workbook aside. Just like when you have been using training wheels to learn to ride a bicycle, the only way to know for sure if you are ready is to try it without the training wheels. The first time I tried continuing my spiritual practice without the Workbook, it was a dismal failure, the equivalent on a bicycle of falling over within one hundred feet. I'd read through the Workbook about six times by then, too! (I had not really tried to follow the practice instructions, however, so it is no wonder that I hadn't formed good habits of practice.) Within a few weeks, I wasn't doing any spiritual practice at all! I realized that I wasn't yet ready to set aside the "training wheels," and I resumed doing the Workbook lessons.

What do I do after the Workbook?

The Manual for Teachers offers very clear instructions for continuing our daily spiritual practice after we have completed the Workbook, in a section titled "How Should the Teacher of God Spend His Day?" (M-16). If you think you are ready to move on without the Workbook, this is where to find your instructions. And if you are wondering whether or not you are ready, reading over these instructions and asking yourself, "Am I ready to do this?" will help you make up your mind.

The section begins by talking about an *advanced* teacher of God. It says, basically, that an advanced spiritual teacher does not need any structure or program; the question of how to spend his day is meaningless, because the advanced teacher lives in constant contact with the Holy Spirit, and simply follows His guidance moment to moment.

However, it goes on to say, the *ordinary* teacher of God—for instance, someone who has just completed the Workbook (and completing the Workbook is a prerequisite to bearing the title "teacher of God")—still *does* need structure. Not as much structure as someone doing the Workbook, but not as little as an advanced teacher. Something in between. This person is not yet ready to live without structure; she or he is still in training, still learning to listen to the Holy Spirit in every moment. The Manual then goes on to tell us what that structure should be, in some detail.

As we have pointed out in our introduction to Part II of the Workbook, and also in "Preliminary Notes on Workbook Practice" in *A Workbook Companion, Volume I,* the instructions given here in the Manual sound remarkably like the fully matured pattern of practice established toward the end of Part I in the Workbook, and carried on through all of Part II. Here they are, as I presented them in Volume I:

The post-Workbook practice, in simple outline, is this:

1. Begin the day right, as soon as possible after waking. "As soon as possible after waking take your quiet time, continuing a minute or two after you begin to find it difficult" (M-16.4:7). The goal in this time is to "join with God." We should spend as long as it takes to do that until it becomes difficult; the length of time is not a major concern (4:4–8).

2. Repeat the "same procedures" at night; just before sleeping if possible (5:1).

3. Remember God all through the day (6:1–14).

4. Turn to the Holy Spirit with all your problems (7:4–5).

5. Respond to all temptations by reminding yourself of the truth (8:1–3; 10:8; 11:9).

It would be good to read over all of Section 16 of the Manual if you are considering post-Workbook practice, and to spend some time carefully studying what it has to say in detail. The outline I have given here just gives the general ideas. It may be enough to let you decide whether you feel ready for carrying out this program.

Are you ready to spend as much time as it takes to join with God every morning and evening? It might be just a few minutes; it might be an hour. Do you feel confident you know what to do in that time, without the Workbook at hand to give you some specific practice instruction? Are you comfortable enough with the basics of Course meditation to undertake it on your own?

Do you feel you have a habit of remembering God all through the day, and will be able to do that without having a specific thought from the lesson for the day to call to mind? (You may pick some thought for yourself from the Text or Workbook, to use like a lesson thought.)

Have you begun to turn to the Holy Spirit with all your problems as a matter of course, as a habit?

Are you able to respond to temptation with the truth on your own? Or would it still be more helpful to you to have a Workbook lesson that gives you some suggestions about doing that?

If your answers to these questions are mostly positive, then you are ready to leave the Workbook behind. If you find yourself mostly answering "No," then you can probably benefit from repeating the Workbook.

Hints for post-Workbook practice

Let me offer some practical hints, if you have decided to move on to post-Workbook practice. I have found it helpful to make a list of useful thoughts from the Course (not just the Workbook), thoughts that I have found effective in responding to temptation, or thoughts that have helped me, in meditation, to move more quickly into that "quiet center." Some people have begun to compile a notebook containing such thoughts or passages from the Course. You may want to categorize these, for instance, passages useful in working on forgiveness; passages useful when in fear; and so on.

If you look through the Text you will find a number of passages that are in italic type. These passages are nearly all different forms of suggested spiritual practices. They will all say something like this:

Whenever you feel troubled by anything, say to yourself...and then comes the part in italics. You may want to make a collection of these passages and then spend several days working with each of them.

You may be studying the Text and be struck by something you are reading, seeing how it applies to a situation in your life. Take that passage and turn it into your own, personalized spiritual practice. Use it to lead in to your meditations; use it for hourly remembrance and for response to temptation.

Speaking of studying the Text, by all means, do study it! Don't just read it, study it. Give yourself plenty of time for such study. I don't really think you can carefully study the entire Text in much less than three years of daily reading and study. I once *read* the entire Text in about two months, but it has taken me the last four years to *carefully study* every chapter. The Circle of Atonement now offers a year-long long-distance text study program. For information on how to join the program, go to www.circleofa.org and look under "continuing education" or call 928-282-0790.

Just because you are not going through the Workbook lessons day after day, don't think that you can't do a lesson every now and then. Sometimes, a particular lesson from the Workbook will come to mind; follow your instinct, and do the lesson.

Do you remember a few lessons, as you went through the Workbook, that seemed particularly effective or powerful for you, so that, perhaps, you wanted to stop and spend a week or two on just one of them? Well, now you can do that! You can set your own program. The point now is to maintain a habit of consistent, daily practice, but you, in conjunction with the Holy Spirit, are now setting your own individualized curriculum.

One of the techniques we practice with in the Workbook is coming up with related thoughts. Often, the thought you choose to practice with may be one of those related thoughts, rather than words that come directly out of the book.

Some days, you may not have any particular words at all to practice with; you may simply use the day to practice constantly seeking and finding the peace of God.

The basic idea for post-Workbook practice is that you can use any of the techniques and practices given anywhere in the Course, and you can focus on whatever you feel you most need, or whatever works best for you.

And remember, the point is to continue with such practices indefinitely until, like the Workbook itself, you no longer need them. Your life will be a continuous holy instant. It may seem impossible, but the Course promises that God will make it possible for you:

> In time, with practice, you will never cease to think of Him, and hear His loving Voice guiding your footsteps into quiet ways, where you will walk in true defenselessness. For you will know that Heaven goes with you. Nor would you keep your mind away from Him a moment, even though your time is spent in offering salvation to the world. Think you He will not make this possible, for you who chose to carry out His plan for the salvation of the world and yours? (W-pI.153.18:1–4)

About the Authors

 Allen Watson is a staff writer and teacher with the Circle of Atonement, and is the author, or co-author with Robert Perry, of several popular books on the Course, as well as numerous articles in Course magazines and newsletters. He is well known around the world for his helpful daily commentaries, which are on the Internet as well as in book form (*A Workbook Companion, Volumes I & II*). Allen is also internationally known as a speaker on the Course. His gifted and spirited writing and teaching help students to unlock the meaning of the Course for themselves.

 Robert Perry has been a student of *A Course in Miracles* (ACIM) since 1981. He taught at Miracle Distribution Center in California from 1986 to 1989, and in 1993 founded the Circle of Atonement in Sedona, Arizona. The Circle is an organization composed of several teachers dedicated to helping establish the Course as an authentic spiritual tradition.

One of the most respected voices on ACIM, Robert has traveled extensively, speaking throughout the U.S. and internationally. In addition to contributing scores of articles to various Course publications, he is the author or co-author of twenty books and booklets, including *Path of Light: Stepping into Peace with* A Course in Miracles. Robert's goal has always been to provide a complete picture of what the Course is—as a thought system and as a path meant to be lived in the world on a daily basis—and to support students in walking along that path.

www.circlepublishing.org

Circle Publishing is a division of the
Circle of Atonement Teaching and Healing Center.

The Circle of Atonement offers a wide range of teaching materials
designed to help the student walk the transformative path of
A Course in Miracles. It offers a vision of the Course that is both
faithful to it and practical for the student. Visit the Circle's website
at www.circleofa.org for a wealth of free materials, including
articles by Robert Perry, Daily Lesson Commentaries by Allen
Watson, and Course Q&A's by Greg Mackie. You may also sign
up to receive the Circle's free e-newsletter, *A Better Way*, or to
receive Allen's Lesson Commentaries or Robert's weekly class
notes by e-mail.

Contact:
The Circle of Atonement
P.O. Box 4238
West Sedona, AZ 86340
Phone: (928) 282 0790
E-mail: info@circleofa.org
www.circleofa.org